SOCIAL AND ENVIRONMENTAL POLICIES IN EC PROCUREMENT LAW

In developing public procurement policy, governments are often concerned not only with value for money but also with promoting their social and environmental objectives.

However, imposing social and environmental requirements makes it harder for some suppliers to participate in public procurement. EC law thus limits the ability of national governments to implement such policies. But how should the balance be struck between these trade concerns and the desire of national governments to use procurement as a policy tool? And should the EC even harness Member States' procurement power to EC-wide objectives, such as green energy policy?

Despite the new provisions included in the EC's new (2004) procurement directives, important issues remain unresolved. This volume focuses on new issues in the field, notably the innovative provisions in the new directives, new academic thinking and areas neglected in the debate, such as the impact of EC law on the Corporate Social Responsibility policies of private utilities.

SUE ARROWSMITH is Professor of Public Procurement Law and Director of the Public Procurement Research Group in the School of Law, University of Nottingham, an Adjunct Professor at Copenhagen Business School and a Foundation Professor of the Chartered Institute of Purchasing and Supply (CIPS). She is also a member of the EC's Advisory Committee for the Opening Up of Public Procurement and editor of the *Public Procurement Law Review*.

PETER KUNZLIK is Professor of Law and Director of the City Law School at City University, where he is pro-Vice Chancellor. He is also a barrister and a non-practising member of Hailsham Chambers, Temple, London.

SOCIAL AND ENVIRONMENTAL POLICIES IN EC PROCUREMENT LAW

New Directives and New Directions

Edited by

SUE ARROWSMITH

and

PETER KUNZLIK

CAMBRIDGE
UNIVERSITY PRESS

CAMBRIDGE UNIVERSITY PRESS
Cambridge, New York, Melbourne, Madrid, Cape Town, Singapore, São Paulo, Delhi

Cambridge University Press
The Edinburgh Building, Cambridge CB2 8RU, UK

Published in the United States of America by Cambridge University Press, New York

www.cambridge.org
Information on this title: www.cambridge.org/9780521881500

First published 2009

Printed in the United Kingdom at the University Press, Cambridge

A catalogue record for this publication is available from the British Library

ISBN 978-0-521-88150-0 hardback

CONTENTS

v

4   **Application of the EC Treaty and directives to horizontal policies: a critical review   147**
SUE ARROWSMITH

7 Disability issues in public procurement   310
ROSEMARY BOYLE

CONTRIBUTORS TO THE VOLUME

SUE ARROWSMITH, Professor of Public Procurement Law, School of Law, University of Nottingham

ROSEMARY BOYLE, Solicitor, Legal Services Office, University of Cambridge

NICHOLAS HATZIS, Lecturer in Law, The City Law School, City University, London

PETER KUNZLIK, Director of the City Law School, City University, London

COLIN MAUND, Chief Executive Officer, Achilles, Abingdon

CHRISTOPHER McCRUDDEN, Professor of Human Rights Law, Oxford University; Fellow, Lincoln College, Oxford

MORITZ GRAF VON MERVELDT, Attorney/Head of Antitrust, Regulatory Affairs, ProSiebenSat.1 Media AG, Berlin

HANS-JOACHIM PRIESS, Partner, Freshfields Bruckhaus Deringer, Berlin

SOPE WILLIAMS, Lecturer in Law, School of Law, University of Nottingham

DANIEL WILSHER, Senior Lecturer in Law, The City Law School, City University, London

PREFACE

Public procurement – the government's activity of purchasing the goods and services it needs to carry out its functions – is a subject of growing interest to academics and in the last two decades has emerged as a distinct area for legal study. Whilst, given the recent nature of this development, many aspects of public procurement law and policy remain unexplored by scholars, the use of procurement as a tool to promote social and environmental objectives – what we call 'horizontal' procurement policy – is one aspect that has always attracted interest. In part, this is because of its intersection with other policy areas such as labour relations, gender equality and environmental and energy policy. In most jurisdictions interest in the use of procurement as a policy tool has been increasing, not least because of its potential role in addressing the pressing issues of climate change and energy security and because increased outsourcing to developing countries has led to a resurgence of interest in the issues of fair working conditions and 'fair trade' in public contracts.

This subject has interested the co-editors of this book for many years. Sue Arrowsmith's interest has arisen from her broader interest in public procurement regulation. She first examined the use and regulation of procurement as a policy tool in the context of the Canadian system in *Government Procurement and Judicial Review* back in 1989 and she has since explored differing national approaches (for example, in the United Kingdom, South Africa and the United States) in research for, amongst others, the UK Office of Government Commerce and the UN, and in the book *Regulating Public Procurement: National and International Perspectives* (2000, with John Linarelli and Don Wallace). She examined the implications of this subject for trade agreements in a 1995 article ('Public Procurement as a Tool of Policy and the Impact of Market Liberalisation' (1995) 111 *LQR* 235) and later developed her ideas on this perspective in her treatises on WTO and EC/UK procurement law which both include extensive chapters on horizontal policies

xvii

(*Government Procurement in the WTO* (2003) and *The Law of Public and Utilities Procurement* (1996, and 2nd edn 2005)). She has also been closely involved in EC policy in her capacity as a long-standing member of the European Commission's Advisory Committee for the Opening Up of Public Procurement. Peter Kunzlik's interest stems from his work in the fields of environmental law and energy policy as well as his specific interest in procurement, both as an academic and (previously) as a practitioner. He has written extensively on the implications of procurement law for environmental and energy policy over the last fifteen years, culminating in his participation in a recent OECD study on environmental issues in procurement (N. Johnstone (ed.), *The Environmental Performance of Public Procurement: Issues of Policy Coherence* (2003)) and recent publications on the new procurement directives. In some respects the editors hold different views on the subject of horizontal policies: at the risk of some oversimplification, Arrowsmith is sceptical of its value in view of the difficulties of implementing policies in an effective way in the real world whilst Kunzlik is in general more sympathetic. However, they have been united in arguing for a flexible approach in interpreting international trade rules that allows considerable discretion for national horizontal policies.

The present book is concerned with the particular issue of horizontal policies under EC law. The first, and hitherto most important, dimension of this issue is that already referred to above, namely the extent to which the law limits the *discretion* of Member States to pursue national policies in order to advance the internal market. In addition, a second and more novel dimension concerns the question of whether EC law should require or encourage Member States to use their procurement power to promote the EC's own policies, such as development of renewable energy sources or gender equality. From both perspectives the subject was a hotly debated and politically contentious one during the legislative procedure for the EC's recent procurement directives. The outcome of this procedure was some new EC provisions to clarify and extend the possibilities for Member States to use procurement as a policy tool, as well as some innovative measures harnessing national procurement power for EC objectives, by requiring states to exclude contractors convicted of corruption and certain other offences and by requiring them to consider accessibility issues in drafting specifications. However, additional proposals from the European Parliament that would have taken the directives even further in both dimensions were rejected, and many issues were left open given the difficulty of reaching agreement. Thus the recent legislation has by no means closed the debate on horizontal policies, but has merely heralded a new phase in its development.

This aim of this book is not to provide a comprehensive account of the law but, as the title indicates, to examine new legal developments and to consider new dimensions of the subject. To this end, we have solicited a series of essays that examine discrete themes relating to the regulation of horizontal policies under EC law.

Firstly, an important aim has been to examine the new provisions in the 2004 procurement directives. This is done, in particular, in several chapters that focus mainly on these new provisions.

One is chapter 7 on disability issues by Rosemary Boyle, which considers (inter alia) the directives' new provisions on accessibility and on reserving contracts for sheltered employment programmes. Whilst generally favouring legal interpretations that offer discretion for Member States in this area, Boyle urges caution in the way in which this is used in practice, drawing upon the US experience to support her argument. Another chapter that focuses on an important new provision is chapter 10 on eco-labels by Dan Wilsher, which examines the new rules on eco-labels in the 2004 directives as well as the implications of the Treaty for this field. After explaining the practical value and use of eco-labels, he explains that there are considerable difficulties in balancing EC and national interest in promoting their use with the needs of the internal market, to which there are no easy short-term solutions. Using the framework set out in previous chapters for analysing EC policy, Wilsher elaborates legal interpretations of the law that could be adopted to address this issue. In addition, chapter 12, by Sope Williams, examines the directives' new requirements for excluding contractors convicted of certain criminal offences. She explores the practical difficulties of applying these provisions, as well as many of the grey areas in the legal rules. She also highlights the provisions' potential significance for any future exclusions policies – for example, in defining the scope of authorities covered and persons to be excluded.

Secondly, we have also included several essays that examine issues that have not yet been much addressed and/or which make significant new contributions to the debate.

Thus in chapter 6 Christopher McCrudden deals with the subject of equality considerations in public procurement. In this chapter he supports the case for an interpretation of EC law that gives a broad discretion to Member States to pursue horizontal policies based, inter alia, on the fundamental principle of equality as a principle of interpretation. He also raises the possibility that the procurement directive's equal treatment principle, when interpreted in light of this principle, might be developed by the ECJ to impose a *duty* to consider equality considerations in public procurement. This analysis forms part of his wider research project on social issues in procurement, published as *Buying Social Justice: Equality, Government Procurement, and Legal Change* (2007).

Chapter 8 by Nicholas Hatzis assesses the impact of EC law on small and medium-sized enterprise (SME) policy in public procurement, explaining the context of this subject and unravelling the way in which various complex rules of EC law apply in this field. Disagreeing with some of the principles proposed by Arrowsmith in chapter 4, Hatzis contends that there are important restrictions on implementing SME policies under the EC Treaty and, in particular, that these cannot form grounds for justification under the Treaty derogations or mandatory requirements. However, he also highlights many ways in which SME policies may still lawfully be pursued.

In chapter 9 Peter Kunzlik considers the increasingly critical issue of using public procurement policies to promote the production of 'green' energy, which is an important plank of EC strategy both in the environmental sphere and in the field of energy security. This chapter examines both the background to this subject and the legal position of green energy policies in procurement. In particular, building on his previous work, he presents a detailed case for an interpretation of EC law that gives considerable flexibility to Member States not merely to favour energy supplied from renewable sources but also to favour the purchase of products that are themselves made with green energy. These possibilities he considers to be based on a general principle that public authorities may favour products produced in a particular way – challenging a view of the Commission that green energy requirements are somehow different from other production-related measures in public procurement.

Chapter 11, by Sue Arrowsmith and Colin Maund, examines an area hitherto largely unexplored, namely the use of horizontal policies by utilities. As they explain, utilities in many sectors have become increasingly concerned with social and environmental issues in the supply chain as part of the general Corporate Social Responsibility (CSR) movement and, to some extent at least, this concern is driven by commercial pressures arising from the need to respond to the concerns of investors, customers and employees. However, many utilities – including private utilities – are regulated by the EC procurement rules that impose constraints not applicable to other commercial companies. As the chapter explains, these issues have been barely touched on in public debate, in guidance from the European Commission or in academic literature. The chapter calls for a debate on the subject and elaborates a framework for that debate. After explaining the background, it explores the legal constraints that exist, including the myriad uncertainties that utilities face. It then highlights the policy issues relevant for addressing this subject, including the Commission's own policy on CSR, the need for utilities to respond to commercial pressures, and the problems caused by increasing globalisation and cooperation in the utility sector which, combined with fragmentation of procurement regimes, create difficulties for global strategy development and collaborative sourcing policies.

Finally, we have also included a chapter (chapter 5) by Hans-Joachim Priess and Moritz Graf von Merveldt on the implications of the state aid rules for horizontal policies, which brings to an English-speaking audience and integrates with the English-language literature important discussions found, in particular, in German literature. They explore the extent to which implementing of horizontal policies through procurement might involve provision of unlawful state aid and how authorities can ensure avoidance of the risks in this area.

All these chapters were presented and discussed at two workshops organised for this purpose as part of the international conference 'Public Procurement: Global Revolution III' at the University of Nottingham in June 2006. This conference, which attracted more than 200 participants from 35 countries and 15 international organisations, provided the opportunity for the authors to debate the issues in this book both with each other and with a diverse audience of academics, practitioners and policy-makers, and we are grateful to all the participants for their input.

Our original plan was to include a single introductory chapter that, drawing on our previous work in this area, would outline the governing rules and principles and set out our own thoughts on key issues, by way of background to the later chapters. However, as we began to write this chapter we came to appreciate more fully that there are some fundamental difficulties in dealing with procurement under the EC's free movement rules and some problems with the ECJ's approach that have potentially important implications for horizontal policies. Most specifically these relate to the characterisation of some public procurement measures as hindrances to trade, the application of the *Keck* jurisprudence to procurement, and the application of the principle of equal treatment without regard to nationality that the ECJ has created in the area of public procurement. These, we realised, were novel and important problems that needed fuller exploration. In addition, we realised that to address these issues properly we needed to elaborate more fully the taxonomy of horizontal policies that we had developed in previous work.

The single introductory chapter has thus expanded into four. Our first chapter explains the phenomenon of horizontal policies and then, drawing on our previous work as well as some chapters of the present book, elaborates certain key themes, trends and principles that we consider central to understanding and developing EC law in this field. It includes an elaboration of our view set out elsewhere on the need for an interpretation that gives significant weight to Member State discretion: this is based on several key principles, namely the equal status of horizontal policies with other procurement policies; the principle (based on the objectives of the EC procurement regime and limited competence of the EC) that it is for Member States to determine the balance between these different policies in procurement; the principle of subsidiarity; the fundamental principle of equality; and the Integration Principle of Article 6 EC. Chapter 2 then provides an overview of the current EC instruments that regulate public procurement, focusing, in particular, on the areas of difficulty in applying the Treaty to public procurement that we referred to above. Chapter 3 sets out a detailed taxonomy of horizontal policies in procurement and chapter 4 then offers a critical review of the impact of the EC regime, in light of the principles highlighted in chapters 1 and 2, and using the taxonomy of chapter 3. These chapters now provide a relatively full contextual and legal background for the later chapters, identifying the key issues emerging from the past and current debate and offering our own perspective on these issues.

We are extremely grateful to Ama Eyo who has worked tirelessly and cheerfully as the research assistant on this project and without whose unstinting efforts it would not have been brought to a (reasonably) timely completion. Sue Arrowsmith would also like to thank the sponsors of the Public Procurement Research Group at the University of Nottingham, Achilles Information Ltd, Bevan Brittan LLP and the Chartered Institute of Purchasing and Supply, whose generosity in providing funds has, inter alia, enabled us to employ a research assistant for the technical work. We also owe specific thanks to Achilles for the additional sponsorship provided to run the 'Global Revolution III' conference. Finally, we would also both like to express our gratitude to everyone at Cambridge University Press, in particular to Kim Hughes, and in particular for their tolerance of our ever-expanding ambitions for this work as it progressed and the consequent impact on timescales and length of this book.

This book is up to date as of 31 December 2007, although in some cases we have also been able to accommodate some later developments.

Sue Arrowsmith and Peter Kunzlik
March 2008

CHRONOLOGICAL TABLE OF CASES

European Court of Justice

Treaties

Directives

Decisions

Council Decision 89/490/EEC, OJ 1989 No. L239/33 347

Council Framework Decision 2000/383, OJ 2000 No. L140 /1 44

Council Decision 2000/819/EC on a multiannual programme for enterprise and entrepreneurship and in particular for small and medium-sized enterprises, OJ 2000 No. L333/84 347

Decision 2001/405/EC establishing the ecological criteria for the award of the Community eco-label for paper products (as amended by Decisions 2005/384/EC and 2007/207/EC), OJ 2001 No. L142/10 412

Council Decision 2001/469 concerning the conclusion on behalf of the European Community of the Agreement between the Government of the United States of America and the European Community on energy-efficient labelling programmes for office equipment, OJ 2001 No. L172/1 382

Decision 2003/68 establishing the European Community energy star board, OJ 2003 No. L67/22 382

Council Framework Decision 2003/568/JHA on combating corruption in the private sector, OJ 2003 No. L192/54 485

Council Decision 2004/579/EC on the conclusion on behalf of the European Community of the United Nations Convention Against Transnational Organised Crime, OJ 2004 No. L261/69 483

Recommendations

Council Recommendation 83/230, OJ 1983 No. L123/40 371

Council Recommendation 88/349, OJ 1988 No. L160/46 378

Resolutions

Council Resolution concerning a Social Action Programme, OJ 1974 No. C13/1 281

Council Resolution on the action programme for SMEs, OJ 1986 No. C 287/1 346

Council Resolution on the development of subcontracting in the Community, OJ 1989 No. C 254/1 358

Resolution of the Council and the Representatives of the Governments of the Member States on a Community programme of policy and action in relation to the environment and sustainable development – A European Community programme of policy and action in relation to the environment and sustainable development, OJ 1993 No. C138/1 375

Regulations

TABLE OF UK LEGISLATION

Statutes

Statutory Instruments

United States

South Africa

WTO Agreement on Government Procurement

Editors' Note – the decision in *Rüffert* v. *Land Niedersachsen*

In April 2008 the Second Chamber of the European Court of Justice (ECJ) gave judgment in the case of *Rüffert* v. *Land Niedersachsen*[1] which may have significant implications for the ability of public authorities to advance certain social goals through the exercise of their procurement function. In brief, the judgment indicated that, in the context of the Posted Workers Directive, it is a violation of the EC Treaty to impose working conditions for those working on public contracts that do not apply to workers in general (that is, to those working on private as well as on public contracts). This raises the possibility that, more generally, the Treaty precludes standards of behaviour being imposed on those who obtain government contracts that do not apply to businesses in general, both in carrying out the contract and in relation to the activities of a government's contractor outside its government contracts. It is a striking feature of the judgment, however, that the ECJ does not refer to its own jurisprudence on public procurement or to the provisions on social and environmental considerations in the Community directives on public procurement. This is in spite of the fact that this jurisprudence and legislation arguably should have been taken into account in the ECJ's decision-making and is potentially affected by the *Rüffert* judgment.

Production of the present book was too advanced at the time of judgment to incorporate an analysis of the *Rüffert* case into the main text. However, the case's potential significance for the subject matter of this book is sufficient to warrant a brief note on its possible implications and on our own response to the judgment.

---

[1] Case C-346/06, *Dirk Rüffert* v. *Land Niedersachsen*, 3 April 2008.

1

The facts and judgment

The *Rüffert* case concerned German legislation which required that public contracts for building works worth more than EUR 10,000 be awarded only to undertakings which agreed to pay staff working on such contracts a minimum wage as prescribed by a collective agreement on 'building and public works'. The law applied equally regardless of whether the contractor in question was a domestic undertaking or an undertaking from another Member State. The ECJ held that Directive 96/71, the Posted Workers Directive,[2] precluded the adoption of such a law. This was because, although the Posted Workers Directive permitted Member States to require the payment of minimum wages as prescribed by 'collective agreements' which had been declared 'universally applicable', the collective agreement in this case did not conform to that requirement: the Court held that since the requirement to pay the minimum wage specified by the agreement applied only to workers engaged on public contracts and not equally to those engaged on private contracts it could not be regarded as having been declared to be universally applicable. Indeed the referring court had itself confirmed that it had not been so declared under German law.

Although the case was concerned specifically with the preclusory effects of the Posted Workers Directive, the reasoning and statements of the Court in reaching this conclusion may, as noted above, have wider implications.

First, before addressing the question raised by the referring court, the ECJ gave a general characterisation of the situation which had arisen in the case by noting that the obligations provided by the German legislation meant that 'construction undertakings from other Member States must adapt the remuneration they pay to their workers to the normally higher level in force at the place [in Germany] where the contract is to be performed. Such a requirement causes those undertakings to lose the competitive advantage which they enjoy by reason of their lower wage costs. Consequently, the obligation to comply with the collective agreements constitutes an impediment to market access.'[3] In this spirit, interpreting the Posted Workers Directive in light of Article 49 EC, the Court went on to hold that by requiring undertakings performing public works contracts to apply the minimum wage laid down by the local law a Member State may be considered as imposing an additional economic

---

[2] The Posted Workers Directive, OJ 1997 No. L18/1.   [3] The *Rüffert* judgment, para. 14.

burden that may impede or render less attractive the provision of services in the host Member State with the result that the measure was therefore capable of constituting a restriction on intra-community trade within the meaning of Article 49 EC.[4] On this reasoning, we should note here that in chapter 2 we argue that not all procurement measures that impede or render less attractive the provision of services in another Member State are potentially to be considered as restrictions on trade and – as is relevant here – that workforce conditions limited to the performance of the public contract awarded (and not extending to the contractor's other business activities) are capable of constituting a restriction on trade *only* when directly or indirectly discriminatory. This issue has not been directly considered by the ECJ, however. Although the Court's language in *Rüffert* may imply, contrary to our view, that such measures *are* potentially caught by the Treaty even when non-discriminatory, it is important to note that *Rüffert* actually concerned a measure that was discriminatory in effect, and that the Court thus did not specifically address the position of non-discriminatory measures (as also in the case of *Contse*,[5] which is discussed in chapter 2). Thus we consider that the position of such non-discriminatory measures still remains open for consideration by the ECJ.

Having concluded that the measure was capable of constituting a restriction on trade under Article 49 EC the Court in *Rüffert* then went on to consider whether legislation such as that in question could be justified by the objective of protection of workers. The Court concluded that it could not because it did not comply with the requirements of the Posted Workers Directive, and especially because it was only applicable to workers (albeit regardless of whether they were nationals of the host state or of another Member State) engaged on public contracts but *not* also to those engaged on private contracts: the file contained no evidence that such protection was necessary for construction workers engaged in the former but not the latter. Nor could the measure be justified as being necessary to further the financial balance of the social security system or the protection of the independence of trades unions.[6]

In summary, therefore, the Court appears to have concluded that both the Posted Workers Directive and Article 49 EC prevent a Member State

---

[4] *Ibid.* para. 37.
[5] Case C–234/03, *Contse SA, Vivisol Srl & Oxigen Salud SA* v. *Instituto Nacional de Gestión Sanitaria (Ingesa)* ('*Contse*') [2005] ECR I–9315.
[6] *Rüffert*, paras. 41 and 42.

from legislating to require that workers engaged on public contracts are
to be entitled to higher standards as regards minimum wages than are
legally applicable to workers engaged on purely private contracts, even
though the rule for public contracts is equally applicable as between
workers of domestic undertakings and those from other Member States.

It is notable that Advocate General Bot took a different view from the
Court, including on the question of justification. Whilst he considered that
the German legislation was to be regarded as restricting intra-community
trade in services he also considered that it was capable of justification as
being for the protection of workers and prevention of social dumping.[7] In
particular, he rejected the view that the legislation could not be justified
because it distinguished between workers and on public and private contracts. In this respect he noted that 'while it is true that the aim of public
procurement is above all to meet an identified administrative need for
works, services or supplies, the award of public contracts also authorises
the attainment of other public interest requirements, such as environmental
policy, or, as in the present case, social objectives'.[8] Further, citing *Beentjes*
and *Nord Pas de Calais*, the Advocate General noted that 'the possibility of
integrating social requirements into public procurement contracts has
already been recognised by the Court ... and is now enshrined in [Article
26 of] Directive 2004/18'.[9]

In chapter 3 we suggested that there are in fact two justifications for the
government to impose standards for the performance of public contracts, or –
more broadly – that are applicable for *firms* working on public contracts, but
not to apply the same measures to the whole private sector.

> One is ensuring that government is associated with the highest possible
> standards. As with policies designed to ensure legal compliance this may
> be done both to set an example – which may encourage wider acceptance
> of the standards – and to avoid public criticism. This justification has
> particular force for policies limited to the contract, but is also relevant
> more generally. The second justification for 'regulation through procure-
> ment' concerns the effectiveness of the policy: procurement is in some
> fields a more effective policy instrument than alternatives, such as crim-
> inal or administrative sanctions, thus justifying a decision to focus limited
> resources on enforcing the policy in this limited field ... This is again
> particularly the case where the policy is limited to the government con-
> tract, but is also of broader relevance.

---

[7] Advocate General's Opinion of 20 September 2007, para. 114.
[8] *Ibid.*, para. 132.   [9] *Ibid.*, para. 133.

Although he does not articulate them in this way, these kinds of considerations would seem to lie behind the more flexible view taken by the Advocate General. The ECJ's judgment in *Rüffert*, on the other hand, appears to reject these as general justifications for measures confined to public contracts in the context of the kind of legislation that was in issue in this case.

However, it can be noted that the Court did leave room for the possibility that it might be possible to justify different treatment of workers on public and private contracts in certain cases: as mentioned above the Court mentioned that there was nothing in the file to indicate why special protection was needed for workers on public contracts, which implies that it might be possible to show this. This raises the possibility that it might be prepared to accept some arguments of this kind – if perhaps not as a justification for all policies limited to public sector contract workers, at least where a specific argument is made based on the particular facts (such as the practical difficulties of enforcing legislation outside the context of public contracts). It remains to be seen how receptive the Court will be to any such specific arguments.

Implications for other social policy measures relating to the contract workforce

The judgment in *Rüffert* seems to indicate at the very least that Article 49 EC and the Posted Workers Directive in principle preclude the government from imposing in public contracts conditions beyond those that apply more generally in the state concerned, when these are conditions of the type covered by the Posted Workers Directive. However, it is not clear how far the principle that the ECJ has applied to the working conditions in issue in *Rüffert* also extends to legislation providing for other forms of social opportunity for workers on public contracts, such as access to training, medical benefits and so on. Nor is it clear how the principle laid down in *Rüffert* might affect measures governing the *composition* of the workforce on government contracts, such as conditions or award criteria that require or encourage government contractors to provide job opportunities for the long-term unemployed or for disabled persons. In chapter 4 of this book we argue that many of these kinds of horizontal policies are lawful under the Treaty: we suggest that even to the extent that they are potentially hindrances to trade they are justifiable on various social and environmental grounds as mandatory or general interest requirements. It might be contended, however, that the Court's reasoning in *Rüffert* as regards Article 49 EC now affects those arguments, and precludes any social opportunity requirement imposed by domestic legislation which applies to workers employed on public contracts only and not also to those engaged on private contracts.

Such a contention, however, sits uneasily with the prior developments that have taken place in the EC regime in relation to horizontal considerations in public procurement. This applies both to the Court's previous jurisprudence on social measures in public procurement – such as the *Beentjes* ruling which contemplates conditions requiring employment for the long-term unemployed in the contract – and with the provisions of the procurement directives, which also specifically contemplate conditions of this kind in the new Article 26 on contract conditions (which codifies *Beentjes*) as well as the possibility of limiting contracts altogether to workshops for those with disabilities. Technically speaking it would not be incompatible with these provisions to conclude that such social policy measures that require contractors to provide various kinds of social benefits are not permitted in public procurement contracts since (as explained in chapter 2 and chapter 4) both the jurisprudence and the directives make it clear that their positive provision for such social measures is always subject to their compatibility with the Treaty. However, there is no doubt that all those involved have assumed throughout that such measures are valid in principle and that the constraints on them merely relate to, for example, the need to formulate them in a non-discriminatory manner so far as possible. It would be remarkable if such measures were to be considered unlawful, and it is for this reason that Advocate General Bot considered the existence of the prior jurisprudence and secondary legislation to be relevant to the question before the ECJ in *Rüffert*. Clearly the Advocate General considered that measures of the kind mentioned above are lawful and considered it inconsistent with that position not to accept justification of comparable measures concerning working conditions.

Since the ECJ in *Rüffert* did not accept the possibility of justification of the legislation in that case, however, does this imply that other social policy measures also cannot be justified where they are limited to public contracts? We would suggest that it does not. We consider that the Advocate General is correct in his implication that such measures may in principle be justified, and that the ruling in *Rüffert* is in fact limited to the context of conditions covered by the Posted Workers Directive.

The fundamental importance of the Posted Workers Directive to the outcome of the case is, however, clear when one remembers that both the operative part of the ruling and the Court's reasoning[10] make explicit that it was the directive which precluded the legislation such as that in issue, albeit that the directive was interpreted in light of Article 49 EC.[11] This might argue for a narrow application of the case to facts in which the directive is relevant since it makes clear that the Court itself approached the case on a basis which focused on an interpretation of the specific directive in issue rather than upon wider principles applicable to free movement in the procurement context more generally. Indeed, in our view, that can be the only explanation for the fact that the Court managed to come to judgment without once mentioning any provision of Community procurement legislation at all, nor any of its previous judgments, such as *Beentjes*,[12] interpreting that legislation, or applying the free movement of goods/ services rules in the procurement context.

In summary, we would thus suggest that the *Rüffert* case does not significantly affect the general arguments that we make in chapter 4 regarding the legality of social and environmental policy measures concerning the performance of government contracts. Rather, it affects only the specific issue of working conditions of a kind covered by the Posted Workers Directive.

We should also recall here that, as mentioned earlier in this note, it is our contention that the issue of justification is not generally relevant in any case for non-discriminatory measures relating to performance of a government contract, on the basis that these cannot be hindrances to trade. If that is correct, the *Rüffert* principle will be relevant only for horizontal measures that are directly or indirectly discriminatory, and will be less important than it would be if all procurement measures affecting the workforce were regarded as potential hindrances to trade.

---

[10] Para. 43 of the judgment.

[11] If we are right in characterising the *Rüffert* decision as depending upon the preclusory effect of a Community directive, that would appear consistent with the approach of the Court in another recent decision, namely *Case C-6/05 Medipac-Kazantzidis* v. *Venizelio-Pananio* ('*Medipac*') [2007] ECR I-455 in which the Court held that a contracting authority was not entitled to reject medical devices which conformed to its invitation to tender on public health grounds without following the harmonised safeguard procedure laid down for such devices by Directive 93/42 (the Medical Devices Directive) which were binding upon the authority in question. Although the Court explained this decision by reference to the principle of equal treatment and transparency, it is clear that any other decision would have permitted the contracting authority to render the safeguard procedure nugatory so far as it applies to public purchases and so undermine the effective application of the directive. The directive was therefore clearly being accorded preclusory effect as regards the contracting authority's conduct within its scope similarly to the way in which Directive 96/71 was considered preclusory in *Rüffert*.

[12] Case 31/87 *Gebroeders Beentjes BV* v. *Netherlands* [1988] ECR 4635, discussed at p. 208 below.

Implications for other types of measures involving regulation by contract

It is finally also necessary to note the potential relevance of the *Rüffert* judgment to horizontal policies that go beyond contract performance – for example, requirements that government contractors should employ a certain proportion of disabled workers in their business as a whole. In chapter 3 we distinguish these measures – which can be broadly characterised as measures that are 'regulatory' – from measures limited to contract performance, such as those in issue in *Rüffert* (see chapter 3, section 3). As chapter 3 explains, measures of this kind (like measures limited to contract performance also) are often concerned merely with using public procurement as an additional tool to enforce standards already imposed on other firms in the market, and to this extent do not seem to be affected by the *Rüffert* judgment. However, such procurement measures may also be used effectively to impose regulatory standards on government contractors in their whole business that do not apply at all to other businesses. We explain in chapter 4 that many measures of this kind are now prohibited by the procurement directives, so that they are not now common in the EC. However, we argue there also that such measures may be compatible with the Treaty and thus lawful to the extent allowed by the directives or where applied to contracts that are not caught by the directives at all. In this respect we suggest that the justifications set out earlier – ensuring that government is associated with high standards, by way of example or for other reasons, and providing an effective method of policy enforcement for some cases – apply in this context also, although not always (as we noted above) to the same degree as with measures limited to contract performance.

Are such measures affected by *Rüffert*? As with measures limited to contract performance, we suggest again that this is not generally the case, on the basis that *Rüffert* is concerned only with the kind of working conditions that are dealt with in the Posted Workers Directive. Thus we consider that only measures relating to these kinds of conditions are affected. We can note that the issue may be important in the context of measures in this group, since (as we explain in chapter 2) we consider that these kinds of measures are all potentially hindrances to trade – at least when general in nature rather than applied to isolated contracts – even when they are non-discriminatory.

Public procurement and horizontal policies in EC law: general principles

SUE ARROWSMITH AND PETER KUNZLIK

1. Introduction

Public procurement is the process whereby government bodies purchase from the market the goods, works and services that they need. Whether buying paper clips, commissioning major projects for the construction of hospitals, schools or offices, or procuring multimillion-pound IT and communications systems, the authorities in question are participating in the public procurement market. It is a market of great economic importance, and in the EC context is of particular concern from the perspective of the single market. In 1994 the market in regulated procurement (including utilities) represented no less than 14 per cent of Community GDP[1] and the UK public procurement market alone has been estimated as worth £117 billion.[2]

In this book we are concerned with the impact of EC law on one facet of public procurement, namely its use to promote social, environmental and other societal objectives that are not *necessarily* connected with the procurement's functional objective, in the sense of acquiring paper clips, an IT system, or whatever. This phenomenon embraces, for example, government policies against buying from suppliers that use child labour, and policies requiring suppliers to provide employment for ethnic minorities or disabled persons. These have commonly been referred to in Europe as 'secondary' procurement

---

[1] European Commission, *The Single Market Review*, sub-series III, *Dismantling of Barriers*, Volume 2, Public Procurement (1997), pp. 171–178. As for the size of global public procurement markets, see D. Audet, 'Government Procurement: A Synthesis Report' (2003) 2 *OECD Journal on Budgeting* 156; and F. Tronfetti, 'Discriminatory Procurement and International Trade' (2002) 23 *The World Economy* 57, 60.

[2] Office of Fair Trading, *Assessing the Impact of Public Sector Procurement on Competition* (September 2004). This excludes purchasing of public corporations.

policies[3] and in the United States as 'collateral' policies.[4] However, for reasons explained below, we prefer the label 'horizontal' policies.

The first, and hitherto most important, dimension of the debate about horizontal policies under EC procurement law concerns the extent to which the law limits the *discretion* of Member States to pursue their chosen policies, in order to advance the internal market. This is an important issue for many Member States, since specific horizontal policies can be politically highly charged. In many countries, for example, it would be regarded as outrageous if government offices were to be furnished using hardwood from non-sustainably managed forests, and if EC laws were to prevent authorities from purchasing only sustainably harvested timber there would thus be widespread outcry. Similarly, one might well expect popular criticism if the EC procurement regime were to prohibit Member States from reserving contracts for workshops for the disabled or from rejecting goods manufactured using child labour. These are but a few of the controversial topics in the debate about the way in which horizontal policies and procurement practices should interrelate.

In addition, a second dimension of the subject is the extent to which EC law does or should *require* or *encourage* Member States to use their procurement power to promote certain policies, notably those of concern to the EC itself, such as development of renewable energy sources or gender equality. This dimension is relatively novel, but potentially important, especially as the EC's most recent procurement directives include for the first time provisions that harness the procurement powers of Member States for EC objectives, by requiring states to exclude contractors convicted of corruption and certain other offences.[5] Similarly, as we shall see, Community measures have been enacted to encourage use of procurement to promote objectives related to energy policy.[6]

Use and regulation of horizontal policies is one of the few areas of EC public procurement law to have attracted wide interest[7] and there is a

[3] Including by the present authors: for early use of this term see, for example, S. Arrowsmith, *Government Procurement and Judicial Review* (Toronto: Carswell, 1988), p. 81, and (in relation to EC law) S. Arrowsmith, 'Public Procurement as a Tool of Policy and the Impact of Market Liberalisation' (1995) 111 *LQR* 235, note 1.

[4] See the standard text, J. Cibinic and R. Nash, *Formation of Government Contracts*, 3rd edn (Washington, DC: George Washington University Law School, 1998), chapter 10.

[5] See section 5.3 below and chapter 12.

[6] Directive 2006/32/EC on Energy End-use Efficiency and Energy Services, OJ 2006 No. L114/64.

[7] Perhaps not only because of the interest of the subject matter but also because of important decisions of the ECJ in cases such as Case C–31/87, *Gebroeders Beentjes BV*

significant legal literature, including in English.[8] This book's aim is not to provide a complete summary or critique, but rather to examine new developments and new thinking. In particular we are concerned to assess the implications of the new (2004) procurement directives and of new developments in jurisprudence; to examine issues so far neglected in the literature; and – in the case of state aids – to bring to an English-speaking audience discussions from elsewhere in the EC. To this end, we have solicited a series of essays that examine discrete aspects of this subject.

The first four chapters of this book, however, provide a general introduction. This first chapter introduces public procurement and the concept of horizontal policies, and then elaborates certain key themes, trends and principles that we consider central to understanding and developing EC law in this field. Chapter 2 then provides an overview of the current EC instruments that regulate public procurement, focusing,

---

v. *Netherlands* ('*Beentjes*') [1988] ECR 4635, Case C–225/98, *Commission* v. *France* ('*Nord Pas de Calais*') [2000] ECR I–7445, Case C–513/99, *Concordia Bus Finland* v. *Helsingin Kaupunki* ('*Concordia Bus Finland*') [2002] ECR I–7213 and Case C–448/01, *EVN AG* v. *Austria* ('*EVN-Wienstrom*') [2003] ECR I–14527.

[8] See, for example, on the legal aspects, Arrowsmith, 'Public Procurement as a Tool of Policy', note 3 above; J. M. Fernández Martín, *The EC Public Procurement Rules: a Critical Analysis* (Oxford: Clarendon Press, 1996), chapters 2 and 3; C. Tobler, 'Encore: "Women's Clauses" in Public Procurement under Community Law' (2000) 25 *ELRev* 618; C. Hanley, 'Avoiding the Issue: The Commission and Human Rights Conditionality in Public Procurement' (2002) 27 *ELRev* 714; J. Arnould, 'A Turning Point in the Use of Additional Contract Award Criteria?' (2001) 10 *PPLR* NA 13; C. McCrudden, 'Social Policy Issues in Public Procurement: A Legal Overview', in S. Arrowsmith and A. Davies (eds.), *Public Procurement: Global Revolution* (London: Kluwer Law International, 1999), chapter 12; P. Kunzlik, 'Environmental Issues in International Procurement', *ibid.*, chapter 11; C. Pitschas and H. Priess, 'Secondary Criteria and their Compatibility with EC and WTO Procurement Law – The Case of the German Scientology Declaration' (2000) 9 PPLR 196; T. Westphal, 'Greening Procurement: An Attempt to Reduce Uncertainty' (1999) 8 PPLR 1; K. Krüger, R. Nielsen and N. Bruun, *European Public Contracts in a Labour Law Perspective* (Copenhagen: DJOF Publishing, 1998); OECD, *The Environmental Performance of Public Procurement: Issues of Policy Coherence* (2003), chapters 5 and 6. On the new directives see, in particular, S. Arrowsmith, *The Law of Public and Utilities Procurement*, 2nd edn (London: Sweet & Maxwell, 2005), chapter 19; J. Arnould, 'Secondary Policies in Public Procurement: the Innovations of the New Directives' (2004) 13 *PPLR* 187; H. Nijiiolt, 'Environmental Provisions in Public Procurement Directive 2004/18/EC' (2004) 21 *ICLR* 268; P. Kunzlik, 'Green Procurement under the New Regime', in R. Nielsen and S. Treumer (eds.), *The New EU Public Procurement Directives* (Copenhagen: DJOF Publishing, 2005), chapter 8; and N. Bruun and B. Bercusson, 'Labour Law Aspects of Public Procurement in the EU', *ibid.*, chapter 7. EC law is also extensively dealt with in C. McCrudden, *Buying Social Justice: Equality, Government Procurement and Legal Change* (Oxford University Press, 2007), chapters 16 and 17.

in particular, on some unexplored areas of difficulty in applying the Treaty to procurement. Chapter 3 sets out a detailed taxonomy of horizontal policies in procurement. Chapter 4 then offers a critical review of the impact of the EC regime, in light of the principles highlighted in chapters 1 and 2, and using the taxonomy of chapter 3. The objectives of these chapters are threefold: to provide the contextual and legal background for the later chapters; to identify the key issues emerging from the past and current debate, including from the later chapters in this volume; and to offer our own framework for future analysis. The subsequent chapters then examine either specific areas of policy or – with chapter 5 on state aid and chapter 11 on utilities – novel issues that cut across different policy areas.

This present chapter first introduces the concept of horizontal policies and explains why we refer to 'horizontal' policies rather than the more traditional 'secondary' policies (section 2). It then examines the role of public purchasing, including horizontal policies, in the internal market, with the aim, inter alia, of reinforcing a basic principle that we will refer to throughout, namely the equal status of horizontal policies and other procurement policies (section 3). Section 4 introduces a general theme that recurs elsewhere, namely whether and how any distinction should be made in government procurement between the government's activity as 'purchaser' and its activity as 'regulator'. The chapter then turns to some key principles of the EC's procurement regime. In this respect it considers, first, the objectives of the regime and the competence of the EC in public procurement (section 5); secondly, some principles of interpretation that are of particular importance for horizontal policies (section 6); and, thirdly, the relationship between primary and secondary Community law in this area (section 7). Section 8 concludes.

2. The concept of horizontal policies, the equal status of horizontal policies and the issue of terminology

As we have seen, this book is concerned with the phenomenon whereby public procurement is used to promote social, environmental and other societal objectives that are not inherently necessary to achieving the functional objective of a specific procurement, but which the procuring body chooses, or is required, to advance in the context of its procurement contracts. This can be elaborated as follows.

Public authorities make purchases in order to advance or pursue their particular activities and policies. Thus, for example, a health authority might procure the construction of a hospital, or purchase surgical or other supplies, not as ends in themselves but to enable it to provide the services – health services – that it has been constituted to deliver. Alternatively, it might make these services available indirectly by procuring the provision of hospital services to the public from a private sector provider. In each case, however, the authority is making a purchase in order to carry out its own particular function. In carrying out their functions, however, public bodies may also wish, or be required, to further other societal objectives. These may include a range of environmental, social or industrial policies – for example, reduction of carbon emissions, the economic development of ethnic minority groups, support for employment of the disabled, or the development of poor regions. If one imagines the specific functions of public authorities as organised into vertical 'silos' these societal objectives can be envisaged as involving cross-cutting, 'horizontal' policies, not *necessarily* arising from the particular function of a given body but which may nonetheless be advanced through the way in which it conducts its activities. Public authorities might wish, or be required, to advance such horizontal policies through their procurement, just as they may seek to do so in the conduct of other activities, such as employment or location decisions.

Such policies in procurement have been commonly referred to in the EC, including by the present authors,[9] as 'secondary policies': the 'primary' objective of a procurement is seen to be the purchase on competitive terms of a product, work or service meeting a particular functional need, and factors relating to horizontal policies are designated as 'secondary' in the sense that they do not relate to this need.

The label 'secondary policies' is, however, problematic for several reasons. In general terms, it may be said that this label tends to detract from an important point of principle that should inform analysis in this area, namely the equal status of horizontal policies and other governmental policies.

First, as Arrowsmith has previously pointed out, the distinction between 'primary' and 'secondary' policies in procurement is far from clear-cut since it 'assumes the prior existence of decisions concerning the levels of purchasing, and the goods and services to be acquired [which] … may themselves be influenced by considerations apart from the acquisition of goods and services to fulfil a specified function'.[10] For

---

[9] See note 3 above.
[10] Arrowsmith, *The Law of Public and Utilities Procurement*, note 8 above, at 19.1.

example, a state may choose to implement public infrastructure projects not merely because of the desire for the infrastructure itself but also because of its potential to boost national employment.

Secondly – and even though this is not necessarily implied by the meaning of the term as it originated – there is a danger that the term 'secondary policies' may carry the connotation that such policies are of secondary *importance* to other matters, and/or are of limited importance. However, this is not necessarily the case. Indeed, horizontal considerations, either in the context of a particular procurement or collectively, can be as important as, or even more important than, functional objectives (and this applies whether or not the horizontal policy is a reason for undertaking that procurement in the first place). This is especially so as horizontal considerations often relate to such vitally important matters such as countering the incipient environmental disaster of climate change, preserving economic and political security in the context of energy security, or promoting human health, equality and dignity.

Thirdly, there is a danger that the term 'secondary policies' might be taken as *de-normalising* the pursuit of horizontal policies in public purchasing, by implying that in some way it is inherently not rational, normal or legitimate. This is a very important point, since it might skew the law's approach: in the trade context this might easily lead to an unwarranted assumption that these policies are suspicious and tend to cloak protectionist practices. These policies, however, are both normal in practice, in the sense that they are a common manifestation of market behaviour in both the public and private sectors, and normal from the perspective of the operation of the market, including in international trade, in that they actually contribute to its effective functioning. This point is elaborated in section 3 below. Further, from the constitutional perspective they represent a reasonable and potentially effective way to implement governmental policy, although (as with all government policy) there must be careful consideration of all the issues, as is elaborated in chapter 3.

These points suggest that it is important to highlight a general governing principle, namely that the starting point in regulating horizontal policies in procurement should be that these policies have equal status with other governmental policies, whether these are procurement policies – such as ensuring that goods are acquired on the best possible terms, or promoting integrity in procurement – or other kinds of policies, such as traditional regulatory measures on consumer protection, the environment etc. Referring to 'horizontal policies' rather than 'secondary policies' can help to ensure that regulators, including the regulators of the internal market, treat these policies on their merits, including a recognition of their equal status, and can thus contribute to a regulatory approach that is sufficiently nuanced to take account of the complexities of the issue. For similar reasons McCrudden, in his essay on equality in chapter 6 of this book, refers to policies related to the subject matter of the contract as 'linkages' rather than secondary policies, drawing on terminology used in the broader debate on equality in government policy-making, although (unlike the present authors) he continues to use the label 'secondary' policies for those extending beyond contract performance.[11]

We should add that the term 'horizontal policies' is not here intended as a term of art – a precise definition – and is certainly not intended to carry any normative connotations or to have any legal significance. There may be some argument about whether 'horizontal' or 'functional' is a suitable term to describe, for example, contract specifications or award criteria that seek to minimise the adverse effects of a product or service purchased on health (for example, product safety requirements) or the environment (for example, requirements for use of recycled materials). Whether EC procurement law does or should recognise any distinction of the kind envisaged above between functional and horizontal objectives and, if so, how the precise distinction is to be made, is, in fact, an important issue and a recurring theme in EC procurement regulation. We revert to this in section 4 below. However, it is not material at this point, since the concept of horizontal policies is intended merely as a broad description of the general subject area covered by this book.

3. Purchasing autonomy, the market mechanism and the internal market

In this section we elaborate the proposition already referred to above that the pursuit of horizontal benefits in purchasing, whether by a public or private purchaser, is normal market behaviour and, moreover, actually contributes to the effective functioning of the market. If this is accepted, regulators should not regard pursuit of horizontal policy objectives as inherently suspicious or illegitimate. On the contrary, they should consider it as entirely permissible unless there is a good reason to curtail it.

On what basis can it be claimed that the pursuit of horizontal policy objectives *is* normal market behaviour? The answer lies in a comparison

---

[11] McCrudden, *Buying Social Justice*, note 8 above, chapter 17, p. 554.

of the purchasing conduct of public purchasers with that of private market participants: the two are very similar. Thus, for example, a private individual may prefer to purchase not just beer, but beer contained in a bottle made using recycled glass; and if enough consumers share that preference, brewers will respond by providing beer in recycled glass bottles to seek competitive advantage. That is how markets work. In addition, private consumers may go further than simply expressing a preference related to characteristics of the products that they purchase, by using their purchasing decisions to signal disapproval of a supplier on matters not directly related to the purchase, as with the past consumer campaign to boycott South African produce in protest against apartheid. Such conduct is not confined to private individuals. Indeed, as chapter 11 further explains, businesses increasingly take account of ethical, social and environmental concerns in the supply chain as part of the Corporate Social Responsibility movement, in part because ethical concerns increasingly underlie the ultimate purchasing preferences of their own customers (as with the retail supply of 'fair trade' products).

Thus, public bodies pursuing horizontal procurement policies are exercising the same sorts of preferences as other purchasers. For example, the functional objective of a public works contract for construction of a school building would be provision of the building on competitive terms. It is not inherent in this functional objective that the school must be built using labour hired according to practices that assist the long-term unemployed. Nonetheless, if the purchaser seeks to assist the long-term unemployed by requiring the successful bidder to use labour from this group on the contract, it is exercising its purchaser autonomy (and power) in the same way as a private purchaser might do. It does not wish to purchase *just* a school. It wants to purchase a school *and* the benefit of advancing its horizontal policy. Furthermore, just as private purchasers may seek to signal approval or disapproval of the character or general business practices of some suppliers, so may public bodies. In the case of construction of a school building, for example, an authority might wish to favour bidders who can demonstrate that their overseas facilities do not employ child labour.

Since the benefits of a horizontal policy can be understood as being simply part of what the purchaser 'wants to buy', it is important to consider the role played by the purchaser's preferences as regards the market mechanism. This can then inform the orientation of the discourse on the way in which horizontal policies should be regulated.

Underlying the economic policy of many modern states is the notion which has enjoyed a wide (though varying) degree of acceptance back to the time of the Enlightenment that welfare is best advanced through the 'Invisible Hand' of the market, that is to say that resources are most efficiently allocated by the myriad of market transactions[12] rather than by governmental planning. The Invisible Hand, in turn, works because market participants transact exchanges on the basis of the values that *they* ascribe to particular purchases, the result being that the price mechanism allocates a particular good to the purchaser that most values it as evidenced by the price it is willing to pay. In order for the Invisible Hand to work a purchaser must be free in principle to determine what it values – that is, what it wishes to purchase and the price it is willing to pay.

Public procurement involves a special type of purchaser, the public body. The critical question is the extent to which the public character of such a purchaser *does* or *should* restrict its purchaser autonomy in ways that might constrain its ability to pursue horizontal policies.

Such constraints clearly exist at the national level since public bodies are constituted within the domestic legal and constitutional order of Member States. Their powers are conferred, and their functions exercised, within the national system. Their purchaser autonomy is constrained by domestic law in order to ensure, for example, that they operate within the scope of their lawfully constituted functions and comply with budgetary and good governance requirements. In addition, domestic law may specifically prohibit or restrict public purchasers from having regard to specific horizontal policies, or from implementing them in specific ways. To the extent that the law limits the purchaser autonomy of public bodies, including their ability to pursue horizontal policies, it is appropriate this should generally be done at the national level, since public bodies should be accountable for the expenditure of *national* taxpayers' money to the *national* electorate, through the democratic process. In terms of the market mechanism this can be rationalised in either of two ways. On the one hand, one can conceive of the state itself as being the ultimate market participant, acting through the agency of the public body engaged in a particular procurement. On this basis restrictions on horizontal procurement policies under domestic law or policy constitute an expression of the purchaser autonomy of the state itself. Alternatively, one might consider that the specific authority rather than

---

[12] Adam Smith, *The Wealth of Nations* (London: Penguin Classics, 1982).

the state as a whole is the purchaser in respect of a particular procurement, so that a restriction under domestic law of that authority's ability to pursue a horizontal policy is a constraint upon its purchaser autonomy and, as such, an interference with the market mechanism – but one justified as an expression of the democratic principle: the government, accountable to the national electorate, chooses to interfere in the market mechanism to advance other values.

The question with which this book grapples is the extent to which *EC law* does or should regulate the purchaser autonomy of public bodies, either by constraining their ability to pursue horizontal policies or by requiring them to do so. The EC is not, of course, in the same position as a Member State in this regard. The procurements with which this book is concerned involve the expenditure not of EC resources, but national resources. Nor is the EC the 'ultimate purchaser'. The only significant capacity in which the Community operates as regards such procurement is that of *regulator* and the primary rationale for its regulation, as elaborated in section 5, is concern for the internal market. This concern itself is rooted in market theory. Whilst the concept of the Invisible Hand explains the market mechanism generally, and emphasises the importance of purchaser autonomy to the optimum allocation of resources, the theory of comparative advantage explains the beneficial effects of international trade and underlies the internal market. According to this theory, international trade provides the optimum outcome for all states, on a 'win-win' basis, when compared to protectionism.[13] By facilitating intra-Community trade, the internal market enhances its Members' prosperity. Furthermore, it affords enterprises the possibility to benefit by economies of scale and scope.

It can be seen that, on the one hand, the autonomy of public purchasers, including with respect to horizontal policies, makes an important contribution to the operation of the market, including the international market, supporting the point made above that horizontal procurement policies are to be given equal weight with other policies and should be permitted unless there is a good reason to restrict them. On the other hand, however, there also is a potential for *conflict* between horizontal procurement policies and single market policy, where restrictions may indeed be in order.

---

[13] David Ricardo, *The Principles of Political Economy and Taxation* (New York: Dover Publications, 2004).

This is found most obviously in the fact that some of the traditional purchasing preferences of governments are actually directed at policies that are diametrically opposed to internal market policy. This applies, for example, when governments decide that national prestige requires that a high profile project be delivered by domestic enterprises[14] or places contracts with national firms to prevent factory closures. In these cases single market policy suggests that the autonomy of the government purchaser should be curtailed.

This is not to say that private parties do not also engage in similar behaviour. Indeed, support for local or national business that is not competitive in world markets is an increasing element of horizontal policies in the private sector, where it is even seen as a part of 'socially responsible' purchasing: for example, some British supermarkets make much of the British origin of their products, especially food products, in response to consumer preferences. However, with some exceptions, the relatively limited impact of such protectionist behaviour, combined perhaps with the additional sensitivities of regulating private purchasing, means that it is not generally seen to be necessary to regulate this behaviour in the private sector.[15]

Apart from these obvious cases, the EC has also chosen to regulate other government purchasing behaviour, relating both to functional and to horizontal policies. One reason is that such behaviour may serve as a cloak for protectionism: for example, a policy of purchasing locally produced food ostensibly adopted to reduce the environmental cost of transport may in fact merely serve as a cloak for supporting local farmers for political reasons. Alternatively, regulation may be considered appropriate because the behaviour in question impedes the single market in other ways: even if a policy of favouring locally produced food is adopted from genuine environmental motives it might be constrained nevertheless because of its enormous impact on imports. Unlike the case in which the horizontal policy is merely concerned to shore up uncompetitive suppliers, in many of these other cases the conduct will serve legitimate national objectives, and thus there is a need to balance the impact of

---

[14] See *Harmon CFEM Facades (UK) Ltd.* v. *The Corporate Officer of the House of Commons* [2002] 2 LGLR. 372, concerning the construction of Portcullis House, the prestige office building for Members of Parliament.

[15] On the application of the EC Treaty to private procurement, see Arrowsmith, *The Law of Public and Utilities Procurement*, note 8 above, at 4.23 *et seq.* (Article 28), 4.33 (Articles 43 and 49), and 4.51 *et seq.* (Article 86); and on the directives, see Arrowsmith, *The Law of Public and Utilities Procurement*, note 8 above, chapters 14 and 15.

constraints on these objectives against the benefit for the single market. In fact, in procurement even the regulation of overt protectionism requires a balancing exercise of this kind since, as explained below, the impact of the mechanism chosen for regulation – transparent contract award procedures – affects the means available to national governments for implementing most of their procurement objectives, including other horizontal objectives (such as gender equality, support for persons with disabilities etc.). For example, the requirement to follow strict transparency rules can reduce the discretion to negotiate with suppliers that some governments consider important for obtaining value for money.[16]

Again, we can note that EC law does not in general perceive the need to regulate private behaviour in the same way – with limited exceptions, including for private utilities (as chapter 11 explains), it does not regulate the way in which the private sector addresses 'horizontal issues'. Indeed, it positively encourages them to do this, through its policy on Corporate Social Responsibility, even though private sector actions, such as requiring compliance with 'fair labour' codes across their suppliers' business, have precisely the same restrictive effect as comparable actions in the public sector.[17] In this respect, the past restrictive attitude of the European Commission towards horizontal policies in the public sector, which is elaborated further below, appears to reflect a kind of 'institutional schizophrenia' on this issue.

In our view, the issue of horizontal policies is most suitably addressed, and the apparent conflict between the approach to public and private sector behaviour minimised, by an approach that starts by recognising the basic autonomy in the market of both public and private sector purchasers, and restricts that autonomy only when there are special reasons to do so. In EC law such special reasons are found in the above-mentioned tendency for governments to favour national industry solely for reasons that are directly contrary to the single market, which does present a significant problem to be addressed by EC law. Beyond this, however, any restraints need to be carefully considered. The various interests that are affected in striking the balance between trade and national autonomy in public purchasing are explored in chapter 3.

---

[16] See Arrowsmith, 'The Problem of Discussions with Tenderers under the EC Procurement Directives' (1998) 7 *PPLR* 65; K. Krüger, 'The Scope for Post-tender Negotiations in International Tendering Procedures', in Arrowsmith and Davies, *Public Procurement*, note 8 above, chapter 10.

[17] See chapter 4, in particular at 4.3.1 and 8.1.6, where it is explained that the Commission argues that such policies in the public sector contravene EC law.

4. Government as purchaser and government as regulator under EC law

A distinction that the present authors[18] and others have sometimes used in analysing public procurement policies is that between the government as a 'purchaser' and the government as a 'regulator'. (We use the term 'purchaser' rather than 'consumer'[19] to reflect the fact that products purchased under public procurement rules are sometimes purchased for resale.) This reflects, broadly, the fact that sometimes the government's concern is merely to acquire a product, work or service that it needs, but that in other cases it also uses its procurement power to 'regulate' behaviour as a substitute for more traditional regulatory techniques. For example, as chapter 3 elaborates, governments have sometimes used exclusion from government contracts as a sanction to push firms to adopt proactive recruitment policies to broaden the ethnic, gender, or religious constitution of their workforce.[20] This use of procurement serves as an alternative, or sometimes additional, means of promoting behaviour that is or might be secured through more traditional sanctions, such as financial or criminal penalties. Similarly, we suggested above that an authority might wish to limit bidders for a school building to those who can demonstrate that their overseas facilities do not employ child labour. Procurement measures are here comparable to some extent with regulatory measures that ban altogether imports of products made in a certain way, although the decision to use procurement may reflect particular concerns, such as the desire for the government to disassociate itself from particular products without forcing its preferences on the private sector. As a generalisation, governments use procurement in a manner akin to regulation on a greater scale than private firms. However, as we have noted, such a phenomenon is not unknown in the private sector as, for example, with the former consumer boycotts of South Africa.

The concepts of 'government as purchaser' and 'government as regulator' can provide a useful shorthand to emphasise the different policy considerations that may arise from different types of procurement measures: on the one hand, those that are limited to acquiring particular

---

[18] For example, Arrowsmith, *The Law of Public and Utilities Procurement*, note 8 above, at 17.8.

[19] A term used by Arrowsmith, *The Law of Public and Utilities Procurement*, note 8 above, at 17.8, and also by McCrudden, for example in chapter 6 (of this book) and in McCrudden, *Buying Social Justice*, note 8 above, chapter 17.

[20] Chapter 3, section 2.2.

items and, on the other, those that share some of the features of regulatory activity. One example, perhaps, is the greater need for procedural safeguards for regulated parties when exclusion from procurement is used as a form of regulatory sanctions.[21] The concept of 'regulation' by contract was highlighted for this purpose by Daintith in an important article in the 1970s, which drew attention to the phenomenon of using procurement in a manner akin to regulation, and the constitutional issues that this raised in the United Kingdom.[22]

From the perspective of internal market rules, we consider that in principle the problem to be addressed, and hence the most important rationale for EC intervention, is the same for both pure public 'purchasing' decisions and for public procurement decisions that have a regulatory element, namely the potential for discrimination and other barriers to trade arising, in particular, from the government's political interests in supporting national industry. However, as we outline below (and elaborate in chapter 4), purchasing and regulatory-type measures may nevertheless require different policy responses for reasons such as their degree of impact on trade and the practical implications of ECJ scrutiny of decisions.

The purchaser/regulator distinction can also be useful for descriptive purposes, to categorise and illuminate different methods of policy implementation. The taxonomy set out in chapter 3 reflects a distinction that might be broadly categorised as one between 'government as purchaser' and 'government as regulator', namely between measures that are concerned solely with the performance of the contract awarded and measures that are not limited to contract performance but directed also at suppliers' behaviour outside the contract. The distinction between contract-related measures and others is employed in that chapter both to illuminate practice and to highlight some of the considerations relevant to policy-making and regulation.

These concepts can also, of course, be used in legal discourse to categorise measures that are, or should be, subject to different legal treatment, arising from these different policy factors. For example, where legal norms applicable to regulatory activity, such as procedural safeguards, seem appropriate only for procurement measures going beyond the contract, their scope can be defined as applicable only to government procurement action taken 'as regulator'.

---

[21] Chapter 3, section 2.2.
[22] T. Daintith, 'Regulation by Contract: the New Prerogative' (1979) 32 *CLP* 41.

The scope of certain EC procurement rules, notably those in the directives, reflects a distinction along broadly these lines: we will see in chapter 4 that the directives and related jurisprudence make it clear that many measures concerned with the contract awarded (government as purchaser) are permitted, whereas many that go beyond it (government as regulator) are not, although (as we will also see) there are also many grey areas. We would contend, however, that at EC level this type of distinction has sometimes distracted policy-makers from addressing the quite complex substantive issues that lie behind the regulation of horizontal procurement measures. In particular, as we elaborate in chapters 4 and 9, this is the case with the Commission. As we explain there, the Commission has made a purchaser/regulator-type distinction to support a narrow interpretation of the directives, suggesting that, in general, measures concerned with the effects of the purchased products *when consumed* by the government are permitted, as they refer to what the government is buying, but that other measures are not, including measures concerned with the 'production' effects of the products supplied (such as pollution caused by manufacture) as well as measures extending to the general business of the supplier. However, rather than questioning the nature of the distinction it has made, the Commission has applied this approach in an illogical manner when it has led to unsatisfactory policy outcomes; thus, it has accepted that an obligation to supply energy from renewable sources (which clearly concerns production methods) may be part of what the government is buying, because of its political importance, but has not accepted the possibility of other requirements concerning production of supplies, even though these cannot be distinguished conceptually from requirements to supply energy produced from renewable sources.[23] McCrudden, on the other hand, employs a purchaser/regulator distinction in a more consistent and considered manner to argue for an interpretation of the directives that is both consistent between different policy mechanisms *and* relatively broad: he suggests that for the most part the directives must be interpreted to allow all measures relating to the 'subject matter' of the contract (that is, all measures whereby the government acts purely as purchaser), but that this concept is to be interpreted broadly in that the purchaser may specify the subject matter. As we elaborate further below, he uses this argument to support both the conclusion that the purchaser may include

---

[23] See, in particular, chapter 4, sections 8.1.6 and 8.2.

requirements concerning methods of production[24] (as the present authors have also previously argued, but the Commission generally rejects)[25] and that the purchaser may exclude firms for inability to meet requirements concerning the contract workforce[26] (which the Commission again rejects).[27]

There are some problems in invoking the purchaser/regulator distinction to analyse the implications of existing EC rules, since the classifications of measures involved are more complex than this twofold categorisation suggests. In fact, different legal rules do, and may, require several different distinctions, all of which sit somewhere on the borderline between what may be characterised as 'purchasing', as opposed to 'regulatory', activity. We will see in the following chapters that a distinction that follows broadly the division between government as purchaser and government as regulator in fact is made for several *different* purposes under EC procurement law, under both the directives and under the Treaty (which McCrudden does not consider); but that in each case the line between government as purchaser and government as regulator may be drawn in a slightly different place, according to the precise considerations involved. Nevertheless it may be useful even as a legal concept, provided that its limitations are recognised and the policy issues involved are carefully addressed.

The taxonomy set out in chapter 3, whilst using this distinction at a broad level, aims to provide a more detailed and nuanced classification of procurement measures that can be used to analyse the reach of specific legal rules and decisions. In particular, it is useful to subdivide measures that are directed solely at contract performance into four categories, namely those relating to consumption (use) of the products/works/ services, those relating to production and delivery, those relating to disposal, and those relating to the contract workforce. Whilst these can all in a broad sense be said to concern the government as purchaser insofar as they are directed at contract performance, it is not clear that they always are, or should be, treated alike under legal rules affecting horizontal policies. Whilst measures in the first of these categories – those relating to consumption effects, such as the environmental impact

---

[24] McCrudden, *Buying Social Justice*, note 8 above, chapter 17, where the concept is also invoked to support, for example, a broad interpretation of permitted award criteria along the same lines as that preferred by the present authors in this and previous works: see chapter 4, section 13 of this book.
[25] See the discussion in chapter 4, section 8.1.6.
[26] See chapter 6.   [27] See chapter 4, section 8.

of using a product – are almost invariably[28] regarded as 'purchasing' decisions, measures relating to the contract workforce are sometimes treated differently; and there often is some uncertainty over how to treat measures relating to production/delivery and disposal, although we argue (both in this book and elsewhere) that generally these should be treated as 'purchasing' decisions, in the sense of being regulated in the same way as measures relating to consumption effects.

More precisely, the purchaser/regulator distinction may be relevant under EC law, first, in applying the EC Treaty, as is discussed in chapter 2 and illustrated in Table 2.1. In this respect the distinction can be employed, first, in deciding which procurement measures are to be characterised as 'hindrances' to trade under the Treaty's free movement provisions. Measures characterised as hindrances to trade require specific justification, including under a proportionality test, if they are to be lawful; those that are not, on the other hand, are excluded from scrutiny, as is explained in chapter 2. We argue that decisions on whether to make a purchase and what to purchase should *not* generally be treated as hindrances to trade, even when they are discriminatory in effect, a position we consider consistent with the case law.[29] We call these decisions 'excluded buying decisions'. This argument is based on practical and constitutional concerns relating to judicial scrutiny at EC level of these decisions, which distinguish them in our opinion from certain measures of a more regulatory nature. In this instance, a distinction between certain activity of the government as a 'buyer' and its other procurement activity, including activity as a regulator, is used to argue for a *lower* degree of scrutiny than is applied to many governmental decisions affecting the single market. However, as chapter 2 will explain, it is not necessarily appropriate to characterise this distinction as one between 'government as regulator' and 'government as purchaser': certain decisions that in general language and for other legal purposes (including under the directives) could be labelled as 'purchasing' decisions probably are (and should be) subject to justification requirements, because of their significance for trade, notably those concerning the

---

[28] An exception is perhaps the Commission's argument in *Concordia Bus Finland*, rejected by the ECJ, that award criteria under the directives cannot concern even all consumption effects, but only those of direct economic advantage to the purchaser: see chapter 4, section 13.

[29] Chapter 4, section 3.1.

workforce used on the contract, such as requirements to employ long-term unemployed persons on the contract work.

In addition, a distinction of broadly this kind could be relevant merely to the treatment of *non-discriminatory* measures under the Treaty. If, contrary to our argument on 'excluded buying decisions', the ECJ does not accept that *all* decisions relating to whether and what to purchase are excluded from the concept of hindrances to trade, we contend in chapter 2 that certainly non-discriminatory procurement measures of this kind should be excluded, for precisely the same practical and constitutional reasons that support limited scrutiny of even discriminatory measures. We argue in chapter 4 that non-discriminatory procurement measures are caught by the EC Treaty *only* when they are regulatory measures of a general nature, and not where they are measures limited to 'purchasing' activity in the sense of being limited to the contract (nor where they are measures going *beyond* the contract that are limited to specific contracts). We also suggest that any exclusion of non-discriminatory procurement measures taken by the government as purchaser rather than as regulator should extend to all measures connected with the contract, including those relating to the workforce.[30]

The distinction between government as purchaser and government as regulator may also be relevant to the Treaty at a different level altogether: the Commission appears to consider that measures of a regulatory nature, in the sense that they are directed at activity beyond the contract, cannot generally be justified when they affect conduct in other Member States, because of their significant impact on trade.[31] This issue is particularly important if, contrary to our own argument, non-discriminatory procurement measures are generally caught by the Treaty. However, we in fact reject the view that measures of this kind cannot be justified: we do not consider the distinction to be relevant at all in addressing this question, as we elaborate in chapter 4.

Finally, so far as the Treaty is concerned, we should note that it is possible that the ECJ might develop a distinction between horizontal measures that relate to the contract and those that go beyond it in considering the legality of horizontal policies under the state aid rules. It is, however, argued in chapter 5 (see section 5.3.4) that this is neither necessary nor appropriate, and this view is shared by the present authors.

---

[30] Chapter 4, section 3.1.

[31] The Commission also considers that this applies to measures concerning production of supplies for the contract because of their *effects*. See chapter 4, section 3.1.

In addition to a purchaser/regulator distinction being relevant under the EC Treaty, as just discussed above, the procurement directives – at least the Public Sector Directive[32] – also contemplate a purchaser/regulator-type distinction, and the debates on the position under the directives have sometimes been couched in this language.[33]

Broadly speaking, as already mentioned, the directives' approach is to allow policies concerning the contract itself, but not those directed at activities beyond the contract. As with the Treaty, a purchaser/regulator distinction is in fact potentially relevant to various different issues, and it is not clear that the ECJ will make the distinction in the same way for all purposes, nor whether it will draw the line in the same place as it does in applying any of the Treaty doctrines.

Under the Public Sector Directive the distinction may be pertinent, first, in deciding what requirements may be included in contracts at all.[34] In this respect, as chapter 4 will explain, Article 26 of the Public Sector Directive appears to allow only terms that relate to 'performance of the contract'. As we will see, it clearly allows terms relating to consumption of the products/works/services and those relating to the contract workforce. It also appears that it allows most types of terms relating to production/delivery and to disposal. However, the precise possibility for terms on these matters has not yet been clarified: in particular, as chapter 4 explains, the Commission appears to reject the general possibility of including terms concerning the production of *supplies* and the ECJ has not yet pronounced clearly on the general principles governing this question. On the other hand, the directive does not appear to allow any terms going beyond the contract, such as requirements that government contractors should abide by fair labour practices across their whole business (that is, regulatory-type procurement measures):[35] these would not be terms relating to contract performance.

Secondly, a kind of distinction between purchaser and regulator is also reflected in both the Public Sector and Utilities Directives' rules on award criteria: these must be linked to the 'subject matter' of the contract.[36] As with the concept of a term that relates to 'contract performance', this again implies some kind of link to the products/works/services being procured. However, the case law again is not clear on the precise line

---

[32] On the Utilities Directive 2004/17, see chapter 11.
[33] See, for example, McCrudden in chapter 6 of this book.
[34] See the discussion in chapter 4, section 8.   [35] See chapter 4, section 8.1.5.
[36] See chapter 4, section 13.

between permitted and non-permitted measures: whilst the ECJ indicates that the subject matter of the contract includes consumption effects and at least some production effects, it is uncertain whether workforce matters form part of the subject matter.[37] We argue in chapter 4 that in fact there is an exact symmetry between measures permitted as contract terms and those permitted as award criteria – that is, that the concepts of 'relating to contract performance' and 'linked to the subject-matter of the contract' are the same. To that extent, a 'purchaser/regulator' distinction may be useful shorthand for expressing what the directives do and do not permit.

In addition, a distinction that could be framed in terms of purchaser/regulator is also relevant under the Public Sector Directive in excluding undertakings. Under this directive it appears that firms may be excluded from contracts for inability to fulfil contract terms related to delivery of the goods, works or services (that is, to deliver what the government is buying) but not for other matters. In this respect, however, the ECJ has taken a narrow view of what the government is 'buying', precluding the possibility of excluding firms in advance on the grounds that they cannot comply with terms relating to the *contract workforce*.[38] We suggest in chapter 4 that it is questionable whether such an approach can be justified on policy grounds. Further, the position of disposal and production or delivery requirements relating to the goods, works or services, as opposed to consumption requirements, is unclear in this respect: certainly the Commission considers some of these requirements, at least, cannot provide the basis for advance exclusions, even though (as with workforce requirements) it may be lawful to include them in the contract. McCrudden has specifically invoked the purchaser/regulator distinction to reject the traditional interpretation that workforce conditions cannot be the basis for exclusion, as well as the Commission's view that precludes exclusion based on certain production and disposal measures: he argues that all four types of terms relating to the goods, works or services give rise to the possibility of advance exclusions, *provided that the government itself regards the benefits under these terms as part of what it is buying under the contract*.[39]

In conclusion, we should be wary of referring to any distinction between the government as purchaser and government as regulator, to

---

[37] *Ibid.*

[38] Unless, of course, these affect the 'buying' element, such as the characteristics of the products/works/services when consumed (for example, concerning the qualifications of the workforce to deliver services of sufficient quality).

[39] See chapter 6.

the extent that this is by no means clear-cut and may conceal various legal and practical complexities that are relevant in regulating horizontal policies. However, provided that the issues involved are properly isolated and addressed, the distinction can sometimes serve as useful shorthand to describe and analyse the position.

We should, finally, note the relationship between the concepts of government as purchaser/government as regulator, on the one hand, and the distinction between functional and horizontal objectives, on the other. As mentioned above, we have used the concept of 'horizontal' policies or objectives, in contrast with 'functional' objectives, in a very broad sense to describe and delimit the subject matter of this book. However, as we mentioned, it is not a precise distinction and is not intended to have legal significance. Whilst this imprecise concept might linguistically be interpreted as conveying the same broad idea as that of government as purchaser (functional activity) and government as regulator (horizontal activity), we employ the concept of horizontal policies in the broadest possible sense to include even procurement measures that are concerned with the consumption impact of products/works/services. This is the case even though for legal purposes these are generally treated in the same way as those features of products/works/services that relate to the purchaser's core objectives – for example, measures laid down by a health authority to specify the number of wards or operating theatres in a hospital – and would thus, under any approach to the purchaser/regulator distinction, be considered to involve government activity as purchaser. The concept of horizontal policies is employed in this broad manner purely for descriptive purposes, to ensure that all subject matter that is potentially relevant to the legal discourse is covered by our analysis. Thus we do not equate the functional/horizontal distinction directly with the purchaser/regulator distinction in any of its forms.

5. Horizontal policies and the objectives and competences of EC procurement regulation

5.1. Introduction

The functioning of the internal market in public contracts is implemented mainly through two sets of provisions.[40] First, there are the free

---

[40] Some other measures are also relevant: see further, Arrowsmith, *The Law of Public and Utilities Procurement*, note 8 above, chapter 3.

movement provisions of the EC Treaty. These prohibit unjustified discrimination in public procurement and certain other restrictions on access and, controversially, have recently been interpreted as also requiring transparency in awarding public contracts. Second, relevant for larger public contracts, is secondary legislation in the form of directives, which require authorities to award these contracts using specific transparent procedures which the directives set out. The current directives are those adopted in 2004, namely Directive 2004/18/EC,[41] which governs most major public contracts (the Public Sector Directive), and Directive 2004/17/EC,[42] which regulates contracts in certain utilities sectors (the Utilities Directive).

5.2. EC law and the discretion of Member States

So far as concerns the *discretion* of Member States to implement horizontal policies – which we have seen is the main dimension of the relationship between EC procurement law and horizontal policies – it is important at the outset to have a clear conception of the precise means through which the EC regime seeks to achieve an internal market in public procurement, and the means by which it *may* do this – that is, the scope of its legal competence. This is essential for understanding the nature and limits of the EC's control over horizontal policies, and for interpreting and developing the EC provisions, yet is often misunderstood.

In the authors' view, the regime that has been developed under the Treaty and directives seeks to develop the internal market through three main means.

The first is simply by prohibiting discrimination in public procurement. This is done by the Treaty itself and also by explicit provisions in the directives, as elaborated below.

The second is by requiring Member States to award contracts through procedures that are *transparent*, to prevent them from concealing discriminatory behaviour, particularly behaviour that is discriminatory in intent. In particular, as elaborated below, the directives limit the discretion of public purchasers by requiring them to hold a competition that is

---

[41] Directive 2004/18/EC of the European Parliament and of the Council on the coordination of procedures for the award of public works contracts, public supply contracts and public service contracts, OJ 2004 No. L134/114.

[42] Directive 2004/17/EC of the European Parliament and of the Council coordinating the procurement procedures of entities operating in the water, energy, transport and postal services sectors ('Utilities Directive'), OJ 2004 No. L134/1.

publicised to all interested suppliers, and is conducted according to rules set out in the directives, with pre-disclosed selection and award criteria, so that discriminatory measures cannot be concealed behind a cloak of subjective decision-making. The implementation of a transparent system of procedures to support the non-discrimination principle has always been the primary aim of the directives.[43] As chapter 2 explains, the controversial requirement for transparency in public contracts under the EC Treaty has been implied by the ECJ for the same purpose, namely to allow monitoring for compliance with non-discrimination rules.[44]

Thirdly, the EC procurement rules are concerned to remove certain restrictions on access to the market – even, in certain cases, non-discriminatory restrictions – that are considered disproportionate in light of their objectives. For example, as chapter 2 explains, the Public Sector Directive contains a limited list of evidence that purchasers may require from firms to assess their technical capacity, in order to limit the burden of participation. The extent to which the Treaty, too, controls non-discriminatory measures is less clear, as is also discussed in chapter 2.

On the other hand, the authors contend that it is *not* an objective of either the EC free movement rules or the directives to ensure that states achieve 'value for money' in purchasing in the sense of obtaining their requirements on competitive terms, or to regulate the balance between such 'value for money' considerations and other considerations, such as process efficiency and – of particular relevance for the present purpose – horizontal policies. Value for money is an important objective – probably the most important objective – of most national regimes on public procurement and also of the procurement rules that international institutions use to regulate aid-funded procurement.[45] These national and

---

[43] The recitals to the first directive on works (Directive 71/305/EEC, OJ 1971 No. L185/5) refers merely to the need for 'co-ordination of national procedures', but later recitals refer to this purpose: see Directive 77/62/EEC, OJ 1977 No. L13/1, stating the need for transparency 'allowing the observance of [the prohibition on measures restricting imports] to be better supervised'; Directive 89/440/EEC, OJ 1989 No. L210/1 (amending Directive 71/305) (need to improve transparency 'in order to be able to monitor compliance with the prohibition of restrictions [on freedom of establishment and freedom to provide services] more closely'); and Case C–44/96, *Mannesmann Anlagenbau Austria AG* v. *Strohal Rotationsdruck GmbH* [1998] ECR I–73, para. 33 (stating that 'the aim' of Directive 93/37/EC is to 'avoid the risk of preferences being given to national tenderers or applicants', cited in many subsequent judgments).

[44] See chapter 2, section 3.2.

[45] See S. Arrowsmith, J. Linarelli and D. Wallace, *Regulating Public Procurement: National and International Perspectives* (The Hague; London: Kluwer Law International, 2000), especially chapters 2 and 3.

international systems generally seek to achieve value for money by requiring public purchasers to use procedures that are broadly similar to those in the EC directives, in particular by requiring a publicly advertised competitive award process. However, value for money is not per se an objective of the EC regime.[46]

There is potential for confusion here as the Commission, when asserting the benefits of EC procurement policy, has increasingly referred to attaining value for money as a benefit of EC rules on procurement and in some cases has even referred to it as an *objective* of the EC regime. Thus in its recent Communication on Corporate Social Responsibility,[47] in the section on public procurement policy, the Commission refers to previous Communications on social and environmental issues in public procurement, stating that these clarify how the EC regime allows public purchasers to take account of such issues '*whilst at the same time ensuring respect of the principle of value for money for taxpayers* and equal access for all EU suppliers'[48] (emphasis added). Similarly, in a 2003 Press Release on remedies the Commission states that 'EU law on public procurement aims to increase competition and transparency in order to create opportunities for businesses, *better value and higher quality services for the taxpayer*'[49] (emphasis added).

Better value for money in public purchasing is certainly one of the benefits intended to *follow from* the internal market, and, in particular, from the procurement directives – for example, because of lower prices obtained from suppliers from other Member States.[50] On the other hand, the EC procurement rules are not directed at achieving value for money per se in a way that is *separate* from internal market objectives, as some of

---

[46] See Arrowsmith, *The Law of Public and Utilities Procurement*, note 8 above, at 3.8 *et seq.*

[47] European Commission, Communication concerning Corporate Social Responsibility: a business contribution to sustainable development, COM (2002) 347 final.

[48] *Ibid.*, p. 22, section 7.5.

[49] European Commission, Public Procurement: Commission consults on how rejected bidders can challenge public procurement decisions, Press Release IP/03/1455.

[50] Such benefits are highlighted on the Commission's SIMAP website page on procurement policy (http://ec.europa.eu/internal_market/publicprocurement/index_en.htm): 'The opening up of public procurement within the Internal Market has increased cross-border competition and improved prices paid by public authorities. There remains potential for significant further competition in procurement markets *and for further savings for taxpayers.*' This recognises the benefits to taxpayers as those flowing from the internal market, not benefits independent of the internal market. Improved value for money for public purchasers will also follow from many other aspects of single market policy, such as policies on technical regulations in products purchased by the public sector.

the statements above might imply. Ensuring the wise expenditure of public money and improving the quality of public services are not per se objectives that the EC is, in general, competent to pursue, and general power to implement policies to this effect cannot be found in the powers to adopt secondary legislation derived from Article 47(2) EC, Article 55 EC and Article 95 EC, on which the procurement directives are based. Saving public expenditure and improving the quality of services simply do not in and of themselves *contribute to* the creation of an internal market.

A more specific argument to support the view that the EC regime is – or, at least, can be – concerned to ensure value for money might be that an internal market can only work if public purchasers behave 'efficiently' in choosing the best supplier. The Invisible Hand can work to allocate resources effectively, including in international trade, only if purchasers that seek value for money actually do so effectively, and only in these circumstances will the most efficient firms survive and develop, ensuring that the benefits of specialisation are realised. While commercial pressure ensures that private sector firms obtain their requirements from the most competitive source, this cannot be assumed to be the case with the public sector, even if it does not engage in discriminatory behaviour; thus it is necessary to regulate award procedures to ensure efficient behaviour. This is perhaps envisaged by the Commission when it refers to the regime's alleged concern with 'the rational allocation of public money through the choice of the best offer presented'.[51]

However, as in Arrowsmith's previous work,[52] we reject this view of EC procurement law as being concerned to ensure value for money in Member States as a substitute for the operation of the market.

So far as the Treaty is concerned, the free movement provisions are concerned only with hindrances to trade – that is, hindrances to suppliers wishing to access the market – not with the competitive behaviour of purchasers. Whilst the Treaty involves positive obligations to advertise as well as negative obligations not to discriminate, the ECJ has stated that the purpose of the positive obligation to advertise is to ensure monitoring of the obligation not to discriminate[53] – it is not to ensure value for money.

---

[51] See, for example, European Commission, Interpretative Communication on the Community law applicable to public procurement and the possibilities for integrating environmental considerations into public procurement, COM (2001) 274 final, p. 4.

[52] Arrowsmith, *The Law of Public and Utilities Procurement*, note 8 above, at 3.8–3.12.

[53] Some subsequent cases indicate that the positive obligations exist to support a broader obligation of equal treatment, but we reject this: see chapter 2. Even if such an obligation does exist, it does not, of course, imply a best value objective.

With regard to the directives, the recitals to the earlier directives, on which the current ones are closely based, indicate clearly that the directives seek an internal market by the means referred to above, namely supporting the obligation not to discriminate through transparency (with competition being a means for creating the transparency needed to prevent non-discrimination, not a means to value for money),[54] and removing barriers that prevent suppliers from other Member States from accessing the market. The issue has never been carefully analysed in the jurisprudence, but the limited role of the directives is supported by the Opinion of Advocate General Jacobs in *SIAC Construction*:[55] 'the main purpose of regulating the award of public contracts in general is to ensure that public funds are spent honestly and efficiently, on the basis of a serious assessment and without any kind of favouritism or quid pro quo whether financial or political. *The main purpose of Community harmonisation is to ensure in addition abolition of barriers and a level playing-field by, inter alia, requirements of transparency and objectivity*' (emphasis added). This contrasts the objective of efficient spending with the more limited internal market objective. This view also finds support in several cases that emphasise the purpose of the directives in preventing discrimination when interpreting the scope of entities and contracts covered: if one aim of the directives was to ensure value for money it would be expected that this would also be taken into account in analysing their scope.[56] The directives' requirements to choose the lowest or most economically advantageous tender, discussed in chapter 2, merely reflect the fact that selection of the best

---

[54] The recitals to Directive 77/62, for example, refer to competition as the means to ensure the transparency that will allow restrictions under the Treaty to be complied with: 'Whereas that prohibition [on free movement in the EC Treaty] should be supplemented by the coordination of the procedures relating to public supply contracts *in order, by introducing equal conditions of competition for such contracts in all the Member States, to ensure a degree of transparency allowing the observance of this prohibition to be better supervised*' (emphasis added).

[55] Case C–19/00, *SIAC Construction* v. *Mayo CC* ('*SIAC Construction*') [2001] ECR I–7725, para. 33 of the Opinion.

[56] Case C–380/98, *R* v. *HM Treasury ex parte University of Cambridge* [2000] ECR I–8035, para. 16, cited in many later cases. Some of these refer to avoiding risk of preference *and* the possibility of a body being guided by considerations other than economic ones (e.g., Case C–470/99, *Universale-Bau* v. *EBS* [2002] ECR I–11617, para. 52; Case C–237/99, *Commission* v. *France* [2001] ECR I–939), but it appears that this refers to non-economic considerations deriving from preference – the actual analysis in the cases focuses on the risk of discrimination.

tender is in fact the objective of procedures in national law, and that this was accepted by Member States when adopting the directives: the directives regulate the process for making the choice, to ensure transparency, but this does not imply that the directives themselves *aim at ensuring efficient expenditure.*[57] Indeed, it seems questionable whether the EC has competence to legislate to ensure value for money under the single market provisions.[58]

What are the implications of this analysis for horizontal policies?

First, it suggests that there is no role for EC rules in ensuring that national resources are spent wisely, and thus no role for the EC in deciding on how to balance value for money – and other national policy considerations, such as procedural efficiency or accountability – with horizontal objectives. These remain in principle matters for Member States to determine, according to their own priorities between these objectives and also their own assessments of the best means to implement those priorities – for example, whether through award criteria or contract conditions (as discussed in chapter 3). There are, in fact, many reasons why Member States may wish to restrict their authorities' pursuit of horizontal policies. In particular, as discussed in chapter 3, Member States inevitably encounter the need for a trade-off between horizontal and other objectives, including value for money – for example, because of a reduced pool of potential bidders, or the cost to suppliers of enhancing their products to meet environmental requirements; and they may regulate horizontal policies in their national systems to ensure that policies are effective and the trade-offs appropriate in light of their own priorities.

---

[57] Arguably a different view is reflected, however, in Recitals 5 and 12 of the Public Sector Directive and Utilities Directive respectively. However, these are not conclusive. They both indicate that the directives seek to integrate environmental protection into the procurement regime as required by Article 6 EC 'whilst ensuring the possibility of obtaining the best value for money'. This does not indicate that achieving value for money is one of the directives' objectives but rather that the directives recognise that environmental protection will, from an authority's point of view, only be one of a range of applicable objectives, chief amongst which, of course, would be value for money, and that the directive is designed to allow *authorities* to balance these.

[58] These may be invoked only to support the four freedoms or to eliminate appreciable distortions of competition: Case C–376/98, *Germany* v. *Parliament and Council* [2000] ECR I–8419. It seems open to question whether legislating for value for money relates to either objective and, if it does, whether doing so would comply with the subsidiarity principle, which applies to single market legislation: see Article 3 of the Protocol (No. 30) to the EC Treaty on the application of the principles of subsidiarity and proportionality (1997) and para. 178, concerned with Article 95 EC.

However, the EC rules do not, and probably cannot, regulate for these reasons, but only in order to promote the internal market.

On the other hand, it also needs to be recognised that measures to implement the internal market could be applied either very narrowly or very broadly, and could in themselves provide a potentially wide tool for limiting Member States' discretion. A strict approach to transparency, for example, could lead to the conclusion that there should be a very narrow scope for implementing horizontal policies, not because of their impact in terms of a higher price, reduced competition or additional procedural costs, but because of the possibility of abuse of discretion to favour national firms. Further, in implementing internal market policy the EC's assessment of the value of horizontal policies for Member States is not immaterial, since the EC may take into account its own appreciation of the importance of these policies in balancing internal market considerations with Member States' interests. However, neither the Community legislator nor the ECJ should impose its own assessment of the values pursued by horizontal policies but at most the EC should concern itself with questions of proportionality.[59]

Clear recognition of this limited role of the EC from a conceptual perspective will at least ensure that the correct considerations are taken into account and that the EC does not overreach its proper role by attempting its own balance between horizontal policies and other policies that are not concerned with the internal market. This is likely to produce an approach that affords greater flexibility to Member States than one under which the EC itself has responsibility for deciding all the trade-offs involved. For example, in applying the equal treatment principle, discussed further in chapter 4, it seems clear that the ability of undertakings to meet horizontal criteria may be considered, in principle, of a weight equal to or greater than their ability to meet financial criteria, in determining whether bidders are in a comparable position.[60] Similarly, in determining the proper scope of discretion under the directives in setting selection criteria or award criteria, the interests of Member States in horizontal policies – and in determining how this is best achieved in their own systems – must be considered of no lesser weight than their interests in obtaining good commercial terms. The

---

[59] Just as under Article 30 EC it is for the Member States to determine the required standard of protection of the stated interests.

[60] See further chapter 4, section 6.

more recent rulings of the ECJ, notably in *Concordia Bus Finland*[61] (allowing environmental award criteria concerned with reducing noise and pollution, which hardly any tenderers could meet) and in *EVN-Wienstrom*[62] (allowing a 45 per cent weighting for an environmental award criterion and emphasising that that weighting is for Member States), which are discussed further in later chapters, are consistent in both their reasoning and their results with this approach; whilst the earlier ruling in *Beentjes*[63] (preventing exclusions for inability to comply with workforce conditions of a social character) is harder to reconcile with it. It is true that both *Concordia Bus Finland* and *EVN-Wienstrom* both concerned horizontal policies in the environmental sphere, the importance of which is specifically highlighted by Article 6 EC (discussed further below); but we would argue that this specific Treaty principle merely confirms the importance of allowing broad Member State discretion in relation to horizontal policies.

Finally, even if, contrary to what has been argued above, it is indeed an objective of EC procurement policy to lay down rules to promote the award of public contracts to the 'best' contractor to counteract the danger of inefficient purchasing, it does not necessarily follow that it is for EC law to balance horizontal and other considerations. This rationale for EC intervention suggests merely that EC law should ensure that procuring entities buy in such a way that the priorities that they have set themselves between financial, horizontal and other considerations are implemented effectively, not that the EC should set those priorities. Such an approach could merely justify more stringent regulation of the *means* for implementing such policies, rather than of the policies themselves.

5.3. The EC's role in promoting or requiring use of horizontal policies

We have so far, in section 5.2, considered the role of the EC in *limiting* the discretion of Member States to implement horizontal policies. In

---

[61] Case C–513/99, *Concordia Bus Finland*, note 7 above; and see further chapter 2, section 3.1. In particular, the ECJ in this case, in para. 56, referred specifically to the directives' objective in removing barriers to free movement to support its conclusion that certain environmental award criteria are allowed, implying that this limited objective does not in principle involve the EC in determining what other objectives Member States may implement in procurement (in particular, environmental objectives).

[62] Case C–448/01, *EVN-Wienstrom*, note 7 above; see, in particular, chapter 4, section 13.

[63] Case 31/87, *Beentjes*, note 7 above. See, in particular, chapter 4, section 8.1.4.

addition, however, there is a second dimension of this subject, namely the role of the EC in harnessing the collective purchasing power of Member States towards the realisation of societal objectives.

In this respect the EC could act, and has acted, through various means. For example, it has sought in a limited way to facilitate the development of small and medium sized enterprises (SMEs) by encouraging their participation in public procurement, as chapter 8 explains. More radically, the 2004 directives have for the first time included provisions that require Member States to use procurement to support certain horizontal objectives. One is a requirement for certain regulated purchasers to exclude from contracts firms that have convictions for corruption, certain types of fraud, money laundering or participation in a criminal organisation. Chapter 12 discusses these provisions, including their more general implications for this 'second dimension' of horizontal policies under EC law. In addition, as discussed in chapter 7 on disability issues, the directives now state that 'whenever possible' technical specifications should take into account accessibility criteria for people with disabilities or design for all users.[64] Proposals were also made during the legislative process for the 2004 directives to include further grounds for mandatory exclusions, in addition to those for corruption etc.[65] And some commentators have proposed that the EC should harness Member States' procurement power to promote EC objectives in areas such as gender equality.[66] Furthermore, Directive 2005/32/EC on Energy End-use and Energy Services[67] (discussed in chapter 9) obliges Member States to take account of energy efficiency in procurement. McCrudden, in chapter 6, has also raised the possibility that the fundamental principle of equality in EC law might be developed in the future by the ECJ to provide for an obligation to take into account gender equality in public procurement, introducing a mandatory, EC-wide, commitment even in the absence of specific secondary legislation.

Of course, as in other areas, the Community's competence to legislate is limited by two legal principles. First, the Community must act within the limits of the powers conferred upon it, and within the limits of the objectives assigned to it, by the Treaty.[68] A corollary of this is that each legislative measure must be based upon one of the authorising provisions

---

[64] Article 23(1) of the Public Sector Directive.   [65] See further chapter 2, section 4.2.
[66] See, for example, Tobler, note 8 above.   [67] OJ 2006 No. L114/64.
[68] Article 5 EC, first paragraph.

of the Treaty. In addition, Community action is subject to the principles of subsidiarity and proportionality as stated in Article 5 EC.[69]

So far as competence is concerned, the 'task' of the Community is defined to cover a wide range of values, many of which are of types that typically underlie horizontal policies in procurement. Thus the task of the Community is to 'promote throughout the Community a harmonious, balanced and sustainable development of economic activities, a high level of employment and of social protection, equality between men and women, sustainable and non-inflationary growth, a high degree of competitiveness and convergence of economic performance, a high level of protection and improvement of the quality of the environment, the raising of the standard of living and quality of life, and economic and social cohesion and solidarity among Member States'.[70] The 'activities' through which the Community is to perform its 'task' also include activities in a wide range of policy areas commonly associated with horizontal policies. As well as the establishment and functioning of the internal market (including free movement of persons)[71] they include, for example, the promotion of coordination between employment policies of the Member States with a view to enhancing their effectiveness by developing a coordinated strategy for employment,[72] a policy in the social sphere,[73] the strengthening of economic and social cohesion,[74] a policy in the sphere of the environment,[75] the strengthening of the competitiveness of Community industry,[76] a contribution to the attainment of a high level of health protection,[77] a contribution to education and training and the flowering of the cultures of Member States,[78] a policy in the sphere of development cooperation,[79] a contribution to strengthening consumer protection,[80] and measures in the spheres of energy, civil protection and tourism.[81]

---

[69] Article 5 EC and Protocol (No. 30), note 8 above. The second paragraph of Article 5 provides that, 'in areas which do not fall within its exclusive competence, the Community shall take action, in accordance with the principle of subsidiarity, only if and in so far as the objectives of the proposed action cannot be sufficiently achieved by the Member States and can therefore, by reason of the scale or effects of the proposed action, be better achieved by the Community'. The principle of proportionality as stated in the third paragraph of Article 5 provides that 'An action by the Community shall not go beyond what is necessary to achieve the objectives of this Treaty.'

[70] Article 2 EC.   [71] Article 3 (1)(a), (c), (d) and (h).

[72] Article 3(1)(i).   [73] Article 3(1)(j).   [74] Article 3(1)(k).   [75] Article 3(1)(l).

[76] Article 3(1)(m).   [77] Article 3(1)(p).   [78] Article 3(1)(q).   [79] Article 3(1)(r).

[80] Article 3(1)(t).   [81] Article 3(1)(u).

Of course, although these policy areas fall within the 'activities' of the EC the Community's competence to legislate in any given case must arise from one or more specific 'legal bases' or 'Treaty bases'. The Treaty bases of the new procurement directives are stated as being Article 47(2), Article 55 and Article 95 EC. Article 47(2) authorises the Community to adopt directives coordinating national laws 'concerning the taking-up and pursuit of activities as self-employed persons' 'in order to make it easier for persons to take up and pursue activities as self-employed persons',[82] and is applied also, in the context of freedom to provide services, by Article 55 EC. Finally, Article 95 EC makes special provision for adopting legislation for the purposes of Article 14 EC – that is, progressively establishing the internal market.[83] Thus (with exceptions) it authorises measures for approximation of Member States' laws 'which have as their object the establishment and functioning of the internal market'.[84] Such approximation measures may include measures concerning health, safety, environmental and consumer protection, in which cases they are to take 'as a base a high level of protection, taking account in particular of any new development based on scientific facts'.[85] We suggested above that the fact that the procurement directives are based on legal bases for internal market measures[86] is one reason why they cannot be regarded as aimed at ensuring value for money in general.

Thus to be well founded the 'affirmative' provisions of the new directives, which seek to advance Community horizontal policies, must fall within the fields of activity in which legislation is authorised by Article 47(2), 55 and 95 EC. In fact, it is questionable whether these 'affirmative' provisions do relate to the establishment and functioning of the internal market. Arguably the mandatory exclusions for corruption etc. relate not to this but to Community policy on combating crime, and those concerning accessibility etc. in technical specifications relate only to aspects of Community social policy.

Before considering whether these specific policies are within the Community's field of competence, it is worth noting the governing principles. First, the decision whether a provision can be based upon a particular Treaty base 'must be based on objective factors which are

---

[82] Article 47(2) is stated as authorising legislation 'for the same purpose' as Article 47(1) which in turn is stated to be for the purpose of 'making it easier for persons to take up and pursue activities as self-employed persons'.
[83] Article 14(1) EC.   [84] Article 55(2).   [85] Article 55(3).
[86] Including measures for freedom of establishment and to provide services.

amenable to judicial review and [which] include the aim and content of the measure'.[87] On the other hand, if a measure 'pursues a twofold purpose or has a twofold component and if one of those is identifiable as the main or predominant purpose or component, whereas the other is merely incidental, the act must be based on a single legal basis, namely that required by the main or predominant purpose or component'.[88] Exceptionally, however, 'if it is established that the act simultaneously pursues a number of objectives or has several components that are indissociably linked, without one being secondary and indirect in relation to the other, such an act will have to be founded on the various corresponding legal bases'.[89] A dual legal basis is not, however, possible where the legislative procedures laid down for each legal base are incompatible.[90]

The Public Sector Directive is stated to be based upon Articles 47(2), 55 and 95 EC. It may, however, be questioned whether the two mandatory horizontal policy elements of the new directives can be said to relate to free movement and the establishment and functioning of the internal market taken in isolation. In *Tobacco Advertising*[91] the Court made clear that Article 95 EC does not provide a general power to regulate the internal market but only a power to adopt measures which have 'the specific object of improving the conditions for the establishment and functioning of the internal market – and that [these] must be designed to remove genuine obstacles to free movement or distortions of competition, not purely abstract risks'.[92] The Court held in that case that a ban on tobacco advertising went beyond the powers of Article 95 EC. Similarly the mandatory exclusion of suppliers having criminal convictions for corruption etc. does not guarantee market access or ensure free movement; on the contrary, it restricts market access to advance the values involved in combating crime and terrorism. Similarly the rule that technical specifications must take account of accessibility does not

---

[87] Case C–94/03, *Commission v. Council* [2006] ECR I–1, para. 34 following Case C–269/97, *Commission v. Council* ('*Titanium Dioxide*') [2000] ECR I–2257. See also Case C–338/01 *Commission v. Council* [2004] ECR I–4829.

[88] Case C–94/03, *Commission v. Council*, note 87 above, para. 35.

[89] *Ibid.*, para. 36. See also Case C–336/00, *Republik Österreich v. Huber* [2002] I–7699; A. Arnull *et al.*, *Wyatt and Dashwood's European Union Law*, 5th edn (London: Sweet & Maxwell, 2006), p. 79.

[90] Case C–338/01, *Commission v. Council*, note 87 above, paras. 17–21 citing *Titanium Dioxide*, note 87 above.

[91] Case C–376/98, *Germany v. Parliament and Council*, note 58 above.

[92] Arnull *et al.*, note 89 above, p. 87.

advance market access for suppliers but a social policy aimed at reducing social exclusion. It is, in fact, quite striking that the directive does not recite that a Community prohibition on participation in public contracts of those convicted of the relevant offences is required to prevent an actual threat to the internal market and free movement, nor that it is possible that Member States may (if left to themselves) deal with the question differently such that differences in national regulation may realistically create the risk of regulatory barriers to cross-border participation in public contracts. Nor do the recitals provide any suggestion that the mandatory accessibility requirement is necessary to deal with an actual or potential disruption of the internal market or barrier to free movement.

Thus it can be argued that these two new sets of provisions could not properly be based on Articles 47(2), 55 and 95 EC taken in isolation.

There is also another argument to consider, however. If a measure pursues two objectives, one of which can be regarded as predominant and the other as merely incidental, then the legislation must only be based on the predominant Treaty base alone. It might be argued that this is the case here, that the directive pursues a 'twofold purpose' serving the ends of free movement and the internal market on the one hand, and the objectives of crime policy (as regards Article 45) or social policy (as regards Article 23(1)) on the other. On this basis, provided that one could regard the crime policy or social policy elements as 'merely incidental' to the directive's predominant purpose then it might be regarded as properly based upon the free movement and internal market legal bases, notwithstanding the presence of the horizontal policy elements relating to crime policy or social policy. However, this can apply only if the horizontal policy element *could* have been properly based upon another Treaty provision.

As regards the accessibility provision, a possible legal basis is found in the provisions on consumer protection. Article 153(1) EC requires the Community to 'contribute to protecting the health, safety and economic interests of consumers' and Article 152(2) requires consumer protection requirements to 'be taken into account in defining and implementing other Community policies and activities' which would include, of course, procurement. Furthermore, Article 153(3) (a) provides that the Community shall contribute to these objectives through measures adopted pursuant to Article 95. Thus the accessibility provisions, in so far as they impact upon 'the health and safety and economic interests of consumers', could properly, perhaps, be based on Article 95 EC in conjunction with Article 153(2) EC. Without appropriate ramps or lifts in public buildings, for example, disabled people might be at greater risk of falling in ways that would detract from their health and safety. Furthermore, lack of accessible design might exclude disabled people from accessing economically valuable public services, such as publicly funded therapeutic, social or other services, and thus impact upon their 'economic interests'. Thus the accessibility provisions might be valid, provided that they are considered 'merely incidental' to the directive's 'predominant' free movement and internal market objectives.

Article 136 EC provides a legal base for social policy legislation in several fields, defined by Article 137(1) EC,[93] and includes at least two fields of potential relevance, namely 'the integration of persons excluded from the labour market, without prejudice to Article 150 [which deals with vocational education]'[94] and 'combating social exclusion'.[95] A requirement to consider accessibility for the disabled might enhance employment in public authority facilities of disabled people, and con-tribute to the combating of social exclusion of disabled people who might otherwise be excluded from access to facilities or services. However, Article 137 EC (which contains two separate bases for Community measures in Article 137 (2)(a) and (b)) also limits the *types* of measure that the Community can take. Article 137(2)(a) only allows the Council to take measures 'designed to encourage cooperation between Member States' and the directives' provisions go far beyond this. Article 137(2)(b), by contrast, does allow the Council to adopt directives but this power is confined to the fields referred to in Article 137(1) (a) to (i), excluding 'the combating of social exclusion', which is provided in Article 137(1)(j). Nonetheless, it does include 'the integration of persons excluded from the labour market' (Article 137(1)(i)) so that to the extent that accessi-bility of design of authorities' procurements will impact on exclusion from public employment it might be covered. However, provisions

---

[93] These fields are defined in Article 137(a) to (k). These are '(a) improvement of the working environment to protect workers' health and safety; (b) working conditions; (c) social security and social protection of workers; (d) protection of workers where their employment contract is terminated; (e) the information and consultation of workers; (f) representation and collective defence of the interests of workers and employer; (g) conditions of employment of third-country nationals legally residing in Community territory; (h) the integration of persons excluded from the labour market, without prejudice to Article 150 [on vocational training policy]; (i) equality between men and women with regard to labour market opportunities and treatment at work; (j) the combating of social exclusion; [and] (k) the modernisation of social protection systems without prejudice to point (c)'.
[94] Article 137(1)(h) EC. [95] Article 137(1)(j) EC.

adopted must be 'minimum requirements for gradual implementation, having regard to the conditions and technical rules obtaining in each of the Member States' and must also avoid imposing administrative, financial and legal constraints in a way that would hold back the creation and development of small and medium-sized enterprises (SMEs). It seems difficult to fit the directives' accessibility provision into this framework, not least because it introduces a rule of immediate rather than gradual application. Article 137(2)(b) seems to be concerned with the development of technical rules of general application, rather than rules relating only to public contracts.

The legal basis of the provisions combating crime is even more debatable. The Community's competence in criminal justice remains constrained and the relevant provision, Article 61 EC of the EC Treaty,[96] only provides (so far as material) that the Council may adopt 'measures to prevent and combat crime in accordance with the provisions of Article 31(e) of the Treaty on European Union'. That provision, in turn, relates only to 'measures establishing minimum rules relating to the constituent elements of criminal acts and to *penalties* in the fields of organised crime, terrorism and illicit drug trafficking' (emphasis added). Since the exclusion from public contracts required by the directives is not imposed by a convicting court, it seems at least arguable that it does not qualify as a 'penalty' under this provision. Indeed, Council Framework Decision 2000/383[97] (on increasing protection by criminal penalties and other sanctions against counterfeiting in connection with the introduction of the euro) which is also based on Article 31(e) TEU (together with Article 34(2)(b)) clearly uses the concept of 'penalties' for punishments handed down in criminal proceedings.[98] Similarly, although constraints upon the market activities of persons convicted of serious crime might be justified to protect consumers, Article 153 EC on consumer protection[99] does not appear relevant: it is hard to see how exclusion of suppliers from public contracts, which by definition are contracts with public authorities rather than consumers, contributes to consumer protection except

---

[96] Part of Title IV of the Treaty on 'Visas, Asylum, Immigration and Other Policies Related to Free Movement of Persons'.

[97] OJ 2000 No. L140 /1.

[98] Cf. Council Framework Decision 2000/383 on increasing protection by criminal penalties and other sanctions against counterfeiting in connection with the introduction of the euro (OJ 2000 No. L140 /1), which is also based on Article 31(e) TEU (together with Article 34(2)(b)) and which provides for penalties in the context of criminal proceedings.

[99] Article 153(4) in conjunction with Article 153(3)(b).

in the most tenuous and tangential way.[100] What, however, of the 'back stop' provision in Article 308 EC? This appears problematic, since it can only apply where a measure is intended to attain one of the objectives of the Treaty. This means that it must be possible to 'connect' the exclusion from public contracts 'to one of the objectives which the Treaty entrusts to the Community',[101] stated in Articles 2 and 3 EC.[102] However, none of these objectives relate to the combating of crime or terrorism.[103]

In addition to the affirmative provisions in the general procurement directives, the Community has already adopted or proposed measures imposing obligations on authorities affecting energy/environmental aspects of their procurement activities.[104] In particular, as mentioned above, and as is discussed in detail in chapter 9, Directive 2006/32 on Energy End-use and Energy Services[105] imposes obligations on Member States to meet indicative energy efficiency targets in the public sector by taking measures listed in the directive, most of which relate to procurement decisions. Similarly, the proposed directive on the promotion of

---

[100] By discouraging enterprises from the offences in question and thus indirectly protecting consumers, to the limited extent that these offences affect consumers. The same objection would apply to Article 153(2) EC providing a legal base for EC measures to contribute to the Treaty's consumer protection objectives by supporting, supplementing and monitoring the policy pursued by the Member States. In any case these exclusions would seem to go beyond 'supporting' etc.

[101] Case T–306/01, *Yusuf* [2005] ECR II–3533, para. 137.

[102] *Ibid.*, para. 139.

[103] As regards terrorism see *Yusuf*, note 101 above, para. 152. It is true that in *Yusuf* the Court nonetheless held that the measure in question could be regarded as valid on the basis of a combination of Articles 60, 301 and 308 EC, but this was because Articles 60 and 301 EC are 'quite special provisions of the EC treaty' since they 'expressly contemplate situations in which action by the Community may be proved to be necessary in order to achieve, not one of the objectives of the Community as fixed by the EC Treaty, but rather one of the objectives specifically assigned to the [European] Union by Article 2 of the Treaty on European Union, viz., the implementation of a common foreign and security policy': *Yusuf*, para. 160 *et seq.* This consideration does not apply in the present case since Articles 60 and 301 EC relate to the interruption of economic relations with third countries pursuant to a common position or joint action under the Treaty on European Union.

[104] European Commission, Proposal for a Directive of the European Parliament and of the Council on the promotion of clean road transport vehicles, COM (2005) 634 final and the Proposal for a directive amending Directive 2002/91 on the energy performance of buildings. See European Commission, Communication Limiting Global Climate Change to 2 Degrees Celsius – The way ahead for 2020 and beyond ('Communication limiting global climate change'), COM (2007) 2 final, p. 12, section 6.3.

[105] Directive 2006/32/EC, note 67 above.

clean road transport vehicles[106] would require Member States to ensure that their contracting authorities procure 25 per cent of the heavy vehicles they purchase as 'clean' (in the sense of low polluting) vehicles, whilst Directive 2002/91 (on energy performance of buildings)[107] provides for improvement of the energy performance of buildings by laying down a framework for calculating buildings' energy performance and obliging Member States to provide for minimum energy efficiency requirements. Each of these measures is based on Article 175 EC, which is the Treaty base for measures intended to achieve the environmental objectives of the Community.[108]

In the social sphere McCrudden, in chapter 6, argues in favour of the existence of a right to equal treatment in the sense of status equality, and, as noted above, suggests that this might even be mirrored by a duty in the procurement context for public authorities to use procurement to advance such equality, given the importance of the equality provisions of the EC Treaty. Such a duty in the directives would, of course, need to be justified in terms of competence, just like any other Community horizontal policy. McCrudden argues that competence exists on the basis that provisions designed to enable particular categories of people to participate in the market can be justified by reference to the internal market legal base. The question here is whether such status equality measures can be regarded as designed to 'remove genuine obstacles to free movement or distortions of competition, not purely abstract risks', as required by the ECJ in *Tobacco Advertising*. Should the Community legislature wish to include more specific social policy measures in the procurement directives in future, it would need to consider whether the internal market provisions do indeed provide an adequate legal basis for such measures and, if not, whether there are other Treaty provisions that can do so.

6. The impact of EC law on Member States' discretion: principles of interpretation

In the analysis above we have so far elaborated two important principles relevant to interpreting the EC procurement regime as it affects

---

[106] European Commission, Proposal for a Directive of the European Parliament and of the Council on the promotion of clean road transport vehicles, COM (2005) 634 final and see Communication limiting global climate change, note 104 above.

[107] Directive 2002/91/EC of the European Parliament and of the Council on the energy performance of buildings, OJ 2003 No. L1/65.

[108] Which objectives are set out in Article 174 EC.

horizontal policies. The first is that the implementation of horizontal policies in public procurement is a legitimate activity that as a starting point should be treated on equal terms with other government policy-making. The second is that the basic discretion to determine the scope of horizontal policies and to balance them against other national policies lies with Member States: both potentially and actually the free movement provisions and main secondary legislation allow only for limited EC intervention, in order to prevent discrimination (including through transparency) and to remove certain obstacles to market access.

In this section, we highlight several further principles that are relevant and important from a legal perspective in addressing horizontal policies, both for the legislative activity of the EC and for judicial interpretation.

First, Article 6 EC provides that environmental protection requirements are to be integrated into the definition and implementation of other Community policies. Amongst other things, this principle can be used to support an interpretation that leaves a broad scope to Member States in implementing environmental objectives through procurement. As is elaborated in chapter 4 and in chapter 9 on energy policy, this has already been central in shaping ECJ jurisprudence. The Court has referred to this principle in interpreting both the Treaty and procurement directives, including in its broad interpretation of national discretion in *EVN-Wienstrom*, referred to above, and in its ruling in *Concordia Bus Finland*, also mentioned above, that certain environmental criteria may be used as contract award criteria under the directives.

Secondly, Article 3(2) EC requires that in all of its activities the Community 'shall aim to eliminate inequalities, and to promote equality, between men and women', and certain aspects of equality, including sex equality and also religious equality, have been recognised as amongst the fundamental rights protected by EC law.[109] McCrudden places significant weight on the status of equal treatment on these grounds as a fundamental principle of EC law in arguing for a broad interpretation of the discretion of Member States when implementing equality policies through procurement. He suggests also in chapter 6 that the principle might even be developed to impose an *obligation* to take into account issues of gender equality in procurement. His arguments on these points, insofar as they affect interpretation of the directives, are elaborated in chapter 6.

---

[109] See further chapter 6 of this book.

So far as Member State discretion is concerned, these provisions raise the possibility of a broader scope for some types of horizontal policies – those concerned with environmental and equality issues – than for others. For example, in *PreussenElektra*[110] a measure promoting renewable energy was held open to justification as a mandatory requirement under Article 30 EC even though it discriminated directly on grounds of nationality and the ECJ had previous held that directly discriminatory measures could not be justified. One possible rationale for this conclusion is that environmental measures are a special case because of Article 6 EC: both the ECJ and Advocate General Jacobs referred to Article 6, although neither made it clear whether environmental measures are a special category or whether the rule that directly discriminatory measures cannot be justified no longer applies.[111] Article 6 or the principle of equality might also be relied on to justify differential treatment under the directives: for example, it might be suggested that there is an exception to the principle in the Public Sector Directive that a supplier can only be excluded in advance for reasons set out in the directive for exclusions connected with contract requirements on environmental or equality issues.[112] The present authors, however, take the view that for most cases, at least, the other principles that we refer to in this chapter justify the broad interpretation of the scope for state discretion put forward in chapter 4, and that the rules on environmental and equality issues merely reinforce the case for a broad approach more generally.

---

[110] Case C–379/98, *PreussenElektra AG* v. *Schleswag AG* ('*PreussenElektra*') [2001] ECR I–2099.

[111] Advocate General Jacobs refers to Article 6 EC and indicates that this might justify treating environmental concerns on the same basis as the interests referred to in Article 36 EC, the original version of which was adopted when environmental concerns were not so significant (paras. 231–232 of the Opinion). The ECJ also mentions Article 6 as one of several considerations that together lead it to the final conclusion that justification is possible (para. 76 of the judgment).

[112] See chapter 4, sections 8.1.6 and 10.2. Such an approach is consistent with the ECJ judgment in Joined Cases C21/03 and C–34/03, *Fabricom* v. *État Belge* [2005] ECR I–1559, which permitted exclusion to ensure equal treatment from a commercial perspective (preventing conflict of interest that might give one party a commercial advantage in tendering or affect the neutrality of specifications). McCrudden, in chapter 6, in arguing that this principle justifies a broad interpretation of the term 'subject matter' of the contract, also does not appear to differentiate between different policy areas for this purpose. However, this might be possible – for example, exclusions to implement certain policies only might be accepted. It is not clear whether McCrudden shares the authors' perspective set out in the text, or whether he would consider certain types of equality to constitute a special case.

A principle of more general relevance that is important for horizontal policies is subsidiarity. Under the second paragraph of Article 5 EC this principle provides that, 'in areas which do not fall within its exclusive competence, the Community shall take action, in accordance with the principle of subsidiarity, only if and in so far as the objectives of the proposed action cannot be sufficiently achieved by the Member States and can therefore, by reason of the scale or effects of the proposed action, be better achieved by the Community'. The principle regulates the scope for legislative action under the Treaty's internal market provisions.[113] As chapter 2 explains, Advocate General Sharpston has invoked it in interpreting the impact of the Treaty's free movement provisions on public procurement,[114] specifically to deny a detailed EC-level transparency obligation for low-value contracts, and it is also relevant for interpreting the procurement directives. Finally, another principle of general significance is proportionality. Like subsidiarity, it regulates the exercise of the EC's legislative powers. In this respect Article 5 EC provides: 'an action by the Community shall not go beyond what is necessary to achieve the objectives of this Treaty'. This principle is also relevant for interpreting EC secondary measures. The authors are not aware of any case in which proportionality has been used as a guiding principle in interpreting the EC Treaty itself. Hartley, however, points out[115] that Article 220 of the EC Treaty provides that 'the Court of Justice shall ensure that in the interpretation and application of this Treaty the law is observed' and if by 'the law' is meant some body of principles outside the Treaty itself (for example, the general principles of law) that might imply that the Treaty could be interpreted in light of the proportionality principle.

These principles and those discussed earlier in the chapter all tend to point to a limited, rather than an intrusive, approach to regulating horizontal policies in public procurement. Chapter 4 examines the way in which these principles may affect the interpretation of Community law in relation to specific issues, and argues that the individual or cumulative effect of these principles supports the existence of a broad national discretion for Member States at several levels. For example, in relation to the Treaty, they are relevant to the suggested conclusion that

---

[113] Case C–376/98, *Germany* v. *Parliament and Council*, note 58 above. See more generally Case C–114/01, *AvestaPolarit Chrome Oy* [2003] ECR I–8725, para. 55.

[114] Case C–195/04, *Commission* v. *Finland*, opinion of 18 January 2007, para. 88.

[115] T. Hartley, *The Foundations of European Community Law: an Introduction to the Constitutional and Administrative Law of the European Community*, 6th edn (Oxford University Press, 2007), p. 132.

measures regulating behaviour outside the contract may be justified, and also to the possibility of justifying measures directed at conduct in another state.[116] In relation to the directives these principles are similarly invoked to support various liberal interpretations including supporting the possibility of: including contract terms concerning the way in which products are produced;[117] using award criteria relating to workforce issues (such as employment of persons with disabilities);[118] excluding suppliers that cannot comply with conditions on workforce matters;[119] and excluding criminal convictions for reasons unrelated to future contract performance.[120]

7. The relationship between primary and secondary Community law: using the directives to interpret the Treaty?

A question of increasing importance in public procurement is the extent to which the ECJ will draw on EC secondary legislation adopted to interpret the Treaty itself, an approach labelled by Treumer and Werlauff as the leverage principle.[121] As they have explained, the ECJ has sometimes used the technical and legal solutions provided in secondary legislation (or proposed legislation) to develop Treaty rules in an extensive way and such that the Court would have reached a different solution in the absence of the secondary legislation. This approach seeks to address objections concerning the impact of the Treaty on Member States' interests by incorporating into primary law the solutions that states have accepted in secondary instruments. In procurement this approach has been used most notably in *Telaustria*[122] and subsequent jurisprudence, discussed in chapter 2, in which the ECJ has drawn inspiration from the procurement directives to hold that the Treaty implies certain 'positive obligations' of transparency applying not only to contracts under the directives but also to other major procurements, such as concessions, that are outside the directives.

This approach has been followed to justify *imposing* specific obligations, as in *Telaustria*. We will see in chapter 2 that in its

---

[116] See chapter 4, section 4.3.1.   [117] See chapter 4, section 8.1.6.
[118] See chapter 4, section 13.   [119] See chapter 4, section 8.1.6.
[120] See chapter 4, section 10.2.
[121] S. Treumer and E. Werlauff, 'The Leverage Principle: Secondary Community Law as a Lever for the Development of Primary Community Law' (2003) 28 *ELRev* 124.
[122] Case C–324/98, *Telaustria* v. *Telekom Austria* ('*Telaustria*') [2000] ECR I–10745; and see also the more recent principle of equal treatment, discussed in chapter 2, section 3.3.

Communications interpreting these 'positive' Treaty obligations the Commission has suggested that the Treaty imposes extensive obligations, parallel to those in the directives. The leverage principle has also been used to define the specific content of those obligations: thus, it appears that derogations to advertising under the procurement directives (for example, for cases of urgency) also set the limits to the Treaty's advertising obligations.[123] On the other hand, it is less clear whether other limitations imposed by the secondary legislator will be accepted: in particular, how far positive Treaty obligations will apply, as is argued by the Commission, to low-value contracts that the legislator deliberately excluded from the directives as being of limited cross-border interest.[124] However, in *Commission v. Finland*[125] Advocate General Sharpston invoked the subsidiarity principle to suggest that the Treaty's positive obligations do not generally apply to individual low-value contracts, given that this contravenes the legislative intention expressed in the relevant secondary instrument.[126]

Based on the same principle of subsidiarity, the leverage principle might potentially also be used to set *limits* to the Treaty's application. Thus, where secondary legislators have deliberately declined to regulate an area, the ECJ could take the view that comparable Treaty obligations, also, should not apply – not merely (as with the derogations example above) to set limits on obligations that would *not* otherwise apply, but actually to limit obligations that *might* otherwise apply. For example, the ECJ has ruled that 'in-house' arrangements – that is, arrangements within a public authority rather than with an outside undertaking – are not regulated contracts either under the directives or under the EC Treaty.[127] In the authors' view, the width of the directives' explicit exemptions for certain arrangements with associated companies, notably a Utilities Directive exemption for contracts awarded to related 'affiliated

---

[123] See, e.g., the opinion of AG Stix–Hackl in Case C–231/03, *Consorzio Aziende Metano (Coname)* v. *Comune di Cingia de' Botti* [2005] ECR I–7287, para. 79; opinion of AG Jacobs in Case C–525/03, *Commission* v. *Italy* [2005] ECR I–9405, paras. 40–49; opinion of AG Sharpston in Case C–195/04, *Commission* v. *Finland* [2007] ECR I–3351, para. 76.

[124] Arguably the case of concessions arising in *Telaustria* itself is different on the basis that that exclusion was not based on a balance of internal market considerations and other legitimate interests.

[125] Case C–324/98, *Telaustria*, note 122 above.

[126] In that case Directive 93/36 on public supply contracts, a predecessor to the Public Sector Directive: para. 88 of the Opinion.

[127] Case C–107/98, *Teckal Srl* v. *Comune di Viano* [1999] ECR I–8121.

undertakings',[128] should be taken into account in defining 'in-house' entities under the Treaty. However, the procurement jurisprudence so far tends towards rejecting this approach.[129]

In the authors' view the ECJ should be very wary of using the leverage principle to create obligations. One reason, emphasised by Treumer and Werlauff, is the legal uncertainty this can create. Another is the relatively permanent character of the Treaty, and the difficulties of amending it. This is particularly important in an area such as public procurement, where both practices and values may change rapidly, as illustrated by the need to introduce extensive revisions to the directives in 2004, and, in the context of this book, the rapidly evolving importance of environmental considerations in public procurement. To develop detailed obligations from general Treaty provisions by judicial interpretation presents the danger of adherence to detailed models that may rapidly become obsolete. On the other hand, it seems more justified to draw inspiration from secondary legislation to *limit* intervention under the Treaty, since if circumstances change in such a way as to warrant more extensive restrictions, this can be done through new secondary legislation.

This issue of the relationship between primary and secondary legislation is potentially important for horizontal considerations in public procurement. The ECJ has yet to clarify how far the various detailed rules of the procurement directives on horizontal policies also apply under the Treaty, but it is possible that, by virtue of the leverage principle, some of these rules will influence the ECJ's interpretation of the free movement provisions. This means, first, that the directives' restrictions on implementing social and environmental policies, which we will see in chapter 4 are quite considerable, might be imported into the Treaty. For example, the ECJ might take the view that the directives' explicit requirements for award criteria and contract conditions to relate to the subject matter/performance of the contract[130] merely reflect the Treaty, with the result that award criteria and conditions for *all* contracts are restricted to those relating to the subject matter (at least when directly or indirectly

---

[128] Article 23 of the Utilities Directive.
[129] See Case C–26/03, *Stadt Halle, RPL Recyclingpark Lochau GmbH* v. *TREA Leuna* [2005] ECR I–1 and Case C–503/04, *Commission* v. *Germany*, ECJ judgment of 18 July 2007, indicating that the rules of secondary legislation in the procurement Remedies Directives (as to which see chapter 2, section 4.1) do not affect the scope of the Treaty, nor the relationship between the Commission and Member States.
[130] See chapter 4, section 8.1.5 and section 13.

discriminatory).[131] At present it is difficult to predict to what extent this will happen, although we have suggested that the ECJ should be wary of doing this. In addition, the ECJ might be reluctant to reject practices that the secondary legislator has assumed to be acceptable, even when these are quite restrictive – for example, set asides for workshops for disabled persons (which are discussed in chapter 7). This, we suggested above, is more justifiable.

8. Conclusions

In this chapter we have introduced the concept of horizontal policies in public procurement. We have also explored a number of general themes and principles that are pertinent to this issue under EC law.

So far as concerns limits on the discretion of Member States, we have argued, in particular, that there are a number of legal principles that, taken together, favour a restrictive rather than intrusive approach to regulation. These are: the equal status of national horizontal policies and other procurement policies (such as value for money); the principle that the discretion to determine horizontal policies and to balance them against other policies (including other procurement policies) lies with Member States; the principle of subsidiarity; and the principle of proportionality. In the particular areas of environmental policy and equality policy we have also seen that the above general principles are supplemented by the Treaty requirement to integrate environmental considerations into Community action and the fundamental principle of equality. Some of the ways in which these principles may and should, in our view, affect interpretation of EC law are elaborated in chapter 4. They also feature prominently in other chapters in this book, both those of the present authors (chapters 9 and 11) and those of others (for example, chapter 6 on equality), although it should be stressed that our views are not necessarily shared by all the authors of the individual chapters. Some of these principles are also relevant to another important issue considered in the present chapter, namely the relationship between primary and secondary Community law. Here we have counselled against importing restrictions from secondary procurement law too readily into primary law.

---

[131] The position of non-discriminatory horizontal requirements depends on whether or not the ECJ treats these as hindrances to trade or involving different treatment of comparable suppliers, as to which see chapter 2, section 3.1.

It is worth mentioning that the present authors in fact maintain different views on the merits of public procurement as a policy tool for national governments, and indeed for the EC itself, in light of the interests considered in chapter 3. At the risk of oversimplification, it can be said that, with limited exceptions, Arrowsmith is sceptical of its value in view of the difficulties of implementing horizontal policies in an effective and balanced way in the real world, whilst Kunzlik is in general more sympathetic. However, this difference does not lead to a divergence of views between us on the appropriate interpretation of EC law, given our common view on the rules and principles discussed in this chapter, as well as our common view on the marginal impact of many of these policies on trade and the problems with judicial scrutiny at EC level, as elaborated in chapter 2. In general, these considerations indicate that the decisions on the value to be given to horizontal policies and how they are to be balanced with other concerns are to be made at Member State level.

A second dimension of Community procurement policy is the possibility for the EC itself to harness Member States' procurement towards Community goals. In this respect, we have also explored the limits on Community action. Here we have stressed that the EC may not itself act to require or encourage use of procurement as a policy tool except within the legal limits of the EC Treaty, which places significant limits on the possibilities for action. Nevertheless, there is scope for Community action in some areas, especially in relation to environmental matters, and the affirmative use of procurement in this particular area is likely to play an increasingly important role.

EC regulation of public procurement

SUE ARROWSMITH AND PETER KUNZLIK

1. Introduction

In this chapter we turn to an overview of the main legal rules applying to EC public procurement. This chapter serves merely as an introduction; the detailed application of the rules to horizontal policies is examined in chapter 4.

EC law takes a graduated approach to regulation, such that we may divide procurement into three categories. The first covers procurement that is outside the EC Treaty altogether, the second procurement that is within the Treaty but outside the procurement directives, and the third procurement within the directives. We will consider each in turn.

2. Procurement outside the scope of the Treaty

A procurement that is outside the EC Treaty is not subject to EC regulation at all. In the context of public contracts, particularly important in this regard is Article 296(1)(b) EC, which excludes from the Treaty certain measures relating to 'the production of or trade in arms, munitions, and war material'. This takes outside the Treaty – and thereby also the procurement directives – public contracts for 'hard defence material' such as weapons and tanks, provided, however, that there is a security justification for exclusion.[1]

---

[1] Case C–24/91, *Commission* v. *Spain* [1992] ECR I–1989, and see European Commission, Interpretative Communication on the application of Article 296 of the Treaty in the field of defence procurement, COM (2006) 779 final. Article 296(1) EC does not exclude other equipment procured by the armed forces. See S. Arrowsmith, *The Law of Public and Utilities Procurement*, 2nd edn (London: Sweet & Maxwell, 2005), at 4.59 *et seq.*; A. Georgopoulos, 'Defence Procurement and EU Law' (2005) 30 *ELRev* 559; M. Trybus, *European Union Law and Defence Integration* (Oxford: Hart, 2005). On recent EC/EU policy in regulating hard defence procurement, see European Commission, Communication to the Council and the European Parliament on the results of the consultation launched by the Green Paper on Defence Procurement and on the future Commission initiatives, COM (2005)

3. Procurement within the Treaty but outside the procurement directives

Contracts within the scope of the Treaty may be outside the procurement directives, either because they are below the financial thresholds or because they are excluded by reason of their subject matter. In such cases the procurement will nonetheless be subject to the EC Treaty and to general principles of Community law derived therefrom.

Although the Treaty does not include provisions specifically dealing with Member States' procurement[2] it generally guarantees the free movement of goods (Article 28), freedom of establishment (Article 43), and freedom to provide services (Article 49), including in public procurement.[3]

We will first examine the impact of these provisions under the well-established principle that they prohibit 'negative' measures – such as preferences for national suppliers – that restrict access to public procurement. We will see, however, that whilst this basic principle is well-established, its application in the context of public procurement presents special difficulties that are significant for, inter alia, horizontal policies, but have not yet been much explored in the literature or jurisprudence.

Having considered this first aspect of the free movement rules, we will then consider certain more novel developments relating to transparency and equal treatment. These indicate, in particular, that the free movement rules also imply certain 'positive' obligations of advertising, competition etc. to support market access.

The other main Treaty provisions[4] affecting horizontal policies, those on state aid, are examined separately in chapter 5.

---

626 final; European Defence Agency, Code of Conduct on Defence Procurement of the EU Member States Participating in the European Defence Agency (November 2005), available at www.eda.eu.int; A. Georgopoulos, 'The New European Defence Agency: Major Development or Fig Leaf?' (2005) 14 *PPLR* 103; A. Georgopoulos, 'The European Defence Agency's Code of Conduct for Armament Acquisitions: A Case of Paramnesia?' (2006) 15 *PPLR* 51. See also Article 197 EC.

[2] Although Article 183(4) deals with contracts financed by the EC in overseas countries and Article 163(2) provides for the EC to encourage enterprises to exploit opportunities from liberalisation of the public contracts market.

[3] See also Arrowsmith, note 1 above, chapter 4.

[4] Other provisions affecting public procurement include Article 86 EC (see Arrowsmith, note 1 above, at 4.51–4.58) and Articles 81 (anti-competitive agreements and concerted practices) and 82 (abuse of a dominant position): see Arrowsmith, note 1 above, at 2.53–2.56.

3.1. 'Negative' obligations

3.1.1. Free movement of goods

Article 28 EC on free movement of goods prohibits 'all quantitative restrictions on imports and all measures having equivalent effect' between Member States, the latter including all trading rules 'which are capable of hindering, directly or indirectly, actually or potentially, intra-Community trade'.[5] Article 28 applies to measures that refer to the government contracts market as well as to measures affecting the domestic market as a whole. It applies to goods supplied under any public contracts, whether primarily for the supply of goods, or primarily for works or services.[6]

The concept of 'measures' in general only encompasses general laws and practices.[7] However, although the point has not been specifically addressed, the ECJ has consistently *assumed* that the Treaty (including Article 28) applies to individual procurement decisions, such as specific contract awards.[8] It is questionable whether this is correct: it is hard to see that procurement should be different in this respect from other governmental activity.[9] However, this approach may have been adopted to allow the ECJ to deal with states that do not regulate procurement through formal rules, but restrict access to the market through persistent practices that may be hard to prove. We will see below that Advocate General Sharpston[10] has recently contemplated that a distinction between individual contracts and general measures may be relevant in applying the Treaty to low-value contracts, so that at least many small contracts will be excluded from individual scrutiny. It would be more appropriate, however, and consistent with general EC law, to consider only general practices as within Article 28.

---

[5] Case 8/74, *Procureur du Roi* v. *Dassonville* [1974] ECR 837.

[6] Case 45/87, *Commission* v. *Ireland* ('*Dundalk*') [1988] ECR 4929.

[7] Case 21/84, *Commission* v. *France* [1985] ECR 1356.

[8] It did so, for example, in Case C–3/88, *Commission* v. *Italy* ('*Re Data Processing*') [1989] ECR 4035 (Article 49 – services); Case C–243/89, *Commission* v. *Denmark* ('*Storebaelt*') [1993] ECR I–3353 (Article 28 – goods); Case C–359/93, *Commission* v. *Netherlands* ('*UNIX*') [1995] ECR I–157 (Article 28 – goods); Case 59/00, *Bent Mousten Vestergaard* v. *Spottrup Boligselskab* ('*Bent Mousten*') [2001] ECR I–9505 (Article 28 – goods); and Case C–324/98, Case C–324/98, *Telaustria Verlags GmbH and Telefonadress GmbH* v. *Telekom Austria AG* ('*Telaustria*') [2000] ECR I–10745.

[9] Arrowsmith, note 1 above, at 4.5–4.6.

[10] In Case C–195/04, *Commission* v. *Finland*, Opinion of 18 January 2007, discussed in section 3.1.2 below.

Article 28 does not merely prohibit discrimination on grounds of nationality, but prohibits 'restrictions' on imports and 'measures having equivalent effect'. If national measures are equivalent in effect to restrictions on imports they may be prohibited if: (a) they discriminate directly against imports as compared to domestic goods;[11] (b) they discriminate indirectly against imports in that, although facially neutral, they in practice have the effect of favouring domestic goods;[12] or (c) even though they do not discriminate (directly or indirectly) against imported goods they nonetheless hinder or restrict imports (for example, even though they restrict domestic products equally).[13] We will examine these three categories separately, focusing, in particular, on the particularities of public procurement that have not been addressed systematically by the ECJ or the literature.[14] Whilst jurisprudence and academic analysis has moved increasingly away from analysing measures in these categories, we will continue to use them since (as we elaborate below) we believe they still have significance for procurement.

Direct discrimination Procurement measures that discriminate directly between imported and domestic goods, by applying different rules to each will generally constitute hindrances to trade under Article 28 EC. An example is provided by *Du Pont de Nemours*[15] in which an Italian law required public bodies to obtain at least 30 per cent of their supplies from certain enterprises established in Southern Italy. As discussed in chapter 4, this infringed Article 28 EC.[16] It seems likely that *all* directly discriminatory measures are hindrances to trade requiring justification. We suggest below that certain procurement measures that place imports at a disadvantage will often fall outside Article 28,

---

[11] See, for example, Case C–263/85, *Commission* v. *Italy* [1991] I–2457 and Case C–21/88, *Du Pont de Nemours Italiana SpA* v. *Unita Sanitaria Locale No 2 Di Carrara* (*'Du Pont de Nemours'*) [1990] ECR I–889.

[12] See, for example, Case 45/47, *Dundalk*, note 6 above.

[13] Case 120/78, *Rewe-Zentrale* v. *Bundesmonopolverwaltung für Branntwein* (*'Cassis de Dijon'*) [1979] ECR 649.

[14] Although this chapter draws on previous analysis of some of these points concerning negative measures in procurement in Arrowsmith, note 1 above, chapter 4.

[15] Case C–21/88, *Du Pont de Nemours*, note 11 above.

[16] *Ibid.*, para. 13. The ECJ considered that such a measure was not justified: see chapter 4, section 3. For further examples of directly discriminatory procurement measures, see Case C–263/85, *Commission* v. *Italy*, note 11 above (national measures requiring contracting authorities to purchase vehicles of domestic manufacture as a condition of eligibility for subsidies); Case C–243/89, *Storebaelt*, note 8 above (clause in a Danish construction contract requiring the use of Danish materials).

including measures concerning the nature and characteristics of products to be purchased. However, even if this is the case, these types of measures will be caught, it is submitted, if they are *directly* discriminatory. Thus, for example, the EFTA court in *Fagtún*[17] – concerning a specification requiring roofing material to be produced in Iceland, purportedly to ensure that it was adequate for Icelandic weather – seemed to assume that all directly discriminatory measures relating to products supplied are hindrances to trade that require justification to be compatible with the Treaty.[18]

Indirect discrimination   As with other government measures, many procurement decisions that have a greater impact on imported products than domestic products will be characterised as hindrances to trade. An example is seen in *Dundalk*.[19] This case concerned a specification requiring pipes for construction works to conform to an Irish standard. This applied to domestic and imported products alike, but had a greater impact on imported products because in practice only one firm, an Irish firm, produced pipes complying with the standard; and it was regarded as involving indirect discrimination that was a hindrance to trade. In chapter 4 we will see that measures concerning the contract workforce that have a greater impact on non-domestic suppliers are also regarded as hindrances to trade, as are restrictions on access to suppliers that implement horizontal policies – for example, preferences for companies whose main operations are in the area of the works procured.[20]

We suggest, however, that some types of procurement decisions are not hindrances to trade even when they have a greater impact on non-domestic products. We will refer to these as 'excluded buying decisions'.

First, we suggest that this is the case for initial decisions on whether to go ahead with an activity – for example, whether to build a public library rather than use the funds for other purposes.[21] Secondly, we suggest this also applies to decisions on what exactly to purchase to meet a

---

[17] Case E–5/98, *Fagtún* v. *Byggingarnefend Borgarholtsskola, the Government of Iceland, the City of Reykjavik and the Municipality of Mosfellsbaer* [1999] EFTA Court Report 51; [1999] 2 CMLR 960.

[18] Although in fact the Court did not seem to regard its directly discriminatory nature as essential to its conclusion that a hindrance existed: see para. 38 of the Advisory Opinion.

[19] Case 45/87, *Dundalk*, note 6 above.

[20] Case C–360/89, *Commission* v. *Italy* [1992] ECR I–3401.

[21] Which could be regarded as benefiting domestic industry more than foreign industry since the economic opportunities from domestic work are likely to be greater than for industry from other Member States even under conditions of genuine EC-wide competition.

requirement – for example, whether to purchase helicopters rather than lifeboats for sea rescue. Here it can be said that the measures do not restrict access to the market, but merely establish what that market is, and thus are not hindrances to trade. In support of this, or as an alternative, it can be argued that there is no discrimination or other unequal treatment: the prohibition on discrimination on grounds of nationality under Article 28 is one manifestation of the equal treatment principle, and suppliers able to supply the authority's requirements are not in a position that is comparable to those who cannot. On the other hand, in the rare cases where decisions on how to meet a requirement are taken out of protectionist *motives* (or appear unrelated to their purported aims) they should be considered as hindrances to trade, since they are then disguised restrictions on access to an existing market.[22]

In addition, we suggest that substantive decisions concerning the features of products procured are also decisions that establish the market rather than restrict access to it, and thus are not hindrances to trade. Again, there is no discrimination or unequal treatment, since suppliers who cannot meet the requirements of the market are not in a comparable position with those who can. Thus the mere fact that a purchaser insists on substantive product characteristics, such as environmental features, which are more common in domestic than imported products, should not be regarded as hindering trade.[23] This reasoning finds support in *Concordia Bus Finland*, discussed below.

Dundalk was, of course, itself a case on product specifications. However, it was a special case, in that products not complying with the standard were excluded from the market even if they were *exactly* equivalent in material respects (quality etc.). Such cases do, it is submitted, involve restrictions on market access: the government is excluding products that meet its needs. By contrast, however, when a government merely sets substantive requirements, such as quality standards, and admits any products that meet them, these should not be treated as a hindrance to trade. Thus if in *Dundalk* the authority had indicated that it would accept pipes made to the Irish standard *or equivalent*, there would be no hindrance to trade. This principle is relevant not merely for specifications on product characteristics

---

[22] As explained in chapter 3, such decisions are sometimes, in practice, influenced by horizontal considerations connected with the development of national industry (they correspond to category 2 in the taxonomy of policy mechanisms set out in chapter 3) and in this case may fall to be justified under the Treaty.

[23] See also, previously, Arrowsmith, note 1 above, at 17.8 *et seq.*

the products in question on safety grounds: rather, they seemed to consider that the authority was required to accept the products as fit for the use in question.[34] Even if the ruling goes further than merely requiring the authority to accept its own specification, however, it might be justified by the specific context of the Medical Devices Directive in establishing harmonised standards that can be rejected by Member States and their authorities only in accordance with the directive's explicit safeguard procedure, and does not necessarily imply that specifications in general are hindrances to trade. Thus the ECJ stated that 'not only the wording of ... Directive 93/32 but also the purpose of the harmonization system established by it preclude a contracting authority from being entitled to reject, outside that safeguard procedure and on grounds of technical inadequacy, medical devices which are certified as being in compliance with the essential requirements provided for by that directive'.[35] The fact that specifications are not generally to be considered as obstacles to trade is reinforced by the fact that the ECJ bases its ruling on this point specifically on the principles of transparency and equal treatment, rather than by referring to restrictions on trade.[36]

If, as suggested, certain 'buying' decisions – 'excluded buying decisions' – are not in principle hindrances to trade, the question arises as to *precisely* which ones. It was suggested above that decisions on *whether or not* to make a purchase, and on *what* to purchase, are excluded buying decisions. So are decisions concerning the 'consumption' characteristics of products, as in *Concordia Bus Finland*. However, it is not clear whether the ECJ would apply this approach to certain other types of decision relating to the contract – other decisions that might be labelled 'buying' decisions – that we referred to in chapter 1, namely decisions concerning production and delivery, or disposal by the supplier.[37] Possibly it would be reluctant to do so, given that some of these measures could in fact have a significant impact on trade – for example, requirements concerning the carbon footprint of products (which could

---

[34] AG Sharpston was explicit about this (paras. 78–79 of the Opinion and para. 123 of the Opinion) and it seems to be implied by the ECJ's reasoning that it would be necessary to invoke the public health derogation to buy products considered by the authority to be safe pending completion of the safeguard procedure in which the Commission would judge this issue.

[35] Para. 50 of the judgment.   [36] Para. 55 of the judgment.

[37] A requirement to manufacture the product in such a way as to ensure efficient disposal (which could be by the authority itself) should be considered to be a consumption characteristic that should not be treated as a hindrance to trade.

significantly favour local production) or requirements to limit pollution in production, which could effectively require production changes affecting a whole factory. So far as concerns the other category of decisions relating to the contract that was mentioned in chapter 1, namely those concerning the contract workforce, the jurisprudence indicates that these *are* hindrances to trade when they are harder to meet for firms for other Member States than for domestic firms. Thus in *Beentjes*[38] and in *Nord Pas de Calais*[39] (cases discussed further in chapter 4) the ECJ stated that award criteria and conditions concerning the use of the long-term unemployed on government contracts could constitute indirect discrimination that violated the Treaty if they were harder for non-domestic suppliers to meet. In addition, the ECJ's ruling in *Contse*,[40] discussed below, suggests that all measures concerning the nature of the supplier, rather than the product or service, may fall to be treated as hindrances to trade where they have a greater impact on non-domestic firms. In that case, which concerned a contract to provide home respiratory treatment and other assisted breathing techniques, the Court considered that various conditions and criteria concerning the provision of the service were hindrances to trade under Article 49 EC that could not be justified. It also seems likely that all procurement decisions unrelated to contract performance – for example, decisions excluding suppliers that invest in particular countries – will be hindrances to trade, in that their effects are akin to the kind of regulatory measures clearly caught under Article 28 (although these effects will be more limited when confined to individual contracts or small numbers of contracts).

It might be objected that the proposed approach endorses a distinction between horizontal policies and 'commercial' policies, with the latter being treated more leniently, contrary to our contention in chapter 1 that the two groups of policies should be treated on an equal footing. However, whilst most policies of the latter type will indeed escape justification and most of the former probably will not, the suggested approach is not based on a distinction of this kind per se, and nor does it result from affording a greater value to commercial policies; it is based on directly relevant, and quite different, policy considerations affecting the respective measures, relating to their impact on trade and the costs

---

[38] Case 31/87, *Gebroeders Beentjes BV* v. *Netherlands* ('*Beentjes*') [1988] ECR 4635.

[39] Case C–225/98, *Commission* v. *France* ('*Nord Pas de Calais*') [2000] ECR I–7445.

[40] Case C–234/03, *Contse SA, Vivisol Srl & Oxigen Salud SA* v. *Instituto Nacional de Gestión Sanitaria (Ingesa)* ('*Contse*') [2005] ECR I–9315.

and suitability of judicial scrutiny of decisions. The suggested distinction also does not imply that horizontal policies should be subject to strict limitations. In fact, it is invoked not to limit national discretion, but rather to *reject* limitations that might otherwise apply to certain procurement decisions, including some relating to social or environmental policies.

It might also be objected that the proposed approach involves uncertain distinctions between different kinds of procurement measures – relating respectively to consumption, production and delivery effects, disposal effects, and workforce conditions – that sometimes have arbitrary effects. Whilst this is a valid point, our approach is still preferable to the alternatives of either substantial judicial intervention in procurement decisions or leaving them free from scrutiny. Chapter 4 suggests that similar distinctions should *not*, however, be made in the context of other EC rules, notably in considering whether purchasers should be able to exclude in advance suppliers that are not able to meet certain social conditions;[41] and we suggest below that a similar distinction also is inappropriate in applying the grounds of justification to procurement policies that *are* hindrances to trade.

To the extent that the ECJ does not ultimately accept our argument for restricted scrutiny of certain procurement measures with a greater impact on imports, under our doctrine of 'excluded buying decisions' similar arguments can still be made for excluding those same measures from the Treaty when they are *not* discriminatory. This issue is considered under the next heading below.

Non-discriminatory measures In some cases measures are hindrances to trade under Article 28 even when they have an equal impact on domestic and imported products. We will refer to these as non-discriminatory measures.[42] The application of Article 28 to non-discriminatory procurement measures is both uncertain and problematic, including for horizontal policies. The importance of this question depends on whether the ECJ accepts our doctrine of excluded buying decisions: if many procurement measures, such as specifications and award criteria concerning product

---

[41] See chapter 4, section 8.

[42] This is convenient shorthand. It should be pointed out, however, that not all measures that cannot be characterised as 'discriminatory' or unequal in their application are in this category – measures that are unequal in their application to domestic and imported products but immune from scrutiny as 'excluded buying decisions' as discussed in the previous section, 'Indirect discrimination', are in a separate category.

characteristics, are not hindrances to trade, the potential impact of the Treaty on non-discriminatory measures will be much less significant than if they are. However, even if the ECJ does accept this doctrine, the treatment of non-discriminatory measures is important for many types of measures not covered by that doctrine – for example, measures governing the contract workforce, measures concerning the qualifications of suppliers, and horizontal measures beyond the contract. This includes, for example, increasingly important provisions on labour conditions in third countries, which may well have an equal impact on domestic and imported products.

At one time the ECJ appeared to be developing a principle that Article 28 applies to *all* national measures that might restrict imports, notwithstanding that they affect domestic products de jure and de facto in exactly the same way. However, this position was reconsidered following the ECJ's decision in *Keck*.[43] Without modification this position would have potentially subjected every element of domestic regulation of markets to challenge if, however non-discriminatory, the rule might adversely affect the actual or potential flow of imports, significantly affecting the remaining regulatory autonomy of Member States while clogging the courts, including the ECJ, with cases having little connection to intra-Community trade. As is well known, the ECJ addressed this problem in *Keck*, and in its following jurisprudence, by distinguishing between domestic measures hindering trade that relate to the characteristics of the products in question, which are covered by Article 28 whether discriminatory or not, and those which merely relate to 'selling arrangements' – for example, rules on opening hours of retail outlets – which will not infringe Article 28 when non-discriminatory.

However, the *Keck* distinction is problematic for several reasons. These arise, in part, from the fact that it is too closely tailored to the specific problem faced in *Keck* and similar cases to serve as the basis of a more general re-calibration of the application of Article 28, including for procurement cases.

First, it fails to reflect the fact that some measures relating to 'selling arrangements', such as restrictions on advertising, restrict marketing of imports more than many rules on product characteristics. The Court may possibly be moving towards a 'more nuanced approach' to 'selling arrangements', whereby they may be caught if they substantially restrict

---

[43] Note 25 above.

access of imports.[44] Advocate General Jacobs has suggested[45] that Article 28 applies to measures involving a *substantial* restriction on market access for imports and that this should be presumed for measures related to the characteristics of products but not for 'selling arrangements'.

Secondly, whilst potentially liberating from Article 28 'selling arrangements' that *may* significantly restrict imports, the *Keck* approach does not liberate other measures that actually have little effect, actual or potential, on imports. Arguably these should not be regulated, since the costs in terms of, first, national sovereignty and, secondly, litigation (including use of ECJ resources) outweigh any benefits for the single market. This is important for public procurement because, if the Court is right that individual procurement decisions are 'measures' under Article 28, many procurement decisions may have no substantial impact, actual or potential, on intra-Community trade. In fact, their effect may be even less than that of the 'selling arrangement' measures which the *Keck* jurisprudence sought to exclude from Article 28. This could be the case, for example, with a requirement for certain design features in an individual building that would better accommodate disabled persons, or a procurement to develop a prototype of a new type of environmentally-friendly vehicle. On the other hand, it must be acknowledged that many procurement measures – including horizontal policies that go beyond the contract, and those that are applied to a range of government procurements – could have a significant trade impact.

It was suggested in the previous section on indirect discrimination that, in line with the approach in *Concordia Bus Finland*, many procurement measures (which we called 'excluded buying decisions') are not hindrances to trade even when they involve a greater burden for imports, for some of the same reasons that lie behind the *Keck* jurisprudence on non-discriminatory measures, namely to avoid a disproportionate burden on the courts, to ensure commercial certainty, and to achieve a suitable balance between trade considerations and national sovereignty. A fortiori, *non-discriminatory* 'buying decisions' should not be treated as hindrances to trade. Further, the award of *every* contract to a tenderer necessarily involves the hindrance or exclusion of other tenderers, or of the works, goods or services they might have supplied. That is the whole

---

[44] Case C–405/98, *Konsumentombudsmannen (KO)* v. *Gourmet International Products AB* [2001] ECR I–1795.
[45] In Case C–412/93, *Société d'Importation Edouard Leclerc-Siplec* v. *TFI Publicité SA* [1995] ECR I–179.

point of competitive procurement – the selection of one product/service or supplier rather than another. If the mere fact that such imports are 'hindered' in this way is enough to trigger Article 28 then *every* procurement decision is prima facie 'prohibited' and requires justification as a step towards exclusion, in spite of the fact that the very point of competitive procurement is ultimately to exclude all but the successful products and suppliers.

In light of these concerns, even if the ECJ were to decide, contrary to the approach in *Concordia Bus Finland*, not to recognise a category of 'excluded buying decisions' and to review procurement measures in general, including contract specifications, it should not, it is submitted, extend this to non-discriminatory buying decisions. Further, the policy considerations just outlined justify excluding *all* non-discriminatory measures from review when these relate to the goods, works or services under the contract, including measures relating to supplier qualifications and measures concerning the contract workforce (which we suggested earlier are not in the 'excluded buying decisions category' when discriminatory in effect). If it is appropriate to regulate non-discriminatory measures, the legislator should adopt detailed rules that provide for legal certainty – as it has done with major contracts in the directives.

As with measures that are discriminatory in effect, these policy considerations against review of non-discriminatory measures would be less weighty if judicial scrutiny were confined merely to procurement measures of a general nature, or (although much less so) at least to individual contracts above the directives' thresholds. However, as suggested above, even if this were the case, the arguments regarding the limited expertise of the ECJ in commercial and procedural matters and legal certainty, especially in light of the possibility of dealing with these issues through secondary legislation, still indicate that limited scrutiny is appropriate.[46]

On the other hand, it seems appropriate to treat even non-discriminatory procurement measures as hindrances to trade to the same extent as more traditional regulatory measures, when these procurement measures are not directed solely at the provision of the goods, works or services under the contract, but are a manifestation of the government's activity as

---

[46] Case C–6/05, *Medipac*, note 31 above, in which the Court held that the contracting authority, a hospital, was not free to reject a particular make of contract product (*in casu*, surgical sutures), is not inconsistent with the general proposition advanced above because, as explained above, the Court came to its conclusion on the basis that the hospital's decision was in breach of a specific directive governing the marketing of such medical products.

regulator. At least this is the case when these are measures that are general in nature, rather than confined to isolated contracts. From a policy perspective, such measures cannot be distinguished from other regulatory measures: on the one hand, the concerns raised above over judicial scrutiny of procurement do not have the same force, whilst, on the other, the rationale for the free movement rules applies equally and the trade impact is comparable. We will see below that the ECJ has generally treated non-discriminatory measures affecting trade in services as hindrances to trade without making any distinction between, for example, selling arrangements and other types of arrangements comparable to the distinction made in relation to trade in goods. In the context of public procurement this means, for example, that a policy of excluding from government services contracts undertakings that do not meet targets for employing persons with disabilities in their business is a hindrance to trade. The position of a similar policy providing for exclusion from supplies contracts is not so clear: such a policy seems to be neither a 'selling arrangement' nor the type of measure treated as a hindrance to trade (such as a measure concerning product characteristics) under the *Keck* jurisprudence. It seems preferable, however, to treat 'regulatory' measures affecting supplies procurement as hindrances to trade: such measures may have a significant trade impact. It is particularly unsatisfactory to adopt a different approach to goods and services in public procurement, since the impact of measures is comparable in each market and, furthermore, individual measures often cover both goods and services.

We have so far considered the issue from a policy perspective, but what is the position of the Community institutions and, in particular, the ECJ?

In the context of horizontal policies the Commission in its Communication on social issues in public procurement takes the view, at least in the context of services, that even non-discriminatory policies may require justification, and does not distinguish between different kinds of procurement measures.[47] Thus the Commission seems to reject any doctrine of excluded buying decisions and to assume that judicial

---

[47] European Commission, Commission interpretative Communication on the Community law applicable to public procurement and the possibilities for integrating social considerations into public procurement, COM (2001) 566 final, pp. 20–21, citing Joined Cases C–369/96 and C–376/96, *Criminal Proceedings against Jean-Claude Arblade* ('*Arblade*') [1999] ECR I–8453.

scrutiny extends to non-discriminatory individual procurement decisions of any kind – at least for services contracts.

However, the jurisprudence itself has not fully clarified the position. In relation to specifications concerning the consumption characteristics of products, the ECJ held in *UNIX*[48] that a requirement to use the 'UNIX' operating system in a contract for an information technology system infringed Article 28 EC even though it did not favour domestic products, since it nonetheless excluded firms using systems other than UNIX which were equally suitable for the purchaser's operational requirements. This ruling effectively applies to non-discriminatory measures the principle of *Dundalk*, that specifications on product characteristics must not be *defined* to exclude products that can meet the purchasing authority's exact operational requirements. However, the case does not necessarily entail inroads on purchaser autonomy in defining required characteristics: it merely indicates (like *Dundalk*) that an authority is constrained in the manner in which it *expresses* its requirement so as not to exclude those products which actually do meet its needs. It is not inconsistent with the proposition that measures *setting the level* of an authority's requirement are not in principle hindrances to trade.

It should also be mentioned that in the context of services procurement the ECJ assumed in *Contse*[49] that non-discriminatory conditions and award criteria relating to service providers were automatically hindrances to trade. However, as explained below, the measures addressed in *Contse* clearly had a greater impact on non-domestic than domestic service providers, so that the ruling does not strongly support any proposition that non-discriminatory measures are generally subject to justification. The opportunity to clarify the position is unlikely to arise in the context of *regulatory* procurement measures – those extending beyond the contract – since (as we will see in chapter 4) for major contracts such measures are largely precluded by the procurement directives.

Thus we consider that the jurisprudence is not inconsistent with our suggestion that non-discriminatory procurement measures are hindrances to trade only where: (i) they exclude those able to meet the government's exact operational requirements, or (ii) they are in the nature of regulatory measures (and possibly only in the latter case where they are general in nature rather than confined to specific contracts).

---

[48] Case C–359/93, *UNIX*, note 8 above. See also Case C–59/00, *Bent Mousten*, note 8 above.
[49] Case C–234/03, *Contse*, note 40 above.

Justifying measures under Article 30 or mandatory requirements   As
mentioned, a measure considered a hindrance to trade is not automatically prohibited: it is permitted if it can be justified either under
one of the explicit derogations from Article 28 set out in Article 30
EC or as a mandatory requirement under the rule of reason in *Cassis
de Dijon*.[50]

Article 30 allows Member States, where there are no Community
measures that fully regulate the area, to derogate from Article 28 on
grounds of 'public morality, public policy or public security; the protection of health and life of humans, animals or plants; the protection of
national treasures possessing artistic, historic or archaeological value; or
the protection of industrial and commercial policy'. Derogation is conditional on showing that any discrimination is justifiable on objective
grounds (for example that it is not 'arbitrary discrimination'), that it does
not imply a 'disguised restriction on trade', and that any restriction on
trade is proportionate in that it is necessary to the end to be achieved and
no more restrictive of trade than necessary.[51] Nonetheless, the Court
recognises that the Member State determines the *standard* of protection
required.[52] A mere assertion that a measure relates to a ground within
Article 30 is not sufficient, as was made clear in the procurement context
in *Re Data Processing*.[53]

The rule of reason in *Cassis de Dijon* provides for broader derogation,
to advance a range of 'mandatory requirements', or essential societal
values, recognised by the ECJ. These include consumer protection,[54]
environmental protection (which may go beyond the 'protection of life
and health of humans, plants and animals' covered by Article 30),[55] the

---

[50] Case 120/78, *Cassis de Dijon*, note 13 above.
[51] See, in procurement, e.g., Case C–234/03, *Contse*, note 40 above, at para. 25 stating that
to be justifiable a measure must 'be suitable for the attainment of the [imperative]
objective' in question and 'must not go beyond what is necessary to attain it'.
[52] 'In the absence of harmonised rules ... recourse to Article 30 EC may entail the
application of different standards in different Member States, as a result of different
national value-judgments, and different factual situations': A. Arnull *et al.*, *Wyatt and
Dashwood's European Union Law*, 5th edn (London: Sweet & Maxwell, 2006), p. 617. See
Case 34/79, *Henn & Darby* [1979] ECR 3795; Case C 94/83, *Albert Heijn BV* [1984] ECR
3263; and Case C–366/04, *Schwarz* v. *Bürgermeister der Landeshauptstadt Salzburg*
[2005] ECR I–10139.
[53] Case C–3/88, *Re Data Processing*, note 8 above.
[54] See Case 120/78, *Cassis de Dijon*, note 13 above, para. 9 and Case 286/81, *Oosthoek's
Uitgeversmaatschaapij BV* [1982] ECR 4575, para. 18.
[55] Case 240/83, *Procureur de la République* v. *Association de défense des brûleurs d'huiles
usagées* [1985] ECR 532.

effectiveness of fiscal supervision[56] and the legitimate interests of economic and social policy.[57] Others may be added by the Court. This 'rule of reason' is also subject to a requirement of proportionality. A view long held was that it could only be applied to measures that do not on their face distinguish between domestic and imported products. As mentioned in chapter 1, however, in *PreussenElektra*[58] the ECJ accepted that *environmental* protection could justify even distinctly applicable measures. However, as explained there, it remains unclear whether the Court's ruling was based on environmental protection being a special case, or a more general acceptance that distinctly applicable measures can be justified under the rule of reason.

The importance of these rules on justification in public procurement depends significantly on how far procurement measures are treated as hindrances to trade in the first place, both where they have a greater effect on non-domestic products, and where they are non-discriminatory, as discussed above.

One area in which this is important is in relation to contract specifications – and other measures, such as award criteria that are directed at defining the products supplied. We have suggested above that to a large extent these do not require justification, even if they are harder for imported products to meet than for domestic products, as they are 'excluded buying decisions'. However, it is not clear whether the ECJ will accept this.

To the extent that entities *do* need to justify specifications, there are questions over how the rules will operate, since they have mainly been developed in the context of regulatory measures. In particular, in that context the ECJ has developed a presumption that products in lawful circulation in one Member State must be admitted to others – that is, that product requirements *prima facie* are not justified where they are not required in the state of origin. In *Dundalk*[59] Advocate General Darmon seemed to consider that this presumption also applies in the context of public procurement specifications.[60] However, in our view, even if specifications must be justified this approach is wholly inappropriate. First, unlike regulatory measures, procurement decisions are directed at securing a product for a specific use, for which the minimum standards set for

---

[56] Case 120/78, *Cassis de Dijon*, note 13 above, para. 9.
[57] Case 155/80, *Oebel* [1981] ECR 1993, para. 12.
[58] Case C–379/98, *PreussenElektra AG* v. *Schleswag AG* [2001] ECR I–2099, discussed in chapter 1, section 6.
[59] Case 45/87, *Dundalk*, note 6 above.
[60] This was also accepted by the Irish Government in argument.

products to enter into general circulation may not be suitable. Secondly, just like private consumers, public authorities have widely differing values and concerns in relation to issues such as health and safety, environmental protection and service levels – reflecting, for example, local priorities – which they may legitimately wish to reflect in specifications. Given this diversity a simple presumption that public authorities should be willing to purchase any product in free circulation is simply inappropriate. Thus, if (contrary to our suggestion) specifications are hindrances to trade that authorities must justify, each case must be assessed on its own merits.

It is necessary to consider, however, the possible implications of *Medipac*, the facts of which were outlined above. We suggested that the case is explained by the fact that an authority cannot reject a product because it does not meet requirements not referred to in the specification. On the other hand, however, the ECJ also indicated that the authority, having initially specified for sutures complying with the Medical Devices Directive, could not, when it became concerned about the safety of particular sutures bearing the CE mark under that directive, simply advertise a new contract with new specifications that excluded the sutures in question: it was required to suspend the procurement and to initiate the safeguard procedure of the Medical Devices Directive by informing the designated national authority.[61] It might be argued that that was tantamount to prohibiting the authority from excluding products that complied with that directive. The case does not, however, support such a proposition. In fact the Court went out of its way to note at the outset that the authority had not 'imposed particular requirements going beyond the *minimum* required by Community law',[62] implying that it might indeed have been possible to specify requirements beyond those required for the CE mark. Be that as it may, in *Medipac* the authority had itself brought the Medical Devices Directive into play by

---

[61] The Court (at paras. 60 and 61) added that during the suspension period, in case of urgency, the authority could take all interim measures necessary to procure the medical devices necessary for its operations providing it could show sufficient urgency and demonstrate that the measures taken were proportionate. Presumably such interim measures would include purchasing a limited supply of sutures through the negotiated procedure as suggested by Advocate General Sharpston at para. 119 of her Opinion of 21 November 2006. Presumably also in this situation the authority would be entitled when purchasing its urgent interim supply to insist upon purchasing products other than those about which it has safety concerns. Otherwise public health would be put at risk pending the outcome of the safeguard procedure.

[62] Para. 41 of the judgment, emphasis added.

referring to the CE mark. By refusing to accept that the sutures were safe the authority was indirectly challenging the product's entitlement to bear the CE mark, and in this respect had usurped the role of the designated national authority under the Directive's safeguard provisions. This explains why the Court emphasised that the hospital 'was not given such competence by the Greek State [and so] … is not entitled to implement on its own the safeguard measures' provided for by the directive[63] and why the authority could not simply restart the procedure with a new specification. Nothing in the judgment precludes an authority (which accepts that all sutures bearing the CE mark are safe) from specifying at the outset higher safety standards than those guaranteed by the mark.

Even if we are wrong, however, and the Medical Devices Directive does preclude state hospitals from specifying sutures which exceed the minimum standards guaranteed by the CE mark, that outcome would depend upon the directive's particular provisions. At its broadest, the ruling would be limited to compliance with harmonisation directives, and would not require authorities to accept products complying with European standards in general, nor create a presumption that authorities must accept products in free circulation. Furthermore, even some harmonisation measures merely set minimum standards, allowing national authorities to require higher standards. Indeed Article 176 EC expressly provides that environmental protective measures adopted by the Community under Article 175 EC do not prevent Member States from maintaining or introducing more stringent protective measures, where compatible with the Treaty and notified to the Commission.

Also important for procurement is the fact that certain procurement decisions may need to be justified by reference to financial considerations, such as limiting expenditure on the product or limiting procedural costs, especially if the ECJ does not accept our view that many award criteria and contract terms do not constitute hindrances to trade. In this context it needs to be mentioned that *De Peijper*[64] suggested that measures may not be justified by the need to lighten the administrative burden or reduce public expenditure unless these would clearly exceed the limit of what can reasonably be required. In light of the policy considerations referred to above, however, and the very purpose of most 'exclusionary' procurement measures as being concerned with

---

[63] Para. 49 of the judgment.
[64] Case 104/75, *Officier van Justitie* v. *De Peijper* ('*De Peijper*') [1976] ECR 613.

obtaining goods and services on the best terms available, this seems clearly an unsuitable test for most purchasing decisions. Indeed, if (contrary to what we suggest) such decisions are not removed from scrutiny altogether, quite the opposite presumption should be adopted, based on the same reasons that we put forward for declining even to treat such measures as hindrances to trade.

The application of these various justifications in the specific context of horizontal procurement policies is elaborated in chapter 4.

3.1.2. Freedom of establishment and freedom to provide services

The EC Treaty provides also for freedom of establishment (Article 43 EC) and the freedom to provide services (Article 49 EC). The former concerns the right of individuals and firms from one Member State to set up in business within another. Article 43 entitles benefiting enterprises[65] to establish subsidiaries, branches and facilities in other Member States. It prohibits government measures which hinder such establishment or which hinder the operations of such enterprises once established in another Member State. Thus, in the procurement context, when an enterprise from one Member State is established in another, Article 43 prohibits government measures in the latter which restrict that enterprise's access to government contracts there – for example, rules that prevent such a Community enterprise from bidding for government contracts.

Article 49, on freedom to provide services, concerns the right of an enterprise from one Member State to provide services in another by means of *temporary* presence there (including the presence of employees) and without having to establish on a permanent or continuing basis (for example, without having to set up a branch or subsidiary). It prohibits a Member State from preventing Community enterprises from other Member States from providing services within its territory, including from restricting their participation in government contracts, whether under a contract for the provision of services or by any other arrangement such as through a joint venture company.[66]

As with Article 28, Article 49 may be infringed by conduct concerning government contracts which discriminates on grounds of nationality either directly (e.g. by giving preferential treatment to domestic bidders or reserving contracts for domestic firms)[67] or indirectly, through

---

[65] See Article 48 EC.
[66] Case C–108/98, *RI.SAN* v. *Comune di Ischia* ('*RI.SAN*') [1999] ECR I–5219.
[67] Case C–360/89, *Commission* v. *Italy* [1992] ECR I–3401.

facially neutral measures which have the practical effect of favouring domestic firms.[68] Examples are measures making it more difficult for enterprises from other Member States to use their own labour force, such as requirements to use local labour.[69] As well as infringing Article 49 EC measures discriminating directly or indirectly on grounds of nationality will also infringe Article 43 where they hinder access to public contracts for Community nationals or enterprises from other Member States which are established in the awarding state.[70] As with free movement of goods, the Court has also held that certain measures that impact equally on domestic and non-domestic firms may infringe Article 49. Indeed, it seems to take the approach that all measures that have an impact on trade in services are prima facie covered;[71] in contrast with its position in the *Keck* jurisprudence governing trade on goods the ECJ has not yet had cause to restrict this general approach.

As with free movement of goods, an important question is whether a requirement 'hinders' freedom of establishment or freedom to provide services simply because some bidders are able to meet the requirement but others – perhaps including enterprises from other Member States – are not. As we have seen, in *Concordia Bus Finland* the ECJ upheld an environmental contract award criterion even though it could only be met by a very small number of firms (including, in particular, one firm associated with the authority itself),[72] and we have argued above in considering free movement of goods that this case indicates that measures concerning the service to be provided or the terms of its provision are not generally hindrances to trade where they are bona fide but 'excluded buying decisions'. On the other hand, as we have seen, the ECJ seemed to indicate in *Beentjes* and *Nord Pas de Calais* that discriminatory measures relating to the contract workforce *are* hindrances to trade that must be justified.

---

[68] See, e.g., Case C–3/88, *Re Data Processing*, note 8 above.

[69] See Case C–243/89, *Storebaelt*, note 8 above.

[70] See, e.g., Case C–3/88, *Re Data Processing*, note 8 above.

[71] See Case C–234/03, *Contse*, note 40 above, discussed above and Case C–384/93, *Alpine Investments BV* v. *Minister van Financien* [1995] ECR I–1141 and Cases C–369/96 and C–376/96, *Arblade*, note 7 above. In Case 94/99, *ARGE Gewasserschutz* v. *Bundesministerium für Land- und Fortstwirtschaft* ('*ARGE*') [2000] ECR I–11037, the Court did not take the opportunity to discuss the extent, if at all, that non-discriminatory measures affecting access to government contracts would in principle be caught by Article 49.

[72] Case C–513/99 *Concordia Bus Finland*, note 26 above.

So far as concerns decisions that are non-discriminatory in effect, we have suggested above, in discussing trade in goods, that these also should not be regarded as hindrances to trade where they relate solely to contract performance. This applies either under the doctrine of excluded buying decisions (which, if it covers certain measures that have a greater impact on service providers from other Member States, will a fortiori cover equivalent measures that are non-discriminatory) or, if this doctrine is not accepted, in any case for measures (such as workforce measures) not covered by that doctrine, by virtue of a separate rule that defines the application of the *Keck* principle to public procurement in a limited way. On the other hand, we suggested that for both services and goods the *Keck* principles should be applied so as to bring within the concept of hindrances to trade all procurement measures of a 'regulatory' nature in the sense of measures that extend beyond the contract, at least where these are general in nature. For example, we suggested that a policy of excluding from government services contracts undertakings that do not meet targets for employing persons with disabilities is a hindrance to trade.

A broader approach that requires justification of *all* procurement measures might find some support in the reasoning in *Contse*,[73] and we have seen above in discussing trade in goods that the Commission also seems to accept that approach. The case concerned a contract to provide home respiratory treatment and other assisted breathing techniques. The ECJ considered that various conditions and criteria concerning the service provision were hindrances to trade under Article 49 EC that could not be justified. These were: a requirement that at the time of tendering the tenderers should have an office open to the public in the capital city of the province in which the service was provided; an award criterion giving preference to tenderers with offices open to the public in other specified towns in the province; an award criterion giving preference to tenderers with oxygen producing, conditioning and bottling plants within 1000 kilometres of that province; and a provision that, in the event of a tie on points under the other award criteria, the contract was to be awarded to the firm previously supplying the service. However, all these measures had a greater impact on non-domestic firms than on domestic firms, and the ruling thus does not necessarily mean that

---

[73] Case C–234/03, *Contse*, note 40 above. Earlier in Case 94/99, *ARGE*, note 71 above, the Court also did not take the opportunity to discuss the extent, if at all, to which non-discriminatory measures affecting access to government contracts would in principle be caught by Article 49.

non-discriminatory measures would be treated in the same way: a case involving measures of this kind would clarify for the ECJ the implications of such an approach, which it might then reject.

Articles 45 EC and 55 EC permit derogations from Articles 43 and 49 respectively on grounds of public policy, public health or public morality[74] and, as with goods, derogation is also possible under a rule of reason for measures protecting imperative public interests recognised by the ECJ – for example, protection of intellectual property, protection of the consumers of services and protection of the environment.[75] As mentioned, it remains unclear whether the rule of reason is capable of being invoked in relation to distinctly applicable measures in general, or only those concerning environmental protection. The importance of these justifications in the procurement context again depends on the extent to which procurement measures are considered hindrances to trade in the first place.

3.1.3. Conclusion

We have seen that the treatment of procurement measures under the free movement rules is at present unclear. Whilst it is sometimes assumed by the Commission and ECJ that any measures that affect access to public contracts are hindrances to trade, there are many policy reasons not to treat 'buying decisions' and regulatory decisions of government in precisely the same way. In particular, we suggest that there is a doctrine of 'excluded buying decisions' whereby certain decisions concerned merely with what the government is buying and the terms of purchase are generally outside the scope of review, an approach supported by *Concordia Bus Finland*. On the other hand, we suggest that procurement measures that are akin to traditional regulatory measures – that is, those going beyond the contract in question, at least when general in nature – should be subject to scrutiny as hindrances to trade in the same way as many other regulatory measures.

From a legal perspective, the outcome of our discussion can be summarised as follows, as also set out in Table 2.1.

---

[74] Furthermore Articles 43 and 49 do not apply to activities 'connected, even occasionally, with the exercise of public authority': Article 45 EC derogating from Article 43; Article 55 derogating from Article 49.

[75] See P. Craig and G. de Búrca (eds.), *EU Law: Text, Cases and Materials*, 3rd edn (Oxford University Press, 2004), pp. 814–819.

Table 2.1: *Impact of the EC Free Movement Rules on Procurement Measures*

Type of measure	Hindrance if direct discrimination	Hindrance if greater impact on imported products/service providers from other Member States	Hindrance if non-discriminatory
Limited to contract (government as purchaser)			
1. Decision to purchase or not to purchase	Yes	No?**	No?
2. Decision on what to purchase	Yes	No?**	
3. Other measures (specification and conditions; award criteria; exclusions etc.), relating to:			
a. Consumption*	Yes (*Fagtún*)	No?** ('excluded buying decision') (*Concordia Bus Finland?*)	No? ('excluded buying decision') (*Concordia Bus Finland?*)
b. Production and delivery*	Yes (*Du Pont de Nemours*)	?	No?
c. Disposal*	Yes	?	No?
d. Workforce doing contract work	Yes (*Storebaelt*)	Yes (*Beentjes; Nord Pas de Calais*)	No?
Beyond the contract (government as regulator)			
e. Nature of undertaking (ethnic group etc.)	Yes	Yes (C-360/89)	Yes
f. Undertaking's behaviour outside the contract	Yes	Yes (C-360/89)	Yes

* Refers only to decision setting level of requirements – Treaty applies where there is restriction deriving from decisions on *how* a particular level of requirements should be met (*Dundalk* etc.). For consumption effects (goods), at least, and services this may apply even when non-discriminatory (*UNIX*).

** Unless there is a discriminatory motive.

1. All procurement measures that discriminate directly against products or services providers of other Member States are hindrances to trade that must be justified under Treaty derogations or as mandatory requirements or general interest requirements (as shown, for example, by *Du Pont de Nemours*).

2. Provided that they do not involve direct discrimination, many procurement measures are not hindrances to trade even when they have a greater impact on products/service providers from other Member States, since they set the market, and do not restrict it – the doctrine of 'excluded buying decisions' (supported by *Concordia Bus Finland*). This applies at least to measures (specifications, award criteria etc.) concerned with consumption effects (for example, the environmental impact of products in use as in *Concordia Bus Finland*) and possibly to some other measures concerned with the contract itself. It does not, however, apply to workforce measures relating to the contract – at least where they are not non-discriminatory – which are hindrances to trade (*Beentjes* and *Nord Pas de Calais*). The 'excluded buying decisions' doctrine is also not applicable when there is a discriminatory motive for the measure, nor when it does not reflect a real operational requirement (*Dundalk* and *UNIX*).

3. Non-discriminatory measures relating to contract performance are not hindrances to trade, either under the excluded buying decisions doctrine, or under a separate rule. However, procurement measures that are not confined to the contract – those of a 'regulatory' nature – *are* hindrances to trade, at least where general in nature.

3.2. The positive obligation of transparency

The traditional understanding of the free movement provisions was that they did not themselves imply transparency, and that thus only contracts subject to the directives attracted transparency obligations. However, in the seminal case of *Telaustria*,[76] concerning a services concession, which is outside the directives, the ECJ held that the Treaty implied an obligation of transparency requiring the advertising of the contract, to ensure that it was possible to monitor for compliance with

---

[76] Case C–324/98, *Telaustria*, note 8 above. The Court's approach was followed by the Grand Chamber in Case C–321/03, *Consorzio Aziende Metano* v. *Comune di Cingia de' Botti* ('*Coname*') [2005] ECR I–7287.

the Treaty's non-discrimination obligation.[77] Although *Telaustria* conceived of the transparency obligation as being derived from the rule against non-discrimination on grounds of nationality, subsequent pronouncements characterised it as a manifestation of a broader principle of equal treatment regardless of nationality, which we discuss further below.

This is highly controversial,[78] and there are also important uncertainties to resolve before its real impact becomes clear.

First, there is lack of clarity over which contracts are covered. *Telaustria* concerned a contract excluded from the directives for historical reasons because of its nature as a concession, rather than its limited importance for trade, and, as noted in chapter 1, the ECJ has drawn inspiration from the secondary legislation on procurement to develop a Treaty regime that fills this perceived 'gap' in the legislation itself ('the leverage principle'). It remains to be seen, however, how far transparency applies to contracts that are excluded because they are below the directives' value thresholds. In *Commission* v. *Finland*[79] Advocate General Sharpston cogently argued that individual low-value contracts should not be open to ECJ challenge under the Treaty because of lack of transparency, although it might be necessary for Member States to enact their own transparency rules that could be challenged. Her argument was based upon four main, and related, points: namely that the Community legislator deliberately chose *not* to apply detailed requirements to low-value contracts; that 'the effects on the fundamental freedoms should be regarded as too uncertain and indirect to warrant the conclusion that they may have been infringed'; that the principle of subsidiarity in Article 5 EC 'dictates that Community law should only impinge on national law to the extent justified by an assessment of costs and benefits';[80] and that a detailed publicity obligation would offend legal

---

[77] Case C–324/98 *Telaustria*, note 8 above, paras. 61–62 of the judgment.

[78] See Arrowsmith, note 1 above, at 4.12 *et seq.*; P. Braun, 'A Matter of Principle(s): the Treatment of Contracts Falling Outside the Scope of the European Public Procurement Directives' (2000) 9 *PPLR* 39; E. Hordijk and M. Meulenbelt, 'A Bridge Too Far: Why the European Commission's Attempts to Construct an Obligation to Tender outside the Scope of the Public Procurement Directives should be Dismissed' (2005) 14 *PPLR* 123; A. Brown, 'Seeing through Transparency: The Requirement to Advertise Public Contracts and Concessions under the EC Treaty' (2007) 16 *PPLR* 1; D. McGowan, 'Clarity at Last? Low-value Contracts and Transparency Obligations' (2007) 16 *PPLR* 274.

[79] Case C–195/04, *Commission* v. *Republic of Finland* [2007] ECR I–3351; Opinion of 18 January 2007.

[80] Case C–321/03, *Coname*, note 76 above, para. 88.

certainty.[81] However, the Court held that the case was inadmissible and so did not address these points.[82] In our view, these arguments are convincing. Further, as argued in chapter 1, there are sound arguments against the very use of the leverage principle, even in the context of major contracts, and especially in such a rapidly changing and technically complex area as procurement. There is also uncertainty regarding 'Part B' services contracts (a concept discussed below): the ECJ ruled in *An Post*[83] that transparency applies to these contracts, but only where they are positively shown to be of 'certain cross-border interest'. However, it remains uncertain how this will operate in relation to different types and value of Part B contracts and in different circumstances.

A second uncertainty concerns the content of transparency under the Treaty, including what is involved in the publicity requirement, and whether transparency includes other obligations.[84] As discussed in chapter 1, the ECJ may draw inspiration from the directives to develop precise and detailed requirements for contracts outside those directives, and the Commission has supported this approach in its Communications.[85] Again, however, as outlined in chapter 1 and for many of the reasons referred to in Advocate General Sharpston's Opinion, this does not seem desirable; and it can be noted that Germany has mounted a legal challenge to the Commission's recent Communication on the Treaty's application to below-threshold contracts.[86]

The *Telaustria* jurisprudence is also problematic in other respects. It has long been held that Articles 43 and 49 do not apply to purely 'internal' situations, for example 'to activities whose relevant elements are confined within a single Member State',[87] including in public

---

[81] *Ibid.*, paras. 89–97.
[82] However, it had previously stated that the 'modest economic interest at stake' with some below-threshold contracts might mean that the effects on the fundamental freedoms are too uncertain and indirect to warrant the conclusion that they have been infringed: *Coname*, note 76 above, para. 20.
[83] Case C-507/03, *Commission v. Ireland* ('*An Post*'), ECJ judgment of 13 November 2007.
[84] See further Brown, note 78 above.
[85] See, in particular, European Commission, Communication on the Community law applicable to contract awards not or not fully subject to the provision of the public procurement directives, OJ 2006 No. C 179/2 and European Commission, Communication from the Commission to the European Parliament, the Council, the European Economic and Social Committee and the Committee of the Regions on Public-Private Partnerships and Community law on public procurement and concessions, COM (2005) 569 final.
[86] In Case T-258/06, *Germany v. Commission*.
[87] Case 52/79, *Procureur du Roi v. Debauve* [1980] ECR 833, para. 9.

procurement.[88] The Court has, however, recently eroded this principle and has been willing readily to find a cross-border element, for example by invoking the right of potential recipients of services outside the Member State in question.[89] Furthermore, although the Court applied the 'internal situation' doctrine to procurement in *RI.SAN*,[90] it declined to do so (without even discussing *RI.SAN*) on materially identical facts in *Parking Brixen*,[91] where it held that a Treaty obligation of transparency applied in a procurement where all the parties to the litigation were from the awarding state. It seems that the conceptual difficulty of relying upon a duty of transparency derived from the non-discrimination rule to this sort of internal situation may have encouraged the court to invoke a different principle – transparency arising from a broader principle of equal treatment regardless of nationality – which is discussed immediately below.

3.3. Development of a general principle of equal treatment in public procurement

As is explained at 4.3.3 below, a principle of equal treatment *regardless* of nationality of bidders was implied by the ECJ into the old procurement directives and is now written expressly into the current directives.[92] According to the ECJ in *Fabricom*,[93] this duty 'requires that comparable situations must not be treated differently and that different situations must not be treated in the same way unless such treatment is objectively justified'. The ECJ has now suggested, in *Parking Brixen*,[94] that the *Treaty itself* also imposes an obligation of this kind. In this case the Court, following the Commission, asserted that the obligation to publicise a services concession derives from a broad Treaty obligation of

---

[88] See Case C–108/98, *RI.SAN*, note 66 above.
[89] See, e.g., Case 352/85, *Bond van Adverteerdes* [1988] ECR 2085; and Case C–51/96 and C–191/97, *Deliège* v. *Ligue Francophone de Judo et Disciplines Associés* [2000] ECR I–2549.
[90] Case C–108/98, *RI.SAN*, note 66 above.   [91] *Ibid.*
[92] Case C–243/89, *Storebaelt*, note 8 above.
[93] Cases C–21/03 and Case C–34/03, *Fabricom SA* v. *Belgian State* ('*Fabricom*') [2005] ECR I–1559, para. 27.
[94] Case C–458/03, *Parking Brixen GmbH* v. *Gemeinde Brixen, Stadtwerke Brixen AG* ('*Parking Brixen*') [2005] ECR I–8585; Case C–410/04, *Associazione Nazionale Autostrasporto Viaggiatori (ANAV)* v. *Commune di Bari, AMTAB Servizio SpA* [2006] ECR I–3303; and Case C–226/04 and C–228/04, *La Cascina Soc. coop. arl., Zilch Srl* v. *Ministero della Difesa & Ministero dell'Economia e delle Finanze, Pedrus Service et al.* ('*La Cascina*') [2006] ECR I–1347.

equal treatment – apparently to reject the argument that there was no violation of the Treaty since all of the parties were domestic firms:[95]

> According to the Court's case-law, Articles 43 EC and 49 EC are specific expressions of the principle of equal treatment (see Case C–3/88 *Commission v Italy* [1989] ECR 4035, paragraph 8). The prohibition on discrimination on grounds of nationality is also a specific expression of the general principle of equal treatment (see Case 810/79 *Überschär* [1980] ECR 2747, paragraph 16). In its case-law relating to the Community directives on public procurement, the Court has stated that the principle of equal treatment of tenderers is intended to afford equality of opportunity to all tenderers when formulating their tenders, regardless of their nationality (see, to that effect, Case C–87/94 *Commission v Belgium* [1996] ECR I–2043, paragraphs 33 and 54). As a result, the principle of equal treatment of tenderers is to be applied to public service concessions even in the absence of discrimination on grounds of nationality.

In our view, this view is incorrect.[96] There is no authority for such a general principle separate from specific obligations such as non-discrimination on grounds of nationality, and no basis to treat procurement as a special case. The Court's reasoning is flawed, involving a non-sequitur: the fact that the principle of non-discrimination on grounds of nationality under the Treaty is one aspect of equal treatment does not entail that all the consequences of the equal treatment principle as manifested in the directives must follow from the Treaty also.

A Treaty principle of this kind would extend the scope for judicial review of procurement beyond a duty to advertise and potentially expose many decisions relating to procurements outside the directives to judicial scrutiny. Thus any measures affecting suppliers differently – for example, on qualifications, award criteria, time limits or procedures used – could be examined to see if they involve different treatment of suppliers in a 'comparable' position and, if so, whether they can be justified,[97] even though the framework provided by the directives within which an

[95] Case C–458/03, *Parking Brixen*, note 94 above, para. 48.
[96] See also M. Krügner, 'The Principles of Equal Treatment and Transparency and the Commission Interpretative Communication on Concessions' (2003) 12 *PPLR* 181; Arrowsmith, note 1 above, at 4.1.6. A different view is put forward by T. Tridimas, *The General Principles of EU Law*, 2nd edn (Oxford University Press, 2006).
[97] Although the extent of this will depend on how a 'comparable' situation is defined: see further S. Arrowsmith, 'The Past and Future Evolution of EC Procurement Law: from Framework to Common Code?' (2006) *PCLJ* 337, pp. 354–359.

obligation of equal treatment might be fleshed out and understood will be absent. In fact, if this approach is followed it would appear that the permissibility of procurement measures under the Treaty, both 'negative' and 'positive', would fall to be analysed not under the *Keck* approach but under a separate principle embracing both discriminatory and non-discriminatory measures alike. To take one example, a decision to exclude from a contract to supply clothing suppliers that cannot comply with fair labour clauses might potentially be regarded as involving different treatment of firms in a comparable position – those that can meet the requirement for clothing – that needs to be justified in light of the social objective that it pursues, even though there is no discrimination on grounds of nationality. This could render redundant any debate over whether non-discriminatory procurement measures – the exclusion of firms that cannot comply with fair labour clauses – are hindrances to trade. This approach is open to objection for the same reasons of legal certainty, practicality, subsidiarity and proportionality that have been discussed earlier in considering reviewability of procurement under more 'traditional' Treaty interpretations.

We consider that the ECJ's approach in *Parking Brixen* is incorrect and should be reconsidered. If this is not done, then the position of procurement measures, including on horizontal policies, will be difficult to predict. In that event, we consider that for consistency the ECJ will need to take the same approach in applying equal treatment as it does under the more traditional approach of addressing hindrances to trade, where the doctrines offer potential for overlap. For example, the Court should not effectively re-examine, under this distinct principle, the issue that was decided (within the scope of the directive) in *Concordia Bus Finland*: it should maintain the approach that in setting award criteria relating to the goods supplied, suppliers that cannot meet the criteria are not in a comparable position with those who can. We also consider that non-discriminatory measures of all kinds should remain free from scrutiny – in effect, that the impact of the doctrine should be confined to the issue of *who* may invoke the positive transparency principle.

The application to horizontal policy measures of the equal treatment principle *in the directives* is considered in chapter 4. If we are wrong in the view expressed above concerning the nature of equal treatment under the Treaty, then the considerations discussed there will be relevant in considering equal treatment under the Treaty, as well as under the directives.

4. Procurement within the scope of a directive

4.1. The history and nature of the public procurement directives[98]

The third category of case concerns contracts *within* the procurement directives, namely Directive 2004/18, covering most public sector procurement – the Public Sector Directive – and Directive 2004/17, the Utilities Directive.

Since it was originally thought that the Treaty did not impose any positive or detailed obligations in awarding contracts – for example, on advertisement or procedures – secondary legislation in the form of 'coordination' directives was considered necessary to flesh out the Treaty rules for the reasons discussed in chapter 1, namely for monitoring and enforcing the prohibition on discrimination, for removing certain barriers to access and for facilitating access (for example, through EC-wide advertising). The directives covered only major contracts, since only these were considered of interest to trade. The first coordination directive, Directive 71/305,[99] dealt with works contracts (construction) and Directive 77/62[100] with supply contracts (goods).

These original directives were often disregarded and in any event covered neither services contracts nor contracts let by most utilities, even public sector utilities. In its White Paper[101] on the completion of the internal market by 1992, the Commission proposed to complete the procurement regime. This led to amendments to the directives and, in due course, consolidation in two new directives, Directive 93/36/EEC[102] on public supply contracts and Directive 93/37/EEC[103] on public works contracts. In addition, coverage was extended by Directive 92/50/EEC[104] to certain (non-construction) services. Regulation was also extended to

[98] See further Arrowsmith, note 1 above, chapter 3, and the works cited there.
[99] Council Directive 71/305/EEC concerning the coordination of procedures for the award of public works contracts, OJ 1971 No. L 185/5.
[100] Council Directive 77/62/EEC coordinating procedures for the award of public supply contracts, OJ 1977 No. L 13/1.
[101] European Commission, White Paper to the Council on completing the Internal Market, COM (85) 310 final.
[102] Council Directive 93/36/EEC coordinating procedures for the award of public supply contracts, OJ 1993 No. L199/1.
[103] Council Directive 93/37/EEC concerning the coordination of procedures for the award of public works contracts, OJ 1993 No. L 199/54.
[104] Council Directive 92/50/EEC relating to the coordination of procedures for the award of public service contracts, OJ 1992 No. L 209/1.

utilities by Directive 90/531/EC,[105] which covered works and supplies; services contracts were added for utilities by Directive 93/38/EC,[106] which replaced Directive 90/531/EC. The Utilities Directives covered, and still cover, not only public utilities but also private utilities that are considered to present a risk of discriminatory behaviour because of the potential for state influence over their purchasing policy. In addition, Remedies Directives 89/665/EC[107] and 92/13/EC[108] were adopted to provide systems of remedies for public and utilities contracts respectively.

This activity resulted in a multiplicity of legislation: three coordination directives covering separate types of contract (works, supply and services), a directive on utilities procurement, and two on remedies. Furthermore, economic and technological developments offered new and efficient procurement techniques that were, however, not easily accommodated within the directives. This situation persisted until 2004 when the Community adopted[109] the new Public Sector Directive and the new Utilities Directive, replacing the previous directives. Each directive, within its field, covers works, supply and services. In addition, each simplifies the regime and modernises it, both by incorporating the accumulated jurisprudence of the ECJ and by making express provision for modern practices, including electronic purchasing.[110] In addition, the principles of equal treatment and transparency[111] have been written expressly into the new text.

As we will see, the main rules comprise: requirements to advertise contracts EU-wide; requirements to follow specified procurement methods and to allow certain minimum time-limits for response; rules

---

[105] Council Directive 90/531/EEC on the procurement procedures of entities operating in the water, energy, transport and telecommunications sectors, OJ 1990 No. L 297/1.

[106] Council Directive 93/38/EEC coordinating the procurement procedures of entities operating in the water, energy, transport and telecommunications sectors, OJ 1993 No. L 199/84.

[107] Council Directive 89/665/EEC on the coordination of the laws, regulations and administrative provisions relating to the application of review procedures to the award of public supply and public works contracts, OJ 1989 No. L395/33.

[108] Council Directive 92/13/EEC coordinating the laws, regulations and administrative provisions relating to the application of Community rules on the procurement procedures of entities operating in the water, energy, transport and telecommunications sectors, OJ 1992 No. O.J. L76/14.

[109] See S. Arrowsmith, 'An Assessment of the New Legislative Package on Public Procurement' (2004) 41 *CMLR* 1; R. Williams, 'The New Procurement Directives of the European Union' (2004) 13 *PPLR* 153.

[110] See Arrowsmith, note 1 above, chapter 18.   [111] See section 4.3.3 below.

limiting selection and award criteria and requiring their disclosure to undertakings; and obligations to provide information.

It has always been clear, as indicated in *CEI and Bellini* and *Beentjes*,[112] that the directives do not provide an exhaustive set of rules governing public procurement: as stated in *Beentjes*, for example, 'the [1971 Works Directive] does not lay down a uniform and exhaustive body of Community rules: within the framework of the common rules which it contains, the Member States remain free to maintain or adopt substantive and procedural rules in regard to public works contracts on condition that they comply with all the relevant provisions of Community law'.[113] In practice, many Member States[114] have additional national rules – for example, to require stricter tendering procedures than the directives. These include national rules on horizontal policies. These may limit such policies, even when the directives allow them; for example, the Local Government Act 1998 in England largely prohibits local authorities from taking into account 'non-commercial' considerations.[115] National rules can also *oblige* authorities to use their procurement to promote particular goals – for example, by requiring contracts to be set aside for sheltered workshops (as discussed in chapter 7). As originally conceived, the directives in fact provided for only a limited degree of regulation, and appeared to leave a significant area of discretion to Member States.

However, despite the non-exhaustive nature of the directives, the reality is that the scope for national discretion is now substantially limited and continues to diminish. Whilst the original system was essentially one of negative harmonisation in which the primary rule, non-discrimination on grounds of nationality, was supported by secondary rules to ensure transparency, the regime is evolving towards a regime of positive regulation with limited national discretion,[116] albeit that, as chapter 1 argued, Member States still retain responsibility in principle over policy on value for money, preventing corruption, accountability

---

[112] Joined Cases 27–29/86, *S.A. Construction et Entreprises Industrielles and others* v. *Société Co-operative 'Association Intercommunales pour les Autoroutes des Ardennes' and others* ('*CEI and Bellini*') [1987] ECR 3347; Case 31/87, *Beentjes*, note 38 above.

[113] Case 31/87, *Beentjes*, note 38 above, para. 20 of the judgment.

[114] For example, the UK has few legislative rules, apart from those implementing the directives: see Arrowsmith, note 1 above, chapter 2.

[115] See Arrowsmith, note 1 above, at 19.65 *et seq.* and also chapter 7 of this book.

[116] Arrowsmith, note 97 above.

and efficiency, as well as over national horizontal policies. This has resulted from a number of strands of development.

First, as we have seen, the directives now embrace norms relating to equal treatment that go beyond non-discrimination on grounds of nationality and provide a positive organising principle for opening up public contracts, as well as a general principle of transparency. The ECJ has used these principles both to interpret the explicit rules of the directives and to imply additional obligations. Both principles provide great scope for the ECJ to step in to decide how to balance the interests involved in the procurement process. In doing so, however, it must bear in mind the principles discussed in chapter 1, including the fact that the balance between horizontal policies and other procurement policies remains primarily a matter for Member States. In fact, as we have seen, and as is discussed further below, these principles do seem to be reflected in the ECJ's approach, in particular in *Concordia Bus Finland*.

Secondly, Member States' discretion has been limited by a tendency of the ECJ to take an approach to interpretation that gives significant weight to internal market considerations at the expense of discretion.[117] In the area of horizontal policies this has been manifested most notably in *Beentjes* and subsequent jurisprudence,[118] in which the ECJ indicated that firms could not be excluded in advance from contracts because of possible inability to comply with certain social and environmental conditions. However, there are now perhaps signs of retreat in decisions such as *Concordia Bus Finland* and *EVN-Wienstrom*, discussed above.

Thirdly, national discretion is restricted by the increasingly detailed and precise rules on award procedures. Thus the 2004 directives include new rules requiring authorities to weight award criteria and to disclose selection criteria that aim to increase transparency,[119] as well as new provisions on issues such as electronic communications, electronic auctions and framework agreements, as outlined below. Whilst the Commission has presented the directives as enhancing flexibility – and indeed they do this in important respects, including for horizontal policies – in many areas they merely confirm and regulate in more detail mechanisms that were probably already permitted under the old

---

[117] Although Treumer points out that for Member States with a strict domestic system the decisions can appear liberal: S. Treumer, 'The Discretionary Powers of Contracting Entities: Towards a Discretionary Approach in the Recent Case Law of the Court of Justice?' (2006) 15 *PPLR* 71.

[118] See chapter 4, section 8.1.4.

[119] See Article 53(2) and Article 44(2) and 44(3) of the Public Sector Directive.

directives.[120] Thus overall the impact of the new directives is, arguably, to limit Member State discretion. Some of these additional rules, such as weighting and disclosure rules, affect implementation of horizontal policies.

Finally, we saw in chapter 1 that the new directives include for the first time explicit provisions *requiring* states to use procurement to support particular policies.

The overall impact of the new directives as regards provisions that are specific to horizontal policies is considered further in the next section.

4.2. Horizontal policies under the directives: legislation, jurisprudence and soft law

The original directives said little about their impact on horizontal policies. Some contained provisions preserving certain existing preferential policies, but on condition that they were compatible with the EC Treaty,[121] which the ECJ, in *Du Pont de Nemours*,[122] ruled not to be the case with regional policies.[123] There was also a provision – still found – concerning subcontracting, to encourage participation by small and medium-sized enterprises.[124] Apart from this, however, the old directives did not deal expressly with horizontal policies, and did not make clear how far these could be implemented through mechanisms such as award criteria and exclusions. Their implications became clear only over time. As their potential impact was increasingly recognised, the legal position became the subject of soft law in the shape of guidance from the European Commission and was also developed in the jurisprudence.

Commission guidance has played a prominent role. In particular,[125] during the legislative process for the 2004 directives, launched in May 2000,[126] the Commission produced two parallel Communications

---

[120] See Arrowsmith, note 109 above.

[121] For example, Article 25(4) of Directive 77/62 and Article 29(a) of Directive 71/305.

[122] Case C–21/88, *Du Pont de Nemours*, note 11 above.

[123] See chapter 4, section 3.   [124] See chapter 8.

[125] Earlier pronouncements include European Commission, Communication on public procurement: regional and social aspects, COM (89) 400 final; European Commission, Green Paper: public procurement in the European Union: exploring the way forward, pp. 39–42; European Commission, Public procurement in the European Union, sections 4.3 and 4.4.

[126] European Commission, Proposal for a Directive of the European Parliament and of the Council on the coordination of procedures for the award of public supply contracts, public service contracts and public works contracts, COM (2000) 275 final; European Commission, Proposal for a Directive of the European Parliament and of the Council coordinating the procurement procedures of entities operating in the water, energy and transport sectors, COM (2000) 276 final.

on horizontal policies. These were the Commission interpretative Communication on the Community law applicable to public procurement and the possibilities for integrating environmental considerations into public procurement[127] (hereafter Communication on environmental considerations), published in July 2001, and Commission interpretative Communication on the Community law applicable to public procurement and the possibilities for integrating social considerations into public procurement[128] (hereafter Communication on social considerations), published in October 2001. These were prompted by increasing demand for guidance, and probably also by the Commission's desire to highlight the positive opportunities for horizontal policies in procurement with the aim, in part, of heading off calls from the European Parliament for a greater role for horizontal policies.

This guidance, however, obviously could offer no legally definitive statement on the basis of which authorities could securely develop their policies or tenderers be certain of their rights. Furthermore, although it had some value as a statement of the Commission's likely 'prosecutorial' policy, its value in other respects has been questionable. This is, first, because the Commission has tended to take a restrictive view of the possibilities for horizontal policies, almost to the point of seeming out of touch with reality. A notable example was its argument in *Concordia Bus Finland*[129] that an authority was prohibited from taking account of emissions limits of buses in a contract for bus transportation services, on the basis that the directives allow only award criteria involving a 'direct economic advantage' and thus preclude such environmental considerations – a viewpoint implicitly rejected by the ECJ, which considered such criteria to be acceptable. It is remarkable that the Commission considered it legally tenable to argue this, in the absence of any clear restriction, in an era of concern over climate change and urban pollution. In some key respects, the Commission's restrictive interpretations have in fact been rejected, as in *Concordia Bus Finland* and also in

---

[127] European Commission, Interpretative Communication on the Community law applicable to public procurement and the possibilities for integrating environmental considerations into public procurement, COM (2001) 274 final. See also Commission Staff Working Document, Buying green! A handbook on environmental public procurement, SEC (2004) 1050.

[128] European Commission, Interpretative Communication on the Community law applicable to public procurement and the possibilities for integrating social considerations into public procurement, COM (2001) 566 final.

[129] Case C–513/99 *Concordia Bus Finland*, note 26 above.

EVN-Wienstrom, discussed below.[130] The guidance does not, therefore, necessarily provide a useful predictor of the outcome of legal challenge.

In addition, the Commission's reasoning has sometimes been so confused as to obscure the content. Often this appears to arise from a sort of 'institutional schizophrenia' in which tensions within the Commission disrupt the coherence of its position, with internal market staff taking a view that favours market considerations and others taking a different line as a result of the higher value that they place on issues such as 'green procurement'. Such divisions are not always addressed and resolved but manifest themselves in muddled guidance – for example, in the case of 'green electricity', as discussed in chapter 9. In other cases the guidance simply fails to address contentious issues. For example, the Communication on environmental considerations refers often to the possibility of including environmental policies if compatible with the EC Treaty, but gives no precise examples.[131] The utility of guidance is also reduced by the time period that elapses between identifying issues of concern and publishing guidance – illustrated, for example, by the omission of any significant consideration for utilities, as discussed in chapter 11.

Judicial adjudication also has significant limitations as a means of elaborating the legal framework for horizontal policies. First, wide variation both in the objectives sought and (as elaborated in chapter 3) the mechanisms for achieving them makes it difficult for jurisprudence to create a coherent framework applicable to the whole area. Secondly, since judicial pronouncement depends on the accident of litigation it is difficult in the short term to develop the law: important issues may simply not be presented for consideration. Thirdly, as we have noted, horizontal policies often require a trade-off between single market concerns, government's obligation to account to the electorate for expenditure, and a whole range of controversial policy objectives. These second two features tend to suggest that judges may not, from a constitutional point of view, be best placed to strike the required balance. The Court's success in carrying out this role has in fact been rather mixed. Perhaps precisely because it has been aware that it has been entering upon sensitive

---

[130] Case C–448/01 *EVN AG* v. *Austria* ('*EVN-Wienstrom*') [2003] ECR I–14527.

[131] See, for example, Communication on environmental considerations, note 127 above, section 1, which merely notes the issue must be considered on a case by case basis. Similarly, as noted in chapter 11 on Utilities, the guidance notes that the position for utilities may be different from that under the Public Sector Directive, but does not mention how.

territory involving political and resource-allocation choices not well suited to judicial decision, some of its judgments have been poorly reasoned.[132]

The absence of specific provision for horizontal policies became increasingly unsatisfactory given changes in society that have increased the prominence of horizontal policies. First, growing awareness of environmental problems, such as climate change, pollution and the conservation of species and eco-systems, has focused attention on the need to facilitate, and even to require, 'green' procurement. These concerns are particularly emphasised in the context of energy procurement, discussed in chapter 9, in which environmental concerns are now coupled with significant concerns relating to energy security. In addition, with globalisation and increased outsourcing to developing countries, 'fair trade' concerns have come to the fore, as noted in chapter 1 and discussed further in chapter 11. With this, demand has grown for public authorities to adopt ethical positions in purchasing, although it is not always easy to disentangle the ethical and protectionist dimensions of this movement.

All these developments, combined with the interest generated by Commission guidance and judicial pronouncements, made it inevitable that the horizontal policies issue would be much debated during the legislative process for the new directives. A result was that the new directives include some new specific provisions on horizontal policies. As Kunzlik argues in chapter 9, in the context of environmental policy these new provisions can be seen to some extent as measures implementing the requirement in Article 6 EC to integrate environmental protection into the definition of Community policies.

First, the Commission itself proposed several provisions that were accepted. For the most part these set out explicitly the pre-existing possibilities for Member States to implement horizontal policies, and, in particular, write in possibilities clarified in jurisprudence. This was in line with the more general policy of writing the jurisprudence into the directives' text, and also seems to have been aimed at heading off more radical amendments that might broaden national discretion. Thus the directives now include express references to the possibility of including environmental specifications and award criteria,[133] specifications relating to access for all users, as discussed in chapter 7, and special contract

---

[132] See, e.g., the discussion of Case C–225/98, *Nord Pas de Calais*, note 39 above, on award criteria, in chapter 4, section 13.

[133] See chapter 4, sections 8.1.3 and 13.

conditions requiring, for example, that contract work be given to unemployed or handicapped persons[134] (as recognised by the ECJ in *Beentjes*). In addition, the directives include certain *restrictions* on horizontal policies, that had either been recognised in the jurisprudence (for example, that award criteria should be limited to the subject matter of the contract)[135] or that the Commission had advocated in its guidance (for example, limiting special conditions to contract performance).[136]

Secondly, the new directives include one important new provision that increases flexibility, namely a provision allowing states to reserve contracts for sheltered employment programmes (see chapter 7). It had become apparent some years ago that such measures were precluded under the old directives, but there was broad consensus for allowing them.

Thirdly, for the first time the directives introduced provisions that *require* Member States to use procurement to promote certain horizontal policies. In this respect, as we have seen in chapter 1, authorities are, first, obliged to exclude from contracts firms convicted of corruption and certain other criminal offences, to support EC policies, and, secondly, must take into account accessibility criteria for people with disabilities and design for all users (again discussed in chapter 7).

As anticipated, the European Parliament, adopted a number of amendments[137] to the Commission's proposals, which would have expanded Member State discretion, or at least implemented an expansive interpretation in grey areas or confirmed existing possibilities. These would have expressly permitted award criteria based on a tenderer's equality policies, and on environmental characteristics, including those relating to production methods of goods.[138] They would also explicitly have allowed exclusion of enterprises which: violate 'international core labour standards' or 'fundamental European legislation relating to employment protection and working conditions';[139] have 'not fulfilled employment protection obligations towards workers and labour law obligations towards their representatives in accordance with applicable

---

[134] See chapter 4, section 8.1.4.   [135] See chapter 4, section 13.
[136] See chapter 4, section 8.1.4.
[137] See Position of the European parliament adopted at the first reading on 17 January 2002 with a view to the adoption of European Parliament and Council Directive.../.../EC on the coordination of procedures for the award of public supply contracts, public service contracts and public works contract, OJ 2002 No. C271/E/176.
[138] *Ibid.*, Article 62(1)(b).   [139] *Ibid.*, Article 53(2)(c).

legal provisions, including those in legislation, collective agreements and contracts' (where established by court judgment);[140] or had failed to meet legal obligations relating to health and safety of workers (even if not established by a court conviction).[141] Further amendments provided for additional *mandatory* exclusions for enterprises guilty of non-compliance with rules 'on collective agreements or other employment–related and social aspects in the country in which they are established or in another relevant country'.[142] In the end, however, these amendments were rejected, some at the conciliation stage. To that extent, the new directives might be seen as a 'victory' for the Commission and its restrictive approach.[143] Nevertheless, as we will see,[144] whilst the Commission has resisted certain express provisions that would have implemented or clarified a broad approach, it is not clear that the ECJ will reject all the possibilities that were the subject of these amendments.

The outcome of the recent legislative activity for Member State discretion is, in summary, as follows. First, *discretion* to implement horizontal policies has been increased in limited respects (notably with sheltered employment programmes). Secondly, some possibilities, and some restrictions, have been expressly confirmed, thus clarifying the legal position – in some cases in favour of horizontal policies (as with environmental award criteria, for example), in some cases against (as with contract conditions going beyond the contract). Thirdly, however, as will become evident, there are still many issues unresolved. These will be important areas for future debate and for future guidance and jurisprudence, especially given the political importance of horizontal policies. Fourthly, as we have noted, the principle of using the procurement power of Member States in a collective manner to support EC policy has been clearly established. As elaborated in chapter 12, this could have significant implications. What is certainly clear is that the recent legislation has by no means closed the debate on horizontal policies, but has merely heralded a new phase in its development.

---

[140] *Ibid.*, Article 53(2)(e).   [141] *Ibid.*, Article 53(2)(h).

[142] *Ibid.*, Article 53(1)(d) (re money laundering) (e) (re fraud and dishonest anti-competitive practices in procurement) (f) (re collective agreements and social aspects) and (g) (re drugs offences).

[143] J. Arnould, 'Secondary Policies in Public Procurement: the Innovations of the New Directives' (2004) 13 *PPLR* 187.

[144] See, in particular, chapters 4 and 9.

4.3. Overview of the Public Sector Directive and its main obligations[145]

4.3.1. Introduction

Having considered the principles that underlie the directives and the historical context, we now turn to an overview of the rules in force. Here we merely provide a preliminary sketch for readers unfamiliar with the directives: chapter 4 elaborates their impact on specific horizontal policies and mechanisms.

As we have seen, the directive governing most public sector contracts is the Public Sector Directive (2004/18), and a separate Utilities Directive (2004/17) regulates contracts in certain utility sectors. To some extent the same rules apply under the two directives, including for horizontal policies – and this is the case with many of the issues discussed in this book. However, there are also important differences, and the Utilities Directive also raises some distinct policy issues, not least because it regulates many private companies as well as public authorities. These issues are discussed by Arrowsmith and Maund in chapter 11, which focuses specifically on utilities. The remainder of this chapter focuses on the Public Sector Directive.

4.3.2. Coverage

The Public Sector Directive applies in principle to works, supply or service contracts for pecuniary consideration between a 'contracting authority' and an 'economic operator'.[146] Contracting authorities are the State, regional and local authorities, and 'bodies governed by public law' and associations formed by such authorities or bodies.[147] A body 'governed by public law' is, broadly speaking, any non-commercial body that is owned, controlled or supervised by another contracting authority – for example, many public universities.[148] The directive provides an

---

[145] For a detailed analysis of the directives in general, see Arrowsmith, note 1 above; and for a briefer but useful account P. Trepte, *Public Procurement in the EU: A Practitioner's Guide* (Oxford University Press, 2007).

[146] The term 'economic operator' refers to a supplier of goods, a contractor as regards works, and a provider of services: Article 1(8).

[147] Article 1(9) of the Public Sector Directive. All Article references hereafter in this chapter are to this directive.

[148] Defined in Article 1(9) as a body established for the specific purpose of meeting needs in the general interest, not having an industrial or commercial character, having legal personality and financed, for the most part, by the State or contracting authorities, or subject to management by such authorities or having an administrative, managerial or supervisory board more than half of whom are appointed by contracting authorities: see Arrowsmith, note 1 above, chapter 5.

extensive (but non-exhaustive list) of 'bodies governed by public law'.[149] Whether a body is covered in a particular state depends entirely on the Community definition in the directive; it is immaterial whether the body is under public law or private law in the Member State concerned.[150]

A contracting authority's contracts are subject to the directive where: (a) they meet or exceed the applicable value threshold, and (b) they are not of a type excluded from the directive.[151] The current threshold under the Public Sector Directive is EUR 133,000 for public supply and public service contracts awarded by central government authorities (listed in Annex IV), EUR 206,000 for supply and service contracts awarded by other authorities, and EUR 5.15 million for works contracts.[152] Authorities are prohibited from splitting contracts to avoid the thresholds,[153] and there are also 'aggregation' rules that require certain similar contracts awarded over a period of time to be aggregated together for threshold purposes.[154] The thresholds are reviewed every two years to align them with the thresholds in the WTO's Agreement on Government Procurement (GPA), which themselves change every two years. The GPA governs access to EC markets of suppliers from certain non-EC countries and alignment is necessary to ensure that non-EC suppliers do not benefit from more favourable thresholds than EC suppliers.

So far as exclusions are concerned, one of the most important is for services concessions, although, as shown in *Telaustria*, these are subject to transparency requirements under the EC Treaty. Works concessions are not excluded entirely but only an obligation to advertise and other very limited obligations apply.[155] Concessions are arrangements whereby the provider of the works/service obtains remuneration by exploiting it[156] – for example, a contract for building and operating a tramway under which the provider is paid from passenger fares. These arrangements can be important for horizontal policies but, as we have seen, there is considerable uncertainty on how they are affected by the

---

[149] Annex III of the Public Sector Directive.

[150] E.g., Case C–283/00, *Commission* v. *Spain* ('*SIEPSA*') [2003] ECR I–11697, para. 74.

[151] See, in particular, Articles 10–18, discussed in detail in Arrowsmith, note 1 above, chapter 6.

[152] Article 7 (a)–(c) as amended by Commission Regulation (EC) No 1422/2007, amending Directives 2004/17/EC and 2004/18/EC of the European Parliament and of the Council in respect of their application thresholds for the procedures for the award of contracts, OJ 2007 No. L317/34. Special thresholds sometimes apply, e.g. for certain defence contracts.

[153] Article 9(3).   [154] Article 9(5) and (7).

[155] Articles 56–61.   [156] Article 1(3) and (4).

Treaty. Other excluded contracts include those for certain sensitive services, such as broadcasting services,[157] and certain contracts concluded with other public bodies.[158]

In addition, for services a distinction is drawn between service contracts listed in Annex IIA ('Part A services') which are subject to the directive's full regulatory regime,[159] and those listed in Annex IIB ('Part B services') which are subject only to rules on technical specifications and post-award notices.[160] However, Part B services may be subject to 'positive' obligations under the Treaty, as we have seen, as well as the general principles of the directives discussed below.

4.3.3. The general principles

As we have mentioned, the directives lay down certain general principles, as well as detailed rules. In this respect the Public Sector Directive states, in Article 2, that 'contracting authorities shall treat economic operators equally and non-discriminatorily and shall act in a transparent way', giving express recognition to principles previously implied into the directive by the ECJ. These principles have been used by the EC both to *interpret* the explicit rules of the directives and also to imply *additional* obligations when no explicit rules exist.

The equal treatment principle was first articulated in 1993 in *Storebaelt*.[161] As noted previously, it was recently defined in *Fabricom* as requiring 'that comparable situations must not be treated differently and that different situations must not be treated in the same way, unless such treatment is objectively justified',[162] and can be invoked by domestic suppliers as well as by suppliers from other Member States.[163] The requirement to act 'non-discriminatorily' appears to be simply one specific manifestation of the general equal treatment principle.[164]

---

[157] Article 16(b).

[158] Article 11 and Article 18. Certain 'in-house' arrangements are outside the concept of a public contract: Case C–107/98, *Teckal Srl* v. *Comune di Viano, Azienda Gas-Acqua Consorziale (AGAC) di Reggio Emilia* [1999] ECR I–8121.

[159] Article 20, subjecting such contracts to the provisions of Articles 23–55 inclusive.

[160] Article 21, subjecting such contracts 'solely' to the provisions of Article 23 (technical specifications) and Article 35(4) (award notices).

[161] Case C–243/89, *Storebaelt*, note 8 above.

[162] Para. 27 of the judgment. See also Advocate General Mischo in Case C–513/99, *Concordia Bus Finland*, note 26 above, para. 149 of the Opinion.

[163] Case C–87/94, *Commission* v. *Belgium* ('*Walloon Buses*') [1996] ECR I–2043.

[164] The ECJ in Case C–513/99, *Concordia Bus Finland*, note 26 above, indicated that compliance with the directive's equal treatment principle includes an obligation to

The ECJ has not defined transparency but, as Arrowsmith has set out elsewhere,[165] in the context of the directives it can be seen to have four facets: publicity for contract opportunities; publicity for the rules governing each procedure (such as the award criteria); rule-based decision-making; and provision for verification and enforcement. The ECJ has applied the principle in many cases in a way that gives effect to one or more of these facets.[166]

4.3.4. The permitted procurement procedures and techniques

The directive requires an authority intending to let a contract to publish an advertisement – a 'contract notice' – in the *Official Journal of the European Union*.[167] The *Official Journal* provides a summary in all official EU languages, and offers access through a searchable electronic database. A notice can be dispensed with only when using the negotiated procedure without a contract notice, a procedure available only in limited cases, such as extreme urgency.

The directive then authorises the use of five procurement procedures, the 'open procedure', the 'restricted procedure', 'competitive dialogue', the 'negotiated procedure' with prior publication of a contract notice, and the 'negotiated procedure' without publication of a contract notice. The general rule is that authorities may use either the open or the restricted procedure. When the open procedure is used any firm may bid;[168] under the restricted procedure any firm may request to participate but the authority may choose only some to bid, using objective criteria discussed below.[169] These are both formal tendering procedures in which there is limited scope for dialogue or amendments to tenders.[170] Competitive dialogue[171] may be used only for particularly complex contracts':[172] it was introduced in 2004 to provide a suitable procedure

---

comply with the non-discrimination principle of the Treaty's free movement provisions: see para. 82 of the judgment and section 3.1 above.

[165] Arrowsmith, note 1 above, at 3.9.
[166] See, for example, *Walloon Buses*, note 163 above (to support conclusion that entities may not use undisclosed award criteria) and Case C–470/99, *Universale-Bau* v. *EBS* [2002] ECR I–11617 (to require disclosure of selection methodology even though not expressly mentioned in the directive).
[167] Article 35(2), Article 29(2), Article 30(1) and Article 33(3)(a).
[168] Article 1(11)(a).   [169] Article 11(b).
[170] On this and other aspects of these procedures, see Arrowsmith, note 1 above, chapter 7.
[171] As to which see generally Arrowsmith, note 1 above, chapter 10; Brown, 'Infrastructure Projects: Competitive Dialogue or Better the Devil you Know?' (2004) 13 *PPLR* 160 and S. Treumer, 'Competitive Dialogue' (2004) *PPLR* 178.
[172] Article 29(1).

for complex privately-financed infrastructure projects, though it is not limited to such cases. In this procedure any firm may request to participate but the authority can again select limited participants, again using the criteria discussed below.[173] The authority then enters into dialogue with the aim of developing one or more solutions capable of meeting its requirements, which are then submitted in the form of final tenders.[174] Negotiated procedures with a notice are those in which the authority chooses several firms to consult (again using the objective criteria set out below) and enters into negotiation of terms.[175] It is available only in limited cases, including when the open or restricted procedure has resulted in irregular or unacceptable tenders,[176] when overall pricing is not possible[177] and for purchasing services where their nature is such that contracts specifications cannot be established with sufficient precision to use open or restricted procedures.[178] A negotiated procedure without a contract notice is available in a narrow range of circumstances, mainly certain cases of extreme urgency, and cases in which there is only one possible contractor.[179]

The directive also now provides expressly for framework agreements,[180] which are convenient arrangements for making repeat purchases. They are not separate award procedures, but a mechanism used within the usual award procedures – usually the open or restricted procedure: they essentially allow authorities to select several firms as framework suppliers for products or services and then place orders with one of these suppliers when a particular need arises. The new directive also includes specific provision for electronic reverse auctions, in which tenderers admitted to an open or restricted procedure bid prices[181] downwards through an electronic device that enables all bidders to see whether they are currently the best bidder;[182] and for a new type of wholly electronic mechanism, the so-called 'dynamic purchasing system', which is a variation on the open procedure.

---

[173] Articles 29(3), 44–52.   [174] Articles 11(c) and 29.   [175] Article 11(d).

[176] Article 30 (1)(a). 'Unacceptable' means under national provisions corresponding with Articles 2, 24, 25 and 27 of the Directive itself.

[177] Article 30(1)(b).   [178] Article 30(1)(c).   [179] Article 31(1)–(4).

[180] See, in particular, Article 5 and Article 32; and generally Arrowsmith, note 1 above, chapter 11.

[181] In theory other elements of the bid that can be quantified in such a way as to enable automatic evaluation can also be revised in the auction, but in the authors' experience this is extremely rare.

[182] See further Arrowsmith, note 1 above, chapter 18 and Arrowsmith, 'Electronic Reverse Auctions under the New EC Procurement Directives' (2005) 14 *PPLR* 203.

4.3.5. Specifications and other contract requirements[183]

In any procurement an authority needs to define its requirements, by providing technical specifications. We have seen that the Treaty precludes any specifications that exclude products or services able to meet the entity's functional requirements – although it is less clear how closely the Treaty controls the authority's discretion to *set* its own functional requirements. In addition, the directive also contains rules on technical specifications.[184]

First, they must be formulated in one (or both) of two ways.[185] The first is by reference to technical specifications as defined by Annex VI. This refers to certain European-level standards (such as national standards that give effect to European standards) or international standards (such as those of the ISO), or, where these do not exist, certain national-level standards. When this approach is used, the reference must be accompanied by the words 'or equivalent' and functional equivalents must be accepted (as also required by the Treaty), although the burden of proving equivalence is on tenderers.[186] The second is in terms of performance or functional requirements.[187] These rules do not appear to affect the purchaser's discretion to set the level of standards to be met, but merely to ensure that requirements are expressed in an accessible manner, and that the authority is prepared to consider all products, works or services that meet its needs.

Specifications also must not generally describe requirements by reference to a specific make or source, or a particular process, or to trade marks, patents, types, or a specific origin or production with the effect of favouring or eliminating certain undertaking of products; in the exceptional cases where this is permissible, the reference must again be accompanied by the words 'or equivalent'.[188]

In addition, Article 23(2) states, rather vaguely, that technical specifications 'shall afford equal access for tenderers and not have the effect of creating unjustified obstacles to the opening up of public procurement to competition'.

Finally, as mentioned, an innovation from the perspective of horizontal policies is the new provision stating that authorities 'whenever possible' should 'take into account accessibility criteria for people with disabilities or design for all users';[189] this is discussed in chapter 7.

---

[183] See further Arrowsmith, note 1 above, chapter 17.
[184] Defined in Article 23(1) and Annex VI; on this definition see further chapter 4 at 8.1.3.
[185] Article 23(3)(a).   [186] Article 23(4).   [187] Article 23(3)(b).
[188] Article 53(8).   [189] Recital 29 and Article 23(1).

4.3.6. Exclusion and selection of tenderers

For several reasons authorities may wish to exclude firms from contracts. The directive significantly limits Member States' discretion in this area. First, it generally permits exclusion only on limited *grounds* listed in the directives, including financial position and technical capability. Secondly, it also controls the *process* of exclusion. These rules ensure that authorities provide fair opportunities of participation and that procedures for assessing qualifications are not unduly burdensome and do not conceal discrimination.

The explicit grounds for exclusion can be divided into four main categories: financial; technical; enrolment on a trade or professional register and possession of a licence; and various grounds relating to 'professional honesty, solvency and reliability'.[190] Authorities can in general exclude firms only on these grounds, as recently confirmed in *La Cascina*.[191]

The first category, financial reasons for exclusion, is dealt with by Article 47,[192] which provides that firms may be excluded because they lack 'financial and economic' standing. This is not defined but clearly refers to whether firms have adequate financial resources to perform. It is for national authorities to determine the standards that firms must meet – for example, the size of turnover required.[193] As regards the proof of standing, the directives list certain evidence which authorities may demand – for example, bankers' statements – and they may also call for other evidence if needed;[194] but firms may also offer other 'appropriate' evidence,[195] to avoid an unreasonable burden.

Secondly, Article 48 provides that firms may also be excluded where they lack the 'technical or professional ability' to perform the contract.[196] As with financial standing the standards for qualification – for example, the amount and type of equipment needed – are for national authorities. Article 48 also lists evidence which authorities may demand as proof – for example, the education and professional qualifications of the contractor and/or its staff.[197] We will see in chapter 4 that there is

---

[190] Joined Cases C–226/04 and C–228/04, *La Cascina*, note 94 above, para. 21 of the judgment.
[191] *Ibid.* [192] See further Arrowsmith, note 1 above, chapter 12, especially 12.4 *et seq.*
[193] See *CEI and Bellini*, note 112 above, paras. 26–28; *Beentjes*, note 38 above, para. 17.
[194] *CEI and Bellini*, note 112 above. [195] Article 47(5).
[196] See further Arrowsmith, note 1 above, chapter 12, especially 12.13 *et seq.*
[197] This is in principle exhaustive: Case 76/81, *S.A. Transporoute* v. *Minister of Public Works* [1982] ECR 417; *CEI and Bellini*, note 112 above; Case C–71/92, *Commission* v. *Spain* [1993] ECR I–5923. However, Article 48(5) may possibly allow some additional criteria and evidence for works and services contracts.

considerable debate over how far certain social and environmental requirements in public contracts can be classified as relating to technical or professional ability.[198] This is important, since it is relevant for whether or not the authority can exclude a firm that it considers will not be able to comply with the social or environmental requirements in question.[199]

Thirdly, Article 45 provides for exclusion on various grounds referring to 'professional honesty, solvency and reliability'. These are where the provider: is bankrupt, subject to a winding up order or similar; has been convicted of an offence relating to the business; has been guilty of 'grave misconduct' relating to the business; has failed to pay tax or social security contributions; or has been guilty of serious misrepresentation in supplying information. These grounds are sometimes relevant to financial and technical capacity (for example, an insolvent firm is un- likely to have adequate financial standing). However, as elaborated in chapter 4, they are not necessarily connected with the ability to perform, and the provisions on criminal offences and grave misconduct may thus provide significant possibilities for implementing horizontal policies.[200]

Fourthly, authorities may require firms to be registered on certain trade or professional registers in their state of establishment (Article 46).[201]

There is, however, an exception to the principle that firms may be excluded only on the grounds above, which allows exclusion to give effect to equal treatment: in *Fabricom* the ECJ recognised the possibility of excluding a supplier for reasons of conflict of interest, to allow autho- rities to give effect to equal treatment.[202]

In addition, in restricted and negotiated procedures and competitive dialogue authorities may, as we have seen, limit the number of those invited to make offers.[203] This must generally be done by using the same criteria as are permitted for the initial exclusion, namely technical capa- city etc.[204]

The directive requires any minimum financial and technical require- ments, as well as the criteria for choosing between qualified firms, to be

[198] See chapter 4, section 8.1.6.   [199] See chapter 4, section 8.1.4.

[200] See chapter 4, section 10.2.

[201] For some Member States that have relevant registers these are listed expressly in Annex IX. Certain special provision is made for states (such as the United Kingdom) where none exist.

[202] Cases C–21/03 and Case C–34/03, *Fabricom*, note 93 above. The ECJ did not clarify whether exclusion is *required* in such a case.

[203] Article 44(3).   [204] Case C–360/89, *Commission* v. *Italy* [1992] ECR I–3401.

stated in the contract notice,[205] to ensure that the criteria used cannot act as a cloak for discrimination.[206] However, it is not necessary to disclose any weightings of the selection criteria.[207]

Finally, we should note that the directive does not expressly require firms to be excluded on the grounds above, but merely permits this in states' discretion and regulates the way that this is done. However, as we have seen, the new directive does now provide some *mandatory* grounds for exclusion, namely for conviction of participation in a criminal organisation, corruption, fraud and money laundering, in order to support EC horizontal policies, as discussed in chapter 12.[208]

4.3.7. Award criteria

Once it has received the final tenders or offers, the authority must award the contract to the tenderer who has submitted the best tender, using one of two bases – the 'lowest price'[209] or the 'most economically advantageous' offer.[210] In the latter case, it may consider criteria such as quality, price, technical merit, aesthetic and functional characteristics, environmental characteristics, running costs, cost-effectiveness, after-sales service, technical assistance, delivery date, delivery period, or period of completion.[211] However, such award criteria must be 'linked to the subject matter of the public contract in question'. This limitation was implied by the ECJ into the old directives in *Concordia Bus Finland*,[212] and is now expressly stated in the directive, in Article 53(1)(a). We will see in chapter 4 that this is an important limitation for horizontal policies, since it precludes award criteria directed at a supplier's behaviour outside the contract. Further, even for criteria that relate solely to the contract, there is some uncertainty over whether all such criteria are permitted – in particular whether authorities may use award criteria relating to the contract workforce and production of supplies – although we argue in chapter 4 that they may, in fact, do so.

For each contract the authority specifies in advance the criteria to be used and the relative weightings assigned to each (apart from exceptional

---

[205] Article 44(2) and (3).
[206] In addition, references required must be stated in the notice or in the documents: Article 47(4) and Article 48(6).
[207] Recital 40.   [208] Article 45(1).   [209] Article 53(1)(b).
[210] Article 53(1)(a). For contracts awarded by competitive dialogue only this latter basis may be used: see Article 29(1).
[211] Article 53(1)(a).   [212] Note 26 above.

contracts) for non-compliance. We include in the present category of the taxonomy, however, only measures supporting norms that apply to all firms in a comparable position, rather than just government contractors. This is done for several reasons, including for convenience of exposition, since in the vast majority of cases procurement policies relating to compliance with legal norms relate to norms of general application and because, from a constitutional perspective, implementing norms only for government contractors presents more features in common with the other policies discussed below, as a regulatory strategy that focuses solely on public procurement. For similar reasons, we also exclude from this first group procurement policies that support norms that are not directly *legally* binding on the contractor under national law – for example, ILO conventions on labour standards that have not been implemented in domestic law. We will see in chapter 4, however, that for policies at the margins of this first group – that is, policies in regulatory legislation that are limited to government contractors, and policies to enforce non-legal norms deriving from an external source – there is debate over whether to treat them in the same manner as the first group under EC law, since they exhibit some common features with that group – such as the external nature of the norm being enforced – even though other features differ.[9]

In terms of the categories discussed in section 3 below, namely policies relating to the contract and policies that go beyond the contract, policies concerned with enforcing general legal norms may apply to both. Thus a requirement to follow health and safety legislation when working on the contract, for example, is limited to the contract. On the other hand, a mandatory exclusion of all contractors convicted of corruption supports anti-corruption legislation as it affects both the contract awarded and other business activity. Similarly, the Northern Ireland government's use of exclusions from government contracts under the FETO also uses procurement to secure compliance with legal requirements affecting all the contractor's business activities.

Regarding the nine policy mechanisms discussed in section 4 below, we can point out that whilst many are potentially applicable for ensuring compliance with general legal norms not all of them are suitable for this purpose. In particular, it is unlikely that authorities will choose to include compliance with the law as an award criterion. It is unlikely, for example, that a government will give extra points in the tender evaluation process

[9] See, for example, chapter 4, section 11.3.

to firms that have no convictions for corruption, while admitting, albeit under a penalty in tender evaluation, firms that do. Rather, authorities that choose to take account of criminal convictions are likely to prefer an approach that involves a contractual requirement for compliance with the law, or exclusion for past non-compliance. However, an element of discretion or judgment may well feature in the way that such requirements are enforced in practice through the selected mechanisms, or the standard of 'compliance' that is set. For example, an authority that includes a contractual requirement to comply with health and safety legislation may take into account the nature and severity of any violations that occur, and the intention or negligence of a contractor, in deciding whether to terminate a contract for violations – and indeed, may be required to do so by the applicable law of the contract.

Procurement policies concerned only with compliance with existing legal norms may be adopted for a number of reasons, more than one of which may apply in a given case.

A first reason is simply to avoid associating the government with unlawful behaviour, both to set an example and to avoid public criticism.

A second is to provide an additional enforcement tool for securing compliance with the general law or penalising legal violations, and for reducing the risk that the contractor will violate the law or otherwise behave in an unreliable or damaging manner when performing government work. The possibility of terminating the contract, for instance, may serve as a more potent tool to induce compliance during the contract work than a remote threat of criminal prosecution. Contractual sanctions may be especially useful if the work will be carried out in another state and the government of the awarding state is concerned about inadequate law enforcement in that former state. Measures to ensure compliance for both these reasons are often considered important for enforcing legal requirements in the procuring entity's own area of activity – for example, a government department responsible for the environment may be particularly concerned not to deal with contractors that have convictions for violating environmental legislation, or with using its procurement power as a tool to enforce environmental laws.

Thirdly, measures directed at legal compliance may be concerned with ensuring a level playing field. This arises from the fact that firms that do not comply with their legal obligations – for example, by paying their taxes and complying with labour law obligations – enjoy an unfair competitive advantage and, if allowed to thrive, may drive legitimate operators out of the market, both for government contracts or more

generally. This has been an important element of recent public procurement reforms in South Africa, for example.[10]

Finally, such measures can help to ensure that government funds are
not used to support criminal or other undesirable enterprises, which may
use government contracts as a means to raise revenue for terrorist or
other criminal activities.[11]

In many countries, including the EC Member States, it is a feature of
the external norms in question that there are mechanisms for judging
compliance – for example, criminal courts or regulatory commissions or
agencies – that are formal and transparent, and follow fair procedures.
Procurement measures based on non-compliance with the law may rely
on these, in that the application of procurement measures, such as
exclusion, is made subject to the existence of criminal convictions or of
other formal determinations of non-compliance. This is the case, for
example, with the EC-wide mandatory exclusion provisions for corruption etc., which apply only where there is a conviction, as discussed in
chapter 12.

Reliance on external adjudication may to some extent meet objections
over the fairness of procedures to the contractor and possible abuse of
discretion for ulterior motives that may apply if the awarding authority
itself is left to decide whether a contractor has violated the law.[12] Such an
approach may also limit the need for the procuring authority to undertake administrative investigations of a contractor's position without the
necessary expertise or resources. However, even when policies are based
on external determinations, such as a criminal conviction, there may be
administrative difficulties, since it may not be easy to obtain evidence of
convictions, especially when dealing in the increasingly global market-
place with firms (domestic or foreign) that may have convictions abroad.
As chapter 12 makes clear, policies based on criminal convictions may
also be difficult for procuring entities to apply if they also involve
excluding related persons and companies (such as subsidiaries) and
there is no formal and external mechanism to identify these companies.
Such difficulties may also hamper the effectiveness of the policies

---

[10] As originally outlined in Green Paper on Public Sector Procurement, GN no. 691, GG17928
of 14 April 1997 (South Africa). For review and discussion, see D. Letchmiah, 'The Process of
Public Sector Procurement in South Africa' (1999) 8 *PPLR* 15.

[11] A consideration behind, for example, the policy of New York discussed by Anechiarico
and Jacobs, note 5 above.

[12] This does not, on the other hand, deal with the possibility of abuse of discretion in
deciding whose convictions should form the basis for exclusion.

involved. To overcome these obstacles to efficient administration and effective policymaking, formal information mechanisms are very useful. Thus in Northern Ireland, for example, the Equality Commission has responsibility for bringing to the authorities' attention violations of FETO that result in exclusions for both the violator and connected firms.[13] Procurement policies concerned with violation of general norms are also sometimes applied, however, without relying on a non-compliance determination under the general legislation itself. For example, the World Bank procurement rules that apply to many contracts financed by the Bank in developing countries now provide for the possibility of excluding contractors that have engaged in corruption, even without a criminal conviction.[14] This raises the question of whether it is appropriate to make a determination that a firm has not complied with legal requirements, and to impose sanctions, without the safeguards of the 'normal' process, such as a criminal trial. To a large extent, the issues are the same here as with any kind of procurement determination involving consequences for contractors – whether this concerns legal violations or other matters, including violation of a horizontal requirement set by the purchaser – namely how to strike a balance between contractor interests and an efficient procurement process. This is discussed further below. With policies based on non-compliance with external norms an additional dimension might be identified, in that the determination of non-compliance may carry a stigma from the fact that the conduct is also condemned by the 'external' normative system (such as the criminal law). However, this occurs in many other situations, such as when civil liability is imposed for conduct that is also criminal, but with a different burden of proof, and seems unobjectionable merely because of this additional dimension. The determination of a violation does not involve the same consequences as a criminal conviction (or other regulatory procedure), and there is thus no prima facie reason to apply the same procedural rules as for criminal proceedings.

We will see in chapter 4 that policies limited to legal compliance are less likely to violate EC law than those that are not. This applies even when they are not directed solely at performance of the contract itself but at – for example – imposing sanctions for past behaviour. In particular, exclusion from contracts based on criminal convictions is permitted in

---

[13] Article 62(3) of FETO, note 6 above.

[14] World Bank, *Guidelines for Procurement under IBRD Loans and IDA Credits* (May 2004), section 1.15.

principle under the EC regime. Probably one reason for this is that exclusions based on norms that are externally set and applied are less open to abuse for discriminatory motives than other grounds for exclusion.[15] Indeed, as we have seen, EC law even *requires* exclusion in the case of convictions for corruption and certain other offences. We will also see that exclusions for serious criminal and regulatory violations are possible even without a conviction.[16] On the other hand, exclusion for non-compliance with policies that are *not* embodied in general regulatory legislation is more problematic.[17]

We should finally add that we include in this category of the taxonomy procurement measures that are designed to support any legal norm applicable to the contractor or the contract work – whether laid down by the awarding state or another state. In general, when procurement policy seeks to support legal norms applicable to performing the contract, these will be the norms of the awarding state: most bidders will be national contractors whose operations are subject to national law. However, when contracts are performed by foreign contractors and/or contract work (such as the manufacture of supplies for the contract) is carried out abroad, legal norms laid down by other countries may apply in addition, or instead. These norms, also, may be the subject of procurement measures; for example, states that include contract terms requiring compliance with health and safety laws governing the contract performance may wish to apply these to contract work carried out abroad that is subject to health and safety laws laid down by the country in which the work is carried out. Where the laws in question are not considered adequate by the awarding state, it might also seek to impose domestic standards on the foreign contractor through procurement measures, such as a contract term to require compliance with the same standards that are imposed by domestic law.[18] States may also wish to adopt policies that take account of compliance with the laws of other countries outside the contract – for example, where authorities exclude firms with

---

[15] See chapter 4, section 11.2.   [16] See chapter 4, section 11.2.

[17] See chapter 4, section 11.3.

[18] This situation we do not consider as falling within the present category of the taxonomy. In theory government might also legislate more generally for foreign firms to abide by domestic legal standards, even outside the context of government contracts. Both cases, of course, raise questions of the permitted reach of regulatory jurisdiction of states under international law on state jurisdiction (as to which see generally V. Lowe, 'Jurisdiction', in M. Evans, *International Law*, 2nd edn (Oxford University Press, 2006), chapter 11) as well as under EC and WTO rules.

convictions for corruption regardless of where the conviction was obtained, or simply where they adopt a policy of excluding all firms with serious criminal convictions of any kind.

2.2 Policies that go beyond compliance with general legal requirements

Many horizontal policies are, on the other hand, designed to provide social or environmental benefits that go beyond merely ensuring that government contractors comply with the general law. Again, such policies may be limited to work done on the contract – for example, an authority may require a contractor to engage a certain proportion of disabled persons, or long-term unemployed persons, in providing services under a government contract, or give preferences through award criteria to firms that do this. Such policies may also extend beyond the contract. For example, to promote gender and racial equality a government might decide to exclude from contracts firms that do not adopt a proactive policy to implement a gender and ethnic balance in their workforce, even though such a requirement is not imposed on firms in general: such a policy has been adopted by the US federal government, for example,[19] and was followed by many local authorities in the United Kingdom in the 1980s.[20] This contrasts with the use of procurement to promote political and religious equality in Northern Ireland, where we have seen that procurement has been used merely to reinforce general legal requirements that apply to all firms.

Sometimes policies of this kind that are limited to government contractors are established without any legislative basis. The fact that

---

[19] The programme also extends to matters of religion, disability and veteran status. Federal contractors (and subcontractors) are prohibited from discriminating on the basis of race, colour, religion, gender, national origin, disability, or protected veteran status, and must also take affirmative measures to ensure equal employment opportunity in their workplaces: see Executive Order 11246, as amended; Section 503 of the Rehabilitation Act of 1973, as amended; and the Vietnam Era Veterans' Readjustment Assistance Act of 1974, as amended, 38 U.S.C. 4212. A good historical review and up to date summary is found in McCrudden, note 8 above, chapter 6.

[20] See Institute of Personnel Management, *Contract Compliance: The United Kingdom Experience* (1987); J. Carr, *New Roads to Equality: Contract Compliance for the United Kingdom?* (London: The Fabian Society, 1987). As will become clear in chapter 4, it now appears that many of the features of these policies may have violated the EC procurement rules; they were in any case curtailed by Section 17 of the Local Government Act 1988, as to which see Arrowsmith, note 1 above, at 19.65 *et seq.* and also the discussion in chapter 7 of this book.

legislation may not be needed but is required for alternative approaches, such as criminal sanctions, or the fact that legislation is needed only in a particular form, such as secondary rather than primary legislation, may be one reason that procurement is chosen as a policy tool, even when it is not otherwise the preferred approach. The decision of the US federal Government to implement equality policies through procurement, for example, appears to have been taken because of the difficulty of putting regulatory legislation of general application through Congress.

Another constitutional consideration that has influenced the use of procurement to affect contractor behaviour is that it may not merely be easier to implement policies through procurement than other methods, but this may be the *only* tool available because of legal constraints on authorities' power. This appeared to be a significant factor in making procurement the policy instrument of choice for local authorities in the UK in the 1980s in areas such as equality and anti-apartheid policy: other approaches, such as adoption of criminal sanctions, were patently beyond their legal powers. This has sometimes given rise to constitutional concerns over whether it is appropriate for such authorities to do directly what they may not do indirectly. In some cases, such as with anti-apartheid policy in the United Kingdom, the courts or legislature have intervened to clarify or provide that such 'indirect regulation' is, indeed, not actually permitted by law.[21] To some extent, however, this approach has been positively endorsed as being within the legitimate remit of local entities by legislation 'mainstreaming' certain policies across all government activity. For example, legislation in the United Kingdom now *requires* all public authorities, including local authorities, to consider various equality matters in the exercise of all their functions, including procurement,[22] although most have no regulatory powers over this subject matter. Such developments have increased the prominence of EC procurement regulation, which, as we will see, may restrict the scope

---

[21] *R* v. *Lewisham LBC, ex p. Shell UK* [1988] 1 All ER 938: see further Arrowsmith, note 1 above, at 19.28–19.29. On this issue in Canada see *Shell Canada Products* v. *City of Vancouver* [1994] 1 SCR 231, noted by S. Arrowsmith (1994) 3 *PPLR* CS 174. For a similar issue concerning the power of the states of the United States of America in excluding from contracts firms that have dealings with certain foreign countries, see *Crosby* v. *National Foreign Trade Council* 120 S. Ct. 2288 (2000) and R. Stumberg, 'Preemption and Human Rights: Crosby v National Foreign Trade Council' (2000) 32 *Law & Pol. Int. Bus.* 109.

[22] See Race Relations Act 1971, as amended by the Race Relations (Amendment) Act 2000. This is, however, subject to the Local Government Act 1988, which contains certain special provisions on race relations matters in Section 18(2), and also to EC law. (See

for national authorities to act under this mainstreaming legislation. It is interesting that concern over implementing through procurement policies that do not directly impact on an authority's broader remit was reflected by the European Commission in its arguments in *Concordia Bus Finland*: it suggested that award criteria should be confined to matters with a direct impact on the procuring authority. However, this was rejected by the ECJ.[23] This was clearly correct, since the desirability of such 'indirect' regulation is of no concern to the EC's single market, but is a matter of the constitutional organisation of functions at national level.

As we have seen, horizontal procurement policies often appear as a form of regulation, and it might be asked whether it is justifiable to use procurement in this way, when the effect is to 'regulate' firms that contract with the government but to leave unregulated other comparable firms that do not. The parallel with other forms of regulation is obviously closer where the government seeks to influence contractor behaviour outside the contract itself. Whilst private individuals generally have no option but to express their preferences for certain behaviour through their purchasing and other similar activities, and thus can only influence the behaviour of a limited number of firms, the government does have the option of broader regulatory measures, which raises the question of whether it is justified to limit 'regulation' to government contractors.

Two justifications, however, can be offered. One is ensuring that government is associated with the highest possible standards. As with policies designed to ensure legal compliance this may be done both to set an example – which may encourage wider acceptance of the standards – and to avoid public criticism. This justification has particular force for policies limited to the contract, but is also relevant more generally. The second justification for 'regulation through procurement' concerns the effectiveness of the policy: procurement is in some fields a more effective policy instrument than alternatives, such as criminal or administrative sanctions, thus justifying a decision to focus limited resources on enforcing the policy in this limited field. As Morris states (in the context of equal opportunities policies): 'the individual complaint and adjudication

---

further Commission for Racial Equality and Local Government Association, *Race Equality and Procurement in Local Government: A Guide to Meeting the Duty to Promote Race Equality*.) See also Disability Discrimination Act 2005, discussed by Boyle in chapter 7 of this book.
[23] See chapter 4, section 14.

model of tackling discrimination is fundamentally flawed by problems of legalism, tortuous procedure and satisfying the legal burden of proof. Contract compliance, in contrast, is not handicapped by these problems. It evades the inherent deficiencies of individual adjudication or institutional investigation.'[24] Further, the close relationship between the government and its contractors can help ensure effective monitoring of policies. This is again particularly the case where the policy is limited to the government contract, but is also of broader relevance.

The use of procurement in a way that goes beyond merely requiring compliance with the general law may give rise to a number of concerns of constitutional principle. This is especially the case when procurement is used to provide sanctions for compliance with normative standards that apply beyond the contract being awarded, akin to regulation.[25] Such concerns may relate to, for example, the democratic legitimacy of regulation through procurement, the adequacy of procedural safeguards for contractors, legal certainty and transparency. We have already seen above that some similar concerns may arise with policies that are limited to compliance with the general law; for example, there may be concerns over procedural safeguards when a procuring authority makes its own determination of whether a contractor has violated the criminal law. However, in practice such concerns tend to arise more frequently with policies that go beyond the limits of the law. One reason for such concerns is that, as mentioned above, regulation through procurement may not require legislation, or at least primary legislation, which tends to provide better for the application of constitutional principles than do administrative processes. A second, related, factor is that where procurement is used merely to enforce legal requirements, use is often made in practice of external mechanisms for adjudicating on compliance, such as the criminal courts, which provide for safeguards for contractors. A third consideration is that the contractual activity of government sometimes is not subject to adequate control under constitutional and administrative law doctrines;[26] for example, in some states there is some uncertainty over how far general administrative law principles concerning due

---

[24] P. Morris, 'Legal Regulation of Contract Compliance: An Anglo-American Comparison' (1990) 19 *Anglo-Am. LR* 87, 88–89.

[25] As highlighted in the UK by T. Daintith, 'Regulation by Contract: the New Prerogative' [1979] 32 *CLP* 41.

[26] See, generally, S. Arrowsmith, 'Government Contracts and Public Law' (1990) 10 *LS* 231 (on common law systems).

process and rationality in decision-making apply to contracting activity.[27] Such concerns do not, however, cast any doubt on the suitability of procurement as a policy tool per se, but merely on the way in which constitutional principles are applied to this method of policy implementation in practice. They merely highlight the need to take special care when implementing such policies to ensure that this is done in accordance with ordinary constitutional values.

In practice many national regimes may, of course, choose to implement horizontal policies in a manner that does address these kinds of constitutional issues,[28] and may use formal instruments – including legislation – to do so, whether or not this is actually required under the constitution. For example, a state may enact legal rules that set out the policy in detail to ensure legal certainty, provide explicitly for transparency in the process, and set out procedural requirements for decisions to safeguard contractors' interests. As mentioned above, one method for addressing some of these concerns is to provide for a body external to procuring entities themselves to take decisions on the status of contractors, such as whether they have violated norms for which they may be excluded from government contracts; this approach is as relevant for violations of norms set solely for government contractors as it is for norms of more general application. An example of a significant body of this kind is the United States Office of Federal Contract Compliance Programs, which has a central responsibility for the government's programmes on affirmative action in the workplace, including decisions on non-compliance by contractors.[29] Central responsibility for making, collating and publicising decisions on contractors' status under horizontal procurement programmes can help to: promote transparency, consistency and effective enforcement; ensure adequate procedural safeguards for contractors, by focusing resources and expertise in one place; and avoid the delays to individual procurements that may occur when decisions are made on an ad hoc basis. This is especially important when decisions involve complex issues such as how non-compliance by one company should affect associated companies or persons.

---

[27] See, for example, S. Arrowsmith, 'Judicial Review and the Contractual Powers of Public Authorities' (1990) 106 *LQR* 277 and S. Bailey, 'Judicial Review of Contracting Decisions' (2007) *PL* 444.

[28] As noted above, norms that are limited in their application to government contractors can be set out in legislation as legally binding obligations, and may even be made subject to sanctions – such as fines – that are additional to any 'procurement' sanctions, such as exclusions.

[29] The Office is part of the US Department of Labor's Employment Standards Administration.

We can note in this respect that some of the concerns that arise from a national perspective also have parallels under EC law – in particular, as we have seen, transparency is a major concern of public procurement in EC law, because of its role in addressing the problem of discrimination – and thus may be affected to some extent by the EC regime.

Finally, we should mention that the participation of foreign firms in public procurement creates some additional complexities for implementing and regulating policies that extend beyond legal compliance. Authorities will need to decide whether to apply their policies to foreign firms and/or to work done abroad, or to confine these to domestic firms and/or work done in the awarding state. We explain in chapter 4 that where a policy seeks to 'buy' through government procurement social benefits such as reduced unemployment, authorities may not wish to pay for this when the benefits will go outside the jurisdiction. Thus they may wish to confine their measures to home suppliers and domestic contract work, or may even prefer to exclude foreign firms or activity, to ensure domestic benefits. It may also seem inappropriate, as well as involving unjustified costs to the domestic regime, to use procurement to 'regulate' firms or activities that are generally outside domestic jurisdiction, if the awarding state does not perceive that it has an interest in these firms or activities. However, as we will see in chapter 4, excluding foreign firms or work done abroad altogether may be problematic under international trade rules (although we suggest that it should in fact be permitted in some cases),[30] while admitting foreign firms or allowing performance abroad, but applying policies only to domestic firms or work, may be seen as creating problems for values of equal treatment under both domestic and international rules. Conversely, for reasons of equal treatment or otherwise, authorities might seek to impose requirements on foreign firms or work done abroad that already apply under general legal norms to domestic activity. How far these choices are limited by EC law is considered further in chapter 4.

3. Policies confined to performance of the contract being awarded and policies that go beyond contract performance

3.1. Introduction

As we have seen, a further distinction that can be made is one between, on the one hand, procurement policies that are concerned only with the

---

[30] See chapter 4, section 4.3.1, 'Justifying contractual requirements that hinder trade'.

work under the contract being awarded, and, on the other, policies that also extend to a supplier's other activities. As was explained in chapter 1, this can be characterised very broadly as a distinction between the 'government as purchaser' and 'government as regulator'. Further, various different policy concerns arise that often correspond broadly with these two groups of measures. However, both in describing and assessing the operation of horizontal policies and in analysing the impact of legal rules, this simple characterisation is often too crude and a more detailed taxonomy is needed that takes into account the dimensions set out in section 2 above, as well as the various sub-divisions set out below.

3.2. Policies confined to contract performance

An example of the first kind of policy, already mentioned, is a contract condition that requires a specified proportion of the contract work to be carried out by persons with disabilities or the long-term unemployed. Such policies relating to the contract may merely seek to ensure that the contractor complies with the law in carrying out the contract work, as discussed in section 2 above – for example, by ensuring the contractor complies with health and safety laws when carrying out the work. However, they may also seek to realise benefits from the work that go beyond those provided for by law – such as the employment of disabled persons beyond any legal requirements.

We have already alluded in chapter 2 to the fact that policies within this group can be subdivided into several further categories that are useful for legal analysis, in particular. The first two correspond completely with the first two mechanisms for implementing horizontal policies that are outlined in section 4 below, whilst the others are subdivisions that are relevant for all or some of the remaining mechanisms (contract conditions, award criteria, exclusions etc). They are as follows:

1. *Decision to purchase or not to purchase* – for example, a decision not to proceed with construction works because of the impact on the environment (see further section 4 (i) below).
2. *Decision on what to purchase* – for example, to purchase helicopters rather than life boats for sea rescue (see further section 4 (i) below).
3. *Policies relating to the contract that are implemented through other mechanisms.*

This third group may in turn be divided into four groups, as reflected in Table 2.1 set out in chapter 2, namely policies relating to: (a) the effect of the products, works or services when consumed, (b) the impact of production or delivery of the products, works or services, (c) the impact of disposal of the products, works or services, and (d) the contract workforce. Policies may, of course, relate to more than one group: a notable example is an award criterion that takes account of the environmental impact of a product across its whole life cycle, to include production, delivery, consumption and disposal (for example, a criterion that takes into account a product's whole carbon footprint). However, it is useful to distinguish the four groups both for purposes of exposition and because distinctions between the different groups are found in law and in the analysis of policy-makers, as explained in chapters 2 and 4.

i) The effect of the products, works or services when consumed

This refers to the effect of the products, works or services when consumed, whether by the authority itself, the public, or other intended beneficiaries. In the social sphere, for example, the government may seek to ensure that they can be used by all groups of employees or by all members of the public, as appropriate. Thus, for example, the government might specify that food served in canteens for government employees, in schools, or in public museums should cater to the needs of all religious groups. As discussed in chapter 7 on disability issues, 'social' specifications are becoming important in promoting accessibility for the disabled; thus governments may, for example, want to specify that buses for public bus services should be accessible to those in wheelchairs, that buildings should include ramps or lifts, or that IT equipment in offices, schools and libraries should be accessible for disabled users. Alternatively, as is also discussed in chapter 7, governments may prefer to incorporate disability considerations through award criteria rather than contractual requirements or may use a combination of both approaches. Examples of this sub-category in the environmental sphere include requirements for vehicles for government use to meet certain standards that limit toxic emissions or noise when the vehicle is used, or award criteria that take this into account.

ii) The impact of production or delivery of the products, works or services

A second sub-category concerns the impacts of the production or carrying out of the products, works or services (but excluding issues relating to the contract workforce, which we treat separately). We include production and delivery in one category here, since in the case of certain works and services production and delivery to the customer are merged. (In the case of supplies, of course, they are generally separate processes altogether.) Measures in this sub-category are particularly important in the context of environmental policy. For example, in relation to the production stage purchasers might specify that products should not be manufactured through a process that pollutes the environment; that products such as paper should be composed of recycled materials; or that products should be obtained from sustainable sources – for example, electricity from renewable sources (as discussed in chapter 9), or timber and timber-products from legal and sustainable sources (as is UK government policy).[31] For works or services authorities might include requirements that limit the environmental impact of delivery, such as requirements not to waste energy during delivery, or not to disturb wildlife. For supplies, they could include requirements to minimise packaging or requirements to limit the adverse impact of delivery – for example, by use of clean transport, measures to limit the risks of chemical spillages or by local production.[32] Social considerations may be implemented through requirements concerning the location of production (for example, a requirement for goods to be locally produced) or the manner of production – for example, in South Africa the government has made use of requirements that specify labour-intensive methods for construction of works, such as rural gravel roads, as a means to enhance employment.[33]

iii) The impact of disposal of the products, works or services

Thirdly, governments might wish to include provisions on disposal of goods, a type of measure that is again particularly relevant for environmental requirements. For example, they may require suppliers to recycle the products supplied after use.

iv) Measures relating to the contract workforce ('workforce measures')

Finally, governments may implement horizontal policies through requirements relating to the composition or working conditions of the contract workforce. Like other procurement measures, workforce measures may be

---

[31] On current policy see HM Government, UK Government Sustainable Procurement Action Plan (2007) available at www.sustainable-development.gov.uk, at 8.8–8.9.
[32] The last is particularly problematic for trade regimes because it may substantially affect trade, but we suggest it is justified in some cases: see chapter 4, section 4.3.1, 'Justifying contractual requirements that hinder trade'.
[33] See Green Paper, note 10 above, pp. 61–65.

limited to ensuring compliance with legal obligations, but frequently governments also take measures going beyond legal compliance. In the United Kingdom, for example, for the early part of the twentieth century central government required fair working conditions for those employed on government contracts that were more favourable than those applying under the general law, and inserted into all contracts terms requiring contractors to meet these higher standards.[34] Contract clauses may also, for example, require contractors to provide work on the contract for those with disabilities, or require that some of the work is subcontracted to small firms; or these considerations may, for example, be taken into account as contract award criteria.

3.3. Policies that go beyond contract performance

For descriptive purposes, policies that go beyond contract performance can be divided into three main groups.

First, they include policies that seek to regulate the contractor's behaviour across its business activity as a whole. Examples that we have already mentioned are policies that exclude from contracts firms that do not develop affirmative action policies to implement equality in their workforce, as with the equality policies of the US federal government and of the Northern Ireland government under FETO that were referred to in section 2 above. Measures excluding from government contracts any firms that invest in the tobacco industry or that have business dealings with 'undesirable' third countries are other examples, a notable illustration of the latter being a previous policy of some US states to exclude contractors that had connections with Myanmar (a policy ultimately declared unconstitutional, however, under US law).[35] Again, some

---

[34] For a summary of the policy see Arrowsmith, note 1 above, at 19.11–19.12, and for detailed analysis see B. Bercusson, *The Fair Wages Resolutions* (London: Mansell, 1978).

[35] Under: An Act Regulating Contracts with Companies Doing Business with or in Burma (Myanmar), chapter 130, 1996 Session Laws, Mass. Gen. Laws Ann., chapter 7 223 (West 1997). On the policy see, for example, S. Cleveland, 'Norm Internalisation and US Economic Sanctions' (2001) 26 *YJIL* 7; P. Fitzgerald, 'Massachusetts, Burma and the World Trade Organization: A Comment on Blacklisting, Federalism and Internet Advocacy in the Global Trading Era' (2001) 34 *CILJ* 1; M. Baker, 'Flying over the Judicial Hump: A Human Rights Drama Featuring Burma, the Commonwealth of Massachusetts, the WTO and the Federal Courts' (2000) 32 *Law & Pol. Int. Bus.* 51. On the legal issues under the US constitution, see *Crosby* v. *National Foreign Trade Council* 120 US S. Ct. 2288 (2000) and for summaries B. Denning and J. McCall, Note in [2000] 94 *AJIL* 750; J. Linarelli, 'Economic Sanctions and the US Supreme Court: Crosby

policies of this kind are limited to legal compliance – to ensuring that the contractor complies with the law in all the contractor's activities, as with the Northern Ireland policy on political and religious discrimination under FETO. However, many policies of this kind also seek to impose standards on contractors' businesses beyond those of undertakings in general – as with the US federal equality policy – or seek other social or environmental benefits not otherwise provided for by law.

A second group of policies going beyond contract performance comprises various policies in which the government does not so much seek to change the behaviour of undertakings,[36] as support or develop economic activity of undertakings with particular characteristics. Common examples are preferences or set-asides to assist businesses owned by ethnic minorities or small businesses (as discussed in chapter 8), or policies to support workshops that provide employment for the disabled (as discussed by Boyle in chapter 7).

Finally, other policies in this category are those under which governments require contractors to provide benefits to the community that are not directly connected with the contract – such as building community facilities, or building in the local area a factory unconnected with the contract. Benefits of this kind are often referred to as offsets.

We include in this category policies that are concerned with the behaviour of contractors *on government contracts in general*, rather than merely with the contractor's performance of a contract being awarded in a particular procurement process. An example would be a policy of excluding from future government contracts any contractor that has violated corruption laws in relation to previous government contracts, even though contractors with other corruption convictions are not excluded.

Policies that are directed at, or affect, behaviour outside the confines of government contracts often impose a greater burden on suppliers than policies limited to the contract, especially when they extend to all the suppliers' activities. As a result, there are also potentially greater costs for

v National Foreign Trade Council' (2001) 10 *PPLR* NA 91 and S. Banerjee, 'The Burma Law Dilemma: The Constitutionality of US State and Local Sanctions in the Sphere of Foreign Commerce: Crosby v National Foreign Trade Council 530 US 2000' (2000) 27 *LIEI* 293. On legality under WTO law, see S. Arrowsmith, *Government Procurement in the WTO* (The Hague; London: Kluwer Law International, 2003), chapter 13 and the other works cited there at pp. 327–328.

[36] Of course, this is not a hard and fast distinction. For example, policies supporting minority-owned businesses may seek to encourage established firms to take minorities into the ownership and management of the business.

the procurement process, both because of the costs of compliance reflected in tenders, and because (especially with contract requirements laid down by government) they may reduce the pool of contractors. From the EC's perspective, we will see in chapter 4 that these policies have given rise to concern because of their relatively greater impact in limiting market access.[37] This difference between policies that are formally limited to contract performance and those going beyond it is, in this respect, a matter of degree, which depends on the nature of the contract: even policies formally limited to contract performance may have a significant practical impact on wider business activity. For example, compliance with a clause requiring supplies to be produced without pollution may effectively require a business to change its production methods for all similar products, or at least for those made in the same factory. Similarly, it may be difficult to limit changes to pay and conditions only to workers on government contracts, either because individual workers are involved in both governmental and non-governmental work, or because it appears inequitable to apply different pay and conditions to similar work within the same organisation.

A key question that has arisen under EC law is how far the two types of horizontal policies outlined above should receive different treatment. At present, it can be said, broadly speaking, that in terms of the scope of discretion of Member States policies that are limited in their focus to the contract being awarded ('government as purchaser') receive more lenient treatment than those that are not ('government as regulator'). However, as chapter 1 explained, in considering the concept of 'government as purchaser' and 'government as regulator', the position is – potentially at least – quite complex, since there are many different legal doctrines that apply, and they do not necessarily all apply in quite the same way.[38]

4. Mechanisms for implementing horizontal policies

As mentioned, a third element of the taxonomy of horizontal procurement policies is the distinction between different mechanisms for implementing these policies. As we will see, many of these mechanisms are appropriate for all types of policies – both those that are limited to compliance with the law and those that are not, and both those that are

---

[37] See, in particular, chapter 4, section 4.3.1, 'Justifying contractual requirements that hinder trade' and chapter 4, section 8.

[38] See chapter 1, section 4.

limited to contract performance and those that are not. However, this is not always the case – for example, it was suggested in section 2 that a contractor's ability to comply with external legal requirements is unlikely to be suitable as an award criterion.

Whatever the mechanism chosen, incorporating horizontal policies into procurement generally involves some costs that must be weighed against the benefits to be achieved.[39]

First, such policies often involve paying higher prices for the goods, works or services and/or involve an adverse impact on other features of a supplier's offer such as service quality. This is not, of course, always the case, and some policies directed at social or environmental goals may even enhance value for money: for example, buying more expensive low-energy light bulbs may save funds in the long term if the extra expenditure is outweighed by lower energy costs, while policies to enhance access of small suppliers without any form of preference (mechanism (ix) below) may lead to better value from greater competition. However, many policies do involve additional costs. These can arise both from the costs to suppliers of providing the social or environmental benefits – for example, the extra costs of features to make buses accessible to wheelchairs, or of providing enhanced working conditions – and because some firms may be deterred from participating altogether, thus reducing competition. In this respect the position is, of course, no different in principle from the purchase of other benefits or features under a contract, such as paying a higher price for more rapid processing with an IT system – although the costs and benefits of certain horizontal policies, notably those that regulate behaviour beyond the contract, may be particularly difficult to establish. We will discuss in more detail below the way in which different policy mechanisms, and different approaches within those mechanisms, may affect the government's ability to identify and control the extent of costs and the value offered by contractors.

A second cost may arise from increased discretion for procuring entities – for example, the discretion to exclude firms that do not meet horizontal requirements, or the extra discretion involved in applying social award criteria. This is not to imply that the discretion involved in such assessments is any greater than that involved in other assessments – for example, of technical capability – but merely that the overall element of discretion may be increased. This will be a greater concern

---

[39] For an excellent review of the evidence on empirical impacts of horizontal policies available in existing literature, see McCrudden, note 8 above, pp. 594–617.

for procurement systems that place significant emphasis on limiting discretion and its potential for abuse as a means of achieving their objectives, whether those objectives are value for money, reducing corruption and/or preventing discrimination on grounds of nationality. As the author has explained elsewhere, the value of limiting discretion as a means of achieving procurement objectives varies greatly between individual states and procuring entities, according to such factors as the extent and nature of the problems involved (such as the extent of corruption), and the knowledge and skills of purchasing officers.[40] As we saw in chapter 2, the EC directives limit discretion in order to deter and monitor discrimination on grounds of nationality; and some of the EC's rules, such as restrictions on advance exclusion from procurement and requirements to disclose criteria in advance, may probably be explained on this basis. Such restrictions may be problematic for those Member States that do not emphasise discretion as a means of achieving national procurement goals, since they impose greater additional constraints on those Member States than apply under purely national rules.

A third type of cost is the cost of checking for compliance, assessing additional award criteria etc., and the cost to firms of complying with additional administrative requirements (which may also deter participation).[41] The potential for horizontal policies to create significant costs if implemented effectively is illustrated by chapter 12, dealing with the EC's mandatory exclusions of contractors convicted of corruption and certain other offences: in particular, it may be difficult to make such policies effective without imposing unreasonable costs on both the administration and suppliers to prevent unscrupulous firms from evading the exclusion rules by setting up new companies.[42]

Finally, the disruption and costs of complaints or legal disputes may be increased by adding horizontal policies into the procurement process.

Both costs and benefits vary according to the mechanism used, as well as other factors, such as the consistency and effectiveness with which the policy is applied and monitored. The costs of the different mechanisms, and the balance of costs and benefits, are relevant for national governments when deciding whether and how to implement horizontal policies.

---

[40] See Arrowsmith, Linarelli and Wallace, note 1 above, pp. 20–23.

[41] For an interesting illustration see P. Wittie, 'Transnational Concerns: Domestic Preferences' (2002) 11 *PPLR* 145, 147–148, considering the US programme of domestic preferences.

[42] See chapter 12, section 5.

As chapter 1 explained, this balance is in principle for Member States to determine; the EC does not in general have the power to regulate procurement to determine the appropriate balance between horizontal policies and other procurement policies, but only to regulate Member States' discretion for the limited purpose of creating an internal market. However, costs and benefits are relevant at EC level to some extent in deciding how to treat horizontal policies under internal market rules: EC law must consider both the adverse impacts on trade of the various policy mechanisms, and – as noted above – the costs for national governments of the loss of discretion in implementing horizontal policies. The choice available between different procurement mechanisms – as well as the availability of policy tools other than public procurement – must also be taken into account in considering the proportionality of Member State action. The main relative advantages and disadvantages of the different policy mechanisms are noted briefly in the following taxonomy of available mechanisms.

The main mechanisms are as follows:

i. The decision to purchase, or not to purchase

As discussed in chapter 1, the very reason that governments make many of their purchases in the first place is to implement industrial or social policies – to provide health facilities, education etc. – or environmental benefits (for example, with the procurement of a recycling plant). In these cases these benefits are the very purpose of purchasing the works, products and services. In addition, however, a decision on whether to make a particular purchase at all may be influenced by social or environmental concerns that are separate from those to be achieved through the use of the products, works or services themselves (the hospitals, schools etc.). These decisions we can consider for the purpose of this book as involving horizontal policies.[43]

First, as we noted in chapter 1, a government's decision to make a purchase of products, works or services may be taken not only because of the benefits from those products, works or services directly, but also because of the other resulting benefits – without these, the purchase might not be made. For example, states often undertake programmes of public works to provide employment and a consequent economic boost in times of high unemployment or recession; in this case both

---

[43] On this point see chapter 1, section 2.

the desire for the buildings or other infrastructure to use for offices, transport etc. *and* the boost to employment may influence the decision to go ahead with the project. A government might also undertake a programme that uses innovative products of some kind – for example, constructing an experimental housing village using environmentally friendly materials and processes – not merely because of the direct benefit (for housing), but to develop the products concerned.

Secondly, a government might decide not to go ahead with a purchase that it *would* otherwise wish to make, because of the social or environmental impacts. For example, it may decide to abandon a plan for a dam because of the adverse impact on the environment; or to scale down the original size of a public housing project because of environmental concerns.

ii. The decision on what to purchase

Assuming that a decision has been made to undertake a particular function or project, the basic means chosen for carrying it out may be influenced by social or environmental concerns, as well as by the direct requirements of the function or project itself. For example, an authority might for environmental reasons decide to construct a video-conferencing facility, rather than to spend money on travel for meetings; or it might decide to purchase helicopters rather than lifeboats for sea rescue, to support a national helicopter industry. Environmental considerations might also influence its decision on whether to provide a tunnel or a bridge as a solution for joining the mainland to an island. The decision on precisely how to implement a project – as well as the decision to undertake it – might also be influenced by the desire to develop new products or services. The solution chosen will generally be written into the contract specification, creating a contractual obligation to deliver it.

There is no bright line between situations (i) and (ii), nor between (ii) and (iii) below. A choice of means may involve a compromise on functionality – for example, video-conferencing may be inferior to meetings in securing effective discussions and improving communication, but chosen for the environmental benefits. Whether a decision to choose a particular means, or to scale down a project, should be classified as a decision not to make a purchase or a decision on *what* to purchase is a matter of degree. Similarly, whether a particular specified requirement is merely a function of a specified product or a different means of meeting a need is also a matter of degree. However, it is a convenient classification for descriptive purposes.

iii. Contractual requirements laid down by the purchaser

Once a decision is made to procure particular products, works or services, entities may seek to implement social or environmental objectives by laying down contractual obligations on these matters in the contract of procurement. These may relate to the contract, or they may go beyond it.

So far as requirements relating to the contract are concerned, we have seen above that these – like many of the other mechanisms discussed below – can be of several types. As explained, they may relate to: consumption effects (such as pollution when a product is used); production or delivery effects (pollution in producing a product); disposal effects (such as whether it can be recycled); or workforce matters (such as the terms and conditions of workers on the contract).

In addition, conditions may be laid down to promote compliance with standards or requirements that are not limited to the contract work. For example, a government requiring its suppliers to implement active fair recruitment policies across their whole business might include an undertaking on this as a contract term; or a contract might include a term that suppliers should deliver any stipulated offsets. Contract terms relating to horizontal policies of this kind will often concern the supplier's future conduct and provide an incentive to compliance with government requirements, as with the examples above. However, a government might also wish to include contractual warranties relating to past conduct – for example, that the contractor has not in the preceding years done business with a particular third country regime, or has not engaged in corruption on previous contracts.

As well as laying down requirements for all tenderers, governments also often include contract terms as part of other policy mechanisms. For example, they might include warranties that the contractor concerned is eligible for a set-aside or award preference, as discussed in relation to mechanisms (v) and (viii) below.

The categorisation above is not intended to suggest anything about how EC law does or should treat different types of contractual requirement. We will see in chapter 4[44] that, in establishing which contractual requirements governments may include, EC law distinguishes between two types: those that concern performance of the contract, which are allowed, and those that do not, which are not. However, there is some debate about how to draw the line, including how to treat requirements

---

[44] See chapter 4, section 8.

concerning the manner in which products are produced.[45] With respect to those requirements that *are* allowed EC law also appears to adopt a further distinction between certain requirements that we will call 'technical' and requirements concerning other matters: with the former group, purchasers may exclude in advance suppliers they consider cannot meet the requirement, whereas with the latter group they may not. Again, the boundaries of the categories are debated. The result is a threefold categorisation: requirements allowable as contract conditions that can also form the basis for advance exclusion; requirements allowable as contract conditions that cannot, however, form the basis for advance exclusion; and requirements that are not allowed at all. How these fit with the descriptive categories above is examined in chapter 4.

Generally requirements will – like the basic features of the project – be included in the contract to ensure that they can be enforced. In many cases, as we have seen, they will be requirements that the contractor is not otherwise obliged by law to meet. In some cases, however, the government may include as contractual conditions requirements already imposed by law, to provide an additional enforcement mechanism or to reinforce the existing requirement. For example, in the UK the Westminster government's standard contract terms include an obligation for contractors to refrain from any discrimination in employment that is forbidden by law, whether on grounds of race, gender, religion, disability, sexual orientation or otherwise.[46] Similarly, a contract term might require a firm to comply with health and safety legislation on a construction site.

As with other aspects of contracts, horizontal requirements should be drafted to maximise the benefits from social or environmental requirements, by giving suppliers the maximum flexibility over *how* to meet the government's functional requirements. For example, under a policy requiring firms to utilise long-term unemployed persons in government works contracts, it may not be appropriate to specify precisely *how* unemployed persons should be engaged (whether as employees, employees of subcontractors etc), but to leave firms free to use the most cost-effective methods, especially since they are likely to have better knowledge of the market. Limiting specifications to functional requirements may,

---

[45] See chapter 4, sections 8 and 14.
[46] See, for example, Model Terms and Conditions for contracts for goods, D2, available at www.ogc.gov.uk.

in fact, itself have industrial, social or environmental benefits that extend beyond the contract, in that this encourages innovation.

The approach of laying down minimum requirements in the contract documents is suitable when for some reason there are overriding requirements that *must* be met. This will be the case, of course, if the specifications merely reflect existing legal requirements. It may also be the case in other situations in which there is reliable information that any additional costs of meeting the requirements are within acceptable limits, or (more rarely) where the government is unwilling to make the purchase without these benefits. (In this case, if the overall price is too high it will not go ahead.) As we have pointed out, such additional costs may arise both because of the extra cost for firms of meeting the requirements and because some firms may be unable to participate at all because they cannot meet them. However, before laying down social or environmental requirements that go beyond the law, it may be useful to consider whether or not it would be better to approach the issue in an alternative way, notably through the use of social or environmental award criteria, mechanism (viii), as discussed below; using award criteria can allow a more precise assessment of the costs, provides a mechanism to limit these costs, and facilitates the best overall combination of social/ environmental benefits on the one hand, and price and other features on the other. We should also note that it is possible, by using suitable award criteria, to assess the costs of certain specific social or environmental requirements that the authority might want to include, by requiring or allowing variant bids. Variants bids are bids that propose a different approach to those suggested in a 'standard' solution laid down by the authority – including because they propose additional features not found in the standard bid, or because they omit certain features found in the standard bid. Allowing or requiring firms to submit variant bids instead of or in addition to a standard bid can allow an authority to assess the additional costs that will be incurred by including the additional/omitted features, by comparing the costs of the variant and standard bids in comparing tenders, and taking these into account in the contract award criteria. This approach can be used to help determine the costs of including social or environmental requirements. Thus an authority might include a requirement for providing specific employment and training for the unemployed in a standard bid, but also allow firms to submit variant bids that do not include such social benefits. The award criteria will then need to include the social benefits provided by the bid, so that if these are considered to outweigh any extra costs the authority can then award the contract to a bid that offers the social benefit rather than one that does not.

On the other hand, it may sometimes be appropriate to require compliance with standards going beyond the law regardless of all these considerations. This is especially the case if these standards have some symbolic importance that might be compromised by an overt trade-off between social/environmental aspects and commercial considerations – for example, where the government is seeking to promote compliance with certain environmental standards by setting an example.

In addition, we can note that in some cases minimum requirements on social or environmental features or benefits may be combined with award criteria that give additional credit to those products or services with *enhanced* environmental or social features. This is discussed further in chapter 7 on disability issues.

As well as including social or environmental requirements to obtain specific social or environmental benefits under the contract, or to limit the adverse impact of the contract, a different – or, often, additional – motive for such requirements is to promote the development and mass production of products with desirable social or environmental features, that can then be used in the wider market. (As noted above, governments may even make initial decisions on what projects to undertake for this same reason.) For example, as discussed in chapter 7, the government may decide to purchase IT equipment with features that make it accessible to disabled users, not merely for the benefit of employees and the public who use this equipment, but also to encourage the development and manufacture of affordable equipment that can be bought by the private sector. This is an additional reason for including such features as mandatory requirements of the specifications rather than merely as award criteria, since it may be necessary to guarantee a market for the products.

There are various means available to secure compliance with contract conditions. First, contractual remedies may be available for a violation (which may, indeed, be the motivation for including the term as part of the contract). Often the remedies are simply those available under general national contract law. These may include a right to terminate the contract, an order to compel performance, and/or a right to compensation for violations. The remedies may depend on how the parties choose to treat a particular requirement. For example, in English law they may choose to state that violating a social or environmental condition will give rise to a remedy of termination; this is done in practice with, for example, obligations to provide timber from legal sources.[47] The applicable general rules – for example, the nature and amount of damages – will vary according to national law. General contractual remedies may, however, be difficult to exercise; for example a damages remedy may require specific and quantifiable damage to the government that is difficult to prove for breach of social conditions, while terminating the contract may be inconvenient in practice because of the costs and delay. For this reason it may be useful to provide for suitable remedies directly in legislation (such as specific financial penalties) as has been done, for example, in South Africa, for enforcing contract specifications concerned with the employment of disadvantaged groups.[48] We will see in chapter 4 that it is not clear how far EC law procurement law limits the exercise of remedies for violating a contractual requirement.[49]

In addition, to secure the benefits involved in the policy authorities will generally wish to reject in advance tenders that do not accept the requirements – and under EC law they are generally required to do so.[50] They may even also wish to exclude tenderers who are willing to accept the requirement, when the authority considers that the tenderer cannot, or will not, actually comply with it; this is especially the case because of the practical difficulties that may exist in exercising remedies for an actual violation. We will see in chapter 4, however, that EC law possibly does not allow such advance exclusion for *all* contractual requirements, including many horizontal requirements, probably because of the fear that such exclusions might be abused to favour national suppliers.[51]

iv. Packaging and timing of orders

Governments may also implement horizontal policy objectives through the way in which their orders are placed on the market, in terms of the way in which requirements are packaged together and/or the timing of those requirements. As discussed in chapter 8, this is one strategy used to promote the participation of small and medium-sized enterprises (SMEs) in public procurement. For example, one reason that governments may let their requirements through framework agreements,[52] that involve awarding small amounts of work over a period of time, is to

---

[47] *Framework for Sustainable Development on the Government Estate*, Part F, available at www.sustainable-development.gov.uk

[48] Preferential Procurement Regulations 2001 pertaining to the Preferential Procurement Policy Framework Act: No 5 of 2000, Regulation 15.

[49] See chapter 4, section 8.1.4.   [50] See chapter 4, section 8.1.3.

[51] See chapter 4, section 8.1.3.   [52] See chapter 2, section 4.3.4.

improve the chances for SME participation. Similarly, a requirement awarded at one time may be divided into separate lots to offer the possibility of tendering either for the whole amount or for small parts, with awards being made on the basis of best overall value for money.

Such approaches may be designed to enhance value for money by widening the market to include more firms – smaller as well as larger. However, they may also seek specifically to support SME development as an industrial policy objective. In this case any costs are mainly administrative costs, namely the additional costs of letting and administering a large number of smaller contracts rather than one large contract – and such costs can be factored into the bid evaluation, if desired. However, such approaches may also be adopted even when it is accepted they may involve higher prices or other loss of value. For example, work may be packaged in small amounts with separate award procedures for each contract, to promote SME participation, even though it is recognised that this may lead to higher prices by deterring larger firms from tendering.

v. Set-asides

Another mechanism for implementing horizontal policies is to limit participation in certain procurements solely to a particular group. This approach has often been used in the context of prison workshops and, as chapter 7 explains, workshops for disabled persons (and the new EC directives now provide expressly for the latter).[53] It has also been used to provide economic opportunities for disadvantaged ethnic groups and SMEs: set-asides are, for example, an important feature of the United States federal government's policies to promote small businesses in general and small businesses owned by disadvantaged persons, in particular.[54] Such policies may be favoured by government both for their high visibility – the public and favoured groups can see specific results in contracts awarded to the beneficiaries – and because their guaranteed and immediate allocation of contracts may produce rapid economic results. Governments can make set-asides more effective through contractual terms, such as a warranty that the contractor is eligible for the set-aside.

---

[53] See chapter 7, section 5.4.
[54] For an outline see J. Cibinic and R. Nash, *Formation of Government Contracts*, 3rd edn (Washington, DC: George Washington University Law School, 1998), chapter 10. Up to date information on these schemes is available at www.sbaonline.sba.gov/.

The costs of set-asides are, however, potentially high, because of reduced competition for contracts, combined with the fact that the favoured groups may not be as competitive as those who are excluded. Governments may be prepared to pay extra costs, or may attempt to eliminate them, by allowing set-asides only when they can be operated on commercial terms. As with policies implemented through contract conditions, the procurement process itself will not provide any precise information on the extra costs incurred. However, governments can to some extent retain the benefits of competition by setting aside just part of procurement, holding a competition for the whole requirement, and then allowing the best bidder from the favoured group to provide the part set aside only if it will improve its offer to match the best terms offered in the competition (the 'offer-back' approach). This approach was used by the UK government, for example, for major contracts awarded to support workshops for the disabled under its old 'Priority Suppliers' scheme.[55]

Another problem with set-asides is that the favoured groups may have insufficient incentives to become competitive in the general market place. If – as is often the case – one objective of the policy is to develop industries or firms that are competitive in the wider market, procurement set-asides may actually be counter-productive In practice, set-asides may also be introduced or maintained as a result of political pressure when they are not needed, leading to costs, but without any concrete benefits.

In some cases, in particular when governments have sought to promote a 'national champion' or to place contracts strategically to maintain competition, contracts have been set aside not merely for a limited group, but for specific firms without competition. Contracts may also be allocated to specific firms in a favoured group without competition in other cases. For example, under the old UK scheme for supporting workshops for the disabled the government allocated low-value requirements to these workshops without competition where it was satisfied that the supply was on commercial terms.[56]

---

[55] This was dropped when it became apparent that it was not compatible with the relevant EC directive, and it is not permitted under the new directive's express provisions on this subject: see chapter 7, section 5.4.
[56] See chapter 7, section 5.4.

vi. Exclusion from contracts for non-compliance with government policies

Another important mechanism for implementing policies through procurement is exclusion from the chance to participate in contracts. Exclusion or the threat of exclusion may be used to encourage compliance with government policies, and/or to penalise past violations.

As with many other procurement mechanisms, such as contractual conditions, exclusion may be employed as an additional measure to support general norms, such as those of the criminal law, that are not limited to government contractors. The EC's mandatory exclusion of firms convicted of certain criminal offences, discussed in chapter 12, is an example of this, as is the Northern Ireland policy of excluding firms that violate obligations not to discriminate on grounds of religious or political belief, discussed in section 2 above. Exclusions may also be used, however, to support norms laid down solely for government contractors. This, we have seen in section 2, is the case with the US federal government policy of excluding contractors that do not implement recruitment policies designed to promote workplace equality.

As with some other mechanisms, exclusion may be limited to supporting compliance with norms relating to the contract awarded: governments may exclude a firm merely to ensure that a contract is awarded only to a supplier that is able to perform certain contract requirements, which could be any of the four types of requirement outlined in section 3 (that is, concerning consumption effects, delivery or production effects, disposal effects or the contract workforce). For example, an authority might decide to exclude a supplier that it does not think will actually be able to meet a contract requirement to ensure that all energy supplied under the contract is from renewable sources. Exclusion may also, however, again be used as a tool to ensure compliance with requirements *not* linked solely to contract performance. These may be requirements applying to all a contractor's business: examples are the EC's mandatory exclusion provisions, which require exclusion for all past convictions for the stated offences, and the US policies promoting workplace equality, referred to above. The government may also wish to use exclusion as sanction for non-compliance with contractual or other requirements merely on previous government contracts – for example, for violation of previous contractual terms on fair working conditions. Failure to comply with past requirements may, of course, be evidence of inability to comply in the future, and past non-compliance might thus be invoked

to exclude for this more limited reason, as well as by way of penalty for
past violations. Governments may also wish to exclude firms not merely
for non-compliance with certain standards but also for other reasons
noted in section 3 above, namely because they wish to confine participation to certain groups of firms, such as small businesses, or workshops for
the disabled, or because such firms cannot meet 'offset' requirements.

We can see that a government may often wish to use both exclusions
and contract conditions together. For example, where a works contract
includes contractual requirements to engage the long-term unemployed
on the contract, both the threat of exclusion from future contracts and
the availability of contractual remedies for violation might be employed
as a means of ensuring compliance.

Exclusions of this kind may result in higher prices and/or a compromise of quality or other terms, both because they may limit competition
and because contractors that do compete may pass on some of the compliance costs to the government. As with set-asides and contractual conditions, it can be difficult to assess the precise costs. Further, the discretion that
exclusions involve may create scope for abuse – for example, they may be
abused to exclude firms that offer competition to a favoured supplier.

Nevertheless, exclusions can be useful. First, they allow governments to
work closely with a limited group of firms on an ongoing basis to improve
practices – for example, on recruitment. Secondly, as with contractual
requirements, they can be used to support existing legal norms, such as
prohibitions on corruption, or other standards (such as on human rights)
where an explicit cost/benefit analysis through the use of award criteria
seems inappropriate because of the moral dimension. As with contract
requirements, however, balancing of the costs and benefits may in practice
occur through the exercise of discretion over whether or not to exclude.
Even mandatory exclusions are often made subject to exceptions for public
interest reasons, as with the EC's mandatory exclusions discussed in chapter
12. Such exceptions could be based on cost considerations – although it is
not clear that this is the case with the EC's mandatory exclusions.[57]

We will see in chapter 4 that exclusions are one of the most problematic aspects of EC law, probably because of a fear that the discretion
that they confer may be abused to favour national suppliers. We have
already noted that, probably for this reason, EC law possibly does not
allow exclusions in all cases, even for the limited purpose of securing
compliance with all social or environmental requirements of the

---

[57] See chapter 12, section 8.

contract.[58] We will also see that EC law does not generally allow exclusion for violation of norms set for government contractors that go beyond the general law, since EC law does not generally allow use of procurement to regulate firms' behaviour.[59] The main exception to this is that exclusions may possibly be used against contractors that have violated external norms, such as those of the criminal law[60] – and, indeed, as we have seen, exclusion is *required* for those convicted of corruption and certain other offences. How far exclusions may be used as a sanction for past violations of the government's own contracts is not entirely clear.[61]

vii. Preferences in inviting firms to tender

Horizontal considerations can also be taken into account in deciding which firms to invite to tender. In some procedures, entities may decide to invite only a limited number of firms from those qualified – for example, when the costs of evaluating many tenders are likely to outweigh the benefits from greater competition. We saw in chapter 2 that under the EC directives the restricted procedure, negotiated procedure and competitive dialogue all allow for this approach. Making this selection on the basis of horizontal considerations can give the relevant firms a much better chance of receiving contracts.

Preferences in selection have often been used to favour firms with certain characteristics unconnected with their ability to perform but related to broader goals. These are perhaps most likely in practice to be concerned with the characteristics of suppliers – for example, selection preferences for firms from poor regions, those owned by disadvantaged ethnic minorities or workshops for disabled persons. However, they could in theory also relate to the firms' relative performance in complying with certain standards, such as fair recruitment standards. They might also be used in favour of firms likely to offer a better performance of the particular contract in respect of its social or environmental objectives – for example, firms that the authority thinks are able to offer better proposals for utilising unemployed persons on the contract, where the quality of such proposals is a contract award criterion.[62] As with award

---

[58] See chapter 4, section 8.1.4.   [59] See chapter 4, section 11.
[60] See chapter 4, section 11.2.   [61] See chapter 4, section 11.2.
[62] As with award criteria, exclusion and contract requirements, preferences concerning performance could relate to consumption effects, production/delivery effects, disposal effects or workforce matters: see section 3 above.

criteria, however, preferences might not be considered suitable for ensuring compliance with external norms, or with policies based on moral principle.

Using this mechanism need not affect other aspects of the procurement, such as price or quality, where it is used only when the qualified firms are otherwise equal. However, there may still be administrative or other costs. It is also possible that non-favoured firms will be deterred from participating because of the reduced chance of success, and that this will affect value for money.

viii. Award criteria

Another common mechanism for implementing horizontal policies is through award criteria – that is, by taking account of industrial, social or environmental considerations when comparing what different bidders can offer.

Award criteria may be used to determine the basic means for implementing a project, in the sense referred to in discussing mechanism (ii) above. Thus, referring again to the example there of a government considering whether to provide a tunnel or a bridge to an island, rather than making this decision itself and writing its choice into the specification issued to bidders, it might leave to bidders the option of proposing different solutions. In such a case the environmental implications of solutions can be taken into account as an award criterion in evaluating proposals.

As with contractual requirements, award criteria, also, will often be limited to the performance of the contract, and as with many other mechanisms may concern all four types of measure outlined in section 3. Thus they might relate to the consumption effects of the product/works/services – for example, a preference for buses that are accessible to wheelchairs; to the production or delivery effects – for example, a preference for products produced from recycled materials; to the disposal effects – for example, a preference for tenderers willing to take back the products for recycling; or to the workforce carrying out the contract – for example, a preference for tenderers offering employment and training to the long-term unemployed. This latter approach has been adopted in Northern Ireland, for example, where the government recently undertook a pilot project to examine the costs and benefit of such an approach: tenderers for selected works and services projects were required to present an employment plan for utilising on the contract persons unemployed for more than three months, the quality of which was taken into

4

Application of the EC Treaty and directives to horizontal policies: a critical review

SUE ARROWSMITH

1. Introduction

Chapter 1 introduced the phenomenon of horizontal policies in procurement and highlighted relevant principles of EC law, in particular, the equal status of horizontal policies with other procurement policies; equal treatment and integration of environmental considerations into EC policies; proportionality and subsidiarity; and the limited relevance of the directives in interpreting the EC Treaty. Chapter 2 provided an overview of the EC procurement regime, whilst chapter 3 set out a taxonomy of policies. The present chapter will now provide a critical review of EC regulation of horizontal policies, drawing on the framework of previous chapters. As well as offering a critical review of the regime, this chapter also provides background for the analysis in later chapters. Conversely, it draws on those chapters to provide a more complete picture of the regime.

This chapter first considers the application of the EC Treaty's free movement rules to horizontal policies (sections 2–4). (As mentioned in chapter 1, the state aid rules are examined separately in chapter 5.) It then examines how national discretion to implement horizontal policies is affected by Public Sector Directive 2004/18/EC, which has a significant impact in this field (sections 5–14). It also notes the extent to which the directive has sought to harness Member States' procurement power in support of the Community's own policy objectives (section 15). Special considerations applicable to Utilities Directive 2004/17/EC, which has been much less explored in previous work, are examined by Arrowsmith and Maund in chapter 11. Finally, the chapter notes briefly the potential impact of the EC's international trade agreements, in particular the World Trade Organization Agreement on Government Procurement (GPA) (section 16).

2. Horizontal policies and the EC Treaty: introductory remarks

We saw in chapter 2 that the EC Treaty's free movement provisions apply in principle to all public procurement. This includes contracts that are outside the directives or only lightly regulated, such as concessions, 'Part B' services contracts and below-threshold contracts.

As mentioned in chapter 1, and elaborated below, under the *directives* the legality of horizontal policies turns to a great extent on whether the governments acts as a purchaser, implementing policies concerned only with performance of its own contracts, or as a regulator, using procurement as a broader policy tool: the directives generally permit the former activity but not the latter. An important theme of the present section is that, in the author's view, the same limitations on policies going beyond the contract do not apply under the Treaty. This conclusion is warranted in light of the principles discussed in chapter 1, including the need to proceed with caution in extending restrictions in secondary legislation to primary Community law. On the other hand, it is argued that a kind of distinction between government as purchaser and government as regulator should be employed to *contain* EC controls on national discretion, in that many policies limited to contract performance are to be excluded from the concept of hindrances to trade under the Treaty, under the doctrine of 'excluded buying decisions' that was elaborated in chapter 2. (See section 4.3.1 below.)

We will consider in turn two policy groups: on the one hand, industrial policies, defined broadly as those that seek to promote or support the development of industry in general, or particular areas or sectors of industry, and, on the other, social and environmental policies.[1] This is not a precise classification, nor exhaustive of possible horizontal policies, but is useful to elucidate the impact of the law. In particular, the Treaty largely prohibits policies in the first group, making it unnecessary to consider separately all the distinctions and mechanisms elaborated in chapter 3. With social or environmental policies, however, a more detailed analysis is required.

3. Industrial policies and the EC Treaty

As mentioned, industrial policies appear largely to be prohibited under the Treaty. However, there are qualifications to this. Further, as

---

[1] S. Arrowsmith, *The Law of Public and Utilities Procurement*, 2nd edn (London: Sweet & Maxwell, 2005), chapter 19.

elaborated below, the author does not consider that such policies can generally be designated as unlawful – as sometimes suggested – merely because they restrict trade and are of an 'economic nature'; a more nuanced analysis is required.

We may begin by noting, first, that procurement policies that aim merely at supporting national industry against foreign competition to preserve employment and profits – 'simple protectionism' – will generally violate the free movement rules. Most policies of this kind are distinctly applicable. We explained in chapter 2 that such policies are hindrances to trade, and it is clear that they cannot be justified under Article 30 EC, Articles 45–46 EC and Article 55 EC, or as general interest requirements: their objectives are directly contrary to those of the free movement provisions of facilitating competition based on comparative advantage. This applies to preferential treatment at main contractor level, such as setting aside purchases for national firms, and at subcontractor level, and to preferences for national labour or products. Thus in *Storebaelt*,[2] for example, the ECJ ruled that it violated Article 28 EC, Article 43 EC and Article 49 EC to include in a contract for building a bridge a 'Danish content' clause requiring the greatest possible use of Danish materials and goods, and Danish labour and equipment – a contention not disputed by Denmark.[3]

Whilst most provisions motivated by simple protectionism are distinctly applicable, they could, however, be indistinctly applicable – for example, preferences for contractors whose main activity is in the awarding state. We argued in chapter 2, based primarily on *Concordia Bus Finland*,[4] that certain 'buying' decisions, those limited to contract performance, are not generally hindrances to trade, even when they have a greater impact on imported products – for example, award criteria that favour non-polluting products.[5] Whilst such decisions *may* be taken with the motive of favouring national industry, this will not generally be so, and we suggested that for various reasons such measures are hindrances to trade only when discriminatory intent is shown. However, whilst jurisprudence and policy support this approach for measures concerning consumption effects (as with *Concordia Bus Finland*), the position may differ for measures concerning production or delivery effects, or disposal

---

[2] Case C–243/89, *Commission* v. *Denmark* ('*Storebaelt*') [1993] ECR I–3353, para. 23.
[3] Which merely disputed the admissibility of the proceedings.
[4] *Concordia Bus Finland* v. *Helsingin Kaupunki* ('*Concordia Bus Finland*') [2002] ECR I–7213.
[5] See chapter 2, section 3.1.1.

effects, two of the other categories of measures identified in chapter 3.[6] In particular, measures that concern the location of production can have a significant impact on trade and can readily be used to disguise simple protectionism, and thus probably should be treated as hindrances to trade. An example might be a requirement for food supplied to be produced within a certain radius of the place of consumption (see section 4 below). It remains to be seen, however, how the ECJ will treat the various kinds of production/delivery/disposal measures. As regards the fourth category in the chapter 3 taxonomy, namely workforce measures, we explained in chapter 2 that the ECJ has considered (in *Beentjes*,[7] *Nord Pas de Calais*[8] and *Contse*)[9] that these are automatically hindrances to trade where they have a greater impact on industry from other Member States. Authorities adopting measures of this kind are thus required to justify them, rather than benefiting from a presumption of legality. It also seems that measures going beyond the contract will be treated as hindrances to trade; this is indicated by *Commission* v. *Italy*,[10] discussed below, in which the ECJ treated as a hindrance to trade an Italian measure giving preference for invitations to tender for certain works contracts to associations and consortia that included undertakings with their main activities in the region of the works.

We have so far considered policies adopted from simple protectionist motives. Policies that seek to promote national industry or some section of it, may, however, have an objective *beyond* merely protecting jobs and profits in a non-competitive industry. Most such policies can be put into one of two categories. One consists of policies that are compatible with the underlying principles of competition based on comparative advantage – for example, infant industry policies for developing industries with a *potential* comparative advantage, policies to preserve competition (by preventing monopolies, for example), or policies to promote small and medium-sized enterprises (SMEs). The other comprises policies with a social or political dimension, such as policies to remove inequalities between groups or to prevent social unrest. As noted above, the existence of direct discrimination *or* the fact that the measure has a greater impact

---

[6] See section 3.1.
[7] Case C–31/87, *Gebroeders Beentjes BV* v. *Netherlands* ('*Beentjes*') [1988] ECR 4635.
[8] Case C–225/98, *Commission* v. *France* ('*Nord Pas de Calais*') [2000] ECR I–7445.
[9] Case C–234/03, *Contse SA, Vivisol Srl & Oxigen Salud SA* v. *Instituto Nacional de Gestión Sanitaria (Ingesa)* ('*Contse*') [2005] ECR I–9315.
[10] Case C–360/89, *Commission* v. *Italy* [1992] ECR I–3401.

on undertakings from other Member States is normally alone sufficient to characterise these types of measures as hindrances to trade that require justification;[11] this is illustrated by *Du Pont de Nemours*[12] and *Commission* v. *Italy*[13] (although, as discussed above, with indistinctly applicable measures there may be an exception for limited 'buying' decisions). A difficult question, however, is when, if ever, such measures can be justified.

In this respect it can, first, be pointed out that policies developing national industry as a means to some *further end* that is itself a ground for justification are, in principle, capable of justification. Thus in *Campus Oil*,[14] the ECJ made it clear that states may support a national industry for security reasons under the public security derogations. In that case it upheld a requirement of the Irish government that importers of refined petroleum products should purchase their oil from an Irish refinery, which was justified under the public security derogation in Article 30 EC by the need to maintain a national capacity in refining oil. This point is particularly important for defence procurement: whilst contracts for defence purposes are in principle subject to the EC Treaty,[15] it will be permitted to place contracts with national suppliers to preserve a national capability where justified for defence purposes.[16]

On the other hand, for public procurement the ECJ appears to have rejected regional development as an objective that can justify a hindrance to trade, even though regional development policy may have important social objectives and is recognised as a policy of the Community and Member States under Article 87 EC. This excludes use of procurement as a policy tool in one area in which it has been important in the past.

---

[11] An argument to the contrary in *Du Pont de Nemours* was rejected.

[12] Case 21/88, *Du Pont de Nemours Italiana SpA* v. *Unita Sanitaria Locale No. 2 Di Carrara* ('*Du Pont de Nemours*') [1990] ECR I–889.

[13] Case C–360/89, *Commission* v. *Italy*, note 10 above.

[14] Case 72/83, *Campus Oil Ltd* v. *Minister for Industry and Energy* ('*Campus Oil*') [1984] ECR 272.

[15] Subject also to Article 296 EC providing a derogation on security grounds for hard defence contracts: see Arrowsmith, note 1 above, at 4.59–4.65; A. Georgopoulos, 'Defence Procurement and EU Law' (2005) 30 *ELRev* 559. It can be invoked only on security grounds and not for economic reasons: Case C–414/97, *Commission* v. *Spain* [1999] ECR I–5585. Much equipment excluded under Article 296 is subject to an open-market regime of the European Defence Agency Code of Conduct: see B. Heuninckx, 'Towards a Coherent European Defence Procurement Regime? European Defence Agency and European Commission Initiatives' (2008) 17 *PPLR* 1.

[16] Either under Article 30 EC or under Article 296 EC.

The issue was considered in *Du Pont de Nemours*.[17] The case arose
from a challenge in the Italian courts to a decision by an Italian health
authority to reserve 30 per cent of its requirement for radiological films
and liquid for firms in the impoverished Mezzogiorno region. The
decision was taken in accordance with a law that required Italian authorities to reserve 30 per cent of their supplies purchases for companies that
were established and had fixed plant in the Mezzogiorno, and which
offered products processed at least partly in that region. Development of
poorer regions is an EC objective and may be pursued through Member
States' own aid to industry in certain cases, even though state aid is
generally prohibited under Article 87(1) EC. This is provided for under
Article 87(3), which allows the Commission to authorise state aid given,
inter alia, 'to promote the economic development of areas where the
standard of living is abnormally low or where there is serious under-
employment' (Article 87(3)(a)),[18] even when the aid distorts the common market. The benefit of eliminating regional inequalities is here
considered to outweigh trade interests. The ECJ ruled in *Du Pont de
Nemours*, however, that the procurement measures hindered trade *and*
could not be justified.[19] As to hindrance to trade, the ECJ concluded
that this existed merely because 'products originating in other Member
States suffer discrimination in comparison with products manufactured
in the Member State in question'.[20] The ECJ regarded the measure as
distinctly applicable, even though a large part of Italian production was
also excluded.[21] As to justification, it was argued that the measure was
justified as a mandatory requirement, since it went beyond 'protectionist
aims' and sought to eliminate the 'social and economic disequilibrium' of
the region. It was suggested that this was a legitimate interest of the Italian
government, and that it was also relevant that this was a Community
objective:[22] the measure was concerned to assist a region with an abnormally low standard of living in accordance with the regional policy envisaged in Article 87(3) EC. The ECJ, however, rejected these arguments,

---

[17] Case C–21/88, *Du Pont de Nemours*, note 12 above.
[18] Regional aid may also be possible under Article 87(3)(c) to facilitate the development of
certain economic activities or of certain economic areas, where it does not adversely
affect trading conditions to an extent contrary to the common interest. There are also
certain types of aid listed in Article 87(2) that are automatically lawful.
[19] See paras. 11–18; confirmed in Case C–351/88, *Laboratori Bruneau Srl* v. *Unita Sanitaria
Locale RM/24 de Monterotondo* [1991] ECR I–3641 concerning the same legislation.
[20] Case C–21/88, *Du Pont de Nemours*, note 12 above, para. 11.
[21] See para. 14 and the discussion of justification below.
[22] Sections 2 and 3 of the report of the judge rapporteur.

simply concluding that general interest requirements can never be invoked to justify distinctly applicable measures.[23]

It is not clear whether this reasoning on justification still applies. As mentioned in chapter 2, following *PreussenElektra*[24] the ECJ seems now to accept that distinctly applicable requirements may be justified, at least in some circumstances. On this basis *Du Pont de Nemours* might be reconsidered. It is also possible to envisage regional policy measures that are *not* distinctly applicable and to which the reasoning in *Du Pont de Nemours* thus does not apply – for example, measures placing contracts with firms with a certain proportion of their business activity in the favoured region, regardless of nationality. The argument that regional aid measures are capable of justification might be supported, as argued in *Du Pont de Nemours*, by the analogy of state aid: if national state aid that distorts competition is sometimes permitted because of regional development considerations, why not procurement measures, also?

However, the state aid provisions can also support the opposite conclusion on the basis that they are intended to define exhaustively when national measures restricting competition may be adopted for regional development purposes, especially as this aid under Article 87 is subject to an explicit control and authorisation of the Commission. This was the viewpoint of Advocate General Lenz in *Du Pont de Nemours*: he considered that general interest requirements may not be invoked where 'the machinery provided for in the Treaty affords a sufficient guarantee of the achievement of the objective pursued'.[25] It seems likely that this approach would be favoured by the ECJ, also, thus ruling out regional development measures in procurement even if they are indistinctly

---

[23] Para. 14. This was in spite of the fact that the relevant directive and its predecessors contained specific provisions preserving regional policy measures, which apparently assumed that some of these were compatible with the Treaty (although stated to be subject to compatibility): see Article 26 of Council Directive 77/62/EEC OJ 1977 No. L13/1 stating the directive was not to prevent implementation of the provisions of a predecessor Italian law and modifications thereto, as amended by Article 16 of Council Directive 88/295/EEC, OJ 1998 No. L127/1 to refer generally to preservation of 'existing national provisions which have as their objective the reduction of regional disparities and promotion of job creation in the most disadvantaged regions and in declining industrial regions'.

[24] Case C–379/98, *PreussenElektra AG* v. *Schleswag AG* [2001] ECR I–2099.

[25] Para. 45 of the Opinion. He also relied on the principle, criticised below, that economic objectives cannot be used for Treaty derogations (para. 42); and in a similar vein stated in para. 45 that a State 'may not rely on mandatory requirements in order to protect its domestic economy'.

applicable, and even if the original reasoning in *Du Pont de Nemours* on distinctly applicable measures no longer applies.

The same reasoning seems applicable to other policies referred to in the state aid provisions – for example, policies to remedy a serious disturbance in a state's economy, for which aid may be authorised under Article 87(3)(b) (although this is rare). More generally, given that the explicit rules on state aid allow Member States to address inequalities in development or deteriorating economic conditions only in carefully defined circumstances, the ECJ is unlikely to accept any argument based on the need to protect industry to avoid social inequality or unrest or political problems. This point is reinforced by the fact that under the original Article 226 EEC there was a specific procedure for the Commission to authorise national protective measures in such cases (for difficulties which were serious and liable to persist in any sector of the economy or which could bring about serious deterioration in the economy of a specific area), applicable only until expiry of the transitional period.

A further question raised by *Du Pont de Nemours* is whether procurement measures promoting regional development – or, indeed, other industrial objectives that may be pursued under Article 87 – may themselves constitute state aid, and may, as such, be authorised by the Commission under Article 87(3). This possibility was, however, ruled out by the ECJ in *Du Pont de Nemours*: the Court stated that, irrespective of whether assistance through procurement can be characterised as aid under Article 87,[26] it cannot be authorised under the state aid rules when (as the court concluded in that case) it violates the free movement rules, and also that qualification as aid would not alone exempt it from the free movement rules.[27] The judgment is not entirely satisfactory, since it does not explain why certain measures (such as financial assistance) that seem to hinder trade *can* be authorised as aid, whilst others (such as procurement) cannot. However, the most likely explanation is that measures cannot be authorised as aid unless they pass a proportionality test *as applied by the ECJ*.[28] Whatever the reason for the conclusion on this point, however, the impact of *Du Pont de Nemours* is to preclude use of

[26] Advocate General Lenz seemed inclined to the view that it could not, although he did not give a definitive view: see paras. 58–59. It would now appear that it can – see chapter 5 by Priess and von Merveldt.

[27] Para. 21.

[28] See A. Doern, 'The Interaction between EC Rules on Public Procurement and State Aid' (2004) 13 *PPLR* 97.

procurement as a tool of regional policy – and the same conclusion would probably apply to the use of procurement to address other policies for which state aid may be given. This position could be supported on the basis that other forms of regional assistance, such as direct financial aid, are generally economically more efficient than targeted procurement. On the other hand, there are certain circumstances in which procurement is, in fact, the optimal instrument for regional aid – for example, to circumvent a corrupt and inefficient bureaucracy as a means of distributing benefits[29] – so that arguably it should be an available instrument *in principle*.

It should be noted that the ruling in *Du Pont de Nemours* that procurement measures directed at regional development may not be *authorised* under the state aid rules does not rule out the possibility that they are aid measures that *violate* the state aid rules, as well as the free movement rules. The extent to which horizontal procurement policies do violate the state aid rules is examined by Priess and von Merveldt in chapter 5.

As for industrial development policies without a wider dimension, the ECJ has frequently stated that the Treaty derogations[30] and general interest requirements[31] cannot justify policies of an 'economic' nature. This was a further reason cited by Advocate General Lenz in *Du Pont de Nemours* for rejecting regional policy measures in procurement.[32] If this is a correct statement of principle, it rules out any policy that hinders trade and has an ultimate objective that relates solely to industrial development, including policies to support the objectives of the single market, such as promoting infant industries, preserving competition or supporting SMEs.

This reasoning was apparently relied on to reject the possibility of supporting SMEs through public procurement in *Commission* v. *Italy*.[33] In that case the ECJ held contrary to Article 49 EC two provisions of an Italian law which required for certain works contracts: (i) that authorities

[29] O. Stehmann and J. Fernández Martín, 'Product Market Integration versus Regional Cohesion in the Community' (1991) 16 *ELRev* 216.
[30] For example, Case 7/61, *Commission* v. *Italy* [1961] English Special Edition 317; Case 352/85, *Bond van Adverteerders* [1988] ECR 2085; Case C-353/89, *Commission* v. *Netherlands* [1991] ECR I-4069; and C-288/89, *Stichting Collectieve Antennevoorziening Gouda and others* v. *Commissariaat voor de Media* ('*Stichting*') [1991] ECR I-4007.
[31] Case C-398/95, *Syndesmos ton en Elladi Touristikon kai Taxidiotikon Grafeion* v. *Ypourgos Ergasias* [1997] ECR I-3091, para. 23.
[32] Paras. 42 and 45 of the Opinion.
[33] See Case C-360/89, *Commission* v. *Italy*, note 10 above.

should stipulate that main contractors should reserve a minimum proportion of the works for undertakings with their registered office in the
region of the works, and (ii) that in deciding which firms to invite to
tender authorities should give preference to associations and consortia
that included undertakings with their main activities in the region. The
Court stated that both measures were discriminatory and a restriction on
trade, the former apparently involving direct discrimination, and the
second indirect discrimination, since Italian undertakings were much
more likely than foreign undertakings to carry on their main activity in
the region.[34] Italy argued that such measures were intended to assist
SMEs, and specifically to offset the disadvantages for SMEs of the
directives' aggregation rules, which tend to encourage larger contracts.[35]
The ECJ dealt with this briefly: it stated merely that such considerations
were not covered by Treaty derogations nor reasons of public interest
that might justify the obstacles to trade[36] and cited two cases in which it
had ruled that non-economic objectives cannot provide derogations.[37]

In the author's view, however, such a general principle is too unso-
phisticated and needs to be nuanced. This so-called principle was first
adopted to preclude economic objectives that were clearly incompatible
with the scheme of the Treaty.[38] It provides a neat way to encapsulate the
principle that Treaty derogations cannot be used to justify objectives that
are 'mere' protectionism or objectives that merely address the broad
social or political consequences of inequality or economic decline in
certain areas or activities. However, other policies that are economic in
the sense of affecting industrial development – or, indeed, other financial
or commercial interests of the state – should not be caught by a general
principle that *automatically* precludes justification.

As Hatzis elaborates in chapter 8, SME development, for example, is an
important element of national and EC policies for ensuring competitiveness, and policies directed at this that hinder trade in the short term
should be assessed on their merits. The decision in *Commission* v. *Italy* is

[34] Para. 12.   [35] On these see section 9 below.
[36] Para. 14. Advocate General Lenz also did not consider this further, and commented only
that there existed no justification under the Treaty derogations: paras. 18 and 23 of the
Opinion.
[37] Case C–353/89, *Commission* v. *Netherlands*, note 30 above, and C–288/89, *Stichting*,
note 30 above, concerning the Treaty derogations on free movement. Reliance by the ECJ
on these cases without further reasoning implies that it based its conclusion both on the
Treaty and on general interest requirements on a general principle precluding derogations concerned with economic objectives.
[38] Case 7/61, *Commission* v. *Italy*, note 30 above.

correct on its facts, as the policy was wholly disproportionate to any objective of SME development – for example, in that subcontracting did not have to be to SMEs and was limited to firms in a particular region – but arguably not all SME policies should be ruled out. Hatzis, on the other hand, takes a different view in chapter 8, arguing that the case precludes SME policies being justified as mandatory requirements.[39] (However, both Hatzis[40] and other commentators, such as Burgi,[41] consider some SME measures, such as division of contracts into lots, are not hindrances to trade at all, and this is also the view of the present author who considers that such decisions are generally 'excluded buying decisions', in accordance with the principles discussed in chapter 2, unless adopted for protectionist reasons.) Similarly, it is submitted that other industrial policies that hinder trade but have objectives compatible with the underlying principles of the single market should be considered on their merits. It is unlikely that many such policies can be justified, especially since Article 157(1) EC entrusts the Community and Member States with securing the conditions for the competitiveness of Community industry '*in accordance with a system of open and competitive markets*', but justification should not be ruled out a priori.

Most industrial development policies involve either direct or indirect discrimination by promoting either particular areas or sectors of national industry[42] or individual national firms.[43] However, not all do so. For example, requiring firms to deal electronically to promote electronic commerce might hinder access to the market but have an equal impact on foreign and domestic industry. Chapter 2 explained that it is not clear how far non-discriminatory procurement measures are hindrances to trade requiring justification,[44] but we suggested that generally they are not. Where justification *is* required, it is likely to be easier for non-discriminatory measures. There is also, of course, scope for promoting industrial development through measures that do not restrict access to markets at all and which thus clearly cannot be regarded as hindrances to trade – for example,

---

[39] See chapter 8, section 3.   [40] See chapter 8.
[41] M. Burgi, 'Small and Medium-Sized Enterprises and Procurement Law – European Legal Framework and German Experiences' (2007) 16 *PPLR* 284.
[42] In *Du Pont de Nemours* the Court ruled that the fact that a policy involves support for an identified part of national industry to the exclusion of other parts, as well as the exclusion of industry of other Member States, does not prevent it from being characterised as distinctly applicable.
[43] A measure directed at one national firm may also be discriminatory on grounds of nationality: see, for example, Case C–353/89, *Commission* v. *Netherlands*, note 30 above.
[44] See chapter 2, section 3.1.

by using broad output specifications to encourage innovative solutions for projects, or by improving transparency to encourage SME participation, as discussed in chapter 8, section 5.

We have so far focused on the means of implementing policies follow-ing the decision to procure. In chapter 3, though, we saw that the potential for horizontal benefits – for example, to national employment – may be the very reason for initiating a procurement. Can this decision be affected by the Treaty? Probably it cannot. In chapter 2 we argued, supported by the *Concordia Bus Finland* case,[45] that many government 'buying' decisions, including on what to buy, are not generally hin-drances to trade: they establish what the market is, rather than restrict access to a market. Thus, in our view, the EC Treaty does not have any impact on such a decision. Of course, even when such a decision is restrictive in effect in the sense that a decision not to procure reduces the available market, it is not likely to have a greater adverse impact on non-domestic firms/products, but even if that is the case – or even if certain non-discriminatory procurement decisions are subject to the Treaty – we do not consider that it is subject to the free movement rules.[46] The same principle applies, we suggested, to a decision on what to purchase to implement a project – for example, a decision to purchase lifeboats rather than helicopters for sea rescue – although this *could* have greater impact on imported products. Of course, a decision to undertake a project, or to use a particular approach (helicopters rather than life-boats) for reasons of industrial or employment policy, might be *imple-mented* through measures that hinder trade – for example, limiting work on the project to national firms. These implementing measures would themselves, however, be reviewable under the free movement rules, as discussed above.

4. Social and environmental policies and the EC Treaty

4.1. Introduction

Other horizontal policies in public procurement mainly relate either to social concerns or, increasingly, to environmental issues. We will con-sider the impact of the Treaty on these policies by looking in turn at the different policy mechanisms set out in chapter 3.

---

[45] See note 4 above.
[46] Chapter 2 suggests that directly discriminatory decisions are hindrances to trade but it is hard to envisage decisions of this kind that fall into this category.

4.2. The decision to purchase or not to purchase and the decision on what to purchase

As we have seen, a decision to undertake, or not to undertake, a procurement in the first place could be made based on horizontal considerations – for example, in the environmental arena, the desire to develop new 'green' products. We have also seen that the means chosen for carrying out a particular function may be influenced by social or environmental concerns – for example, a decision to construct a video-conferencing facility, rather than to spend money on travel for meetings. As discussed in section 3 in the context of industrial development, we would argue that decisions of this kind establish the market, rather than restrict access to it, and are not subject to the free movement rules.

4.3. Contractual requirements laid down by the purchaser

4.3.1. Requirements confined to contract performance

We have seen in chapter 3 that one major mechanism for promoting social and environmental policies is the use of contractual requirements relating to contract performance. We will consider in some detail the Treaty's impact on such requirements, as they are important in practice. Many of the points below also apply *mutatis mutandis*, however, to other mechanisms.

Requirements limited to compliance with general legal requirements
We saw in chapter 3 that contract requirements sometimes merely reiterate general legal obligations governing contract performance, such as those on workforce health and safety.

These, as we saw, will normally be legal requirements of the *awarding state* – for example, legislation on health and safety standards for the contract workforce. Provided that it is lawful for the awarding state to require undertakings to observe the regulatory legislation (an issue discussed below), then procurement measures, such as contract conditions, that provide for compliance, including by non-domestic firms, *may* be lawful.[47] It cannot be assumed that such measures are *automatically* permitted, however: in general, measures for ensuring compliance with regulatory provisions, as well as the substantive provisions themselves,

---

[47] This possibility is referred to in Article 27 of the Public Sector Directive, as to which see 8.1.1.

must be justified under a proportionality test where they constitute hindrances to trade.[48]

Our analysis in chapter 2 suggests that many of these measures should not in fact be considered as hindrances to trade. In particular, they will not generally have any greater impact on non-domestic products or firms, and we suggested in chapter 2 (section 3.1) that non-discriminatory procurement measures relating to the contract are not generally hindrances to trade. Further, we also suggested in chapter 2 that some procurement measures, even if they have a greater adverse impact on imported products, are not generally hindrances to trade because they establish the market, and do not restrict it.[49] These we referred to as 'excluded buying decisions', and we suggested that they include, at least, decisions relating to the consumption effects of the products (for example, requirements for products to comply with general legal standards on acceptable pollution levels).

However, even to the extent that such contract conditions *are* hindrances to trade, it is submitted that the government's interest in ensuring legal compliance by its own contractors, as discussed in chapter 3[50] – for example, to encourage by example and to disassociate itself with unlawful behaviour, and to ensure a level playing-field – will often make it possible to justify such contract-specific measures, including the possibility of terminating contracts for a violation. We consider this possible for all measures that relate to contract performance in the sense of our taxonomy in chapter 3. We will see below that the Commission has argued that it is not generally possible to justify measures relating to production of supplies. However, we reject that argument below in considering contract requirements going beyond legal compliance, and a fortiori those arguments also apply to requirements that are limited to compliance with the general law.

A wide view of equal treatment under the Treaty as concerned with equal treatment between all contractors and extending to non-discriminatory requirements might suggest that even procurement measures concerned solely with the compliance of domestic contractors with domestic law might be subject to scrutiny and justification. However, this broad view was rejected in chapter 2[51] – and this consequence of such a broad view illustrates the deficiencies of that broad approach.

[48] Case C–113/89, *Rush Portuguesa* v. *Office national d'immigration* ('*Rush Portuguesa*') [1990] ECR 1417.
[49] See again chapter 2, section 3.1. [50] See chapter 3, section 2.1.
[51] See chapter 2, section 3.3.

When it is *not* lawful to require undertakings from other Member States to observe the regulatory provisions themselves, it might be argued that procurement measures to enforce them also infringe the Treaty. However, the position is unclear. In *Alsace International Car Service*[52] the European Court of First Instance ruled that the Parliament would not have violated the procurement directives' equal treatment principle in awarding the contract to a group of taxi firms even if such firms enjoyed tax advantages under their national (French) legislation that violated EC law. One reason given was that any such unlawful measures were not attributable to the Parliament itself. This might support a general principle that the illegality of a regulatory provision from an external source does not affect the legality of the related procurement measures, and it is necessary instead to challenge the regulatory provision directly. However, this might not apply to regulatory measures enacted by the awarding state itself. It is submitted that in this situation the position will depend on the precise connection between the procurement measures and the general measures. Thus, the fact that competition for the contract is affected by the legislation (as in *Alsace International Car Service*) should not affect the legality of the procurement, and (in our context) a general requirement to comply with legislation – for example, on working conditions – should not be unlawful merely because some of that legislation is unlawful. However, a contract requirement to comply with a specific piece of unlawful legislation, or an action to enforce a specific act of non-compliance, *should* itself be considered unlawful. It is suggested that in this case the procurement measure is a hindrance to trade even if it is not the kind of measure that would normally be treated as such in accordance with our analysis in chapter 2; its character as such derives from the fact that it is merely a direct application of an unlawful regulatory measure.

Contractual requirements might also require compliance with applicable legal norms laid down by a state other than the one awarding the contract – either another Member State, or a third country. This is often relevant when an undertaking performs contract work outside the awarding state, and is subject to legal rules laid down by the state in which the work is carried out. Such requirements seem permissible under the same principles as requirements that concern the laws of the awarding state. As explained in chapter 3, authorities have legitimate concerns

---

[52] Case T–139/99, *Alsace International Car Service* v. *European Parliament* ('*Alsace International Car Service*') [2000] ECR II–2849.

in ensuring that their undertakings comply with applicable law in other countries, including to ensure reliability, to avoid associating themselves with illegal behaviour and to ensure a level playing field. It can be pointed out that the directives assume in the context of advance exclusion from contracts that such concerns are valid, in that they expressly allow purchasers to exclude firms that are in violation of tax or security laws in other Member States, or that have committed criminal offences outside the awarding state.[53] However, if the regulatory legislation itself contravenes EC law, possibly the procurement measure would not be unlawful: the 'non-attribution' approach taken in *Alsace* seems relevant, and the illegality should be addressed through action against the Member State adopting the legislation.

Requirements that go beyond compliance with general legal requirements
Are such requirements hindrances to trade?   As we saw in chapter 3, contracts also often contain requirements relating to social or environmental matters that are not concerned merely with legal compliance, but seek further social or environmental benefits from the contract, or to minimise its adverse impact. These may concern the consumption impact of the products, works or services supplied, their delivery or production effects, their disposal effects, or the contract workforce.

In chapter 2, as just noted, we suggested that there are certain 'excluded buying decisions' that are not hindrances to trade, even when they have a greater impact on non-domestic firms/products,[54] and that these include contract requirements relating to consumption effects – for example, a requirement that buses used in a contract for a public bus service should not exceed certain levels of pollution, akin to the award criteria used in *Concordia Bus Finland*. If that view is correct, government purchasers enjoy a broad discretion to set requirements on social and environmental matters, including requirements that exceed those in mandatory and voluntary European standards. Similarly, it seems justified under the Treaty to define levels of environmental protection by reference to national eco-labels, provided that the purchaser also indicates that it will accept equivalents – an issue considered further in chapter 10 on eco-labels. However, it must be acknowledged that it

---

[53] See chapter 2, section 4.3.6. The mandatory exclusions for corruption etc also require exclusions in such a case: see chapter 12.

[54] See again chapter 2, section 3.1.

is not clear how this doctrine stands in light of the ECJ's ruling in *Medipac*[55] – although we argued in chapter 2 that it is not inconsistent with that ruling – and it is possible that even social and environmental specifications relating to consumption effects require justification. Further, even if there are some 'excluded buying decisions', it is unclear, as we saw in chapter 2, whether the doctrine covers all 'buying' decisions, including those relating to production, delivery and disposal. These are particularly important in the context of environmental policies. If they are not covered by a doctrine of 'excluded buying decisions' contract requirements on these matters will require specific justification under the Treaty derogations or mandatory requirements.

In addition, one group of requirements subject to scrutiny consists of requirements relating to the contract workforce. The ECJ has indicated that, as with industrial policies relating to the contractor, these are hindrances to trade if they have a greater impact on undertakings from other Member States. This point was made in *Beentjes* in 1988.[56] The case arose from a request for a preliminary ruling from a review body in the Netherlands. Beentjes had submitted the lowest tender for a public works contract, but had been excluded, one reason being that the authority had included a condition that the contract workforce should be made up of at least 70 per cent of long-term unemployed persons, employed through the regional unemployment office, and Beentjes was not in a position to comply. The ECJ indicated that this was not a lawful ground for exclusion because it was not listed in the relevant directive.[57] In addition, the ECJ stated that the requirement could infringe the prohibition on discrimination based on nationality if 'such a condition could be satisfied only by tenderers from the State concerned or indeed if tenderers from other Member States would have difficulty complying with it'[58] (although the Court left the national court to decide if this particular policy was discriminatory).[59] *Beentjes* indicates that the approach of *Du Pont de Nemours* and *Commission* v. *Italy*, of characterising as a hindrance to trade any measure that has a greater impact on non-domestic goods or undertakings, applies also to measures relating to the contract workforce.

---

[55] C–6/05, *Medipac-Kazantzidis AE* v. *Venizelio-Pananio* ('*Medipac*') [2007] ECR I–4557.
[56] Case 31/87, *Beentjes*, note 7 above.   [57] See the discussion at 8.1.4.
[58] Para. 30. Oddly, the ECJ referred to Article 12 EC rather than the free movement provisions.
[59] In fact, the obligation to use the regional unemployment office may have rendered the condition unlawful in light of *Rush Portuguesa*, note 48 above.

The ECJ took the same approach in *Nord Pas de Calais*,[60] discussed later, which concerned award criteria (rather than conditions) relating to the contract workforce. This reflects the ECJ's approach to discrimination in the context of traditional 'regulatory measures', whereby mere differences in impact are considered automatically to hinder trade and policy reasons for different treatment are addressed at the level of justification.

Thus, whilst some buying decisions that reflect horizontal considerations (particularly those concerning consumption effects) are possibly not hindrances to trade, others, namely workforce requirements and, possibly, production, delivery and disposal requirements, are potentially caught when they are distinctly applicable or – as indicated in *Beentjes* – when they have a greater impact on non-domestic industry.

An unresolved question, however, is one alluded to briefly above in the context of industrial policy, namely how far contract conditions are caught even if they have an equal impact on domestic and non-domestic industry. We saw in chapter 2 that the European Commission in its Communication on social issues in procurement takes the view that non-discriminatory measures *are* caught,[61] but the point has not been clarified in jurisprudence. We argued in chapter 2 that the free movement provisions do not, in fact, generally catch non-discriminatory procurement measures that relate to contract performance: these are to be treated in the same manner as 'selling arrangements' under the *Keck* jurisprudence. This argument is based on many of the same policy considerations that support the existence of the doctrine of 'excluded buying decisions', and will be particularly important if that doctrine is not accepted. Many horizontal policies concerning social and environmental issues are, in fact, equal in their impact on different Member States and this is therefore an important issue. If non-discriminatory policies are not caught by the free movement rules, then Member States will be free to implement these policies as they think fit. If such policies are caught, however, they must be justified under the somewhat complex and uncertain principles discussed below. It will, however, generally be easier to justify non-discriminatory policies than those that are discriminatory.

Finally, we should recall that chapter 2 suggested that even with 'excluded buying decisions' distinctly applicable requirements and those adopted from discriminatory motives *are* hindrances to trade. So

---

[60] Case C–225/98, *Nord Pas de Calais*, note 8 above, para. 50 of the judgment.
[61] Chapter 2, section 3.1.1, 'Non-discriminatory measures'.

also are *all* requirements that do not establish operational requirements, but exclude products, services or firms that can meet the government's requirements, as shown in *Dundalk*[62] and *UNIX*,[63] discussed in chapter 2 – and (regardless of the treatment of other types of non-discriminatory procurement decisions, as discussed above) this applies even when the measures have an equal effect on domestic firms/products and others. Thus a contract specification that not merely limits the permitted levels of pollution from buses purchased but also specifies the technical means to achieve this when other means would serve just as well is a hindrance to trade. Requirements in these categories are unlikely to be justified.

Justifying contractual requirements that hinder trade   Horizontal requirements that *are* hindrances to trade must be justified under Treaty derogations or as general interest requirements. Many interests that are the subject of horizontal policies are in fact interests recognised under these provisions – for example, promoting equal opportunities (a fundamental principle of EC law, as explained in chapter 6), protecting workers,[64] providing employment opportunities for persons with disabilities, addressing long-term unemployment,[65] and reducing pollution and promoting energy from renewable sources.[66] There is, however, as yet little indication from the ECJ on how it will balance such interests against trade concerns in public procurement, especially when the policies concerned have an impact outside the awarding state that does not affect that state directly.

It is submitted that the considerations outlined in chapter 1 have an important role here. First, the ECJ must have regard to the equal status of horizontal policies with other procurement policies, the principles of subsidiarity and equality, and the Article 6 EC Integration Principle.

---

[62] Case 45/87, *Commission of the European Communities* v. *Republic of Ireland* ('*Dundalk*') [1988] ECR 4929.

[63] Case C–359/93, *Commission* v. *Netherlands* ('*UNIX*') [1995] ECR I–157.

[64] As recognised, for example, in Case 279/80, *Criminal Proceedings against Webb* [1981] ECR 3305, para. 19; Case C–113/89, *Rush Portuguesa*, note 48 above, para. 18.

[65] In particular, it should not be ruled out as an 'economic objective' that cannot form a ground for justification: see section 3 above. The European Commission in its Interpretative Communication on the Community law applicable to public procurement and the possibilities for integrating social considerations into public procurement, COM (2001) 566 final ('Communication on social considerations'), suggests (footnote 62) that such a condition is justified provided that it does not (contrary to the position in *Beentjes*) require recruitment through a local office.

[66] See further chapter 9.

Secondly, it must keep in mind the limited objectives of EC procurement policy and the EC's limited competence which, as chapter 1 explained, mean that it is for Member States to determine the balance between horizontal and other policies in procurement, including the 'commercial' aspects. In chapter 1 we also argued that it is not appropriate to conclude from the fact that certain limitations on horizontal policies apply under the directive that these apply under the Treaty. All these considerations favour a flexible approach to horizontal policies. How they might affect certain concrete issues is elaborated below.

It is also appropriate to recall here that, as chapter 2 explained, there is debate over how far *directly* discriminatory measures can be justified as general interest requirements, rather than merely under the explicit Treaty derogations.[67] However, we suggested there that *PreussenElektra* now indicates that this is possible for *all* directly discriminatory requirements.

In the following discussion we will first focus on policies that we believe are hindrances to trade, in particular workforce measures. We will then consider briefly justification of conditions relating to consumption effects since, although we take the view that these are not hindrances to trade, the ECJ may take a different view.

A first important issue is whether the policy can be promoted through means other than procurement that are less restrictive of trade[68] – for example, criminal sanctions, training programmes or subsidies to particular social groups (although these may be precluded by the state aid rules discussed in chapter 5). Chapter 3 observed that procurement may be favoured as a policy tool above more economically efficient alternatives because the political processes are more convenient.[69] It may also be preferred because its costs are less visible: these costs may, for example, be hidden in higher prices paid for goods, whilst payments for training or subsidies are clearly identifiable. However, these political concerns probably should not be taken into account in deciding whether a policy is justified under the free movement provisions. This consideration will be more important for policies that extend beyond the contract than for those restricted to the contract, but may also be relevant for the latter – for example, in considering whether it is justified to require firms to engage the long-term unemployed on contract work.

It is also necessary to consider whether the policy can be implemented equally or more effectively through less restrictive procurement

---

[67] Chapter 2, section 3.1.   [68] See chapter 2, section 3.1.   [69] Chapter 3, section 2.2.

mechanisms.[70] Chapter 3 explained that award criteria can have certain advantages over contract conditions as a national policy mechanism, including because they allow a more explicit and transparent balancing of costs and benefits. They may also be less restrictive of trade. However, there are cases in which contractual requirements seem justified: they may be the only way to avoid associating the authority with certain behaviour and to set an example, and – in terms of concrete benefits – it may be the only way that a contracting authority can guarantee a particular result. In assessing contract conditions it also must be kept in mind that the balance between the benefits of horizontal policies and their financial costs is for national authorities to determine, and not for the EC, as chapter 3 explained. This is illustrated by the *EVN-Wienstrom* case on award criteria,[71] discussed further below, where the ECJ indicated that states may adopt a 45 per cent weighting for environmental criteria since this balance – even under the directives – is for national authorities.[72] So far as the use of conditions for exemplary purposes is concerned, it is worth noting that Directive 2006/32[73] on Energy End-use and Energy Services, discussed further in chapter 9, explicitly recognises the importance of the 'exemplary' role of public procurement and the scope for pursuing this through contract specifications (although the directive is itself, of course, lawful only if compatible with the Treaty).

To comply with the Treaty, Member States may also need to give attention to the precise way in which conditions are formulated. For example, arguably it violates the Treaty to require entities to use long-term unemployed persons in a specified manner on the contract, without allowing suppliers to propose their own alternative, and equally effective, strategies for utilising the long-term unemployed.[74] In effect, this is an application to workforce conditions of the principles of *Dundalk* and *UNIX* that require states to permit any tenders that can meet their substantive requirements. With environmental policies the

---

[70] See Case C–324/93, *R v. Secretary of State for the Home Department, ex parte Evans Medical and MacFarlan Smith* ('Evans Medical') [1995] ECR I–563, concerning the possibility of protecting security interests in procurement (relating to the diversion of drugs) by a less restrictive approach than limiting access to the competition.
[71] Case C–448/01, *EVN AG v. Austria* ('EVN-Wienstrom') [2003] ECR I–14527.
[72] See section 13 below.
[73] Directive 2006/32/EC of the European Parliament and of the Council on energy end-use efficiency and energy services and repealing Council Directive 93/76/EEC, OJ 2006 No. L114/64.
[74] Specifying a particular method might be justified, however, to provide a particular training that would better prepare the workers to re-enter the job market.

proportionality principle may similarly demand that, wherever possible, entities address the environmental impact of products through their whole life cycle, allowing undertakings more choice in formulating their tenders to meet the authority's concerns. For example, there is arguably a presumption against setting conditions that relate solely to disposal or place of production, when other elements, such as transportation, are significant for the same objective (such as limiting the authority's carbon footprint). Of course, as well as minimising the impact on trade, such a whole life cycle approach is generally required from a national perspective to ensure effective and efficient implementation of the authority's own policy.

Proportionality may also require that policies with a discriminatory effect be reformulated when their objectives can be achieved without discrimination. For example, it may not be lawful to require contractors to comply with specified national Codes, or other standards widely used only amongst national firms, on issues such as fair recruitment policies for the contract work, when a contractor complies with similar Codes in its state of origin or has its own effective policies. Policies formulated to avoid indirect discrimination by allowing contractors to implement 'equivalent' approaches may, as we have seen, not even require justification, on the basis that non-discriminatory measures are not hindrances to trade. If, however, they *are* hindrances to trade then, subject to the discussion below concerning work outside the awarding state, it seems that such non-discriminatory policies may be justified. A solution that would facilitate use of public procurement to support workforce policies whilst greatly limiting any trade impact would be to develop European standards on workforce issues.[75]

Another issue arises when a state is interested in 'buying' social benefits – for example, job opportunities for disabled persons – only for its own residents. To require contractors to provide opportunities for persons in the awarding state *only* may involve significant discrimination against non-domestic firms. However, governments may be unwilling to pay the additional costs of procuring social benefits when these will accrue to persons outside the state, as where a non-national undertaking wins a contract and performance is not by its nature tied to a location in the awarding state (often the case with supplies and services contracts).

[75] On this see C. McCrudden, *Buying Social Justice: Equality, Government Procurement and Legal Change* (Oxford University Press, 2007), pp. 606–608, concerning the impact of a common standard developed by local authorities within the United Kingdom.

On the other hand, a Member State may be unwilling to avoid discrimination by applying social requirements *only* to domestic firms or to work on its own territory, as this may place domestic firms at a visible disadvantage,[76] and also discourage them from carrying out work in the home state. If it is not possible or desirable to limit the benefits of policies to the awarding state, however, this may reduce the incentive to pursue social benefits through procurement, to the detriment of the relevant social groups throughout the EC.

This issue is relevant in the context of reserving procurements for sheltered workshops for persons with disabilities. We will see in chapter 7 that it has sometimes been assumed, and is stated in the Commission guidance,[77] that it is not, in fact, allowed to reserve contracts solely for domestic workshops. In the author's view, however, taking into account the principles set out in chapter 1, this is justified on the basis that this policy area is primarily a matter for Member States and they should not effectively be deprived of the use of procurement as a tool to pursue it; and also by the need to ensure a stable supply of work for specific workshops that cannot be guaranteed where competition is required. This, it is submitted, provides another example, along with the green energy policy accepted in *PreussenElektra*,[78] of a distinctly applicable policy that can be justified without relying on a specific Treaty derogation. This view is also accepted by Boyle in chapter 7 (although, as chapter 7 explains, the directives rule out this possibility for workshops covered by the directives).

These kinds of problems do not, of course, arise when policies are concerned mainly to ensure that the government sets an example to the private sector, or that it does not support 'undesirable' contractors with government funds. However, they are a concern when the aim is to produce specific and concrete social benefits through the contract, as in the examples above.

---

[76] The same issue arises, of course, with regulatory legislation, as has often been discussed, but the effects may be greater in procurement since the cost is often immediate and visible, being tied to a specific contract that is subject to competition between undertakings from different states. In addition, if, contrary to the argument made in chapter 2, the Treaty contains an equal treatment principle in public procurement not limited to non-discrimination based on nationality, it may be unlawful to apply more onerous conditions to domestic suppliers. However, if it is lawful to apply to domestic suppliers legislation that does not apply to others arguably it is also possible to apply to them 'regulatory' measures limited to government procurement.

[77] European Commission, Communication on social considerations, note 65 above, p. 18.

[78] Note 24 above, discussed in chapter 2.

Should states, on the other hand, decide to implement policies that offer benefits open to all, a question then arising is whether it is even permitted to impose conditions relating to a contract workforce in another Member State (such as a requirement to engage persons with disabilities). This issue is discussed further below, although it can be mentioned here that the directives' provisions on set-asides for sheltered workshops assume that this is possible. To ensure coherent and effective social policies on such issues, an EC-wide approach is arguably necessary in an EC-wide market – for example, a common policy *requiring* all states to reserve certain contracts for sheltered workshops. However, this is problematic because of the different procurement and social priorities of Member States, and because there is no Community competence in some of the relevant areas, as discussed in chapter 1.

As just mentioned, another issue of difficulty concerns the fact that when contract activities, such as production or disposal of products, are carried out abroad, contractual requirements could (as with measures limited to legal compliance) affect an EC contractor's activities outside the awarding state – either in another Member State, or in a third country. This is not significant for works. However, it is important for supplies, since supplies offered by firms from other Member States will often be manufactured outside the awarding state, and it is also important for many services contracts, especially white-collar services – for example, contracts for call-centre services or software design. The issue does not arise much outside public procurement, since states do not generally seek to regulate matters outside their territory. May an authority lay down contract conditions that govern activity taking place in another country, including in another Member State? The issue is particularly important if, contrary to our argument in chapter 2, non-discriminatory policies are generally covered by the Treaty.

With worker protection policies, where the work is carried out in the contractor's home state and that state is another EC Member State, such policies may generally be justified only when the workers' interests are not adequately protected by the home state's rules, and it is difficult in practice to show this.[79] The relevant jurisprudence makes it difficult to justify any requirements on pay and conditions of work. However, it is

---

[79] For the jurisprudence see C. Barnard, *The Substantive Law of the EU: The Four Freedoms* (Oxford University Press, 2004), pp. 352–353. The Communication on social considerations, note 65 above, p. 21 suggests that a purchaser could not, for example, require adherence to local collective agreements.

less clear that this will also be true of other 'workforce' policies, such as contract conditions promoting employment of persons with disabilities or measures to promote gender equality. The Commission's guidance indicates that perhaps these are not problematic: it states that conditions may concern 'the obligation to recruit, for the execution of the contract, a number of disabled persons over and above what is laid down by national legislation in the Member State where the contract is executed or in the Member State of the successful tenderer'.[80] The guidance does not deal explicitly, however, with the case of work *carried out* in another Member State (or even the case in which workers are recruited in the home state and posted abroad), so it is not clear whether the Commission considers such clauses permissible in that case.[81] The directives' provisions on set-asides for sheltered employment (discussed in chapter 7) seem, however, to assume that they are; if set-asides are permitted then a fortiori it seems possible to include a contract condition on the same matter. As noted above, if measures relating to work outside the Member State are not permitted, states may be discouraged from implementing social policies through procurement because of the disadvantage to domestic undertakings, unless, as we have in fact argued, it is permitted to confine benefits to the home state.[82]

Like workforce conditions, conditions relating to production effects may also affect activity in another Member State. These are particularly important for environmental policy – for example, requirements for

[80] European Commission, Communication on social considerations, note 65 above, p. 17.
[81] On this the Commission also states: 'it would appear more difficult to envisage contractual clauses relating to the manner in which supply contracts are executed, since the imposition of clauses requiring changes to the organization, structure or policy of an undertaking established on the territory of another Member State might be considered discriminatory or to constitute an unjustified restriction on trade': Communication on social considerations, note 65 above, p. 18. It is not clear if the Commission's concern is simply with the fact that a procurement measure might affect activity in another Member State, or the fact it might affect activity outside the contract, or both. If the former, the Commission may take the view that measures relating to work in another Member State are not generally permitted. If so, then the point is pertinent not only for supply contracts, but also for services contracts which are sometimes performed outside the awarding state. However, it seems more likely that the Commission's concern is with the impact of measures outside the contract, discussed below.
[82] Since it does not violate equal treatment to require compliance with national legislation in the state of work, we suggested above that it is also acceptable to confine procurement compliance policies to the awarding state only. However, whilst this might make it possible to implement measures through contract conditions (applicable to domestic activity only) it is difficult to see how such policies can operate through award criteria.

energy produced from renewable sources or timber from sustainable stocks, or conditions that manufactured goods must be produced using environmentally-friendly techniques.

The legality of contract conditions (and other procurement measures) relating to production effects, specifically those relating to production of energy from renewable sources, is considered in chapter 9 on green energy. More generally, however, we can note that the possibility of procurement measures directed at these effects is accepted in *EVN-Wienstrom* in which, as we have seen, the ECJ recognised the possibility of using award criteria relating to the 'green' origins of electricity supplied under a public contract, including from another Member State. In the author's view this possibility is not confined to environmental measures. Although the Integration Principle of Article 6 EC, which was referred to in *EVN-Wienstrom*, could provide special support for recognising production conditions relating to environmental matters, this narrow approach is not justified. As argued in chapter 1, this principle and also the principle of equality merely reinforce the need for an interpretation of EC law that gives broad scope to the possibility of implementing horizontal policies, which is justified also by other, more general, principles such as the equal status of horizontal policies and other procurement objectives and subsidiarity. If certain procurement measures that hinder trade are a suitable and proportionate means to implement renewable energy policy, which is important to the EC, there is no reason to rule out a priori justification of comparable measures (with comparable restrictive effects) that pursue other policies that may be just as important to national governments. *EVN-Wienstrom* concerned award criteria but (as also suggested in chapter 9) it is no less relevant for contract conditions: these can provide a more effective method to achieve their objective given their ability to guarantee a market.

The Commission has taken a narrow view on this question in relation to supply contracts. Thus it states:

> it would appear more difficult to envisage contractual clauses relating to the manner in which supply contracts are executed, since the imposition of clauses requiring changes to the organisation, structure or policy of an undertaking established on the territory of another Member State might be considered discriminatory or to constitute an unjustified restriction on trade.[83]

---

[83] Communication on social considerations, note 65 above, p. 18.

This suggests a concern with the significant impact on trade that such conditions might have: it assumes that conditions directed at activity beyond the contract are not lawful because of their wide impact, and that even conditions directed only at the contract being awarded are precluded where they have an indirect impact beyond the contract. However, this view is hard to reconcile with the jurisprudence on green energy – and, indeed, on the EC's own initiatives on green procurement discussed in chapter 9. It also seems contrary to the assumption in the new directives that set-asides for sheltered workshops are permitted. In fact, the Commission accepts the possibility of measures relating to the politically important issue of green energy procurement, and has attempted to reconcile its broader – negative – views on production-related measures under the Treaty and directives by suggesting that green energy measures are not solely production measures but relate *to the characteristics of the product itself*.[84] Clearly, however, this is not the case, as the author and her co-editor have pointed out previously,[85] and as is elaborated below (section 8.1.6) and in chapter 9 on green energy. It is also relevant, particularly in light of the Integration Principle, that a coherent approach to implementing environmental objectives through procurement sometimes demands that authorities consider the overall environmental impact of a product across all stages of its life: when production is a significant element it is arbitrary not to consider it, and an inability to do so may preclude any effective policy. In our view any general presumption against the legality of production-related requirements must thus be rejected. The implications of these views in the specific context of green energy are elaborated further in chapter 9, which argues that it is lawful to require not merely the supply of green energy but also the supply of products made using green energy.

We should also point out that if, contrary to our argument above, there is a presumption against measures affecting production of supplies in another state, issues of legality may arise also for certain works and services contracts. The Commission's concern with supply contracts arises because, first, it may be impossible to identify precisely which work relates to the order of the public purchaser (whose order may be

[84] See further 8.1.6 below. There is some ambiguity over whether this means that such conditions cannot be included at all or merely that they are special conditions rather than technical requirements, but it seems the former is intended.
[85] For example, Arrowsmith, note 1 above, at 19.44 and P. Kunzlik, 'Making the Market Work for the Environment: Acceptance of (Some) "Green" Contract Award Criteria in Public Procurement' (2003) 15 *JEL* 175, 192.

fulfilled from general stock), and, secondly, it may be difficult to confine the impact of the purchaser's requirements to that order: for example, limiting pollution may be feasible only for a factory as a whole, or the contract workers subject to workforce requirements may also work on other contracts during the same period. Thus the activity of the whole undertaking or unit is affected, involving a greater impediment to trade. However, the same considerations may apply, for example, with the services of a call centre or software design company, where the contract workers may work also for other customers. Conversely, some requirements relating to production of supplies may not present these problems, such as where a unit operates solely to supply a particular authority's requirements. The position is, of course, complicated by the fact that the effect of any particular condition will depend on the way in which a particular supplier's business is organised, and this may vary between suppliers.

A related question is the position of policies affecting activities in a third (non-EC) country. This is becoming important, since with increased outsourcing to developing countries policies are increasingly concerned with labour standards of third countries. This is a major concern of utilities pursuing a Corporate Social Responsibility agenda, as examined in chapter 11, but is also an issue for other regulated authorities. Since such policies may affect EC contractors carrying out work in third countries (either directly or, more likely, through subcontractors), as well as contractors from third countries, the EC Treaty is relevant. In principle, it seems that the same rules apply as apply to activities in other Member States, except that there is no presumption that the relevant interests are adequately protected by local laws. Thus we consider, for example, that requirements for firms to supply only products made under certain fair labour conditions can be justified in principle – not only, in appropriate cases, by their concrete benefits, but also by an authority's desire to disassociate itself with exploitative behaviour, in response to public opinion or by way of example. (As we have noted, the 'exemplary' role of public authorities in procurement policy is explicitly recognised in Directive 2006/32[86] on Energy End-use and Energy Services, which is discussed in chapter 9.) Further, it seems unarguable that such requirements can be included when purchasing certain products for resale – for example, to employees in a workplace café who demand products made under fair labour conditions. In the case of the

---

[86] Note 70 above.

exemplary role of government and purchase for resale, at least, there is no alternative mechanism for achieving the relevant objectives. However, as discussed above, where a policy is discriminatory, the authority must consider whether it could be implemented through non-discriminatory means. We cannot in this short account examine the specifics of the complex question of labour-related policies.[87] However, one might expect that policies referring to accepted standards, such as ILO labour standards, will be easier to justify than those that do not, a point considered further in chapter 11 on utilities.

Policies affecting activities outside the awarding state are also particularly likely to be affected by the WTO Agreement on Government Procurement (GPA), considered in section 16 below. As we explain, the GPA's constraints are in many ways similar to those of the EC rules, but they differ in some respects and may impose some additional constraints. We need to note here that there are some rulings that cast doubt on the possibility of measures directed at production effects of products produced outside the 'regulating' state.[88] Whether the GPA in principle precludes conditions dealing with production in government contracts has not been the subject of specific rulings. However, the better view – as with EC law – is that even if the GPA rules out procurement measures that seek to regulate activity outside the contract, it does not rule out measures limited to performance of the contract in the sense of our taxonomy in chapter 3, including those on production.

In view of its current importance, it is also worth mentioning specifically the position of procurement policies relating to the authority's carbon footprint. Such policies may have a significant trade impact, and may also readily be abused for protectionist reasons. Nevertheless, they relate to important interests and in light, in particular, of the Integration Principle in Article 6 seem capable of justification. However, to justify such requirements authorities may need to show that they form part of a coherent overall policy (which is not, for example, limited to products that

---

[87] See further, for example, H. Nielsen, 'Public Procurement and International Labour Standards' (1995) 4 *PPLR* 94; K. Krüger, R. Nielsen and N. Bruun, *European Public Contracts in a Labour Law Perspective* (Copenhagen: DJOF Publishing, 1998); H. Randall and L. Smith (eds.), *Local Government Contracts and Procurement* (London: Butterworths, 2002), chapter 16; N. Bruun and B. Bercusson, 'Labour Law Aspects of Public Procurement in the EU', in R. Nielsen and S. Treumer (eds.), *The New EU Public Procurement Directives* (Copenhagen: DJOF Publishing, 2005), p. 117.

[88] See, in particular, S. Arrowsmith, *Government Procurement in the WTO* (The Hague: Kluwer Law International, 2003), chapter 13 (in particular pp. 346–348) and the literature cited there.

happen to be important for the local or national economy). It will probably be difficult to justify requirements that are directly discriminatory – for example, requiring food to be grown in the awarding state – as opposed to requirements that focus more directly on environmental damage. Further, a policy referring solely to the distance travelled, rather than the actual environmental impact of transportation, might not be accepted: products transported long distances in bulk by water, for example, could have a smaller carbon footprint than products brought a shorter distance by air or road. A measure that focuses only on one aspect of the life cycle, such as production, might also be challenged: the damage from transporting produce from developing countries might be more than outweighed by the low carbon footprint of the farmer. It is also arguable that such policies are permitted only to the extent that they take into account any measures taken to offset the environmental impact.

We suggested in chapter 2, based on *Concordia Bus Finland*, that contract conditions relating to consumption effects, and possibly certain other effects, are not generally hindrances to trade but excluded buying decisions. However, we also acknowledged that this is not wholly clear, and that the ECJ ruling in *Medipac* might provide support for a different approach that requires purchasers to justify all contract conditions, or at least those that are discriminatory in effect. The standard of scrutiny that might apply in this event was discussed in section 3.1 of chapter 2. We suggested there that even to the extent that justification is required, a purchaser in fact has a very broad discretion in setting its operational requirements, to reflect its preferences as a purchaser; and in light of the equal status of horizontal policies and other procurement policies it seems clear that this applies to social and environmental requirements. This is reflected in the ECJ decision in *EVN-Wienstrom*,[89] discussed in section 13 below, in which the ECJ allowed a 45 per cent weighting for environmental award criteria. Chapter 2 also argued that this discretion includes the possibility to set contract standards relating to social and environmental matters that are higher than those in non-mandatory European standards or in directives, including New Approach Directives, that set standards for admission into free circulation.

This standard of scrutiny is also examined in chapter 10 in relation to eco-labels. In this respect, we suggested earlier that if requirements relating to consumption effects are not hindrances to trade, purchasers can rely on national eco-labels to define and explain their level of

---

[89] Note 71 above.

environmental requirements (although they must admit any products that meet the same level of requirements, even without the label). However, as Wilsher explains in chapter 10, if environmental specifications require justification, 'reliance on the national eco-label might be open to challenge on the basis that its criteria were faulty on scientific grounds or that other criteria would better achieve the same or better environmental protection' or even because the ECJ considers that levels of environmental protection sought are disproportionate. As with other contract requirements, it might be particularly difficult to justify reference to eco-labels when this has a discriminatory effect.

Finally, we will see in section 8 below that the procurement directives restrict not only the substance of contract conditions, but also the means of enforcement, especially in that they appear to limit the possibility for excluding undertakings that cannot meet certain social or environmental conditions.[90] It might be argued that similar restrictions apply under the Treaty, on the basis that the authority's objectives can be met without advance exclusions, but instead by exercising contractual remedies if a violation occurs, as under the directives – an approach less restrictive of trade and less open to abuse for protectionist reasons. However, we reject this view: as chapter 3 explained, this is often a less effective means of enforcement. As chapter 1 explained, the courts should be slow to import the directives' restrictions into the Treaty, and given the equal status of commercial objectives – which *can* form the basis for exclusion – and horizontal objectives there is no ground for limiting advance exclusion under the Treaty. (In fact, as explained in section 8 below, we consider that the arguments just mentioned may even support a different interpretation of the directives, in line with that suggested by McCrudden in chapter 6 on equality issues; but this is not per se material to the position under the Treaty itself.)

4.3.2. Contractual requirements going beyond contract performance

We have so far considered contractual requirements governing contract performance but, as we have seen, a purchaser may also wish to include requirements that go beyond this – for example, to require the contractor to adhere to certain environmental or labour standards across its whole business. These may be standards set out in general laws or standards

---

[90] See section 8.1.4 below.

going beyond the law. The considerations discussed above are relevant in assessing these requirements, but additional points also apply.

First, whilst certain measures limited to contract performance might be categorised as 'excluded buying decisions' that are not generally considered as hindrances to trade, we have suggested, on the other hand, in chapter 2, that all kinds of measures that go *beyond* contract performance *are* hindrances to trade – at least when discriminatory in effect. Thus we saw that in *Commission* v. *Italy*[91] a preference for firms with their main activities in the area of the works was held to be a hindrance to trade (and one that could not be justified). Similarly, discriminatory measures that regulate the behaviour of undertakings – for example, a requirement that contractors should sign up to national Codes on treatment of their general workforce – will be hindrances to trade. The position of *non-discriminatory* measures going beyond the contract is, as we also saw in chapter 2, less clear. We suggested, however, that these are probably hindrances to trade, at least where general in nature. On this basis, a general policy requiring contractors for certain services contracts to apply fair working conditions across the workforce would be considered a hindrance to trade even if non-discriminatory, although a requirement included simply in an individual contract might not. We also mentioned in chapter 2 that the position may possibly differ for goods, based on the *Keck* jurisprudence, indicating that only certain types of non-discriminatory measures relating to supplies are hindrances to trade (in contrast with *Alpine Investments* indicating that *all* measures affecting trade in services are hindrances to trade).[92] On this basis, the above requirement for a contractor to apply fair working conditions across the workforce would be a hindrance to trade in a services contract, but not in a supply contract, although the impact on trade is greater in the latter case. Clearly this would be unsatisfactory, however, and we argued in chapter that no distinction is to be made between goods and services.

Secondly, we need to recall the point discussed in section 4.3.1 above that the Commission's Communication on social considerations seems to indicate that there is a presumption, at the very least, against justifying policies that extend beyond the contract.

In this respect, measures limited to compliance with legal obligations – for example, exclusion of firms convicted of criminal offences – are likely

---

[91] Case C-360/89, *Commission* v. *Italy*, note 10 above, discussed in section 3 above.
[92] See chapter 2, section 3.1, non-discriminatory measures.

to be less contentious than those that are not, whether adopted to ensure the reliability of suppliers, or for the other legitimate national policy reasons considered in chapter 3 (limiting support for undesirable contractors, deterring violations etc.). It can be noted that the procurement directives assume that authorities can be concerned with legal violations outside their own contracts, and probably not only for ensuring reliable performance of contracts but for the other reasons just mentioned above.[93] As mentioned earlier, measures merely to support compliance with the law do not create the same potential for abuse as measures that involve a Member State setting its own standards of behaviour, through public procurement measures, for contractors from other Member States.

What, however, of policies that are not limited to legal compliance? This is a very important issue if non-discriminatory horizontal measures are caught by the Treaty. If policies of this kind are caught by the Treaty and also cannot be justified, regulated purchasers will generally be unable to use procurement to promote ethical supplier behaviour or to avoid association with unethical suppliers, such as those using child labour in developing countries.

We have noted in the previous section that, leaving aside legal compliance (which the Commission does not discuss), Commission guidance indicates that procurement measures are not generally permitted where they are directed at, or affect, a firm's activities beyond the contract awarded, at least outside the awarding state. Further, as discussed in section 5, the Public Sector Directive appears to prohibit contract conditions that go beyond the contract, based on the same concern that any policy affecting non-contract work is unduly restrictive of trade.

In the author's view, however, a broader approach is warranted under the Treaty in light of the principles discussed in chapter 1 concerning the equal status of horizontal and other procurement policies, the importance of environmental considerations and equal treatment, and subsidiarity. In particular, there should be no presumption against policies that extend beyond the contract. The court should not be too quick to find that alternative measures were possible and should not rule out policies even when the aim is merely to avoid associating government with undesirable conduct and to set an example. This applies even for policies prohibited under the directives which, as argued in chapter 1, are not significant in interpreting the Treaty. The directives in any case

---

[93] See section 10.2 below.

assume that some measures extending beyond the contract are lawful, since they specifically allow purchasers to reserve contracts for sheltered workshops based on the nature of the organisation.[94]

EVN-Wienstrom[95] might possibly be read to support the view that measures beyond the contract are difficult to justify, but the author does not consider that it endorses such a restrictive approach. In that case the ECJ ruled that a measure to promote development of renewable energy beyond the contract violated the directives' equal treatment principle. The case arose out of a call for tenders by Austria for purchasing electricity. The estimated amount of energy to be supplied under the contract was 22.5 GWh and it was a qualification condition that tenderers could supply at least this amount from renewable sources. In addition, to encourage an increase in the market supply of green energy, one award criterion was the amount of green energy that the tenderer could supply in excess of 22.5 GWh, weighted at 45 per cent. The other criterion was price, with a weighting of 55 per cent. Thus the award criteria gave preference to tenderers who could supply more green electricity than the amount to be supplied under the contract. As already mentioned, the ECJ considered that it did not violate the Treaty or directive to include this weighting for the environmental criterion *in so far as it related to the electricity supplied under the contract*. However, the ECJ also ruled that the criterion concerning the *total* amount of energy produced from renewable sources was unlawful, as it was not linked to the contract's subject matter as the directive requires (see section 13 below). In addition, both Advocate General Mischo and the ECJ stated that the criterion involved 'unjustified discrimination'. This was because it favoured large suppliers above small suppliers who were all equally able to meet the requirements of the contract[96] (large suppliers being able to produce more electricity as green energy simply because of their greater production capacities).[97] According to the Court: 'Such a limitation on the circle of economic operators in a position to submit a tender would have the effect of thwarting the objective of opening up the market to competition pursued by the directives.'[98]

---

[94] Rather than merely referring to the possibility of requiring the contract work to be performed by those with disabilities.

[95] Note 71 above.   [96] Para. 69 of the judgment and para. 72 of the Opinion.

[97] Advocate General Mischo stated that the size of an enterprise was not a reason that could amount to objective justification. However, this reasoning seems incorrect since the renewable energy policy, not size, was the purported justification.

[98] Para. 69.

This might indicate that the ECJ will be unwilling to accept measures unrelated to contract performance. However, the decision is better explained on narrower grounds. First, the difference in treatment between large and smaller suppliers is relevant to the availability of less trade-restrictive measures; it might have been equally (or more) effective to consider the amount of green energy produced *in proportion* to overall amount of electricity generated, to encourage all suppliers to produce green energy. Thus it may violate the proportionality principle on its facts. Secondly, the reasoning focuses on equal treatment under the directives, not the Treaty. Under the directives it indeed violates equal treatment when suppliers are treated differently for reasons prohibited under the directives themselves – and since the *directive* prohibits conditions, exclusions or award criteria unrelated to the contract, this condition violated equal treatment. However, this may not apply under the Treaty.

It is thus submitted that there is no presumption under the Treaty against requirements that extend beyond contract performance, even if the directives do not allow them. Each requirement, of course, needs to be assessed on its merits, but it is suggested that some such requirements are permitted, both to promote concrete benefits, and to set an example and to avoid associating the government with undesirable undertakings. For example, allocation of government contracts might well be used to promote development of green energy using policies that are less arbitrary than that in issue in *EVN-Wienstrom*; and government contracts can arguably be used to promote fair labour standards and equal opportunities outside government contracts as well as within them, although subject to limitations concerning, for example, recognition of equivalent policies, as discussed in section 4.3.1 above.

Again, it is relevant to note that (as discussed in section 8 below) the procurement directives restrict not only the substance of contract conditions, but also the means of enforcement, especially in apparently limiting the possibility for excluding undertakings that cannot meet certain social or environmental conditions. As with conditions limited to legal compliance, however, and for the same reasons (as discussed at 4.3.1 above), we reject the view that the Treaty similarly limits the possibility of exclusion where an entity considers firms cannot meet such conditions.

Finally, again the permitted scope policies of a regulatory nature – especially those affecting activities outside the awarding state – could be affected by the World Trade Organization's Agreement on Government Procurement (GPA) or by other international law rules. The GPA only generally applies at present to contracts covered by the procurement directives, which, as we will see below, already largely prohibit policies going beyond the contract, so that this issue is unlikely to be important. However, it might become important should the EC wish to revise the directives. Further, in addition to the possible impact of the GPA, there is scope to argue that procurement measures regulating the behaviour of non-nationals outside the regulating state might exceed state jurisdiction under rules of international law.[99] It is not yet established how international law rules on jurisdiction apply to various regulatory policies instituted through public procurement or through other state measures that do not involve traditional regulatory sanctions (such as conditions attached to funding), or to measures that regulate through limiting access to trade.

4.4. Packaging and timing of orders

We saw in chapter 3 that horizontal policies can be implemented through the timing and packaging of orders; in particular, orders may be split or spread out to promote participation of SMEs. These issues are discussed further in chapter 8 on SMEs. As mentioned in section 3 above, such measures are covered by the doctrine of 'excluded buying decisions' elaborated in chapter 2, except when adopted for protectionist reasons – for example, where below-threshold orders are split deliberately to avoid publicity obligations. Thus we take the view that such policies are generally allowed. As mentioned above, Hatzis in chapter 8 also considers that such measures are not hindrances to trade.

4.5. Set-asides

We saw in chapter 3 that another means for promoting horizontal policies is by setting aside contracts for particular groups. The ECJ ruling in *Du Pont de Nemours*, discussed in section 3, which concerned a set-aside for firms in Italy's Mezzogiorno region, confirms that set-asides involving direct discrimination are hindrances to trade.[100] Set-asides involving indirect discrimination are also hindrances to trade, as

---

[99] For summary and critique of jurisdiction under international law, see V. Lowe, 'Jurisdiction', in M. Evans, *International Law*, 2nd edn (Oxford University Press, 2006), chapter 11.

[100] See section 3 and also Case C–360/89, *Commission* v. *Italy*, note 10 above, in which a directly discriminatory requirement for contractors to reserve a proportion of works for undertakings with their registered office in the region of the works was a hindrance to trade.

indicated by *Commission* v. *Italy*, which was also discussed in section 3. In that case the ECJ treated as a hindrance to trade an Italian measure giving preference for invitations to tender for certain works contracts to associations and consortia that included undertakings with their main activities in the region of the works; a fortiori a set-aside for such firms would be a hindrance to trade. As with other measures, it is not clear how far non-discriminatory set-asides are caught by the Treaty. We saw in chapter 2 that the position may be different for goods and services and also that non-discriminatory procurement measures may perhaps be caught only when general in nature. However, there is no clear ruling.

In considering whether set-asides are justified under the Treaty or by general interest requirements, many of the same considerations apply as with contract conditions, as discussed at 4.3 above. Set-asides have a particularly restrictive effect on the market: they totally shut out many suppliers, who may be unable to meet the relevant conditions (as with set-asides for businesses owned by women or ethnic minorities), or unable to do so without radical changes to the business (for example, changing location). However, this does not per se preclude justification: it is merely one factor relevant in determining whether the objective sought might be pursued by less restrictive means (through procurement or otherwise). Where this is not the case the policy may be justified. This may be the case with set-asides for sheltered workshops, as discussed in chapter 7, which the directives assume to be compatible with the Treaty. However, where the aim of a policy is to develop businesses that are competitive in the wider economy, other means, such as award criteria, may be equally or more effective. The relative merits of set-asides and award criteria in this respect were discussed in chapter 3. Hatzis argues in chapter 8 that the proportionality test in fact rules out set-asides for SMEs on the basis that they are not indispensable to SME policy.[101] Arguably use of set-asides is in fact limited to providing work opportunities for groups that are not expected to compete in the general market, such as those with disabilities.

As with contract requirements, set-asides that are discriminatory in effect might need to be reformulated in a non-discriminatory manner. We suggested in section 4.2 above, however, that – contrary to assumptions made when adopting the directives – set-asides for sheltered workshops can be justified, even when limited to national suppliers. Sheltered workshop policies may also have a discriminatory effect where a state's

---

[101] See chapter 8, section 3.

definition of sheltered workshop covers workshops found in that
Member State but not elsewhere – for example, where a Member State
reserves contracts for facilities in which 90 per cent of the employees
have disabilities, but workshops in other states are organised with a lower
proportion of disabled employees. This issue is discussed by Boyle in
chapter 7. In light of the principles discussed in chapter 1, the author
shares Boyle's view in that chapter that policies with a discriminatory
effect can be justified when based on some demonstrable reason, such as
maximising the opportunities available to disabled persons.

In chapter 8, Hatzis argues that set-asides for SMEs violate the Treaty's
equal treatment principle, which he considers is not limited to discrimination on grounds of nationality and allows distinctions between suppliers only to the extent that they are concerned with the supplier's ability
to carry out the relevant economic activity. This argument, if correct,
would also preclude many other set-asides. However, as elaborated in
chapter 2, the author rejects the view of equal treatment under the Treaty
as being independent from discrimination based on nationality. Further,
even if it is, equal treatment should not be interpreted as allowing only
distinctions that are concerned with the supplier's ability to perform the
activity: this requires a distinction between the 'commercial' aspects of
procurement, and the social/environmental aspects, and accords to the
former a superior status, an approach which we rejected in chapter 1.

4.6. Exclusion from contracts for non-compliance with government policies

4.6.1. Provisions limited to compliance with general legal requirements

We saw in chapter 3 that governments may wish to exclude firms from
contracts either to encourage compliance with horizontal policies or as a
sanction for past non-compliance, and may wish to do this to support
norms laid down in general law, such as the criminal law.

The most limited exclusions are those concerned to ensure compliance with the general law (such as environmental regulations) in performing the contract, by excluding firms considered to present a risk of
non-compliance. The other main mechanism for ensuring that firms
comply with the law in performing contracts is the contractual condition.
Contractual requirements have already been discussed in section 4.3 and
since similar considerations apply to exclusions readers are referred to

that section. We suggested there that, in general, contract conditions may require compliance with applicable laws, whether these be national laws or applicable laws of other states. We also noted that exclusion is, however, a mechanism that is more restrictive of trade than a simple contract condition: it precludes any chance to demonstrate actual compliance, and also confers a discretion that might be abused. We also noted that the Public Sector Directive has generally been interpreted as allowing contractual requirements on a broader basis than exclusions and, in particular, as prohibiting authorities from excluding firms that those authorities think cannot comply with certain social and environmental requirements (called 'special conditions'), which possibly includes even some requirements that apply under the general law. However, we rejected the view that such 'non-commercial' exclusions are also precluded by the Treaty, given the equal status of horizontal and other procurement policies elaborated in chapter 1 and our view that the directive is not relevant here for interpreting the Treaty (see 4.3.1). The importance of this issue depends, of course, on the extent to which exclusions for anticipated non-compliance with the law are considered to be hindrances to trade. If, as chapter 2 argues, measures relating to consumption effects and/or non-discriminatory measures are not caught by the Treaty at all, most exclusions of this kind will not need justification. However, if we are wrong about this the issue will take on more importance.

Governments also sometimes wish to exclude firms for *past* non-compliance with the law, either in performing government contracts or more generally; this may be a means of promoting compliance with the law in government contracts themselves, or as part of a broader policy of supporting the norms in the legal provisions in question. We will see below that the directives assume – correctly in our view – that such exclusions are often permitted (specifically for criminal convictions, grave misconduct and non-compliance with tax and social security obligations), at least where the exclusions aim to ensure legal performance of the contract, and probably even when they have broader objectives.

4.6.2. Provisions that go beyond compliance with general legal requirements

Governments may also wish to exclude firms from participation to support social or environmental policies beyond those required under the general law.

Exclusions for anticipated non-compliance in contract performance
These may, first, be limited to the contract in question, most notably
where the government wishes to exclude a firm that it considers unable to
comply with social or environmental requirements in carrying out the
contract. As with policies concerned with legal compliance, the considerations under the Treaty are largely the same as those that apply in assessing
the legality of the contractual requirements themselves, as discussed in
section 4.3.1 above. It was explained that contractual requirements that go
beyond the law but are limited to matters relating to contract performance
are generally permitted, as even if hindrances to trade they can often be
justified (although we saw that the Commission has expressed doubts over
conditions governing production of supplies). It was also suggested that
many such requirements are not even hindrances to trade, either on the
grounds that they are 'excluded buying decisions' – for example, specifications concerned with the pollution or noise effects of products – or because
they are individual non-discriminatory measures outside the Treaty. The
same will apply for exclusions that support these contractual requirements –
for example, a decision to exclude an undertaking because it does not have
the expertise to implement requirements to limit environmental damage in
carrying out the works. Thus some of these exclusions, it is suggested, also
are not hindrances to trade.

To the extent that they *are* hindrances to trade, however, they can
often be justified. For example, since (as outlined at 4.3.1 above) a
government-wide requirement to utilise long-term unemployed persons
on a works contract is probably a hindrance to trade, excluding a firm
that cannot meet this is probably also a hindrance to trade, but such
exclusion is justified by the policy that justifies the contract requirement
itself. As with policies limited to legal compliance, we have already
rejected the view that an advance exclusion is an enforcement mechanism that violates the proportionality test (even though the procurement
directives may limit the exclusion mechanism): we consider that simply
including the condition and the possibility for contractual remedies is
not generally an adequate means for securing the authority's objectives.
This point has already been discussed at 4.3 above.

**Exclusions that are not limited to performance of the contract being
awarded** Governments also sometimes wish to exclude undertakings
for their *past* non-compliance with government policies.

As with policies concerned only with compliance with the general law,
exclusion might be limited to non-compliance with policies relating to

work under government contracts – for example, non-compliance with past contract conditions requiring utilisation of the long-term unemployed on contract work. Arguably such an exclusion is generally to be treated under the Treaty in the same manner as an exclusion to ensure compliance with a future contract, as discussed above, both in terms of conceptual analysis (whether or not it is a hindrance to trade, for example) and in terms of concrete outcome (whether or not it is permitted). Thus if a decision to exclude for anticipated non-compliance with specifications on consumption effects, such as a requirement for quiet buses, is (as we argue) an 'excluded buying decision', so also is a decision to exclude for past non-compliance with such a requirement. Similarly, if – as we suggest – a decision to exclude for anticipated non-compliance with a condition for utilising the long-term unemployed is a hindrance to trade that can generally be justified, so also is an exclusion for past non-compliance. It is worth noting that exclusions based on specific past conduct are perhaps less open to abuse than exclusions based on anticipated non-compliance, since they are based on a specific past act. As discussed at 10.3, the directives in fact provide for exclusion in certain cases that are not limited to legal compliance (including for certain violations of past contracts classified as 'grave misconduct'), thus assuming these comply with the Treaty.

We have also seen that exclusions may support broader policies that seek to regulate firms' general behaviour – for example, governments might exclude firms that apply 'unfair' labour conditions in any of their factories. We discussed at 4.3.2 the position where the government uses contractual requirements in this way, and similar considerations apply to exclusions. As we have seen, policies that discriminate directly or are harder to meet for products or firms from other Member States are probably hindrances to trade that must be justified. There is uncertainty over non-discriminatory policies, which may include some 'fair labour' policies, but possibly these, also, require justification as 'regulatory' measures, even if it is not necessary to justify non-discriminatory policies limited to government contracts themselves. We saw, also, that the Commission has doubted the possibility of justifying regulatory policies implemented through procurement where they affect activities outside the awarding states,[102] which would severely limit use of procurement as a regulatory tool (especially if the Treaty covers non-discriminatory

---

[102] The Commission considers this issue only in relation to contractual requirements affecting activities outside the contract, but a fortiori its reasoning applies to exclusions.

measures) – but we rejected this view. It is suggested, again, that exclusions can be justified on the same basis as contractual requirements, in light of their importance in ensuring that policies are effective. Again it should be reiterated that the directive provides for exclusion in certain cases that are not limited to legal compliance, namely where there is grave misconduct, assuming thus that at least *some* exclusions not limited to legal compliance comply with the Treaty. (On the other hand, the Public Sector Directive does not allow contractual requirements of a regulatory nature, and, as we will see at 10.3, also does not allow exclusions of a regulatory nature as a general rule.)

4.7. Preferences in inviting firms to tender

In assessing the legality of using horizontal considerations to select firms to tender, similar considerations arise as with exclusions, as just discussed at 4.6 above. Thus criteria that are hindrances to trade when used to exclude undertakings will also be hindrances to trade when used to select between qualified firms. Similar considerations will also apply to justification, although here it is also relevant to consider the more limited impact of preferences on the market, and their more limited effect in promoting domestic goals. As we saw in section 3 and in section 4.3 above one of the key cases concerned with the definition of hindrances to trade and with the justification on economic grounds is *Commission* v. *Italy*,[103] which in fact concerned criteria for selecting firms to tender.

4.8. Award criteria

4.8.1. Award criteria confined to contract performance

Award criteria, as we have seen,[104] are likely to be used only for social and environmental polices that go beyond legal requirements. Thus our discussion of award criteria will focus on these policies.

As with other mechanisms, award criteria may, first, be limited to the way in which the contract is carried out. They may be concerned with the same issues as contract requirements and, indeed, may be used as an alternative or alongside them, as discussed in chapter 3 – for example, where the contract includes minimum requirements for accessibility of IT products and also gives credit in the award phase for accessibility features beyond the minimum. The principles that govern contract

---

[103] Note 10 above.   [104] See chapter 3, section 2.

requirements seem in general relevant to award criteria that deal with the same matters. Thus we suggested at 4.3.1 that the jurisprudence on award criteria is relevant also to considering the legality of contractual requirements, and we discussed the key cases on award criteria in that section. However, as with preferences, their different impact on trade, on policy implementation and on other procurement objectives, in comparison with other mechanisms, is relevant.

To recap: we suggested, first, that many measures – whether contract requirements, award criteria or other measures – will be 'excluded buying decisions' that are not generally hindrances to trade. This applies at least to measures on consumption effects. We suggested at 4.3.1 that this argument is supported by *Concordia Bus Finland*, which is a case on award criteria. Thus genuine preferences of the authority that are reflected in the award criteria, such as a price preference for products that do not pollute the environment when used or which are accessible to disabled persons, should not need justification, although we have seen that it is not wholly clear whether the ECJ will accept this, at least for measures with discriminatory effect. On the other hand, even measures concerning consumption effects will be hindrances to trade where these involve direct discrimination, have discriminatory motives or exclude products with equivalent features to those specified, under the principle of *Dundalk* and *UNIX*. These cases should apply equally to award criteria, and the same approach should be applied in determining what is 'equivalent' for this purpose.

We also saw in section 4.3.1 that workforce conditions *are* hindrances to trade, at least where they have a greater impact on other Member States, based on *Beentjes* (which concerns contract requirements) and *Nord Pas de Calais* (concerning award criteria). The classification of indirectly discriminatory measures concerning production, delivery and disposal is, on the other hand, unclear.

As with contract requirements, for all award criteria there is uncertainty over how to treat non-discriminatory measures, but, as with contract requirements, we suggest that criteria relating solely to individual contracts are not hindrances to trade, even if they are not excluded buying decisions. Thus, for example, one-off preferences for firms utilising the unemployed for work on a contract are arguably not hindrances to trade unless they have a discriminatory effect.

When criteria need justification, the considerations that apply to contractual requirements, which were discussed in detail at 4.3.1, are again relevant.

We suggested there that many horizontal policies will generally be capable of justification, although care may be needed to avoid discrimination when this is not necessary to achieve the policy objective. We saw also that the Commission has questioned whether entities can justify measures affecting production in another Member State, at least those having an impact beyond the contract, notably those concerning the production of supplies. However, we rejected this view. In particular, the possibility of justifying production measures was accepted in *EVN-Wienstrom*, which was actually a case concerning award criteria (in that case concerning production of green energy).

More generally, we also noted that in the context of award criteria the ECJ seemed to accept in *EVN-Wienstrom* that states enjoy a broad discretion in weighting different criteria, a principle that we suggested applies to all social and environmental criteria.

A final consideration is that award criteria may have a less restrictive effect on trade, and provide a more proportionate and effective approach, than other mechanisms, especially for policies directed at promoting long-term economic development of certain groups. Thus award criteria might sometimes be easier to justify than contractual requirements or exclusions.[105] However, this depends on the facts of each case.

4.8.2. Award criteria that are not confined to contract performance

Award criteria may also go beyond the way in which the contract is carried out. When award criteria concern the firm's behaviour outside the contract – for example, its wider policies on the environment or its efforts at fair recruitment – relevant considerations are again similar to those applying to contractual requirements. As with contractual requirements, it appears that criteria that have a greater impact on products or services from other Member States will always need to be justified. The position is less clear for non-discriminatory criteria, but again we suggest that these are hindrances to trade only when they relate to the characteristics of products or are general in nature.

When policies going beyond the contract do need justification the considerations discussed at 4.3.2 above for contractual requirements again are relevant, with one of the most important issues again being the possibility of justifying policies that are directed at activities outside the awarding state. We saw at 4.3.2 that *EVN-Wienstrom*, which was a case on award criteria of this kind – namely, criteria that favoured firms

---

[105] See Case C–324/93, *Evans Medical*, note 70 above.

producing renewable energy even beyond the contract requirements – might indicate reluctance by the ECJ to accept criteria going beyond the contract even under the Treaty. However, it was suggested that the decision can be explained on other grounds.

4.9. Measures for improving access to government contracts

Finally, it can be pointed out that measures for ensuring wide access to government contracts by simplifying procedures or providing training will not generally be hindrances to trade. Such measures are often directed at improving access to contracts for SMEs, and are considered further by Hatzis in chapter 8.

4.10. Proving compliance with social and environmental measures under the EC Treaty

We have so far examined the Treaty's constraints on substantive measures. It also needs to be mentioned briefly that constraints exist on the means of proof of compliance with those measures that authorities may require from suppliers. Requiring particular methods of proof, such as particular certifications, may be a hindrance to trade that cannot be justified. Authorities' objectives of securing compliance can often be met by allowing use of other reasonable methods of proof, and this would also be less restrictive of trade; and hence it may violate the proportionality test to insist on particular means of proof. This may apply even if other methods would involve greater cost or inconvenience to the authority – for example, where examining dossiers provided by individual suppliers on their products would be more burdensome than requiring a certificate of compliance from a third party. As we noted in chapter 2, in De Peijper,[106] the ECJ indicated that measures may not be justified by the need to lighten the administrative burden or reduce public expenditure unless these would clearly exceed the limit of what can reasonably be required. Whilst we suggested that this doctrine is not relevant for substantive decisions in procurement, concerning the nature of the purchase and terms of the contract, it may be relevant for proof of compliance with standards set.

A requirement to accept a particular means of proof will be a hindrance to trade when the means specified is more burdensome for

---

[106] Case 104/75, Officier van Justitie v. De Peijper ('De Peijper') [1976] ECR 613.

non-domestic firms or products – for example, where it requires a national certification.[107] However, as with other procurement measures it is not clear how far the Treaty applies to non-discriminatory requirements. We will see below that the procurement directives specifically prohibit authorities from requiring Eco-management and Audit Scheme (EMAS) certificates or quality assurance certificates based on European standards as means for proving compliance with environmental management requirements or quality assurance requirements, to the exclusion of 'equivalent' means of proof. A requirement for these certificates is likely to be non-discriminatory, however, and whether it also violates the Treaty to require such certificates thus depends on how far the Treaty applies to non-discriminatory measures, as discussed in chapter 2.

4.11. Disclosure obligations under the EC Treaty

Finally, we can note that the EC Treaty obligation of transparency, which was discussed in chapter 2, may place on authorities certain disclosure obligations relating to use of social or environmental criteria – for example, to disclose award and selection criteria in advance. As explained in chapter 2, section 3.2, neither the scope of the transparency obligation nor its contents are yet clear. In chapter 1 (section 7) we mooted the possibility that the ECJ might develop this in line with the explicit provisions of the directives (which, as discussed further below, require, for example, disclosure of the weighting of award criteria), but we suggested that this would not be appropriate. It currently remains unclear how far the Court will go in this direction.

5. Horizontal policies and the Public Sector Directive: introductory remarks

So far as the Public Sector Directive is concerned, we have already explained that its main impact is to *restrict* the scope for horizontal policies. We will see that the directive's procedural rules have a significant impact on the mechanisms available for implementing horizontal policies, which are considered in turn below. In particular, it can be said, although at the risk of some oversimplification, that the directive limits the government's ability to use procurement to act as a 'regulator', rather

---

[107] Case 76/81 *S.A.Transporoute* v. *Minister of Public Works* (*'Transporoute'*) [1982] ECR 417.

than merely as a purchaser, in the sense discussed in chapter 1.[108]
Justifications for this restrictive approach, although never clearly articulated by the ECJ, appear to be the adverse impact on market access of
regulatory measures in procurement, and the fact that broad discretion
provides opportunities for abuse to favour particular firms or products.
As chapter 1 anticipated, we will see that the precise boundary between
purchasing behaviour, which is permitted, and regulatory behaviour,
which is prohibited, is unclear, in the same way the purchaser/regulator
boundary is uncertain in various contexts under the EC Treaty. It will be
argued below that the directive should favour a coherent approach and,
in particular, that the line between permitted and prohibited measures
should be drawn in the same place in the context of contract requirements, selection criteria and award criteria. Drawing on the principles
discussed in chapter 1, we will also argue that various uncertainties in the
directives should be resolved through an interpretation that favours
Member States' discretion to use procurement for horizontal objectives.

We also need to make one more preliminary remark, concerning the
relationship between the directive and the Treaty. Recital 6 states:
'Nothing in the directive should prevent the imposition or enforcement
of measures necessary to protect public policy, public morality, public
security, health, human and animal life or the preservation of plant life,
in particular with a view to sustainable development, provided that these
measures are in conformity with the Treaty.' McCrudden, in chapter 6
(section 5), has characterised this as a 'Treaty-based exception'. This
provision might provide the basis for an argument that authorities may
derogate even from the explicit restrictions of the directives where these
are utilised to further the interests referred to in this recital (which are
those listed also in the explicit derogations from the Treaty's free movement provisions). For example, although (as explained in section 13
below) the directive generally requires award criteria to be linked to the
subject matter of the contract, it might be argued that this limit could be
disregarded for criteria concerned with these interests when such criteria are
compatible with the Treaty. Thus it might be argued, for example, that –
contrary to the apparent view of the ECJ in *EVN-Wienstrom* (see section 13
below) – award criteria concerned to promote supply of green energy
in a supplier's business *outside* the contract might be permissible under
the directive (although in that case the actual policy would not have met
the proportionality requirement, as discussed at 4.3.2 above). On this

---

[108] See chapter 1, section 4.

view, the directive's explicit rules are not seen exhaustively to regulate the possibility of using procurement to promote certain national interests, balancing those interests against trade concerns, but leave this open to Member States. The possibility of invoking public health interests by way of exception to the directive's rules on advertising and competition seemed to be accepted in *Medipac*, a case discussed in detail in chapter 2 (section 3.1.1), although not essential for the ruling in that case.

If correct, this view has potentially very significant implications for horizontal policies. This is especially the case if the first part of this chapter is correct in arguing that many of the explicit restrictions of the directive, notably those on policies going beyond the contract, do *not* apply by virtue of the Treaty itself but only because of the directive's express limitations. Its main importance will be found in the area of environmental policies, including green energy, which can be linked to health and/or public security, two of the listed derogations.

However, we do not think that the Treaty derogations can be invoked in this way. The explicit rules in the text of the directive do appear to regulate the balance of various interests in public procurement – trade interests and other interests – in such a way as to remove Member State discretion over this balance in relation to certain policy-mechanisms, such as award criteria that go beyond the subject matter of the contract. To this extent we consider that the Treaty derogations do not apply because there is exhaustive harmonisation of the specific subject matter (use of certain procurement mechanisms in question to implement national interests). However, the explicit rules of the directive do still leave a significant area of discretion to implement these interests (for example, in excluding firms that cannot supply safe products to government) and it is this that the recital refers to: it indicates that there is a residual area of discretion in procurement in these matters that the directive is not intending to harmonise. This has clearly been assumed in the jurisprudence, in cases such as *EVN-Wienstrom*, where the ECJ has resolved issues of horizontal policies simply by reference to the restrictions in the directives without considering if the measures in question might be 'saved' by compatibility with the Treaty. Whilst the recital's wording does seem to indicate that *nothing* in the directive affects the freedom to take measures in procurement to pursue these interests where compatible with the Treaty, it can be pointed out that this is a statement only in the recitals and not a specific exception in the text, and cannot be considered to give such a general exemption when this conflicts with the directive's explicit textual rules.

If we are wrong on this, however, then there is considerable scope to argue that the explicit rules discussed below do not affect states' ability to implement the specific horizontal policies referred to in the recitals.

6. The principles of equal treatment and non-discrimination in the directive

As chapter 2 explained, Article 2 of the directive states three general principles: transparency, equal treatment and non-discrimination.

It was suggested in chapter 2 that the last refers to non-discrimination on grounds of nationality, a principle already applicable to many entities under the EC Treaty. The impact of the non-discrimination obligation in the Treaty itself was considered above. To recap, most procurement measures that have a greater impact on industry from other Member States than on national industry, and possibly some non-discriminatory measures, are hindrances to trade that will violate this obligation unless justified on various public interest grounds. However, we suggested above that many social and environmental policies are open to justification (although many industrial policies are not). We also suggested that there is a significant category of 'excluded buying decisions', which covers, at least, decisions directed at the social and environmental impact of products when consumed, that are not generally hindrances to trade and will violate the Treaty only when they involve direct discrimination or a discriminatory motive.

We also saw in chapter 2 that the principle of equal treatment, defined in *Fabricom*, entails that 'comparable situations must not be treated differently and that different situations must not be treated in the same way, unless such treatment is objectively justified',[109] and that this is concerned not only with differences of treatment based on nationality, but also with other unjustified differences in treatment (including between national suppliers). This raises the possibility that differentiation between suppliers and products for reasons of social or environmental policy might need justification under the directives, even when non-discriminatory. This would be the case if such differentiation involves different treatment of 'comparable' situations. We suggested that many non-discriminatory decisions in procurement are *not* generally caught by the EC Treaty since they

---

[109] Joined Cases C21/03 and C–34/03, *Fabricom v. État Belge* ('*Fabricom*') [2005] ECR I–1559, para. 2. See also Advocate General Mischo in Case C–513/99, *Concordia Bus Finland*, note 4 above, para. 149 of the Opinion.

are not generally hindrances to trade, and an equal treatment principle extending beyond non-discrimination on grounds of nationality does not apply. However, it is necessary to consider whether they might be caught by the broader principle of the directive.

In considering how to apply the directive's equal treatment principle we can note, first, that in deciding which situations are 'comparable' it is necessary to have regard to the purpose of equal treatment in this context. This was stated in *Storebaelt* as to 'ensure the development of effective competition', leading to selection of the best bid.[110] This means that the principle generally forbids different treatment of firms in a comparable competitive position – for example, by allowing one firm that has submitted a tender, but not another, to amend its tender.[111] Conversely, it also indicates that distinctions based on competitive advantage do not involve different treatment of comparable situations, since the situations are not comparable. We can also expect that if, as argued above, certain 'excluded buying decisions' are outside the obligation not to discriminate on grounds of nationality, then those measures also will not violate the more general equal treatment principle, of which the former obligation is one manifestation.

Taking these points into account, from a legal perspective it appears that, as with the Treaty, certain buying measures do not involve different treatment between *comparable* situations. This conclusion and the reasoning above are supported by *Concordia Bus Finland* and, in particular, the Opinion of Advocate General Mischo. In that case, as previously discussed,[112] the ECJ indicated that award criteria concerning the environmental characteristics of buses for a public bus service (their pollution and noise levels) were not discriminatory, either under the equal treatment principle of the directives, which was the subject of the question to the ECJ, or under the EC Treaty, which the ECJ considered was to be analysed in the same way. Advocate General Mischo stated that distinctions based on these matters do not violate equal treatment since those able to supply products with these characteristics are *not in a comparable situation* with those who cannot. Under the rationale of *Storebaelt*, it can

---

[110] *Storebaelt*, note 2 above, para. 33. This does not necessarily imply that this is the objective of the directives per se, merely that this is normally the main purpose of national procedures and is provided for in the directives in the context of setting out transparent procedures for states to implement their objectives: see chapter 1, section 5.2.

[111] Case C–87/94, *Commission* v. *Belgium* ('*Walloon Buses*') [1996] ECR I–2043. See generally Arrowsmith, note 1 above, at 7.7–7.9.

[112] Chapter 2, section 3.1.

be said that the distinctions are distinctions based on the different competitive position of firms/products in light of the government's requirements. Thus there is no need to justify specifications and award criteria relating to the goods, works or services that reflect genuine preferences of the procuring entity on the social and environmental impact of their purchasers – or at least those relating to consumption.[113]

Distinctions relating to other matters, however, will probably be considered as giving rise to different treatment of comparable situations, in the same way that they are regarded as hindrances to trade under the Treaty. This will apply to some measures limited to contract performance. Specifically, as discussed in section 4.3.1 above, workforce matters relating to the contract are classified as hindrances under the EC Treaty where they have a greater effect on non-domestic industry – for example, in *Beentjes* – and thus will probably be considered to involve different treatment of comparable situations that must be justified under the directive's equal treatment principle. We saw above that it is unclear how far measures relating to production and delivery and to disposal are hindrances to trade under the Treaty, and it is likewise unclear whether they involve different treatment of comparable situations under the directive. Measures that extend beyond contract performance that have a discriminatory effect are probably all caught by the Treaty and, hence, also involve different treatment of comparable situations under the equal treatment principle. However, the question has limited importance since, as elaborated below, most of these measures are anyway ruled out by the directive's specific rules.[114]

---

[113] Some situations that otherwise might not be comparable might be treated as such where the distinction is made in violation of proportionality. Thus in *Fabricom*, note 109 above, the ECJ indicated that it was permitted in principle to exclude firms involved in preparatory work for a tender, which cannot necessarily be considered in a comparable position to those that have not been involved in such preparatory work because of the risk of conflict of interest. However, the Court also ruled that it was not permitted to exclude firms that could positively prove there was no risk to competition from their participation in preparatory work, as the objective sought could be achieved by the less restrictive means of excluding only those who could not show that there was no risk. However, this was not concerned with firms' relative competitive position and, in particular, was not concerned with what the authority was buying.

[114] It is less clear how far equal treatment applies to measures that are not 'excluded buying decisions' but are non-discriminatory in effect. These might violate equal treatment under the directive when pursued through a mechanism prohibited by the directive: see the discussion of *EVN-Wienstrom* at 4.3.2 above. This issue is important mainly for workforce conditions relating to the contract since other horizontal measures that are

7. The decision to purchase or not to purchase and the decision on what to purchase: impact of the directive

We suggested in section 4.2 above that a decision to undertake or not to undertake a purchase in the sense of the chapter 3 taxonomy, including a decision made for social or environmental reasons, is not reviewable under the EC Treaty. It appears, likewise, that such a decision is not affected by the procurement directives, which are concerned merely with the manner in which an entity obtains its requirements, and not with what those requirements are. This is also the view stated by the European Commission:

> The first occasion for taking into account environmental considerations relative to a public contract, is the phase *just before the public procurement directives will be applicable*: the actual choice of the subject matter of the contract or, to simplify the question 'what do I, public authority, wish to construct or purchase?'[115] (emphasis added)

8. Contractual requirements laid down by the purchaser: impact of the directive

8.1. Requirements confined to contract performance

8.1.1. Requirements limited to compliance with general legal requirements

The Public Sector Directive does not generally limit the scope for contractual requirements obliging compliance with external legal obligations that govern contract performance – for example, terms requiring compliance with regulations on the safety of the products/supplies or on the safety of the workforce undertaking construction work, or with legal rules on the origins of timber. Thus such contractual requirements may generally be included if they comply with the Treaty.

It is submitted that this is the case for all measures classified in our chapter 3 taxonomy as measures relating to contract performance,

---

not 'excluded buying decisions' (i.e. those beyond the contract) are generally prohibited by the directive's specific rules, as discussed further below.

[115] European Commission, Interpretative Communication on the Community law applicable to public procurement and the possibilities for integrating environmental considerations into public procurement, COM (2001) 274 final ('Communication on environmental considerations'), p. 4. See also the almost identical statement in the Communication on social considerations, note 65 above, p. 6.

including workforce and production/delivery measures. As we will see at 8.1.2, the Commission has argued that some contract requirements relating to production of supplies do not relate to performance of the contract under Article 26 on special conditions and thus are prohibited, and this argument might also extend to requirements limited to legal compliance. However, we reject this argument at 8.1.2 for measures going *beyond* legal compliance and, a fortiori, it must also be rejected for measures limited to legal compliance.

As for enforcement, section 8.1.3 explains that there are different categories of contractual requirements, some of which can be enforced through advance exclusion from contracts (which we call technical requirements) and some of which cannot (special conditions). As outlined there, it is not clear how clauses requiring compliance with the law are to be treated in this respect, and, in particular, whether the fact that they are concerned merely with external obligations is significant for enforcement.

We can also note that Article 27(1) of the Public Sector Directive provides that an authority *may* state in the contract documents (or be obliged by a Member State to state) the bodies from which firms may obtain information on 'obligations relating to taxes, to environmental protection, to the employment protection provisions and to the working conditions which are in force' where the contract works or services are to be carried out and which are applicable to performance. This is no doubt also permitted for other legal obligations and merely emphasises the point in the context of workers' protection etc.[116] In addition, authorities supplying this information *must* ask firms to indicate that they have taken the obligations into account when drawing up tenders (Article 27(2)). The explicit references to taxes and environmental protection were added in 2004, reflecting the increased prominence of environmental considerations in the new directive and mirroring explicit references to environmental considerations in other provisions, such as those on specifications (see 8.1.3) and on award criteria (see section 13). However, a proposed amendment from the European Parliament making it compulsory to supply the above information was not included.

---

[116] Similarly, the limitation to works and services does not preclude clauses relating to the production and delivery of supplies; the provision merely focuses on the most important situations.

8.1.2. Requirements that go beyond compliance with general legal requirements: introduction

Social and environmental requirements relating to contract performance in the sense of our chapter 3 taxonomy are (subject to one possible exception discussed below) generally permitted under the directive, provided that they comply with both the Treaty and the directive's explicit rules. The directive treats these requirements, however, in two different categories. The first we will label 'technical requirements' (reflecting the fact that the directive refers to the concept of 'technical' capability to indicate ability to fulfil them). The second category we label 'special conditions', following the terminology of the directive itself, as discussed in section 8.1.4 below. The difference between the two categories lies in enforcement: it is probably permitted to exclude undertakings in advance if it is considered they will not comply with technical requirements – even undertakings that accept those requirements – whereas a priori exclusion is probably not allowed for anticipated non-compliance with special conditions, as elaborated in 8.1.6.

There is one view, apparently favoured in the Commission guidance, that there is an exception to the general principle above, in that certain requirements relating to production of goods supplied (which relate to contract performance in our taxonomy) are not lawful under the directive. This is elaborated at 8.1.6 below. If this view is correct, there are then three possible categories for social and environmental requirements that relate to contract performance within our taxonomy:

(i)   technical requirements, which are permitted conditions for which advance exclusion is allowed;
(ii) special conditions that are permitted but for which no advance exclusion is allowed; and
(iii) prohibited requirements, that are not permitted at all.

However, as elaborated in section 8.1.6, we reject this view: we consider that the only requirements not permitted are those directed *beyond* the goods, works or services provided under the contract – for example, requiring suppliers to pay fair wages even to workers not engaged on government contracts.

We will consider first the possibility of social or environmental requirements as technical requirements (8.1.3) and then the possibility of including social or environmental requirements as 'special conditions' and the rules applying to those conditions (8.1.4). Next, we will consider briefly the existence of a category of prohibited requirements (8.1.5).

Finally (8.1.6) we will consider how to draw the line between these three categories, including whether any are to be classified as prohibited requirements.

8.1.3. Requirements that go beyond compliance with general legal requirements: technical requirements

The first group of requirements to consider is those we have labelled 'technical requirements'. We use this term to refer to those contract requirements that entities may include in their contracts *and* which may form the basis for a priori exclusion of firms that cannot meet them, on the basis that those firms lack technical or professional ability under Article 48 of the directive. This category clearly includes many specifications that refer to social or environmental features of the products, works or services provided. It probably includes – to use examples from the Commission's guidance – requirements that food served in employee canteens should cater for all religious groups, or that paper should be made from recycled materials or window frames out of wood.[117]

The possibility of including contract requirements that relate to accessibility and environmental performance is specifically highlighted in the directive's definition of technical specifications in Annex VI, point 1(a). For example, 'technical specification' in the context of a works contract is defined as:

the totality of the technical prescriptions contained in particular in the tender documents, defining the characteristics required of a material, product or supply, which permits a material, a product or a supply to be described in a manner such that it fulfils the use for which it is intended by the contracting authority. These characteristics shall include *levels of environmental performance, design for all requirements (including accessibility for disabled persons)* and conformity assessment, performance, safety or dimensions, including the procedures concerning quality assurance, terminology, symbols, testing and test methods, packaging, marking and labelling and production processes and methods. They shall also include rules relating to design and costing, the test, inspection and acceptance conditions for works and methods or techniques of construction and all other technical conditions which the contracting authority is in a position to prescribe, under general or specific regulations, in relation to the finished works and to the materials or parts which they involve. (emphasis added)

---

[117] The last two examples are put forward as acceptable specifications in the Communication on environmental considerations, note 115 above, p. 9.

'Technical specification' in the case of public supply or service contracts (Annex VI, point 1(b)) means:

> a specification in a document defining the required characteristics of a product or a service, such as quality levels, *environmental performance levels, design for all requirements (including accessibility for disabled persons)* and conformity assessment, performance, use of the product, safety or dimensions, including requirements relevant to the product as regards the name under which the product is sold, terminology, symbols, testing and test methods, packaging, marking and labelling, user instructions, production processes and methods and conformity assessment procedures. (emphasis added)

These definitions are similar to those in the pre-2004 directives, except for the new references to environmental and accessibility considerations. These probably do not involve any substantive change – such requirements could be included under the old directive – but appear to have been added (as also with new provisions on award criteria discussed in section 13) merely to emphasise the scope for implementing social and environmental policies, and to highlight the directive's 'positive' aspects from this perspective. We should note here that the definitions are not included primarily for defining the type of contractual requirements permitted, but to define the scope of various rules in the directive for controlling the way in which certain technical requirements are presented, as discussed below. However, the specific references to social and environmental requirements are relevant for supporting an interpretation that certain requirements of this kind are permitted, especially given that this definition was reworded in Directive 2004/18 for the specific purpose of indicating the scope for including such requirements in public contracts.

As mentioned, the directive in addition includes a specific provision *requiring* that entities consider accessibility requirements in their specifications, as discussed in chapter 7.

As explained in chapter 2, Article 23 of the directive contains various rules controlling specifications. These apply to technical requirements in the contract, including social and environmental requirements, whenever these fall within the definition of technical specifications. This will be the case with most, if not all, technical requirements on social or environmental matters.[118] We saw that these rules in Article 23

---

[118] It may be that the concept of technical and professional capability is limited to ability to comply with terms that form part of the technical specifications. Arguably these

require states to define their requirements by reference to certain listed specifications – notably, national standards implementing European standards and international standards – *or* by reference to performance or functional requirements, and generally preclude references to goods of a specific make or source or to a particular process (Article 23(8)). These rules appear to serve two purposes, namely: (i) to ensure, as required by the Treaty, that Member States do not exclude firms or products that can meet their substantive requirements (achieved by using performance/ functional specifications or indicating that entities will accept 'equivalents' where listed specifications are used) and (ii) to ensure that the specifications can be easily understood (achieved by using either performance/functional requirements or listed specifications that are familiar or readily accessible). We should also note another transparency requirement of Article 23, namely that the technical specifications must be 'set out in the contract documentation, such as contract notices, contract documents or additional documents'.

An exception to some of the above rules appears to apply under Article 23(6), a special provision on eco-labels. This is examined by Wilsher in chapter 10 on eco-labels. It expressly permits entities to define the environmental characteristics of products by reference to eco-labels, including purely national eco-labels, when drawn up following certain procedural requirements concerned with transparency and broad participation of stakeholders. As Wilsher argues in chapter 10, this appears to provide an exception to the directive's general rules for presenting the entity's technical requirements. However, as he also explains, this rule will not exempt entities from the usual requirement to accept products that are equivalent to those that comply with the eco-label.

The above rules on specifications do not, on the other hand, appear to restrict states' discretion to specify *what* social or environmental features they require or the *level* of requirements, such as the acceptable level of pollution from a product's use. Social or environmental requirements may be included even when the entity uses a standard specification that does not include such requirements: Article 23(3)(d) states that the listed specifications and performance/functional specifications may be used in

concepts are also connected in the sense that inability to comply with terms that are part of the technical specifications in all cases involves an absence of technical or professional capability (giving rise to the possibility of exclusion, as discussed below). However, it is also arguable that the concept of technical specifications extends also to terms that are not considered relevant for assessing technical/professional ability, namely special conditions: see further 8.1.4 below.

combination. There also appears to be nothing in the directive to prevent
states from specifying for higher standards than those in a listed specification, such as a European specification – for example, a higher level of
environmental protection. The extent to which the Treaty limits the level
of permitted requirements was discussed in section 4.3.1 above where we
argued, first, that many technical specifications are excluded buying
decisions, resulting in a wide discretion for the procuring entity and,
secondly, that, even when justification of specifications is required, the
Treaty, like the directives, does not limit discretion over the level of
requirements.

Control over the content of specifications beyond that found in the
Treaty might possibly be derived from Article 23(2), which states that
technical specifications 'shall afford equal access for tenderers and not
have the effect of creating unjustified obstacles to the opening up of
public procurement to competition'. A broad interpretation might allow
the courts to review social or environmental (or other features) of
specifications to determine whether they are justified in light of their
impact on trade. The better view, however, is that this provision merely
introduces the directives' more detailed provisions on specifications set
out above, and does not impose separate obligations. This view is supported by Recital 59:

> The technical specifications drawn up by public purchasers need to allow
> public procurement to be opened up to competition. *To this end*, it must
> be possible to submit tenders which reflect the diversity of technical
> solutions. Accordingly, it must be possible to draw up the technical
> specifications in terms of functional performance and requirements,
> and, where reference is made to the European standard or, in the absence
> thereof, to the national standard, tenders based on equivalent arrange-
> ments must be considered by contracting authorities. (emphasis added)

This treats the explicit rules on performance standards and the obligation to accept 'equivalent' tenders as rules that implement the general
principle of 'the opening up of public procurement to competition'.[119]

The extent to which the directives (or Treaty) limit the power to reject
products or services that are approximate, but not precise, equivalents of
those in national eco-labels is considered further by Wilsher in chapter 10.

---

[119] On the other hand, if, contrary to our argument above and in chapter 2, a broad view is
taken of the Treaty that specifications (at least non-discriminatory specifications) are
hindrances to trade, this provision might simply reiterate this.

We can also note that the directive makes explicit provision for use of variants, which we saw in chapter 3 can sometimes provide a useful means for authorities to establish the cost of including social or environmental obligations in a project and to decide whether or not to include such requirements. In this respect, Article 24 of the directive provides that authorities may authorise variants where the criterion for an award is the most economically advantageous tender (Article 24(1)). They must indicate in the notice whether variants are accepted and cannot accept them where not positively indicated in the notice (Article 24(2)). They must also indicate in the contract documents the minimum requirement that variant bids must meet and any special requirements that apply (Article 24(3)).

How may an entity ensure that the appointed supplier will comply with technical requirements?

First, in procedures under the directives, tenderers must accept the mandatory requirements, including those on social and environmental matters. Those that do not may be rejected. Indeed, those that do not accept fundamental requirements *must* be rejected, under the equal treatment principle.[120]

It may be, though, that even when a firm is willing to accept the social or environmental requirements laid down the purchaser believes that there is a risk the firm will not comply and wishes to exclude it. As mentioned above and as is elaborated in section 8.1.4, the directive appears to distinguish in this respect between technical requirements and special conditions, permitting exclusion for anticipated non-compliance only with the former. This is the key difference between the two categories of conditions into which social or environmental requirements may fall. The extent to which specific social and environmental requirements are technical requirements that can form the basis of exclusion rather than special conditions that cannot is considered at 8.1.6 below.

Finally, another issue is the position of a supplier who is awarded a contract and then violates a contractual requirement. In principle, it seems the position depends mainly on national law rules on contractual remedies, although EC law will impose some constraints – for example, the non-discrimination principle will prohibit more favourable treatment of national suppliers in the way in which remedies are exercised. To the extent that the authority can exclude the supplier in advance for anticipated non-compliance, as with technical requirements, there is no objection to a remedy allowing termination of the contract for actual non-compliance.

---

[120] *Storebaelt*, note 2 above.

We have seen in chapter 2 that the Public Sector Directive contains detailed rules on evidence that authorities may require from undertakings for assessing their ability to comply with technical requirements.[121] Of particular note in the present context is Article 48(2)(f), stating that for works and services contracts purchasers may call for an indication of the environmental management measures that firms will apply when performing the contract. This was probably possible under the pre-2004 directives and thus serves again to highlight pre-existing possibilities. Also noteworthy is Article 50, requiring purchasers referring to certification requirements on environmental management standards to refer to the EC Eco-management and Audit Scheme (EMAS) or to European or international standards or certifications, but also to accept other 'equivalent' evidence offered of compliance with the standards. This parallels the explicit provision on accepting 'equivalents' that applies in relation to substantive requirements under Article 23, and also probably reflects a general Treaty requirement to accept any adequate evidence of compliance with requirements, as discussed at 4.10.[122]

8.1.4. Requirements that go beyond compliance with general legal requirements: special conditions

A second category of requirement comprises 'special conditions'. In this respect Article 26 of the directive contains an explicit new provision:

> Contracting authorities may lay down special conditions relating to the performance of a contract, provided that these are compatible with Community law and are indicated in the contract notice or in the specifications. The conditions governing the performance of a contract may, in particular, concern social and environmental considerations.

This clarifies that conditions of this kind are permitted. In this respect, the provision writes into the directive a rule established in *Beentjes*.[123] In

---

[121] As well as for deciding which firms to invite to tender: see section 12.
[122] A similar provision applies to quality assurance standards under Article 49.
[123] Note 7 above. The original version of this provision was contained in Article 23(3) of the Proposal, stating: 'Contracting authorities may require particular conditions concerning performance of the contract, provided that those conditions are compatible with Community law'; the Explanatory Memorandum states that Article 23 'reiterates the principles inherent in the current directives, and therefore does not change the existing arrangements': see European Commission, Proposal for a Directive of the European Parliament and of the Council on the coordination of procedures for the award of public supply contracts, public service contracts and public works contracts, COM (2000) 275 final.

that case the ECJ ruled that Member States may apply conditions relating to employment of the long-term unemployed on the contract, which the Court referred to as 'specific additional conditions' – and thus indicated as being distinct from technical requirements. Recital 33 gives examples of possible special conditions:

> Contract performance conditions are compatible with this directive pro-vided that they are not directly or indirectly discriminatory and are indicated in the contract notice or in the contract documents. They may, in particular, be intended to favour on-site vocational training, the employment of people experiencing particular difficulty in achieving integration, the fight against unemployment or the protection of the environment. For instance, mention may be made, amongst other things, of the requirements – applicable during performance of the contract – to recruit long-term job-seekers or to implement training measures for the unemployed or young persons, to comply in substance with the provisions of the basic International Labour Organisation (ILO) Conventions, assuming that such provisions have not been implemented in national law, and to recruit more handicapped persons than are required under national legislation.

As is apparent from the text of Article 26 cited above, the Article permits special conditions only when stated in the contract notice or specifications.

Are special conditions subject to the controls in Article 23 outlined at 8.1.3 above? The relationship between the concept of 'technical speci-fications' in Article 23, on the one hand, and the two categories of technical requirements and special conditions, on the other, is unclear. One view could be that all measures within the definition of technical specifications are also matters of technical or professional ability under Article 48 (i.e. technical requirements) rather than special conditions, in which case, as explored below, the definition of technical specifications is significant in drawing the line between them. Another view, however, is that some or all terms that are special conditions also form part of the 'technical specifications'. If so, special conditions will, like technical requirements, certainly be subject to the Article 23 controls. However, even if the former view is correct, the ECJ may still apply the Article 23 controls to special conditions by analogy.

How may the purchaser secure compliance with special conditions? As already explained in section 8.1.3 purchasers may, and indeed must, *reject* tenders that do not comply with fundamental requirements, and this will include non-compliance with special conditions, as well as technical requirements.[124] However, as we have mentioned, when the tenderer accepts a requirement but the purchaser wishes to exclude the tenderer because of the risk of non-compliance, a distinction may need to be made between technical requirements, where the tenderer may be excluded, and special conditions, where, arguably it may not. This is the view taken by the European Commission.

This view is based on an interpretation of rather unclear provisions in the Public Sector Directive. As outlined in chapter 2, the directive sets out several grounds for exclusion, including absence of technical or professional ability, absence of economic and financial standing and criteria relating to 'personal position', such as criminal convictions.[125] In *Beentjes*,[126] decided in 1988, the ECJ considered whether an authority could reject a tender for a works contract because of the tenderer's inability to comply with a requirement for using long-term unemployed persons to do the contract work. The judgment itself is unclear on this: the ECJ merely stated that the requirement did *not* relate to technical ability or financial standing[127] but nevertheless could be included in the contract if compatible with the Treaties,[128] but the Court did not state expressly whether or not it could provide the basis for exclusion. The case was interpreted by the Commission, however, in line with the Opinion of Advocate General Darmon,[129] as meaning that inability to comply with such a condition *cannot constitute grounds for exclusion*,[130] since it does not relate to one of the express grounds for exclusion, and that these are the *only* permitted grounds. The present author's view at the time of the judgment, on the other hand, was that since the ECJ did *not* state that anticipated non-compliance cannot provide grounds for exclusion, and the Court also emphasised the framework nature of the directives, the case did *not* in fact preclude exclusion for non-compliance, but supported quite the opposite view, namely that exclusion is possible; and also that this is desirable.[131] However, the reasoning in the later case of

---

[124] As also stated by the European Commission, Communication on social considerations, note 65 above, p. 16, citing *Storebaelt*.

[125] See chapter 2, section 4.3.6.   [126] Note 7 above.   [127] Para. 28.

[128] Paras. 29–31 and 37.   [129] Para. 39 of the Opinion and also para. 43.

[130] This interpretation was put forward soon after the judgment in European Commission, Communication on social and regional aspects of public procurement, COM (89) 400 final, point 47, and is repeated in the more recent Communication on social considerations, note 65 above, p. 16.

[131] S. Arrowsmith, *Public Procurement in the European Community: Volume II: A Guide to the Procurement Cases of the Court of Justice* (Earlsgate Press, 1992), pp. 78–79.

Commission v. *Italy*[132] supports the interpretation that exclusion is not possible. In that case the ECJ ruled that entities may select undertakings to participate in restricted procedures only on the basis of the criteria listed in the directives, which are exhaustive. This case concerned the selection of firms from amongst those meeting minimum requirements (the issue discussed in section 12 below), rather than ability to comply with basic requirements and, furthermore, did not cite *Beentjes*. However, the reasoning was that only the grounds listed in the directive can form the basis for exclusion.[133] The principle that the stated grounds for exclusion are exhaustive has subsequently been accepted in *ARGE*[134] and *La Cascina*,[135] endorsing the reasoning that lies behind *Commission* v. *Italy*. On the basis of *Commission* v. *Italy* and these later cases the present author has in more recent work accepted the principle that anticipated non-compliance with special conditions cannot provide grounds for exclusion, and this is also accepted by many other commentators.[136]

The principle remains open to criticism, however. Advocate General Darmon in *Beentjes* did not offer any policy reason for it. In light of the purpose of the directives of implementing transparent procedures to support open markets, as discussed in chapter 1, the rationale would appear to be to remove the possibility that entities might abuse the discretion to exclude to favour a national supplier. The effect, however, is to elevate in importance the policies reflected in technical requirements above the policies reflected in special conditions. This seems unjustified in light of the principles set out in chapter 1, namely the equal status of horizontal policies and other procurement policies, and the principle that it is for Member States to balance the various non-trade considerations involved in procurement. Discretion to exclude for anticipated non-compliance with a special condition is no more susceptible of abuse than discretion to exclude relating to technical requirements. Further, exclusion is important given the difficulties of enforcing many requirements through contractual remedies such as termination and damages, as discussed in chapter 3. Thus – as the

---

[132] Case C–360/89, *Commission* v. *Italy*, note 10 above.   [133] See, in particular, para. 20.

[134] Case C–94/99, *ARGE Gewässerschutz* v. *Bundesministerium für Land- und Forstwirtschaft* ('*ARGE*') [2000] ECR I–11037, para. 27.

[135] Joined Cases C–226/04–C–228/04, *La Cascina* v. *Ministero della Difesa* ('*La Cascina*') [2006] ECR I–1347, para. 22.

[136] For example, P. Trepte, *Public Procurement in the EU: a Practitioner's Guide* (Oxford University Press, 2007) at 5.61–5.62 and S. Treumer, 'The Selection of Qualified Firms to be Invited to Tender under the EC Procurement Directives' (1998) 7 *PPLR* 147, 148.

present author argued after *Beentjes* – technical specifications and special conditions should be treated alike for the purpose of exclusions.

Are there any recent legal developments or alternative arguments to support this approach?

A first possibility arises from the principles elaborated in chapter 1 and, in particular, developments in those principles since *Commission* v. *Italy*. Of particular relevance are the development of equality as a fundamental principle of Community law, as elaborated by McCrudden in chapter 6, and the Integration Principle of Article 6 EC. These might support a change to the previous interpretation of the directives, based on the need to give greater weight now to the interest in including social and environmental considerations in procurement. This argument would also be bolstered if a principle of proportionality of Community action were relevant for inter-preting the directives, as contemplated in chapter 1.

In addition, it is necessary to take into account the fact that (as discussed in chapter 2) in *Fabricom* the ECJ implicitly recognised the possibility of exceptions to the principle that the listed grounds for exclusion are exhaustive – in that case for exclusion of conflict of interest, to give effect to equal treatment. If there is an exception for exclusions to implement equal treatment, equally an exception might exist for exclusions for social and environmental policies. At the very least, this could be done for policies covered by Article 6 EC and the fundamental principle of equality – an approach that clearly still recognises the 'exceptional' character of non-listed exclusions. However, we argued in chapter 1 that the scope of Member State discretion should not be interpreted differently according to the content of the policies in issue, but, rather, that arguments based on Article 6 EC and equality as a fundamental principle merely provide additional support for a liberal approach to Member State discretion.

A second possibility is elaborated by McCrudden in chapter 6.[137] There he argues essentially that exclusion for anticipated non-compliance with a condition is permitted whenever a Member State *decides to make the conditions part of the subject matter of the contract*, because compliance will then be a matter of technical capacity.[138] According to McCrudden,

---

[137] And see also McCrudden, *Buying Social Justice*, note 75 above, chapters 16 and 17. McCrudden takes the view that these are not to be termed 'special conditions' under Article 26: see McCrudden, *Buying Social Justice*, note 75 above, pp. 538–543.

[138] That the purchaser may make such requirements part of technical capacity is implicit in the discussion in chapter 6, section 4 and is elaborated further in McCrudden, *Buying Social Justice*, note 75 above, pp. 538–543.

the Court in *Beentjes* 'was not deciding ... whether the reduction in unemployment through the use of unemployed persons could be a permissible subject matter of the contract, only that it was not the subject matter of the contract *in this particular case*'.[139] This argument allows Member States to exclude for anticipated non-compliance, in recognition of the principles outlined in chapter 1, yet is also consistent with the reasoning in the current jurisprudence. This raises the question, however, of what evidence authorities may call for to prove capacity, since the evidence listed in the directive for this is exhaustive, yet is not apt for establishing compliance with many social conditions. It remains to be seen whether such arguments will be accepted by the ECJ.

Even if the Commission's restrictive interpretation is accepted, Member States can exclude firms that they do not expect to comply whenever the firm has been guilty of significant non-compliance in previous contracts: as explained below, this probably amounts to 'grave misconduct', which is a ground for exclusion. This possibility can be used to enable purchasers to exclude when they fear non-compliance, and fear of exclusion could also provide a significant incentive for firms to comply with special conditions.

If it is correct that Member States *cannot* exclude more generally for anticipated non-compliance with special conditions, the question arises whether terminating contracts for non-compliance with these conditions is also ruled out. The directives do not expressly regulate the contract administration phase, but the EC regime clearly has an impact on this phase that may affect contractual rights. Such an effect is sometimes implied from the directive – for example, to prohibit substantial changes to the terms set in the competition[140] – and also results from the obligation to terminate certain contracts awarded in violation of EC procurement rules.[141] The ECJ has not yet, however, considered whether the directive limits contractual remedies, which under national law might include termination and/or damages. However, as we have noted, their exercise will be subject to the relevant equal treatment and

[139] See chapter 6 at p. 297.
[140] See, for example, V. Auricchio, 'The Problem of Discrimination and Anti-competitive Behaviour in the Execution Phase of Public Contracts' (1998) 7 *PPLR* 113; Arrowsmith, note 1 above, at 6.5–6.17.
[141] See, in particular, Case C–503/04, *Commission* v. *Germany*, ECJ judgment of 18 July 2007.

non-discrimination principles[142] so that, for example, violations by national suppliers must not be treated more leniently than violations by firms from other Member States. It is also arguable that if a priori exclusion is not generally permitted for anticipated non-compliance with special conditions, and is permitted for past violations of special conditions only for deliberate and/or serious violations – as discussed at 10.3 – then it is implied that entities can *terminate* existing contracts only for serious and/or deliberate violations: otherwise an entity could terminate a contract with a supplier, only to find it has no grounds to exclude that supplier from tendering for the replacement contract. However, a more suitable approach is to interpret grave misconduct as covering any violation that has previously led to termination or, alternatively, to imply into the directive a right to exclude a supplier from a contract that it has previously held and that has been lawfully terminated. Such a limited right of exclusion is not as open to abuse as a general right of exclusion for anticipated non-compliance, since it is based on specific past conduct.

In practice, there are significant constraints on termination, which may involve delays and other costs, especially with works contracts. These will be increased by the directive's own requirements to tender the replacement contract, although purchasers may sometimes be able to use the negotiated procedure without a notice for 'extreme urgency'.[143]

8.1.5. A third category: social and environmental conditions that may not be included as contract requirements ('prohibited requirements')

A third category of conditions consists of conditions that the directives do not allow. We will refer to these as 'prohibited requirements'.

The existence of this category appears to be confirmed by Article 26 of the Public Sector Directive. As explained, as well as clarifying that certain conditions *may* be included, stating that entities 'may lay down special conditions relating to the performance of a contract', Article 26 also appears to rule out by implication conditions that do *not* relate to performance, or at least to assume that such requirements are implicitly

---

[142] These are also important for utilities that are not covered by the EC Treaty's free movement rules, in covering the ground of those Treaty rules.
[143] See chapter 2, section 4.3.4.

prohibited:[144] if conditions unrelated to performance are possible, the Article would not mention contract performance. This is the view of the European Commission: in its Communications prior to the Public Sector Directive, the Commission appeared to take the view that Member States may only include conditions relating to performance[145] and, in the Explanatory Memorandum to the original Proposal for the directive, stated that Article 26 (Article 23(3) of the Proposal) was intended to 'reiterate' existing principles.[146] This view also finds support in the fact that award criteria are expressly limited to the subject matter of the contract: as discussed in section 13, it is illogical to allow contract requirements that go beyond contract performance but not to allow award criteria of that kind, since – as discussed in chapter 3 – award criteria are often a more efficient policy tool and less restrictive of trade than contract requirements. (Conversely, we also argue in section 13 below that the policy of the directives requires that the concept of subject matter of the contract should be expansively interpreted in the context of award criteria, to cover all issues that could be addressed through special conditions.)

These restrictions on contract conditions and award criteria can be seen as manifestations of a general approach in the directive of allowing governments to implement social and environmental policies as a purchaser, but limiting use of procurement as a tool of regulation. This approach is also carried through to exclusion and selection of tenderers, processes which must be linked to a firm's ability to deliver certain contractual requirements, as discussed in sections 10, 11 and 12 below. The policy behind this approach seems to be to reduce the restrictive effect on trade of using procurement as a regulatory tool and possibly to limit opportunities for abuse of discretion.

This approach generally rules out, first, any condition not concerned with the goods, works or services provided (those classified in our chapter 3 taxonomy as 'Contractual requirements going beyond contract

---

[144] Technical specifications and other technical requirements, discussed at 8.1.3 above, are by definition limited to contract performance, as indicated by the fact that the permitted evidence listed is limited to evidence relevant for contract performance.

[145] In particular, in its Communication on environmental considerations, note 115 above, p. 19, the Commission states that 'such a requirement should be defined in such a way that it has a bearing on the performance or execution of the contract'.

[146] European Commission, Proposal for a Directive of the European Parliament and of the Council on the coordination of procedures for the award of public supply contracts, public service contracts and public works contracts, note 127 above, pp. 23–24.

performance'): for example, that the contractor should not have investments in tobacco companies, or should deal in its business only with 'ethical' suppliers.

A second consequence of this approach is that it rules out any conditions that are concerned with performance *in the sense of our chapter 3 taxonomy*, but are not concerned with 'performance' of the contract *in the sense of Article 26*. Which conditions relate to performance in the sense of Article 26 is considered in section 8.1.6 below. A strict interpretation is that certain requirements that *are* related to contract performance within the chapter 3 taxonomy, notably those concerning production of supplies, are *not* related to contract performance within Article 26, and are thus ruled out. However, as will be explained we reject that view, and consider that Article 26 permits all conditions that are concerned with contract performance within the chapter 3 definition.

A quite different interpretation of Article 26 is that the explicit provision permitting certain conditions – those relating to contract performance – clarifies that certain conditions are allowed but, since it does not prohibit them explicitly, does not also rule out other conditions. In other words, the provision clarifies in a positive way the possibilities for including social or environmental conditions, as recognised in the jurisprudence (which has been concerned so far only with performance-related conditions); it does not, on the other hand, impose any restrictions. In this respect it merely reflects, in particular, the statement in Recital 5, that in light of Article 6 EC the directive 'clarifies how authorities may contribute to environmental protection and sustainable development'. In particular, it might be argued that, although the Commission considers them to have been prohibited under the old directives, the possibility of non-performance related conditions is not clear from the ECJ jurisprudence, and that the legislature intended to leave that question open.

Apart from the Explanatory Memorandum mentioned above, the legislative history of the provision throws little light on this issue:[147] whether the provision has any restrictive effect was hardly touched on, but to the extent that it was, it seems to have been assumed that permitted conditions are limited to contract performance,[148] as intended by the

---

[147] This history is usefully set out in J. Hebly (ed.), *European Public Procurement: History of the 'Classic' Directive 2004/18/EC* (Alphen aan den Rijn: The Netherlands, 2007), pp. 711–726.

[148] The Committee of the Regions, Opinion of the Committee of the Regions on the Proposal for a Directive of the European Parliament and of the Council on the

Commission. This interpretation seems more likely to be the one adopted, in light both of the wording and the historical context.

8.1.6. Classification of social and environmental requirements that go beyond legal compliance: technical requirements, special conditions or prohibited requirements?

As we have just seen, the Public Sector Directive appears to recognise three categories of requirements:[149] technical requirements that can both be included in the contract and provide grounds for exclusion for anticipated non-compliance; conditions relating to performance of the contract within Article 26 ('special conditions'), which are permitted but cannot be used for advance exclusion; and (probably) prohibited requirements, that cannot be included at all because they do not 'relate to contract performance' within the meaning of that concept under Article 26. For some requirements it is reasonably clear to which category they belong, but with others the position is uncertain. This issue of classification is discussed below, by reference to the various measures set out in the chapter 3 taxonomy, namely those concerned with consumption effects, production/delivery, disposal and workforce matters. A summary is provided in Table 4.1 on page 216.

In the author's view, there is symmetry between the types of measures relating to contract performance that may be included as contract requirements, and the types of measures that may be included as award criteria. More precisely, it is submitted that the scope for including social or environmental award criteria is precisely the same as the scope for implementing the same policies through contract requirements: matters

---

coordination of procedures for the award of public supply contracts, public service contracts and public works contracts and the Proposal for a Directive of the European Parliament and of the Council coordinating the procurement procedures of entities operating in the water, energy and transport sectors, OJ 2001 No. C 144/23, at 2.7; and the Committee on the Environment, Public Health and Consumer Policy, Opinion of the Committee on the Environment, Public Health and Consumer Policy published in Committee on Legal Affairs and the Internal Mark: Report on the proposal for a directive of the European Parliament and of the Council on the coordination of procedures for the award of public supply contracts, public service contracts and public works contracts, FINAL A5-0378/2001, Part 2, p. 138, Article 23(3). Both suggested deleting reference to performance of the contract because they considered it to impose inappropriate restrictions (in the former case regarding the provision as going beyond the restrictions existing in Community law), thus clearly regarding it as restricting these types of conditions to those related to the contract.

[149] Other types of terms that the authority may include in the contract will be on numerous matters such as the terms of payments due, confidentiality etc.

Table 4.1: *Impact of the Public Sector Directive's Rules on Contract Requirements*

	Technical requirement (permitted, but no advance exclusion for absence of technical or professional ability)	Special condition (permitted, but no advance exclusion for absence of technical or professional ability?)	Prohibited condition
Type of measure			
Limited to contract (government as purchaser)			
a. Consumption impact	Yes		
b. Production and delivery	Yes, for some (at least delivery of works and services)	Yes, for some	? for some (Commission view of most requirements concerned with production of supplies)
c. Disposal	?	?	
d. Workforce doing contract work		Yes	
Beyond the contract (government as regulator)			
e. Nature of supplier			Yes (subject to rules on sheltered employment)
f. Supplier behaviour outside the contract			Yes

that cannot be included as contract requirements (whether as technical requirements, special conditions or otherwise) cannot be award criteria, and matters that can be contract requirements can be award criteria. Certainly, there is a strong argument for the latter proposition, since, as discussed in chapter 3,[150] award criteria frequently provide a more efficient and less trade-restrictive policy mechanism than contract requirements. (As we will see in section 13, however, the Commission takes a different view, rejecting certain social award criteria that can be included as special conditions.) However, it is suggested also that anything that can be included as an award criterion is also possible as a contract condition: it is illogical to distinguish between the two since their effect can be almost identical given that, as we will see in section 13, award criteria can be given a very significant weighting, which may render it effectively impossible for undertakings to win contracts without providing social or environmental benefits. Thus it is submitted that any matters that relate to contract performance under Article 26 on special conditions are also matters 'linked to the subject matter of the public contract' under Article 53 on award criteria (a provision discussed in section 13 below). In light of this symmetry between award criteria and contract requirements, the jurisprudence on award criteria is relevant for determining what contract requirements are allowed, and will be examined accordingly.

How then are various measures to be classified? As noted above, in some cases classification is uncontroversial.

First, certain requirements, such as those relating to consumption effects, seem definitely to be technical requirements – for example, requirements for food to be organically grown (where this affects the product content and hence health impact), requirements that pollution or noise from buses should not exceed a specified level (which we have seen were accepted as *award criteria* in *Concordia Bus Finland*) and requirements for low-energy light bulbs.

Secondly, conditions relating to the contract workforce (recruitment of long-term job-seekers, recruitment of more handicapped persons than required by national law etc.), on the other hand, as listed in the recitals to the directive and indicated by *Beentjes* (as discussed at 8.1.4), are generally in the second group. Perhaps the main area of controversy relating to this group concerns requirements relating to the workforce producing products supplied – for example, that the workforce should enjoy fair labour conditions. It is explained below that the Commission apparently considers that requirements concerned with production of supplies are prohibited, presumably on the basis that they do not relate to contract performance, and this view might also extend to the conditions

---

[150] Chapter 3, section 4, point viii.

of the workforce producing supplies. There is, however, no legal authority for this view. It is submitted that in fact the concept of contract performance more naturally includes conditions of this kind, and also that the principles elaborated in chapter 1, notably the equal status of horizontal policies with other procurement policies, subsidiarity and the principle of equal treatment on grounds of gender etc., support a conclusion that such requirements are permitted under Article 26 of the Public Sector Directive. We have already argued in section 4.3.1 – again contrary to the Commission – that such conditions are not generally ruled out by the EC Treaty.

For the other requirements outlined in chapter 3, relating to delivery/production and disposal, the position is also uncertain: there is no clear indication on how to treat them in either the directive or jurisprudence.

One issue that has been uncontroversial is treatment of measures to reduce the environmental impact of performance of works and services contracts, such as requirements not to disturb tides or to waste water or energy in carrying out construction, or to use environmentally-friendly products in providing cleaning services. The Commission's view is that these fall within the first group (technical requirements): they can be included in the contract and suppliers that cannot meet them can be excluded.[151] This view also finds support in Article 48(2)(f), stating that to determine technical capability entities may demand evidence of an undertaking's environmental management measures relating to contract performance when awarding works and services contracts.

The position of measures concerned with production of *supplies* also has not been addressed directly in the jurisprudence. In *EVN-Wienstrom*, the ECJ accepted the possibility of *award criteria* concerning the extent to which electricity supplied under a contract is produced from renewable sources.[152] Given the symmetry suggested above between award criteria and contract requirements this case implies, it is submitted, that contract *requirements* for energy to be supplied from renewable sources are also permitted (although not whether such requirements are technical requirements or special conditions, a point considered below). However, there is still controversy over the general position of

---

[151] European Commission, Communication on environmental considerations, note 115 above, p. 7. The Commission states that conditions on these matters may be included as they are part of the 'definition of the subject matter of the contract', implying that exclusion is possible, since technical capacity refers to the ability to provide the subject matter.

[152] Note 71 above, para. 34, discussed further below.

the provisions relating to employment protection and working conditions in force at the place where the work, service or supply is to be performed' (Article 55(1)(d)). This was the result of an amendment to the Commission's original proposal inserted by the Parliament at first reading,[162] and was accepted by the Commission as merely clarifying the pre-existing position.[163] As the Commission indicates,[164] this provision implies that if the tender is low because these employment protection measures etc have not been taken into account the tender may be rejected: if it could not be rejected, there would be no purpose in seeking explanations. In the author's view,[165] Article 55 does not create grounds for rejecting tenders: rejection is governed by the directive's general rules on exclusion and selection, outlined above, and on award criteria,[166] which apply in the same way both where there is an abnormally low tender and where there is not. Thus Article 55(1)(d) merely confirms a *general* rule, not confined to low tenders, that states can reject tenders that it appears will not comply with legislation on employment and working conditions,[167] as well as

---

[162] Position of the European Parliament adopted at first reading on 17 January 2002 with a view to the adoption of European Parliament and Council Directive .../.../EC on the coordination of procedures for the award of public supply contracts, public service contracts and public works contracts, OJ 2002 No. C271 E/176.

[163] European Commission, Amended Proposal for a European Parliament and Council Directive concerning the coordination of procedures for the award of public supply contracts, public service contracts and public works contracts, COM (2002) 236 final, at 3.2.

[164] *Ibid.*, at 3.2. See also the European Commission, Communication on social considerations, note 65 above, p. 15.

[165] This view was also put forward by the Presidency in debate: Council of the European Union, Outcome of proceedings from working party on public procurement, 4/5 October 2001, extracted in Hebly, note 147 above, p. 1354, comment under Article 54.

[166] The provision on abnormally low tenders applies both where an authority is considering rejecting a tender because it considers the tenderer cannot perform, and where the risk of non-performance means that the bid is less advantageous under the award criteria: Arrowsmith, note 1 above, at 7.143.

[167] In the debate referred to in note 165, the Presidency stated that the power to reject for social dumping followed from other provisions and is not limited to abnormally low tenders. On the other hand, it is not clear that the Commission takes the same view in its Communication on social issues, note 65 above. Whilst, as indicated, the Commission accepts that states may reject tenders that are abnormally low because the tenderers have not addressed compliance with social legislation, it is not clear that the Communication accepts that anticipated non-compliance with social legislation more generally may provide a ground for rejection: the Communication addresses compliance with social legislation in the context of exclusion for convictions or past gross misconduct, and of verifying tenders for compliance, but does not mention the point in discussing exclusion for absence of technical capacity (section 1.3.2 of the Communication on social issues).

other legislation.[168] As mentioned at 8.1.1, Article 27 of the directive
provides that a purchaser may state, or be obliged to state, where a
tenderer may obtain information on obligations relating to taxes, environmental protection, employment protection provisions and working
conditions (Article 27(1)), and that entities providing such information
must request tenderers to take them into account (Article 27(2)). This
provision does not indicate whether or not a purchaser can exclude a
firm that it considers will not comply, but Article 27(2) does state that it
is without prejudice to the application of Article 55.

8.2. Contractual requirements going beyond contract performance

We have focused above on requirements that relate to contract performance. In doing so we explained that the directive envisages three types
of contract conditions relevant for horizontal policies, namely technical
requirements, special conditions and prohibited requirements, and that
requirements concerning contract performance in the sense of our
chapter 3 taxonomy fall into the first two categories.

On the other hand, it appears that requirements that we classified in
chapter 3 as going beyond contract performance will be classified as
requirements that go beyond performance in the sense of Article 26 of
the directive, and hence will be prohibited. This will no doubt apply to all
requirements that are not limited in their terms to conduct connected with
the goods, works and services. As noted above, this will include a condition
that the contractor should not have any investment in tobacco companies
or should only deal with 'ethical' suppliers. Also in this category would be a
requirement for an electricity supplier to produce electricity from renewable energy sources for other customers: as explained in section 13 below,
in *EVN-Wienstrom* the ECJ ruled that the extent to which an electricity
supplier supplies other customers with 'green' energy is not a lawful award
criterion as it does not relate to the subject matter of the contract, and a
similar policy instituted through a contract requirement also seems unlawful. This accords with the author's view outlined at 8.1.6 above that there is
a symmetry between matters permitted as contract requirements and
matters permitted as award criteria.

---

[168] McCrudden, *Buying Social Justice*, note 75 above, pp. 552–554, suggests that exclusion
of abnormally low tenders is possible for non-compliance with Community legislation
on equality. On the basis of the argument in the text above this applies regardless of
whether this legislation falls within the concept of 'working conditions' in Article 55,
which is purely illustrative and deals anyway only with abnormally low tenders.

9. Packaging and timing of orders: impact of the directive

It can be noted, first, that the directives do not deal specifically with the packaging or timing of contracts, and thus have limited impact in this area.

It needs also to be mentioned, however, that there is one way in which the directive has an important impact on packaging of requirements, which affects small and medium-sized enterprises (SMEs). To prevent regulated entities from avoiding the directives by splitting their purchases to bring them below the thresholds, the directives contain 'aggregation rules' which require entities to add together the value of certain separate purchases in deciding if the thresholds are met.[169] For example, for supplies entities must (broadly speaking) add together the value of all similar supplies bought over a year or at the same time to determine whether thresholds are met, even if bought under separate contracts.[170] This does not mean that the entity may not *buy* the supplies under separate contracts rather than one large contract; it merely means that all the contracts must be awarded using the directive's procedures. The result in practice, however, is that an entity is likely to use either a single contract or a framework agreement, since it is disproportionately costly to run a separate tender under the directive for each small contract. These rules also make it less feasible for entities deliberately to split contracts into small amounts to support SMEs – although use of lots or multi-supplier frameworks can alleviate this problem, and there are also limited exceptions to aggregation rules to allow some lots to be awarded outside the directive.[171] Hatzis further examines the directive's impact on SME policies in chapter 8.

10. Exclusion from contracts for non-compliance with government policies: impact of the directive

10.1. Introduction

Section 8 has already considered the position when Member States seek to exclude a firm from contracts because they believe it will not comply with social or environmental requirements under that contract. Chapter 3 explained that states may also, however, wish to exclude firms from

---

[169] Article 9(3), (5) and (7) of the Public Sector Directive. For details see Arrowsmith, note 1 above, at 6.148–6.159.
[170] Article 9(5) and (7) of the Public Sector Directive.
[171] Article 9(5) of the Public Sector Directive.

government contracts as a sanction for the firm's failure to comply with social or environmental standards in the past, or as an incentive to compliance in the future.

The starting point in considering such exclusions is the rule discussed at 8.1.4 above, that the Public Sector Directive allows exclusion only on listed grounds and, by way of exception, for ensuring equal treatment. As chapter 2 outlined,[172] the listed grounds are: absence of economic or financial standing to perform the contract (Article 47);[173] absence of technical or professional ability to perform the contract (Article 48);[174] certain grounds relating to an undertaking's 'personal situation', such as the existence of criminal convictions (Article 45); and absence of registration on certain professional or trade registers (Article 46).

10.2. Exclusion for non-compliance with general regulatory requirements

As with other policy mechanisms, exclusion for non-compliance might in practice be concerned only with violations of norms set in *other* regulatory provisions, such as in the criminal law. When procurement is used in this limited way, it appears that the directive does not impose significant limitations of substance, but only transparency requirements.

The main relevant provisions are Article 45 on the undertaking's 'personal situation'. This lists various optional grounds for exclusion,[175] which the ECJ has summarised as being concerned with 'professional honesty, solvency and reliability'.[176] They include:

i) the fact that the firm 'has been convicted by a judgment which has the force of *res judicata* in accordance with the legal provisions of the country of any offence concerning his professional misconduct' (Article 45(2)(c)); and

---

[172] See chapter 2, section 4.3.6.
[173] That these provisions refer to capacity to undertake the contract is confirmed by Article 44(2) stating that minimum levels of capacity and information sought must be related to and proportionate to the subject matter of the contract.
[174] Again, the fact that these provisions refer to capacity to undertake the contract is confirmed by Article 44(2) referred to above in note 173.
[175] In Joined Cases C–226/04–C–228/04, *La Cascina*, note 135 above, the ECJ made it clear that it is for Member States to decide whether to apply each of these grounds, and that they may be applied less stringently than is allowed by the directive: see para. 21.
[176] *Ibid.*

ii) the fact that the firm has been 'been guilty of grave professional
misconduct proven by any means which the contracting authority
can demonstrate' (Article 45(2)(d)). This can probably be relied on
to exclude those who have committed a criminal act but not
been convicted, when the misconduct is 'grave', as is stated by the
Commission,[177] although it may not cover all criminal acts: arguably
there must be misconduct which is culpable, and possibly serious
in its effects. This provision also seems capable of covering non-
compliance with other external norms – for example, non-compliance
with rules that attract administrative sanctions or with professional
codes of ethics.

The recitals mention several possibilities for using these provisions to
support social and environmental policies. Thus Recital 43 indicates that
'non-compliance with environmental legislation or legislation on unlawful agreements in public contracts which has been the subject of a final
judgment or a decision having equivalent effect may be considered an
offence concerning the professional conduct of the economic operator
concerned or grave misconduct' and that 'non-observance of national
provisions implementing the Council Directives 2000/78/EC [OJ 2000
No. L303/16] and 76/207/EEC [OJ 1976 No. L39/40 as amended] concerning equal treatment of workers, which has been the subject of a final
judgment or a decision having equivalent effect may be considered an
offence concerning the professional conduct of the economic operator
concerned or grave misconduct'. Recital 34 refers to the fact that non-
compliance with laws and collective agreements concerning employment
conditions and safety at work may be grave misconduct or an offence
concerning professional conduct.

These provisions can be relied on to exclude firms that have engaged
in the conduct in question during past performance of government
contracts, whether in contravention of contract conditions or not – for
example, firms that have not paid their contract workers the minimum
wages required by law, or that have been involved in serious violations of
social or environmental conditions in past contracts. However, they are
by no means limited to violations during past contract performance.

It is not entirely clear whether these provisions are directed solely at
the ability of the excluded firm to perform the contract, by creating a
presumption that the firm is not reliable or honest, and thus cannot be

---

[177] European Commission, Communication on social considerations, note 65 above, p. 11.

trusted to perform effectively and legally. Certainly this is one purpose
of these provisions, and authorities need not demonstrate that the particular conviction or misconduct creates a doubt on this issue[178] – for
example, it seems lawful to exclude any firm with significant criminal
convictions. However, if the *only* objective of the provision is to allow
exclusion of unreliable firms, exclusions that are clearly directed at
horizontal policies *unconnected* with performance might be prohibited.
For example, this might be the case where a government department
responsible for environmental issues refuses contracts to firms with
convictions for even minor environmental violations, in order simply
to enhance compliance with the regulatory rules for which it is responsible and to avoid any association with such firms.

The better view, however, is that this is permitted. This finds support
in *La Cascina*, in which the ECJ stated that Member States may decide
not to apply the 'professional honesty, solvency and reliability' criteria,
or to apply them with varying degrees of rigour, 'according to the
legal, economic or *social* considerations prevailing at national level'[179]
(emphasis added). Further, in labelling the provisions as concerned with
'professional honesty, solvency and reliability', the ECJ treats reliability
distinctly from 'professional honesty'. The latter concept indicates that
violating certain norms is unacceptable and exclusion from government
contracts a legitimate response independent of reliability. This response
could be for one of a number of reasons outlined in chapter 3: to support
particular horizontal policies in a concrete way through additional
incentives and sanctions, to disassociate the authority from criminal or
unethical behaviour, or to remove funds from firms involved in illegal
activity. Exclusion can also be part of a policy to prevent firms from
gaining an unfair competitive advantage that might arise from
non-compliance with legal rules, as indicated by Advocate General
Poiares Maduro in *La Cascina*.[180] The reasons for making such an
exception to the usual rule that entities may not exclude for reasons
unrelated to performance can be found both in the strength of these
special reasons for allowing exclusion, and also the fact that exclusions
are less open to abuse when the grounds of exclusion are defined by

---

[178] See, for example, E. Piselli, 'The Scope for Excluding Providers who have Committed
Criminal Offences under the EU Procurement Directives' (2000) 9 *PPLR* 267;
D. Triantafyllou and D. Mardas, 'Criteria for Qualitative Selection in Public Procurement:
A Legal and Economic Analysis' (1995) 4 *PPLR* 145, 246.
[179] Joined Cases C–226/04–C–228/04, *La Cascina*, note 135 above, para. 23.
[180] *Ibid.*, para. 24 of the Opinion.

pre-existing legal norms (which must themselves, of course, comply with Community law). This interpretation is also buttressed by the principles discussed in chapter 1, in particular the equal status of social and environmental policies with other procurement policies, subsidiarity, the equal treatment principle in the social field and Article 6 EC on environmental considerations.

In addition to the general exclusions for criminal convictions and grave misconduct authorities may exclude a firm that:

i) 'has not fulfilled obligations relating to the payment of social security contributions in accordance with the legal provisions of the country in which he is established or with those of the country of the contracting authority' (Article 45(2)(e)); or

ii) 'has not fulfilled obligations relating to the payment of taxes in accordance with the legal provisions of the country in which he is established or with those of the country of the contracting authority' (Article 45(2)(f)).

According to *La Cascina*, these provisions allow exclusion only for current non-compliance and not for past non-compliance (such as late payment).[181] However, arguably authorities can exclude under the more general provisions discussed above where firms have criminal convictions relating to non-payment, or where past non-payment is sufficiently serious to constitute grave misconduct.

Several uncertainties surround these provisions. One is the extent of transparency obligations. So far as the contract notice is concerned, Annex VII item 17 requires information in the notice on selection criteria relating to 'personal situation'. However, Recital 40 indicates that this only requires a 'general reference in the contract notice to the situations set out in Article 45', which may indicate either that the authority must simply refer to Article 45 or that it must refer to the specific grounds in Article 45 that it will use. Under the general transparency principle, however, it is arguably necessary to formulate more precisely the way in which these provisions will be applied, whether through national legislation, in published guidance or in the contract documents – for example, to specify the kind of convictions that will provide grounds for exclusion, how recent convictions must be etc.[182]

---

[181] *Ibid.*, para. 33 of the judgment.

[182] This could be supported by reference to Article 45(2) stating that 'Member States shall specify, in accordance with their national law and having regard for Community law,

This can provide a safeguard against abuse to favour national firms. The ECJ's recent ruling in *La Cascina*, concerning exclusion for non-compliance with tax obligations, suggests that the Court may take a strict approach. In that case it ruled that Member States must set the time by which tax payments must have been made or by which any relevant 'regularisation' of the situation must have occurred to avoid exclusion: this could be at the date for lodging the request to participate; the date for issuing invitations to participate; the date for tenders; the date at which tenders are considered; or the date for award.[183] However, the Court stated that, based on transparency and equal treatment, this date must be determined with certainty and made public.[184]

Another important uncertainty is the extent to which the provisions authorise exclusion of firms because of the convictions, misconduct etc. of associated companies or individuals (for example, directors). The issues that arise here are considered in chapter 12 dealing with manda-tory exclusions for certain offences.[185]

Finally, as mentioned above, for certain offences in which there is a Community interest, the directives now actually *require* Member States to exclude convicted firms. The relevant provisions are examined in chapter 12.

10.3. Exclusion for non-compliance with standards that go beyond regulatory requirements

What if Member States wish to use exclusions from government con-tracts to induce compliance with standards that go beyond those required by law?

First, exclusion may be a useful sanction for past violations of special conditions. Entities may not exclude firms in advance for anticipated non-compliance with such conditions but may they, however, exclude for past violations? This is probably permitted in certain cases: in *Commission* v. *Spain*, Advocate General Gullman stated that an authority might be able to exclude under the grave misconduct provision for

---

the implementing conditions of this paragraph'. However, this could also refer simply to the fact that states have a broad discretion over implementing the provisions.

[183] Joined Cases C–226/04–C–228/04, *La Cascina*, note 135 above, para. 31.

[184] *Ibid.*, para. 32.

[185] Although the approach of the two sets of provisions will not necessarily be the same, given their different nature as optional and mandatory provisions.

deliberate omission to perform 'contracts awarded'.[186] Arguably, however, a deliberate violation must also be serious in impact to warrant exclusion. It is also unclear how far the Advocate General contemplated exclusion for non-performance of contracts awarded by others, although there seems no reason to distinguish according to the awarding authority. The only relevant consideration is surely the nature of the targeted behaviour. To the extent that exclusion is indeed possible for contractual violations, this can provide one tool for excluding firms that the entity fears will not comply with conditions, and can also provide an incentive to comply.

In addition, an entity might wish to require undertakings to adhere in their business as a whole to certain social or environmental norms that are not embodied in general law, such as proactive fair recruitment policies. Exclusion for not doing so is not generally possible, however. This follows from the principle allowing exclusion only for the reasons stated in the directive which, as we recalled, for the most part refer only to financial and technical capability to perform. Where the authority's requirements go beyond those required by law, the only possible ground for exclusion appears to be grave misconduct. This might be relied on to exclude for violations of certain objective norms that are not actually legal requirements, such as violations of professional codes. It does not, on the other hand, appear to give scope for setting general standards of behaviour for government contractors that are independent of external norms, whether set by regulatory authorities or by individual authorities.

Thus it is not generally possible to implement social or environmental standards that use exclusion from government contracts as the sole means of enforcement (rather than merely using exclusions to supplement existing criminal law provisions), except in those limited cases in which violation of the norm constitutes grave misconduct. Thus Member States may probably not implement contract compliance regimes similar to, for example, the US regime to promote affirmative action in recruitment referred to in chapter 3,[187] even though (as explained there) there are sometimes good reasons for a regulatory approach based solely on contract compliance, such as the greater effectiveness of an approach that involves working closely with limited firms. This rule in the directive effectively precludes contract compliance as an option for implementing government policy as an alternative to other tools, because of the impact

---

[186] Case C–71/92, *Commission* v. *Spain* [1993] ECR I–5923, para. 95 of the Opinion.
[187] Chapter 1, section 2.1.

on trade. Given that, as chapter 2 explained,[188] domestic firms benefit from equal treatment under the directive, states cannot avoid these strictures by limiting exclusions to domestic undertakings.

11. Set-asides: impact of the directive

As we have seen, social policies, in particular, are sometimes implemented by setting aside contracts for limited groups – for example for firms owned by disadvantaged ethnic minorities. The Public Sector Directive does not generally allow such set-asides, however. This follows from the principle recalled at 10.1 above, that exclusion is permitted only on grounds listed in the directive. This also means, as Hatzis notes in chapter 8 (section 3), that authorities may not set aside contracts for SMEs, even if this is permitted under the EC Treaty.[189]

There is, however, one major exception, introduced in 2004: Article 19 of the Public Sector Directive now allows Member States to reserve contracts for workshops or programmes where most of the employees are handicapped persons. This is the one case in which there is broad consensus that the restrictive impact on trade of reserving contracts for a limited group is justified by the social benefits. The provision is examined by Boyle in chapter 7 on disability issues.

12. Preferences in inviting firms to tender: impact of the directive

What about taking into account social or environmental considerations in deciding which qualified firms to invite to tender?

The scope for this also appears limited since, as chapter 2 explained, the directive allows entities to take into account in selecting firms to tender only those same criteria permitted for exclusion. This principle was set out by the ECJ in *Commission* v. *Italy*,[190] already considered in section 3. The ECJ ruled that the provision in that case, providing for authorities to give preferences in inviting tenders for certain works contracts to associations and consortia that included undertakings with their main activities in the region of the works, violated not only the Treaty but also the relevant directive, since entities must select invitees based *only* on economic and financial grounds, or 'personal position'

---

[188] See chapter 2, section 4.3.3.   [189] See chapter 8, section 3.
[190] Case C–360/89, *Commission* v. *Italy*, note 10 above.

(that is, the Article 45(2) criteria, such as grave misconduct). Thus, for example, in the same way that the entity cannot exclude firms from consideration because they do not adopt proactive fair recruitment policies, so also it cannot give preference to firms that do so in choosing between qualified firms. Further, although, as mentioned, entities may set aside contracts for sheltered employment purposes, arguably they may not take into account that a tenderer provides sheltered employment when selecting tenderers for a regular competition. Nor may they select for ability to comply with special conditions. However, they may select on the basis of social or environmental considerations relating to technical capability. For example, they may take account of relevant past experience in environmental management when the contract includes technical requirements of an environmental nature such as limiting disturbances to wildlife when executing public works.

13. Award criteria: impact of the directive

Regarding award criteria, it will be recalled that awards must be made to the tender that is the lowest priced or the tender that is 'the most economically advantageous from the point of view of the contracting authority' (Article 53(1)). Article 53(1)(a) sets out a non-exhaustive list of criteria for judging the latter, namely 'quality, price, technical merit, aesthetic and functional characteristics, environmental characteristics, running costs, cost-effectiveness, after-sales service and technical assistance, delivery date and delivery period or period of completion'. In interpreting this provision in the context of horizontal criteria it is important to note that the directive's first recital emphasises the intention to clarify ECJ case law:

> This directive is based on Court of Justice case-law, *in particular case-law on award criteria, which clarifies the possibilities for the contracting authorities to meet the needs of the public concerned, including in the environmental and/or social area.* (emphasis added)

It can be seen, first, that Article 53 refers expressly to the possibility of using 'environmental characteristics' as award criteria. The old directives did not expressly refer to this possibility, but it was confirmed in *Concordia Bus Finland*.[191] That case, as we have seen, concerned a tender for operating a bus network, where the procuring entity had allocated

---

[191] Case C–513/99, *Concordia Bus Finland v. Helsinki*, note 4 above.

points in the evaluation for tenders offering buses with levels of nitrogen oxide emissions and noise below defined levels. The ECJ ruled that such environmental criteria were permitted. It expressly rejected an argument that the criteria must be of a purely economic nature referring, *inter alia*, to Article 6 EC on integrating environmental considerations into Community policy.[192] It is also important that in allowing such criteria the ECJ implicitly rejected a Commission argument that environmental protection criteria can be included only when they provide a direct economic advantage to the authority relating to the works/supplies/ services, which in the Commission's view could not include criteria relating to externalities such as the impact of pollution on the population. Article 53 now expressly confirms the interpretation that certain environmental criteria are permitted and, as with the express references to environmental specifications set out at 8.1.3 above, also serves to draw attention to the possibility of using environmental criteria.

Since the listed criteria are not exhaustive, there is also room for using certain social criteria, even though these are not mentioned. For example, as elaborated in chapter 7 on disability issues, entities may include criteria relating to the accessibility of buildings or IT equipment.[193]

Environmental and social criteria can be included either by allocating points to tenders meeting certain minimum criteria (as in *Concordia Bus Finland*) and/or by allocating variable credit (possibly up to a certain limit) according to the extent to which the different tenderers provide social/environmental benefits.[194]

Whilst social and environmental award criteria are permitted they must, however, comply with the various rules that govern all award criteria, including rules on advance disclosure and weighting (as set out in chapter 2), non-discrimination and equal treatment, and certain other limitations.

The most important limitation, highly significant for horizontal policies, is that criteria must be 'linked to the subject-matter of the public contract in question' (Article 53(1)(a)). This phrase did not appear in the old directives, but in its decision under those directives in *Concordia Bus Finland* the ECJ ruled that: 'Since a tender necessarily relates to the subject-matter of the contract, it follows that the award criteria which may be applied in accordance with that provision must themselves also

---

[192] *Ibid.*, para. 57.   [193] Chapter 7, section 4.3.
[194] On these different approaches see chapter 3, section 4 (viii), 'Award criteria'.

be linked to the subject-matter of the contract.'[195] Article 53 of Directive 2004/18 now states this expressly. The ECJ gave no reason relating to the old directives' wording why a tender necessarily relates to the subject-matter of the contract, nor any policy reason why this should be the case, in particular why the limited purpose of the directive in removing barriers to free movement and the Integration Principle of Article 6 EC do not permit a broader view of award criteria. The reasons behind such a limitation seem, however, to be the restrictive effect on trade of broader criteria, and possibly the fear of abuse of any broad discretion – the same justifications that apparently lie behind the decision to limit contract conditions to the performance of the contract (discussed at 8.1.5), and to limit grounds for exclusion and selection to those related to contract performance (discussed in sections 10.3, 11 and 12 above).

In the same way that these limitations on contract conditions and on exclusion and selection preclude policies that are not concerned solely with the supplies, works or services provided, so this requirement for a link to the subject matter of the contract rules out award criteria that go beyond a concern with the supplies, works or services under the contract, a manifestation of the directive's general approach in permitting procurement policies implemented as 'purchaser', but not those implemented as 'regulator'. In the context of award criteria this is illustrated by *EVN-Wienstrom*.[196] As explained in section 4.3.2, this case concerned a procurement of electricity by the Austrian state under the old Supply Directive 93/36, which required electricity supplied to be from renewable sources. The state also included an award criterion favouring tenderers who could supply to the market from renewable sources *more* electricity than the amount required under the contract. The ECJ ruled that the criterion violated the directive, as it was not linked to the subject matter of the contract as required by *Concordia Bus Finland*. This will remain the case under the explicit requirement for a link to the subject-matter of the contract under Article 53(1)(a) of the current Public Sector Directive. It can be noted that a proposed amendment by the European Parliament to allow authorities to include the tenderer's equal opportunities policy as an award criterion, even – apparently – outside performance of the contract, was eventually rejected.[197]

---

[195] Note 4 above, para. 59 of the judgment.   [196] Note 71 above.

[197] Note 167 above, Article 62(1)(b). This rejection does not of itself indicate that Article 53 does not permit such policies but this is clear from the requirement of a link to the subject matter of the contract.

States may wish to use for award criteria, as contract requirements, all types of measures set out in chapter 3, namely measures concerned with consumption effects, production/delivery effects, disposal effects, and workforce matters. Although *Concordia Bus Finland* and the new directive have established that certain environmental criteria are permitted and that these must relate to the subject matter of the contract, the precise scope for including all these measures as award criteria is still not clear.

We discussed in section 8 how far, in the context of horizontal policies, the directive allows different types of measures as *contract requirements*. It was suggested there that there is symmetry between measures that may be included as contract requirements and those that may be included as award criteria: matters that cannot be included as contract requirements cannot be award criteria, and matters that can be contract requirements (whether as technical requirements or special conditions) can also be award criteria. For that reason the jurisprudence on award criteria (in particular, *Concordia Bus Finland* and *EVN-Wienstrom*) were referred to in that section in considering contract requirements. However, the position is not entirely certain from the jurisprudence, and it is thus necessary to outline what jurisprudence does exist on award criteria, and how it relates to the jurisprudence and legislation examined above in the discussion of contract requirements.

First, so far as concerns award criteria on *consumption effects*, *Concordia Bus Finland* itself indicates that these are allowed: the criteria in that case on pollution and noise levels of buses related to the impact of consumption of products in use.

Secondly, with regard to *production and delivery effects*, as we saw in section 8, the ECJ ruled clearly in *EVN-Wienstrom* that the directive allows a state to consider as an award criterion whether or not electricity supplied is from renewable sources.[198] Whilst the directive prohibited the criterion in that case because it was concerned with the sources of the tenderers' production of electricity *beyond* that supplied under the contract, the Court made it clear that such a criterion is not ruled out when limited to the electricity supplied under the contract itself.[199] It can be noted that the European Parliament had proposed amendments to refer

---

[198] Note 71 above, para. 34.
[199] If this were *not* considered as linked to the subject matter of the contract, there would be no room for such a criterion – contrary to the possibility indicated by the ECJ in the passage quoted.

explicitly to the possibility of including environmental criteria relating to production methods,[200] which were not eventually included; but this does not necessarily imply that such criteria are *not* included and the possibility of some criteria relating to production, including production of supplies, is confirmed by *EVN-Wienstrom*.

The ECJ does not in *EVN-Wienstrom*, however, propose any principle to determine precisely when delivery or production effects will be permitted award criteria and when, if ever, they will not. It was explained in section 8.1.4 above that the position is also not wholly clear as regards the possibility of including production and delivery effects as *contractual requirements*. It was argued there, however, that all measures directed at contract performance within the meaning of our chapter 3 taxonomy are permissible,[201] and that, contrary to the Commission's view, this generally includes measures relating to production of supplies. It is submitted, similarly – and for similar reasons – that all measures of this type are also permitted as award criteria. This is justified in light of the general principles discussed in chapter 1, specifically the equal status of social and environmental policies with other procurement policies, the principle of subsidiarity and, given the importance of production and delivery measures in the environmental field, the Integration Principle in Article 6 EC. A broad view is also taken by Kunzlik in chapter 9 on green energy, who also suggests in that context that award criteria may even refer to whether products supplied on government contracts have themselves been produced using electricity from renewable sources (although subject to the important constraints that application of the criteria must be capable of verification, as discussed below).

Thirdly, with regard to disposal effects, there is no clear indication in legislation or jurisprudence on how to treat these. As discussed in section 8.1, it seems that these are permitted either as technical requirements or as special conditions, and thus should also be permitted as award criteria.

---

[200] Article 62(1)(b) of the Position of the European Parliament adopted at first reading on 17 January 2002 with a view to the adoption of European Parliament and Council Directive .../.../EC on the coordination of procedures for the award of public supply contracts, public service contracts and public works contracts, note 167 above and Article 56(1) of the Position of the European Parliament adopted at second reading on 2 July 2003 with a view to the adoption of European Parliament and Council Directive 2003/.../EC on the coordination of procedures for the award of public works contracts, public supply contracts and public service contracts, OJ 2004 No. C74 E/286.

[201] Although it was suggested that it is not clear whether they are technical requirements or special conditions.

Finally, it is necessary to consider workforce measures. May a Member State, for example, award additional points in the tender evaluation to firms offering employment to disabled persons or the long-term unemployed? This is a matter of controversy, but, as the author has argued elsewhere,[202] the better view is that such criteria are allowed.

First, this interpretation is supported by the principle of symmetry of contract requirements and award criteria outlined above since, as section 8 explained, workforce matters may be the subject of special conditions.

In addition, the possibility of including 'workforce' award criteria is specifically supported by *Nord Pas de Calais*.[203] That case arose out of a practice in the Nord Pas de Calais region in France of referring in contract notices for public works contracts to the ability of firms to combat local unemployment as an 'award criterion'. The ECJ stated that a policy combating unemployment could in principle be an 'award criterion', subject to compatibility with the non-discrimination rules.[204] (In fact, the criterion in question apparently violated the rules since it referred to local unemployment.) However, the meaning of the ruling is disputed because of the Court's reasoning and the circumstances of the case. First, the Court relied on its previous decision in *Beentjes* on special conditions. However, as we have seen, *Beentjes* did not suggest that the directives permit *award criteria* on workforce matters, but concerned special conditions. The Court did not refer to the difference. However, this reference to *Beentjes* in a case on award criteria could in fact be considered as supporting the symmetry principle in the sense that anything permitted as a special condition is automatically permitted as an award criterion. Secondly, it should be mentioned that the Commission guidance does not consider *Nord Pas de Calais* to support the general use of workforce criteria,[205] but suggests that it endorses workforce criteria only *if the economic aspects of the tenders are equal.* However, although it appears that the criterion was operated in this way in the case considered by the Court, it is surely significant that the Court does not mention this, implying that the principle stated in the judgment is not confined to these circumstances. Further, it is hard to see how such a specific

---

[202] Arrowsmith, note 1 above, at 19.58–19.60.

[203] Case C–225/98, *Nord Pas de Calais*, note 8 above.   [204] *Ibid.*, para. 54.

[205] European Commission, Communication on social considerations, note 65 above, pp. 14–15. This approach has been accepted, for example, by Northern Ireland in a pilot project for using procurement to find work for the unemployed: see A. Erridge and S. Hennigan, 'Public Procurement and Social Policy in Northern Ireland: The Unemployment Pilot Project', in K. Piga and G. Thai (eds.), *Advancing Public Procurement* (Boca Raton: PrAcademics Press, 2006), chapter 13.

and limited rule can be derived from the text of the directive. Thus the Commission's interpretation cannot be sustained.

In relation to production/delivery, disposal and workforce matters, it might be argued that there is some difference between the permitted scope of award criteria, on the one hand, and contract requirements, on the other, in view of the different language used: under Article 53 award criteria must be 'linked to the subject-matter' of the contract whilst permitted contract requirements, specifically under Article 26 on special conditions, are those 'relating to performance' of the contract. Thus it could be suggested – as by Arnould, for example[206] – that the concepts of the subject matter and performance are different, and, in particular, that measures classed as special conditions, as opposed to technical require-ments, when included as contract requirements are not part of the subject matter for the award criteria rule. A reason for such a narrow approach to award criteria could be to limit the scope of discretion to exclude firms to prevent abuse, as with the rule that undertakings cannot be rejected for anticipated non-compliance with special conditions. This is reflected in the Opinion of Advocate General Alber in *Nord Pas de Calais*: he considered that the social consideration in that case was *not* a permitted award criterion, since *Beentjes* intended to preclude such a criterion affecting the selection of the winning undertaking.[207] This may also lie behind the Commission's preference for an interpretation that limits the impact of *Nord Pas de Calais* in permitting social award criteria, as discussed in the previous paragraph. However, this argument is relevant only to excluding firms when the authority considers that those firms will not meet social undertakings offered in their own tender; it is not an argument not to allow Member States to take into account as award criteria the extent of the social (or environmental) commitments offered in the tender. It should be noted that as with environmental production measures, the European Parliament at its second reading voted for an amendment stating that the award criteria linked to the subject matter could include 'the tenderer's policy in relation to people with disabilities' and 'its equal treatment policy'.[208] However, as with the proposed amendment on production methods, rejection of this

---

[206] J. Arnould, 'Secondary Policies in Public Procurement: The Innovations of the New Directives' (2004) 13 *PPLR* 187, 191 and 194–195.

[207] Note 8 above, para. 49 of the Opinion.

[208] Article 56(1) of the Position of the European Parliament adopted at second reading on 12 July 2003 with a view to the adoption of European Parliament and Council Directive 2003/.../EC on the coordination of procedures for the award of public works contracts,

provision does not indicate positively that such criteria are not permitted but merely reflects the inability of the Community institutions to reach agreement. The broad interpretation of permitted award criteria offered above that would allow workforce criteria to be used is supported by the principles discussed in chapter 1, namely the equal treatment of horizontal policies with other procurement policies, subsidiarity, equality and the Integration Principle of Article 6 EC. It is also required by the fact that, as chapter 3 explains, award criteria provide a mechanism to implement horizontal policies that offers a better balance between costs and benefits than the mechanism of contract requirements and is also less restrictive of trade. The different terminology in Article 53 and Article 26 is explained merely by the accident of historical development, namely that the jurisprudence that led to Article 53 (*Concordia Bus Finland*) concerned a supply contract, for which the term 'subject matter' is more apt, whilst the jurisprudence that led to Article 26 (*Beentjes*) concerned works, for which the terminology of 'performance' is more natural.

In addition to the requirement that award criteria must be limited to the subject matter of the contract, the jurisprudence has also established certain other conditions governing award criteria:[209] in particular, they must not give unfettered discretion,[210] they must be objective and quantifiable,[211] and their application must be capable of verification.[212] These conditions impose some limits on use of social and environmental criteria. For example, Kunzlik argues in chapter 9 that the verification requirement limits scope for policies favouring products using only electricity from renewable sources.[213]

Within the limits set above, however, the ECJ appears to accept a broad scope for horizontal award criteria, at least for certain policies. This is indicated by *EVN-Wienstrom*. In that case the authority had used

---

public supply contracts and public service contracts, note 200 above. The full history of Article 53 is usefully set out in Hebly, note 147 above, at 1257–1309 and is also recounted in the context of horizontal criteria by, for example, McCrudden, *Buying Social Justice*, note 75 above, 456–466.

[209] These are discussed in detail in Arrowsmith, note 1 above, at 7.110–7.115.

[210] See, in particular, *Beentjes*, note 7 above, para. 26; Case C–19/00, *SIAC Construction v. Mayo CC* ('*SIAC Construction*') [2001] ECR I–7725, para. 37; Case C–513/99, *Concordia Bus Finland*, note 4 above, para. 61.

[211] Case C–513/99, *Concordia Bus Finland*, note 4 above, para. 66.

[212] Case C–448/01, *EVN-Wienstrom*, note 71 above, paras. 51–52.

[213] See chapter 9, section 9.1.

16. The impact of the Government Procurement Agreement and other international trade agreements

Finally, it is appropriate to mention briefly the possible impact of the EC's[223] international trade agreements with third countries,[224] in particular the World Trade Organization's Agreement on Government Procurement (GPA).[225] Under this agreement the EC has opened up significant parts of its government market[226] to a number of countries that include its major trading partners, notably the United States, Japan and Canada. The GPA imposes a non-discrimination obligation towards the other Parties, as well as a requirement to follow transparent award procedures which follow a similar pattern to those of the directives (although generally closer to those of the Utilities Directive than the Public Sector Directive).

In principle the EC directives govern access to procurement markets of EC Member States, whilst the GPA applies only as between the EC Member States and other GPA parties. In (very) limited respects the GPA procedures were previously more stringent than those of the directives, leading to the anomalous position that in certain respects non-EC suppliers enjoyed better safeguards for access to EC procurement than EC suppliers. To remove this anomaly, Directive 97/52/EC on the public sector[227] and Directive 98/4 on utilities[228] amended the directives to align them with the GPA. To cover any discrepancies not specifically rectified a general provision (now in Article 5 of the Public Sector

---

[223] There is debate over the division of competence between the EC and its Member States in relation to these agreements, including the GPA, that need not be considered here: see Arrowsmith, note 1 above, at 20.2–20.6 and (on the GPA specifically) 20.11.

[224] See generally Arrowsmith, note 1 above, chapter 20 and J. Schnitzer, 'The External Sphere of Public Procurement Law: Bi-regional Trade Relations from the Perspective of the European Community' (2005) 14 *PPLR* 63.

[225] See Arrowsmith, note 88 above; A. Reich, *International Public Procurement Law: the Evolution of International Regimes on Public Purchasing* (The Hague: Kluwer Law International, 1999); B. Hoekman and P. Mavroidis (eds.), *Law and Policy in Public Purchasing: The WTO Agreement on Government Procurement* (Ann Arbor: University of Michigan Press, 1997); and R. Anderson, 'Renewing the WTO Agreement on Government Procurement: Progress to Date and Ongoing Negotiations' (2007) 16 *PPLR* 255.

[226] On coverage see Arrowsmith, note 1 above, at 20.10–20.13 and the works cited there.

[227] Directive 97/52/EC amending Directives 92/50/EEC, 93/36/EEC and 93/37/EEC concerning the coordination of procedures for the award of public service contracts, public supply contracts and public works contracts respectively, OJ 1997 No. L328/1.

[228] Directive 98/4/EC amending Directive 93/38/EEC coordinating the procurement procedures of entities operating in the water, energy, transport and telecommunications sectors, OJ 1998 No. L101/1.

Directive) provides that in awarding contracts covered by the GPA Member States shall apply in their relations conditions as favourable as those which they grant to third country undertakings in implementing the GPA.

Although it is unlikely, Member States might possibly adopt horizontal policies that are compatible with the detailed procedures of the directives but violate the GPA.[229] For example, it is not entirely clear that the current text of the GPA allows exclusion on such a broad basis as appears in the directives for firms with criminal convictions;[230] and the GPA might also impose additional limits on horizontal policies that affect suppliers' activities outside the territory of the awarding state.[231] In such cases EC suppliers will also be able to invoke the GPA limitations, relying on Article 5. However, the impact of the GPA rules on horizontal policies is even less clear than that of the EC rules, so that the possibility of any difficulties arising are perhaps more theoretical than real. Perhaps the main importance of the GPA is that it reduces the flexibility available to the EC to modify its policies in future. It seems, however, that the recent addition to the directives of set-asides for sheltered employment programmes can be reconciled with the GPA, since the GPA has an explicit exception for programmes relating to the products or services of handicapped persons.[232]

---

[229] On the GPA's rules on horizontal policies see generally Arrowsmith, note 88 above, chapter 13; S. Arrowsmith, 'Public Procurement as a Tool of Policy and the Impact of Market Liberalisation' (1995) 111 *LQR* 235; Krüger, Nielsen and Bruun, note 87 above, especially chapter V; P. Kunzlik, 'Environmental Issues in International Procurement', in S. Arrowsmith and A. Davies (eds.), *Public Procurement: Global Revolution* (London: Kluwer Law International, 1999), chapter 11; C. McCrudden, 'Social Policy Issues in Public Procurement: A Legal Overview', in S. Arrowsmith and A. Davies (eds.), *Public Procurement: Global Revolution* (London: Kluwer Law International, 1999), chapter 12; C. McCrudden, 'International Economic Law and the Pursuit of Human Rights: A Framework for Discussion of the Legality of "Selective Purchasing" Laws under the WTO Procurement Agreement' (1999) 2 *JIEL* 3; C. Pitschas and H. Priess, 'Secondary Criteria and their Compatibility with EC and WTO Procurement Law – The Case of the German Scientology Declaration' (2000) 9 *PPLR* 171; C. Spennermann, 'The WTO Agreement on Government Procurement – A Means of Furtherance of Human Rights' (2001) 4 *Zeitschrift für europa-rechtliche Studien* 43; S. Griller, 'International Economic Law as a Means to Further Human Rights? Selective Purchasing under the WTO Agreement on Government Procurement' (2003) *Schriftenreihe der Österreichischen Gesellschaft für Europaforschung* 267; McCrudden, *Buying Social Justice*, note 75 above, chapter 15.

[230] See Arrowsmith, note 88 above.   [231] *Ibid.*

[232] Article XXIII(2). See also chapter 7, note 92.

5

The impact of the EC state aid rules on horizontal policies in public procurement

HANS-JOACHIM PRIESS AND MORITZ GRAF
VON MERVELDT

1. Introduction

The question as to whether and, if so, how the EC rules on state aid affect the application of horizontal policies in public procurement is highly controversial and, regrettably, still subject to a considerable degree of legal uncertainty. In essence, the argument turns on the question whether a Member State purchasing goods or services within a public procurement procedure grants an unjustified economic advantage to the successful bidder when it awards the contract on the basis of horizontal criteria. It is generally assumed that by doing so the procuring entity usually pays a higher price than it would have had to pay without the use of the horizontal policy. Arguably, this overcompensation would put the bidder at a competitive advantage vis-à-vis its competitors thus resulting in a distortion of competition. On the other hand, however, it is obvious that the application of the EC state aid rules to horizontal policies would *de facto* put an end to the use of horizontal policies in public procurement. Procurement measures involving state aid would have to be notified to the European Commission (the Commission) under Article 88 EC Treaty and could not be implemented before the Commission had cleared the measures – a procedure that may last several years.[1] This chapter aims to summarise the debate and to provide a clearer picture as to what policies the Member States are entitled to pursue without falling foul of the EC Treaty's rules on state aid.

---

[1] A. Doern, 'The Interaction between EC Rules on Public Procurement and State Aid' (2004) 13 *PPLR* 97.

2. The concept of state aid

Article 87(1) EC Treaty provides that 'any aid granted by a Member State or through State resources in any form whatsoever which distorts or threatens to distort competition by favouring certain undertakings or the production of certain goods shall, insofar as it affects trade between Member States, be incompatible with the Common Market'. The concept of state aid is not defined in the EC Treaty itself. However, the wording of Article 87(1) EC Treaty indicates a wide reading ('any aid') and the European Court of Justice (ECJ) has adopted a broad interpretation accordingly. According to the case law of the ECJ, the concept of aid not only embraces positive benefits, such as subsidies, but also encompasses measures which, in various forms, mitigate the charges which are normally included in the budget of an undertaking and which, without therefore being subsidies within the strict meaning of the word, are similar in character and have the same effect.[2] The relevant test is whether the recipient has received an economic advantage, which it would not have obtained under 'normal market conditions'.[3] In the view of the ECJ, it is immaterial in which particular form an advantage is granted. Whether or not a measure constitutes aid depends rather upon its effects.[4] Likewise, the objectives pursued by the Member State granting the aid, or its motives, are also irrelevant for the purpose of assessing whether or not a measure constitutes state aid.[5]

3. The case law of the European Courts and the case practice of the Commission

Consequently, Article 87(1) EC Treaty has been applied to a large variety of measures such as the privatisations of public undertakings,[6] the

---

[2] Case 30/59, *De gezamenlijke Steenkolenmijnen in Limburg* v. *ECSC High Authority* [1961] ECR 3; Case C–387/92, *Banco Exterior de España* v. *Ayuntamiento de Valencia* [1994] ECR I–877, para. 13; Case C–200/97, *Ecotrade* v. *Altiforni e Ferriere di Servola* [1998] ECR I–7907, para. 34.

[3] Case C–342/96, *Spain* v. *Commission* [1999] ECR I–2459, para. 41.

[4] Case T–14/96, *BAI* v. *Commission* ('*BAI*') [1999] II–139, para. 81; Case T–106/95, *FFSA* v. *Commission* [1997] ECR II–229, para. 125.

[5] Case C–480/98, *Spain* v. *Commission* [2000] ECR I–8717, para. 16; Case 310/85, *Deufil* v. *Commission* [1987] ECR 901, para. 8.

[6] European Commission, XXIII Report on Competition Policy 1993, para. 403.

sale of public land,[7] capital injections to stated-owned companies[8] and state guarantees granted to undertakings in difficulties.[9] Given the wide definition of the concept of aid, it hardly seems surprising that the reverse situation where a Member State is not acting as an investor or seller, but rather as a purchaser of goods or services, does not escape the scope of the general prohibition on state aid set out in Article 87(1) EC Treaty.

3.1. The case law of the ECJ

So far, the ECJ has not had to decide the question of the extent to which horizontal policies in public procurement involve unlawful state aid. The question of the application of the state aid rules in a procurement context was raised in two cases concerning Italian rules reserving a proportion of public supply contracts to undertakings established in the Mezzogiorno. In both cases, the Italian Government argued that the procurement measures should qualify as lawful state aid. However, the ECJ did not consider whether the rules in question constituted state aid, because it was already established that they infringed Article 30 EC Treaty (now Article 28 EC Treaty).[10]

3.2. The case law of the CFI

It fell to the European Court of First Instance (CFI) to first openly address the interplay between public procurement and the state aid rules. In *BAI*, the CFI held that the fact that a Member State acted as a purchaser of goods or services would not preclude the application of the EC state aid rules to that conduct.[11] In this case, the Basque Provincial Council

---

[7] European Commission, Communication on state aid elements in sales of land and buildings by public authorities, OJ 1997 No. C209/3.

[8] Case C–305/89, *Italy* v. *Commission* [1991] ECR I–1603; European Commission, Position on the application of Articles 92 and 93 of the EC Treaty to public authorities' holdings in company capital, Bulletin of the European Communities 9/84, 104; European Commission, Communication to the Member States – Application of Articles 92 and 93 of the EEC Treaty and of Article 5 of Commission Directive 80/723/EEC to public undertakings in the manufacturing sector, OJ 1993 No. C307/3.

[9] European Commission, Notice on the application of Articles 87 and 88 of the EC Treaty to State aid in the form of guarantees, OJ 2000 No. C71/14.

[10] Case C–21/88, *Du Pont de Nemours Italiana SpA* v. *Unita Sanitaria Locale No 2 Di Carrara* ('*Du Pont de Nemours*') [1990] ECR I–889, para. 21; Case C–351/88, *Laboratori Bruneau* v. *USL RM/24 di Monterotondo* [1991] ECR I–3641, para. 7.

[11] Case T–14/96, *BAI*, note 4 above, para. 71.

had purchased 46,500 travel vouchers for shipping passages between Portsmouth and Bilbao within a period of three years. The objective of the measure was to distribute the vouchers among certain low-income groups and groups covered by social and cultural programmes, including school groups, young people and the elderly. Initially, the Provincial Council had purchased a significantly smaller number of vouchers (26,000). However, the agreed price had been higher than the commercial tariff. Following an intervention of the Commission, the price was lowered, whereas the volume of the purchased vouchers almost doubled. The Commission subsequently found that the modifications implemented by the Provincial Council had brought the measure outside the ambit of Article 87(1) EC Treaty.

The CFI disagreed, arguing that it was immaterial for a finding of state aid whether or not an agreement was reciprocal, i.e. that the Member State had received a consideration for awarding the contract. The CFI confirmed that 'according to settled case-law, Article 92(1) [now Article 87(1)] makes no distinction according to the causes or aims of the aid in question, but defines it in relation to its effects'.[12] Accordingly, the CFI held that the real question was whether the consideration paid adequately reflected the market value of the goods or services procured. The CFI stated that the Commission had failed to establish that the purchase of the travel vouchers was 'in the nature of a normal commercial transaction'.[13] The fact that following the Commission's initial intervention the price per voucher had been reduced to even less than the official price did not lead to a different conclusion given the long-term nature of the contractual obligation, as well as the fact that the number of vouchers purchased apparently far exceeded the actual demand. Furthermore, the CFI ruled that, given its effects-based approach, the cultural and social aims pursued by the Spanish authorities played no part in the characterisation of the measure in the light of Article 87(1) EC Treaty.[14]

The CFI has subsequently affirmed the *BAI* judgment and further clarified the case law on those public procurement situations that may be relevant under the EC state aid rules.[15] In *Thermenhotel*, the CFI said that an agreement entered into 'on purely economic grounds' would

---

[12] Case T–14/96, *BAI*, note 4 above, para. 81.   [13] *Ibid.*, para. 75.   [14] *Ibid.*, para. 81.
[15] Joined Cases T–116/01 and T–118/01, *P & O European Ferries (Vizcaya), SA and Diputación Foral de Vizcaya v. Commission* ('*P&O*') [2003] ECR II–2956, para. 114 *et seq.*; Case T–158/99, *Thermenhotel Stoiser Franz and others v. Commission* ('*Thermenhotel*') [2004] ECR II–1.

not awarded to the offeror submitting the most economically advantageous bid.[33]

5.2. Determination of the market price

A measure can only constitute state aid if it confers an economic advantage upon the recipient. As mentioned above, the relevant test for this is whether the recipient would have also obtained the benefit under 'normal market conditions'.

5.2.1. The 'market economy test'

In this respect, the most important conclusion to be drawn from the *BAI* case law of the CFI is that the relevant yardstick for assessing public procurement measures – and thus also the use of horizontal policies – will be the same as it is for other state measures. By asking whether or not a procurement measure was in the nature of a 'normal commercial transaction', the CFI in *BAI* obviously applied the so-called 'market investor test'.[34] This test was originally applied by the European courts and the Commission to assess whether capital injections made to public undertakings by a Member State amounted to state aid, i.e. whether the measure conferred an economic advantage upon the provider which it would not have obtained under normal market conditions and thus qualified as state aid.[35] The argument runs on the following line: if a prudent private investor would have also made the investment in question, it could be safely assumed that an equivalent measure adopted by a Member State would not constitute unlawful state aid. In the subsequent case practice, the market investor test was applied in an adapted form to

---

[33] *Ibid.*, 11 *et seq.*

[34] E.g. in Report XXIII on Competition Policy (1993) the Commission dealing with privatisations of public assets used very similar language. It argued that 'sales on conditions that are not customary in comparable transactions between private parties' should be notified to the Commission for examination, para. 403.

[35] Case C-256/97, *DM Transport* [1999] ECR I-3913, para. 22; cf. Case C-342/96, *Spain* v. *Commission* [1999] ECR I-2459, para. 41; Joined Cases C-296/82 and C-318/82, *Netherlands and Leeuwarder Papierwarenfabriek* v. *Commission* [1985] ECR 809; Case C-323/82, *Intermills* v. *Commission* [1984] ECR 3809; Case C-234/84, *Belgium* v. *Commission* [1986] ECR 2263; European Commission, Position on the application of Articles 92 and 93 of the EC Treaty to public authorities' holdings in company capital, Bulletin of the European Communities 9/84, 104; European Commission, Communication to the Member States – Application of Articles 92 and 93 of the EEC Treaty and of Article 5 of Commission Directive 80/723/EEC to public undertakings in the manufacturing sector, OJ 1993 No. C307/3.

evaluate privatisations of public undertakings[36] and the sale of public land and buildings under the EC state aid rules.[37] In these cases it was asked whether a (hypothetical) prudent private seller would have been willing to accept the price for which the public asset was sold. If so, the measure would not be deemed to constitute aid.

According to the CFI in *BAI*, the same test also applies in the reverse procurement situation. The private investor test or – more aptly named – the market economy test is thus not confined to public funding, but rather a generally applicable tool for evaluating economically beneficial public measures.[38] Accordingly, a purchase made by a Member State does not constitute aid where a prudent private purchaser would have bought the relevant goods or services under the same conditions. If this question is answered negatively, for example, because a private purchaser would consider the relevant product to be too expensive, the procurement measure can be deemed to overcompensate the provider and be caught by the EC state aid rules.

In *BAI*, the CFI moreover provided an example for a situation in which there is no need to apply the market purchaser test. In the event that the procuring Member State has no actual need for the goods or services procured, it should indeed be safe to assume that a prudent private purchaser would not have considered the purchase; hence there is no sense in asking whether the purchase itself was made under market conditions.[39]

5.2.2. What would a private purchaser do?

The critics of horizontal criteria point at the market investor test in order to establish that the use of horizontal criteria in a procurement situation can involve state aid. Generally, a private investor cannot be assumed to pursue horizontal policies given that they are by definition of a non-economic nature. Prima facie it would thus seem that the award of a contract involving horizontal criteria would be unlikely to reflect the actual market value of the goods or services in question. On the basis of this proposition, it has been submitted that the application of horizontal criteria in a procurement context would automatically lead to

---

[36] European Commission, XXIII Report on Competition Policy 1993, 403.
[37] European Commission, Communication on state aid elements in sales of land and buildings by public authorities, OJ 1997 No. C209/3.
[38] R. D'sa, 'When is Aid not State Aid? The Implications of the English Partnerships Decision for European Competition Law and Policy' (2000) 25 *ELRev* 139.
[39] Case T–14/96, *BAI*, note 4 above, para. 79.

an increase of the purchase price for the goods or services procured.[40] A private purchaser would not be willing to pay such a surcharge resulting from the application of horizontal criteria. Thus, the award of the contract on the basis of a (non-economic) horizontal criterion is said to grant an economic advantage to the provider where a competing offer not fulfilling the relevant horizontal criteria was economically more advantageous.[41] The economic advantage would then be the difference between the price for the offer fulfilling the horizontal criteria and the excluded competing offer which did not comply with such criteria and which would therefore have been chosen by a private purchaser.[42] In effect, Member States applying horizontal policies would simply be paying individual undertakings to comply with its policies, thereby favouring them to the detriment of their non-compliant competitors.[43]

The consequences of this line of argument would be far-reaching. Community supervision of state aid is based on a system of *ex ante* authorisation. If procurement measures and the use of horizontal criteria were to fall under this system, the Member States wishing to award a contract would be obliged to notify the proposed measure to the Commission prior to its implementation. Article 88(3) EC Treaty prohibits the implementation of the measure until the Commission has authorised it (standstill obligation). Any aid that is granted in the absence of the Commission's approval is automatically categorised as unlawful aid. The Commission is under an obligation to order the recovery of the economic advantage.[44] Moreover, an infringement of the standstill obligation may result in the nullity of the grant under national law, which could not be remedied even if the Commission subsequently authorised the grant.[45] Thus, the obligation to notify and the standstill obligation would, if the use of horizontal criteria in procurement constituted state aid, de facto lead to a situation where horizontal criteria could not effectively be taken into account when awarding contracts even in those cases where the procuring entity has complied with all the requirements of procurement law.[46]

[40] Dreher/Haas/von Rintelen, note 25 above, 32 *et seq.*
[41] *Ibid.* 25; Dippel/Zeiss, *NZBau* (2002), 377.
[42] Dreher/Haas/von Rintelen, note 25 above, 26.   [43] Bartosch, *EuZW* (2001), 229, 231.
[44] Article 14 of Council Regulation (EC) No 659/1999 laying down detailed rules for the application of Article 93 of the EC Treaty, OJ 1999 No. L.83/1.
[45] This is, for example, the case in Germany: Bundesgerichtshof (Federal Supreme Court), Case XI ZR 53/03, *EuZW* (2004), 252.
[46] Doern, note 1 above.

5.2.3. Which private investor?

These consequences already indicate that it may not be appropriate to compare procurement measures using horizontal criteria with the conduct of a private purchaser that decides on purely economic grounds. Indeed, such an argument seems flawed: whilst it is true that a private investor or purchaser cannot generally be assumed to pursue horizontal policies, it is also not possible to assume that a private purchaser would never do so. As has been discussed in chapter 1, a private purchaser might well, for example, be willing to accept a higher price for environmentally friendly products. He may even refuse to buy from certain providers on purely moral grounds, as consumer boycotts have compellingly shown in the past. This kind of purchasing by private firms or individuals is becoming increasingly common with the development of the concept of Corporate Social Responsibility, as is discussed in chapter 11 of this book.

It is recognised under the EC state aid rules that a state measure must not be compared to the conduct of a private investor pursuing short-term aims. Rather, it is possible to compare the conduct of the Member State with the conduct of a long-term investor who is prepared to accept short-term losses in order to achieve his long-term objective, or who is even only seeking to protect his image.[47] Of course, this argument alone does not suffice to bring horizontal criteria outside the ambit of Article 87(1) EC Treaty because horizontal policies are generally of a macro-economic nature. A private investor or purchaser that pursues macro-economic objectives that do not bring about any individual long-term benefit to him cannot be a proper yardstick for the assessment of state aid.[48] The ECJ has made it clear that under the market economy test only such benefits can be taken into account which are directly enjoyed by the acting entity and not just the general public.[49] Nevertheless, this case law shows that there can be different types of private purchasers and that there is no obvious conclusion that only those private investors who do not pursue horizontal policies may be taken as a yardstick.

---

[47] Case C–303/88, *Commission* v. *Italy* [1991] ECR I–1433, para. 22; Joined cases T–129/95, T–2/96 and T–97/96, *Neue Maxhütte Stahlwerke GmbH and Lech–Stahlwerke GmbH* v. *Commission* [1999] ECR II–17, para. 109, 122 *et seq.*
[48] Doern, note 1 above.
[49] Case C–278/92, *Spain* v. *Commission* [1994] ECR I–4103, para. 22.

5.2.4. Which horizontal criteria?

It is important to note that Member States can promote 'horizontal', i.e. non-economic, objectives, and are often even obliged to do so. In this respect the Member States are, in principle, free to choose the tools by means of which they want to achieve those objectives and this also includes procurement measures. (As has been discussed in chapters 1 and 2, under other provisions of the EC Treaty and under the procurement directives, Member States have significant flexibility to pursue horizontal objectives through public procurement – although the directives and Treaty do also impose significant constraints.)[50] It follows that a procurement measure also does not necessarily constitute aid simply because a contract was awarded on the basis of horizontal criteria. A Member State is, of course, free to purchase, for example, environmentally friendly goods if it deems fit, just like a private investor or purchaser. The fact that such a procurement measure may be motivated by a horizontal policy is irrelevant for the assessment under state aid law.[51] Otherwise, public procuring entities would even have to refrain from making purchases that are motivated by horizontal policies: for example, it would not be possible for a public entity to purchase low fuel consumption vehicles in order to protect the environment, because this measure would automatically put the manufacturers of high fuel consumption vehicles at a competitive disadvantage.

This leads us to conclude that as long as a horizontal policy such as, for example, the protection of the environment is related to the subject matter of the awarded contract, it will not involve state aid within the meaning of Article 87(1) EC Treaty, provided that the goods are purchased at a market price.[52] It is irrelevant in this respect whether the market price for the product in question is higher than the price for its 'conventional' substitute (as it generally will be). Rather, the higher price paid by the procuring entity merely reflects the specific features of the procured product.[53] This will apply even if, contrary to what we argue below, it is the case that other horizontal criteria are otherwise to be treated somehow as a 'special case' in the context of the state aid rules.

---

[50] See generally chapters 1 and 2 of this book.
[51] Case C–56/93, *Belgium* v. *Commission* [1996] ECR I–723, para. 79; Doern, note 1 above, p. 110.
[52] Doern, note 1 above; Dreher/Haas/von Rintelen, note 25 above, 7 *et seq.*
[53] Eilmansberger, *WuW* (2004), 384, 389; Krohn, *Öffentliche Auftragsvergabe und Umweltschutz*, 171 *et seq.*

On the other hand, if, as we argue below, *all* horizontal policies are to be addressed by considering simply what price a private purchaser would have paid for the goods, works or services *together with the benefit of the horizontal policies* it will not be necessary to make a conceptual distinction between policies related to the subject matter and other policies – effectively the same test applies in both cases. We include this point regarding policies relating to the subject matter merely in case the ECJ does not accept our approach.

If the ECJ were to adopt a different approach, so that it is indeed relevant whether or not a horizontal measure relates to the subject matter, then it becomes necessary to consider how the line is to be drawn between measures that relate to the subject matter and those that do not. It was explained in chapter 1 (section 4), that a distinction of this kind, which is sometimes characterised as one between the government acting as purchaser and government acting as regulator, is made in various contexts in EC procurement law, and that the line is not necessarily to be drawn in the same place. We will not consider in further detail here how any such line might be drawn in the context of state aid, since we prefer an approach that does not require such a distinction. However, it is no doubt the case that at the very least measures concerned with the 'consumption' effects of the products, works and services supplied (as with the example of low fuel consumption vehicles) will be considered to relate to the subject matter, and that measures that are wholly unrelated to contract performance – such as criteria concerned with a supplier's general business practices – will not relate to the subject matter.

5.2.5. Which benchmark?

A horizontal criterion which is *not* performance-related, on the other hand, *per definitionem* reduces the number of potential bidders and could therefore selectively favour the undertaking that is awarded the contract.[54] Here, it would seem that the above-cited critics of horizontal criteria have a point in arguing that the use of horizontal policies involves state aid, if a private purchaser decides on purely economic grounds to buy a less expensive but equivalent product instead.

However, not only is this argument based on a flawed proposition, namely that a private purchaser cannot be assumed to consider horizontal policies, it is also circular: by taking a public procurement procedure without horizontal criteria as a benchmark to decide whether the use

---

[54] *Ibid.*, p. 172.

of horizontal policies involves state aid, the outcome is predetermined. According to that benchmark, a procurement measure using horizontal criteria would in effect only fall outside the ambit of the state aid rules, if compliance with the horizontal criteria were *not required*. Under such a test, a procurement measure based on horizontal criteria will always constitute aid where the successful offer is more expensive than competing offers not complying with the horizontal criteria.

It must be kept in mind that under the EC rules on state aid, only the selective grant of an economic advantage putting the recipient at a more advantageous position vis-à-vis other bidders qualifies as state aid under Article 87(1) EC Treaty. However, this will only be the case if the recipient is *overcompensated* for the delivery of the goods or services – that is, where the equilibrium between the price paid and the good delivered is spoiled. As long as the increase in price caused by the application of horizontal criteria corresponds with higher operating expenses incurred by the provider who is awarded the contract, no such overcompensation exists: then, the margin of the provider remains unaffected by the use of the horizontal criteria.[55] Consequently, the award of the contract will not confer a competitive advantage upon the provider that could be said to lead to a distortion of competition.

It follows from all this that the relevant question is *not* whether a private purchaser who does not pursue horizontal policies but who only takes into account economic criteria would also have purchased the goods or services at the same price. The relevant question, rather, is whether a private undertaking *pursuing* a horizontal policy would have paid the same price for the relevant goods or services.[56]

This line of argument is supported by a recent judgment of the ECJ: in the *Altmark* case, the ECJ confirmed that a relevant economic advantage could only occur if the recipient was overcompensated. With regard to public subsidies intended to enable the operation of regional scheduled road transport services, a service in the general economic interest within the meaning of Article 86 (2) EC Treaty, the ECJ held that such

---

[55] Eilmansberger, 'Überlegungen zum Zusammenspiel von Vergaberecht und Beihilferecht', *WuW* (2004), 384, 387; Pünder, 'Die Vergabe öffentlicher Aufträge unter den Vorgaben des europäischen Beihilferechts', *NZBau* (2003), 530, 532.

[56] S. Arrowsmith, *The Law of Public and Utilities Procurement*, 2nd edn (London: Sweet & Maxwell, 2005), at 19.38; Eilmansberger, note 55 above, 384, 388; *Pünder*, note 55 above, 532; Krohn, note 53 above, 175; Jennert, 'Vergabefremde Kriterien – keine Beihilfen, sondern gemeinwirtschaftliche Pflichten', *NZBau* (2003), 417, 418; H. Priess, *Handbuch des europäischen Vergaberechts*, 3rd edn (Köln/Berlin/München, 2005), p. 29.

subsidies would not be caught by Article 87(1) EC Treaty where 'the compensation does not exceed what is necessary to cover all or part of the costs incurred in discharging the public service obligations, taking into account the relevant receipts and a reasonable profit for discharging those obligations'.[57]

This statement indicates that the mere fact that a Member State faces a higher price for goods or services in order to promote horizontal policies would not suffice to bring the measure within the ambit of Article 87(1) EC Treaty.[58] If the procuring entity receives 'value for money', the use of horizontal policies will not involve state aid.

5.2.6. Which procedure?

The critics of the use of horizontal criteria, however, point out that it is a generally accepted rule that a 'sufficiently well-publicised, open and unconditional bidding procedure' rules out a finding of state aid. Following on from this, the critics argue that by using horizontal policies the procuring entity would deviate from the procedural rules laid out in the law by rendering the tender 'conditional'. It has been submitted that using horizontal criteria in a procurement context entails a deviation from this rule. In view of this it could be argued that a contract which is awarded on the basis of horizontal criteria could confer an economic advantage upon the provider.[59]

However, this line of argument is also flawed as it disregards the case practice of the European Commission on this subject. The requirement to hold a tender procedure has been developed by the Commission to create a clear set of rules that would allow the procuring entities to assess when a notification would become necessary under the EC state aid rules. In its Communication on the sale of public land and buildings,[60] the Commission held that such a sale 'following a sufficiently well-publicised, open and unconditional bidding procedure, comparable to an auction, accepting the best or only bid is by definition at market value and consequently does not contain state aid'.[61] Later, the Commission applied

---

[57] Case C–280/00, *Altmark Trans and Regierungspräsidium Magdeburg* v. *Nahverkehrsgesellschaft Altmark GmbH* ('*Altmark*') [2003] ECR I–7747, para. 95.
[58] Arrowsmith, note 56 above; Eilmansberger, note 55 above, 384, 388 *et seq.*; Pünder, note 55 above, 530, 532; Krohn, note 53 above, 173 *et seq.*
[59] Dreher/Haas/von Rintelen, note 25 above, 34.
[60] European Commission, Communication on state aid elements in sales of land and buildings by public authorities, OJ 1997 No. C209/3.
[61] *Ibid.*, para. II.1.

similar criteria with regard to privatisation of public companies.[62] Today, the principles set out in the notice can be considered to apply to all measures potentially involving state aid *mutatis mutandis*. In the view of the Commission, 'an offer is "unconditional" when any buyer, irrespective of whether or not he runs a business or of the nature of his business, is generally free to acquire the land and buildings and to use it for his own purposes'. Arguably, it could be doubted whether a public procurement measure could still be considered to be 'unconditional' if it was based on horizontal criteria. In the case of *Gröditzer Stahlwerke*[63] for example, the Commission argued that the bidding procedure had not been 'unconditional' and thus involved state aid because the parties were asked to submit detailed commitments regarding jobs to be created or saved and future investment and financing.

However, it is not possible to conclude from this that the use of horizontal criteria automatically renders a procurement measure 'conditional' thereby bringing it within the ambit of Article 87(1) EC Treaty. Despite the statement in *Gröditzer Stahlwerke*, the Commission has also made it clear that it would accept restrictions that are imposed for 'the prevention of public nuisance, for reasons of environmental protection or to avoid purely speculative bids'.[64] In its Communication on the sale of public land and buildings,[65] the Commission stated that if the future owner of the acquired land or building was to assume special obligations, the offer could still be regarded as 'unconditional … only if all potential buyers would have to, and be able to, meet that obligation, irrespective of whether or not they run a business or of the nature of their business'.[66] In addition, the Commission pointed out that there was no obligation to carry out a bidding procedure. A sale made on the basis of an independent expert evaluation would also not involve state aid. The Commission clarified that even the application of 'special obligations' would not alter

---

[62] European Commission, XXIII Report on competition policy 1993, para. 403. However, there is no obligation upon the Member States to organise formal invitations to tenders or to apply the rules governing open invitations to tender with regard to the sale of public assets: cf. European Commission, Decision of 11 April 2000 on the aid granted by Italy to Centrale del Latte di Roma, OJ 2000 No. L265/1, para. 88.

[63] European Commission, Decision of 8 July 1999 on State aid granted by Germany to Gröditzer Stahlwerke GmbH and its subsidiary Walzwerk Burg GmbH, OJ 1999 No. L292/27, para. 87.

[64] European Commission, Communication on state aid elements in sales of land and buildings by public authorities, note 60 above, para. II.1 lit. b.

[65] *Ibid.*   [66] *Ibid.*, para. II.1 lit. c.

this finding if such obligations related to the land and buildings at issue, and not to the purchaser or his economic activities.[67]

It can be concluded from this practice that by requiring a bidding procedure to be 'unconditional', the Commission simply wants to ensure that the measure was not applied in a *discriminatory* manner – that is, that it is not targeted at specific investors. Obviously, the Commission is of the opinion that the terms 'unconditional' and 'non-discriminatory' are interchangeable.[68] The application of non-discriminatory horizontal policies does not therefore render an offer conditional thereby triggering the notification requirement under Article 88 EC Treaty.

The subsequent practice of the Commission confirms this reading of its guidelines: in the *Centrale del Latte di Roma* case,[69] the Commission had originally raised concerns under the state aid rules, because the privatisation in question had been subject to certain conditions, namely the maintenance of certain numbers of jobs and continuing purchase of supplies of raw materials from local producers, which might have resulted in a higher price than would have been the case if those conditions had not been applied.[70] However, the Commission then went on to say that

> as regards the conditions governing the sale, the Commission notes, first, that the sale of public assets on special conditions is acceptable under Community law where those conditions do not discriminate among the potential buyers. In the sale in question, none of the conditions (safeguard-ing of jobs, implementation of a business plan, obligation to buy at least 80% of raw materials from local producers, and obligation not to transfer the place of production for five years) discriminates among the potential buyers.[71]

In the *London Underground* case, the Commission did not even men-tion the term 'unconditional'. It stated that if infrastructure arrange-ments are concluded 'after the observance of an open, transparent and non-discriminatory procedure, it is, in principle, [the case] that the level of any public sector support can be regarded as representing the market price for the execution of a project' and would consequently not involve

---

[67] *Ibid.*, para. II.2 lit. c.   [68] Koenig/Kühling, note 27 above, 779, 782.
[69] European Commission, Decision of 11 April 2000 on the aid granted by Italy to Centrale del Latte di Roma, OJ 2000 No. L265/1.
[70] *Ibid.*, para. 82.   [71] *Ibid.*, para. 91.

state aid.[72] With regard to horizontal criteria, it would follow from this that there are no objections under EC state aid rules as long as the application of such criteria does not result in discriminatory treatment of bidders.

The case law of the ECJ with respect to the use of horizontal criteria in procurement proceedings points in the same direction: in *Concordia Bus Finland*,[73] the ECJ clarified that there was nothing in the law that could be interpreted 'as meaning that each of the award criteria used by the contracting authority to identify the economically most advantageous tender must necessarily be of a purely economic nature'.[74] As has been discussed in chapter 4 (section 13 of that chapter), in effect, the ECJ thereby permitted the use of horizontal criteria, such as environmental protection, on the following three conditions. First, the award criteria must be 'linked to the subject-matter of the contract'.[75] Second, the relevant criteria must be expressly mentioned in the contract documents or tender notice and, finally, it must comply with 'all the fundamental principles of Community law, in particular the principle of non-discrimination'.[76] In *EVN-Wienstrom*,[77] also discussed in chapter 4, the ECJ confirmed this ruling and held that

> it follows that the Community legislation on public procurement does not preclude a contracting authority from applying, in the context of the assessment of the most economically advantageous tender for a contract for the supply of electricity, a criterion requiring that the electricity supply be produced from renewable energy sources, provided that the criterion is linked to the subject-matter of the contract, does not confer an unrestricted freedom of choice on the authority, is expressly mentioned in the contract documents or contract notice, and complies with all the fundamental principles of Community law, in particular the principle of non-discrimination.[78]

It is interesting to note that, in both cases, the ECJ apparently did not see any need to reflect on the question whether the use of horizontal criteria constituted state aid within the meaning of Article 87(1) EC Treaty.

---

[72] European Commission, Decision No. N 264/2002, London Underground Public Private Partnership, OJ 2002 No. C 309/14, para. 79.

[73] Case C-513/99, *Concordia Bus Finland* v. *Helsingin Kaupunki* ('*Concordia Bus Finland*') [2002] ECR I-7213.

[74] *Ibid.*, para. 55.   [75] *Ibid.*, para. 59.   [76] *Ibid.*, para. 62 *et seq.*

[77] Case C-448/01, *EVN AG* v. *Austria* ('*EVN-Wienstrom*') [2003] ECR I-14527.

[78] *Ibid.*, para. 34.

6. Conclusions

Looking at the case law and previous practice, it becomes apparent that the underlying principles of the EC public procurement and state aid rules are identical.[79] It is the objective of the public procurement rules as well as of EC state aid law to prevent distortions of competition. Consequently, as long as the award of a contract on the basis of horizontal criteria is the result of free competition, the measure would not involve state aid unless the criteria are applied in a discriminatory manner.[80] Only in this situation would the award of the contract on the basis of horizontal criteria not be the result of undistorted competition. It is not then possible to assume that the transaction has been concluded under 'normal market conditions'. Hence, the procurement measure could only be implemented following a notification to the Commission which, in effect, means that the measure in its originally envisaged form cannot be carried out at all.

If, on the other hand, a procurement measure has been preceded by a 'sufficiently advertised open tender procedure', it can be deemed to be a 'normal commercial transaction' and, consequently, not to involve state aid[81] – provided, of course, that the contract has been awarded to the economically most advantageous offer.[82]

However, while an open tender thus provides a 'safe harbour' with regard to the EC state aid rules, this does not mean that the award of a contract without an open tender would necessarily involve state aid. A bidding procedure is only one of a number of tools for determining whether or not a contract was awarded under market conditions. The Commission made this clear for example in its Communication on state aid elements in the sales of land and buildings, where it accepted that the market value could also be established on the basis of an independent expert evaluation using generally accepted market indicators and valuation standards.[83] Hence, there can be no presumption that a measure will

---

[79] Koenig/Kühling, note 27 above, 779, 780.

[80] Arrowsmith, note 56 above, at 19.39; Eilmansberger, note 55 above, 384, 389; Jennert, note 56 above, 417, 419.

[81] Joined Cases T–116/01 and T–118/01, *P&O*, note 15 above, para. 118; Eilmansberger, note 55 above, 384, 386; M. Stemkowski and M. Dischendorfer, 'The Interplay between the EC Rules on Public Procurement and State Aid' (2002) 11 *PPLR* 47; Lübbig, *EuZW* (1999), 672.

[82] Case C–280/00, *Altmark*, note 57 above, para. 93.

[83] European Commission, Communication on state aid elements in sales of land and buildings by public authorities, OJ 1997 No. C209/3II.2 lit. a.

involve state aid only because a contract has been awarded following a restricted or even a negotiated procedure.

As previously mentioned, it is only overcompensation that would render a measure unlawful. However, as long as the award of the contract is the result of a genuinely competitive process, the purchase price can be deemed to be the market price and would thus not involve state aid. Arguably, as long as the Community directives on public procurement are complied with, there can be no finding of state aid.[84] While a restricted procedure by definition excludes a number of potential bidders by reference to their general characteristics, it nevertheless ensures effective competition, as it requires the invitation of sufficient offers that can then be compared with each other. Thus, like an open tender, a restricted procedure can also be sufficiently open, transparent and non-discriminatory to prevent a finding of overcompensation.[85] The negotiated procedure, on the other hand, is less likely to provide a 'safe harbour' as a comparison between various offers will only be possible if there has been a call for competition beforehand.[86] Finally, it must be noted that there is no presumption that a measure involves state aid, even if it has not been awarded in an open, transparent and non-discriminatory procedure. The only, albeit significant, consequence is that the measure is taken outside the procedural 'safe harbour'. This applies even where the procurement measure was based on horizontal criteria.[87] It has been submitted that such a deviation from the accepted rule should lead to a reversal of the burden of proof, which would be shifted to the procuring entity.[88] A reversal of the burden of proof would widen the scope of the EC state aid rules. As a result the standstill obligation set out in Article 88(3) EC Treaty would apply even to a measure in relation to which there is merely uncertainty as to whether or not it involves state aid. Hence, an implementation without the authorisation by the Commission would automatically render the pro-curement measure illegal regardless of whether or not the authorisation were later granted. In effect, a measure involving horizontal criteria could for practical reasons never be implemented, even if the measure were perfectly legal under the EC procurement rules and did not overcom-pensate the provider.[89] This result would be inappropriate.[90] However,

---

[84] Arrowsmith, note 56 above, at 4.41.   [85] *Ibid.*
[86] *Ibid.*   [87] Arrowsmith, note 56 above, at 4.43.
[88] Dreher/Haas/von Rintelen, note 25 above, 34 *et seq.*   [89] Doern, note 1 above, at 116.
[90] Arrowsmith, note 56 above, at 4.43; Pünder, note 55 above, 530, 534.

while there is no reversal of the burden of proof, procuring entities must nevertheless be aware that they carry the factual risk whether their own legal assessment of the measure is accurate. As a practical consequence, procuring entities are advised to err on the side of caution and to avoid a negotiated procedure where horizontal criteria are involved.

6

EC public procurement law and equality linkages: foundations for interpretation

CHRISTOPHER McCRUDDEN

1. Introduction

The particular issue that is the focus of this chapter is how governments use their purchasing power to advance conceptions of social justice, particularly equality and non-discrimination. The term 'linkage' is used throughout this chapter to describe this use of procurement.[1] This chapter attempts to set out the foundations for a new interpretation of the EC procurement directives,[2] as they apply to the contested ground of what I call 'procurement linkages'. This chapter is extracted from a more detailed exposition of the legal issues involved, not only in the EC context but also more broadly.[3]

My argument in this chapter is that three aspects of Community law relating to procurement need to be borne in mind when interpreting the procurement directives in the context of procurement linkages: the overall limits of the procurement directives deriving from the Treaty, the

---

[1] 'Linkage' is used in preference to the concept of 'conditionality', with which it shares certain similarities, because the diversity of ways in which procurement and social justice have been brought together goes beyond simply awarding contracts on certain conditions, and extends to include, for example, the definition of the contract, the qualifications of contractors, and the criteria for the award of the contract. 'Linkage' is also used in preference to 'secondary criteria' because we shall see subsequently that social justice issues can be part of the subject matter of the contract. This issue of terminology is also discussed in chapter 1 of the present book, section 2, where the editors also reject the use of the term 'secondary', preferring instead to refer to 'horizontal policies'.

[2] The current directives are Directive 2004/18/EC of the European Parliament and of the Council on the coordination of procedures for the award of public works contracts, public supply contracts and public service contracts ('Public Sector Directive') OJ 2004 No. L134/114 and Directive 2004/17/EC of the European Parliament and of the Council coordinating the procurement procedures of entities operating in the water, energy, transport and postal services sectors ('Utilities Directive') OJ 2004 No. L134/1.

[3] C. McCrudden, *Buying Social Justice: Equality, Government Procurement and Legal Change* (Oxford University Press, 2007).

importance of 'equal treatment' as the basis of both EC states' equality law and procurement law, and the importance of viewing the procurement directives as engaging with a policy instrument that is based on freedom of contract, raising the importance of what is meant by the 'subject matter of the contract'.

2. Some preliminary points

Several important developments have occurred that challenged an approach to the interpretation of EC procurement law that sees linkages as simply constraints on a Community policy of open markets adopted at the behest of purely national interests. Too often, in the past, the relationship between domestic procurement linkages and EC law has been viewed as a battle between Community policy (in the shape of procurement reform) versus domestic policy (in the shape of status equality). The Community has now developed its social dimension to a greater degree. In some areas, notably in the area of status equality, the Community has adopted significant legislation. Social policy has come to play a central role in building Europe's economic strength, through the development of what came to be identified by Community institutions as a unique social model. Economic progress and social cohesion came to be regarded as complementary pillars of sustainable development and both are at the heart of the process of European integration. There has been an increasing emphasis in the Community on social and equality rights, particularly in the workplace. As sustainable development has moved beyond environmental issues into social issues, status equality has been increasingly identified as an element, as it has been too in the growing movement for corporate social responsibility. Increasingly, at the Community level, and also at the national level in several states, status equality has become 'mainstreamed', meaning that the need to further status equality has come to be seen (at least at the rhetorical level) as something to be integrated into a wide range of policies and institutional practices. The importance of these developments is that the tensions between the social and economic perspectives of procurement can no longer be translated as simply equating to Member State versus EC level policy clashes; the social dimension is now increasingly dominated in certain areas by EC level policy.

However much the social dimension of the Community waxes and wanes politically, *legally* there is now no reason to see the resolution of conflicts between EC social and economic policies as inevitably leading to the economic dominating the social. There is no priority given, for example, to the provisions enabling procurement legislation to be enacted over the provisions enabling status equality legislation to be enacted. Instead, three fundamental aspects of Community law relating to procurement need to be borne in mind when interpreting the procurement directives in the context of procurement linkages: the overall limits of the procurement directives deriving from the Treaty, the importance of equal treatment as the basis of both EC states' equality law and procurement law, and the importance of viewing the procurement directives as engaging with a policy instrument (public procurement) that is based on freedom of contract, raising the importance of what is meant by the 'subject matter of the contract'. The next three sections consider each of these issues.

From the point of view of interpreting EC procurement law, each of these developments is important. Taken together, they require a revised approach to the interpretation of EC procurement law as far as the use of procurement linkages is concerned. What is needed, in light of these developments, is an interpretation of the procurement directives that is true to the text of the directives, reflects the evolving ECJ case law, but crucially does not incorporate into the interpretation process other assumptions that are currently legally unsustainable. What is necessary is an interpretation of the procurement directives in particular that views EC law as one harmonious whole, giving appropriate weight to all of EC law, without assuming any particular priority or hierarchy. Is this possible? My argument is that it is not only possible, but is the only appropriate way of interpreting the directives. To interpret the directives otherwise is, quite simply, legally incorrect. This approach is one that is entirely consistent with the approach adopted by the ECJ. We are consistently urged by the ECJ to regard EC law as a body of law that should be interpreted as a harmonious whole. It is clear that the time has long passed when particular areas of EC law, such as procurement law, should be regarded as hermetically sealed from other areas of EC law or indeed from international law more generally. In presenting this revised approach, I am conscious that I am, of course, building on the work of others.[4]

---

[4] There has been a stream of academic analysis that has interpreted the directives and the ECJ case law to permit social linkages. See generally S. Arrowsmith, *The Law of Public and Utilities Procurement*, 2nd edn (London: Sweet & Maxwell, 2005); C. Tobler, 'Encore: "Women's Clauses" in Public Procurement under Community Law' (2000) 25 *ELRev* 618; C. Hanley, 'Avoiding the Issue: The Commission and Human Rights Conditionality in Public Procurement' (2002) 27 *ELRev* 714; K. Krüger, R. Nielsen and N. Bruun, *European Public Contracts in a Labour Law Perspective* (Copenhagen: DJØF Publishing, 1998). An

This chapter is primarily concerned with the relationship between procurement and status equality, especially when procurement is used to put into effect the principles that underpin the EC status equality directives. However, first, it is nonetheless instructive that the directives continue to exclude some services, 'which are especially sensitive from a cultural and social point of view',[5] allowing contracting authorities to choose the award procedure they wish to apply.[6] Second, procurement in the broadcasting context is excluded on the grounds that 'for these kinds of contracts, it must be possible to take into account aspects of cultural or social significance'.[7] Those legislating the directives were, therefore, clearly willing and able to balance social and economic considerations in deciding on coverage. It is clearly recognised that procurement decisions are affected by social considerations and the directives have accommodated that political reality. The question is: to what extent?[8]

3. Equal treatment as the basis of EU status equality law and procurement law

The principle that links and underpins each of these two sets of legal obligations (the relationship between the law of the EC governing public procurement – in particular, the new procurement directives – and the law regarding status equality) is the principle of 'equal treatment'. The ECJ has developed a jurisprudence that subjects the exercise of Community competence to the requirement that it complies with 'general principles'

extensive bibliography of academic writing on procurement linkages is included in the helpful overview by S. Whitton, 'On the Pursuit of Non-economical Policies in the EU Law of Public Contracts, with Special Focus on Case-law and Forthcoming Directive 2004/18/EC', University of Warwick, unpublished paper, 22 February 2005.

[5] J. Arnould, 'Secondary Policies in Public Procurement: The Innovations of the New Directives' (2004) 13 *PPLR* 187, 192.

[6] Annex IIB of the Public Sector Directive; Annex XVIIB of the Utilities Directive.

[7] Arnould, note 5 above, p. 192.

[8] In addition to the literature cited above, the following have also discussed related issues: N. Bruun and B. Bercusson, 'Labour Law Aspects of Public Procurement in the EU', in R. Nielsen and S. Treumer (eds.), *The New EU Public Procurement Directives* (Copenhagen: DJØF Publishing, 2005), chapter 7; P. Kunzlik, 'Green Procurement under the New Regime', *ibid.*, chapter 8; S. Hjelmborg, P. Jakobsen and S. Poulsen, *Public Procurement Law – the EU Directive on Public Contracts* (Copenhagen: DJØF Publishing, 2006), pp. 204–226; C. Bovis, *Public Procurement in the European Union* (Basingstoke: Palgrave Macmillan, 2005), pp. 95–117.

of EC law.[9] This has implications for equality and discrimination in several principal ways. Despite the existence of numerous provisions of the Treaty 'that provide for the principle of equal treatment with regard to specific matters',[10] the ECJ has held that the principle of equality is one of the general principles of EC law. Within the sphere of EC law, this principle of equality precludes comparable situations from being treated differently, and different situations from being treated in the same way,[11] unless the treatment is objectively justified.[12] The ECJ has recognised, for example, that the principle that everyone is equal before the law is a basic principle of EC law.[13] Why did the Court find it necessary to hold that equality is a general principle of EC law? Tridimas observes: 'It may be that those [specific] provisions do not guarantee equal treatment in all cases so that the development of a general principle is necessary to cover the lacunae left in written law.'[14]

In the public procurement context, the obvious starting point for understanding the meaning and implications of the 'equal treatment' dimension of the procurement directives is to be found in those aspects of the Treaty that protect the 'four freedoms'. There are several EC Treaty provisions in which the principles of non-discrimination or equality are expressly mentioned. These are regarded as specific enunciations of the general principle of equal treatment.[15] The principal examples are Article 12 EC (formerly 6) (discrimination on the grounds of being a national of one of the Member States is prohibited), Article 18 EC (formerly 8a) (every citizen of the Union has the right to move and reside

---

[9] See, in general, T. Tridimas, *The General Principles of EC Law* (Oxford University Press, 1999), chapter 2. See also 'Equality' in A. G. Toth, *The Oxford Encyclopaedia of European Community Law*, Vol. I (Oxford: Clarendon Press, 1990), pp. 188–201.

[10] Tridimas, note 9 above, p. 40.

[11] Case 106/83, *Sermide SpA v. Cassa Conguaglio Zucchero* [1984] ECR 4209, para. 28. See also Opinion of AG Van Gerven delivered on 15 September 1993 in Case C–146/9, *Koinopraxia Enoseon Georgikon Synetairismon Diacheiriseos Enchorion Proionton Syn. PE (KYDEP) v. Commission* [1994] ECR I–4199.

[12] See Case C–189/01, *Jippes v. Minister van Landbouw, Natuurbeheer en Visserij* [2001] ECR I–689, para. 129 and Case C–149/96, *Portugal v. Council* [1999] ECR I–8395, para. 91.

[13] Case 283/83, *Racke v. Hauptzollamt Mainz* [1984] ECR 3791; Case 15/95, *EARL de Kerlast v. Union régionale de coopératives agricoles* [1997] ECR I–1961; Case 292/97, *Karlson* [2000] ECR I–2737.

[14] Tridimas, note 9 above, p. 41.

[15] Case 1/72, *Frilli v. Belgium* [1972] ECR 457, para. 19; Joined Cases 103 and 145/77, *Royal Scholten-Honig (Holdings) Ltd v. Intervention Board for Agricultural Produce* [1978] ECR 2037, para. 26.

freely within the territory of the Member States, subject to certain limitations), Article 34(2) EC (formerly 40(3)) EC (non-discrimination between producers and consumers in the context of the Common Agricultural Policy), Article 39 EC (formerly 48) (non-discrimination as between workers who are nationals of the host state and those who are nationals of another Member State), Article 43 EC (formerly 52) (equal treatment as between nationals and non-nationals who are established in a self-employed capacity in a Member State), Article 49 EC (formerly 59) (equal treatment for providers of services) and Article 90 EC (formerly 95) (non-discrimination in the field of taxation as between domestic and imported goods).[16] 'Probably the most obvious and central manifestation of the non-discrimination principle in EC law has been in the context of prohibiting discrimination on grounds of nationality or origin.'[17] A considerable body of secondary legislation has further supplemented these provisions.[18] One way of viewing the procurement directives is that they are instances of equal treatment in this sense.

   If we are to take the approach of the ECJ seriously, however, that is too limited an interpretation. For the Court, equal treatment precludes comparable situations from being treated differently, and different situations from being treated in the same way,[19] unless the treatment is objectively justified.[20] This is a general principle, not limited simply to securing non-discrimination on grounds of nationality. The case in which the ECJ first articulated the idea that the principle of equal treatment 'lies at the very heart of the [procurement] directive'[21] illustrates the point. In the Storebaelt case,[22] the Court held that 'observance of the principle of equal treatment of tenderers requires that all the tenders comply with the tender conditions so as to ensure an objective comparison of the

---

[16] Article 18 EC.
[17] G. de Búrca, 'The Role of Equality in European Community Law', in A. Dashwood and S. O'Leary, The Principle of Equal Treatment in EC Law (London: Sweet & Maxwell, 1997), p. 20.
[18] For example Council Regulation (EEC) 1612/68 on the free movement of workers within the Community, OJ 1968 No. L257/2.
[19] Case 106/83, Sermide SpA v. Cassa Conguaglio Zucchero [1984] ECR 4209, para. 28. See also Opinion of AG Van Gerven delivered on 15 September 1993, Case C–146/91, Koinopraxia Enoseon Georgikon Synetairismon Diacheiriseos Enchorion Proionton Syn. PE (KYDEP) v. Commission [1994] ECR I–4199.
[20] See for example Case C–189/01, Jippes v. Minister van Landbouw, Natuurbeheer en Visserij [2001] ECR I–5689, para. 129 and Case C–149/96, Portugal v. Council [1999] ECR I–8395, para. 91.
[21] Case C–242/89, Commission v. Denmark ('Storebaelt') [1993] ECR I–3353.
[22] Ibid., para. 39.

tenders submitted by the various tenderers'.[23] It therefore considered that the principle of equal treatment precluded *Storebaelt* from taking into consideration a tender where the tender did not comply with the fundamental conditions stipulated by the authority in the tender documents.[24] This aspect of the case had nothing to do with non-discrimination on the basis of nationality. An interpretation of equal treatment that regards it as simply another way of expressing a prohibition of discrimination on grounds of nationality therefore misunderstands the complexity of the concept, as used by the Court. The question that the Court requires to be addressed is the broader one that concentrates on preventing comparable situations from being treated differently, and different situations from being treated in the same way. The issue then becomes one of determining when the situations are 'comparable'. In the *Storebaelt* case, the Court emphasised the importance of 'the development of effective competition in the field of public contracts'[25] and this has led Arrowsmith to suggest that tenderers are 'comparable' when the entities are in a 'comparable competitive position'.[26]

3.1. Conceptions of equality and non-discrimination

Equality and non-discrimination are complex concepts, with considerable debate about their meanings and justification. In order to better understand the variety of different ways in which legal measures advancing equal treatment currently operate, four categories[27] of, or approaches to, equality and non-discrimination may usefully be identified. Several caveats are necessary regarding these distinctions. First, the categories are constructed to try to make sense of a sometimes bewildering range of legal material; these categories have received no judicial approval. Second, these categories are not watertight, but porous, with developments in one category influencing approaches in others. Third, these categories attempt to describe the current approaches to equality and non-discrimination, rather than to provide a normative analysis of these approaches.

3.1.1. Equality and equality as 'rationality'

The first approach is where the principle of non-discrimination (interpreted as the limited principle that likes should be treated alike, unless

---

[23] *Ibid.*, para. 37.   [24] *Ibid.*, para. 43.   [25] *Ibid.*, para. 33.

[26] Arrowsmith, note 4 above, at 7.7 and also chapter 4 of the present book, section 6.

[27] We will use the terms 'category', 'approach' and 'meaning' interchangeably in this chapter. No significance should be attached to this.

there is an adequate justification for not applying this principle) is a self-standing principle of general application, without specific limitation on the circumstances in which it is applicable, and without limitation on the grounds on which the difference of treatment is challengeable. In many jurisdictions, this approach to equality is particularly associated with constitutional guarantees.[28] This approach is essentially rationality-based. Under this approach, then, discrimination is merely an example of irrationality, with no greater moral or legal significance than if the government decided to allocate houses only to those with red hair. This approach is often apparent in the interpretation of constitutional provisions guaranteeing non-discrimination in general terms.

However, non-discrimination is often tied to some more specific context. There are, essentially, two methods of limiting the prohibition of discrimination, and they operate both separately and together. One method is where the prohibition of discrimination is limited to particular subject areas, such as employment, or to certain rights, such as freedom of speech. A second approach is where the right to non-discrimination is limited to certain grounds or statuses, such as sex, race, religion, disability, etc. These two different approaches give rise to important differences in methods, aims and justifications for legal intervention, giving rise to two further approaches of non-discrimination, additional to 'equality as rationality'.

3.1.2. Equality and equality as protective of other 'prized public goods'

In the second approach, the non-discrimination principle becomes an adjunct to the protection of particularly prized 'public goods', including human and other rights. The principle is essentially that such 'prized public goods' should in principle be distributed to everyone without distinction. In the distribution of the 'public good', equals should be treated on a non-discriminatory basis, except where differences can be justified. In this context, the focus is on the distribution of the public good, rather than the characteristics of the recipient. The courts will scrutinise public authorities' (less frequently, private bodies')[29] actions in a more intense way than under the first approach, when the actions of the public authority give rise

---

[28] See in general the Council of Europe's Constitutional Law Bulletin, which is a good source of case law on the constitutional principle of equality.

[29] The extent to which norms applying to states give rise to state responsibility where third parties within the state act contrary to the norm is left to one side.

to discrimination (defined essentially as treating someone differently) in these circumstances. Under this approach, discrimination is objectionable because it is an unacceptable way of limiting access to the 'prized public good'.

3.1.3. Equality as preventing 'status-harms' arising from discrimination on particular grounds

In the third approach to non-discrimination, the focus of attention turns instead to the association between a limited number of particular characteristics (such as race, gender, etc.) and the discrimination suffered by those who have, or who are perceived to have, those characteristics, irrespective of whether the decision might be justified as rational. The courts will scrutinise public authorities' (and others') actions in a more intense way than under the first approach where the public authorities' actions discriminate against individuals with those particular characteristics. In this context, however, the meaning of discrimination expands beyond the principle that likes should be treated alike to embrace also the principle that unlikes should not be treated alike. This approach is essentially aimed at preventing status-harms arising from discrimination on particular grounds.

The third approach also differs from the second in being less concerned with the importance of the good being allocated and more concerned with the use of actual or imputed identity in a wide range of situations. In the second approach, the harm to be prevented lies in the arbitrary allocation of something that in principle all should have. In the third approach, the harm lies in the use made of particular statuses to affect the allocation of a wide range of opportunities, which may or may not reach the importance of rights, but where the use of those characteristics is unacceptable in such decisions. In this third approach to non-discrimination, the focus of attention shifts from the importance of the 'public good' (particularly the human right in issue) and turns instead to the association between a limited number of particular characteristics (such as race, gender, etc.) and the discrimination suffered by those who have, or are perceived to have, those characteristics, where the public authorities' actions discriminate against individuals with those particular characteristics.

In several ways, the third category of discrimination and equality is more complex than the first and second categories discussed previously, and this greater complexity has resulted in the emergence of legal issues that are so far relatively underdeveloped in the context of discussions about the other categories. Unlike under the second approach, it does not apply as a penumbra of all major areas of rights (indeed many fundamental rights are not included within the coverage of anti-discrimination law). In another respect, of course, the approach taken under this third approach is considerably broader in scope, covering both public and private sector actors operating in those areas covered, whereas to a considerable extent the first and second approaches apply largely to the public sector.

3.1.4. Equality as proactive promotion of equality of opportunity between particular groups

In the fourth approach, certain public authorities (less frequently private bodies) are placed under a duty actively to take steps to promote greater equality of opportunity (the legal meaning of which is yet to be fully articulated) for particular groups. The concept of equal treatment here goes beyond any of the concepts of discrimination characteristic of the previous approaches and involves not only a duty on the public authority to eliminate discrimination from its activities, which is seen as merely one example of where equality of opportunity is denied, but actively to take steps to promote greater equality of opportunity through its activities. Under this approach, a public authority to which this duty applies is under a duty to do more than ensure the absence of discrimination from its employment, educational, and other specified functions, but also to act positively to promote equality of opportunity between different groups throughout all policy making and in carrying out all those activities to which the duty applies.

3.2. Equal treatment in Community law

These various distinctions help us to understand what is going on in Community law. There are two important dimensions to the meaning of equal treatment in Community law as propounded by the ECJ. In one dimension, the non-discrimination principle is a general principle of rationality, or becomes an adjunct to the protection of particularly prized 'public goods' (the first two dimensions of equality discussed in the previous paragraphs). The principle is essentially that such 'prized public goods' should in principle be distributed to everyone without arbitrary distinction. In the distribution of the 'public good', equals should be treated on an equal basis, except where differences can be justified. In this context, the focus is on the distribution of the public good, rather than the characteristics of the recipient. Under this approach, not according equal treatment is objectionable because it is an unacceptable way of limiting access to the 'prized public good'. This is generally the view that characterises the approach to the meaning of equal treatment in the context of the 'four freedoms' in EC law. It is also the way in which the concept of equal treatment has thus far been used in the context of procurement. The 'prized public good' in the case of procurement is access to a competitive procurement market across Europe.

In a second dimension of EC law, however, the focus of attention of the meaning of 'equal treatment' turns instead to the association between a limited number of particular characteristics (such as race, gender, etc.) and the consequences suffered by those who have, or who are perceived to have, those characteristics. This approach is essentially aimed at preventing status-harms arising from discrimination on particular grounds (the third of the approaches discussed previously).

It is important, however, not to over-emphasise the differences between the first and second dimensions of the equal treatment principle in Community law. In the EC, rights to equality (in respect of equal pay between men and women) and non-discrimination (in respect of nationality) were both originally conceived as legal instruments to ensure the establishment and proper functioning of the common market.[30]

Subsequent political and legislative developments reflect broader social considerations, leading to the recognition of new rights in a range of areas, including on gender equality as part of a strategy of building a social dimension to Community policy,[31] especially during the 1970s.[32]

Simultaneously, existing rights, such as the right to equal pay, were remodelled on the basis of both economic *and* social considerations.[33]

---

[30] See especially Article 12, Article 39(2) and Article 141 EC (formerly Article 7, Article 48 (2) and Article 119 EEC). Implicitly the principle of non-discrimination also appears in Article 28, Article 43 and Article 49 EC (formerly Article 30, Article 52 and Article 59 EEC). Cf. G. More, 'The Principle of Equal Treatment: From Market Unifier to Fundamental Right?', in P. Craig and G. de Búrca (eds.), *The Evolution of EU Law* (Oxford University Press, 1999), pp. 521–535; G. de Búrca, note 17 above, pp. 13–34.

[31] The adoption of Council Directive 76/207/EEC, on the implementation of the principle of equal treatment for men and women as regards access to employment, vocational training and promotion, and working conditions, OJ 1976 No. L39/40 is an example. Cf. Council Resolution concerning a Social Action Programme, OJ 1974 No. C13/1.

[32] J. Kenner, *EU Employment Law. From Rome to Amsterdam and Beyond* (Oxford: Hart Publishing, 2003), pp. 23–69; R. Nielsen and E. Szyszczak, *The Social Dimension of the European Union*, 3rd edn (Handelshøjskolens Forlag, 1997), pp. 25–28.

[33] See Case 43/75, *Defrenne v. Sabena* ('*Defrenne*') [1976] ECR 455.

More widely still, this reflects the evolution of the Community from an economic to a markedly more encompassing organisation. Within this expanded scope for a broader social discourse, the right to equal treatment was gradually emancipated from the need to be formally legitimated only by economic justifications. A parallel development took place with other rights – and measures setting out such rights – in the broader social policy area.[34] Article 13 EC appears to be part of a yet further development in Community law towards recognising the right to equality and non-discrimination as an 'autonomous principle', i.e. a human right that is of value independently of the economic or social benefits that it may bring.[35] However, this development is also somewhat hesitant and halting: the limitation of the Employment Discrimination Directive to employment and occupation, i.e. the restriction of the material scope within which the right to non-discrimination can be exercised, shows that the right to equal treatment is still not completely autonomous.[36] Rather, its protection in Community legislation is still largely determined by the existence of a social and economic nexus. In the EC context, this issue is, in part, also related to the complex question of how far the jurisdiction of the EC extends to non-economic issues; the extension of the scope of the Race Directive is not uncontroversial from this perspective.

In its second dimension, then, several different reasons underpin the importance of equal treatment in the EC context, but one of these reasons

---

[34] Compare, for instance, the Preambles to the Acquired Rights Directive and the Collective Redundancies Directive in their original and amended versions twenty or so years later. See Council Directive 77/187/EEC, on the approximation of the laws of the Member States relating to the safeguarding of employees' rights in the event of transfers of undertakings, businesses or parts of undertakings or businesses, OJ 1977 No. L61/26 and cf. Council Directive 98/50/EC amending Directive 77/187/EEC on the approximation of the laws of the Member States relating to the safeguarding of employees' rights in the event of transfers of undertakings, businesses or parts of businesses, OJ 1988 No. L201/88; and Council Directive 75/129/EEC on the approximation of the laws of the Member States relating to collective redundancies, OJ 1975 No. L48/29 and cf. Council Directive 98/59/EC on the approximation of the laws of the Member States relating to collective redundancies, OJ 1998 No. L225/16.

[35] More, note 30 above, pp. 547–548. For interesting explorations of the relationship between social and fundamental rights in the EU context, see S. Fredman, 'Transformation or Dilution: Fundamental Rights in the EU Social Space' (2006) 12 *ELJ* 41; S. Prechal, 'Equality of Treatment, Non–Discrimination and Social Policy: Achievements in Three Themes' (2004) 41 *CMLR* 533.

[36] L. Waddington, *The Expanding Role of the Equality Principle in European Union Law* (Florence, EUI, 2003), p. 29.

is the importance of competition not being stifled by the use of ascriptive criteria to exclude people from being able to participate in economic relationships, such as employment. The 'business case' for status equality is, indeed, based on the argument that discrimination on the basis of race etc. is anti-competitive. In fact, there is a long tradition of viewing anti-discrimination law in this light outside the EC,[37] and in the EC the relationship of gender equality with the operation of the market goes back to the original Article 119 EEC on equal pay in the Treaty of Rome.[38] There is, therefore, some overlap between addressing status equality and promoting competitive markets.

This is not to say that the second dimension of equal treatment is simply the same as the first dimension, just that it overlaps to an extent.[39] In fact, the second dimension of equal treatment has an increasingly important role in EC law.[40] Initially, the approach of the Court was somewhat hesitant. Although in the third *Defrenne* case[41] the ECJ recognised that the elimination of sex discrimination formed part of fundamental rights, the Court declined to widen the scope of Article 119 (now 141), which provides for equal pay between men and women, to require equality in respect of other working conditions. In the *Grant* case (regarding discrimination on grounds of sexual orientation), the Court was cautious in drawing on the apparent logic of this position to reach conclusions that were, in the Court's view, beyond the existing European political consensus.[42] In the *Razzouk* case, however, after reiterating that freedom from sex discrimination is a fundamental right, the Court held that it must, therefore, be upheld in the context of relations between the institutions and their employees. The Court held, therefore, that, in interpreting the Staff Regulations, the requirements of the principle of equal treatment 'are in no way limited to those resulting from Article 119 [now 141] of the EEC Treaty or from the Community directives adopted

---

[37] C. McCrudden, *Anti-Discrimination Law* (Aldershot: Dartmouth, 1991), Introduction.

[38] On labour law (including women's equality) having a dual economic and social aspect, see Case 43/75, *Defrenne*, note 33 above, para. 12 where it was stated that Article 119 pursues a double aim, which is at once economic and social.

[39] For that reason, Christine Breining-Kaufman's analysis of the differences between a trade view of equality and a human rights view is too starkly drawn. See C. Breining-Kaufman, 'The Legal Matrix of Human Rights and Trade Law: State Obligations versus Private Rights and Obligations', in T. Cottier, J. Pauwelyn, and E. Bürgi (eds.), *Human Rights and International Trade* (Oxford University Press, 2005), pp. 95, 103–104.

[40] Tridimas, note 9 above at 69.

[41] Case C–149/77, *Defrenne v. Sabena* [1978] ECR 1365.

[42] Case C–249/96, *Grant v. South West Trains Ltd* [1998] ECR I–621.

in this field'.[43] So too, equality as a fundamental right played an important role in *P* v. *S and Cornwall CC*,[44] which considered whether discrimination on the grounds of gender reassignment was prohibited under EC law. For Tridimas, the case 'provides a prime example of the way the Court views the principle of equality as a general principle of EC law transcending the provisions of Community legislation'.

Perhaps the most dramatic example of this interpretation of 'equal treatment', and of its far-reaching consequences, occurred in the *Mangold* case.[45] According to Article 1, 'the purpose of ... [the Employment Discrimination] Directive [2000/78] is to lay down a general framework for combating discrimination on the grounds of religion or belief, disability, age or sexual orientation as regards employment and occupation, with a view to putting into effect in the Member States the principle of equal treatment'.

The significance, for the operation of the equality directives, of recognising equal treatment as a general principle can be seen in *Mangold*, which involved the issue, inter alia, of the application of the Employment Discrimination Directive's prohibition of age discrimination in Germany. A major problem standing in the way of the application of the directive appeared to be that the time limit for transposition of the age discrimination provisions of the directive had not yet passed for Germany. The ECJ, however, did not find this to be an insuperable barrier. Crucially for our purposes,[46] the ECJ stated that the principle of non-discrimination on grounds of age must be regarded as a general principle of Community law (drawing on international human rights instruments, inter alia). This is an important aspect of Community law regarding status equality (the same reasoning would, presumably, apply to discrimination on the basis of the other statuses listed in Article 13 EC, as well as gender), and it provides a vital link with the law regarding public procurement, which the ECJ has also said is based on the concept of 'equal treatment'.

---

[43] Joined Cases 75 and 117/82, *Razzouk and Beydoun* v. *Commission* ('*Razzouk*') [1984] ECR 1509, para. 17. See also Case C–37/89, *Michel Weiser* v. *Caisse Nationale des Barreaux Français* [1990] ECR I–2395.

[44] Case C–13/94, *P* v. *S and Cornwall CC* [1996] ECR I–2143.

[45] Case C–144/04, *Mangold* v. *Rudiger Helm* ('*Mangold*') [2005] ECR I–9981. Note, however, that the current status of this aspect of *Mangold* is uncertain, following the criticism of the judgment by Advocate General Mazál in Case C–411/05, *Palacios de la Villa*, 15 February 2007.

[46] Case C–144/04, *Mangold*, note 45 above, paras. 74–77.

3.3. Status equality and procurement law: the same principle of equal treatment?

The second dimension of equal treatment in Community law has been largely, if not entirely, ignored by the Commission in current interpretations of the procurement directives, for reasons that are not at all clear. The ECJ has made clear, after all, that the protection of fundamental rights is one of the general principles of EC law, that the requirements flowing from the protection of fundamental rights in the Community legal order are binding on the EC institutions, that they are also binding on Member States when they implement EC rules,[47] and that among the fundamental rights protected by the ECJ, particular aspects of equality have been identified. These include religious equality[48] and the prohibition of sex discrimination.[49] More broadly, the Court has held that fundamental rights 'include the general principle of equality and non-discrimination'.[50]

Although not legally binding, the recitals to the directives are relevant to the issue.[51] Recital 2 of the Public Sector Directive and Recital 9 to the Utilities Directive both state that the directives are 'based on' several principles that 'derive' from the four freedoms set out in the Treaty, including 'the principle of equal treatment [and] the principle of non-discrimination'. Four points are immediately apparent: first, that non-discrimination appears to be a concept that is separable from equal treatment with the latter being a broader concept (a point made clear in Recital 9 of the Utilities Directive, which states that 'the principle of non-discrimination is no more than a *specific expression*' of the principle of equal treatment). Second, there is no apparent limit to the scope of the principle of equal treatment as applying only to equal treatment on the basis of nationality. When the directives wish to make clear that only non-discrimination on the basis of nationality is to be included, then they say so explicitly.[52] Third, the procurement directives are not a complete instantiation of the appropriate relationship between the 'equal treatment' principle and public procurement; they do not incorporate

---

[47] Case C–442/00, *Rodríguez Caballero* [2002] ECR I–11915, para. 30.
[48] Case 130/75, *Prais v. Council* [1976] ECR 1589.
[49] Case C–149/77, *Defrenne*, note 41 above, paras. 26–27. See C. Docksey, 'The Principle of Equality between Women and Men as Fundamental Right under Community Law' (1991) 20 *ILJ* 258.
[50] Case C–442/00, *Rodríguez Caballero*, note 47 above, para. 32.
[51] Arrowsmith, note 4 above, at 12.43.
[52] For example, Article 3 of the Public Sector Directive.

the whole of the equal treatment principle; the equal treatment principle more broadly should be integrated into their interpretation. Fourth, there is nothing in the procurement directives that should lead anyone to suppose that equal treatment in its first dimension only is appropriate to be taken into account. As Recital 2 of the Public Sector Directive explicitly states: the provisions of the directive 'should therefore be interpreted in accordance with both the aforementioned rules and principles and other rules of the Treaty'. The same must surely apply to the Utilities Directive.

3.4. *Obligations to promote status equality in the procurement directives*

The analysis so far suggests that there are likely to be situations where the aim of the directives and the aim of status equality law will overlap to such an extent that they pursue the same policy objective of reducing barriers to competition, and that the concept of equal treatment goes further in promoting status equality. What are the implications for the interpretation of the directives?[53] Both Article 2 of the Public Sector Directive and Article 10 of the Utilities Directive state clearly and simply: 'Contracting authorities shall treat economic operators equally and non-discriminatorily and shall act in a transparent way.' The directives then proceed to set out various ways in which these principles should be implemented in specific situations. With the exception of Article 3 of the Public Sector Directive, these requirements to act in a non-discriminatory way, or to treat economic operators equally, are not stated only to require non-discrimination or equality on grounds of nationality,[54] or to restrict its interpretation to include only the first dimension of the meaning of equal treatment. There appears no reason, in the light of the ECJ's case law on equal treatment in the Treaty, to narrow the meaning of the directives in this way. It therefore appears that there is both a general obligation to accord equal treatment to economic operators under the directives and more specific obligations of the same kind applicable to

---

[53] I do not here discuss the issue of the implications of the principle of equal treatment for procurement outside the existing procurement directives: see M. Krügner, 'The Principles of Equal Treatment and Transparency and the Commission Interpretative Communication on Concessions' (2003) 12 *PPLR* 181; S. Arrowsmith and P. Kunzlik, chapter 1 of this book.

[54] For example, the following provisions in the Public Sector Directive: Article 29(3); Article 29(6); Article 29(7); Article 30(3); Article 42(4); Article 72.

more specific situations, and that these require non-discrimination and equality on the basis of race, gender, etc.

Indeed, to the extent that the directives require 'equal treatment' and not just 'non-discrimination', they may go further in some respects. Where do the differences between non-discrimination and equal treatment lie? The best way to consider the difference is to view non-discrimination as giving rise to a negative obligation, whereas equal treatment involves the taking of action by the Member State (as under the fourth approach to equality sketched out previously). Is there a positive obligation on Member States to further the principle of equal treatment? Krügner considers that such an obligation should be derived in part from Article 10 EC and the principle of effectiveness (*effet utile*) that derives from it. Article 10 provides: 'Member States shall take all appropriate measures, whether general or particular, to ensure fulfillment of the obligations arising out of this Treaty or resulting from action taken by the institutions of the Community. They shall facilitate the achievement of the Community's tasks. They shall abstain from any measure which could jeopardise the attainment of the objectives of this Treaty.' Taken together with the ECJ case law, he concludes that 'Member States may have to take positive measures in order to guarantee the full scope and effect of Community law',[55] including the principle of equal treatment.

If there is a positive duty to promote equal treatment under the procurement directives (and that is unclear at the moment), then that would be an important development. Some of the voluntary initiatives in Britain, where public bodies attempt to diversify their supplier base by undertaking positive action to encourage black and minority owned businesses to tender for public contracts, could then be seen as attempts by a Member State to fulfil its positive obligation to further the principle of equal treatment under the directives. There would, however, be limits on how far EC Member States can embrace the type of affirmative action carried out in other states in this regard, such as the United States, Malaysia and South Africa, as EC equality law imposes limits on affirmative action that are narrower than those drawn elsewhere.[56]

---

[55] Krügner, note 53 above, p. 194.
[56] See, e.g., Case C–319/03, *Briheche v. Ministre de l'Intérieur* [2004] ECR I–8807; Case C–476/99, *Lommers v. Minister van Landbouw* [2002] ECR I–2891; Case C–407/98, *Katarina Abrahamsson and Leif Anderson v. Elisabet Fogelqvist* [2000] ECR I–5539; Case C–158/97, *Badeck* [2000] ECR I–1875; Case C–409/95, *Marschall v. Land Nordrhein-Westfalen* [1997] ECR I–6363.

3.5. Equal treatment as an interpretative principle

Beyond this context, where else would my argument that the directives be interpreted in the light of the principle of equal treatment, including both its dimensions, be of importance? It is clear from much of the legal writing on the directives that there are significant issues of interpretation that are likely to face contracting authorities and others in the next few years. With relatively few exceptions, where a question of interpretation has arisen that might go either to uphold the use of procurement linkages, or against such linkages, the interpretation advanced has more often seemed to be driven by pragmatic and policy considerations, with an absence of reference to principle. My principal suggestion is that understanding that the use of procurement linkages to advance status equality is a way of delivering a Community policy, part of the conception of equal treatment regarded by the ECJ as a fundamental interpretative principle of EC law, will allow an interpretation that is much more favourable to allowing such linkages than one that ignores such an understanding.

Conflicts between status equality linkages in procurement can come into conflict with obligations to promote competitive procurement markets in the Community. But when we recognise that both are aspects of the same fundamental principle of equal treatment, the principle enunciated by the German Constitutional Court in its interpretation of rights conflicts in German constitutional law is of considerable relevance: 'This conflict … is to be resolved on the principle of practical concordancy, which requires that no one of the conflicting legal positions be preferred and maximally asserted, but all given as protective as possible an arrangement.'[57] It is at this point that the further principle widely utilised by the ECJ as a method of harmonising apparently conflicting provisions, and mentioned specifically in the recitals (Recital 2 to the Public Sector Directive; Recital 9 to the Utilities Directive) as a principle governing the interpretation of the procurement directives, comes into play, i.e. the principle of proportionality. This helps because it means that the procurement directives should be interpreted as not going further than is necessary to serve legitimate policies, particularly if to do so would undermine the furtherance of another fundamental EC policy, to achieve status equality.

[57] 'Classroom Crucifix', 93 BVerfGe 1 (1996), translated and reproduced in D. Kommers, *The Constitutional Jurisprudence of the Federal Republic of Germany*, 2nd edn (North Carolina: Duke University, 1997).

4. Freedom of contract and the subject matter of the contract

An examination of the effect of the procurement directives on the ability of contracting authorities to incorporate procurement linkages must appreciate that there is an earlier stage in contracting, about which the directives have very little to say, when the contracting authority is deciding what, exactly, it is that it wants to contract for. In broad terms, a 'government contract' arises between a public body and a supplier or contractor when there is an agreement between them enforced by the law or recognised by the law as affecting the rights and duties of the parties.[58] There are many legal restrictions on the principle of freedom of contract that apply to both public contracts and private contracts; these are usually governed by domestic law. Sometimes, for example, public contracts are subject to greater restrictions on freedom of contract than private contracts because the market disciplines that apply in the case of private contracts do not necessarily apply in the case of public contracts, and because we sometimes require public bodies to meet a higher level of ethical standards than private contractors. Do the EC procurement directives, or Community law more generally, impose restrictions on the freedom of contract of parties in a public contract? The answer is quite clearly 'yes', in that (as we have seen) both the Treaty and the directives impose an obligation that economic operators be accorded 'equal treatment', and this prohibits public authorities discriminating against, for example, foreign contractors. As the Commission's Communication on environmental considerations in procurement put it:

> A contracting authority, as a public body, has to observe the general rules and principles of Community law. More precisely, these are the principles regarding the free movement of goods and services as laid down in Articles 28 to 30 (formerly 30 to 36), and 43 to 55 (formerly 52 to 66) of the EC Treaty. This implies that the subject matter of a public contract may not be defined with the objective or the result that access to the contract is limited to domestic companies to the detriment of tenderers from other Member States.[59]

---

[58] G. Treitel, 'Contract: General Rules', in P. Birks, *English Private Law*, Volume II (Oxford University Press, 2004), at 8.01.

[59] European Commission, Interpretative Communication on the Community law applicable to public procurement and the possibilities for integrating environmental considerations into public procurement ('Communication on environmental considerations'), COM (2001) 274 final, p. 12.

Does Community law go further than that in limiting freedom of contract? As we have seen, Community law is particularly concerned with the *way* in which public contracts are dealt with; is it also concerned with limiting *what* can be contracted for, provided equal treatment is accorded? The question is a crucial one because if the answer is 'no', then there seems little under Community law to prevent a public body from specifying that a particular social policy goal is *that for which the public body is specifically contracting*. In its two Communications,[60] on environmental and social considerations in procurement, the Commission made clear that, apart from the issue of equal treatment, Community law did not regulate what could be contracted for. 'The public procurement directives do not prescribe in any way what contracting authorities should buy and are consequently neutral as far as the subject matter of a contract is concerned.'[61] The Communication on social considerations states: 'In general, any contracting authority is free, when defining the goods or services it intends to buy, to choose to buy goods, services or works which correspond to its concerns as regards social policy ... provided that such choice does not result in restricted access to the contract in question to the detriment of tenderers from other Member States.'[62] Even more clearly, the Commission's *Handbook* on green procurement states: 'In principle [public authorities] are free to define the subject matter of the contract in any way that meets [their] needs. Public procurement legislation is not much concerned with what contracting authorities buy, but mainly with how they buy it. For that reason, none of the procurement directives restrict the subject matter of a contract as such.'[63]

Indeed, apart from these general statements making clear the extensive freedom to contract that applies, the Communication on social considerations specifically states, in an important footnote, that 'certain ... contracts targeted at a particular social category have, *by their very nature*, a social objective (for example, a contract for training for long-term unemployed persons). Another example is contracts for the purchase

[60] *Ibid.*; European Commission, Commission interpretative Communication on the Community law applicable to public procurement and the possibilities for integrating social considerations into public procurement ('Communication on social considerations'), COM (2001) 566 final.
[61] Communication on environmental considerations, note 59 above, p. 12.
[62] Communication on social considerations, note 60 above, p. 7.
[63] European Commission, *Buying Green!: A Handbook on Environmental Public Procurement* ('*Handbook*') (Luxembourg: Official Publications of the European Communities, 2004), p. 14.

of computer hardware/services adapted to the needs of disabled persons.'[64] If the contracting authority defines the subject matter of the
contract to be the production of widgets, then no social considerations
are involved. If the subject matter of the contract is defined, however, to
be the supply of food to state schools in a way that caters to a broad mix
of pupils of differing faiths (or none), then the ability to supply halal meat
will be an aspect of the subject matter of the contract.

As we shall see, this broad interpretation of what can constitute the
subject matter of the contract gels perfectly with, and is further borne out
by, the approach taken in the directives as to what can constitute a
technical specification. Of course, as the Communication on environmental considerations also makes clear, the directives kick in after the
decision is made as to what it is that is being contracted for, so that,

> After having made the first choice on the subject matter of the contract,
> the public procurement directives oblige contracting authorities to specify
> the characteristics of the subject in a manner such that it fulfils the use
> for which it is intended by the contracting authority. To this end, the
> directives contain a number of provisions relating to common rules in the
> technical field, to be specified in the contract documents relating to each
> contract.[65]

It is also clear that the subject matter of each contract and the criteria
governing its award must be clearly defined.[66] We will be much concerned with these issues subsequently. For the moment, however, all that
concerns us is whether the directives limit what can be contracted for
and, apart from the issue of equal treatment and compliance with the
provisions of the Treaty, the answer appears to be that the directives do
not limit what can be contracted for.

Can we go further? Can we have mixed purpose public contracts, in
which the contracting authority wants to achieve two objectives, rather
than one, where one objective is the purchase of an everyday item (such
as the supply of pencils), and the second is the achievement of a social
aim (such as equal status)? Can a contracting authority, for example, say
that the subject-matter of the contract is (a) the supply of widgets, (b) *by
a workforce made up of those drawn from the unemployed*? The answer

---

[64] European Commission, Communication on environmental considerations, note 59 above,
footnote 15 (emphasis added).
[65] *Ibid.*, note 59 above, p. 9.
[66] Case C–87/94, *Commission* v. *Belgium* [1996] ECR I–2043, paras. 51–53, and Case
C–324/98, *Telaustria* v. *Telekom Austria* ('*Telaustria*') [2000] ECR I–10745, para. 61.

appears to be 'yes'. Indeed, it would be surprising if contracts could not be used as such multi-purpose vehicles, when we consider the complex subject matter of some Public Private Partnership contracts. Why might there be any argument that this is not permissible? The first response is sometimes simply disbelief that such a simple solution to such an apparently difficult and long running issue is possible under Community law. But that is hardly an argument against the approach suggested here. Describing the incorporation of social issues into procurement as involving the use of 'secondary' considerations is potentially misleading. If the subject matter of the contract can itself be the delivery of the social policy, then social issues are no longer 'secondary' to the contract, but central to it, and the use of the term 'secondary' in this context to describe them is misleading.

Some previous commentators did, in fact, address this point.[67] Krüger, Nielsen and Bruun argued in 1998: 'It is perfectly acceptable to award contracts for the erection or supply of facilities for more atypical functions such as bettering conditions for immigrants or national minorities, women's paid labour market participation, district areas in situations where no commercial aspects apply.'[68] They continued:

> Contracts subject to procurement procedure rules could however also be aimed at national policy objectives such as … securing employment or aiming at environmental preservation. Or contracts could have twofold purposes with public policy objectives integrated in more conventional best value for money purchase … The scope of discretion left to the contracting entities in matters of objectives, purpose and aims of public contracts is wide. The object of the contract and the more specific commitments under the contract in question are to a large extent left untouched by the procurement regulations.[69]

A second objection to the approach advocated here may be that the incorporation of such considerations as primary elements of the subject matter of the contract is so liable to abuse that it should be stopped, but that argument (apart from being based on arguable empirical assumptions) has no legal basis on which to hang its scepticism about the incorporation of such social policy considerations. There is nothing in the directives that seeks to prevent contracting authorities from doing things that, in policy terms, we might think of as stupid, or unacceptable

---

[67] Krüger, Nielsen and Bruun, note 4 above, p. 139.
[68] Ibid.   [69] Ibid., pp. 140–141.

for political reasons. Krüger *et al.* pointed to a potential argument against this wide interpretation, referring to 'the underlying need for maximum transparency injected into the final award. Transparency in this rather blunt form [commercial objectives] might justify award evaluations which render otherwise acceptable Community objectives as illegal.'[70] Allowing them to be included as award criteria might 'compromise an efficient ex post review of the decisions taken at the end of the procedure'. But, provided transparency is ensured in other ways, there is no a priori reason to resort to the blunt approach, where to do so would limit so substantially the policy space available to Member States.

A third argument against the permissive approach to the subject matter of the contract advocated here is more complex, relating to the basis on which a contract exists or not. In English law, for example, it is probably not possible to contract with someone simply to obey the law because there is no consideration by the party promising to obey the law since they are under a legal obligation to do so in any event. But that is a question of domestic law, not (at least so far) a matter of Community law. Nevertheless, to avoid such an issue arising as a matter of Community law, it may well be better therefore to require that the 'social' subject matter of the contract is one that obliges the other party to go further than simply obeying the law.

Even if the directives are not intended to operate as a mechanism of quality or price control and recognise the parties' freedom of contract with respect to the essential features of their bargain, there remains an important distinction between the term or terms which express the substance of the bargain and 'incidental' (if important) terms which surround them. A fourth response may be that in most cases what a public authority is attempting to do is simply to place incidental, if important, social side constraints on the operation of a contract whose substance is primarily about something else, such as the delivery of widgets. This is, no doubt, correct but does not respond to the issue I am raising here. This is: is it *possible* for a contracting authority to specify a social objective as the subject matter of the contract? I am not addressing the empirical question of whether that is what contracting authorities are currently doing. The point does remind us, however, that if the contracting authority does want the social objective to be part of the subject matter of the contract, it will need to make clear that this is precisely what it wants to achieve, because the default position of observers may well be

---

[70] *Ibid.*, p. 153.

that, if it does not do this, the social consideration will be regarded as 'secondary', in the sense of being a mere incidental side constraint.

Does the case law of the ECJ dealing with public procurement support or challenge the permissive interpretation of the subject matter of the contract discussed above? Two cases in particular may seem to create problems for this interpretation. The first is the *Beentjes* case, which was discussed also in chapter 4.[71] The proceedings concerned a decision to award a public works contract. Beentjes had submitted the lowest bid, but the contract had been awarded to another bidder. Several reasons were given for preferring the other bid, including that Beentjes was not able to employ long-term unemployed persons. The awarding authority had stated this as a necessary condition. Beentjes challenged the decision contending that the Works Directive precluded the contracting authorities from taking account of this consideration. The Court concluded that the condition relating to long-term unemployed people was not precluded by the directive. However, the Court held further that the policy could only be lawful if it was consistent with Treaty principles, which excluded practices operating in a discriminatory manner.

There are several major uncertainties concerning the meaning and implications of the decision of the ECJ in the *Beentjes* case. Two major interpretations are possible. One possible interpretation is that the Court permitted the incorporation of the social policy where the authority lays down a social policy specifically as part of the *contractual conditions* which must be complied with by the contractor. An alternative interpretation would read the case as permitting the contracting authority to decide not to award a contract to a contractor for a reason *other* than failure to agree to a contractual condition. The function of the directive, on this interpretation, is to lay down mandatory procedural requirements relating to some aspects of the contracting process, but otherwise to leave discretion to contracting authorities as to whom to award the contract. Under this interpretation, contractors could be rejected, for example, because of anticipated failure to meet a desired policy aim specified by the contracting authority. It is unclear whether the Court adopted the first or the second interpretation discussed above. On the one hand, it has been argued that *Commission* v. *Italy* implies that the first interpretation of the directive discussed above is correct. Otherwise

---

[71] Case C–31/87, *Gebroeders Beentjes BV* v. *Netherlands* ('*Beentjes*') [1988] ECR 4635; see also chapter 4, section 8.1.4.

an inconsistency between it and the *Beentjes* case would arise.[72] It should be noted also that it is the first interpretation that the Commission appears to adopt in its Communication following the decision in *Beentjes*.[73]

If the first interpretation is correct, there remain several issues. First, may a contracting authority, which specifies achievement of a social policy as a contractual requirement, take agreement to comply with the contractual condition into account in deciding to whom the contract should be awarded? Second, may a contracting authority, which specifies achievement of a social policy as a contractual requirement, reject a tender where the tenderer agrees to carry out the conditions of the contract, but the contracting authority considers that the tenderer may be unable to do so? On the one hand, a limited future-oriented approach does not seem consistent with the *Beentjes* case itself. On the other hand, some have argued that the second interpretation only allows the determination of a contract once failure to comply with a contractual term is established, and not in anticipation of inability to comply. The Commission's Communication stressed that the *Beentjes* approach must not be interpreted as effectively allowing the application of a criterion of award not specified in the directives.[74] As Winter argues:

> a careful analysis will be necessary to ascertain whether a contractual condition should in reality not be characterised as an unlawful criterion of award. This would be the case if the contract notice, rather than requiring the successful tenderer to employ a specific number of unemployed persons, would indicate that the contracting authority is to choose between tenders taking into account the proposals of tenderers to use unemployed persons in the performance of their contract *or their ability to employ* such persons.[75]

On this interpretation, the sanction for failure to meet the condition specified will be not to award future contracts to that contractor. Indeed, failure to meet a contractual condition might well amount to professional misconduct sufficient to refuse to consider the tenderer in future.

---

[72] S. Arrowsmith, 'Public Procurement as an Instrument of Policy and the Impact of Market Liberalisation' (1995) 111 *LQR* 235.

[73] European Commission, Communication on public procurement: regional and social aspects, COM (89) 400 final, p. 7.

[74] *Ibid.*

[75] J. Winter, 'Public Procurement' (1991) 28 *CMLR* 774. See also W. van Gervan, 'General Report to the 14th FIDE Congress', in FIDE, *L'Application dans les États Membres des Directives sur les Marchés Publics* (FIDE, 1990), p. 333.

If the first interpretation is accepted, we need to consider also the implications of this approach for the question of what may be taken into account in the context of suitability criteria. May these contractual conditions be taken into account in *selecting* contractors? In the light of what has been said above concerning suitability criteria, the answer would seem to be that they may not be taken into account in the context of suitability. However, we have not yet considered one element in the directive relating to suitability. The Public Sector Directive clearly envisages the rejection of contractors in the context of suitability who do not have the required 'technical capacity'. 'Technical capacity' relates to the ability to carry out the contractual conditions of the contract. If these contractual conditions include certain social policy objectives, then 'technical capacity' may include the ability to carry out these social objectives. If so, contractors may legitimately be excluded under selection criteria also for anticipated failure to meet such conditions, as well as in the context of the application of the award criteria. Otherwise, it might be said, we would be left in the position whereby it would be permissible to exclude for likely failure to meet a contractual condition when awarding the contract, but not at the stage of shortlisting potential contractors.

The major legal problem with this argument lies in the *Beentjes* case itself. For in its judgment the Court stated that the ability to comply with the condition relating to the long-term unemployed was not a matter of technical capacity.[76] It has been argued that this statement by the Court strengthens the argument that the second interpretation is the one that the Court intended to adopt. For if the Court was intending to permit such policies, however they were implemented (i.e. whether or not by contractual requirement), then ability to comply would not be a matter of technical capacity.[77] As Arrowsmith has observed in the past, there was a considerable degree of apparent illogicality about the legal position before the reform efforts of the late 1990s: 'to the extent that social and environmental policies may be taken into account, Member States should be permitted to call for the evidence necessary to apply these policies, and if it is to be permitted at all to include social conditions relating to the

---

[76] Case 31/87, *Beentjes*, note 71 above, para. 28.
[77] S. Arrowsmith, 'Restricted Awards Procedures under the Public Works Contracts Regulations 1991: A Commentary on *General Building and Maintenance* v. *Greenwich Borough Council*' [1993] 4 *PPLR* CS92, at CS 100.

contract, it should be permitted to exclude firms that cannot meet them'.[78]

There is, however, a third interpretation of *Beentjes* that appears to resolve the difficulties. This interpretation distinguishes between conditions that put into effect the subject matter of the contract, and those that do not. *Beentjes* falls into the latter category. Such conditions do not need to relate to the subject matter of the contract. They operate post-award only; provided the contractor or supplier agrees to operate the condition if awarded the contract, then the ability to comply with the condition is not subject to pre-award scrutiny, and can play no part in the award of the contract itself. This is what the Court decided the local authority was able to do in *Beentjes*. However, there is another type of condition that puts into effect the subject matter of the contract. This is not the *Beentjes* case. Otherwise the Court would not have gone out of its way to stress that the condition was not a matter of technical capacity. The Court was not deciding, therefore, whether the reduction in unemployment through the use of unemployed persons could be a permissible subject matter of the contract, only that it was not the subject matter of the contract *in this particular case.*[79]

Is there any better *legal* argument against the broad approach to the concept of the subject matter of the contract suggested above? Arguably, the approach that leaves open the definition of the subject matter in the way suggested might be criticised as based on a common law approach to contracts. Perhaps a different approach may be taken to this issue depending on whether the starting point is a common law or civil law mentality. It is arguable that if we were to take a civil law approach, then, putting the matter simplistically, central to our understanding of the subject matter of this particular contract will have been an earlier choice on what *general* type of contract is involved. This idea of contracts being classifiable on the basis of their general objective, an approach based on the idea of 'nominate' contracts, is then likely to lead one to consider that certain types of conditions in any particular contract are not central to that general type of contract, and therefore cannot be part of the subject matter of that contract. So, classifying a contract as one for sale of goods

---

[78] S. Arrowsmith, 'The Community's Legal Framework on Public Procurement: "The Way Forward" at Last?' (1999) 36 CMLR 13, 48.

[79] Arrowsmith, note 4 above, at 19.57–19.59 reaches a similar conclusion regarding the potential breadth of award criteria, even with an acceptance of the narrow view of *Beentjes*.

will generate an expectation that certain elements of the contract are central to sales contracts, whilst other terms will not be. Thus, this initial classification process is a vital part of the process of understanding what will be considered by the courts to be central to assessing the subject matter of the contract. One way of describing this process might be to say that the classification of the contract as a particular type of nominate contract generates a set of abstract expectations as to what is central to that contract. In the common law, on the other hand, except where statute has intervened, the concept of nominate contracts is much less prevalent, and therefore what constitutes the subject matter of the contract is something that is much more up to the parties in any particular case to determine, rather than one affected by a earlier choice of which nominate contract is involved.

Is there any evidence that this 'civil law' approach,[80] if that is what it is, is one that should be given to the meaning of the subject matter of the contract under Community law? One argument that comes close to this approach is based on the distinction between works, supply, service, and utility contracts specified in the directives. Does this classification generate an approach akin to the nominate contracts of civil law? In other words, does the classification of contracts into works, supply or service contracts lead to a requirement that only certain issues can be part of the subject matter of the contract? There is some support for such an approach in at least one of the Commission's Communications. The Communication on environmental considerations, for example, says (just before referring to the distinction between works, supplies and services contracts): 'The possibilities for the taking into account of environmental considerations differ according to the different types of contracts.'[81] But any sense that this means that what can be included within the agreed subject matter of a contract is limited *legally* by the nature of the contract as dealing with works, services or supplies is rebutted by the later statement, dealing with supply contracts, which says: 'Supply contracts relate, generally, to the purchase of final or end products. Therefore, *apart from the basic and essential choice of the subject matter of the contract ("what shall I purchase?")*, the possibilities to take into account environmental considerations in addition to this choice are not as extensive as for

---

[80] See B. Nicholas, *The French Law of Contract*, 2nd edn (Oxford University Press, 1992), which has been a prime source of information on this.
[81] Communication on environmental considerations, note 59 above, p. 7.

works and service contracts.'[82] The phrase emphasised in the quotation indicates that the 'common law' approach is the one assumed to operate in this context. It is clear also from the case law of the ECJ that the subject matter of the contract determines the classification as works, supplies, or services, and not the other way round.[83]

In any event, we should be sceptical about dividing the civil from the common law approach so rigidly. It is clear that the approach to the subject matter of the contract suggested above is entirely consistent with the law of France, for example. The new French Procurement Code of 2006[84] provides various ways to integrate environmental and social agendas into procurement. The first approach is essentially to 'mainstream' public policy concerns into the planning process of public procurement. The Code stresses, for example, that one of the ways of addressing the goal of achieving sustainable development is to build in the issue of sustainable development right at the beginning of the project, regarding one of the purposes of the contract as being the achievement of such sustainable development. Article 5 of the Code, indeed, imposes on the public body the duty to take into account concerns of sustainable development, defined as development that meets the needs of the present without compromising the capacity of future generations to answer theirs. Thus, it is at the first stage of the procurement process (the definition of the subject matter of the contract) that the Code envisages that the public body should consider the possibilities of integrating requirements in terms of the environment, and cost implications of doing so.

What of the case law of the Court of Justice in other areas of Community law? Does this assist our understanding of what meaning we should attach to the 'subject matter of the contract' in the procurement context? The issue of what constitutes the subject matter of the contract arises in at least two other areas of Community law. It arises, first, in the context of the Unfair Terms Directive, where the 'main subject matter of the contract' is exempted from the restrictions that otherwise apply, in order to allow the retention of the freedom of contract of the parties.[85] In addition, the issue

---

[82] *Ibid.*, p. 8.   [83] Case C–340/02, *Commission* v. *France* [2004] ECR I–9845, para. 35.

[84] Décret n° 2006–975 du 1er août 2006 portant code des marchés publics, JORF n° 179 du 4 août 2006, 11627, available at www.legifrance.gouv.fr

[85] See, in general, the useful discussions in The Law Commission, Consultation Paper No. 166; The Scottish Law Commission Discussion Paper No. 119: Unfair Terms in Contracts, A Joint Consultation Paper; The Law Commission (LAW COM No. 292) and The Scottish Law Commission (SCOT LAW COM No. 199), Unfair Terms in Contracts, February 2005, Cm 6464.

of what constitutes the subject matter of the contract arises in Article 82 EC. This states that 'any abuse by one or more undertakings of a dominant position within the common market or in a substantial part of it shall be prohibited as incompatible with the common market in so far as it may affect trade between Member States'. Such abuse may consist in various activities: directly or indirectly imposing unfair prices or other unfair trading conditions; limiting production, markets or technical development to the detriment of consumers; or applying dissimilar conditions to equivalent transactions with other trading parties. Or, of most interest from our point of view, it may consist in making the conclusion of contracts subject to acceptance by the other parties of supplementary obligations *which have no connection with the subject matter of such contracts*. In neither of these contexts is there case law of the ECJ that would prevent the adoption of the broad approach to the concept of the subject matter of the contract advocated above in the context of the procurement directives.

5. Overall limits of the procurement directives: the limits of the Treaty

In most cases the legal tensions arising out of the use of status equality linkages in procurement can be resolved within the four corners of the procurement directives, interpreted in accordance with the general principles of Community law. There is, however, an additional method of addressing the issues. The procurement directives are anyway subject to a Treaty-based exception that nothing in the directive 'should prevent the imposition or enforcement of measures necessary to protect public policy, public morality, public security, health, human and animal life or the preservation of plant life, in particular with a view to sustainable development, provided that these measures are in conformity with the Treaty'.[86] When will a measure adopted by a Member State be regarded as 'necessary' to protect 'public policy', 'public morality', or 'public security'? This is now an area of considerable activity by the ECJ and only the bare outlines of some of the issues can be discussed here. There is considerable uncertainty about the weight the Court gives respectively to economic rights and human rights where they conflict.[87]

---

[86] Recital 6 of the Public Sector Directive; Recital 13 of the Utilities Directive.
[87] Craig and de Búrca, note 30 above, p. 347. For a more detailed discussion see J. Weiler, 'Fundamental Rights and Fundamental Boundaries: On the Conflict of Standards and Values in the Protection of Human Rights in the European Legal Space', in J. Weiler, *The Constitution of Europe* (Cambridge University Press, 1999), pp. 102–129.

In *Gebhard*,[88] the Court clarified the test for justifying national requirements impacting on the right of establishment. In general, where the taking-up or the pursuit of a specific activity is subject to certain conditions in the host Member State, a national of another Member State intending to pursue that activity must in principle comply with them. The Court mentions 'provisions laid down by law, regulation or administrative action justified by the general good, such as rules relating to organization, qualifications, professional ethics, supervision and liability'.[89] However, national measures 'liable to hinder or make less attractive the exercise of fundamental freedoms guaranteed by the Treaty' must fulfil four conditions in order to be compatible with Community law: 'they must be applied in a non-discriminatory manner; they must be justified by imperative requirements in the general interest; they must be suitable for securing the attainment of the objective which they pursue; and they must not go beyond what is necessary in order to attain it'.[90]

What then could constitute 'imperative requirements in the general interest'? In the *Guiot* case,[91] the Court considered this question in the context of national legislation that required an employer to pay employer's contributions to the social security fund of the host Member State in addition to the contributions already paid by him to the social security fund of the State where he was established. Since such legislation placed an additional financial burden on the employer, the employer was at a disadvantage compared with employers established in the host State, and it was therefore liable to restrict the freedom to provide services. However, the Court held that 'the public interest relating to the social protection of workers in the construction industry may ... because of the conditions specific to that sector, constitute an overriding requirement justifying such a restriction on the freedom to provide services',[92] although that was not the case where the workers in question enjoyed essentially the same protection by virtue of employer's contributions already paid by the employer in the Member State of establishment.

---

[88] Case C–55/94, *Gebhard v. Consiglio dell'Ordine degli Avvocati e Procuratori di Milano* ('*Gebhard*') [1995] ECR I–4165.

[89] *Ibid.*, para. 35.

[90] *Ibid.*, para. 37. See also Case C–19/92, *Kraus v. Land Baden–Württemberg* [1993] ECR I–1663, para. 32.

[91] Case C–272/94, *Guiot and Climatic SA* ('*Guiot*') [1996] ECR I–1905.

[92] *Ibid.*, para. 16. In Case C–222/95, *Société Civile Immobilière Parodi v. Banque H. Albert de Bary et Cie* [1997] ECR I–3899, the Court held that consumer protection could constitute a public interest ground for this purpose: para. 32.

The *Arblade* case[93] gave the Court the opportunity to re-examine the application of Articles 59 and 60 (now, Articles 49 EC and 50 EC) to the posted worker issue, in the light of these jurisprudential developments. The issues were similar to, but went beyond, those raised in the *Guiot* case. Arblade and Leloup, two companies established in France, carried out works in connection with the construction of a complex of silos for the storage of sugar in Belgium, employing workers ordinarily employed in France. In the course of checks carried out on the site in 1993, Belgian inspectors requested the firms to produce various social documents required under French law that certified compliance with social legislation. Their failure to do so resulted in a prosecution, during which the companies argued that the legal requirements were contrary to Community law. The social legislation requirements contested were wide-ranging: an obligation to pay the workers the minimum remuneration fixed by the collective labour agreement applicable in Belgium; the obligation to pay employer's contributions to social security schemes; the obligation to draw up documents such as labour rules, a special staff register, and an individual account for each worker; the obligation to keep such documents available, throughout the period of activity within the territory of the first Member State, on site or in an accessible and clearly identified place within the territory of that State; and the obligation to retain such documentation for a period of five years after the employer has ceased to employ those workers in the first Member State at an address within that Member State.

The Court took the opportunity to give a wide-ranging judgment, upholding some elements of the legislative requirements, and condemning others. For our purposes, some general principles emerge that are of considerable importance. First, as had already happened in the *Reisebüro Broede* case,[94] the Court essentially amalgamated the two tests in *Vander Elst*[95] and *Gebhard*, regarding the former as another way of stating some of the implications of the latter.

Second, the Court addressed the relationship between the concept of 'overriding reasons relating to the public interest' and the concept of 'public order'. The referring court had asked whether, as some of the

---

[93] Joined Cases C–369/96 and C–376/96, *Criminal Proceedings against Jean-Claude Arblade* ('*Arblade*') [1999] ECR I–8453.
[94] Case C–3/95, *Reisebüro Broede v. Sandker* ('*Reiseburo Broede*') [1996] ECR I–6511, para. 28.
[95] Case C–43/93, *Vander Elst v. Office des Migrations Internationales* ('*Vander Elst*') [1994] ECR I–3803.

national rules were contained in 'public order legislation', this affected the extent to which they were contestable under Articles 59 and 60. The Court understood the term 'public order' as 'applying to national provisions compliance with which has been deemed to be so crucial for the protection of the political, social or economic order in the Member State concerned as to require compliance therewith by all persons present on the national territory of that Member State and all legal relationships within that State'.[96] The Court did not consider that because the national rules were categorised as public order legislation, this meant that they were 'exempt from compliance with the provisions of the Treaty; if it did, the primacy and uniform application of Community law would be undermined'.[97] 'The considerations underlying such national legislation can be taken into account by Community law only in terms of the exceptions to Community freedoms expressly provided for by the Treaty and, where appropriate, on the ground that they constitute overriding reasons relating to the public interest.'[98]

Third, although the social protection of workers is capable of amounting to an 'overriding public interest',[99] provisions in national criminal law safeguarding this interest 'must be sufficiently precise and accessible that they do not render it impossible or excessively difficult in practice for such an employer to determine the obligations with which he is required to comply'.[100] Where they result in additional economic costs to the out-of-state service provider, because, for example, contributions are required to be paid in the host Member State and the employer is already required to make equivalent contributions in the firm's state of establishment, they need to satisfy two tests: do the contributions payable in the host State 'give rise to any social advantage for the workers concerned', and, second, do the workers concerned already enjoy protection that is 'essentially similar' to that which the rules of the host Member State seek to ensure?[101]

This last point was of particular relevance in *Mazzoleni*.[102] The firm involved was established in France and employed workers as security officers in a shopping mall in Belgium. Some of the workers were employed full-time in Belgium, while others were employed there for only some of the time and also worked in France. Belgian government inspectors

[96] Case C–3/95, *Reisebüro Broede*, note 94 above, para. 30.
[97] *Ibid.*, para. 31.   [98] *Ibid.*, para. 31.   [99] *Ibid.*, para. 60.
[100] *Ibid.*, para. 43.   [101] *Ibid.*, para. 53.
[102] Case C–165/98, *Mazzoleni* v. ISA ('*Mazzoleni*') [2001] ECR I–2189.

established that the firm was paying its workers working in Belgium below the minimum rates of pay established by the relevant collective agreement governing the private security industry. This case differed from *Arblade* in two important respects. First, it did not concern the construction industry, unlike several of the previous cases discussed already. Second, the evidence presented to the Court indicated that the firm, operating in a frontier region, was sending workers on a continuing basis to Belgium, but with some of its employees carrying out their work in the host country on a part-time basis and for very brief periods, unlike the circumstances in the previous cases, where employees were sent out of the state in which the firm was established to work on projects which were time limited. The Court accepted that these differences were important and, whilst adhering to the general principle of *Arblade* and its predecessors, and accepting also that imposing a minimum wage was for the legitimate purpose of protecting workers, it focused on the question of whether the application of those rules was 'necessary and proportionate for the purpose of protecting the workers concerned'.[103] Although leaving the determination of that issue to the national authorities in this case, the Court indicated some of the relevant factors that should be taken into account in determining the issue. In particular, it pointed to the importance of considering whether there was a disproportionate administrative burden imposed on this employer by the rules, and whether the objective of ensuring the same level of welfare protection for the employees of such service providers as that applicable in the territory of the host state to workers in the same sector 'may be regarded as attained if all the workers concerned enjoy an equivalent position overall in relation to remuneration, taxation and social security contributions in the host Member State and in the Member State of establishment'.[104]

The principle of *Arblade* was followed and applied in several cases subsequently.[105] Of these, the *Finalarte* case[106] considers an important additional point. The case concerned the application of the German legislation on the posting of workers[107] in the context of entitlement to

---

[103] *Ibid.*, para. 34.   [104] *Ibid.*, para. 35.
[105] Case C–493/99, *Commission* v. *Germany* [2001] ECR I–8163; Joined Cases C–49/98, C–50/98 to C–54/98 and C–68/98 to C–71/98, *Finalarte Sociedade de Construção Civil Ld* ('*Finalarte*') [2001] ECR I–7831; Case C–164/99, *Portugaia Construções Ld* [2002] ECR I–787; Case C–79/01, *Payroll Data Services (Italy) Srl* [2002] ECR I–8923.
[106] Joined Cases C–49/98, C–50/98 to C–54/98 and C–68/98 to C–71/98, *Finalarte*, note 105 above.
[107] Arbeitnehmerentsendegesetz, 26 February 1996, BGBl. I, p. 227.

paid holidays in the construction industry. Among the many issues raised by the national court, it pointed out that it appeared from the explanatory memorandum of the law 'that the declared aim of that law is to protect German businesses in the construction industry from the increasing pressure of competition in the European internal market, and thus from foreign providers of services'.[108] The response of the Court was measured. On the one hand, the preparatory materials were relevant but not dispositive of the purpose of the legislation: 'whilst the intention of the legislature, to be gathered from the political debates preceding the adoption of a law or from the statement of the grounds on which it was adopted, may be an indication of the aim of that law, it is not conclusive'.[109] The test that should be applied is whether, 'viewed objectively, the rules in question in the main proceedings promote the protection of posted workers'.[110] To do this 'it is necessary to check whether those rules confer a genuine benefit on the workers concerned, which significantly adds to their social protection. In this context, the stated intention of the legislature may lead to a more careful assessment of the alleged benefits conferred on workers by the measures it has adopted.'[111] Do the legal requirements 'in fact pursue the public interest objective of protecting workers employed by providers of services established outside Germany'?[112]

Applying the principles that derive from these cases to measures included within public procurement by Member States that aim to further status equality, it would appear that the fact that these measures mesh with and further the principle of status equality adopted in the various status equality directives would considerably lessen the likelihood that they would be considered to be discriminatory between Member States. To the extent that they could be regarded as creating a non-discriminatory barrier to trade, the issue will be whether despite this, they are justified on the basis of the protection of an overriding public interest, especially as they further a Community objective.

What of potential conflicts between EC law on procurement and other (non-EC) sources of status equality, such as domestic legislation going beyond existing EC status equality requirements? The *Omega* case is relevant here.[113] The Court of Justice (First Chamber) considered

---

[108] Joined Cases C–49/98, C–50/98 to C–54/98 and C–68/98 to C–71/98, *Finalarte*, note 103 above, para. 38.
[109] *Ibid.*, para. 40.   [110] *Ibid.*, para. 41.   [111] *Ibid.*, para. 42.
[112] *Ibid.*, para. 49.   [113] Case C–36/02, *Omega* [2004] ECR I–9609.

whether restrictions on a commercial activity by Germany on grounds of 'dignity' were consistent with Articles 49 to 55 EC on the freedom to provide services and Articles 28 to 30 EC on the free movement of goods. Omega, a German company, had been operating an installation known as a 'laserdrome', normally used for the practice of 'laser sport' in Bonn. The equipment used by Omega included equipment supplied by the British company Pulsar. Having noticed that the object of the game played in the 'laserdrome' included hitting sensory tags placed on the jackets worn by players, the Bonn police authority issued an order against Omega on 14 September 1994, forbidding it from 'facilitating or allowing in its ... establishment games with the object of firing on human targets using a laser beam or other technical devices (such as infrared, for example), thereby, by recording shots hitting their targets, "playing at killing" people', on pain of a fine for each game played in breach of the order.

In domestic proceedings, the German courts held that the commercial exploitation of a 'killing game' in Omega's 'laserdrome' constituted an affront to human dignity, a concept established in the first sentence of paragraph 1(1) of the German Basic (Constitutional) Law. The Bundesverwaltungsgericht referred the following question to the ECJ for a preliminary ruling: 'Is it compatible with the provisions on freedom to provide services and the free movement of goods contained in the Treaty establishing the European Community for a particular commercial activity – in this case the operation of a so-called "laserdrome" involving simulated killing action – to be prohibited under national law because it offends against the values enshrined in the constitution?' As interpreted by the ECJ, this involved two issues:

> whether the prohibition of an economic activity for reasons arising from the protection of fundamental values laid down by the national constitution, such as, in this case, human dignity, is compatible with Community law, and, second, whether the ability which Member States have, for such reasons, to restrict fundamental freedoms guaranteed by the Treaty, namely the freedom to provide services and the free movement of goods, is subject ... to the condition that that restriction be based on a legal conception that is common to all Member States.

Prior case law had established that where a Member State put in place obstacles to freedom to provide services on the basis of national measures which were applicable without distinction, these were permissible only if those measures were justified by overriding reasons relating to the public interest, were such as to guarantee the achievement of the intended aim and did not go beyond what is necessary in order to achieve it. The particularly important issue that the ECJ considered in the *Omega* case was whether a common legal conception in all Member States is a precondition for one of those States being enabled to restrict at its discretion a certain category of provisions of goods or services protected by the EC Treaty.

Article 46 EC allowed restrictions justified for reasons of public policy, public security, or public health. In this case, the documents before the Court showed that the grounds relied on by the Bonn police authority in adopting the prohibition order expressly mentioned the fact that the activity concerned constitutes a danger to public policy. The ECJ considered that 'the concept of "public policy" in the Community context, particularly as justification for a derogation from the fundamental principle of the freedom to provide services, must be interpreted strictly, so that its scope cannot be determined unilaterally by each Member State without any control by the Community institutions ... Thus, public policy may be relied on only if there is a genuine and sufficiently serious threat to a fundamental interest of society.' However, 'the specific circumstances which may justify recourse to the concept of public policy may vary from one country to another and from one era to another. The competent national authorities must therefore be allowed a margin of discretion within the limits imposed by the Treaty.'[114] The Court:

> recalled in that context that, according to settled case-law, fundamental rights form an integral part of the general principles of law the observance of which the Court ensures, and that, for that purpose, the Court draws inspiration from the constitutional traditions common to the Member States and from the guidelines supplied by international treaties for the protection of human rights on which the Member States have collaborated or to which they are signatories. The European Convention on Human Rights and Fundamental Freedoms has special significance in that respect.[115]

The Court accepted that, as argued by the Advocate General in the case, 'the Community legal order undeniably strives to ensure respect for human dignity as a general principle of law'.[116] The Court accepted that: 'There can therefore be no doubt that the objective of protecting human dignity is compatible with Community law, it being immaterial in that

---

[114] *Ibid.*, para. 31.   [115] *Ibid.*, para. 33.   [116] *Ibid.*, para. 34.

respect that, in Germany, the principle of respect for human dignity has a particular status as an independent fundamental right.' The Court continued: 'Since both the Community and its Member States are required to respect fundamental rights, the protection of those rights is a legitimate interest which, in principle, justifies a restriction of the obligations imposed by Community law, even under a fundamental freedom guaranteed by the Treaty such as the freedom to provide services.'[117] However, 'measures which restrict the freedom to provide services may be justified on public policy grounds only if they are necessary for the protection of the interests which they are intended to guarantee and only in so far as those objectives cannot be attained by less restrictive measures'.[118]

It was not 'indispensable' for the restrictive measure issued by the authorities of a Member State 'to correspond to a conception shared by all Member States as regards the precise way in which the fundamental right or legitimate interest in question is to be protected'.[119] The 'need for, and proportionality of, the provisions adopted are not excluded merely because one Member State has chosen a system of protection different from that adopted by another State'.[120] The Court 'noted that, by prohibiting only the variant of the laser game the object of which is to fire on human targets and thus "play at killing" people, the contested order did not go beyond what is necessary in order to attain the objective pursued by the competent national authorities'.[121]

6. Conclusion

In this chapter, I have considered three fundamental aspects of Community law relating to procurement: the importance of equal treatment as a basis of both EC status equality and procurement law, the overall limits to the procurement directives provided by the Treaty, and the importance of the subject matter of the contract. All these are relevant to the interpretation of the detailed provisions of the directives. However, it is the third issue (the meaning of the subject matter of the contract) that may prove to be of most analytical importance for assessing the legality of procurement linkages furthering equal status goals.

[117] *Ibid.*, para. 35.   [118] *Ibid.*, para. 36.   [119] *Ibid.*, para. 37.   [120] *Ibid.*, para. 38.
[121] This chapter was completed before the important decisions of the ECJ concerning the interpretation of the Posted Workers Directive in the context of Article 19 EC: Case C–346/06, *Rüffert* v. *Land Niedersachsen* (3 April 2008); Case C–341/05, *Laval un Partneri* (18 December 2007); Case C–438/05, *Viking Line APB* (11 December 2007); C–319/06, *Commission* v. *Luxembourg* (19 June 2008).

Space does not permit a full explanation of the implications of this argument. In my book, I argue that the provisions of the directives that are most relevant to the issue of linkage can best be seen as divided into two groups: those where equal status is part of the subject matter of the contract, and those where it is not. In the first group of provisions, we see government acting as a consumer, *buying* social justice. In the second group are the various provisions of the directives that permit procurement linkages irrespective of whether equal status is part of the subject matter of the contract. In this context, we see government acting as a regulator, *requiring* social justice.

Disability issues in public procurement[1]

ROSEMARY BOYLE

1. Introduction

The Public Sector Directive 2004/18/EC for the first time takes explicit account of disability and environmental issues and includes provisions on accessibility and employment of disabled people. Some other social issues, for example race,[2] have not fared so well, perhaps reflecting which groups were most effective at lobbying. The European Disability Forum (EDF) put a great deal of effort into lobbying.

This chapter explains how disability issues could be taken into account prior to the 2004 directive and examines the additional flexibility the 2004 directive provides. It also considers briefly what lessons may be learned from the United States' experience, both for EC policy and for Member States implementing national policies within the EC regime. This includes exploring the extent to which affirmative action through procurement – 'contract compliance' – can be pursued in the context of disability issues, in a way that goes beyond the needs of the particular disabled users of the item procured, and whether this is desirable. In this respect it is suggested that effort should focus on developing well-focused specifications rather than aggressively pursuing contract compliance. The chapter also considers whether any provisions in the 2004 directive *require* purchasers to pursue affirmative action.

The discussion proceeds as follows. First, to set the context, the chapter looks briefly at disability legislation in the EC (using the UK as an example of legislation common across the EC) and in the United States (section 2); and at the UK experience generally of contract compliance (section 3). There then follows a discussion of how the new directive addresses

---

[1] I am glad to acknowledge the assistance of Sue Arrowsmith and John Colling and the analysis of the 2004 directives by the European Disability Forum at www.edf-feph.org/en/policy/publicpro/pubpro_news.htm.

[2] Racial equality is not mentioned in the recitals to the Public Sector Directive.

disability issues. This involves considering the possibilities for taking account of disability issues under the previous directives and the way in which these are clarified and improved under the 2004 directive (section 4). The analysis then turns (in section 5) to the three sets of innovative provisions, namely: new provisions on reference to disability issues in contract specifications; the provision for reserving contracts for sheltered employment; and explicit rules on social conditions for contracts.

The chapter focuses specifically on the Public Sector Directive. However, the new provisions are also included in the new Utilities Directive, and much of the analysis is also relevant to that directive.[3]

2. Disability laws at European and national level and in the United States

EC measures to promote gender equality were first adopted in the 1970s. The 1996 Resolution[4] on equality of opportunity for people with disabilities called upon Member States to ascertain whether their policies took account of the need to eliminate obstacles to full participation in social life by disabled people and to educate public opinion to be receptive to the abilities of disabled people. Article 13 of the EC Treaty (1997), introduced by the Treaty of Amsterdam, specifically empowered the Community to combat discrimination based on sex, race or ethnic origin, religion or belief, disability, age or sexual orientation.

This theme was returned to in 1999[5] to further emphasise promotion of employment opportunities[6] for people with disabilities and the possibilities offered by the information society. In 2000, Directive 2000/78/EC[7] established a general framework for equal treatment in employment

---

[3] On this directive see chapter 11 of the present book.

[4] The Resolution of the Council and of the Representatives of the Governments of the Member States meeting within the Council on equality of opportunity for people with disabilities, OJ 1997 No. C12/1.

[5] Council Resolution on equal employment opportunities for people with disabilities, OJ 1999 No. L372/3.

[6] The economic nexus referred to here (the role of disabled people as employees) and in the procurement directives' provisions on reserved contracts is interesting. The development of equality legislation mirrors the recent active phase of globalisation and may be seen as an aspect of the identification of people as 'consumers' who have money and 'rights'. The corresponding role of people as 'producers' has received less attention.

[7] Directive 2000/78/EC establishing a general framework for equal treatment in employment and occupation, OJ 2000 No. L303/16. See D. Hosking, 'Great Expectations: Protection from Discrimination because of Disability in Community Law' (2006) 31 ELRev 667.

and occupation. These measures set the framework for action across the EC and seem to have resulted in considerable harmonisation.

In the UK the Disability Discrimination Act (DDA) was passed in 1995 ahead of the EC lead in 1999. Its scope was broader than the EC employment equality directives, moving beyond employment equality also to promote equality in provision of public services. It made it unlawful (from December 1996) for service providers to treat disabled people less favourably than others for a reason related to disability. In particular, this meant non-discrimination in employment, access to goods, facilities and services, in the management, buying or renting of land or property and in the provision of education.

As a result, all UK service providers of whatever size, including public bodies, must consider making changes to physical features that make it difficult for disabled people to use their services (whether provided free or otherwise). Since October 1999 entities have had to make reasonable adjustments for disabled people, such as providing extra help or changing methods of service provision, and since October 2004 have had to make reasonable adjustments to the physical features of premises to overcome physical barriers to access. A complaint may be made to an industrial tribunal over discrimination relating to employment[8] or the county court over discrimination in the provision of goods or services.[9] Contravening PSV (public service vehicles) or rail accessibility regulations of the Secretary of State may lead to criminal proceedings.[10]

In 2005 the Disability Discrimination Act 2005 (DDA 2005) was introduced to amend the DDA 1995 and extended its scope from 5 December 2006. It echoes the kind of provisions seen in the Race Discrimination Act 2004. However, it has a more direct reference to procurement, particularly specification of contract requirements, because it requires public providers to make reasonable adjustments to make their goods, facilities and services accessible to disabled users. The Act is backed up by a statutory code of practice[11] which emphasises the need to consult disabled people.[12] The Act imposes a positive duty on public authorities and bodies.

---

[8] Section 8 DDA 1995.   [9] Section 25 DDA 1995.
[10] Sections 40, 46 and 48 DDA 1995.
[11] Disability Rights Commission, 'The duty to promote disability equality: statutory code of practice' ('the Code') available at www.equalityhumanrights.com. The Commission has now been closed and its responsibilities transferred to the new Equality and Human Rights Commission which commenced operation on 1 October 2007.
[12] *Ibid.*, para. 2.52 *et seq.*

The 2005 Act, reinforced by the Code, requires that public authorities carrying out their functions must have due regard to the need to:

   i) promote equality of opportunity between disabled persons and other persons;
  ii) eliminate discrimination that is unlawful under the Act;
 iii) eliminate harassment of disabled persons that is related to their disabilities;
  iv) promote positive attitudes towards disabled persons;
   v) encourage participation by disabled persons in public life; and
  vi) take steps to take account of disabled persons' disabilities, even where that involves treating disabled persons more favourably than other persons.

'Due regard', as stated in the Code,[13] means that authorities should give due weight to the need to promote disability equality in proportion to its relevance. It requires more than simply giving consideration to disability equality. Further, equality for disabled people may mean treating them 'more favourably'.[14] The Code[15] recognises, however, that 'it will not always be possible for authorities to adopt the course of action which will best promote disability equality, but public authorities must ensure that they have due regard to the requirement to promote disability equality alongside other competing requirements'. The Code therefore envisages a proportionate rather than absolute obligation.

In addition specific duties are placed on each public authority, in particular to produce and implement a disability equality scheme to demonstrate how it will fulfil its duties.

A public authority includes any person certain whose functions are functions of a public nature,[16] a definition that includes (and goes beyond) contracting authorities under the Public Sector Directive.[17] The Code[18] considers that a public authority includes any person exercising a 'public function' which would otherwise be exercised by the state, including functions delegated or contracted. Thus a contractor to a public authority

---

[13] *Ibid.*, para. 1.14.   [14] *Ibid.*, para. 1.10.   [15] *Ibid.*, para. 2.37.
[16] Section 2 of the DDA 2005 which amends the DDA 1995 by inserting a new Section 21A into that Act. There is no list of public bodies covered, only a list of some which are excepted (Parliament and the security services). None of the excepted bodies appear in Schedule 1 to the Public Contracts Regulations (England, Wales, Northern Ireland) S.I. 2006/5.
[17] As to which see chapter 2, section 4.3.2.   [18] Note 11 above, para. 5.1 *et seq.*

will be subject to the Act in performing contracted out functions, but not in other aspects of its business.

The 2005 Act is enforced principally by the Equality and Human Rights Commission (which has replaced the former Disability Rights Commission), which can serve a compliance notice on the public authority.[19] The Code also highlights the possibility of judicial review proceedings by interested persons or groups.[20]

Similar laws have been introduced in other Member States.[21]

In the United States, the Americans with Disabilities Act[22] is wide-ranging legislation intended to make society more accessible to people with disabilities. The measures promote equality in employment; access to public services, to buildings serving the public (including facilities such as restaurants and stores, as well as privately owned transportation systems), and to telecommunications (any public telephone service must have a telephone relay service for those using devices for the deaf); and prevention of harassment. In addition Section 508 of the Rehabilitation Act[23] requires that all information technology bought by the federal government be accessible. More precisely, this requires that when developing, procuring, maintaining or using electronic equipment and information technology each federal department or agency shall ensure, unless an undue burden would be imposed, that the technology allows disabled employees and members of the public to have access to and use of information and data comparable to that of other persons. Where an undue burden would be imposed, the government must provide an alternative means of access. In addition, an Access Board issues standards, including technical and performance criteria, to implement these obligations. These are incorporated into the Federal Acquisition Regulations and procurement policies, and the directives of departments and agencies. If a department or agency takes the view that complying with the standards in a procurement would impose an undue burden, this must be documented. The standards require the agency to buy the 'best' accessible technology if

---

[19] Section 49E of DDA 1995 Act inserted by Section 3 of DDA 2005.
[20] Note 11 above, para. 6.5.
[21] The following is a useful link to disability issues worldwide: www.stammeringlaw.org.uk/ links.htm#europe; for Germany: www.cirnetwork.org/idrm/reports/compendium/ germany.cfm; for France: www.handicap.gouv.fr; and for the Netherlands: www.cgb.nl/ cgb190.php.
[22] 42 USC § 12101.   [23] 29 USC § 794(d).

there is no fully compliant product.[24] The regulations are enforceable by administrative complaint and through the courts.

The US federal legislation may be regarded as the advance guard in pursuit of disability equality.[25] Section 508 of the Rehabilitation Act, in particular, provides a useful parallel indicator of where EC law might travel and the problems of an ambitious, as opposed to pragmatic, legislative steer. US experiences, highlighted in a recent article by Yukins,[26] provide an interesting case study for the EC and suggest several important lessons which have a particular bearing on the discussion in this chapter.

First, as Yukins highlights, the standards laid down by government or interest groups have often been highly aspirational and not practical. As he states in relation to the best accessibility standard: 'what this goal (of best accessibility) means is anyone's guess … It demonstrates a key weakness … though the standards speak in the hopeful, mandatory language of the civil rights community, in practice the standards must work through the precise language of the procurement system … the hopeful standards raise, in essence, the risk of a protest in every procurement.'[27]

Secondly, such unclear law leads to uncertainty, with purchasers unwilling to rely on the legal provisions unless forced to in court.[28] Therefore, thirdly, procurement obligations require precise, objective measures. Lack of clarity means poor enforcement: 'the procurement system demands precise, objective measures to ensure that procurements are fair, competitive and transparent'.[29]

Fourthly, 'Section 508's lesson is that implementing social goals through the procurement process is inherently difficult and expensive'[30] and 'as the economic assessment made plain, Section 508 made no sense in terms of a simple dollar-and-cents, cost/benefit analysis; other, less direct, benefits have to be taken into account to rationalise the rule, and the salient indirect benefit seem to be the accessibility gains for those *outside* the Government (service)'.[31] Finally, competing priorities of social policy and value for money place an enormous burden on the system in terms of complexity,

---

[24] C. Yukins, 'Making Federal Information Technology Accessible: A Case Study in Social Policy and Procurement' (2004) 33 *PCLJ* 667, at 695.

[25] European Blind Union, 'Disability Specific Directive', available at www.euroblind.org/fichiersGB/2005dsd.htm, states that 'disabled people look with envy to the legislation in the Americans with Disabilities Act and want a Europeans with Disabilities Act and ask for disability specific comprehensive non-discrimination legislation'.

[26] See further Yukins, note 24 above, p. 667 *et seq.*

[27] *Ibid.*, p. 695, on what the goal of best accessibility means.

[28] *Ibid.*, p. 702.   [29] *Ibid.*, p. 695.   [30] *Ibid.*, p. 671.   [31] *Ibid.*, p. 689.

cost and conflict.[32] One may conclude that conflicts between social policy and value for money need to be resolved clearly at a political level and then implemented via explicit legal rules.[33]

With these considerations in mind, we may now turn to efforts at EC level to pursue disability equality goals through procurement.

3. Contract compliance – the United Kingdom experience[34]

Domestic law sets out what may, must or must not be done in procurement. A freedom (but not an obligation) provided by EC law for an authority may be curtailed by domestic law. An example of how an authority may be free to pursue social considerations at EC level but be constrained by domestic legislation and regulation is found in the experience of UK local government. This discussion will be referred to later, in illustrating how domestic concerns may affect the scope for implementing the provisions in the Public Sector Directive on reserving contracts for entities providing employment for persons with disabilities.

In the 1980s, it was common for local authorities, particularly those controlled by the Labour Party, to pass 'Fair Wages Resolutions' requiring that council contracts should include a term requiring contractors to pay 'fair wages'.[35] At this stage most council contracts were for construction and maintenance services and represented, along with the in-house labour forces, a significant weapon on the local political scene. Policies then began to extend beyond fair wages resolutions to areas of broader concern, which some took the view were not within the appropriate remit of local government – for example opposition to the South African apartheid regime and equality in terms of sexual orientation. This led Mrs Thatcher's Conservative government to enact certain prohibitions in the Local Government Act 1988. This Act provided, inter alia, that local authorities were not to pursue certain

[32] *Ibid.*, pp. 697–699.
[33] *Ibid.*, p. 702 implies that it was the unwillingness of Congress to examine the economic implications which led it to pass much such sweeping social legislation: it simply ignored the question of cost.
[34] See in general S. Arrowsmith, *The Law of Public and Utilities Procurement*, 2nd edn (London: Sweet & Maxwell, 2005), chapter 19, particularly at 19.2 *et seq* and 19.65.
[35] Fair Wages Resolutions began life as a central government measure but were carried on in local government after being abandoned by central government in 1983. See B. Bercusson, *The Fair Wages Resolutions* (London: Mansell, 1978); O. Kahn-Freund, 'Legislation through Adjudication: The Legal Aspects of Fair Wages Clauses and Recognised Conditions' (1948) 11 *MLR* 274; and for a brief summary Arrowsmith, note 34 above, at 19.11–12.

specified[36] 'non commercial considerations' when letting contracts, in particular 'workforce considerations' (terms of employment, composition of the work force and promotion, transfer and training etc. opportunities).[37]

Interestingly, measures concerning race relations remained possible. This was an established feature of domestic law and the Department of the Environment, then responsible for local government, published six 'approved questions' which could be asked.[38] Section 18 of the 1988 Act specifically permitted authorities to ask these questions. However, since, as discussed in chapter 4, the EC procurement rules do not generally allow undertakings to be excluded or selected to tender on grounds relating to race relations issues per se, but only for past professional misconduct and non-compliance with domestic legislation,[39] authorities had to limit themselves to race relations questions concerned only with these matters. Professional misconduct had to be judged by reference to standards established in the tenderer's own Member State because it would generally constitute discrimination on grounds of nationality to judge a contractor by standards it might not know about and did not have to meet at home.[40]

It would equally have been possible under the EC rules to have had regard to disability issues. However, doing so would have contravened the 1988 Act. There was no provision permitting questions in relation to equality other than race. The Local Government Best Value (Exclusion of Non-commercial Considerations) Order 2001[41] changed this, permitting investigation of workforce matters where relevant to best value when 'directly relevant to the delivery of the service in question'. However, as explained in section 4 below, it is hard to reconcile the reservation of contracts for sheltered workshops or employment programmes with the 1988 Act, even as modified by the 2001 Order.

4. Pre-existing possibilities for considering disability issues under the procurement directives

4.1. Introduction

As chapter 2 explained, in 2004 the EC revised its directives on public procurement into two new directives, the Public Sector Directive (the

---

[36] In Section 17(5) of the Local Government Act 1988.
[37] Section 17(1) of the Local Government Act 1988. See also Arrowsmith, note 34 above, at 19.67 et seq.
[38] These were set out in the Department of the Environment Circular 8/88.
[39] See, in particular, chapter 4, section 10.3, and also 4.2.1 below.   [40] See 4.2.1 below.
[41] SI 2001/ 909, issued by the Secretary of State pursuant to Section 19 of the 1988 Act.

focus of this chapter) and the Utilities Directive.[42] As highlighted above, one of the directives' new features is confirmation of the scope for taking forward disability issues and, indeed, encouragement to do so.[43] We will now consider what was possible prior to the 2004 Public Sector Directive and highlight where the previous possibilities have now been clarified or improved.

4.2. Qualification and selection of firms to tender in restricted and negotiated procedures and (admission to) the open procedure

4.2.1. Criteria for exclusion

As explained in earlier chapters,[44] authorities may in general exclude undertakings from procurements only on the grounds stated in the directive, which do not generally allow exclusion for reasons unrelated to a firm's technical or financial capability to deliver the goods, works or services. This means that, for example, failure to adopt a proactive approach to recruiting the disabled in a contractor's general business would not provide grounds for exclusion, since this does not relate to the ability to deliver (and nor would it fall under the provision on grave misconduct, discussed below).

However, as also explained there, by way of exception to this, under both the old directives and the current Public Sector Directive (Article 45) authorities may exclude any firm that has been guilty of grave misconduct or convicted of an offence relating to professional mis-conduct. These provisions may be used to exclude firms for past non-compliance with norms relating to disability issues. Misconduct must, however, be judged by reference to standards established in the under-taking's own Member State because it would contravene the free move-ment rules to judge a contractor by standards it might not know about and did not have to meet in its home state.[45] Thus, it is submitted, a failure by a non-UK contractor to put in place a Disability Equality Scheme of the kind required in the UK cannot be considered grave misconduct in the absence of violation of the laws of the home state.

---

[42] See chapter 2, section 4.1.

[43] It is apparent from the EDF website that considerable lobbying by the EDF took place during the legislative process, in conjunction with other social issue lobbyists. Their impact is clear: equal treatment issues are highlighted in several places in the procure-ment directives.

[44] See chapter 2, section 4.3.6 and chapter 4, section 10.3.

[45] On whether such standards may be included as contract terms, see chapter 4, section 4.3.1.

By way of example, it is useful to consider how this may operate in relation to UK contractors. Section 2 above outlined the various measures and enforcement procedures applicable under the Disability Discrimination Acts: although some criminal offences are created, in the main civil, tribunal or administrative procedures are contemplated for violating the Acts' provisions. Any violation of the Act proven in proceedings against a service provider, or any breach of the Code proven against a public authority – which can include a public contractor – might be sufficiently serious to constitute grave professional misconduct. Grave misconduct might be shown where a complaint against a contractor's employee is upheld and the employer does not take appropriate action. An example might be if the driver of a public service bus became impatient at the slowness of a disabled person to board, made disparaging comments and recklessly closed the vehicle doors on the disabled person. Such action might lead to the driver being prosecuted for assault. In such a case the employer should take appropriate action in respect to prevent a repeat, for example through retraining or perhaps dismissal. Failure to do so might demonstrate participation in unfavourable treatment of a disabled person in relation to that person's disability, contrary to the 1995 Act, or failure to fulfil the duty on a public authority (a provider of public bus services) to eliminate harassment and promote positive attitudes towards disabled persons under the 2005 Act (see section 2.2 above).

4.2.2. Criteria for selection

As was also explained in earlier chapters, in deciding which of the qualified and interested firms should be invited to tender in restricted procedures, negotiated procedures and competitive dialogue authorities may only take account of the criteria for qualitative selection set out in the Public Sector Directive, in particular those relating to the supplier's personal situation, and economic and technical capability.[46] As explained there, as with criteria for excluding contractors as unqualified, these selection criteria must be related to contract performance. Under these principles, it could be appropriate to consider, for example, contractors' relative experience in dealing with information technology accessibility issues when procuring library equipment, or their experience in design for disability when procuring construction of public buildings. On the other

---

[46] Articles 45–48 of the Public Sector Directive: see chapter 2, section 4.3.6 and chapter 4, section 12.

hand, the merits of different contractors' policies in recruiting disabled persons in their business could not be relevant for selecting between qualified undertakings.

4.3. Specifications

4.3.1. The possibility for specifications relating to accessibility and the limits of discretion

It has always been the case that any relevant functional or performance requirements, including those relating to disability, can be included in a specification and the definition of technical specifications in the Public Sector Directive now highlights this possibility. Thus, 'technical specification', in the context of a works contract, is defined in Annex VI as:

> the totality of the technical prescriptions contained in particular in the tender documents, defining the characteristics required of a material, product or supply, which permits a material, a product or a supply to be described in a manner such that it fulfils the use for which it is intended by the contracting authority. These characteristics shall include levels of environmental performance, *design for all requirements (including accessibility for disabled persons).*[47] (emphasis added)

A similar definition of 'technical specification', with a parallel reference to accessibility, also applies to supply and services contracts.[48]

The explicit references to accessibility were included for the first time in the 2004 directive. As chapter 4 notes (see section 8.1.2), this probably does not, however, involve any substantive change: requirements on these matters could be included under the old directives, and when included were probably also part of the definition of 'technical specifications'. However, the new explicit reference clarifies the position, if clarification was needed. By drawing attention to the possibility, it also encourages purchasers to think about and include clear specifications on accessibility. Recital 46 also emphasises the possibility of including accessibility requirements in the specification: 'a contracting authority may use criteria aiming to meet social requirements in response to particular needs – *defined in the specification of the contract* (emphasis

---

[47] The words 'shall include' do not mean that requirements *must* be imposed in relation to all the characteristics referred to (which is an issue for national policy) but that where such requirements are included they are within the concept of technical specifications.

[48] See chapter 4, section 8.1.3.

added) – of particularly disadvantaged groups of people to which those receiving/using the works, supplies or services which are the object of the contract belong'.

In addition to the long-established possibility for authorities to *choose* to include specifications that take account of disability issues there is also now a new provision in Article 23 that appears to *require* authorities to consider including such provisions. This is considered in section 5.2 below. The points made below about the way in which specifications are set and the limits of an authority's discretion in this are equally relevant in that context.

Under these provisions an authority clearly may set accessibility requirements to meet the needs of users of a service or building – for example, by specifying for ramps and lifts to make public buildings accessible, or by specifying that IT equipment should have features that make it accessible for all those likely to use it, including those with disabilities.

Achievements in some sectors show what was already possible under the old rules. Even before the new directive raised the profile of disability issues much good work was done, for example, to make library services more accessible, especially in respect of information technology. For example Warwickshire libraries[49] already have a number of facilities. Magnification of a portion of the screen into a window is available. This can be moved around the screen by clicking and dragging. An on-screen keyboard display can be used by people with limited mobility who find it easier to use a mouse click than to depress keys. Terminals provide various accessibility accessories and some are larger than normal (19 and 21 inch screens). Talking webpage browsers are provided so that webpages can be read aloud and text size can also be increased. 'Trackballs' are also in use in several Warwickshire libraries, which help people who have difficulty using a mouse. Keyboard skins fit over the keyboards and are designed to help people with impaired vision see the keys more easily. There is also JAWS and ZoomText software: the former includes an internal software speech synthesiser to enable information from the screen to be read aloud and also outputs to refreshable braille displays, whilst ZoomText is a screen magnifier with a range of magnifications and colour filtering. In the higher education sector, Newcastle's Robinson

---

[49] www.warwickshire.gov.uk/Web/corporate/pages.nsf/Links/630BD455B4E7BCAB80256 C7C004474A3.

Library, for example, announces on the web[50] that it provides a PC with JAWS and ISS docking stations allowing connection to the University network from a laptop. All computers linked to the Windows 2000 campus network have an accessibility shortcut on the common desktop, which links to Microsoft accessibility features including TextHelp Read and Write. Large screen monitors, large character keyboards and wireless networking are also available.

Individual initiatives are already being built on by the creation of more structured approaches at regional level in the UK. One example is the work of Cambridge OnLine City.[51] Cambridge OnLine describes itself as 'a volunteer based charity that has been providing accessibility services and training to both individuals and organisations for the last ten years'. It has just been appointed 'Accessibility Champion' for the East Region of England. Its website announces:

> This prestigious contract is a huge success for Cambridge OnLine because the ICT Hub (an organisation dedicated to helping the voluntary and community sector improve its capability) have recognised the work we have been doing over the last ten years – especially our work supporting our partner organisations, and helping disabled and disadvantaged people to access computers and the Internet. We will receive Home Office funding to promote and distribute ICT Hub produced accessibility resources and services to voluntary and community organisations in the region.

These kinds of initiatives are already well underway, and testify to the social inclusion agenda being pursued at national level and enshrined in the Disability Acts before the 2004 directive.

We have so far considered specifications designed to ensure accessibility of goods and services to users. However, the beneficial effects of specifications to make products and services accessible are not necessarily confined simply to the contract requirement itself: such activity also raises the profile of disability issues for suppliers generally and product-based standards can gradually emerge, fuelled by the public sector lead. Another way of promoting development of relevant products is to develop national standards. The old Disability Rights Commission pioneered, with the British Standards Institute, guidance on developing accessible websites. It emphasises the need to involve disabled people in the

---

[50] www.ncl.ac.uk/library/accessibility_computing.php.
[51] www.cambridgeonline.org.uk/ERAC.htm.

requirements, design and testing process.[52] The US experience suggests that it is also important to work with suppliers and be aware of what standards already exist. Indeed the US experience raises the question of whether the government should define the standards or allow the commercial sector to come forward with them. The 'Bobby program' was a case in point. This programme was regularly used in the US across the commercial and government spheres to check websites for accessibility, but predated the federal standard. When the Access Board, the body responsible for defining accessibility standards, later came to define the relevant accessibility standard, it did so without regard to emerging proprietary standards and this meant that the manufacturer of the Bobby programme had to develop a different, less useful version, to enable it to supply to federal agencies.[53]

Merely specifying accessibility standards relevant for users may have the effects of raising the profile of accessibility standards and promoting the development of relevant equipment. However, the desire to achieve these effects may also be a motive for specifying such features in government contracts even when they are *not* required by users. For both reasons a purchaser might, for example, wish to specify that *all* software bundled with PCs sold to the authority should include as standard talking webpage browsers, even if most of the users will not actually need these features.

It might be argued that to specify such requirements contravenes the directive. Such an argument could be supported by analogy with the explicit rules that prohibit special conditions (that is, conditions not related to technical characteristics) that do not relate to performance of the contract, the prohibition on excluding firms for reasons unconnected with contract performance, and the explicit rules that prohibit award criteria that are not linked to the contract's subject matter.[54] By specifying features that it does not require as user, the government seeks to achieve a benefit that is connected with its own requirements or their delivery. Under the rules on exclusions and award criteria just mentioned it is obviously unlawful to exclude suppliers on the basis of the proportion of their equipment that is supplied to the market as a whole

---

[52] Website accessibility guidance PAS78 (BSI publicly available specification) available at www.equalityhumanrights.com/en/publicationsandresources/Disability/Pages/Website accessibilityguidance.

[53] See Yukins, note 24 above, at 693.

[54] See chapter 4, sections 8.1.3, 10.3 and 13 respectively.

with 'accessibility' features, or to take this into account as an award criterion. On the other hand, it clearly appears lawful to specify for accessibility features for potential users even when there is only a small chance that they will be used in practice, since, as chapter 1 argued, Member States have a broad discretion in balancing value for money and social considerations in procurement.[55]

4.3.2 Describing accessibility requirements to the market

In addition to the substantive rules on what may be included in regulated contracts, the directives contain rules on how a procuring entity should *describe* its requirements to the market.

Prior to 2004, the directives were rather inflexible on this. In particular, the previous directives required specifications to be drawn up by reference to European specifications (national standards implementing a European standard, European technical approvals or common technical specifications), whenever relevant, or, where the procurement was covered by the Government Procurement Agreement,[56] European standards implementing international standards. In practice, it was often difficult to identify all the relevant European specifications. Where these existed purchasers could use other specifications only in exceptional cases – for example, where necessary for reasons of incompatibility.[57]

As noted in chapter 4, the 2004 directive is more practical and flexible.[58] Article 23 allows purchasers to choose between two methods. First, the purchaser may refer to certain specifications defined in Annex VI, with preference for national standards implementing European standards. In such cases the purchaser must also indicate that it will accept any product, works or services 'equivalent' to those complying with the specified standard. Alternatively, the purchaser may draft the specifications by reference to performance or functional requirements. The one aspect where the new rules might appear less flexible than the old directives is that in the past reference to specific make or source or of a particular process was permitted where authorities were unable to give a description of the subject of the contract using specifications which were sufficiently precise and intelligible, where accompanied by the

---

[55] See chapter 1, section 5.   [56] See further chapter 4, section 16.
[57] See the discussion in Arrowsmith, note 34 above, at 17.20 *et seq.*
[58] See chapter 4, section 8.1.3 and for a full discussion Arrowsmith, note 34 above, at 17.55.

words 'or equivalent'.[59] The equivalent provision in Article 23(8) states that this is exceptional. This may make it problematic to refer to the kind of proprietary standards which have emerged, such as JAWS, even for explanatory purposes.

It must be emphasised that when defining specifications, realistic and achievable goals should be set. For example, little will be achieved by a generalised reference to complying with the authority's generally worded policy that purchasing must contribute to sustainability or equality. For a busy procurement officer including such a reference can seem like a quick way of nodding towards the organisation's policy. However, it can easily be ignored or passed over as too vague by a bidder. It is much better to specify, for example, that in a procurement of IT equipment the tender must identify which parts of the offering meet specified accessibility requirements.

4.3.3 Verification of compliance with accessibility requirements

It is also important to remember that the ECJ has ruled a contracting authority may not use an award criterion that it neither intends nor is able to verify.[60] This probably applies also to specifications, thus precluding a vague and generalised reference to general policy on equality.

EDF recommends putting in place in every case a procedure for verifying a tenderer's ability to deliver the accessibility requirements. Is this, however, appropriate?

This can be considered by reference to the example of IT procurement. A new library system for self-scanning of library books, for example, might include a requirement that at least 20 per cent of terminals can be used by people with sight or physical disabilities. What would a verification procedure involve? If the equipment already exists, the authority might require a sample to examine. On the other hand, if it is designed and built as part of the supply, the authority would assess the proposed solution on a technical but theoretical basis. It would be wise – in both cases, but particularly the second – to make payment dependent on demonstration and testing of the equipment. It would be unlikely in the second case, however, that it would be possible to test the proposed

---

[59] See, for example, Article 10(6) of Directive 93/37/EEC concerning the coordination of procedures for the award of public works contracts, OJ 1993 No. L199/54 (public works contracts).

[60] Case C–448/01, *EVN AG* v. *Austria* ('*EVN-Wienstrom*') [2003] ECR I–14527. Arrowsmith, note 34 above, at 7.116, takes the view that the *EVN-Wienstrom* judgment should not be interpreted to mean that there must be a full verification in each case.

equipment in any real sense before awarding the contract. In addition, if the accessibility requirements were not considered central to the contract, it would be likely that the tender evaluation would concentrate on other aspects of the specification and the accessibility requirements would be verified on delivery and testing, not prior to award; in practice, an authority is unlikely to verify every aspect of a contract in advance. A procurement professional will apply experience and judgment to assess what can be learnt from references and site visits and whether the specification makes technical sense and appears to have been properly costed. Singling out one aspect of procurement (accessibility) and requiring special verification in every case is not appropriate: it is not generally desirable to fetter the discretion and expertise of purchasing professionals through rigid rules of this kind. A better balance of costs and benefits is more likely to result if such decisions are made on an individual basis.

4.4. A balanced score sheet or pass/fail?

One of the uncertainties highlighted by Yukins in relation to Section 508 of the US Rehabilitation Act is how to take account of disability factors.[61] An authority needs to decide whether these should feature as part of a balanced score sheet aiming to secure value for money overall – that is as an award criterion, as discussed in section 4.5 below, or as a 'pass/fail' measure – that is as a mandatory part of the technical requirements (or as a special condition, as discussed in section 5.3 below).

A mandatory specification might require that all IT for a new library should be accessible for deaf, blind and/or physically disabled users. If the bidder cannot meet that requirement, its tender will be rejected. Alternatively, it might be required that a percentage of PCs must accommodate the needs of specified disabled users, but that credit will be given for extending this beyond the specified percentage (a mandatory specification combined with an award criterion) or merely that accessibility of the equipment will be one factor in judging the most advantageous tender (an award criterion only). An award criterion relating to accessibility might be used where the authority is prepared to commit a fixed budget for the IT refurbishment and wishes to select the bidder that can offer the best value for money or most accessibility (depending on its priorities, expressed through weighting the award criteria). As mentioned in

---

[61] Yukins, note 24 above, p. 670.

chapter 3, an award criterion can also provide a mechanism to balance the benefits of accessibility with the cost, and to identify any costs.[62] Any pass/fail mechanism for accessibility will need to be clear about what standards are to be used and what range and severity of disabilities are to be accommodated. It will also need to be far-sighted: the authority must be confident that the solutions that could be offered by bidders would not offer better value or overall accessibility. For example an offer might fail to feature some of the mandatory accessibility criteria but provide a better range of desirable features. If the authority wanted to pursue such a bid,[63] re-tendering would probably be required.[64] In general caution is required when defining a specification as mandatory.

Under the directive itself (subject to the discussion below on Article 23),[65] the choice of mechanism (balanced score sheet or pass/fail) is for the discretion of the authority, unless the Member State concerned makes accessibility requirements mandatory for certain procurements. For example, a requirement to make reasonable adjustments to the physical features of public buildings for disabled users is required by UK legislation under the DDA 1995.[66]

4.5. Award criteria

The new directive's rules on award criteria – that is, the criteria used to compare the merits of the different offers – are set out in Article 53, and were discussed, in particular, in chapter 4, section 13.

These rules allow award criteria concerning accessibility issues that relate to the subject matter of the contract. It was argued in chapter 4 (section 8) that anything that can be included as a *technical requirement* the authority will be able to include, instead or in addition, as an award criterion. Thus – to refer to an example given in section 4.4 above – an invitation to tender might require that a percentage of PCs must accommodate the needs of specified disabled users, but that credit will be given for extending this beyond the specified percentage. Whether it is desirable to deal with such issues through specifications, award criteria or both was considered in section 4.4 above.

---

[62] See chapter 3, section 4, especially 'viii. Award criteria'.
[63] Bids not complying with fundamental requirements cannot be accepted: Case C–243/89, *Commission* v. *Denmark* (*'Storebaelt'*) [1993] ECR I–3353.
[64] See Arrowsmith, note 34 above, at 7.157 *et seq.*
[65] See 5.2 below.   [66] See 5.2 below.

An authority may also wish to consider as a criterion the extent and manner in which persons with disabilities are to be employed on the contract work. As discussed in chapter 4, section 8, the jurisprudence is not entirely clear as to whether 'workforce' matters relating to those engaged *on the contract work itself* are permitted award criteria,[67] but the better view – as Arrowsmith argued in chapter 4 (in sections 8 and 13) – is that these are indeed permitted criteria.

To ensure the best balance between costs and benefits and the most efficient utilisation of persons with disabilities, as well as to allow an authority to assess the cost of including contract conditions on disability in the workforce, it may again be preferable to allow contractors to suggest their own conditions, or at least to choose whether to accept those suggested by the authority, and to consider this in applying the award criteria, rather than to impose set conditions as mandatory (especially as contractors may have better knowledge of the market).[68] Thus, for example, an authority could offer a price preference in the evaluation for each per cent of the contract workforce that is made up of persons with disabilities, or for each contractor employing above a specified proportion of disabled persons.

As chapter 4 explained (in section 13), criteria *not* connected with the subject matter of the contract cannot be used. Thus an authority may not take into account as award criteria how much of a supplier's equipment supplied to the market as a whole has 'accessibility' features, or contractors' general policies towards recruiting persons with disabilities.

Whilst, as we have seen, the directives' definition of technical specifications now makes explicit reference to the possibility of including accessibility requirements, Article 53 does not specifically mention accessibility as a possible *award criterion*. This has prompted EDF to suggest that in implementing the directives States should make specific reference to social criteria in their national legislation setting out the permitted award criteria: Belgium has already included social and ethical criteria in the corresponding article in its national procurement legislation, as have several regions. There is some wisdom in this approach: it makes it crystal clear to authorities that accessibility may be an award criterion and to remind them to consider including it. However, it is certainly not necessary in order for authorities to be permitted to use such criteria. The list of permitted criteria in Article 53(1)(a) is illustrative only[69] and thus, even though it does not

---

[67] See chapter 4, section 13.   [68] See chapter 3, section 4, especially 'viii. Award criteria'.
[69] Case C– 19/00, *SIAC Construction* v. *County Council of the County of Mayo* [2001] ECR I–7725.

mention accessibility criteria, these can be employed where connected with the subject matter of the contract.

4.6. Compliance with national legislation on disability issues

Recital 34 clarifies and reminds purchasers that national laws apply during the performance of a contract '*providing that such rules and their application comply with Community law*' (emphasis added). Obviously these will include any relevant rules on disability issues. Article 27 also clarifies that authorities may state in the contract documents[70] the bodies from whom information may be obtained about obligations relating to employment protection and working conditions in force in the place where the contract will be carried out. Where any such obligations are relevant, it is important in practice for non-discrimination that bidders are alerted to these and this also ensures that non-domestic firms cannot claim they were unaware of their obligations. Where these details are referenced, bidders must confirm that their bid takes account of the legislation and bidders not accepting these obligations can be rejected.[71] On the other hand, as chapter 4 discussed (sections 8.1.1 and 8.13), it is less clear whether a tender can be rejected because the authority believes the tenderer will not comply, when the tenderer indicates that it has considered and accepted the requirements.

The EDF suggests that: 'whenever legislation at national or regional level imposes obligations on accessibility (for the built environment, products, services, etc.) we recommend including a cross reference to that'. In addition, the EDF suggests that the cross reference belongs in procurement legislation. Arguably, however, the most effective place to make such a cross reference is in the contract documents, since this draws the matter directly to bidders' attention.

5. Innovative provisions in the Public Sector Directive

5.1. Introduction

It is now necessary to consider the new possibilities introduced or high-lighted by the Public Sector Directive. There are three main features in the directive which promote disability equality, namely the provisions on

---

[70] One of EDF's recommendations is that authorities should be *obliged* to reference the relevant legislation.

[71] See chapter 4, section 8.1.1.

technical specifications, the provisions on 'special conditions' and the provisions on reserved contracts. These are considered in turn.

5.2. Technical specifications

We have already seen that the definition of technical specifications now includes an explicit reference to the *possibility* for including in the specification reference to accessibility for disabled users. This was discussed in section 4.3.1, where it was suggested it does not change the legal position, but merely emphasises this possibility for Member States.

In addition, however, the directive also includes an apparently *mandatory* requirement to address accessibility issues in drafting specifications. In this respect Article 23 states that whenever possible these technical specifications should be defined so as to take into account accessibility criteria for people with disabilities or design for all users.

This provision was added at the request of the European Parliament. It was felt to be consistent with EU policy towards the disabled and politically would have been difficult to oppose. However, it is not quite clear what it means in legal terms.

Arrowsmith has previously pointed out the difficulties in construing these provisions.[72] A first issue is whether the EC has the legal competence to adopt these provisions at all and, if so, whether an adequate legal basis has been given for including them in the directives. Both questions are discussed in chapter 1 of this book. There Arrowsmith and Kunzlik consider (in section 5.3 of that chapter) that it is arguable that the answer to both questions is in the affirmative, but that this is by no means clear.

A second issue is whether, even if they are lawfully adopted, they are – as Arrowsmith has argued – merely an exhortation to act. The present author shares the view that this is indeed the case, for several reasons. The first is the wording 'wherever possible', combined with the nature of the decision to be made (balancing costs and social considerations). Secondly, regarding this as a mandatory obligation would make it difficult to give it any content without unduly fettering the authority's discretion in balancing costs and benefits. Thirdly, Recital 3 states that the provisions should comply as far as possible with current national procedures and practices. This clarifies that one should be cautious in using the directive as a spear to force an authority to go beyond domestic legislation. There is a clear contrast between the specific wording and

---

[72] Arrowsmith, note 34 above, at 17.75.

mechanisms of the US legislation in Section 508 of the Rehabilitation Act (see section 2.3 above) and the indirect and limited wording in Article 23.

It might alternatively be argued, however, that rather than creating a binding obligation to act in a particular way in particular circumstances, the provision merely creates a binding obligation to *give consideration* to accessibility issues, leaving broad discretion to the authority in balancing cost and accessibility: in other words, there is a legally binding obligation, but one that is violated only if it is shown that the authority has not even addressed its mind to the issue.

The author also rejects the view put forward by McCrudden in chapter 6 of this book that the general principle of equal treatment in procurement might extend to a *positive* obligation to use procurement to promote equal treatment in areas such as gender equality – which could also extend to the area of disability considered in this chapter. In particular, it can be pointed out that whilst Article 12 imposes a direct obligation prohibiting discrimination on grounds of nationality, Article 13 addresses other equalities by empowering the Council to take action. In this context, and taking into account again Recital 3 referred to above, if the procurement directives intend to impose a positive obligation in this field – one that is not related to their primary internal market objective – this would be expected to be done through more explicit provisions.

5.3. Contract compliance – the pursuit of social priorities through contract conditions

The second innovative feature of the directive is Article 26 expressly allowing authorities to lay down conditions relating to social considerations, as discussed in chapter 4, section 8.1.4. To recap, this states that authorities may lay down special conditions relating to the performance of a contract, provided that these are compatible with Community law and are indicated in the contract notice or specifications. The conditions governing the performance of the contract may include social and environmental considerations.

As explained in chapter 4, the flexibility offered by this provision probably is not new; it is intended to clarify the ruling in *Beentjes*, which accepted such conditions. However, it is important for establishing the possibility very clearly, and also, in the author's view, in confirming the Commission's previously stated view that such conditions must be confined to contract performance.

As chapter 4 explained, conditions can be used to impose a contractual obligation to comply with existing legal requirements, whether at EC level or those of domestic law, including by requiring that contractors observe disability legislation in contract performance. An authority may, in addition, however, wish to impose conditions that go beyond any pre-existing legal requirements. In the context of disability issues it might, for example, seek to include a requirement for the contractor to engage a certain number or percentage of disabled persons – beyond that required by law – on the contract work. In this respect, Recital 33 specifically mentions the possibility of including conditions requiring contractors to recruit more handicapped persons than are required under national legislation, indicating that the legislature specifically envisaged such conditions when including the new Article 26.

Another possibility might be a requirement that a percentage of contracts are executed by sheltered workshops as a subcontractor, without specifying which parts. This might lead to a better result than if the authority decided in the abstract that a particular contract requirement was or was not suitable for such treatment. From a practical point of view this approach leaves the decision about how best to deploy disabled labour to the person best able to decide – a contractor experienced in delivering the works, product or services – avoiding the risk that unsuitable aspects might be made the subject of a requirement or suitable ones overlooked. From a legal point of view, it might be useful for any special condition to deploy the approach to disability and sheltered workshops used in Article 19, unless some other internationally recognised definition emerges. As explained below, the criteria for such workshops referred to in the directive may end up creating de facto Europe-wide standards, such that requirements based on those criteria would be unlikely to involve unlawful discrimination on grounds of nationality.

There are some possible legal objections to requirements about the percentage of the contractor's workforce who must be disabled and deployed in performance of the contract, especially if this does not correspond to what can be done without disproportionate financial cost. As chapter 4 explained, contract conditions that are problematic to implement in practice may possibly infringe the Treaty's free movement principles as restrictions on trade, even if not discriminatory. As discussed in chapter 4, the Commission considers that conditions relating to the way in which supply contracts are executed are particularly problematic from this perspective, since they may require changes to the organisation, structure or policy of an undertaking.[73] However, it would seem inconsistent to allow Member States to reserve contracts solely for sheltered employment programmes, but not to allow them to require subcontracting to such programmes or direct employment of disabled persons, which is less restrictive than a total reservation; thus, as Arrowsmith argues in chapter 4, the correctness of the Commission's approach is debatable. As regards the possibility for specifying precisely how disabled persons should be engaged – for example, whether as subcontractors or employees – following the *Siemens* case,[74] it is questionable whether it is open to a contracting authority to specify how a contractor should organise its own workforce: as Arrowsmith has stated, 'it is not clear that a purchaser is actually permitted either to require subcontracting as such or to require that the contractor engage certain numbers of disabled persons. Rather, arguably, it is necessary under the directive and Treaty, reflecting the principle of proportionality, that the contractor should be permitted to decide how to organise the work on the contract, and that any contract condition concerning the employment of disabled persons must leave the option to the main contractor itself of how precisely to employ those persons – for example, whether as subcontractors or directly.'[75]

5.4. Reserved contracts

5.4.1. The context

A third innovative provision in the new directive is Article 19, which allows Member States to reserve contracts for sheltered employment facilities providing employment for persons with disabilities.

The UK's experience can illustrate the kind of concerns this provision seeks to address. In the UK, the ability of local government to pursue

---

[73] See European Commission, Interpretative Communication on the Community law applicable to public procurement and the possibilities for integrating social considerations into public procurement, COM (2001) 566 final, p. 17 discussed in chapter 4, section 4.3.1.

[74] Case C–314/01, *Siemens AG Österreich* v. *Hauptverband* [2004] ECR I–2549: see Arrowsmith, note 34 above, at 12.59 *et seq*. See also the Opinion in Case C–176/98, *Holst Italia SpA* v. *Comune di Cagliari* [1999] ECR I–8606, para. 18: 'the requirement for a specific legal structure in order for a contract to be awarded could therefore be perceived as an unjustified restriction on the right of economic operators to compete under the same conditions'. See also N. Hatzis, chapter 8 of this book, section 4.2, discussing the issue in relation to policy on small and medium-sized enterprises.

[75] S. Arrowsmith, 'Implementation of the New EC Procurement Directives and the *Alcatel* Ruling in England and Wales and Northern Ireland: A Review of the New Legislation and Guidance' (2006) 15 *PPLR* 86, 143.

social policies through procurement was sharply curtailed by the Local Government Act 1988 (see section 3 above) and central government itself also turned away from such policies from the 1980s (although more recently they have again come more to the fore).[76] However, even during this time central government continued to use procurement to combat religious and political discrimination in Northern Ireland[77] and, relevant to the current discussion, to support persons with disabilities and those in prisons, by placing contracts with workshops employing those groups through the Priority Suppliers Scheme.

The Priority Suppliers Scheme was operated by the Supported Employment Procurement and Consultancy Service (SEPAC) for what was formerly the Department of Employment. It allowed government departments, and in particular the Ministry of Defence, to give domestic prison workshops and workshops for the disabled an opportunity to match the best bid for supplies contracts. For contracts put out to tender this was done through the 'offer-back' process, whereby these workshops (which were invited to tender where possible) were offered part of the requirement if they were able to match the best tender received. For smaller contracts, these workshops were allocated the work provided that it could be done on 'commercial terms'. Prior to 1991 the UK had not yet met its obligations to implement the procurement directives through national legislation. However, the Treasury was conscious both that the limitation of the Priority Suppliers Scheme to UK workshops might be questionable under the EC Treaty, and that the 'offer-back' process might violate the relevant directive (which, as now, required supplies contracts to be awarded to the best tenderer and did not include a possibility for a supplier amending its tender to match other tenders).[78] Treasury officials therefore sought an informal understanding with SEPAC that departments should be advised that, for contracts above the threshold, the directive's procedures should take precedence. When the relevant directive, the Supplies Directive, was finally implemented in the Public Supply Contracts Regulations 1991,[79] the regulations did not make any provision for the scheme.

---

[76] See generally Arrowsmith, note 34 above, at 19.2–19.12.
[77] Fair Employment and Treatment (Northern Ireland) Order 1998 SI 1998/3162 and the general discussion in Arrowsmith, note 34 above, at 19.9.
[78] In accordance with the rules on award criteria discussed in chapter 4, section 14.
[79] SI 1991/2679.

In 1992 the Commission asked Member States if they had any preference schemes they would like to list in the Supplies Directive when it was consolidated in 1993.[80] This was shortly after the *Du Pont de Nemours* case in which the ECJ ruled that an Italian scheme giving preference to suppliers in deprived regions of a Member State contravened Article 30 EC and could not be justified under the EC Treaty provisions on state aid.[81] Listing in the Supplies Directive was conditional on any preference scheme being compatible with the Treaty. As the Treasury had doubts about the Priority Suppliers Scheme's compatibility with the EC Treaty it did not raise it – although arguably such a scheme is in fact justifiable under the Treaty, even in the form it took at that time, as Arrowsmith argues in chapter 4.[82]

Some time later, Remploy, a non-departmental public body which receives an annual government grant to provide a specialist recruitment service for people with a health condition or disability, found itself increasingly exposed to competition from Central and Eastern Europe, particularly on textile products such as uniforms and protective clothing. It looked to the Priority Suppliers Scheme for protection only to find it was not listed as an exception to the Supplies Directive. Remploy then raised this issue with Michael Portillo, then Secretary of State for Employment, asking how this had happened during his time as the responsible Minister at the Treasury. He expressed concern to the press that the Commission had intervened. This was apparently a surprise to the Commission who said the UK could have a preference scheme for disabled workshops, but only if operated on an EC-wide basis. This raised the prospect of having to give preferential treatment to workshops in other Member States, although the government perceived its concerns as being mainly with promoting employment opportunities for persons with disabilities in the UK. This illustrates a more general problem with horizontal policies in procurement that was discussed in chapter 4, namely how to reconcile, on the one hand, the EC's interest in opening contracts to trade with, on the other, the fact that many of the social policies implemented through procurement remain to an extent a legal and/or practical concern of Member States at national level.[83]

---

[80] Directive 93/36/EEC coordinating procedures for the award of public supply contracts, OJ 1993 No. L199/1.

[81] Case C–21/88, *Du Pont de Nemours Italiana SpA* v. *Unita Sanitaria Locale No. 2 Di Carrara* [1990] ECR 889.

[82] Chapter 4, section 4.3.1, 'Justifying contractual requirements that are hindrances to trade'.

[83] See chapter 4 at 4.3.1.

In the end Ministers decided to replace the Priority Suppliers Scheme by an EC-wide scheme, the Special Contracts Arrangement (SCA), but only for contracts below the threshold (and therefore less likely to be suitable for cross-border bidding). This was introduced by the Secretary of State for Employment in November 1994. In contrast with the previous scheme, it also did not apply to prison workshops. All suppliers registered under the arrangement were non-profit distributing companies that had at least 50 per cent of the workforce registered as severely disabled. Each company's disabled employees were to make a genuine contribution to the business and all disabled staff were paid a wage equivalent to that paid to those who were non-disabled.

5.4.2 Overview of the directive's new provisions

The Commission proposed the provision for reserved contracts in the Public Sector Directive at Belgium's request. Belgium seems to have taken a strong position on disability issues. The UK chose not to oppose what was essentially an enabling provision and indicated an intention to make it available to contracting authorities.

Article 19 of the Public Sector Directive is the main provision allowing reservations. Recital 28 gives the context:

> Employment and occupation are key elements in guaranteeing equal opportunities for all and contribute to integration in society. In this context, sheltered workshops and sheltered employment programmes contribute efficiently towards the integration or reintegration of people with disabilities in the labour market. However, such workshops might not be able to obtain contracts under normal conditions of competition. Consequently, it is appropriate to provide that Member States may reserve the right to participate in award procedures for public contracts to such workshops or reserve performance of contracts to the context of sheltered employment programmes.

Article 19 (supplemented by Annex VIIa) allows contracting authorities to reserve tenders for sheltered employment workplaces, thus giving authorities scope to support employment opportunities for disabled people through sheltered or supported employment. Sheltered workshops and/or sheltered employment programmes are those where most of the employees are disabled and cannot work under normal conditions. If a contracting authority decides to reserve a tender to sheltered workshops or sheltered employment programmes, it must specify this in the contract notice.

5.4.3. The discretion of Member States and procuring entities, and the example of the United Kingdom

As a first point, it can be noted that it is for Member States to decide how far to allow their authorities to use the provisions. Probably they may decline to allow authorities to use them at all or impose conditions on their use. This is in line with the general approach of the directives to social policies in procurement. As already noted above, these generally remain within the discretion of Member States – although several measures, including the new directive's provisions on accessibility in specifications, now provide limited exceptions to this approach.[84] However, it is, on the other hand, also probably open to Member States themselves to *require* contracting authorities to use the provisions.

In the UK, the consultation paper issued by the Office of Government Commerce (OGC) prior to implementing the 2004 directives stated that the government intended to implement the Article in full 'in line with the policy line agreed at the time of the negotiations on this Article in Brussels'.[85] It continued:

> This is a significant social issue. There is already a similar scheme operating in the UK for below the threshold contracts (Special Contracts Arrangements). However, by extending the scope to 'above the threshold' contracts, this provision could further benefit sheltered organisations. Having said this, it must be remembered that such organisations will only have a certain capability and capacity to meet the requirements of public sector contracts. It is therefore anticipated that realistically this provision will only affect a relatively small proportion of public sector contracts.[86]

As stated in the consultation paper, and in line with its general approach to 'permissive' provisions in the procurement directives, under the Public Contracts Regulations 2006,[87] which implement the directive, the UK has conferred upon authorities the full flexibility allowed by the directive for using the provisions but has not required them to do so. However, although there is no legal obligation to use the

---

[84] Chapter 1, section 5.

[85] OGC, Consultation Document: the approach to implementation of the new Public Sector Directive, May 2004 available at www.ogc.gov.uk/documents/PublicSector ConsultationDoc2004.pdf, p. 9.

[86] *Ibid.*

[87] SI 2006/5. Different regulations apply in Scotland: see Public Contracts (Scotland) Regulations, SSI 2006/1.

provisions, in its guidance on 'Supported Factories and Businesses',[88] the OGC has urged authorities to use them. The guidance provides that contracting authorities should aim to have at least one contract with a supported factory or supported business. This may be for a niche product or service not provided by existing major contracts. In addition, main contractors should be encouraged to use supported employment organisations as subcontractors on public sector (and other) contracts. The use of supported employment subcontractors helps private sector organisations to meet their Corporate Social Responsibility targets.[89] In addition to reserving contracts (and the SCA 'offer-back' procedure which continues), authorities should ensure that there are no barriers to the participation of supported factories and businesses in procurement exercises more generally, in competition with other suppliers and service providers.[90]

This more positive stance, perhaps a result of responses to the consultation paper, involves some changes of emphasis from the 2004 consultation, which emphasised the limited capacity and therefore small number of contracts which would be affected. The guidance also, however, reminds authorities that 'the Government's procurement policy is that all public procurement of goods and services is to be based on value for money'. This presumably has to be read as 'value for money within the social priorities and agendas also set by Government'.

The 2006 guidance may be taken as support for local authorities deciding that letting a reserve contract contributes to its obligation to secure best value.[91] However, the domestic legislation that gives local authorities their legal power to act, and which supports the duty of best value, has a narrow rather than a broad and supranational focus. There is thus some tension between the discretion under the EC regime and the domestic best-value legislation. For example, the 2001 Order in permitting regard to workforce considerations requires that these be directly relevant to service delivery. Equally, section 1 of the Local Government Act 2000, which confers on local authorities a general power to promote economic, social or environmental well-being, must be exercised for the benefit of the local authority area. Reserved contracts under the Public Sector Directive, however, have to be open to all bidders, not just

---

[88] OGC, Supported Factories & Businesses: OGC guidance on reserved contracts in the new Procurement Regulations, January 2006, available at www.ogc.gov.uk/documents/supported_factories_and_businesses.pdf.
[89] Ibid. p. 4.   [90] Ibid.   [91] Section 3 Local Government Act 1999.

local or national contractors: thus letting a reserved contract would contribute to an area's well-being not directly but in general terms through signalling a clear local commitment to disability equality. Exercise of the reserved contracts provisions therefore does not necessarily sit well with other legislation. However, using reserved contracts could form part of a local authority's Disability Equality Scheme (see section 3 above).

It is interesting to note that, whilst Article 19 encourages reserving contracts for the disabled sector, in principle under the directives and the Treaty if a Member State's social objectives can be achieved by different means that are less restrictive of trade that should be done. One route is to provide a subsidy. However, that might in itself amount to state aid, which may explain why the new directive includes a specific provision.[92]

5.4.4 Obligation to follow the normal tendering rules and to open reserved procurements to all Member States

A second issue is the procedural rules to be followed. As the response to the OGC consultation[93] emphasised, Article 19 does not dispense with the need for reserved contracts to be advertised in the *Official Journal* and awarded using the usual award procedures of the directive, which are open to participation by suppliers from all Member States. Thus a supported company from Belgium could compete for a contract in the UK or in Poland, for instance.

5.4.5 Eligible workshops and programmes

A third issue is the type of workshops and programmes eligible to benefit. Article 19 states simply:

---

[92] See Arrowsmith, note 34 above, at 19.35 on the question of whether preferences for workshops should in principle be achieved by less trade restrictive means. See also Interpretative Communication integrating social considerations into public procurement, note 73 above, p. 13 stating that use of quotas for reserved contracts would have been incompatible with the previous directives and the Agreement on Government Procurement. However a different view seems to be expressed at p. 18. The correct view may be that the GPA contemplates that signatories can 'reserve' contracts under Article XXIII.2 which allows an exception for certain measures relating to the products or services of handicapped persons. See also general discussion on social policies and state aid in Arrowsmith, note 34 above, at 19.38–39 and chapter 5 of this book.

[93] OGC, Response to Consultation: Draft Regulations implementing the new Public Sector and Utilities Procurement Directives, December 2005 available at www.ogc.gov.uk/documents/OGC_Response_2005.pdf.

> Member States may reserve the right to participate in public contract
> award procedures to sheltered workshops or provide for such contracts
> to be performed in the context of sheltered employment programmes
> *where most of the employees concerned are handicapped persons who, by*
> *reason of the nature or seriousness of their disabilities, cannot carry on*
> *occupation under normal conditions.* (emphasis added)

This general wording creates problems for authorities in trying to
decide which organisations are eligible. 'Most of' can probably be understood as 'more than 50 per cent'.[94] However there is no definition of
'handicapped persons'. At EC level the Framework Directive,[95] although
it deals with the concept of discrimination in Article 1, does not provide
any definition of disability. Whilst this does not matter in a directive
which seeks to galvanise Member States to take action, it means that
there is no EC-wide definition to refer to in the context of reserved
contracts. The potential for divergent views in defining the concept of
disability could be seen in the statement on the UK Disability Rights
Commission former website that, based on research, around one in five
people of working age are considered by the Government and by the
DRC to be 'disabled'.[96] It is likely, however, that a much narrower range
of persons is covered by the reserved contracts provisions.

In fact, however, a definition of disability based on the nature of the
disabilities suffered does not seem central under Article 19. What is
important is how this condition affects the person's ability to carry on
an occupation under normal conditions.

There is, however, also no definition of 'normal occupation conditions'. Arguably this is a factual question to be determined in the light of
social and economic conditions. A problem arises, though, in applying
this concept in Member States with divergent conditions. For example,
one Member State – say an EC State of long standing – may actively
encourage its more capable disabled persons to integrate within the
workforce, because this enables them to integrate better into society,
whilst another – perhaps a new Member State – does not. The normal
occupation conditions in the former Member State may provide much

---

[94] Case C–380/98, *R* v. *HM Treasury ex parte University of Cambridge* [2000] ECR I–
8035 where the words 'for the most part' in a different context in the procurement
directives (the definition of 'body governed by public law') were interpreted as meaning
'more than 50 per cent'.

[95] Directive 2000/78/EC establishing a general framework for equal treatment in employment and occupation, OJ 2000 No. L303/16.

[96] www.drc-gb.org/your_rights/are_you_being_discriminated_ag/definition_of_disability.aspx

more support for persons to carry on occupations than those of the latter. Workshops in states where favourable conditions exist may thus be staffed by less capable handicapped people than those in other states, and thus may find it harder to compete. On the other hand, the need for workshops to compete effectively may lead them to discourage more capable handicapped people from moving on, to improve their chances of winning public contracts. Correspondingly an authority may feel the need to make sure the playing field is level. It is not clear how for this is permissible. Has 'normal occupational conditions' an objective meaning or is it to be judged by reference to conditions in the bidder's own state?

In the UK, as may happen elsewhere, the government has drawn on domestic disability legislation in implementing the provisions. Thus Regulation 2(1) of the Public Contracts Regulations defines a disabled person as any person recognised as disabled within the meaning of the DDA 1995,[97] and also provides that disability has the same meaning as in that Act. Section 1(1) of the DDA 1995 provides that a person has a disability where he has a 'physical or mental impairment which has a substantial and long-term adverse effect on his ability to carry out normal day-to-day activities', and section 1(2) provides that a disabled person is a person who has a disability. However, as required by the directive, the reserved contract provisions are to apply only when the disability leads to inability to take up work in the open market (Regulation 17(1)). Like Article 19 of the Public Sector Directive, the regulation does not address the practical problems of comparisons across Member States.[98]

So far as the '50 per cent' condition is concerned, in Member States or individual programmes where this condition is not currently met, the directive may have the effect of encouraging reorganisation to meet the minimum 50 per cent condition, so that these programmes may take advantage of Article 19.

It is not clear whether individual Member States may reserve contracts solely for workshops with participation of disabled persons *above* this minimum of 50 per cent. To require contracts to be open to *all*

---

[97] It is also stated in these provisions that 'disabled persons' shall be interpreted accordingly.

[98] The term 'open labour market' has been used rather than 'occupation under normal conditions' and the word 'severity' of the disability rather than 'seriousness', but these changes of wording do not elaborate the definitions but merely rephrase them.

programmes meeting the 50 per cent condition creates greater scope for cross-border competition, since it is more likely that workshops from other Member States will meet the condition. Further, allowing Member States to impose more stringent requirements could provide an opportunity for Member States *deliberately* to restrict participation, effectively, to domestic workshops, contrary to the intention of the directive. On the other hand, there may be sound policy reasons for organising and supporting workshops staffed with a much higher proportion of disabled persons, and not to allow legislation to restrict participation to these workshops might render them unable to obtain contracts. It is submitted that such a policy should be recognised as lawful under both the Treaty and the directives if justified on its facts; the mere fact that the conditions are more difficult to comply with for workshops from other Member States does not per se rule out a policy under equal treatment principles.[99]

Overall, however, and regardless of the legal position on whether Member States may impose more stringent conditions than a 50 per cent requirement, it can certainly be expected that the provisions will have an effect of promoting a more harmonised approach to the organisation of programmes for disabled persons.

There is no requirement in Article 19 that the sheltered workshops and programmes be certified as such or that they must be run by the state or a non-profit organisation or that particular standards of care or employment conditions must be observed. Exploitation of vulnerable workers may be a possibility. On the other hand, it may be the practice in some Member States or programmes to provide enhanced working conditions for disabled workers, beyond those required by law. Continued willingness to do this may, however, be affected by competitive pressure from programmes in other countries. As chapter 4 explained, the free movement rules mean that it might not be permissible to require higher standards to be observed by bidders from other Member States than is required in those states by law.

It may be that the problems identified above prove theoretical rather than real. Authorities may develop mechanisms which prove robust in requiring bidders to demonstrate that they are indeed sheltered workshops and that the working conditions comply with local laws. Conditions in programmes in less affluent Member States may gradually improve and, in the meantime, disabled people in the less affluent states will have a greater

---

[99] Chapter 4, section 4.

chance of improving their life opportunities, enhancing progress towards the goal of social cohesion.

Alternatively, authorities may prefer for administrative convenience or other reasons to reserve only below-threshold contracts. This would be an obvious approach for UK authorities; this is how the Special Contracts Arrangement scheme operated prior to the introduction of the new reserved contracts provisions. As chapter 2 explained, however, recent ECJ jurisprudence indicates that obligations of transparency and, possibly, competition may possibly apply to below-threshold contracts, and, if so, these may affect the possibility for reserved contracts and 'offer-back' schemes in this area.[100] How the courts will deal with sheltered work programmes in this context remains to be seen.

Recital 28 also specifies that authorities may request companies who win a bid to perform their contract in the context of a sheltered employment contract. How this may be done depends on the extent to which it is permissible to require subcontracting, as discussed above.

6. Conclusion

This chapter has explained that the rules in place prior to the Public Sector Directive provided scope for pursing accessibility issues, particularly via the drafting of specifications and award criteria, and that good specifications and award criteria are the most useful way to push forward disability equality through procurement. The directive helpfully clarifies the freedom to pursue accessibility issues, and also prompts authorities to incorporate them into the process.

This chapter also argues that the new rules do not lay down mandatory requirements about the extent to which accessibility issues must be pursued or require accessibility to feature as a mandatory aspect of the specification. The chapter also draws on the US experience of pursuing disability equality through procurement to argue that, although (despite its shortcomings) Section 508 of the US Rehabilitation Act has prompted real progress in accessibility both in government and across society, experience suggests that legislators should be cautious about *requiring* disability issues to be pursued through procurement. Legislators need to be clear both about what they wish to achieve and the cost in terms of value for money and uncertainty. In particular, symbolic as opposed to

---

[100] Chapter 2, section 3.2.

precise legislation causes uncertainty. This is important in the EC context where procurement is already highly regulated.

Finally, this chapter has explained that the new provisions on reserved contracts, together with the possibility of requiring subcontracts to be executed by disabled people, provide new possibilities to extend employment opportunities for disabled people. There are, however, some uncertainties over what may be done and Member States may be deterred from using these provisions by the requirement for EC-wide competition. The newly clarified provision for prescribing special conditions, together with the re-enacted provision which allowed authorities to promote compliance with domestic law as to working conditions, may be useful, particularly in conjunction with the reservation of contracts and subcontracting of work for execution by disabled people. Again, however, there are uncertainties over what is permitted.

It now remains to be seen what use will be made in practice of the opportunities that have been introduced or highlighted in the 2004 procurement directives.

8

The legality of SME development policies under EC procurement law

NICHOLAS HATZIS

I. Introduction

The attainment of certain industrial objectives is one of the main 'horizontal policies' for which Member States have sought to use their purchasing power. In the past, public procurement was used to support domestic industry, in most cases through a 'buy national' strategy, protection of national enterprises from foreign competitors or the promotion of a 'national champion' in a particular sector of the economy.[1] More recently, the issue of the participation of small and medium-sized enterprises (SMEs) in the market for public contracts has received considerable attention. The concern expressed is that although SMEs are the backbone of the European economy they do not win public contracts in a percentage analogous to their share of the overall economic activity in the Community. This chapter examines the legality under EC law of various measures that can be used to increase participation of small and medium-sized economic actors in the procurement market. After a discussion, in section 2, of the reasons which may support a policy in favour of SMEs, section 3 focuses on the practice of reserving for them specific contracts by excluding larger firms. Then, section 4 addresses the question whether an awarding authority can request a main contractor to subcontract part of the work to SMEs, and section 5 focuses on the measures which can help adapt procurement processes to their specific needs.

---

[1] See generally S. Arrowsmith, 'Public Procurement as an Instrument of Policy and the Impact of Market Liberalisation' (1995) 111 *LQR* 235; J. Arnould, 'Secondary Policies in Public Procurement: The Innovations of the New Directives' (2004) 13 *PPLR* 187; S. Arrowsmith, *The Law of Public and Utilities Procurement*, 2nd edn (London: Sweet & Maxwell, 2005) at 19.3–19.5.

2. The role of SMEs

Two types of reasons are usually put forward to explain the need for increased participation of SMEs in the government contracts market.[2] The first relates to the advantages for the procuring entity and the overall public procurement process. Justifications of this type focus on SMEs' capacity for innovation as smaller firms can be more dynamic and inventive than larger, established economic actors[3] because their organisational simplicity and lack of bureaucratic structure allow them to be more flexible and respond more quickly to the needs of the market.[4] They also focus on the potential increase in the amount and quality of competition for public contracts as new SME players enter the market offering better products and services.[5] The second category of reasons, by contrast, emphasises the advantages for the small or medium-sized firms themselves of participating in the procurement market and the benefits that this can achieve for society in general. In essence, if SMEs are given increased access to the large, stable and rather lucrative procurement market they can increase their profitability, gain confidence and grow. This, in turn, means that economic activity at the local level is strengthened, which in turn leads to job creation. Ultimately this is thought to revitalise the local economy and to promote social and economic cohesion[6] which is not merely a political aspiration but a Community policy referred to as such in the EC Treaty.[7]

The concern of the Community institutions for small and medium-sized businesses can be traced back to the early stages of the development of the common market. In a number of documents,[8] the European

---

[2] G. O'Brien, 'Public Procurement and the Small or Medium-Sized Enterprise' (1993) 2 *PPLR* 82; A. Erridge, 'Involvement of SMEs in Public Procurement' (1998) 7 *PPLR* 37. For a discussion of the German experience with SMEs against the background of Community law, see M. Bürgi, 'Small and Medium-Sized Enterprises and Procurement Law – European Legal Framework and German Experiences' (2007) 16 *PPLR* 284, where a distinction is made between measures that aim at counteracting the structural difficulties the SMEs face ('SME-fair' measures) and those that introduce a direct preference for SMEs against other undertakings ('SME-favouring' measures).

[3] Erridge, note 2 above, p. 41.   [4] O'Brien, note 2 above, p. 83.   [5] *Ibid.*

[6] O'Brien, note 2 above, p. 83; Erridge, note 2 above, p. 41.

[7] Article 2 EC Treaty states that 'the Community shall have as its task ... to promote throughout the Community ... economic and social cohesion' while more detailed provisions can be found in Articles 158–162.

[8] See among others Council Resolution on the action programme for SMEs, OJ 1986 No. C287/1; European Commission, Draft Resolution of the Council concerning the

have stressed the importance of SMEs for
… le that they can play in strengthening the
… nd the need for Community-wide initia-
… development. In July 2000, the Council
… r Small Enterprises and in December
… rogramme on entrepreneurship and
… contribution of SMEs to the promo-
…, discusses the difficulties they face
… where measures can be taken; these
… f businesses in a knowledge-based,
… ification of the administrative and
… to Community support networks
… environment for SMEs through
… European Investment Fund. The idea that
und … Community's approach is that European enterprises, in
orde … remain competitive in a globalised economy based on knowledge, need to go beyond traditional business practices and structures and
concentrate on research and innovation, with small and medium-sized
economic actors being particularly well placed to do this.

In the context of public procurement, the Commission has explained
that the need to encourage participation of SMEs in the market should be
reconciled with the objective of the relevant Community legislation of
'ensuring so far as possible [that] all business, large and small should
have access to public contracts on an equal footing'[10] and that measures
aimed at improving the position of SMEs should not 'discriminate
against larger enterprises'.[11] The Commission, therefore, has rejected
policies which discriminate in favour of SMEs, such as set-asides or
regional preferences, concentrating instead on measures which facilitate

action Programme for SMEs, COM (86) 445 final; Council Decision 89/490/EEC on the
improvement of the business environment and the promotion of the development of
enterprises, and in particular small and medium-sized enterprises, in the Community,
OJ 1989 No. L239/33; European Commission, Communication on the implementation
of an integrated programme in favour of SMEs and the craft sector, COM (94) 207 final;
Council Resolution on the coordination of Community activities in favour of small and
medium-sized enterprises and the craft sector, OJ 1996 No. C130/1.
9 Council Decision 2000/819/EC on a multiannual programme for enterprise and entrepreneurship and in particular for small and medium-sized enterprises, OJ 2000
No. L333/84.
10 European Commission, Communication to the Council: Promoting SME Participation
in Public Procurement in the Community, COM (90) 166 final, p. 2.
11 *Ibid.*, p. 3.

their access to award procedures and reduce participation costs.[12] In the 1996 Green Paper on procurement the Commission identified as a key issue the need to determine 'how the correct application of public procurement law can be pursued while implementing other community policies, in particular with regard to policy on small and medium-sized enterprises'.[13] It further discussed a number of difficulties encountered by SMEs in the preparation of bids and at the contract award phase and suggested solutions which mainly relate to the availability of information, technical assistance and training.[14] The new directives, however, contain no specific provisions on SMEs.

3. Set-asides

3.1. Contracts above Community thresholds

Set-asides are the most drastic measure a contracting authority may adopt: certain contracts are reserved for SMEs and every non-small or medium-sized undertaking is excluded.[15] This practice creates a 'captive market'[16] for the benefit of a particular category of providers; in other words, the market is insulated from competition, so that the contracts are awarded to providers which would not have been able to win if the usual commercial criteria applied. It is clear that, in projects falling within the ambit of the directives, set-asides are unlawful. As explained in earlier chapters, with limited exceptions (for example, for set-asides for sheltered workshops and employment programmes) candidates may, generally, only be excluded from contracts under the Public Sector Directive[17] by reference to their suitability to perform the contract, and, in particular, by reference to their economic and financial standing

---

[12] *Ibid.*, p. 4. See also European Commission, Public Procurement: Regional and Social Aspects, COM (89) 400 final. The situation is different in the United States where the Federal Acquisition Regulations explicitly provide in Part 19 for total or partial set-asides for small businesses. When a contracting authority has designated a contract or a class of contracts as a set-aside all bids from non-small businesses are rejected. Undertakings which can benefit from this scheme include veteran-owned small business, service-disabled veteran owned small business, Historically Underutilised Business Zone (HUBZone) small business, small disadvantaged business and women-owned small business concerns.

[13] European Commission, Green Paper: Public Procurement in the European Union: Exploring the Way Forward ('Green Paper'), COM (96) 583 final.

[14] Discussed below under section 5.   [15] Arrowsmith, note 1 above, at 19.15.

[16] A term used by the European Commission: see Green Paper, note 13 above, p. 39.

[17] SMEs issues will rarely arise in the utilities sector.

and their professional and technical knowledge and ability.[18] Under these provisions the size of a tenderer may not be the basis for its exclusion, and, accordingly, set-asides for SMEs are not allowed.[19]

3.2. Equality under the Treaty

As has been explained in chapter 2, the procurement directives do not apply to contracts falling below specified thresholds, which may be particularly important for SMEs, nor to certain other arrangements, such as concessions. However, even for contracts outside the directives obligations apply under the Treaty, including an equal treatment principle.

Does the Treaty allow contracting authorities to adopt a policy of set-asides and reserve contracts for SMEs while excluding all other economic operators if these contracts are below Community thresholds? The answer to this question seems to depend on one's conception of the principle of equality under the Treaty and the obligations that flow from it. As explained in chapter 2, the Commission seems to favour the view that equality and non-discrimination under the Treaty have the same content with the requirement to treat providers equally contained in the directives.[20] Therefore, the Treaty is interpreted as imposing on contracting authorities obligations which are similar to those imposed by the directives. Article 2 of the Public Sector Directive and Article 10 of the Utilities Directive provide that 'contracting authorities shall treat economic operators equally and non-discriminatorily and shall act in a transparent way'. This is a general provision which applies across the board, directs contracting authorities to treat providers equally and prohibits discrimination whether it is based on nationality or any other

[18] Articles 47–52 of Directive 2004/18/EC of the European Parliament and of the Council on the coordination of procedures for the award of public works contracts, public supply contracts and public service contracts ('Public Sector Directive') OJ 2004 No. L134/114; Articles 51–54 of Directive 2004/17/EC of the European Parliament and of the Council coordinating the procurement procedures of entities operating in the water, energy, transport and postal services sectors ('Utilities Directive') OJ 2004 No. L134/1. See also chapter 2, section 4.3.6.

[19] The United Kingdom's Forum of Private Business has been recently lobbying the European Commission to opt out of WTO's Government Procurement Agreement in order to be able to introduce provisions making set-asides for SMEs lawful. See P. Snell, 'SMEs call for opt-out' *Supply Management*, 2 November 2006 (available online at www.supplymanagement.co.uk).

[20] European Commission, Public Procurement in the European Union, COM (98) 143, p. 8; European Commission, Interpretative Communication on Concessions under Community law, OJ 2000 No. C121/2, para 3.1.1.

ground.[21] This argument, as we saw in chapter 2, has now been endorsed by the ECJ in its decisions in *Parking Brixen*[22] and in *ANAV*.[23] If the equality and non-discrimination obligations deriving from the Treaty have similar content with the corresponding obligations in the procurement directives[24] then even contracts below Community thresholds may be subject to an onerous equality requirement which considerably restricts the discretion of contracting authorities and leaves no room for set-asides. An alternative view, favoured by (inter alia) Arrowsmith and Kunzlik in chapter 2, is that equal treatment in the procurement directives is different from equal treatment in the Treaty; the crux of the argument is that in the latter case equality is a requirement of Community law which operates through specific provisions that outlaw discrimination based on enumerated grounds, such as nationality. Thus, although the Treaty provisions on free movement of goods and services and freedom of establishment clearly prohibit both direct and indirect discrimination against providers or products from other Member States, it is wrong to adopt a broad interpretation of the principle of equality in relation to contracts below Community thresholds (or otherwise excluded from the scope of the directives) and read into the Treaty additional equality requirements which can only be derived from the procurement directives.[25] If this view is correct, then a policy of reserving contracts for SMEs could be lawful provided that it does not discriminate against SMEs from other Member States.[26]

In the present author's view, however, there is considerable merit in the Court of Justice's view in *Parking Brixen* and *ANAV* in favour of a robust understanding of equality, which goes beyond nationality discrimination. The conclusion in these cases is further reinforced by the fact

---

[21] Arrowsmith, *Law of Public and Utilities Procurement*, note 1 above, at 7.6–7.11.

[22] Case C–458/03, *Parking Brixen* v. *Gemeinde Brixen* ('*Parking Brixen*') [2005] ECR I–8612.

[23] Case C–410/04, *ANAV* v. *Comune di Bari* ('*ANAV*') [2006] ECR I–3303.

[24] As to which see chapter 4, section 6.

[25] See also P. Braun, 'Matter of Principle(s) – The Treatment of Contracts Falling Outside the Scope of the European Public Procurement Directives' (2000) 9 *PPLR* 39; Arrowsmith, *Law of Public and Utilities Procurement*, note 1 above, at 4.16.

[26] Erridge, note 2 above, p. 49 states: 'Set asides are legal under European legislation for contracts below European thresholds. However, this use must not discriminate against SMEs from other Member States ... if there was a change in policy by the Commission to allow certain contracts to be set aside for SMEs by including size of the company as criteria for excluding tenderers the directives could be amended without contradicting Treaty obligations i.e. non discrimination on the grounds of nationality.' This passage implies that he considers the prohibition of nationality discrimination as the only obligation imposed by the principle of equal treatment under the Treaty.

that equality has been accorded by the Court of Justice the status of a general principle of Community law.[27] Initially, references to non-discrimination appeared in the Treaty in relation to nationality and free movement, the treatment of men and women, agriculture and taxation.[28] Although the case law on equal treatment lacks consistency,[29] the Court has made clear that the principle is binding both on Community institutions and the Member States when acting within the scope of Community law and prohibits the treatment of comparable situations in a different manner or the treatment of different situations in the same manner unless this can be objectively justified.[30] If equality was relevant for issues covered by the Treaty only when a specific provision was engaged then there would have been no need for the Court to find recourse in a general principle of equality. It is because these provisions leave gaps in the protection of the various instances of the right to equal treatment that the Court developed the general principle of equality;[31] therefore, it seems inappropriate to limit its scope to discrimination based on nationality.[32]

The role of equality in the regulation of economic activities by Community law is also relevant for one's understanding of equal treatment in the Treaty and, accordingly, of the obligations it imposes on contracting authorities. This role was explained by Advocate General Tesauro in the following terms:

> the principle of equal treatment is fundamental not only because it is a cornerstone of contemporary legal systems but also for a more specific reason: Community legislation chiefly concerns economic situations and activities. If, in this field, different rules are laid down for similar situations, the result is not merely inequality before the law, but also, and inevitably, distortions of competition which are absolutely irreconcilable with the fundamental philosophy of the common market.[33]

---

[27] P. Craig and G. de Búrca, *EU Law Texts, Cases and Materials* (Oxford University Press, 2003), p. 387; T. Tridimas, *The General Principles of EU Law* (Oxford University Press, 2006), p. 60.

[28] The Treaty of Amsterdam added Article 13 concerning Community action to combat discrimination based on a number of grounds. See Craig and de Búrca, note 27 above, p. 388.

[29] C. Barnard, 'The Principle of Equality in the Community Context: *P, Grant, Kalanke* and *Marschall*: Four Uneasy Bedfellows?' (1998) 57 *CLJ* 352.

[30] For a recent statement of this principle by the Court's Grand Chamber, see Case C–313/04 *Franz Egenberger GmbH* v. *Bundesanstalt für Landwirtschaft und Ernährung* [2006] ECR I–6331, para. 33. See also Tridimas, note 27 above, p. 62.

[31] Tridimas, note 27 above, 62.   [32] McCrudden, chapter 6 of this book.

[33] Case C–63/89, *Assurances du Crédit* v. *Council and Commission* [1991] ECR I–1799, 1829, discussed by Tridimas, note 27 above, p. 75.

The dimension of equality emphasised here is that of participation and rationality:[34] economic actors have a right to participate in the economic life of the Community on an equal footing and Community institutions and Member States are prevented from treating them differentially when this is not justified by objective reasons. Advocate General Tesauro's reference to distortions of competition stemming from discriminatory treatment of economic players in the internal market should be read under the light of the general provisions on competition in the internal market. Article 3.1(g) of the Treaty states as one of the activities of the Community the creation of 'a system ensuring that competition in the internal market is not distorted' while Article 157 provides that the design of the Community's industrial policy shall be 'in accordance with a system of open and competitive markets'. When some economic actors are subjected to arbitrary discrimination in relation to a certain activity or are prevented from participating in the activity altogether they suffer harm as individuals and, at the same time, the competitive elements of the market are seriously undermined. In the procurement field, the very purpose of set-asides is to forestall competition. As we have seen, a policy of set-asides in favour of SMEs is adopted in order to hand over part of the procurement market to tenderers who would not have been able to win the contracts if the usual competitive terms applied by excluding all other tenderers. Of course, not every exclusion of potential providers constitutes discrimination. For instance, the exclusion of a candidate who lacks the necessary technical capacity or expertise does not violate his right to be treated equally since it is based on an objective ground related to his suitability to carry out the work.

In set-asides, however, the exclusion of certain actors is based on their size, a ground totally unrelated to the economic activity in which they wish to engage or to their capacity to do so. It seems, therefore, that if one adopts a more comprehensive approach to the principle of equality under the Treaty, which goes beyond nationality discrimination, set-asides for SMEs are unlawful even for below-threshold contracts and others outside the scope of the directives.

3.3. Discrimination and indistinctly applicable measures

Even if set-asides are not altogether prohibited by the Treaty, contracting authorities, when designing and administering a policy of reserved

---

[34] Tridimas, note 27 above, p. 60.

contracts for SMEs, must not discriminate against products or providers from other Member States. The most obvious conduct covered is direct discrimination,[35] but as was explained in chapter 2 the Treaty also prohibits certain indistinctly applicable measures which, although they apply to both foreign and domestic products and providers of services, tend, in practice, to prejudice the former. We also saw in chapter 2 that the Treaty covers certain procurement measures that are not even discriminatory in their effects, although how far this extends beyond measures relating to the characteristics of products bought is not entirely clear.

It has been convincingly argued by Arrowsmith and Kunzlik in chapter 2 that a cautious approach is necessary when assessing the potential discriminatory effect a procurement measure may have on foreign products or undertakings, and that it would be a mistake to treat features inherent in the nature of competitive markets as a sign of discrimination. For instance, a tender notice may contain a condition that the goods to be purchased must be delivered by the provider to the site of use; a foreign undertaking, which may have to bear additional transportation costs, will find itself in a less favourable position than a domestic undertaking and because of the added costs may be discouraged from tendering. This condition, though, should not be treated as indirectly discriminatory or as a prohibited hindrance to trade because any disadvantage suffered by the foreign provider is inherent in the concept of a competitive market. In other words, discrimination refers to distortions of competition and not practices related to its actual operation in a certain market.[36] It follows, then, that procurement measures which reflect ordinary commercial decisions can fall outside the ambit of the Treaty altogether, in which case there is no need to examine whether they can be justified under the criteria laid down by the Court.[37]

It is submitted that this approach, although appropriate for measures such as those described above, can never be applied to set-asides, even when they genuinely apply to both foreign and domestic products and providers, because their very aim is to restrict competition in the market for government contracts. Put differently, set-asides are exactly the opposite of ordinary commercial decisions within the framework of a competitive market, since contracts are reserved for undertakings which cannot win them in the course of ordinary business where commercial criteria apply.

---

[35] See the discussion in chapter 2, section 3.1.1.
[36] See chapter 2, section 3.1.1.   [37] *Ibid.*

Given the distortion of competition that set-asides entail and their potential effect on the procurement market, they should always fall within the
ambit of the Treaty.

Moreover, a set-aside can constitute an indirectly discriminatory measure. Small and medium-sized businesses may be less well-equipped and
lack the technical or financial capacity to engage in cross-border trade. A
policy which reserves certain contracts for SMEs in general (that is, irrespective of their nationality) can result in the exclusion of large, foreign firms
which are most likely to be able to pursue and perform a contract abroad,
whilst including those foreign providers (foreign SMEs) who are least able to
do so – benefiting mainly national firms in the form of national SMEs.

Of course, as chapter 2 explains, a measure that restricts trade may
survive the Court's scrutiny if it is covered by one of the derogations of
Article 30 or a mandatory requirement and is proportionate to the aim it
pursues.[38] It is very doubtful, however, whether set-asides can satisfy
either of these requirements. Firstly, Article 30 derogations constitute an
exhaustive list which does not include industrial policy, so it is necessary
to have recourse to mandatory requirements. It is unclear whether the
promotion of SMEs' participation in government contracts can in principle be considered a valid reason that can justify indistinctly applicable
measures such as set-asides in the field of public procurement. However,
the judgment in *Commission* v. *Italy*[39] seems to negate such a possibility.
The case concerned an Italian law which made it obligatory for the main
contractor to subcontract part of the work to undertakings whose registered office was in the region where the work would be carried out. One
of the arguments relied upon by the Italian government was that the
measure was intended to offset the disadvantages small and medium-
sized firms faced because of the way this law grouped together, under a
single contract, various works; if these were separated, the argument
continued, they would be of interest only to local undertakings, but the
grouping prevented them, in effect, from tendering. The Court rejected
this argument, stating that 'such considerations are matters neither of
public policy, public security or public health … nor reasons of overriding public interest which might justify the obstacles in question'.[40] If

---

[38] Craig and de Búrca, note above 27, p. 626; C. Barnard, *The Substantive Law of the EU*
(Oxford University Press, 2004), pp. 64 and 108.

[39] Case C–360/89, *Commission* v. *Italy* [1992] ECR–I 3401. The case is discussed in more
detail in section 3 below.

[40] *Ibid.*, para. 14.

the strengthening of the role of SMEs does not constitute a public policy objective which supports state interference with the freedom to provide services, then one may conclude that neither is it a valid mandatory requirement justifying restrictions on free movement of goods.

Arrowsmith suggests, in chapter 4 (section 3 of that chapter), that policies for the promotion of SMEs can be justified under the heading of mandatory requirements and that *Commission* v. *Italy* is to be explained as a case in which the measure concerned did not pass the proportionality test. However, in my view, if, in that case, the Court were actually preoccupied with proportionality it would have stated so explicitly. When it declares a national measure incompatible with Community law on proportionality grounds, the Court first confirms, expressly or indirectly, the legitimacy of the aim pursued and then, in assessing its proportionality, states that it goes beyond what is necessary for the achievement of this aim. This is a well-established mode of reasoning used by the Court to examine interferences with the exercise of the fundamental freedoms. In *Commission* v. *Italy*, though, it focused not on whether the national measure was the least restrictive but on the *aims* (i.e. offsetting the disadvantages for SMEs) put forward by Italy to justify it, and expressly stated they were covered neither by the derogations enumerated in the Treaty nor by overriding public interest reasons.

Secondly, measures caught by the Treaty can only be saved if they are proportionate to the aim pursued. Proportionality is a two-pronged test comprising suitability and necessity:[41] on the one hand means must relate to ends, in the sense that the measure in question must be capable of achieving the desired goal; on the other, the means used to achieve it must be the least restrictive. Proportionality has proved to be a powerful tool in the hands of the ECJ which has used it to scrutinise national measures that undermine the common market through a rigorous application of, mainly, the second part of the test.[42] Set-asides will satisfy the suitability prong, as they can clearly achieve the goal of increasing SMEs' participation in public procurement, but can hardly overcome the hurdle of necessity, since it can be reasonably argued that they are not

[41] T. Tridimas, 'Proportionality in Community Law: Searching for the Appropriate Standard of Scrutiny', in E. Ellis (ed.), *The Principle of Proportionality in the Laws of Europe* (Oxford: Hart Publishing, 1999) pp. 68–69; Barnard, note 38 above, p. 112.

[42] The relationship between proportionality and Member States' competence to adopt regulatory measures is discussed in G. Bermann, 'Proportionality and Subsidiarity', in C. Barnard and J. Scott (eds.), *The Law of the Single European Market: Unpacking the Premises* (Oxford: Hart Publishing, 2002).

indispensable parts of a policy to support SMEs, which can be realised through other, less onerous, measures.[43]

3.4. Affirmative action

Finally, it is worth examining whether set-asides can be saved as a form of positive discrimination in favour of SMEs,[44] on the basis that small and medium-sized businesses, while representing a very significant part of the economic activity in Europe, face structural difficulties in their effort to enter the procurement market that can only be uprooted by remedial measures in the form of positive action by the contracting authorities. This approach is problematic for two reasons. Firstly, there is no basis in primary or secondary Community law for reverse discrimination in the field of industrial policy. Article 2(8) of the Equal Treatment Directive[45] provides that 'Member States may maintain or adopt measures within the meaning of Article 141.4 of the Treaty with a view to ensuring full equality in practice between men and women.' Similarly, Article 141.4 states that 'with a view to ensuring full equality in practice between men and women in working life, the principle of equal treatment shall not prevent any member state from maintaining or adopting measures providing for specific advantages in order to make it easier for the underrepresented sex to pursue a vocational activity or to prevent or compensate for disadvantages in professional careers'. Both provisions refer to gender equality and there is nothing to suggest that they can be read expansively to imply that reverse discrimination is an acceptable Community policy even in relation to aims not explicitly mentioned in Community legislation. In fact, Article 141.4 makes clear that reverse discrimination is an exception to the principle of equal treatment,[46] and, accordingly, it should be interpreted narrowly.

Secondly, even in the field of equality between men and women the Court has found policies which give automatic priority to women to be contrary to the principle of equality. In *Kalanke*[47] it held that a Bremen

---

[43] Arrowsmith, *Law of Public and Utilities Procurement*, note 1 above, at 19.32.

[44] On positive discrimination in Community law, see generally Tridimas, note 27 above, p. 111 and Barnard, note 29 above, p. 366.

[45] Directive 2002/73/EC amending Council Directive 76/207/EEC on the implementation of the principle of equal treatment for men and women as regards access to employment, vocational training and promotion, and working, OJ 2002 No. L269/15.

[46] Tridimas, note 27 above, p. 114.

[47] Case C–450/93, *Eckhard Kalanke v. Freie Hansestadt Bremen* ('*Kalanke*') [1995] ECR I–3051.

law providing that when two equally qualified candidates applied for the same post in a sector where women were underrepresented the female candidate was to be preferred violated the Equal Treatment Directive. The judgment was criticised for adopting too narrow a view of equality,[48] and in *Marschall* v. *Land Nordrhein-Westfalen*[49] the ECJ backtracked from *Kalanke*, holding that a provision which again gave priority to women candidates was compatible with Community law because this time it included a proviso that the appointing authority would take into account any special reasons which could lead to the appointment of the male applicant. Subsequently, the Treaty of Amsterdam added article 141.4 on reverse discrimination. Yet, the Court has continued to scrutinise strictly national measures that lead to automatic appointments of members of certain favoured groups. In *Abrahamson and Anderson*[50] it dealt with a Swedish law providing that candidates from the underrepresented group would be preferred, even when their qualifications were inferior to those of other candidates, if their appointment could be objectively justified. The Court found the law to be disproportionate to the aim pursued because the selection was ultimately based on the fact that one of the candidates belonged to a particular group. Set-asides involve the same automatic preference for certain providers that was condemned by the Court of Justice in *Kalanke* and *Abrahamson and Anderson*. When a contracting authority reserves contracts for businesses that qualify as small and medium-sized it gives, in effect, unconditional priority to providers belonging to a particular category defined by the firms' size.[51]

4. Subcontracting

4.1. Rationale for SMEs' involvement

Subcontracting is the most important and realistic way of promoting SMEs' participation in public procurement. The contract is awarded to a

---

[48] S. Moore, 'Nothing Positive from the Court of Justice' (1996) 21 *ELRev* 156; S. Prechal, 'Case Note' (1996) 33 *CMLR* 1245.

[49] Case C–409/95, *Hellmut Marschall* v. *Land Nordrhein-Westfalen* [1997] ECR I–6363.

[50] Case C–407/98 *Katarina Abrahamsson and Leif Anderson* v. *Elisabet Fogelqvist* [2000] ECR I–5539 discussed by Tridimas, note 27 above, p. 117.

[51] Erridge, note 2 above, p. 48 suggests that 'government policy needs to go further and introduce some sort of positive discrimination to assist SMEs in public procurement as can be seen in the United States' without, however, discussing specific measures or the legality of positive discrimination policies under the Treaty and their relationship with the principle of equal treatment.

large firm which outsources part or parts of it to smaller providers or purchases from them goods or services. Although being a subcontractor is not as visible or lucrative as being the main provider, undertakings without the experience, resources or technical knowledge and capacity required for large and complex procurement projects can still benefit significantly from their participation in the procurement market through subcontracting. In a well-functioning market for subcontracting there seem to be benefits for all the players involved: contracting authorities can have the assurance which a large and experienced firm can offer without sacrificing the innovation potential associated with small and medium-sized businesses; large contractors can use the additional resources and expertise of subcontractors; and SMEs have access to stable business ventures and the opportunity to forge links with large firms.[52] In practice, subcontracting is very common in the procurement world and constitutes an important contribution of SMEs in this form of economic activity.[53]

Even before the completion of the single market the Community institutions had emphasised the importance of subcontracting for the development of a competitive entrepreneurial culture in Europe and the improvement of the position of SMEs. For instance, in a 1989 Resolution[54] the Council noted that the use of external sources was becoming a strategic choice for main contractors and that it was necessary to improve the availability of information regarding cross-border subcontracting opportunities; pointed out that the special case of public procurement had to be studied in depth; and called upon the Commission to 'pursue, in concert with the Member States, its general role of instigating, initiating and coordinating measures aimed at creating a propitious environment for subcontracting'.[55] The Commission, in turn, in its Communication 'Towards a European Market in Subcontracting'[56] explained that it is necessary to achieve an equilibrium between firms of different sizes and that there is a crucial link between subcontracting and SMEs, given the predominant role they play in this area, suggesting a number of measures, mainly in relation to the availability of

---

[52] *Ibid.*, p. 41.

[53] Writing in 1993, O'Brien, note 2 above, p. 86 states that when the direct and indirect participation of SMEs in all procurement sectors is added together it does not fall short of the SMEs' overall share of economic activity.

[54] Council Resolution on the development of subcontracting in the Community, OJ 1989 No. C254/1.

[55] *Ibid.*   [56] SEC (91) 1286 final.

information, in order to strengthen a European, cross-border market for subcontracting.

The recitals to the new directives state that 'in order to encourage the involvement of small and medium-sized undertakings in the public contracts procurement market, it is advisable to include provisions on subcontracting'[57] and Article 25 of the Public Sector Directive and Article 37 of the Utilities Directive provide that 'in the contract documents, the contracting entity may ask, or may be required by a Member State to ask the tenderer to indicate in his tender any share of the contract he intends to subcontract to third parties and any proposed subcontractors'.

4.2. Prohibited and compulsory subcontracting

Given the important benefits SMEs can enjoy from participating in the subcontracting sector, it is reasonable for contracting authorities to encourage subcontracting by providing information about relevant opportunities or facilitating cooperation between undertakings. However, the most obvious measure a contracting authority may take is to require the main contractor to outsource part of the work to a small or medium-sized business. The Court of Justice has not yet had the chance to deal with such a policy, but it is possible to examine its legality by drawing on the principles the Court applies in cases dealing with the permissibility of subcontracting.

Ballast Nedam Groep[58] concerned the question whether a public authority could exclude a firm from the procedure for awarding a public works contract because, being a holding company, it would not execute the work itself but through one of its subsidiaries. The Court noted that it was for the awarding authority 'to check the suitability of contractors in accordance with the criteria of economic and financial standing and of technical knowledge or ability'.[59] However, it continued, the sole purpose of these criteria was to provide for an objective assessment of the candidate's capacity to perform the contract and concluded that 'a person who will have the contract carried out through agencies or branches or will have recourse to technicians or outside technical divisions, or even a group of undertakings, whatever its legal form, may seek to be awarded public works contracts'.[60] The rule was extended by the

---

[57] Recital 43 of the Utilities Directive and Recital 32 of the Public Sector Directive.

[58] Case C–389/92, *Ballast Nedam Groep NV v. Belgian State* ('*Ballast Nedam Groep*') [1994] ECR I–1289.

[59] *Ibid.*, para. 16.   [60] *Ibid.*, para. 13.

Court in *Holst Italia*[61] which differed from *Ballast Nedam Groep* in two respects: the procedure related to a public service, and not a works contract and the tenderer in question was not a holding company that relied on a subsidiary which it controlled, but was itself a subsidiary seeking to rely on the resources of its parent company. In his Opinion, Advocate General Léger dismissed quickly the first distinction, stating that the subject matter of the contract was irrelevant to the question whether a candidate should be under an obligation to fulfil the technical and financial conditions himself or not. With regard to the second point, he noted that the objective of the Community procurement rules 'dictates an interpretation favourable to *the general access of undertakings to public contracts,* provided that their selection is made on the basis of proof of the competence actually available to the undertaking and on the solidity of the guarantees which they offer' (emphasis added).[62] In *Ballast Nedam Groep,* he continued, the Court took no account of the power the holding company had over its subsidiary, but, on the contrary, emphasised that what really mattered was the availability of review procedures to ensure that the external resources were indeed available, and not the legal organisation of the candidate. Following his Opinion, the Court held that 'a party cannot be eliminated from a procedure for the award of a public service contract solely on the ground that that party proposes, in order to carry out the contract, to use resources which are not its own but belong to one or more other entities'.[63]

The issue of direct prohibition of subcontracting came before the Court in *Siemens.*[64] The case concerned the procedure for an electronic data processing system where the invitation to tender and the tender documents contained a clause that only 30 per cent of the services could be subcontracted provided that the fundamental parts of the service would be performed by the tenderer, and the Court was asked to clarify the scope of the *Holst Italia* judgment in relation to restrictions on subcontracting. Advocate General Geelhoed explained that there was a distinction to be made between prohibitions at the phase where the suitability of tenderers was to be assessed and those related to the performance of the contract after it had been awarded. In the first case,

---

[61] Case C–176/98, *Holst Italia SpA v. Comune di Cagliari ('Holst Italia')* [1999] ECR I–8607.

[62] *Ibid.,* para. 44 of the Opinion of the Advocate General.

[63] *Ibid.,* para. 26 of the judgment.

[64] Case C–314/01, *Siemens v. Hauptverband der österreichischen Sozialversicherungsträger ('Siemens')* [2004] ECR I–2549.

the effect of *Holst Italia* was to prevent contracting authorities from excluding tenderers merely because they do not have themselves the capacity to carry out the contract and intend to use subcontractors. On the other hand, restrictions on subcontracting for the performance of the contract after an award has been made can be legitimate, because here the contracting authority has not had the chance to assess the reliability of the proposed subcontractors when examining the bids; thus, by imposing restrictions on subcontracting it does not exclude candidates because they rely on the resources of other entities, but is rather trying to ascertain whether these entities can be relied upon to perform the contract. The Court endorsed the Advocate General's reasoning and concluded that the case fell under the second category of restrictions on subcontracting.

There are two important points which consistently come up in the above cases. Firstly, the Court is at pains to make clear that contracting authorities are entitled to examine whether the main contractor actually has at his disposal the resources and expertise of the firms he intends to use as subcontractors and to review their credentials in order to make certain that the contract will be performed, the onus of proving the availability of these additional resources resting with the tenderer.[65] Secondly, the intention to outsource part of the job to another entity is not sufficient to exclude a candidate from the procurement procedure. The interplay between these rules became evident in *Siemens*, and especially in the Court's distinction between restrictions on subcontracting at the award phase and those concerning the performance of the contract after the award has been made: the former are unacceptable because they relate to the *way* a bidder proposes to carry out the contract; the latter are legitimate since they refer to the bidder's *ability* to perform satisfactorily. The underlying principle is that a contracting authority cannot restrict the form in which the service is provided by reference to criteria which are irrelevant to the tenderer's capabilities.[66] Consequently, a prohibition of subcontracting which does not relate to the reliability of the firms involved is unlawful. Similarly, compulsory subcontracting should also be unlawful.

The closest the Court has come to examining compulsory subcontracting was in *Commission* v. *Italy*,[67] a case which lends further support

---

[65] Case C–176/98, *Holst Italia*, note 61 above, para. 29.
[66] Arrowsmith, *Law of Public and Utilities Procurement*, note 1 above, at 12.59.
[67] Case C–360/89, *Commission* v. *Italy*, note 39 above.

to the above conclusion, despite the fact that it contains no definitive statement of the law. The Commission brought infringement proceedings against Italy in relation to a law which provided that in some works contracts the successful tenderer had to subcontract part of the work to local firms with a registered office in the region where the work was to be executed. Advocate General Lenz stated that there were two possible categories of victims of this provision, i.e. foreign undertakings which could be used as subcontractors and main contractors who are able and wish to carry out the work themselves without relying on subcontractors. Given that the former group was clearly discriminated against, he refrained from examining the situation of the latter, an approach also followed by the Court. There is no doubt, however, that the second situation also constitutes a violation of the Treaty, if the actual effect of the provision is to favour national main contractors by allowing only them to carry out the work without the use of subcontractors.[68] It is less clear whether the same can be said if the rule in question operated in a genuinely non-discriminatory manner and applied equally, in law and in fact, to both foreign and domestic tenderers, imposing on all of them the obligation to outsource part of the work regardless of whether this is commercially justified. The better view is that such a rule is also unlawful because it affects the way the service is provided and constitutes an unjustifiable restriction of competition.[69] Support for this conclusion can be found in Advocate General Lenz's rejection of the Italian government's argument that subcontracting was, in any case, beneficial for tenderers from other Member States as it was easier for them to entrust part of the work to local firms. He stated that 'it is difficult to see why … it should always necessarily make better economic sense to instruct an undertaking established in the relevant region',[70] which implies, firstly, that economic justifiability is relevant for the assessment of the legality of a rule requiring subcontracting and, secondly, that economic justifiability cannot be determined in the abstract but only by reference to specific contracts.

Ballast Nedam, Holst Italia, Siemens and *Commission v. Italy* all concerned disputes about the interpretation and application of the procurement

---

[68] S. Arrowsmith, 'European Communities: The Legality of Secondary Procurement Policies under the Treaty of Rome and the Works Directive' (1992) 1 *PPLR* 408, 412.

[69] Arrowsmith, *Law of Public and Utilities Procurement*, note 1 above, at 12.60.

[70] Case C–360/89, *Commission* v. *Italy*, note 39 above. Opinion of the Advocate General, para. 16.

directives, and it is not clear whether they would have been decided in the same way had the relevant contracts been below thresholds and, thus, covered by the Treaty. Yet, the principles they establish seem relevant for public procurement in general. The pernicious effect of prohibited or compulsory subcontracting is that it affects how the contract is to be performed in a way that is irrelevant to the tenderer's capability and seriously undermines competition in the public procurement market. This is what led Advocate General Léger to argue in *Holst Italia* against restrictions on subcontracting and in favour of 'general access of undertakings to public contracts' and there is no reason to assume that general access is desirable only for contracts above thresholds but not for those governed by the Treaty. Similarly, the reference of Advocate General Lenz in *Commission* v. *Italy* to whether subcontracting is a sensible business choice lends support to the view that compulsory subcontracting is incompatible with the Treaty. The underlying idea is that in a well-functioning, competitive procurement market it is for the undertakings themselves, and not the contracting authority, to decide whether subcontracting is economically sensible. If economic justifiability is a relevant consideration when assessing the legality of compulsory subcontracting this should be true of both directive-governed and Treaty-governed procurement, as it is hard to see why undertakings bidding for contracts above thresholds should be allowed to subcontract when they think it is economically sensible to do so, but those bidding for contracts falling within the scope of the Treaty should be compelled to subcontract. Moreover, in *Commission* v. *Italy* the Court found that the Italian law on subcontracting violated not only Directive 71/305 but also (the old) Article 59 of the Treaty, which suggests that the principles underlying the Treaty and the directives are not dissimilar.

The combined effect of the Court's case law on subcontracting seems to be that the awarding authority cannot restrict the form in which the service is to be provided. One aspect of this rule is that a contracting authority cannot require the main contractor to outsource part of the work as this constitutes an interference with competition in the procurement market; it is, instead, for each candidate to decide whether the use of subcontractors makes economic sense in relation to a particular contract.

Finally, in cases where the Community legislature has wished to make compulsory subcontracting an option it has done so explicitly. Thus, Article 60 of the new Public Sector Directive provides that the contracting authority may require works concessionaires to subcontract up to

30 per cent of the work for which the concession contract is to be awarded. If it intended to give awarding authorities a general discretion to require subcontracting in procurement, or to do so in favour of SMEs, it could have adopted an express provision. The fact that it did not supports the position that compulsory subcontracting is prohibited, unless expressly authorised.

5. The design of the procurement process

5.1. Identifying design defects

In 2004 a long and very detailed report on 'The access of SMEs to public procurement contracts',[71] which had been commissioned a year earlier by the European Commission, was published. In what is probably the first ever in-depth, comprehensive study of the role of SMEs in the procurement market, the authors discuss, among other issues, the structure of the market and the way it affects small and medium-sized undertakings, as well as SMEs' views on the factors that hinder their access to government contracts and the measures which can render public procurement more SME-friendly.

The participating undertakings[72] identified 'design problems'[73] as the main obstacle they face in their effort to bid for public contracts. There are four issues raised by more than 10 per cent of the participants: inadequate information in the invitation to tender, excessive administrative burdens, unclear wording in the invitation to tender and short time span to draw up a tender. Additional points of concern were the high financial requirements and qualification levels, the required certification, the insufficient possibilities to ask questions about the proposal and the large size of the projects.[74] In essence, these complaints boil down to two main problems. Firstly, the quantity and quality of information about procurement projects is often not adequate. A potential provider needs not only to know about the contracts put out to tender

[71] European Commission, The access of SMEs to public procurement contracts, Final Report ('Report on Access') available online at http://ec.europa.eu/enterprise/entrepreneurship/craft/craft-studies/documents/public-procurement-finalreport.pdf.
[72] The study is based on information provided by small and medium-sized enterprises that had tendered for and won a public contract, so the views of unsuccessful undertakings or those which did not tender at all are not represented. However, it is reasonable to assume that at least some of the problems they face, and which prevented them from winning the contract or deterred them from tendering altogether, are similar.
[73] Report on Access, note 71 above, p. 118.   [74] Ibid., p. 94.

but also to be able to assess after reading the tender notice whether it makes sense for the firm to draw up a bid or not. It is worth noting that 80 per cent of the participants stated that getting public contracts was not accidental but part of their strategy,[75] which makes the need for a continuing flow of information even more pressing, as without enough information it is impossible to have an effective and realistic business plan. Secondly, procurement processes are very often too complicated for SMEs. Larger undertakings are usually better placed in relation to the preparation of bids requiring the submission of complex documentation in a short time than small or medium-sized firms which may lack the expertise or resources to do so.

A further issue which can make a significant difference for SMEs is the size of the contract. Packaging various works under a single contract may be justified by reasons of efficiency, such as minimising the administrative costs of the contracting authorities, or may be a requirement of Community procurement law. A large contract, though, may deter small and medium-sized undertakings from tendering. Moreover, smaller firms, even when they decide to tender, will often lack the technical capacity and knowledge or the financial standing necessary to win a large, complex project. In fact, the contracting authorities that participated in the study identified as their main concern in their dealings with SMEs whether they have the means to deliver the required services or products.[76]

5.2. SME-friendly procurement

Before considering the measures which can help tackle the problems described above it must be pointed out that the correct application of the Community rules on public procurement can have a particularly beneficial effect for small and medium-sized firms, as their chances of winning a contract are far better when the procurement market functions in an open, transparent and non-discriminatory way. By contrast, however it is a common practice for contracting authorities to use the negotiated procedure even when this is not justified under Community law.[77] As the Commission has correctly pointed out, the first victims of this phenomenon are SMEs trying to penetrate the market for public contracts.[78]

---

[75] *Ibid.*, p. 90.   [76] *Ibid.*, p. 124.
[77] European Commission, Green Paper, note 13 above, p. 10.
[78] European Commission. Promoting SME Participation in Public Procurement in the Community, COM (90) 166 final, p. 5.

Indeed, the negotiated procedure constitutes a derogation from the principle that the procurement market should be open and function transparently and, by its very nature, restricts competition; its excessive use is not only a serious barrier to entry into the market but also perpetuates the view that it is safer for a contracting authority to deal with established, known firms instead of giving a chance to smaller economic actors.

When it comes to specific measures in favour of SMEs the provision of adequate information seems to play a fundamental role. SMEs themselves have identified prior information notices and pre-selection procedures as elements which can improve the flow of information and widen their access to government contracts.[79] They have also suggested that external help and training for smaller economic actors is necessary to help them overcome their difficulties with the administrative side of preparing bids.[80] A relevant issue raised by many SME participants was the need for better and more frequent use of electronic communication which may include central announcement of invitations to tender on the internet, sending offers and requesting additional information by email and setting up a search engine in order to retrieve the relevant information.[81] Contracting authorities have acknowledged these concerns with 57 per cent of them stating that they take measures to improve the accessibility of smaller firms to the procurement market;[82] their efforts focus mainly on giving more and better information (25 per cent), simplifying procurement rules (16 per cent) and reducing administrative requirements (13 per cent).

The great majority of contracting authorities (85 per cent) also consider the possibility of breaking up projects into smaller lots.[83] However, this method is not as frequently applied as this percentage would suggest, the reasons being the legal complications involved in the division of work, the high coordination costs and the need to have one overall solution.[84] This is an understandable approach as the division of large contracts into lots may indeed increase the administrative costs of the contracting authorities and must be done in a way that respects the aggregation rules of EC procurement law.[85] However, the latter leaves

---

[79] Report on Access, note 71 above, p. 151.

[80] *Ibid.* See also the discussion on information, technical assistance and training for SMEs in O'Brien, note 2 above, p. 87.

[81] Report on Access, note 71 above, p. 95.   [82] *Ibid.*, p. 124.

[83] *Ibid.*, p. 120.   [84] *Ibid.*, p. 121.

[85] As to which see Arrowsmith, *Law of Public and Utilities Procurement*, note 1 above, at 6.148–6.150.

some room for procurement through several smaller contracts,[86] while the additional costs related to the administration of the various lots may be outweighed by the beneficial impact the greater participation of SMEs can have on the procurement market, the increased competition and the improvement in value for money through the bids of smaller undertakings.[87]

The division of contracts into lots will be legal only if both SMEs and large firms are allowed to tender for the whole contract or parts of it, and the award is made to the best overall bid. This policy makes it easier for smaller undertakings to participate in the procurement market, as they can bid for only parts of a large project, without undermining competition since the award is to the best overall offer (i.e. taking into account the flexibility and innovation benefits SMEs may be able to offer) regardless of the size of the firm that made it.[88] Otherwise the division of contracts will constitute an artificial interference with competition which cannot be justified.

6. Conclusion

Public procurement is an area where political visibility is high, so it may be tempting for public authorities to exaggerate the lack of participation of small and medium-sized firms and adopt measures which compromise value for money in order to discriminate in their favour. This is a tendency which should be resisted. Thus, the rejection of set-asides and preference schemes for projects falling within the procurement directives is a sensible choice; a comprehensive conception of the right to equal treatment under the Treaty leads to the conclusion that the same approach is also appropriate for contracts which are not governed by the directives, but which are subject, nevertheless, to the general principles of Community law. On the other hand, measures which facilitate the participation of smaller firms in the procurement market as subcontractors are lawful, but these cannot go as far as making subcontracting compulsory. The division of large contracts into smaller lots is another lawful option, provided that it complies with the aggregation rules and does not lead to excessive administrative costs. In any case, the focus

---

[86] *Ibid.*, at 6.157–6.159.   [87] *Ibid.*, at 19.25.

[88] On these types of measures see also the discussion in chapter 3 of this book, section 4, 'iv. Packaging and timing of orders'.

of the initiatives to improve access of SMEs in the market for public contracts should be on the barriers which prevent undertakings that have the required capacity from winning contracts or tendering altogether. This is a field where contracting authorities can play an important role by making procurement processes more straightforward and transparent, providing adequate information and offering training and assistance in the preparation of bids.

9

The procurement of 'green' energy

PETER KUNZLIK

1. Community energy policy

The context in which energy procurement takes place is complex, implicating at least three areas of European policy: energy, environmental and public procurement. Furthermore, energy policy is a field which deals with issues now recognised as being amongst the most urgent facing the Community but which has until now found no 'bespoke' legal basis within the Treaty.[1] Energy policy measures must, therefore, be based on other Treaty provisions, notably those relating, on the one hand, to the internal market and, on the other, to environmental protection.

Until the coming into force of the Treaty of Lisbon one cannot, therefore, simply look to the EC Treaty to ascertain the objectives of Community energy policy. Instead one must examine a number of instruments which have mapped out the energy challenges which face Europe and the Community's emerging response. These suggest that European energy policy has, in particular, three key objectives.[2] These

---

[1] The Treaty of Lisbon (The Treaty of Lisbon amending the Treaty on European Union and the Treaty establishing the European Community, signed at Lisbon 13 December 2007, OJ 2007 No. C306/1) will, if/when it enters into force for the first time establish a specific treaty basis for energy policy. It will insert a new Article 176A EC stating that: 'in the context of the establishment and functioning of the internal market and with regard for the need to preserve and improve the environment, Union policy on energy shall aim, in a spirit of solidarity between Member States, to: (a) ensure the functioning of the energy market; (b) ensure security of energy supply in the Union; (c) promote energy efficiency and energy saving and the development of new and renewable forms of energy; and (d) promote the interconnection of energy networks'. See however L. Hancher, 'The New European Community Constitution and the European Energy Market' (2004) 11 *IELTL* 222 on this issue.

[2] These are in turn, of course, included in the 'aims' of energy policy proposed by the Lisbon Treaty: see proposed Article 176A of the Treaty of Lisbon, note 1 above. Similarly, had the abortive European Constitution been adopted, Article III – 256 would have provided that the 'aim' of European energy policy would be to '(a) ensure the functioning of the energy market; (b) ensure security of energy supply to the Union, and (c) promote energy efficiency and saving

are: (i) the maintenance of security of supply;[3] (ii) maintenance and improvement of European competitiveness through further development of the internal energy market;[4] and, (iii) last but absolutely not

and the development of renewable forms of energy'. See L. Hancher, note 1 above, p. 222 and G. Rashbrooke, 'Clarification or Complication? The New Energy Title in the Draft Constitution' (2004) 22 *JENRL* 373. In the absence to date of a treaty basis for energy policy, the Community has sought to elucidate a comprehensive energy policy through other means. Part Two of the Presidency Conclusions of the Brussels European Council of 23/24 March 2006, Doc. No. 7775/06 identifies the same 'three main objectives' of an energy policy for Europe, namely improving security of supply, ensuring competitiveness and protecting environmental sustainability and the proposed policy is set out in European Commission, An Energy Policy for Europe, COM (2007) 1 final, pp. 3–5 which describes the three objectives as being 'sustainability', 'security of supply' and 'competitiveness'. See also European Commission, Green Paper – European Strategy for Sustainable, Competitive and Secure Energy, COM (2006) 105 final.

[3] See European Commission, Energy Policy for Europe, note 2 above, p. 3, which states that 'Europe is becoming increasingly dependent on imported hydrocarbons. With "business as usual" the EU's energy import dependence will jump from 50% of total EU energy consumption today to 65% in 2030. Reliance on imports of gas is expected to increase from 57% to 84% by 2030, of oil by 82% to 93%.' See also European Commission, Green Paper – Towards a European Strategy for the Security of Energy Supply, COM (2000) 769 final. Community measures related to energy security include: Directive 2004/67/EC concerning measures to safeguard security of natural gas supply, OJ 2004 No. L127/92; Council Regulation 2964/95 introducing registration for crude oil imports and deliveries in the Community, OJ 1995 No. L310/5; Directive 2006/67/EC imposing an obligation on Member States to maintain minimum stocks of crude oil and/or petroleum products, OJ 2006 No. L217/8 and Directive 73/238/EC on measures to mitigate the effects of difficulties in the supply of crude oil and petroleum products, OJ 1973 No. L228/1, implemented by Council Decision 77/706 on the setting of a Community target for a reduction in the consumption of primary sources of energy in the event of difficulties in the supply of crude oil and petroleum products, OJ 1977 No. L292/9 and Commission Decision 79/639 laying down detailed rules for the implementation of Council Decision 77/706/EEC, OJ 1977 No. L183/1. On the question of energy security globally, see B. Barton, C. Redgewell, A. Ronne and D. Zillman (eds.), *Energy Security: Managing Risk in a Dynamic Legal and Regulatory Environment* (Oxford University Press, 2004).

[4] See the European Commission, Annual Report on the Implementation of the Gas and Electricity Internal Market, COM (2004) 863 final; European Commission, Communication from the Commission to the Council and European Parliament, Completing the internal energy market, COM (2001) 125 final; European Commission, Second Report from the Commission to the Council and the European Parliament on the state of liberalisation of the energy markets, COM (1999) 198 final. The Community has adopted several legislative measures in this regard. Thus Decision No. 1364/2006 of the European Parliament and of the Council laying down guidelines for trans-European energy networks and repealing Decision 96/391/EC, OJ 2006 No. L262/1 and Decision No 1229/2003/EC of the European Parliament and of the Council laying down a series of guidelines for trans-European energy networks and repealing Decision No. 1254/96/EC, OJ 2003 L176/11. As regards electricity see, in particular, European Commission, Proposal for a Directive of the European Parliament and of the Council concerning measures to safeguard security of electricity supply and infrastructure investment, COM (2003) 740 final; Directive 2003/54/EC of the European Parliament and of the Council

least, contributing to environmentally sustainable development and, in particular, reducing emissions of greenhouse gases so as to combat climate change.[5] The radical changes that will have to take place within the European economy if these objectives are to be achieved should not

concerning common rules for the internal market in electricity and repealing Directive 96/92/EC – Statements made with regard to decommissioning and waste management activities, OJ 2003 No. L176/37; Regulation 1228/2003 of the European Parliament and of the Council of 26 June 2003 on conditions for access to the network for cross-border exchanges in electricity, OJ 2003 No. L176/1. See also European Commission, Report on the experience gained in the application of the Regulation No. 1228/2003 on Cross-Border Exchanges in Electricity, COM (2007) 250 final. So far as natural gas is concerned, see Directive 2003/55/EC of the European Parliament and of the Council concerning common rules for the internal market in natural gas and repealing Directive 98/30/EC, OJ 2003 No. L176/57; Regulation 1775/2005 of the European Parliament and of the Council on conditions for access to the natural gas transmission networks, OJ 2005 No. L289/1; and Council Recommendation 83/230 on the methods of forming natural gas prices and tariffs in the Community, OJ 1983 No. L123/40. The European Council of 23/24 March 2006 called for the adoption of a priority (network) interconnection plan, as to which see European Commission, Communication to the Council and the European Parliament – Priority Interconnection Plan, COM (2006) 846 final. More generally, see Directive 94/22/EC of the European Parliament and of the Council on the conditions for granting and using authorisations for the prospection, exploration and production of hydrocarbons, OJ 1994 No. L164/3; Council Directive 2003/92/EC amending Directive 77/388/EEC as regards the rules on the place of supply of gas and electricity, OJ 2003 No. L260/8; Sixth Council Directive 77/388/EEC on the harmonisation of the laws of the Member States relating to turnover taxes – Common system of value added tax: uniform basis of assessment, OJ 1977 No. L145/1; Directive 90/377/EC concerning a Community procedure to improve the transparency of gas and electricity prices charged to industrial end-users, OJ 1990 No. L185/16; Commission Decision 2003/796 establishing the European Regulators Group for Electricity and Gas, OJ 2003 No. L296/34; Council Decision 1999/280/EC regarding a Community procedure for information and consultation on crude oil supply costs and the consumer prices of petroleum products, OJ 1999 No. L110/8; and Commission Decision 1999/566 on a Community procedure for information and consultation on crude oil supply costs and the consumer prices of petroleum products, OJ 1999 No. L216/8. See also P. Cameron, 'The Internal Market in Energy: Harnessing the New Regulatory Regime' (2005) 30 *ELRev* 631; M. Roggenkamp, A. Ronne, C. Redgewell, and I. del Guayo (eds.), *Energy in Europe, National, EU and International Law and Institutions* (Oxford University Press, 2001) and F. Botchway, 'Contemporary Energy Regime in Europe' (2001) 26 *ELRev* 3.

[5] See, for example, European Commission, Communication on limiting Global Climate Change to 2 degrees Celsius – The way ahead for 2020 and beyond ('Communication on limiting global climate change'), COM (2007) 2 final; European Commission, Communication on winning the battle against global climate change, COM (2005) 35 final; European Commission, Communication on strengthening environmental integration within Community energy policy, COM (98) 571 final; European Commission, Communication to the Council on a partnership for integration: a strategy for integrating the environment into EU policies, COM (98) 333 final; European Commission, Communication on climate change – the EU approach to Kyoto, COM (97) 481 final; and European Commission, Communication on the energy dimension of climate change, COM (97) 196 final. See also Commission Decision 280/2004 concerning a mechanism for monitoring Community greenhouse gas emissions and for implementing the Kyoto Protocol, OJ 2004 No. L49/1; Decision 2002/358 concerning the Community's approval

be underestimated. Indeed, the Commission considers that, to be successful, Europe's energy policy will have to involve 'catalysing a new industrial revolution' towards a low carbon economy.[6] Furthermore, although this chapter focuses on aspects of internal policy it should not be forgotten that these same objectives are also being pursued by the Community internationally.[7]

2. The implications of energy policy for procurement

What then are the implications of these objectives for energy procurement? I would suggest that they urgently emphasise the need to facilitate the procurement by public authorities of renewable 'green' energy (i.e. electricity from renewable sources)[8] and of energy-efficient

of the Kyoto protocol to the UN Framework Convention on Climate Change, OJ 2002 No. L130/1; and Directive 2003/87/EC establishing a scheme for greenhouse gas emission allowance trading within the Community and amending Council Directive 96/61/EC, OJ 2003 No. L275/32. The Community documents referred to under notes 8 and 9 below also emphasise the environmental imperative underlying the need to increase use of energy from renewable sources and to improve energy efficiency.

[6] European Commission, Energy Policy for Europe, note 2 above, para. 3.

[7] *Ibid.*, which identifies a number of specific targets for international negotiation including the achievement in international negotiations 'of a 30% reduction in greenhouse gas emissions by developed countries by 2020 compared to 1990' noting that 'global greenhouse gas emissions in 2050 must be reduced by 50% compared to 1990, implying reductions in industrialised countries of 60–80% by 2050'. Furthermore, the Community is moving towards the development of 'a common external policy to support energy policy objectives' as to which see Presidency Conclusions of the Brussels European Council, note 2 above, para. 46 and 'Towards an EU External Energy Policy – The 2006 Brussels Conference, 20th and 21st November 2006', available at ec.europa/external_relations/energy/energy_conference/index.htm. Thus, the Energy Policy for Europe, note 2 above, indicates that one of the policy's priorities is to develop 'an international Energy Policy that actively pursues Europe's interests' (section 3.9). This is noted to be one of the six key areas to be developed according to the proposal for a comprehensive energy policy by the European Commission in its Green Paper – European Strategy for Sustainable, Competitive and Secure Energy, note 2 above.

[8] See European Commission, Communication on the Share of Renewable Energy in the European Community, COM (2004) 366 final; European Commission, Communication on the support of electricity from renewable sources, COM (2005) 627 final; European Commission, Communication on the implementation of the Community Strategy and action plan on renewable energy, COM (2001) 69 final; European Commission, Energy for the Future: Renewable Energy Sources – White Paper for a Community strategy and action plan, COM (97) 599 final; and European Commission, Energy for the Future: Renewable Sources of Energy – Green Paper for a Community Strategy, COM (96) 576 final. The 'energy' theme of the Proposal for a Decision of the European Parliament and of the Council concerning the seventh framework programme of the European Community for research, technological development and demonstration activities (2007 to 2013), COM (2005) 119, Annex 1,

products.[9] This is because, of the three energy policy objectives two, namely security of supply and environmental sustainability, seem to lead to identical conclusions as to patterns of purchasing. Just as environmental sustainability militates in favour of expanded use of renewables so the need for enhanced security of supply requires, amongst other things, that Europe diversify its energy sources away from oil and gas which it has to import from third countries whose internal policies or trading policies may threaten security of European supply.[10]

To cut fossil fuel use, the Community has already taken some legislative steps and has undertaken to obtain 12 per cent of its energy from renewable sources by 2010.[11] The Commission now proposes 'a binding target of increasing the level of renewable energy in the EU's overall mix from less than 7% today to 20% by 2020'.[12] In essence it is seen as vital that the Community move from being a carbon-based to a hydrogen-based fuel economy. At the same time, given Europe's precarious

point 5 has as its objective the development 'of a more sustainable [energy system] based on a diverse portfolio of energy sources ... combined with enhanced energy efficiency, to address the pressing challenges of security of supply and climate change, whilst increasing the competitiveness of Europe's energy industries'.

[9] See European Commission, Communication on limiting Global Climate Change, note 5 above, European Commission, Communication – Action Plan for energy efficiency: Realising the Potential ('Action Plan for energy efficiency'), COM (2006) 545 final and European Commission, Green Paper: Energy Efficiency or Doing More with Less, COM (2005) 265 final which describes options for saving 20 per cent of energy consumption by 2020 through changes in demand and energy efficient technology. See also European Commission, Action Plan to improve energy efficiency in the European Community, COM (2000) 247; European Commission Communication on energy efficiency in the European Community – Towards a Strategy for the rational use of energy, COM (1998) 246 final; and Council Resolution on energy efficiency in the European Community ('Resolution on energy efficiency'), OJ 1998 No. C394/1.

[10] The Commission notes that 80 per cent of energy consumed in the Community comes from fossil fuels and that 'a significant and increasing proportion of this comes from outside the EU'. It considers that dependence on imported oil and gas (currently stated to be 50 per cent) could rise to 70 per cent by 2030: European Commission, Energy for the Future: Renewable Energy Sources – White Paper for a Community strategy and action plan, note 8 above, section 1.1.2.

[11] Ibid., which laid down a Community strategy for the use of energy from renewable sources. Pursuant to this approach the Community has adopted Directive 2003/30/EC on the promotion of biofuels or other renewable fuels for transport, OJ 2003 No. L123/42 and Directive 2001/77/EC on the promotion of electricity from renewable energy sources in the internal electricity market ('Directive 2001/77/EC'), OJ 2001 No. L283/33 (discussed below). It has also set national targets for the proportion of electricity generated by non-fossil fuel renewable sources. See European Commission, Communication on the Share of Renewable Energy in the European Community, note 8 above. See also C. Markus, 'Environmental Aid in the European Energy Market: *veni, vidi, vici*' (2002) 9 *IELTR* 237, 238–240.

[12] European Commission, Energy Policy for Europe, note 2 above, p. 14.

dependence upon imported fuels, reduction in demand through greater energy efficiency can assist in managing energy security risks.[13] So the imperative of seeking to achieve security of supply militates in favour of diversification of fuel sources including greater use of renewables *and* in favour of policies to achieve greater energy use efficiency.

Looking at the position from a purely environmental perspective, one quickly comes to the same conclusion. Amongst the most pressing environmental imperatives concerning energy policy are the needs to address climate change through reduced reliance upon hydrocarbons, diversification of energy sources to non-carbon sources, including renewable energy, and the need to achieve greater energy efficiency.[14] The latter has a clear part to play both in slowing down the rate of depletion of natural fuel resources and, to the extent that hydrocarbon fuels continue to be used, in reducing (or at least helping to constrain increases in) carbon emissions.

Thus the EC's energy and environmental policies both emphasise the need to enhance use of renewable energy sources and improve energy efficiency in order to achieve vital environmental goals but also to achieve the economically and *politically* imperative objective of energy security, an objective which has in recent years become a major national security concern.[15]

---

[13] Member States have undertaken to save 1 per cent of their final energy consumption each year for nine years by expanding use of energy-efficient and cost-effective lighting, heating, hot water, ventilation and transportation; see Directive 2005/32/EC establishing a framework for the setting of ecodesign requirements for energy-using products and amending Council Directive 92/42/EEC and Directives 96/57/EC and 2000/55/EC of the European Parliament and of the Council, OJ 2005 No. L191/29 discussed below. An example of a measure based upon the need to use energy more efficiently is Directive 2004/8/EC on the promotion of cogeneration based on a useful heat demand on the internal energy market amending Directive 92/42/EEC, OJ 2004 L52/50, which is intended to facilitate installation and operation of 'electrical cogeneration plants', i.e. plants which produce electricity and usable heat in one process to save energy and reduce emissions.

[14] See European Commission, Communication on the energy dimension of climate change, note 5 above.

[15] That energy supply can be a matter of national security was recognised in Case 72/83 *Campus Oil Limited* v. *Minister for Industry & Energy* [1984] ECR 2727. More recently it has been recognised in more overtly geopolitical terms, for example, by NATO which instituted an Energy Security Forum in Prague on 22–24 February 2006. The strategic significance of oil security was evidenced by the fact that the forum was addressed by General Charles F. Wald, Deputy Commander, HQ, US European Command: see www.energy-security.org. For appraisals of the political significance of the energy security question see also Paul Gallis (Specialist in European Affairs at the Foreign Affairs, Defense, and Trade Division of the Congressional Research Service), 'CRS Report for Congress: NATO and Energy Security',

Of course the third objective of Community energy policy, to enhance European competitiveness by liberalising the European energy market, reminds us that competition in the internal market is the preferred mechanism for achieving an economically efficient allocation of scarce energy resources in Europe. Furthermore, at a time of possible shortage and insecurity of supply, the internal market may have even greater importance than elsewhere in avoiding 'beggar my neighbour' national policies or the fragmentation or partitioning of the Community through the restrictive business practices of incumbent participants.[16] In some part, therefore, the challenge facing the Community is to enhance security of supply and environmental sustainability without doing so in such a way as might, by creating scope for discriminatory or anti-competitive practices, damage the nascent internal energy market. This might be thought to imply at least a potential tension between specific environmental policy goals in the energy field and the need to protect the internal market.

3. The implications of environmental principles for procurement

The overall direction of Community environmental policy has been elaborated through successive action programmes on the environment, the Fifth and Sixth of which have expressly referred to the role to be played by environmentally sensitive procurement. The Fifth Programme, 'Towards Sustainability' (1992–1999),[17] noted the 'shared responsibility' of public and private actors for environmental protection and, in that context, emphasised that public bodies' purchasing and consumption

available at www.usembassy.it/pdf/other/RS22409.pdf. See also UK Foreign and Commonwealth Office Reports 2005, 'Energy Security', available at www.fco.gov.uk/Files/ KFiles/10deprep05_energysecurity.pdf; cf. L. Guruswamy, 'Energy and Environmental Security: The Need for Action' (1991) 3 *JEL* 209.

[16] There are already concerns about anti-competitive characteristics of the internal energy market for gas and electricity, including over high levels of concentration at the wholesale level, vertical foreclosure and inhibitions to market integration. The Commission has undertaken an inquiry: see European Commission, Inquiry pursuant to Article 17 Regulation No 1/2003 into the European gas and electricity sectors (Final Report), COM (2006) 851 final.

[17] Resolution of the Council and the Representatives of the Governments of the Member States on a Community programme of policy and action in relation to the environment and sustainable development – A European Community programme of policy and action in relation to the environment and sustainable development, OJ 1993 No. C138/1.

decisions could make a significant impact on the environment, especially given the size of the public contracts market, so that environmental factors should be integrated into procurement decisions. The Sixth Action Programme, 'Environment 2010: Our Choice'[18] develops this theme further. It establishes 'Integrated Product Policy' (IPP) as the centrepiece of the Programme, a policy which it says 'will address ways to improve the environmental performance of products *throughout their lifecycle*'[19] (emphasis added), namely at both the production and consumption stages (consumption including use, but also disposal, reuse and recycling). Indeed the Policy is stated to be intended to 'comprise action on economic incentives for environmentally friendly products, enhancing "green demand" through better consumer information, *developing an objective basis for green public procurement*, and action to encourage more environmentally friendly design'[20] (emphasis added). Furthermore, the Commission's Green Paper on Integrated Product Policy[21] argues that public authorities must act as leaders in the process of green management and 'in changes of consumption towards greener products'.

4. Resolving procurement–environment tensions in the energy context

As we have seen, a tension is sometimes thought to exist between the needs of energy/environmental policy and market efficiency. This certainly has been the case in respect of certain specific green procurement techniques. Three factors, however, help to create a conceptual framework within which such tensions might be resolved.

First, although the Treaty does not provide a specific basis for energy policy, it does do so for environmental protection. The key provisions provide that the 'task' of the Community includes 'the promotion of sustainable development of economic activities' and 'a high level of protection and improvement of the quality of the environment'.[22] But the Treaty goes much further than this. Article 6 EC lays down the 'Integration Principle' requiring that

---

[18] European Commission, Communication on the sixth environment action programme of the European Community – Environment 2010: Our future, Our choice. The Sixth Environment Action Programme, COM (2001) 31 final.

[19] *Ibid.*, p. 17.   [20] *Ibid.*

[21] European Commission, Green Paper on Integrated Product Policy, COM (2001) 68 final.

[22] Article 2 EC.

environmental requirements must be integrated into the definition *and implementation* of other Community policies in particular with a view to promoting sustainable development. (emphasis added)

As its wording suggests, Article 6 EC is not merely programmatic; it imposes legal obligations.[23] It has, therefore, had powerful effect[24] and the Commission has explicitly set out a series of principles for further integrating environmental considerations into energy policy.[25]

Second, in the energy field, it is simply not possible to conceptualise environmental protection as something only tangentially linked to substantive policy (in the way, for example, that some would regard environmental protection as of dubious relevance to public procurement). Energy policy is absolutely central to the most pressing of environmental problems (namely climate change). Environmental protection and energy policy are inescapably two sides of the same coin.

Thirdly, of the three objectives of Community energy policy, security of supply and environmental protection are also, as we have seen, mutually reinforcing in that both emphasise the imperative need for growth in the production and consumption of renewables and for enhanced energy efficiency. This is of real importance because, although the very concept of 'sustainable development' implies that economic growth and environmental responsibility can coexist, vested interests are usually able to portray environmental protection as being in some way inimical to economic growth or efficiency. So far as energy is concerned, however, the fact that security of supply is one of the EC's most pressing economic issues, impacting on both economic performance and national security, completely changes the nature of the debate. Favouring renewable sources of energy and the pursuit of energy efficiency can no longer be marginalised into an environmental 'silo': they are essential to *economic* and *national* security.[26]

---

[23] Advocate General Jacobs' Opinion, para. 231, in Case C–379/98, *PreussenElektra AG v. Schleswag AG ('PreussenElektra')* [2001] ECR I–2099.

[24] See in particular Case C–448/01, *EVN and Wienstrom v. Austria ('EVN-Wienstrom')* [2003] ECR I–14527; Case C–513/99, *Concordia Bus Finland v. Helsinki ('Concordia Bus Finland')* [2002] ECR I–7213; Case C–2/90 *Commission v. Belgium ('Belgian Waste')* [1992] ECR I–4431 and Case C–379/98, *PreussenElektra*, note 23 above.

[25] See European Commission, Strengthening environmental integration within Community energy policy, COM (98) 571 final, and Report from the Council to the Helsinki European Council on a strategy for integrating environmental aspects and sustainable development into energy policy, European Bulletin, 12–1999, 1.2.121.

[26] See note 15 above.

5. Community trends that will impact on energy procurement and the procurement of energy-consuming goods, works and services

Before considering energy procurement under the public procurement regime, it is worthwhile to notice some policy developments that will inevitably affect public authorities in their procurement role.

5.1. Community policy on renewable energy

First, as we have seen, Community energy policy anticipates increased use of energy from renewable sources. From a specifically procurement point of view, as long ago as 1988 the Council called upon Member States

> to examine the need to set up agencies, in those Member States where there are none, to promote the use of new and renewable energy sources in order to advise *contracting public authorities*, local authorities and small and medium-sized businesses in the planning of feasibility studies and on the technical and financial aspects of implementing projects to exploit these sources.[27]

This clearly anticipated that contracting authorities had a role in providing demand for 'green' electricity.

Secondly, reflecting the Integration Principle itself, the Council has stated that it 'believes that it is ... highly desirable to build renewables into other Community policies, where it is appropriate to do so'.[28] 'Other policies', as under the Integration Principle itself, would include procurement policy.

Thirdly, the Community has long recognised that if the use of renewable energy is to grow it is necessary to support the emergence of a market for such energy, including by ensuring that purchasers can guarantee that the energy they purchase *is* from renewable sources.[29] This led to Directive

---

[27] Council Recommendation 88/349 on developing the exploitation of renewable energy sources in the Community, OJ 1988 No. L160/46.

[28] Council Resolution on renewable sources of energy, OJ 1998 No. C198/1, para. 16. See also para. 19 on the need to integrate environmental protection into the Community's other policies.

[29] Council Resolution on renewable sources of energy, OJ 1997 No. C210/1, para. 7 provides that 'in order to stimulate the market for renewables, appropriate regulatory measures encouraging market participants to buy energy produced from renewable resources may be introduced'. See also Council Resolution on renewable sources of energy, note 28 above, para. 10: 'the development of Community-wide standards and certification schemes will assist the market penetration of renewables, in view of the significant actual and potential market for environmentally-friendly energy sources, industries and technologies'.

2001/77/EC on the promotion of electricity produced from renewable energy sources in the internal electricity market.[30] Its purpose is 'to promote an increase in the contribution of renewable energy sources to electricity production in the internal market for electricity and to create a basis for a future Community framework'.[31] In adopting the directive, the Community recognised 'the need to promote renewable energy sources *as a priority* measure given that their exploitation contributes inter alia to environmental protection, sustainable development, security of supply and to the meeting of Kyoto targets'.[32] The directive requires Member States to set national indicative targets for consumption of electricity produced from renewable sources,[33] and to 'take appropriate steps to encourage greater consumption of electricity produced from renewable sources in conformity' with those targets.[34] These targets are to be consistent with the Community's climate change commitments under the Kyoto Protocol.[35] The Commission is to assess the extent to which national targets are consistent with the Community's global indicative target that energy from renewables should constitute 12 per cent of gross Community energy consumption by 2010.[36]

A key feature of the directive is that it requires Member States to adopt schemes to guarantee the origin of energy from renewable sources.[37] These are to operate according to 'objective, transparent and non-discriminatory criteria laid down by each Member State'[38] and the guarantees are to be issued on request[39] by one or more designated national bodies.[40] This is intended to facilitate trade in energy from renewables, and to assist consumers seeking to purchase such electricity.[41] Such a guarantee of origin must:

---

[30] Article 1 of Directive 2001/77/EC, note 11 above. See also P. Del Rio and M. Gual, 'The Promotion of Green Electricity: Europe's Present and Future' (2004) 14 *European Environment* 219.

[31] *Ibid.*

[32] *Ibid.*, Recital 1. Recital 2 also describes the promotion of electricity from renewable sources as a 'high priority'.

[33] *Ibid.*, Article 3 and Recital 5.

[34] *Ibid.*, Article 1(1). For a brief examination of the UK's renewable energy policy and the UK Renewables obligation (the requirement that electricity suppliers supply a percentage of their electricity from renewable sources), see B. Allen and J. Zerk, 'An Obligation on Producers to Generate Green Electricity' (2006) 160 *Environment Information Bulletin* 12.

[35] Article 3(2) and Recital 6 of Directive 2001/77/EC, note 11 above.

[36] *Ibid.*, Article 3(4) and Recital 7.   [37] *Ibid.*, Article 5 and Recital 10.

[38] *Ibid.*, Article 5(1).   [39] *Ibid.*, Article 5(1).   [40] *Ibid.*, Article 5(2).

[41] *Ibid.* As regards the need for such a guarantee of origin see 'Pressure Builds for Green Power Accreditation System', ENDS Reports (2005) 361, 29.

specify the energy source from which the electricity was produced, specifying the dates and places of production, and in the case of hydroelectric
installations, indicate the capacity; serve to enable producers of electricity
from renewable energy sources to demonstrate that the electricity they sell
is produced from renewable energy sources within the meaning of the
directive.[42]

The directive requires the mutual recognition of such certificates
'exclusively as proof' of the above elements and refusal to recognise
such a guarantee (for example, on grounds that it was obtained by
fraud) must be based on 'objective, transparent and non-discriminatory
criteria'.[43] Although it was thought too early to consider a Community
level framework for support schemes[44] for renewable energy sources, the
directive provides for the Commission to monitor national schemes and
if necessary to propose such a framework.[45] The directive also requires
Member States, without prejudice to maintenance of the reliability and
safety of the grid, to take the necessary measures to ensure that system
operators in their territory guarantee the transmission and distribution
of electricity produced from renewable sources. It also makes clear that
they may also provide for priority access for such electricity to the grid.[46]

Clearly Directive 2001/77/EC does not itself deal specifically with the
regulation of the public procurement of energy. Nonetheless, it seems to
have an overwhelming importance for procurement. Since the Community
has taken legislative steps to create a new market in energy from renewable
sources, and has linked this to the Community's achievement of a target for
use of such energy, it is simply not credible to contend that contracting
authorities are to be excluded from that market. Instead, for contracting
authorities, as for other purchasers, the practical possibility of specifying
electricity from renewable sources or of favouring its purchase through
award criteria[47] is *enhanced* by ensuring that 'green' electricity can be
authoritatively identified as such.

---

[42] *Ibid.*, Article 5(3) of Directive 2001/77/EC, note 11 above.
[43] *Ibid.*, Article 5(4), which also provides that the Commission may 'compel' a refusing
party to recognise a guarantee of origin.
[44] For example, green certificates, investment aid, tax exemptions or reductions, tax
refunds and direct price support schemes.
[45] Recitals 14–16 of Directive 2001/77/EC, note 11 above.   [46] *Ibid.*, Article 7.
[47] When the 'economically most advantageous' basis of award is used.

5.2. Energy-use standards

Quite apart from the extent to which the procurement regime should permit authorities an area of *discretion* to undertake environmentally sensitive purchasing of energy, the likely direction of policy is that *mandatory* standards will be developed (for example, as regards energy efficiency) that will apply to categories of product whether purchased by private or public persons. Notable amongst such measures are provisions concerning the energy efficiency of domestic refrigeration appliances,[48] hot-water boilers,[49] energy performance of buildings,[50] and energy efficiency requirements for ballasts for fluorescent lighting.[51] In addition, Directive 2005/32/EC[52] establishes a framework for setting eco-design requirements for energy-using products. It does not itself lay down mandatory provisions for specific products but rather defines the principles, conditions and criteria for framing such provisions. The Commission will introduce eco-design requirements for fourteen 'priority product groups' during 2007–2012, and these include a number of products commonly purchased by public authorities – for example, imaging equipments (including photocopiers) and office and street lighting.[53] Such measures are to be supported by a Community framework for the taxation of energy products and electricity.[54]

[48] Directive 96/57/EC on energy efficiency requirements for domestic household electric refrigerators, freezers and combinations thereof, OJ 1996 No. L236/36.

[49] Directive 92/42/EEC on efficiency requirements for new hot-water boilers fired with liquid or gaseous fuels, OJ 1992 No. L167/17.

[50] Directive 2002/91/EC on the energy performance of buildings, OJ 2003 No. L1/65.

[51] Directive 2000/55/EC on energy efficiency requirements for ballasts for fluorescent lighting, OJ 2000 No. L279/33.

[52] Directive 2005/32/EC establishing a framework for the setting of ecodesign requirements for energy-using products and amending Council Directive 92/42/EEC and Directives 96/57/EC and 2000/55/EC of the European Parliament and of the Council, OJ 2005 No. L191/29.

[53] See European Commission, Communication on Limiting Global Climate Change, note 5 above, section 7.1.1.

[54] Directive 2003/96/EC on restructuring the Community framework for the taxation of energy products and electricity, OJ 2003 No. L283/5. This extends the Community system of minimum rates of taxation of mineral oils to coal, natural gas and electricity when used as motor or heating fuels, and electricity. It reduces distortions between oil and other energy products whilst encouraging efficient use of electricity and reducing greenhouse gas emissions, and authorises Member States to protect the environment by giving tax advantages to businesses taking measures to reduce emissions. See also European Commission, Green Paper on market-based mechanisms for environment and related policy purposes, COM (2007) 140 final.

5.3. Energy-use labelling

The Community is also providing labelling standards to assist purchasers, private or public, to identify energy-efficient products.[55] Of particular importance is the Energy Star Programme, a joint US–EU programme to coordinate energy efficiency labelling programmes for office equipment.[56] This programme is likely to become of particular importance for public purchasers in light of Directive 2006/32 on Energy End-Use and Energy Services, discussed below.

5.4. A Community horizontal policy on energy?

Finally, and of most direct importance to public procurement, the Community has imposed and is considering imposing energy-related *obligations* of varying degrees of intensity on Member States *as regards the performance of the public sector* which are bound to affect procurement practice.

The first such provision is Directive 2006/32/EC[57] on Energy End-use and Energy Services, the legal basis of which is Article 175(1) EC, which provides for legislation to achieve the environmental objectives of the Treaty. Its purpose is stated to be 'to enhance the cost-effective improvement of energy end-use efficiency in the Member States'[58] by

---

[55] See Directive 92/75/EEC on the indication by labelling and standard product information of the consumption of energy and other resources by household appliances, OJ 1992 No. L297/16.

[56] See Council Decision 2001/469 concerning the conclusion on behalf of the European Community of the Agreement between the Government of the United States of America and the European Community on energy-efficient labelling programmes for office equipment, OJ 2001 No. L172/1. This is implemented by Regulation 2422/2001 on a Community energy-efficient labelling programme for office equipment, OJ 2001 No. L332/1 and by Decision 2003/68 establishing the European Community Energy Star Board, OJ 2003 No. L67/22. For the controversy over the legal basis of conclusion of the agreement, see A. MacGregor and E. Brown, 'ECJ Pronouncement on the Correct Legal Basis for the Conclusion by the European Community of the EU-US Energy Star Agreement' (2003) 9 *ITLR* 63.

[57] Council Directive 2006/32/EC on energy end-use efficiency and energy services and repealing Council Directive 93/76/EEC, OJ 2006 No. L114/64. The Commission is proposing to amend this directive to 'improve coherence of national public procurement guidelines on energy efficiency'. European Commission, Action Plan for energy efficiency, note 9 above. European Commission, Communication on limiting Global Climate Change, note 5 above, section 7.1.4, suggests that the Commission's proposals will seek increased coherence in national procurement guidelines and in 'existing Community guidelines'.

[58] *Ibid.*, Article 1.

(a) providing the necessary *indicative targets* as well as mechanisms, incentives, and institutional, financial and legal frameworks to remove existing market barriers and imperfections that impede the efficient end use of energy; (b) creating the conditions for the development and promotion of a market for energy services[59] and for the delivery of other energy efficiency improvement measures to final consumers.[60]

The directive is considered to serve the need to improve energy security,[61] the 'promotion of the production of renewable energy',[62] and the 'mitigation of ... greenhouse gas emissions and thereby ... the prevention of dangerous climate change'.[63] Recalling the Community's 1998 commitment 'to improve energy intensity of final consumption by an additional percentage point per annum up to the year 2010',[64] it provides for the adoption of national 'indicative targets to promote energy end-use efficiency and to ensure the continued growth and viability of the market for energy services'.[65] The key provision in this regard is Article 4 requiring Member States to:

adopt and aim to achieve an overall national indicative energy savings target of 9% for the ninth year of the application of the directive, to be reached by way of energy services and other energy efficiency improvement measures. Member States shall take cost-effective, practicable and reasonable measures designed to contribute towards achieving this target.[66]

The 'indicative' nature of the target is emphasised, and this means that the directive 'entails no legally enforceable obligation for Member States to achieve it'.[67] Equally, however, Member States are free to set themselves a national indicative target higher than 9 per cent.[68]

---

[59] Defined in Article 3(e) of Council Directive 2006/32/EC on energy end-use efficiency and energy services, note 57 above.

[60] *Ibid.*

[61] *Ibid.*, Recital 1 and, as regards reduction of dependence upon energy imports, see Recital 3.

[62] *Ibid.*, Recital 1.   [63] *Ibid.*, Recital 2.

[64] *Ibid.*, Recital 10, referring to the Resolution on energy efficiency, note 9 above.

[65] Ibid., Recital 11.

[66] Ibid., Article 4.1 provides for the target to be set and calculated according to a methodology in Annex I, and the comparison energy savings based on conversion factors in Annex II; examples of eligible improvement measures are contained in Annex III and a framework for measuring and verifying savings in Annex IV. It is to be transposed by 17 May 2008. The directive also provides for intermediate national targets for the third year of application: see Article 4.2.

[67] *Ibid.*, Recital 12. Note that, when pursuing energy efficiency, 'substantial negative environmental impact should be avoided': see Recital 15.

[68] *Ibid.*, Recital 13.

The directive also adopts a number of approaches intended to affect both the supply and demand sides of the energy services market.[69] As regards the demand side, the directive foresees the public sector having an 'exemplary role'. Thus:

> the public sector[70] in each Member State should ... set a good example regarding investments, maintenance and other expenditure on energy-using equipment, energy services and other energy efficient improvement measures. Therefore, the public sector should be encouraged to integrate energy efficiency improvement considerations into its investments, depreciation allowances and operating budgets. *Furthermore, the public sector should endeavour to use energy efficiency criteria in tendering procedures for public procurement , a practice allowed under Directive 2004/17/EC ... coordinating the procurement procedures of entities operating in the water, energy, transport and postal services sectors, and Directive 2004/18/EC ... on the coordination of procedures for the award of public works contracts, public supply contracts, and public services contracts, the principle of which was confirmed by the judgment of ... the Court of Justice in Case C–513/99 [Concordia Bus Finland].* (emphasis added)[71]

This 'exemplary role' includes, but is not limited to,[72] the taking of a number of specific measures. Article 5 provides that

> Member States shall ensure that the public sector fulfils its exemplary role in the context of this directive ... Member States shall ensure that energy efficiency improvement measures are taken by the public sector, focussing on cost-effective measures which generate the largest energy savings in the shortest span of time. Such measures shall be taken at the appropriate national, regional and/or local level ... *Without prejudice to national and Community public procurement legislation*:
>
> – *at least two measures shall be used from the list set out in Annex VI;*
> – Member States shall facilitate this process by publishing guidelines on energy efficiency and energy savings as a possible assessment criterion in competitive tendering for public contracts
> – Member States shall facilitate and enable the exchange of best practices between public sector bodies, for example *on energy-efficient public procurement practices*, both at the national and international level. (emphasis added)[73]

---

[69] *Ibid.*, Recital 7.   [70] 'Public sector' is not defined.
[71] Recital 7 of Council Directive 2006/32/EC, note 57 above.
[72] *Ibid.*, Recital 8.   [73] *Ibid.*, Article 5.1.

Furthermore, Member States are required to assign administrative, management and implementing responsibility 'for the integration of energy efficiency improvement requirements as set out' in Article 5(1) to a specific organisation.[74] Since Article 5(1) explicitly refers, as we have seen, to the role of pursuit of energy efficiency in public procurement, this appears to mean that a specific national body must be charged, inter alia, with oversight of compliance with Article 5 as regards public procurement.

We have seen that Article 5(1) requires Member States to ensure that energy efficiency improvement measures by the public sector shall, subject to Community and national procurement law, include at least two measures listed in Annex VI, entitled 'List of eligible energy efficient public procurement measures'. This states that:

> Without prejudice to national and Community public procurement leg-islation, Member States shall ensure that the public sector applies at least two requirements from the following list in the context of the exemplary role of the public sector as referred to in Article 5:
>
> (a) requirements concerning the use of financial instruments for energy savings, including energy performance contracting,[75] that stipulate the delivery of measurable and pre-determined energy savings (including whenever public administrations have outsourced responsibilities);
>
> (b) *requirements to purchase equipment and vehicles based on lists of energy-efficient product specifications of different categories of equipment and vehicles* to be drawn up by the authorities and agencies referred to in Article 4(4)[76] using, where applicable, minimised life-cycle cost analysis or comparable methods to ensure cost-effectiveness;
>
> (c) *requirements to purchase equipment that has efficient energy consumption in all modes, including in standby mode,* using, where applicable, minimised life-cycle cost analysis or comparable methods to ensure cost-effectiveness;

---

[74] *Ibid.,* Article 5.2.

[75] i.e. 'a contractual arrangement between the beneficiary and the provider ... of an energy efficiency improvement measure, where investments in that measure are paid for in relation to a contractually agreed level of energy efficient improvement'; Article 3(j) 'Energy efficiency improvement measures' are defined in Article 3(h).

[76] The national bodies responsible for overseeing the framework set up to achieve indicative energy savings targets.

(d) *requirements to replace or retrofit existing equipment and vehicles with [certain specified equipment]*;

(e) requirements to use energy audits and implement the resulting cost-effective recommendations;[77]

(f) *requirements to purchase or rent energy-efficient buildings or parts thereof, or requirements to replace or retrofit purchased or rented buildings or parts thereof in order to render them more energy-efficient.*
(emphasis added)

Of these measures, those listed at (b), (c), (d) and (f) clearly require implementation through procurement practices and policies. The fact, however, that these provisions are 'without prejudice' to national and Community public procurement legislation', stated in Article 5(1) and repeated in Annex VI, means that these provisions do change EC procurement legislation, either expansively or restrictively.

On the other hand, the Community policy-maker is at least considering *mandatory* energy efficiency obligations on public authorities as regards some other aspects of procurement activity. Following the Green Paper, 'Doing More with Less – the Green Paper on Energy Efficiency',[78] which discussed using public procurement 'to kick-start new energy efficient technologies, such as more energy efficient cars and IT equipment',[79] a directive has been proposed on the promotion of clean road transport vehicles[80] (based on Article 175(1) EC which authorises legislation to achieve the Community's environmental objectives). If adopted this would require Member States to ensure that 25 per cent of road transport vehicles with a technically permissible maximum laden weight of more than 3.5 tonnes, and which are purchased or leased in a given year by public bodies[81] and operators providing transport services under concession or permission from a public body, are clean vehicles.[82] This is intended 'to contribute to reduce pollution and energy

---

[77] Energy audit is defined in Article 3 (l).

[78] European Commission, Green Paper: Energy Efficiency or Doing More with Less, note 9 above, see section 4.3.

[79] *Ibid.*, 'Introduction'.

[80] European Commission, Proposal for a Directive of the European Parliament and of the Council on the promotion of clean road transport vehicles, COM (2005) 634 final.

[81] 'Public bodies' are State, regional or local authorities, bodies governed by public law (as defined in Article 2(a) in a similar manner to the same term in the Public Sector Directive), associations of these, and public undertakings (Article 1). A 'clean vehicle' is a new road transport vehicle complying with an enhanced environmentally friendly vehicle ('EEV') standard as defined in Article 1(c) of Directive 2005/55/EC.

[82] Note 80 above, Article 3.

consumption and favour a faster market introduction of these vehicle technologies'.[83] Indeed, the Commission now proposes in the period 2007–2012:

> to strengthen its efforts to develop the market for cleaner, more energy-efficient, smarter and safer vehicles through public procurement and awareness raising. The Commission will also facilitate cooperation between manufacturers, local and regional authorities, and other entities with large vehicle fleets and car-sharing organisations, with a view to encouraging these buyers to collectively acquire less polluting and energy-efficient vehicles at lower cost through joint procurement and the exchange of information.[84]

Similarly, additional obligations may be put upon public bodies as regards the energy-efficiency of buildings. Thus, the Commission proposes

> an expanded role for the public sector to demonstrate new technologies and methods. During 2009, an assessment of the costs and benefits of expanding the role of the public sector to demonstrate new energy-efficient and renewable technologies and methods will be carried out with a view to amending the [Energy Performance of Buildings Directive (2002/91)] to include such an obligation in Article 7.3.[85]

As the above provisions suggest, as the Community's need to produce and consume energy from renewable sources and to improve energy efficiency becomes ever more urgent, it has become less tenable to leave public procurement policy in this area purely to the discretion of national

---

[83] *Ibid.*, Recital 10.

[84] European Commission, Communication on Limiting Global Climate Change, note 5 above, section 7.3.1.

[85] Ibid. This is also included as a proposed measure in the Action Plan for energy efficiency, note 9 above, Annex section 1. The proposed amendment is based on Article 175 EC authorising legislation to achieve the Community's environmental objectives. In addition, the Commission proposes to: (i) support energy-efficient procurement in the public sector by improving the 'coherence of national public procurement guidelines on energy efficiency' (*ibid.*, Annex, section 1, sixth bullet); (ii) produce a reference document on energy efficiency (*ibid.*, section 7.5.2); (iii) promote several financial mechanisms including 'public-private energy efficiency funds and finance packages for SMEs and public sector [sic] for energy audits and specific energy efficiency investments' (*ibid.*, Annex, section 4, sixth bullet); and (iv) bring forward proposals to assist authorities improve their energy efficiency including through 'standardised energy audits, guidelines as to how to promote energy efficient products for enterprises and public authorities, best practices and benchmark guidelines and education and training for energy managers'. See Communication on Limiting Global Climate Change, note 5 above, section 7.3.1.

authorities. Nonetheless, and surprisingly, a degree of uncertainty still remains as to the precise legal basis on which authorities are themselves entitled, as a matter of their own purchasing autonomy, to insist on purchasing 'green' energy, or to favour products which, throughout their *whole* life cycle, have low energy use.

6. The discretion of contracting authorities to pursue environmental objectives

The tension between environmental policy and economic efficiency has long shaped the discourse about green procurement. This is because the greater the discretion for public authorities to base purchasing on environmental criteria the greater, it is thought, is the danger that they will engage in discriminatory practices under the cloak of environmentalism. The key question is where the balance is to be drawn. To what extent should the autonomy of Member States to pursue environmentally sensitive purchasing be constrained in order to guard against economic nationalism? It is helpful first to seek guidance in the principles underlying EC procurement policy.[86] Chapter 1 explained that this policy is based on non-discrimination, equal treatment and transparency; that the implementation of both commercial and horizontal procurement objectives, and the balance between the different objectives, is still in principle a matter for Member States: and that horizontal policies have an equal status under the Community regime with other procurement policies.

Chapter 1 also explained that the procurement regime is as much subject to the Integration Principle as other Community policies. In fact, however, the Integration Principle was hardly applied in terms of the *definition* of Community procurement policy until the 2004 directives;[87] the previous directives did not directly address the extent and manner in

---

[86] Note that a public contract for electricity constitutes a public *supply* contract: Directive 2004/18/EC of the European Parliament and of the Council on the coordination of procedures for the award of public works contracts, public supply contracts and public service contracts ('Public Sector Directive'), OJ 2004 No. L134/114 defines supply contracts as those for the supply of 'products' (a term not defined), but 'electricity constitutes goods for the purposes of Title I in Part Three of the EC Treaty': the Opinion of Advocate General Jacobs in *PreussenElektra*, note 23 above, para. 197. In Case C–448/01, *EVN-Wienstrom*, note 24 above, the ECJ assumed that a contract for electricity was subject to the old Supply Directive and this was not questioned.

[87] Directive 2004/17/EC coordinating the procurement procedures of entities operating in the water, energy, transport and postal services sectors ('Utilities Directive'), OJ 2004 No. L.134/1 and the Public Sector Directive, note 86 above.

which states could take environmental issues into account. This left a gap which the Commission sought to fill through guidance documents.[88] These tended to be restrictive in nature.[89] Fortunately, in the important cases of *Concordia Bus Finland* and *EVN-Wienstrom*,[90] the ECJ took a more liberal view and filled the gaps in the legislative framework in such a way as to ensure that environmental protection could indeed be integrated into the implementation of procurement policy in a meaningful way. The 2004 directives borrow directly from this case law and integrate environmental protection principles into the definition of the procurement regime, including through specific reference to environmental award criteria.[91]

It is within this context that we must consider the discretion that Member States have to favour environmentally responsible procurement related to energy. The key questions concern the extent of discretion to purchase (i) energy-efficient products, (ii) electricity generated from renewable energy sources, and (iii) products that are themselves manufactured using such 'green' electricity.

7. Procurement of energy-efficient products

First, given the needs of energy security and to reduce greenhouse gas emissions, it is imperative that the procurement regime should, to the fullest extent possible, recognise the right to procure works, supplies and services which are energy efficient at the consumption stage. This is non-controversial. As chapter 4 (section 13) explained, at the award

---

[88] European Commission, Communication on Public Procurement: regional and social aspects, COM (89) 400 final; European Commission, Green Paper on Public Procurement in the EU: exploring the way forward, COM (96) 583 final, section VI; European Commission, Communication on Public Procurement in the European Union, COM (98) 143 final, replaced by European Commission, Interpretative Communication on the Community law applicable to Public Procurement and the possibilities for integrating environmental considerations into public procurement ('Communication on environmental considerations') COM (2001) 274 final.

[89] See e.g. P. Kunzlik, 'Green Procurement under the New Regime', in R. Nielsen and S. Treumer (eds.), *The New EU Public Procurement Directives* (Copenhagen, DJØF Publishing, 2005) and P. Kunzlik, 'The Legal Dimension of Greener Public Purchasing', in N. Johnstone, *The Environmental Performance of Public Procurement: Issues of Policy Coherence*, (Paris, OECD, 2003), pp. 153–219.

[90] Case C–513/99, *Concordia Bus Finland* and Case C–448/01, *EVN-Wienstrom*, note 24 above.

[91] Recital 1 of the Public Sector Directive, note 86 above, and Recital 1 of the Utilities Directive, note 87 above.

stage states clearly may adopt criteria favouring products that are energy efficient in consumption, provided these are appropriately defined and applied. It is also clear (as chapter 4 again explained) that public contracts may include contractual requirements for energy efficiency of goods when consumed – even the Commission has always accepted this possibility.[92] The purchase of such products will be made much easier by the advent of the EU Energy Star Programme and, as we have seen, is one of the ways in which public sector bodies will play their 'exemplary role' under Directive 2006/32/EC.[93]

8. Procurement of electricity from renewable sources of energy

Second, the needs of energy security and the vital objective of combating climate change mean that the procurement regime should also accept to the widest extent possible states' right to favour the purchase of electricity from renewable rather than fossil fuel resources.

8.1. Contract award criteria in electricity supply contracts favouring electricity from renewable sources of energy

When an authority awards a public contract on the 'most economically advantageous' basis it has a great deal of scope to favour electricity from renewable sources. In the past, the Commission argued that this was not the case. It considered that award criteria could only relate to environmental protection where the criteria provided an economic advantage, directly, to the contracting authority, which was specific to the works, supply or services in question. In the Commission's view such criteria could not relate to either production or consumption *externalities* since these criteria would not provide any direct economic advantage to the authority. On this basis criteria favouring energy from renewable resources because it was less polluting to the environment, or to avoid depletion of natural resources, would not be permissible.

---

[92] See, for example, Communication on environmental considerations, note 88 above, Part II, para. 1.2.

[93] See Annex VI (b), (c) and (f) of Council Directive 2006/32 on energy end-use efficiency and energy services, note 57 above. For an interesting analysis as to the extent to which energy efficiency is now a basis for European regulation (including in the public procurement sector), see V. Bruggeman, 'Energy Efficiency as a Criterion for Regulation in the European Community' (2004) 13 *EELR* 140.

The Commission's view did not, however, survive the ECJ's decision in *Concordia Bus Finland*.[94] As chapter 4 explained (in section 13), in the context of a public service contract for the provision of bus transportation services the Court accepted award criteria relating to levels of noise and nitrous oxide emissions from the tenderers' respective bus fleets, implicitly rejecting the Commission's position as regards externalities put forward in that case. It seemed clear after *Concordia Bus Finland* that, in contracts for the supply of energy, award criteria which favour energy from renewable resources would in principle be permissible so long as they complied with various general requirements for award criteria laid down in that case. As chapter 4 also explained,[95] this was confirmed in *EVN-Wienstrom*[96] even though on the facts the particular criteria were not accepted as they went beyond the subject matter of the contract.

8.2. Electricity supply contracts – specifications requiring electricity to be produced from renewable energy sources

A question still not directly addressed by the ECJ, however, is whether authorities letting electricity supply contracts may *require* the provision of energy from renewable sources, rather than merely favouring this through award criteria. The Commission's latest guidance suggests that this is indeed permissible[97] and this must be right. The imperative need to expand production and consumption of energy from renewable sources, both as a question of energy security and to reduce carbon emissions, implies no other outcome, especially in light of the Integration Principle in Article 6 EC.[98] A fortiori this is the case when considered in light of Directive 2001/77/EC[99] which as we saw sets targets for growth in the use of renewable energy. Further, by providing

---

[94] Note 24 above. [95] See chapter 4, sections 8 and 13.
[96] Case C–513/99, note 24 above, para. 34.
[97] Communication on environmental considerations, note 88 above, Part II, section 1.2; and European Commission, *Buying Green!: A Handbook on Environmental Public Procurement* ('*Handbook*') (Luxembourg: Official Publications of the European Communities, 2004), paras. 3.4.2 and 3.4.3.
[98] In *PreussenElektra*, the ECJ considered that a national measure to increase use of renewable energy could relate to the 'protection of human, animal and plant life' under Article 30 EC.
[99] Directive 2001/77/EC, note 11 above.

a definition of 'electricity from renewable sources'[100] and for a guarantee of origin, the directive helps provide a clear objective basis on which to frame requirements for renewable energy.

The only reason why there has been doubt about the matter is that although the Commission accepts that green electricity might be specified it does so on a conceptual basis that is so flawed that it obfuscates the true position.

The Commission's starting point is that authorities may *not* include in their specifications prescriptions which relate to the 'production processes and methods' (PPMs) by which a product is made unless they affect a characteristic of the end-product in use.[101] This seems to have been based upon an interpretation of the definition of 'technical specifications' in Annex III to the old Public Supply Directive which defined the term as meaning:

> the totality of the technical prescriptions contained in particular in the tender documents, defining the characteristics required of a material, product or supply, which permits [it] to be *described in a manner such that it fulfils the use for which it is intended by the contracting authority.* These shall include levels of quality, performance, safety or dimensions, including the requirements applicable to the material, the product or the supply as regards quality assurance, terminology, symbols, testing and test materials, packaging, marking and labelling. (emphasis added)

---

[100] Defined in Article 2(c) as 'electricity produced by plants using only renewable energy sources, as well as the proportion of electricity produced from renewable energy sources in hybrid plants also using conventional energy sources and including electricity used for filling storage systems, and excluding electricity produced as a result of storage systems'. 'Renewable energy sources' are 'renewable non-fossil energy sources (wind, solar, geothermal, wave, tidal, hydropower, biomass, landfill gas, sewage treatment plant gas and biogases' (Article 2 (a)). 'Biomass' is defined in Article 2(b).

[101] See, for example, Communication on environmental considerations, note 88 above, Part II, para. 1.1. Westphal defends this approach in, 'Greening Procurement: An Attempt to Reduce Uncertainty' (1999) 1 *PPLR* 1, 10. In his view 'some seek to stretch the term "life cycle assessment" to cover the production process'. He argues that it is more efficient to achieve environmental objectives through other policies and that to do this through procurement enlarges the purchaser's job beyond identifying the most economically advantageous tender. However, taking account of production impacts as part of life cycle analysis is an orthodox approach and a central plank in the Community's own environmental policy. See, for example, European Commission, Communication to the Council and European Parliament, Integrated Product Policy – Building on Environmental Life Cycle Thinking, COM (2003) 302 final, and the Green Paper on Integrated Product Policy, note 21 above.

In the Commission's view the fact that specifications could prescribe primary materials to be used 'if this contributes to the characteristics of the product ... in such a manner that it fulfils the *use* for which it is intended by the contracting authority'[102] meant that they could not lay down environmental requirements relating to the *production* stage of a product's life cycle when these did not impact upon the characteristics of the product at the consumption stage. This would rule out a requirement for green electricity since this would, par excellence, be a PPM requirement affecting *only* production characteristics.

The Commission's approach is, however, problematic. It seems to be based on an assumption that the definition of 'technical specification' was intended to prohibit a priori certain types of requirements falling outside the definition of 'technical specifications' (such as, according to the Commission, certain PPM requirements). However, had the old directives been intended to provide an a priori prohibition of certain types of requirement they could have expressly said so. In fact they did not. Furthermore, the term 'technical specifications' in the old directives seemed to serve a quite different objective: the directives laid down provisions applicable to 'technical specifications' which were intended to prevent discrimination and to ensure transparency (similar to the purpose of the provisions in Article 23 of the current Public Sector Directive)[103] and it seems that the term 'technical specification' was deployed simply to define the scope of these non-discrimination and transparency requirements, not to prohibit other requirements. A concern for the effectiveness of the non-discrimination and transparency rules suggest that one should seek a wide, rather than a narrow, interpretation of the definition of that term.[104] As I have argued elsewhere, the definition appears to have been sufficiently widely worded to include PPMs not affecting consumption characteristics[105] – an interpretation which will enhance non-discrimination and transparency.[106]

In my view, therefore, origin-neutral PPM requirements in specifications were never prohibited as such by the old directives. Furthermore,

---

[102] Communication on environmental considerations, note 88 above, Part II, section 1.1.

[103] See chapter 2, section 4.3.5 – although note that the content of these provisions has been amended in the 2004 directive.

[104] Chapter 4 suggested that the 'control' rules of Article 23 might also apply by analogy to 'special conditions' (addressed below) but this does detract from the present argument concerning the purpose of the definition of 'technical specifications'.

[105] See, for example, Kunzlik, 'Green Procurement under the New Regime', note 89 above.

[106] Cf. P. Trepte, *Regulating Procurement* (Oxford University Press, 2004), p. 201.

the Commission's contrary view created great difficulty in the context of requirements that electricity be derived from renewable sources. These are PPM prescriptions which affect the production but *not* the consumption characteristics of the electricity in question: once it is in the grid (and when considered from a purely *consumption* point of view) electricity of different origin is indistinguishable in its characteristics. This is precisely why, in *PreussenElektra*,[107] when discussing the difficulty of envisaging a European market in electricity from renewable sources, the ECJ alluded to the difficulty for customers of knowing whether such electricity is in fact generated in that way. It is also precisely why the Community has had to provide for issuing guarantees of origin for such electricity.[108] Thus a principled application of the Commission's basic position on PPMs would mean that such a specification would *not* be lawful. Yet, in *PreussenElektra*[109] the ECJ itself had emphasised the importance of promoting electricity from renewable sources. In such circumstances the Commission had little choice but to accept that it *is* permissible to specify the supply of electricity from renewable energy sources. To do so, whilst at the same time maintaining its stance against the permissibility of PPM requirements that do not affect consumption characteristics, it invented what I call the 'Invisibility Fallacy'.

This is that PPM requirements which at first sight may appear not to affect the consumption characteristics of an end product may nonetheless be regarded as doing so because the required effect may be 'invisible'. Taking the case of 'green electricity' specifically, the Commission has stated that it is permissible to specify the supply of electricity from renewable sources since the green source 'invisibly' affects the characteristics of the electricity at the consumption stage: 'The production process covers all requirements and aspects related to the manufacture of the product which contribute to the characterising of the product without the latter being necessarily visible in the end-product.'[110] This is, however, absurd. Whereas in some cases an environmental PPM requirement might relate to an 'invisible' characteristic of the end product – a consumption characteristic which, *although objectively present* cannot be seen – this is simply not the case with a requirement for 'green' electricity. From the point of view of consumption

---

[107] Case C–379/98 *PreussenElektra*, note 23 above.
[108] See Directive 2001/77/EC, note 11 above.
[109] Case C–379/98 *PreussenElektra*, note 23 above.
[110] Communication on environmental considerations, note 88 above, Part II, section 1.2.

characteristics, electricity from renewable sources and electricity generated from fossil fuels are indistinguishable. There are *no* consumption
characteristic differences between them, visible or invisible. As regards
'green' electricity the 'invisibility' theory was therefore simply fallacious.

Latterly, as was perhaps inevitable in light of the ECJ's pronouncements in *EVN-Wienstrom* – and perhaps in recognition of the weakness
of the Invisibility Fallacy itself – the Commission has revised its public
analysis but, sadly, has done so in a way that muddies the waters even
further. It still maintains that PPM specifications must affect, visibly or
invisibly, the consumption characteristics of the procured product but
has expanded the category of factors which it considers might be taken as
producing the necessary 'invisible' effect. Thus, the Commission reiterates that (even under the new directives),

> since all technical specifications should bear a link to the subject matter of
> the contract, you can only include those requirements which are related to
> the manufacturing of the product and *contribute to its characteristics*,
> without necessarily being visible.[111]

It then goes on to provide a revisionist version of the Invisibility
Fallacy as follows:

> You can for example ask for electricity produced from renewable energy
> source ... although green electricity is not physically different from
> electricity produced from conventional sources, and makes the lights
> work in exactly the same way. *However, the nature and value of the end
> product has been modified by the process and production method used. For
> example, electricity produced from a renewable source will in principle be
> more expensive, but cleaner, than electricity from a conventional source.*[112]

This reasoning tortures logic almost as much as the original
Invisibility Fallacy itself. This is because the Commission has expanded –
without acknowledging the sleight of hand involved – the concept of
'invisible' characteristics at the consumption stage to include factors
extraneous to the characteristics of the product as such but which relate
to its position in the market. It has done this by asserting that 'the nature
and value' of electricity is affected by the manner in which it is generated.
Since, as the Commission now admits, the physical characteristics of the
electricity are not so affected this must mean either that patterns of
demand justify treating green electricity as different from electricity

---

[111] European Commission, *Handbook*, note 97 above, section 3.4.2.   [112] *Ibid.*

from fossil fuels (such demand affecting 'the value' of the electricity) or that authorities can specify green electricity because from a social/environmental point of view it is beneficial (that is, that the 'value' of green electricity is not a market value but a societal/environmental value).

Both possibilities are problematic. It would be odd if patterns of demand could be considered to affect the consumption characteristics of a product as such – whether 'visibly' or 'invisibly'. It is tantamount to saying that if there is specific demand for green electricity arising from its distinctive manner of production then such electricity may be specified – whereas the very fact that authorities wish to specify such electricity is itself evidence of such demand! On this basis the mere fact of demand by contracting authorities for any product produced according to any sufficiently specified PPM – whether affecting the actual characteristics of the product in the consumption stage or not – would be permissible. If that is indeed the case, as I argue, the distinction between specifying PPMs that affect the consumption characteristics of the procured product and those that do not is entirely otiose and positively misleading.

Furthermore, if specification of green electricity is considered justified by virtue of the fact that such electricity is a different product to conventional electricity because it is (assumed to be) more expensive, that would suggest that it might cease to be permissible to specify green electricity if the price difference were eliminated (perhaps because insecurity of supply increases the price of fossil fuels and technological advances reduce the cost of renewable energy). The Commission's reasoning therefore takes us into the realms of *Alice in Wonderland*.

As to the alternative interpretation of the Commission's current approach, namely that authorities can specify green electricity because it is beneficial from a social/environmental point of view, this would be consistent with the Commission's statement that green electricity can be distinguished from conventional electricity because it is 'cleaner' and is attractive from an environmental and energy policy perspective. However, this is inconsistent with the Commission's continued insistence that PPM specifications must affect the characteristics of the product at the consumption stage. At the consumption stage 'green' electricity and electricity from fossil fuels are indistinguishable in terms of their polluting effects: only at the *production* stage is electricity from renewable sources less polluting.

Thus the distinction between PPMs affecting consumption characteristics and those which do not is emptied of substance. If the revised Invisibility Fallacy permits specification of green electricity because it is assumed to be more expensive or cleaner than conventional electricity why can it not also apply to production requirements relating to other products (such as the working conditions of those producing the products) which, although they do not affect the consumption characteristics of the products themselves, may result in cleaner production or higher prices?

Accordingly, it is simply not tenable to say that requirements for green electricity are permitted because of some 'invisible' consumption characteristic of such electricity. Instead, such a specification is in principle permissible for the simple reason that nothing in the directives or Treaty prevents states from assigning value to the environmental performance of the product concerned at the *production* stage.

The Commission's basic stance against PPM requirements which do not affect consumption characteristics was developed in the context of the pre-2004 directives. Its public guidance maintains the same stance under the new directives. The latter do, however, now explicitly integrate environmental factors into the 'definition' of procurement policy, including in the context of technical specifications. In particular, the new Public Sector Directive breaks new ground by referring expressly to environmental requirements in such specifications. Article 23(3) requires that technical specification must be formulated in one of four ways. The first option, stated by Article 23(3)(a), is 'by reference to technical specifications as defined in Annex VI' and to certain technical standards. The definition in Annex VI paragraph 1(a) in turn defines 'technical specification' (for public supply or services contracts) as

> a specification in a document defining the required characteristics of a product or service, such as quality levels, *environmental performance levels*, design for all requirements, [and] ... *production processes and methods*.[113] (emphasis added)

The words emphasised in italics above are nowhere defined in the directive. They are not qualified in such a way as to exclude PPM requirements that affect the 'characteristics' of the end product at the production stage but are unrelated to its consumption characteristics. Similarly the term 'production processes and methods' is not qualified. In my view, therefore, the 2004 directive supports the proposition that states may specify for electricity produced from renewable sources – or

---

[113] A similar definition is provided by Annex VI, para. 1(a) for public works contracts.

for any other PPM affecting the production characteristics of the product even if not affecting its consumption characteristics.[114]

A possible objection to this view might be that the Council rejected a specific European Parliament amendment to the Public Sector Directive to clarify that contracting authorities can prescribe environmental PPM requirements relating to the full life-cycle of a product and that thus the legislature specifically decided to exclude the possibility. However, scrutiny of the legislative history precludes such a conclusion. The amendment would have resulted in the following text (the amending words are shown in italics): '[Specifications] may also be formulated in *terms of* performance *requirements*, of functional requirements *or of requirements with regard to the environmental impact of the product throughout its lifetime.*'[115] The Council's position, as indicated in its Common Position,[116] was *not* simply to reject the Parliament's objectives out-of-hand. Instead the position was stated as follows:

> The Council has not been able to accept the wording of the EP amendment. However, by re-structuring the introduction of the paragraph and adding a general justification, the wording should now meet some of the preoccupations of Parliament, *to allow* references to production processes etc. for obvious technical reasons. Moreover, Annex VI has also incorporated a reference to 'production processes'. (emphasis added)[117]

Furthermore, inconsistently with its current public rejection of PPM requirements that do not affect consumption characteristics, the Commission itself emphasised that the final text does permit environmental PPM requirements. Thus, when commenting on the Council's common position adopted on the proposal for the directive, the

[114] The same appears to be true of specifications under Article 23(3)(b) formulated 'in terms of performance or functional requirements [which] ... may include environmental characteristics'. The concept of 'environmental characteristics' is not qualified or restricted. Arguably the drafting suggests that 'performance' means something different to 'functional' and thus that environmental characteristics may relate to *environmental* performance unconnected to functionality.
[115] Position of the European Parliament adopted at first reading on 17 January with a view to the adoption of European Parliament and Council Directive.../.../EC on the coordination of procedures for the award of public supply contracts, public service contracts and public works contracts, OJ 2002 No. C271E/176.
[116] Common Position (EC) No. 33/2003 with a view to adopting Directive 2003.../.../EC of the European Parliament and of the Council on the coordination of procedures for the award of public works contracts, public supply contracts and public service contracts, OJ 2003 No. 147E/1.
[117] *Ibid.*, as regards amendments 47 and 123.

Commission stated that 'the text would ... allow contracting authorities to require specific environmentally friendly production methods – such as organic production for foodstuffs for schools'.[118] Strikingly, the example given here is of a PPM requirement that does not *necessarily* affect consumption characteristics.

Further, Parliament sought to amend the list of award criteria permitted for assessing the 'economically most advantageous' tender by including expressly the words 'production methods'. When commenting on the Council's common position the Commission argued that this amendment was otiose since the term 'production methods' was (and still is) included in the definition of 'technical specification' in Annex VI: since such *'production methods are explicitly recognised in Annex VI as possible technical specifications, there is nothing to prevent these same specifications from constituting award criteria. It would therefore be otiose to mention them explicitly among the examples of criteria, which are anyway not an exhaustive list'*[119](emphasis added).

The Commission thus portrayed the scope to refer to 'production methods' as the same for award criteria and technical specifications and, as we know from *EVN-Wienstrom*, contract award criteria can in principle include PPMs ('green' electricity in that case) which do not affect the consumption characteristics of the end product. This arguably shows that the references to 'production processes' in Annex VI, and the other Council amendments to which the text cited refers, were considered to achieve the same objective as the Parliamentary amendment, i.e. to permit specifications to refer to environmental PPMs including those that do not affect consumption characteristics.

Possibly the Commission's restrictive approach in the guidance is based upon a simple assumption that PPM specifications in general are so damaging to trade that they cannot be left simply to general principles of equal treatment – and indeed may be based on a tacit interpretation of the EC Treaty as prohibiting such specifications. However, this view of the Treaty must be rejected: even if in the present state of the

---

[118] Public Procurement: Commission welcomes conciliation agreement on simplified and modernised legislation, IP/03/1649.

[119] European Commission, Opinion of the Commission pursuant to Article 521(2), third paragraph, point (c) of the EC Treaty on the European Parliament's amendments to the Council's common position regarding a proposal for a Directive of the European Parliament and of the Council on the coordination of the procedures for the award of public works contracts, public supply contracts and public service contracts, COM (2003) 503 final.

jurisprudence such specifications (even if non-discriminatory) must be considered a hindrance to trade, they should be regarded as justified to the extent that they relate to environmental protection concerns – an approach supported by the Integration Principle. This application of the Treaty to PPM requirements is discussed further in chapter 4.[120]

In summary, therefore, I contend that states may include a requirement for the supply of electricity from renewable energy sources not because of the mythical 'invisible' characteristics of green electricity but because environmental PPM specifications which affect only the production characteristics of the product in question are in principle permissible under the directives and Treaty: they are only precluded if, in the context of a particular procurement, they are so drafted or applied as to infringe one of the more specific prohibitions of the directive or Treaty.

As chapter 4 (section 8.1.3) explained, the effect of including a contract requirement is, first, that a bid that does not accept it will be non-compliant and must be rejected; and, secondly, that failure to provide energy from a renewable source will be a breach of contract. In addition, it is submitted that authorities may exclude firms in advance that do not have the ability to comply with a requirement on providing energy from renewable sources, even if the firm indicates that it will accept the obligation to do so.

It might be objected that this last conclusion is called into question by Article 48 of the Public Sector Directive, which lists the evidence that may be required from suppliers as the basis for exclusion. Article 48(2)(f) permits the authority to require information about bidders' 'environmental management measures' but this refers only to works and services contracts, and not supply contracts. It might therefore be argued that PPM requirements for electricity supply contracts cannot form the basis for exclusion. Such an argument would, however, be based on an incorrect assumption: although Article 48(2)(f) does not apply to supply contracts, several other provisions of Article 48 enable an authority to seek to obtain information that is relevant for excluding bidders who cannot meet a requirement for green electricity. One is Article 48(2)(h), which allows recourse to a statement of the available plant or technical equipment (wind or water turbines, solar generation plant, biomass generators etc.). An authority would also be able to require that a supplier provide certificates of origin under Directive 2001/77/EC on renewable energy since these seem to qualify as 'certificates drawn up by

---

[120] See chapter 4, section 4.

official quality control institutes or agencies of recognised competence attesting the conformity of products clearly identified by reference to specifications or standards' as mentioned in Article 48(2)(j)(ii). It might also require bidders to provide a list of principal deliveries of such energy over the last three years, as permitted by Article 48(2)(ii).

8.3. Special conditions requiring electricity to be supplied from renewable energy sources

We have seen in chapter 4 (section 8.1.4) that Article 26 of the Public Sector Directive confirms that contracting authorities may lay down special conditions relating 'to the performance' of their contracts and that these 'may in particular, concern ... environmental considerations'. In the author's view this category of special conditions is distinct from that of technical specifications in that terms that are special conditions do not form part of the technical specifications.[121] If, contrary to the view expressed in section 8.2 above, requirements for energy to be produced from renewable sources cannot be regarded as part of the technical specifications they would seem to be permitted as special conditions: they can arguably be regarded as 'relating' to 'the performance of the contract'.

It was suggested in section 8.2 above that if a requirement on supplying energy from renewable sources is part of the technical specifications, then tenderers that the authority considers are unable to meet that requirement can be excluded. As we have seen in chapter 4, however, it appears that bidders possibly cannot, on the other hand, be excluded on the grounds of their lack of ability to observe terms that are special conditions – although even this is controversial.[122] However, as chapter 4 (section 8.1.4) explained, an authority that considers that a tenderer cannot meet a special condition is entitled (and indeed required) to exclude any bid which does not accept the condition as non-compliant; and a successful tenderer which fails to honour any such condition will be in breach of contract. Furthermore, a condition could be included in the contract to require that the supplier provide a certificate of origin for the electricity supplied pursuant to Directive 2001/77/EC.

---

[121] Chapter 4, section 8.1.3 suggested that the precise relationship between technical specifications and special conditions is not clear: on other possible interpretations see chapter 4, section 8.1.4.

[122] See chapter 4, section 8.1.4 above.

Failure to provide such a certificate would itself be a breach of contract and would make apparent the substantive failure to deliver green electricity.

9. Procurement of goods produced using electricity from renewable energy sources

The third and most controversial conclusion that I would draw from the Community's energy and environmental policies is that the procurement regime should, to the fullest extent possible, recognise the right to procure works, supplies and services that are *themselves* produced/provided using electricity from renewable sources.

9.1. Award criteria favouring products produced using energy from renewable sources

Whether states can adopt contract award criteria favouring products (other than electricity) made *using* electricity from renewable sources has not yet been addressed by the ECJ. The outcome would seem to depend on what is meant by 'the subject matter of the contract' and upon the precise relationship required between the production process to which the contract award criterion relates and the procured product itself. One can imagine two quite different approaches.

On the one hand, one might consider that an award criterion in a contract for the supply of a product (say, a widget) favouring products produced using electricity generated from renewable resources is essentially the same as an award criterion in an electricity supply contract that the electricity be derived from renewable sources. In these cases the 'subject matter of the contract' might be considered to be the supply of widgets and the supply of electricity respectively. In each case the tenderer will gain an advantage if the product purchased (widgets in the one case, electricity in the other) is produced using green energy. If the specification of electricity from renewable energy sources is indeed permissible (since it is 'linked to the subject matter of the contract') why is the requirement that widgets be produced using only electricity from renewable sources not also considered to be 'linked to the subject matter of the contract'? In some respects the two cases are close parallels: in order to foster green energy the authority has, in each case, chosen to specify a product (in one case electricity and in the other case widgets) produced by the use of energy from renewable resources.

A contrasting approach, however, might distinguish the two cases according to the relationship between the energy input and the end product. On that basis the position as regards the contract to supply electricity might be characterised as follows: an energy source (fossil fuel, biomass, water, wind, etc.) is subjected to a process (combustion, water turbine generation, wind turbine generation) to produce electricity which is *itself* the end product. In the case of production of a different product (the widget) an energy source (as above) is subjected to a process (as above) to produce one product (electricity) which is *not* the end but is rather an input into a further end product (the widget). In the latter case the criterion as to use of renewable energy might be distinguished from that in the former case: it might be said not to be sufficiently 'linked to the subject matter of the contract' because it does not relate directly to production of the end product but to the production of the intermediate product (electricity) which is then used to produce the end product but which forms no part of it.

It would be unfortunate if the Court were to take the second, restrictive, approach outlined above. It is important that the ECJ's language in *Concordia Bus Finland* and in *EVN-Wienstrom* requires only that the requirement merely be 'linked' to the subject matter of the contract, a reasonably wide formula, and not that it be 'directly' linked. Furthermore, from an environmental and energy policy point of view it is highly desirable, or even essential, that a growing proportion of products produced in the Community are made using electricity from renewable sources. On this basis it ought, in my view, to be permissible for award criteria to favour goods produced using only energy from renewable sources. It would clearly not, on the other hand, be permissible to adopt criteria favouring tenders who use renewable energy in the production of goods that are not the subject of the contract or favouring tenderers who use renewable energy in other aspects of their business not directly and specifically involved in producing the product procured.[123]

Further, a restrictive approach may nonetheless be possible in individual cases. Many products involve multiple components and electricity inputs at many stages in the production process. It is conceivable that for

---

[123] See, in particular, Case C–448/01, *EVN-Wienstrom*, note 24 above, where the conditions were unlawful because they related to capacity to supply electricity from renewable sources to third parties; and generally chapter 4, section 13. To qualify as technical specifications conditions must specify the characteristics required of the products to be supplied, rather than characteristics of the supplier.

some products at least the practical impossibility of establishing whether every component has been manufactured using only green electricity might be such as to confer 'an unlimited discretion' on the contracting authority and, as such, would not be permitted under EC law.[124] In *EVN-Wienstrom* the Court held that if an authority uses an award criterion as regards which it 'neither intends, nor is able, to verify the accuracy of the information supplied by the tenderers, it infringes the principle of equal treatment, because such a criterion does not ensure the transparency and objectivity of the tender procedure'.[125] This would, however, need to be determined on a case-by-case basis so that it should not be assumed, a priori, especially in the case of simple products, that it is never possible to develop a sufficient checking mechanism.

9.2. Specifications requiring that products to be supplied must themselves be made using only electricity from renewable energy sources

A separate question is whether an authority may also *specify* that the products supplied other than electricity (e.g. widgets) are produced using only energy from renewable sources. This question is also not yet resolved.

If one were to apply the Commission's Invisibility Fallacy in this context, one might conclude that in some cases such a specification would be permissible. In fact, it is difficult to see how the Commission could assert the Invisibility Fallacy in its revised form to permit the specification of green electricity without also accepting that it might equally permit specifications which require that other products must be made using energy from renewable sources. Thus one might argue that the fact that a product is to be made using only electricity from renewable resources would increase its price by comparison with the like product made using conventional electricity so that it is 'invisibly' different at the consumption stage from such products; or that it is 'cleaner' and so has a different 'value' (economically or environmentally) from the like conventional product. Desirable as these outcomes might be we should, however, reject the Invisibility Fallacy rather than build upon it.

Rather, the starting point should be that, in principle, states can specify environmental PPM requirements that do not affect the

---

[124] Case 31/87, *Gebroeders Beentjes BV* v. *Netherlands* [1988] ECR 4635, para. 26.
[125] Case C–448/01, *EVN-Wienstrom*, note 24 above, para. 51.

consumption characteristics of the product in question so long as they do not infringe the specific prohibitions of the directive or Treaty. The Public Sector Directive is, however, based upon the principles of the *Concordia Bus Finland* and *EVN-Wienstrom* case law.[126] Thus it may be that whether a specification that the procured product must be made using 'green' electricity is permissible depends upon whether it is 'linked to the subject matter of the contract'. This may in turn depend upon whether such a specification can be considered as materially the same as a specification in an electricity supply contract requiring the supply of electricity from renewable sources. If so it would seem in principle to be lawful for the same reasons as is the latter type of specification; and, similarly, it is submitted that an authority could exclude suppliers it considers unable to comply. If, on the other hand, it can be distinguished (as discussed above in the context of award criteria) on the basis that the prescription merely relates to an input creating an intermediate product (the electricity) then the outcome may be different. Once more, however, just as with award criteria, the practical difficulty in a specific case of checking that goods supplied have indeed been made using only electricity from renewable resources may transgress the rules of equal treatment and transparency and, effectively, confer an unlimited discretion on the contracting authority, and thus be unlawful.

9.3. Special conditions requiring that products to be supplied must themselves be made using only electricity from renewable energy sources

If the ECJ were to hold that a requirement for goods supplied to be produced using only energy from renewable sources cannot form part of the authority's 'technical specifications', it might be possible to include it as a special condition under Article 26 of the directive, which we have seen confirms the permissibility of special conditions (specifically including those concerning 'environmental considerations') 'relating to the performance of the contract'. Such a requirement arguably 'relates' to performance of the contract since it relates specifically to the goods supplied. Nothing in Article 26 narrows the meaning of the word 'relating' in such a way as to preclude such an interpretation: it does not require, for example, that the condition must relate to characteristics in use of the contract goods themselves. Such a condition would be lawful if

---

[126] Recital 1 of the Public Sector Directive.

it meets the various other requirements of the Treaty and directives, including (as discussed in section 9.2) the possibility for verification. As outlined at section 8.3 and discussed in chapter 4 (section 8.1.4) the main consequence of classifying the term as a special condition would be to remove the possibility of authorities excluding tenderers in advance for their inability to comply when those tenderers are prepared to accept the requirement.

10. Conclusions

What conclusions can be drawn from the above as regards the extent to which the Community regime allows public authorities to favour the purchase of 'green' energy? First, as regards the use of environmental contract award criteria, in rejecting the Commission's narrow approach that requires economic advantage to the authority, the ECJ in *Concordia Bus Finland* and *EVN-Wienstrom* struck an entirely appropriate balance between environmental considerations and energy policy (including security of supply), on the one hand, and trade concerns. It is important when interpreting the principles expounded in these cases to remember that the judgments represented an expansive approach to green purchasing and a rejection of the Commission's restrictive approaches.

Second, it is unfortunate that the Court has not yet had an opportunity to address the question of environmental specifications. Although even the Commission accepts that specifying in a contract for the supply of electricity from renewable resources is permissible, it is so wedded to the Invisibility Fallacy that its confused (and confusing) reasoning obscures rather than clarifies the legal position. A Court decision sweeping away the Commission's interpretation and making it clear that renewable energy can be specified in contracts for electricity without recourse to the metaphysics of 'invisible' characteristics would be greatly welcomed. It would clarify that states may do the very thing which Community environmental and energy policy both make imperative – and which Directive 2005/32 has been adopted to facilitate. It would hardly be a revolutionary step given that the Court in *EVN-Wienstrom* accepted in principle the legitimacy of contract award criteria (in electricity supply contracts) which favoured the supply of green electricity.

Whether the Court will be willing to sanction award criteria favouring, or specifications requiring, that products *other* than electricity be made using energy from renewable sources is somewhat more difficult. The

Court has a great deal of room for manoeuvre in either direction. In deciding what approach to take the Court will have to weigh in the balance the imperative needs of energy and environmental policy and the needs of the open procurement system. However, given the urgent need to increase Community production and consumption of renewables – from an energy security, national security and environmental point of view – and the dire consequences for Europe if it does not meet that challenge, one would hope that the Court would be slow to adopt a restrictive approach.

10

Reconciling national autonomy and trade integration in the context of eco-labelling

DAN WILSHER[1]

1. Introduction and overview

This chapter considers the extent to which reference to eco-labelling schemes can be used to guide the purchase of goods and services under the EC Treaty and the procurement directives.[2] Eco-labelling refers to schemes in which products and services meeting specified high environmental standards are recognised by a standard-setting body. The products and services may then be sold on the basis that they are less harmful to the environment than rival products.

Eco-labelling standards could, in principle, be used to set either product specifications or award criteria. As chapter 1 discussed, the ECJ decisions in *Concordia Bus Finland*[3] and *EVN-Wienstrom*[4] appear to allow a large margin of discretion to purchasers, subject to transparency and non-discrimination principles, to pursue environmental policies through appropriate award criteria.[5] However this does not address a more serious problem, namely the transaction costs and complexity of

---

[1] The author would like to thank Professor Peter Kunzlik for all his help and encouragement which is greatly appreciated, and Professor Sue Arrowsmith for her input which helped shape his thinking.

[2] Directive 2004/17/EC of the European Parliament and of the Council coordinating the procurement procedures of entities operating in the water, energy, transport and postal services sectors ('Utilities Directive') OJ 2004 No. L134/1; Directive 2004/18/EC of the European Parliament and of the Council on the coordination of procedures for the award of public works contracts, public supply contracts and public service contracts ('Public Sector Directive') OJ 2004 No. L134/114.

[3] Case C–513/99, *Concordia Bus Finland* v. *Helsingin Kaupunki* ('*Concordia Bus Finland*') [2002] ECR I–7213.

[4] Case C–448/01, *EVN AG* v. *Austria* ('*EVN-Wienstrom*') [2003] ECR I–14527.

[5] Case C–234/03, *Contse* v. *Insulad* ('*Contse*') [2005] ECR I–9315, although not concerning environmental procurement, may, however, qualify these earlier decisions by requiring more by way of justification, at least for services under Article 49 EC: see further the text below.

devising such criteria. Contracting authorities may not be expert in setting ecological standards. The costs and complexity of setting such standards on a case-by-case basis would render widespread green procurement a non-starter. The orthodox answer in procurement terms would be for authorities to refer to an international technical standard. However, there is very little international standardisation on eco-labelling for products.[6]

By contrast, there are, however, long-standing and demanding national eco-label systems in many Member States. These would provide an accessible and credible basis for developing environmental specifications and award criteria. However, such systems reflect national traditions and values. National firms have had many years both to shape the standards to which eco-labels relate and to shape their own production processes accordingly. At first sight, therefore, reference in tender specifications to national eco-labels threatens to produce the very kind of trade barrier that the ECJ decision in *Cassis de Dijon*[7] was directed against. However, it is suggested below that this is not the case and that under the EC Treaty the purchaser is and should be free to set specifications or award criteria that refer to eco-label standards.

However, for contracts falling under the procurement directives the position is more complex. Reflecting both its concern over the alleged protectionist effects of eco-labelling specifications and demands from the European Parliament for encouraging green procurement, the European Commission ('Commission') fashioned a novel approach for the directives. This took the form of special provisions which elaborate a set of – largely procedural – preconditions on the eco-labelling standard-setting *process* rather than prescribing the nature of the standard itself. Thus instead of requiring that eco-label standards be shown to be necessary and proportionate in terms of the principle of *Cassis de Dijon*, the standard-setting process must itself meet minimum requirements of openness to stakeholders and scientific validity.[8] It is, however, unclear

---

[6] The International Standards Organisation has a suite of environmental standards but these relate not to products but rather to project management. See ISO 14000.

[7] Case 120/78, *Rewe-Zentrale* v. *Bundesmonopolverwaltung für Branntwein* ('*Cassis de Dijon*') [1979] ECR 649.

[8] The conditions reflect the academic work by M. Maduro, *We the Court: The European Court of Justice and the European Economic Constitution, a Critical Reading of Article 30 of the EC Treaty* (Oxford: Hart Publishing, 1998), who argues that the European economic constitution should embody political principles that serve to protect cross-border trading interests, as discussed further at 5.1.1 below.

what these rules demand of the contracting authority (rather than the
eco-labelling body). If they require an investigation of the extent to
which the framing of each eco-label complied with the access/scientific
validity requirements then this would be absurdly costly and difficult. If,
however, authorities can broadly presume compliance by eco-labelling
bodies, the directive is workable. This would put the burden on ten-
derers/producers to show defects in the eco-label system and to press for
improvements principally by lobbying. Only in extreme cases should it
be inappropriate for a contracting authority to rely upon an eco-label
standard set by a labelling body that has broad procedural and scientific
credibility. This would be a powerful incentive towards allowing reference to national eco-labelling standards as a form of 'exceptionalism'
within the EC procurement regime.

2. What are eco-labels?

The term 'eco-label' is not defined in EC law but has emerged from
practice at Member State and, later, EC levels. Eco-label systems involve
products being voluntarily tested against ecological criteria concerning
the life cycle of products of that kind. Matters like the release of carbon
dioxide during production, the presence of certain non-biodegradable
chemicals, recycling potential and sustainability of materials used are
included in the eco-label standard.[9] In this sense, eco-labels go much
further in environmental terms than the rather narrow concept of 'technical specifications' in the directives. These refer to 'characteristics
required of a material, product, supply or service, which permits this
material, product, supply or service to fulfil the use for which it is
intended by the contracting authority'.[10] By contrast, eco-labels can be
used to specify an ecological standard which considers life cycle impacts
after and before use. The existence of such an eco-label therefore gives
the contracting authority another and more powerful tool for promoting
environmental goals going beyond its use characteristics.[11]

Products meeting the rules of an eco-label scheme are entitled to
display a distinctive logo which guarantees to consumers/procurers that

---

[9] The Global Eco-labelling Network provides information on national schemes. See www.
gen.gr.jp.
[10] See Annex VI of the Public Sector Directive and Annex XXI of the Utilities Directive.
[11] J. Arnould, 'Secondary Policies in Public Procurement: The Innovations of the New
Directives' (2004) 13 *PPLR* 187.

the products have been produced according to the criteria. The Commission appears to take a broad view of what falls within the directives' concept of eco-labels. In its *Handbook*[12] it refers to standards set for organic food labels and energy labels as being included.[13] There is thus potentially an open-ended and evolving set of standards that fall within the concept. The line between eco-labels and other technical specifications may in fact be blurred. On the Commission's view, performance measures that have any environmental dimension might be considered eco-labels regardless of their designation. The Commission has said that European technical standards created by the European Committee for Standardisation (CEN) are beginning to incorporate green standards.[14] This is of some consequence because 'eco-labels' (however defined) benefit from a more liberal regime than other kinds of technical standards as discussed below. The International Standards Organisation now has its ISO 14000 which also could be viewed as an eco-labelling system but its standards relate to broader environmental management rather than specific product requirements. They do not yet meet the need within Europe for a range of products with superior environmental performance.

Clearly this is an area for great debate and divergence in terms of ecological standards. The ranking of factors by importance and the benchmarks set for these is not a matter upon which there is agreement within the EC. Some states, like Germany,[15] have had schemes for many years, covering thousands of products. Their standards have evolved with the involvement of a wide range of (largely local) stakeholders, including scientists, local green groups and industrialists and consumer recognition is high.[16] Other states like the United Kingdom have no general eco-label scheme and do not intend to introduce one although the government has announced a plan for greener procurement through other means.[17] The pattern of development of eco-labels at national level reflects local environmental concerns and variations including, for

---

[12] European Commission, *Buying Green!: A Handbook on Environmental Public Procurement* ('*Handbook*') (Luxembourg: Official Publications of the European Communities, 2004).

[13] *Ibid.*, p. 25.

[14] European Commission, Integration of environmental aspects into European standardisation, COM (2004) 130 final.

[15] The Blaue Engel scheme began in 1978 and appears to have been the world's first.

[16] See German presentation to the EU coordination committee which notes 82 per cent recognition in surveys.

[17] Information obtained from Charles Cox, UK Department for Environment, Fisheries and Rural Affairs. The UK does operate labelling rules relating to organic foods which follow the EU scheme in this area.

example, climatic variation. This means that the properties of, for example, paint must be different in Northern and Southern Europe.

The EC has been active in this field since 1992 when the eco-label scheme was created.[18] Since then types of products awarded the EU logo include floor coverings, tissue papers, paints and varnishes and even televisions.[19] The scheme operates through the EU Eco-labelling Board (EUEB) which comprises representatives from the national eco-labelling bodies, industry and environmental groups. The EUEB considers criteria for each product group and, after a consultation, the Commission drafts a Decision which adopts these.[20] Since 2002 there has also been a Cooperation and Coordination Management Group to promote harmonisation, mutual recognition and joint marketing activities between the different eco-label schemes.[21] Harmonisation is very far off. However, there is a renewed effort to encourage producers to obtain the EU eco-label alongside their national one and to build consumer recognition.[22]

In summary, eco-labelling schemes have grown enormously at national level over the last thirty years. Their aims are clearly multifaceted. Green groups have sought to build alliances with industry to drive up ecological standards and expectations. Industry has reaped profits from consumers' readiness to pay a premium for products easily identified as 'green'. Government has used eco-labelling to demonstrate its environmental commitment in standard-setting. However, given that the whole scheme is voluntary on the part of producers and consumers, it is market-driven and not regulatory. Only if private and public parties choose to buy and sell eco-labels will any environmental improvements occur.

Diversity in eco-labelling does bring benefits. Harmonisation tends to stifle innovation in a fast-moving area. Green standards are constantly evolving and national schemes appear much more nimble in achieving consensus than EU schemes. Furthermore, the general thrust of the

---

[18] Council Regulation (EEC) No. 880/92 on a Community eco-label award scheme, OJ 1992 No. L99/1.

[19] See www.europa.eu for full details of the available schemes.

[20] See, for example, European Commission, Decision 2001/405/EC establishing the ecological criteria for the award of the Community eco-label for paper products (as amended by Decisions 2005/384/EC and 2007/207/EC), OJ 2001 No. L142/10.

[21] www.europa.eu/environment/ecolabel/documents contains full minutes of the meetings.

[22] See the discussion in F. Iraldo, W. Kahlenborn, F. Rubick, D. Scheer, B. Nielsen and A. Petersen, *Final Report: Evaluation of EMAS and Eco-label for their Revision* (Berlin, IÖW Publications, 2005), research commissioned by the European Commission, which looks at ways to improve the eco-label scheme.

recent EU constitutional settlement over trade and the environment has emphasised Member States' right to set higher standards.[23] Diversity and more national autonomy have been stressed over harmonisation and environmental ceilings.[24] Eco-labels are clearly much prized and represent one important aspect of these higher or diverse national standards. The problem is how to encourage and protect these positive features while also encouraging cross-border influences which could drive up standards, increase innovation, reduce costs and result in a soft harmonisation.[25] Ultimately green procurement by both public and private sectors could thereby expand to the benefit of the environment. The effect of the procurement directives on these questions is considered below.

3. The effect of the EC Treaty: is procurement by reference to eco-labels consumption or regulation?

When the state itself procures goods by reference to national eco-labels it might be viewed as simply another consumer. However, there are difficulties with this view. National eco-labels will tend to be held by national producers. The standards they embody will reflect national debates and attitudes to the environment going back some time. There is clearly a danger that procurers may simply reach for the standard with which they are most familiar. They may wish to easily demonstrate to their users and stakeholders that they buy green, and well-known national eco-labels will be the easiest way of doing this. The problem would most clearly arise where a contracting authority does not exercise any real judgment over its environmental criteria but simply reads off the national eco-label specification. Such practices will tend to favour national producers or at least maintain national partition of procurement markets. Including a provision allowing for equivalent tenders will not be a solution whilst divergences remain so great amongst eco-label standards. Producers largely tailor their products to national standards.[26] The costs of making equivalent products and demonstrating their equivalence may be

---

[23] See the revisions to Article 95(4) and (5) EC Treaty allowing higher environmental and other standards to be maintained or introduced even after EC harmonisation measures.

[24] See S. Weatherill, 'Harmonisation: How Much, How Little?' [2005] *EBLR* 533. See also Article 95 and Article 179 EC Treaty on environmental standards.

[25] See C. Barnard and S. Deakin, 'Market Access and Regulatory Competition', in J. Scott and G. de Búrca (eds.), *The Law of the Single European Market* (Oxford, Hart Publishing, 2002).

[26] See S. Weatherill and P. Beaumont, *EU Law* (Penguin Books, London, 1999), chapter 17.

excessive in relation to the market size. Economies of scale will not occur. These concerns echo in part those that drove the *Cassis de Dijon* decision which sought to force negative integration by judicial review of national product standards. It is against this background that we must analyse the effect of the EC Treaty (as opposed to the directives) on procurement by reference to eco-labels.

We need therefore to consider how far reference in procurement to national eco-labelling standards can be considered similar to the barriers to trade attacked in *Cassis* and its progeny. This raises the question discussed in chapter 2 – should procurement decisions be viewed in the same way as the regulatory choices that *Cassis de Dijon* was designed to control? This author favours the answer given there by Arrowsmith and Kunzlick; in general terms 'buying' decisions should not be brought within the *Cassis* jurisprudence. The reasons for this are explored below.

The starting point, however, must be the ECJ decision in *Dundalk*[27] which seemed to assume, although not to decide definitively, that a single procurement decision can be a measure having equivalent effect to a quantitative restriction (MEQR) under Article 28 EC.[28] The facts of that case amounted to indirect discrimination because the tender required a national standard pipe to be supplied without permitting an international equivalent.[29] We can see that, in the present context, restricting a tender specification to that of a national eco-label without providing for an equivalent would meet the same fate. This said, the *Dundalk* approach largely preserves Member State purchaser autonomy, seeing the authority as having discretion to specify its own needs. The only constraint is that it must not discriminate directly or indirectly in defining the means by which those needs are met.

This discrimination approach to Article 28 only takes market integration so far. As noted above, the problem identified by the *Cassis de Dijon* decision was that of mandatory product standards rules operating as regulatory barriers to trade. European countries had acquired centuries worth of product specification rules which had the effect of partitioning the market along national lines. Sometimes these were laudable but on

[27] Case C–45/87, *Commission v. Ireland* ('*Dundalk*') [1987] ECR 783.
[28] See the discussion in S. Arrowsmith, *The Law of Public and Utilities Procurement*, 2nd edn (London: Sweet & Maxwell, 2005), at 4.5–4.6 and 4.8.
[29] The ECJ said such a term 'may cause economic operators who produce or utilise pipes equivalent to pipes certified as complying with Irish standards to refrain from tendering', para. 19. An Irish firm was the only firm whose pipes had been held compliant by the Irish standards body, making apparent the provision's discriminatory effect.

other occasions they were simply the detritus of past lobbying and bore little relation to any discernible public interest.[30] The landmark decision in *Cassis de Dijon*[31] held that, where goods were sold lawfully in one Member State, other Member States had a burden of justifying the prohibition of their sale by reference to 'mandatory requirements' of public policy. It is crucial to note, however, that *Cassis de Dijon* required goods to have been lawfully approved for sale in other Member States before traders could rely upon Article 28. Even more importantly, the underlying premise for this condition was that all Member States could be trusted, prima facie, to allow only safe products onto the market for purchase. This judicially mandated 'mutual recognition' aimed to remove the 'dual burden' of regulation in successive Member States. There are two reasons to reject its applicability to procurement by reference to eco-labels. First, the premise simply does not hold in relation to the environmental life-cycle impacts of products. There is no reason to think that because a product is lawfully sold in one Member State it should be presumed to be 'eco-friendly'. The absence of EU-wide proper mandatory ecological standards for products is the whole reason for voluntary eco-labelling systems; the existing regulatory practices permit environmentally unsound and unsustainable products. Second, reference to an eco-label standard in a specification does not *prohibit* the marketing of products in a Member State. It should be viewed as simply one of the preferences expressed by a state purchaser engaged in an act of *consumption* not *regulation* of the market. It should therefore fall under the doctrine developed by the ECJ in *Keck*. Thus only a specification that discriminates directly or indirectly in the *Dundalk* sense by referring to a national eco-label without provision for an equivalent should breach Article 28.

---

[30] Weatherill and Beaumont, note 26 above, chapter 17.

[31] Even under the decision in *Cassis de Dijon*, extra regulatory restrictions might, however, be justified if shown to advance a recognised public interest (which would include environmental protection) and to be necessary and proportionate to achieving that end. The ECJ thus abandoned the use of discrimination analysis in favour of necessity/ proportionality when testing the compatibility of national measures with Article 28. In the environmental sphere this was dramatically illustrated by *Danish Bottles* in which the ECJ ruled that Danish rules requiring manufacturers of drinks to use specified bottle sizes was disproportionate in its effects on trade and was therefore unlawful. The ECJ effectively held that the level of environmental protection sought by Denmark was excessive when set against its effect on the single market. See Case C–302/86 *Commission* v. *Denmark* ('*Danish Bottles*') [1988] ECR 4607.

However, the question remains to be definitively decided. Clearly it is *possible* to characterise procurement of green products by reference to eco-labelling as constituting regulatory choice (although, as chapter 1 noted, private purchasers, also, increasingly implement such horizontal purchasing policies). If this view were taken the ECJ might require an authority to justify its environmental policy by showing how the restrictions on trade are necessary and proportionate in terms of environmental outcomes.[32] As chapter 2 explained, the recent *Contse*[33] ruling seems to follow this general approach in relation to public procurement of services under Article 49 EC. The ECJ applied its long-standing *Gebhard* formula to procurement.[34] Under this doctrine national measures liable to hinder or make less attractive the exercise of fundamental freedoms guaranteed by the Treaty require the state to show that the measures are necessary and proportionate to securing legitimate policy objectives, including environmental protection. On the facts, certain features of the specification were held liable to 'hinder' tenders from non-national companies and subjected to vigorous judicial review.[35] That decision seems to view procurement authorities as *regulators* and hence subject to more vigorous review on necessity/proportionality grounds.[36] The only limit to the reach of the Treaty (at least under Article 49 EC) appears to be that specifications must at least 'hinder or render less attractive' foreign bids. This may entail, as it did in *Contse*, some form of 'obvious' arbitrariness or discrimination. However, if it does, it is far from clear that judges can use forensic methods to review aspects of a tender alleged to render it 'less attractive' to tenderers. Losing tenderers will always complain about aspects of the design they found harder to fulfil. The courts would then be placed perilously close to

---

[32] Case C–112/84, *Humblot* v. *Directeur Services Fiscaux* [1985] ECR 1367. Case C–132/88, *Commission* v. *Greece* [1990] ECR I–1567. As regards such taxes, however, the state engages with the market only in its capacity as a regulator and not as a participant in the market itself (as to which see chapter 1). This is the approach in relation to Article 90 and discriminatory taxes where the ECJ has been rigorous in reviewing progressive environmental taxes.

[33] Case C–234/03, *Contse*, note 5 above.

[34] Case C–55/94, *Gebhard* v. *Consiglio dell' Ordine degli Avvocati e Procuratori di Milano* [1995] ECR 4165.

[35] The trigger for Article 49 is that the requirements 'hinder or render less attractive' tenders but, as chapter 3 observed, the features of the tender that the ECJ seized upon to bring Article 49 into play in *Contse* were those that discriminated indirectly.

[36] The actual wording of the formula in *Gebhard* does not refer to proportionality but only suitability and necessity but in the *Cassis de Dijon* line of cases this distinction has not been followed.

deciding what authorities' needs or priorities should be, negating the necessary purchaser autonomy of authorities as market participants. Furthermore, as Arrowsmith and Kunzlik argue in chapter 2, this aggressive view of procurement as regulation and of courts as supervisors of such regulatory choices does not sit well with the ECJ's recent case law on environmental procurement in *Concordia Bus Finland* and *EVN-Wienstrom*. These cases view procurement authorities as *consumers*, largely free from judicial review, save on discrimination and transparency grounds. This author considers that this approach should apply to purchasing by reference to national eco-label standards so long as provision is made for equivalent foreign standards. We now turn to those cases.

4. The case law under the old procurement directives

The issue of green procurement had raised problems for many years prior to the 2004 Directives because of the Commission's argument that specifications must provide 'direct' economic benefits to the contracting authority.[37] Eco-labelled products will by their nature tend to produce some benefits for purchasers but more will come from reductions in externalities throughout the life cycle of products. We saw in chapter 2, section 14, that the ECJ rejected the Commission's view decisively in *Concordia Bus Finland* and *EVN-Wienstrom*.[38] However, as we have seen, it is necessary that criteria be 'linked to the subject-matter of the contract, do not confer an unrestricted freedom of choice on the authority, are expressly mentioned in the contract documents or the tender notice and comply with all the fundamental principles of EC law, in particular the principle of non-discrimination'.[39]

This last limitation is important because it singles out non-discrimination and thus refers back to the *Dundalk* principle. The ECJ noted that 'the principle of equal treatment lies at the very heart of the public procurement directives, which are intended in particular to promote the development of effective competition in the fields to which they apply'.[40] However, as chapter 2 explained,[41] the ECJ refused to rule that this principle had been breached simply because only a small number of

---

[37] European Commission, Interpretative Communication on the Community law applicable to public procurement and the possibilities for integrating environmental considerations into public procurement, COM (2001) 274 final.

[38] Case C–513/99, *Concordia Bus Finland*, note 3 above, para. 57.

[39] *Ibid.*, para. 64.   [40] *Ibid.*, para. 81.

[41] Chapter 2, section 3.1.1.

firms could meet the criteria (including one owned by the authority itself). This might also apply to eco-labelling standards which, although in principle capable of being met equally by domestic and foreign suppliers, might in fact only be met by a small number of (possibly national) suppliers given the small size of some of these markets.

As we again saw in chapter 4 (section 13), in *EVN-Wienstrom* the ECJ went further and rejected an argument that the weighting of ecological factors is generally reviewable on grounds of economic benefit, ruling that the weighting is in principle for authorities.[42] The ECJ further made it strikingly clear that the *Cassis de Dijon*-style regulatory review was being rejected when it stated that *even if the environmental objective is not promoted by the criteria* that is not incompatible with EC law.[43] These cases concerned award criteria but there is no reason to suppose that the principles they established are not also applicable to environmental technical specifications.[44]

The Commission's *Handbook* appears to endorse this when it makes clear that 'in principle you are free to define the subject of the contract in any way that meets your needs. Public procurement legislation is not much concerned with what contracting authorities buy, but mainly with how they buy it. For that reason, none of the procurement directives restrict the subject matter of a contract as such.'[45] The Commission then explains that this freedom is not unlimited and that safeguards consist of the Treaty rules on non-discrimination which means that 'you have to ensure that the contract will not affect access to your national market by other EU operators' and that 'the technical specifications used to define the contract must not be defined in a discriminatory way'.[46] These cases and the Commission's guidance give powerful impetus to the idea that procuring authorities have a large degree of autonomy in specifying their environmental requirements through reference to eco-labelling standards.

4.1. Eco-labelling and the case law of the ECJ under the old directives and the EC Treaty: a summary of possible approaches

We may now summarise possible interpretations of this complex and confusing body of case law upon a contracting authority's power to set

[42] Case C–448/01, *EVN-Wienstrom*, note 4 above, para. 39.
[43] *Ibid.*, para. 53. See also para. 72 where the ECJ stated that the fact that that criterion does not necessarily serve to achieve the objective pursued is irrelevant in that regard.
[44] See further chapter 9.   [45] See European Commission, *Handbook*, note 12, p. 14.
[46] *Ibid.*

eco-labelling specifications or award criteria in tender documents. We can assume that the ECJ's position will not differ under the 2004 directives. There are three different perspectives which exhibit increasing levels of judicial control over contracting authorities.[47]

4.1.1. A discrimination test

As regards Article 28, *Dundalk* and *Concordia Bus Finland* seem to imply that public authorities are free to determine their environmental standards as consumers. They are sovereign subject to limiting specifications to matters 'linked' to the subject matter of the contract, provided that the rules are transparent and non-discriminatory. The use of a national eco-label standard can satisfy these conditions provided that suppliers can gain access to the standard, the standard itself is clear and suppliers can use alternative means to prove that they meet it. This would position procurement policies as one of the 'market circumstances'[48] that firms encounter when doing business in other Member States. We saw in chapter 2 that, in order to confine Article 28 within rational boundaries, the ECJ in the *Keck* line of jurisprudence has limited its scope by developing special rules to deal with *regulatory rules* relating to 'selling arrangements' such as, for example, advertising restrictions and opening hours. Procurement policies can also be seen to fall into this class of measure. They do not operate to ban the sale of any products and therefore seem to be unlike *Cassis de Dijon* product rules. The *Keck* decision, although not specifically addressing the point, ought therefore to be applicable. Under that doctrine, direct or indirect discrimination is required to engage Article 28 where non-product rules are in question. Such discrimination can include making it more difficult for importers to market their goods by comparison with domestic producers.[49] Importantly the burden is on importers to demonstrate discrimination where a tender relates to functional or performance criteria, including environmental criteria.

---

[47] See the discussion in Arrowsmith, note 28 above, at 17.8–17.10, which sets out a general account of the relationship between the goods provisions of the Treaty and procurement. She proposes four different models. My account is similar but attempts to locate the issues in the specific context of the law on eco-labelling and environment.

[48] See E. White, 'In Search of Limits to Article 30 EEC Treaty' (1989) 26 *CMLRev* 235.

[49] Case C–405/98, *Gourmet International Products* [2001] ECR I–1795.

4.1.2. A mutual recognition/proportionality test

This approach derives from one of the key ideas underlying the *Cassis de Dijon* case law – mutual recognition. If applied to procurement it might mean that reference to a national eco-label is viewed as a regulatory barrier to trade. Goods lawfully sold in other Member States should be presumed to be marketable in all Member States. For eco-labelled products, however, this approach makes little sense because the whole point is that they are a special product group with unique characteristics. Mutual recognition could not require non-recycled paper to be treated the same way as recycled paper merely because of its functional characteristics. However, the *Cassis de Dijon* principle might bite as regards mutual recognition of other Member States' eco-labels as being equivalent to those of the national authority. This would be based upon the prima facie presumption that eco-labelling standards across the different Member States are equivalent. Green producers would thereby avoid the 'dual burden' of having to apply for a new eco-label for each Member State. Instead, the burden would fall upon the contracting authority to show that the national eco-label was more demanding and that this higher standard was necessary to protect the environment. This might be complex and would involve comparing incommensurate values as each label focuses on different aspects of environmental protection.[50] This approach is clearly at odds with the traditional view expressed in *Dundalk* that the burden is on the *supplier* to show equivalence.

4.1.3. A market access/proportionality test

By contrast the *Contse* approach allows the greatest potential for judicial review. As chapter 2 has noted, it is not clear that it would apply to a tender for goods, because the ECJ has not aligned its case law under Article 28 with that relating to the other free movement provisions. Assuming *Contse* does apply, specifying a national eco-label standard or equivalent would raise costs for some (particularly foreign) companies because they would have to demonstrate equivalence. This might be enough to cross the *de minimis* threshold and thereby 'hinder or make

---

[50] Imagine two products which have different levels of performance on matters such as carbon emissions, biodegradability, use of recycled materials and toxicity. There is no accepted scale by which to compare these different environmental 'values'. We cannot therefore say that one product is environmentally equivalent to another. The relative weight to be given to such matters by different labelling schemes will reflect local assessments and influences.

less attractive' tendering. As noted above, however, this is a very uncertain area, particularly as most measures engaging the test have in practice been indirectly discriminatory anyway. Once this threshold is crossed, the authority would then face the burden of justifying its regulatory choices. The goal of environmental protection would be legitimate, but what about the means? Reliance on the national eco-label might be open to challenge on the basis that its criteria were faulty on scientific grounds or that other criteria would better achieve the same or better environmental protection. This could become very burdensome for the public authority faced with a supplier who points out flaws in the eco-label specification. The *Danish Bottles*[51] case shows the ECJ was prepared to conclude that levels of environmental protection sought by a regulator are excessive or disproportionate. It remains to be seen, however, whether recognition that contracting authorities are acting as consumers rather than regulators will produce a less intrusive approach by the ECJ to use of eco-labels. Arguably it should do so, as Arrowsmith and Kunzlik argue in chapter 2 in relation to the general issue of purchaser autonomy.

4.2. Conclusions on the EC Treaty

It is concluded that none of these three positions prevent use of national eco-labels in procurement but they do have significantly different administrative costs for contracting authorities and might inhibit the wider adoption of eco-labels. The administrative costs relate to the nature of the burden of justification and whom it falls upon. The likelihood that contracting authorities will employ eco-label criteria will decline as the transaction costs of doing so rise. We need to be careful not to raise the cost of green procurement to such a level that it becomes impractical. Like Arrowsmith and Kunzlik, this author would like to see the ECJ make clear that the *Concordia Bus Finland/Keck* approach is preferred, including for eco-labelling specifications. The alternative would bring the ECJ into the arena of vigorous judicial review on necessity and proportionality grounds of every aspect of every tender specification. This is both impractical and undemocratic. It would totally denude authorities of discretion in ways which are inconsistent with the *Cassis de Dijon* and *Keck* bifurcation of Article 28. Only measures which render marketing of a product illegal (and thus deny any access to the market) are caught by

---

[51] Case C–302/86, *Danish Bottles*, note 31 above.

Cassis de Dijon. These are either quantitative restrictions or product rules.[52] All other rules are beyond Article 28, even if they make marketing more difficult, unless they discriminate against imports. Consumers, including public authorities, must be allowed a wide choice of products but they should be free to make that choice. Only where a public body discriminates in its choice should Article 28 bite. However, in relation to services under Article 49, the ECJ's general case law points towards a market access test. *Contse* seems to require that courts protect market access by reviewing the rationality (or proportionality) of any aspect of tender designs which renders access by foreign companies difficult. That will make national eco-labelling standards more difficult to employ because it increases the risk of challenge.

In this regard it should not be forgotten that eco-labelling schemes have been developed and encouraged at both national and EC level to create a market-based mechanism to help assure environmental protection. This was thought superior to the alternative of developing more radical legislative or regulatory approaches. Indeed eco-labelling is likely to be less obstructive to intra-Community trade than such approaches precisely because it is less intrusive into the purchaser autonomy of market participants, whether public or private. In such a context it would be unfortunate unduly to inhibit eco-labelling approaches by contracting authorities as this might (given the size of the public procurement market) undermine their efficacy and thereby suggest greater recourse to traditional 'command-and-control' environmental measures.

5. Eco-labelling under the new procurement directives: enabling green procurement or a super-hurdle?

If the matter were left there, then we could debate the correct approach within the wider context of the proper role of Articles 28 and 49 and green procurement. However, eco-labelling was felt to merit particular treatment within the directives. The same rules were inserted for both the Utilities and Public Sector Directives and the discussion below will refer to the latter only for ease of exposition. These extra measures reflect a mixture of the Commission's efforts at restricting the scope for national favouritism in the use of such labels and, on the other hand, the

---

[52] Product rules are those which prohibit marketing of a product unless it conforms to regulations regarding its composition, ingredients, packaging or labelling. The concept relates to any physical aspect of the product itself.

Parliament's desire to make it clear that procuring authorities can rely on them. Given these competing goals, the overall effect is slightly schizophrenic.

In outline, we can make three points. First, the directives are enabling of procurement by reference to eco-labels because they allow reference to national standards when *describing* requirements, even where international or European standards exist for the same subject matter. As chapter 2 explained (section 4.3.5), the directives do not generally permit this approach to describing requirements, but, when European or international standards exist, require description by reference to those standards and/or to performance or functional requirements. The eco-label provisions constitute a significant exception to the usual hierarchy within the directives. Second, these provisions also appear to allow the standards within the national eco-labels to set the *substantive* environmental performances required by authorities. This is important because it means authorities do not have to give extensive consideration to difficult questions of environmental policy such as the appropriate level of performance required.[53] Third, by contrast, the provisions are restrictive to the extent that they impose procedural standards of transparency on all eco-labels as a precondition for their use in procurement. This was not the case before and, potentially, authorities might not use some national eco-labels any longer because they do not meet these standards.[54] Previously, where no European standard existed, any national standard could be used if 'or equivalent' was included in the specification. Much, however, turns upon how the transparency rules are interpreted.

We can now explore the provisions themselves, and some of their instructive drafting history.

5.1. Eco-labels and technical specifications

The new provisions on eco-labels actually derived from an amendment proposed by the Parliament to the Commission's original drafts of the

---

[53] They would largely be subject to the EC Treaty obligations of non-discrimination and transparency.

[54] National eco-labels cover many more products than the European eco-label and have high levels of consumer recognition. The curtailment of authorities' ability to use them could thus be serious.

2004 directives. In 2001, the Parliamentary Committee on Environment, Public Health and Consumer Policy proposed amendments to Article 24(3) on drafting technical specifications so that they should be formulated by reference to 'national standards implementing European standards, European technical approvals, *European eco-labels ... or pluri-national or national eco-labels that require certification by third parties or environmental management systems*'[55] (emphasis added).

The Committee said that the amendment was 'extremely important and makes it clear that contracting authorities may draw up technical specifications by reference to eco-labels which have been adopted in accordance with the provisions of EC law or are developed in open, transparent, non-discriminatory procedures involving all stakeholders'.[56] The Committee was keen to point out that it would be inconsistent for Directorate General Internal Market to ignore a key policy of Directorate General Environment:

> The award of eco-labels constitutes a binding EC system designed to promote environmental protection and sustainable development in accordance with the Treaty. It is anomalous that the Commission's proposal makes no mention of the use of eco-labels in technical specifications. The criteria for the award of eco-labels are developed on the basis of open, transparent and non-discriminatory procedures involving the participation on an equal footing of all parties concerned.[57]

The problem for the Parliament was that its amendments did not require that the eco-label system meet these transparency tests. Rather it appeared to assume that national eco-label schemes did so. The Commission took the initiative to fill this gap and revised its draft directive[58] to include this. The final provision reads:[59]

---

[55] Committee on the Environment, Public Health and Consumer Policy, Opinion on the proposal for a European Parliament and Council Directive on the coordination of procedures for the award of public supply contracts, public service contracts and public works contracts, COM (2000) 275, Amendment 8.

[56] *Ibid.*   [57] *Ibid.*

[58] European Commission, Amended proposal for a European Parliament and Council Directive concerning the coordination of procedures for the award of public supply contracts, public service contracts and public works contracts, COM (2002) 236 final.

[59] Article 23(3)(b) of the Public Sector Directive says that performance or functional requirements may be used and that these may include 'environmental characteristics'. When laying down these it is permissible to use any eco-label specification which meets the four conditions set in Article 23(6).

Article 23 (6) of the Public Sector Directive

Where contracting authorities lay down environmental characteristics in terms of performance or functional requirements as referred to in paragraph 3(b) they may use the detailed specifications, or, if necessary, parts thereof, as defined by European or (multi-) national eco-labels, or by any other eco-label, provided that:

- those specifications are appropriate to define the characteristics of the supplies or services that are the object of the contract,
- the requirements for the label are drawn up on the basis of scientific information,
- the eco-labels are adopted using a procedure in which all stakeholders, such as government bodies, consumers, manufacturers, distributors and environmental organisations can participate, and
- they are accessible to all interested parties.

Authorities may indicate that the products and services bearing the eco-label are presumed to comply with the technical specifications in the contract documents; they must accept any other appropriate means of proof, such as a technical dossier of the manufacturer or test report from a recognised body.

The provisions[60] are in principle a major step forward because they allow explicit reference to eco-labelling schemes both at EU, multinational (the Nordic countries share a scheme) and even national level when setting specifications. Given that reference to national standards is such a bête noire for DG Internal Market this was a major concession. Clearly the more general rule under Article 23(2)(a) of the Public Sector Directive is that if a contracting authority wishes to refer to technical specifications it must first utilise national standards that implement European standards and various other harmonised standards. Only if none of these exist can national standards be employed. Thus, performance and functional requirements may be exceptionally redefined by reference to eco-label specifications. There is no hierarchy in favour of European or other common standards.

Despite the permission to have recourse to national standards, the principle of alternative means is alive and well. Two distinct, but

---

[60] This approach, on procedures for adoption and the scientific foundations of the standard, resembles the approach under the World Trade Organization's Agreement on Technical Barriers to Trade and under its Agreement on Sanitary and Phytosanitary Measures: see M. Matushita, T. Schoenbaum and P. Mavroidis, *The World Trade Organization* (Oxford University Press, 2006), p. 475.

connected, issues arise here. First, the Commission makes it clear that 'you can never require tenderers to be registered under a certain eco-label scheme'.[61] This is correct, since authorities must accept tenders which achieve standards 'equivalent' to those underlying the eco-label scheme.[62]

The second issue concerns the question whether, if a tender does not achieve exact equivalence, the authority's decision to exclude it may be reviewed for proportionality. This author does not favour such a test for the reasons set out in section 4.1 above in discussing the Treaty. However, the Commission's views on this are ambiguous. It accepts that authorities can refer to eco-labels for 'the underlying specifications ... when defining performance-based or functional environmental requirements'.[63] However, the position is then made unclear by the statement that 'it is, however, not permitted to set a requirement for companies to possess a certain eco-label or be (fully) compliant with a certain eco-label'.[64] This seems to imply that a tenderer who could not meet the specification of the eco-label could challenge it in some way. This is ambiguous and unhelpful. One view is that it suggests a requirement that authorities weigh up a non-compliant tender in some kind of proportionality exercise. That would be impractical and cut down national discretion too much. The place for debate about specifications is the eco-label forum itself, not with the contracting authority.

5.1.1. Meeting the procedural standards for use of eco-labels as technical specifications

Before eco-labels may be used as the basis of technical specifications or award criteria, they must meet four conditions. Each presents serious problems of interpretation.

The first condition is that the eco-label specification must be 'appropriate'. This is very unclear. It may simply be a reference to the condition held to apply in *Concordia Bus Finland*, and now stated expressly in Article 53 of the Public Sector Directive, that award criteria must be linked to the subject matter of the contract. It might conceivably be

---

[61] See European Commission, *Handbook*, note 12, p. 19. This reflects the prohibition in Article 23(8) of the Public Sector Directive: 'Unless justified by the subject-matter of the contract, technical specifications shall not refer to a specific make or source, or a particular process, or to trademarks, patents, types or a specific origin or production with the effect of favouring or eliminating certain undertakings or certain products.'

[62] Case C–45/87, *Dundalk*, note 27 above, and Article 23(3)(b) of the Public Sector Directive.

[63] See European Commission, *Handbook*, note 12, p. 19.   [64] *Ibid.*

argued that 'appropriate' may involve rather more than this, on the basis that, even if there is a link, using a particular specification may still be 'inappropriate'. This might be where the environmental benefit is rather remote or intangible. However, the directive contains nothing to support this interpretation and for contracting authorities to investigate the 'appropriateness' of each specification in a national eco-label scheme would involve heavy costs with uncertain outcomes. Furthermore, rather than importing such an additional constraint, the word 'appropriate' may simply mean that a requirement must comply with all other conditions laid down by the directive.

The second condition, which states that the eco-label specification must be drawn up 'on the basis of scientific evidence', is also unclear. This perhaps reflects a suspicion in the Commission that ecological criteria could be manipulated to favour national producers without giving demonstrable environmental benefits. The condition does not say how far a contracting authority must investigate for itself the science behind the specification. On the face of it, it cannot simply assume adequacy of the science. Furthermore, what kind of evidence is sufficient? Much ecological science depends on value judgments about risk, worth of species, cost/benefits and so on. Eco-labels reflect these as much as they do scientific evidence. In fact, the precautionary principle is recognised in EC law. This allows action to restrict an activity that may be harmful to the environment even before definitive scientific proof is obtained. However, it is very difficult to operate, because it does not provide enough clarity in individual cases.[65] These questions are very complex for specialist environmental agencies. Contracting authorities will find it difficult to know what is required by the condition that an eco-label be based upon scientific evidence.

The third condition states that the eco-label standard must have been set following a procedure in which all stakeholders could participate. This is interesting because it reflects the constitutional dimensions inherent in the *Cassis de Dijon* decision. The work of Maduro, now Advocate General at the ECJ, explored this in detail.[66] He argued that the ECJ's jurisprudence on Article 28 up to *Keck*[67] was based upon the

---

[65] See Article 174 EC Treaty which states that Community policy 'shall be based on the precautionary principle'. The Court of First Instance discussed the principle in Case T–13/99, *Pfizer Animal Health* v. *Council* [2002] ECR II–3302.

[66] Maduro, note 8 above.

[67] Joined Cases C–267 and C–268/91 *Keck and Mithouard* [1993] ECR I–6097.

notion that there was a political gap in the EC's regulatory structure. The
Member States regulate product markets without taking into account the
interests of producers and consumers in other Member States. Given
the predominance of national politics and national interest groups, this is
not surprising. However, in a quasi-federal EC this was unacceptable.
There had to be a mechanism for bringing those cross-border trading
interests into the equation faced by national regulators. Maduro argues
that this was the proper purpose of *Cassis de Dijon*. The ECJ assumed the
political role of ensuring a fair balance between the needs of each
Member State and that of the EC as a whole. It did this by ensuring
that regulatory barriers were scrutinised in proportionality terms for
their effects on trade. However, he argues for a limited role for the ECJ
which 'should not second-guess national regulatory choices but should
instead seek to ensure that there is no under-representation of the
interests of the nationals of other Member States in the national political
process'.[68] He argues for a nuanced approach to Article 28 which supports the requirement for discrimination to be shown unless there is
reason to think that the (non-discriminatory) rule has been adopted
without representation of cross-border interests. One might well add
that if the ECJ should indeed refrain from second-guessing Member
States' regulatory choices, then how much more should it refrain from
second-guessing their choices as market participants?

The requirement that an eco-label be adopted following a procedure,
and using criteria, which are accessible to all stakeholders, seems to be
another solution to this problem of under-representation. It also appears
unique in EC law to the knowledge of this author.[69] We will assume for
the moment that the eco-label is not prone to this defect of potential
'nationalism'. The Member State eco-label must allow sufficient access to
national and cross-border interest groups in order that it meet these
minimum democratic safeguards within the expanded EC polity. This
also reflects principles of participation recognised by administrative law
which emphasise the importance of the opportunity to be consulted on
proposed regulatory rules. The idea is in some respects a sound one. If
parties have a chance to influence the debate on the criteria for the
eco-label there is less danger that the standard will merely reflect national
traditions or industrial interests. It may also include more informed

---

[68] Maduro, note 8 above, p. 173.

[69] It seems, however, to reflect regulatory techniques adopted by the WTO: see note 60
above.

scientific thinking. However, the process is still not perfect; cross-border interests may have less bargaining power with national regulators than domestic counterparts.

From the perspective of contracting authorities, however, the provision is troubling. It is not clear if each eco-label must be scrutinised retrospectively to ensure that its procedural process was open – a difficult exercise involving complex paper trails. Also it is not certain which stakeholders must be consulted or the form that this should take. It might be enough that the eco-label body publicised the proposed standard in trade, environmental and other journals. However, rather more active involvement might be required from stakeholders to show that the standard was not simply the result of insiders colluding. The contracting authority will find it impossible alone to answer these questions. There will no doubt always have been some stakeholders unhappy about the criteria set and their access to the process.[70]

The fourth condition is that the eco-label criteria must be 'accessible' to all interested parties. Accessibility could take many forms but publicly available rules on what the eco-label requires are clearly essential. Any scheme where covert rules exist will fail to meet this test. The rules would also need to be easy to interpret and apply, employing terms and concepts understood in scientific and industrial culture across the EC. Use of obscure terms which are difficult to transpose for producers would not be accessible. However, we must be careful not to impose impossibly

---

[70] Maduro says that 'Rules on the characteristics of products tend to affect divergent national and foreign interests. It is sufficient to think of all national measures that regulate the composition of traditional national products or which correspond to the particular forms of production established in a particular Member State. However, in the case of product requirements of a technical nature (such as rules on additives for example) which are not part of national production habits, the same risk does not arise. Legislation aiming to regulate a recently discovered environmental or health risk would be included in this category' (Maduro, note 8 above, p. 174). He continues by saying that under his proposal the ECJ will 'only review national regulatory policies where there is a suspicion of representative malfunction in the national political process with regard to nationals of other Member States' (174). The question arises as to which side of the line an eco-labelling scheme would fall. This author would suggest that this is where Maduro's work becomes impractical because it is actually rather difficult to distinguish between rules which are likely to reflect national interests and those that are not. To take eco-labelling criteria as an example, the method for setting such criteria will include reference to ecological science, ethical values, industry views and environmental group pressure. These may lead to criteria which favour national production habits because of domestic industry being a stakeholder but they also appear to concern scientific data that Maduro argues does not lead to an exclusion of values and interests shared across Europe.

onerous obligations on eco-labels that may have limited resources. Translation into other languages must be for each tenderer. There are also genuine differences between different Member States' environmental cultures. Accessibility should not require 'harmonisation' of all concepts. There must remain a burden on producers to seek clarification where the meaning of technical terms is doubtful.

5.1.2. A practical solution: a presumption of adequacy for certain eco-label schemes

The high degree of uncertainty introduced by the conditions in Article 23(6) of the Public Sector Directive will require some form of judicial resolution. The effect of referring to eco-label specifications that do not meet the conditions will be to render them invalid. A court faced with litigation on the compatibility of an eco-label scheme with Article 23(6) will need to make a reference to the ECJ. In broad terms, the best policy for interpreting Article 23(6) is to allow contracting authorities to make a presumption that certain eco-labels are generally compatible with the provision because of the way they are operated. The Commission itself implies as much in its *Handbook*. In discussing eco-labels, it refers to 'some interesting European and national eco-labels' (specifically the German 'Blue Angel' and Scandinavian 'Nordic Swan') which 'meet high standards of transparency and scientific rigour in terms of setting criteria and are non-discriminatory'.[71] This endorsement refers to some of the conditions set out in Article 23(6). It may be that this is a solution to the uncertainty in that certain eco-labelling bodies are considered to operate broadly in a manner which complies with the conditions. This would remove the burden for procurers of investigating each eco-label standard. However we may still need several test cases to work through each of the four conditions discussed above. The interesting feature is that the Commission does not seem to doubt that even long-standing eco-labels in which national interest groups no doubt dominated in the past satisfy the conditions by being transparent, rigorous and open to participation.[72]

Of course, progressive judicial recognition of the legitimacy of specific eco-label schemes will take time and be subject to the accident of litigation. Furthermore, it might prejudice the emergence of newer, and perhaps better, eco-label schemes simply because until such a new

---

[71] See European Commission, *Handbook*, note 12 above, p. 20.

[72] *Ibid.*, p. 21 where the Commission emphasised the role of third-party certification.

scheme is judicially recognised it will be legally more secure for authorities to continue referring to older schemes which have been judicially approved. If reference to eco-labels is to be widely adopted by contracting authorities, the ECJ ought to recognise a very substantial margin of discretion on their part; a decision to refer to a particular eco-label should not be insecure unless there is evidence of bad faith or manifest error.

As to eco-labels that fail to meet the standards of Article 23(6), the Commission singles out eco-labels that do not define environmental performance but rather relate to general management of the company and/or concern ethical or other similar issues. As noted above, the Commission's *Handbook* endorses, on the other hand, single-issue labels which relate, for example, to energy use such as the 'Energy Star' or EU organic or energy labels.[73] These appear to be assumed to fall within the 'eco-label'. What about food? Organic food standards for the EU are laid down in Regulation 2092/91 but the *Handbook* says authorities can make their requirements even stricter and that this might include purchasing only varieties in season 'in the area' at the time to reduce transport costs.[74] This is interesting because it appears to allow indirect discrimination against non-local producers. The reduction in 'food miles' is an adequate justification for this approach. This again signals a greater recognition of environmental values by the Commission.

The Commission does not rule out the possibility that private labels may comply with the Article 23(6) conditions. These include the Pan European Forest Certification Council and some organic labels. The *Handbook* notes that 'depending on their accessibility and the way they are adopted these labelling schemes may or may not conform to the guidelines.'[75] This represents a significant and welcome change of position from previous communications in which the Commission displayed a much more hostile attitude to private labels.[76] These labels can be innovative and flexible, driving up industry standards more quickly. There should be no need for the state to be involved so long as transparency and access are assured.

---

[73] Discussed further p. 382 above.
[74] European Commission, *Handbook*, note 12 above, p. 24.   [75] *Ibid.*, p. 21.
[76] European Commission, Interpretative Communication on the Community law applicable to public procurement and the possibilities for integrating environmental considerations into public procurement, COM (2001) 274.

In summary, the *Handbook* seems to imply a rather more generous approach than the directives might first indicate. The broad-brush idea of allowing certain bodies to be validated such that their eco-labels are presumed to comply with Article 23 is sound. However, there would no doubt have to be some scope for challenging the criteria relating to a particular product for failure of participation or scientific rigour in a particular case. The presumption must be rebuttable if Article 23 of the Public Sector Directive is not to be denuded of its purpose in protecting transparency and stakeholder interests. Finally, the *Handbook* is only the opinion of the Commission and is not binding on the courts.

5.2. Eco-labels and award criteria

Given the complexity of using eco-labels in technical specifications, award criteria might be a better place to employ them. However, here too, the position is not totally clear. The directives do not specifically refer to eco-labels in relation to award criteria. As chapter 2 explained, Article 53 of the Public Sector Directive states that the award shall be based on lowest price or most economically advantageous tender 'from the point of view of the contracting authority' and that in the latter case the criteria used 'shall be various criteria linked to the subject-matter of the public contract … for example … environmental characteristics'. The European Parliament had suggested amendments which were broader in a number of respects, including removing the requirement for economic advantage to be 'from the point of view of the contracting authority', thus allowing wider ecological gains. In light of the case-law, however, this amendment may have been unnecessary because, as we have seen, in *Concordia Bus Finland*, the ECJ accepted under the old directives criteria relating to environmental externalities (air and noise pollution) which conferred no direct economic advantage. Since Recital 1 recites that the directive is based upon this case law the same principle would apply under the current directive.

The Parliament also said the permissible award criteria should include 'environmental and health impacts including production methods'.[77] This would have allowed reliance upon eco-label life cycle standards more readily. The amendments were not accepted but it is still possible to view reliance on eco-labels as implicitly allowed because 'environmental characteristics' is ambiguous and the *Concordia Bus Finland*

---

[77] Note 55 above, Amendment 18.

decision held that benefits did not need to accrue directly to the authority. Furthermore, as discussed in chapter 4, in *EVN-Wienstrom* the ECJ recognised, as regards an electricity supply contract, the permissibility of an award criterion relating to production processes and methods of electricity to be supplied to a contracting authority (i.e. a criterion that favoured electricity generated from renewable energy sources). If requirements relating to production processes and methods are permissible as contract conditions and as award criteria, what is the point in denying contracting authorities the right to refer to eco-labels reflecting full life-cycle environmental impacts of the products concerned?

This is of some importance where the eco-label market is a narrow one with few producers. Here use of an eco-label technical specification might lead to a small number of compliant tenders and suspicions about the level of openness of the tender. However, in such cases, the requirement that suppliers be entitled to demonstrate that they achieve 'equivalent' standards to those of the eco-label ought to be sufficient to protect market access. On the other hand, as chapter 3 explained, it is possible that using the award criteria approach allows that authority to better assess and implement an appropriate balance between ecology and value for money. The number of compliant tenders is likely to be higher. The author has indeed seen examples of purchases which gave weight to eco-labelled products but did not require this as a specification.[78]

6. Conclusions

The author has made informal enquiries with some eco-labelling scheme coordinators across Europe and they appear content that the directives do represent an open door for green procurement. They have been encouraging reliance upon their own national schemes but also European and other national schemes where there are overlaps in quality. The suggestion is that the directives provide a measure of clarity in an area which before was uncertain. Contracting authorities sometimes referred to national eco-labels but were unsure about the precise legality of this. They now seem more content that reference to, particularly national, eco-labels is lawful under the new directives. This solves the basic problem of use of national standards being inherently troublesome from the EC discrimination perspective. Particularly in relation to award

[78] This was the approach in a Nordic school purchase: see O. Solevag, *Purchasing and Environmental Issues– a Study from Norway*, available at www.bergfald.no

criteria, eco-labels could be a straightforward and useful method of increasing green procurement. Using eco-labels to set technical specifications is potentially more complex for the reasons stated above. Much depends upon how rigidly the procedural rules in Article 23(6) of the Public Sector Directive are interpreted.

However, the market integration side of the equation is less satisfactory. Green procurement at national level is clearly good but an EC-wide market would be better from the perspective of economies of scale. There is a danger that the Commission's attempts to inject transparency and stakeholder input into the eco-labelling schemes will not be an adequate means of creating this single market in green goods. The political bargaining power of cross-border companies may be weak. They may find it impossible to influence eco-label specifications in the face of national interest groups. At a basic level, it is not clear how stakeholder interests should be incorporated into the process. The convergence of standards that one would like to see may not occur. Although national autonomy to express green preferences is important, the European environment as a whole is affected by production of goods and services. Green procurement needs to expand Europe-wide to have maximum environmental benefit and that requires some degree of convergence in standards. Whilst some environmental impacts are localised, many are not. Allowing national autonomy in this area may not adequately deal with environmental issues (such as carbon emissions) that are truly cross-border.

The directives may have failed to inject sufficient cross-border influence into the standard-setting process for national eco-labels. However, much will depend upon the intensity and constructiveness of bargaining between interest groups within the eco-labelling process, both at EC and national levels. The directives do not legislate for the level of engagement with stakeholders and indeed it is hard to see how legislation could do so without becoming cumbersome. The Commission could, however, use its influence to assist cross-border interest groups which are experiencing difficulty in securing good access to a foreign eco-label forum. Whilst its interpretations of directives are not binding, its view might be influential with national standards agencies. Litigation to secure access is another alternative but seems less likely to be taken up for reasons of cost and reputation damage. If good quality access for pan-European stakeholders occurs, then one would hope that there might be benefits for the European environment. National schemes may continue to converge through removing minor differences in specification and a pan-European market may develop to the benefit of consumers and the environment. This model envisages a growing European polity developing through access to national fora for out-of-state interests. We already see that such a European 'polity' has developed through the participation of stake-holders in the EU eco-label process. Indeed, if the EU labelling scheme becomes more widely known and credible then reliance upon national labels may fall away.

11

CSR in the utilities sector and the implications of EC procurement policy: a framework for debate

SUE ARROWSMITH AND COLIN MAUND[1]

1. Introduction

Corporate social responsibility (CSR) is one of the major developments affecting business over the last decade. CSR has been defined by the European Commission as 'a concept whereby companies integrate social and environmental concerns in their business operations and in their interaction with their stakeholders on a voluntary basis'.[2] Starting with roots in a variety of separate pressures upon corporations to become more socially responsible, CSR is now a major driver behind business decisions. From the 1990s it is issues relating to the supply chain that have come to the forefront.[3] Most large western organisations have been able to clean up their own backyard, ensuring that within their own boundaries issues like human rights, labour standards, environmental care and occupational health are being dealt with through programmes aimed at ensuring consistency of treatment and minimum standards.

---

[1] The authors would like to thank Professor Jeremy Moon, Director of the International Centre for Corporate Social Responsibility, Nottingham University Business School, for his valuable assistance, and Ciara Kennedy-Loest of Lovells, with whom we have had useful discussions.

[2] European Commission, Promoting a European framework for Corporate Social Responsibility, COM (2001) 366 final, a definition taken up in the European Commission, Communication concerning Corporate Social Responsibility: a business contribution to sustainable development ('Communication on CSR'), COM (2002) 347 final. Other terms are also sometimes used to emphasise various facets of the concept: in particular, the term Business Social Responsibility is found, especially to indicate that the subject examined embraces small businesses. Since this article is concerned with EC regulation we will use the term CSR, and use it to cover all business, since the Commission uses it in this sense. On the definitional issues see further J. Moon, 'Corporate Social Responsibility: An Overview', in *The International Directory of Corporate Philanthropy* (Europa Publications Limited, 2002), pp. 3–4.

[3] See generally D. Vogel, *The Market for Virtue: the Potential and Limits of Corporate Social Responsibility* (Washington, DC: Brookings Institution Press, 2005), in particular chapter 4.

However, with the growth and complexity of supply chains and the move to global sourcing, it has become increasingly difficult to ensure similar conduct further down the supply chain.

One sector affected, like others, by these developments, and in which CSR issues have recently come to the fore, is the utilities sector. In addressing supply chain issues, however, many utilities are faced with legal constraints that do not apply to other private firms,[4] namely the restrictions of the EC Utilities Directive (Directive 2004/17).[5] As chapter 2 explained, this directive regulates the procurement of many public and private utilities, with the aim of opening their procurement markets to EC-wide competition. In doing so, the directive imposes significant restrictions on the policies that utilities can adopt on supply chain issues. The European Commission itself in its 2002 Communication on CSR has endorsed a strategy to promote CSR policies at EC level,[6] which calls for the integration of CSR considerations into Community policies. However, there has been no serious consideration either within the EC or in academic literature of the implications of the Utilities Directive for CSR and of its interface with EC initiatives on CSR.

This chapter explains the directive's implications for CSR measures in the supply chain, and the policy issues that these raise. The main aim is to stimulate a debate on this subject at EC level, and to set out a framework for that debate. At a practical level, the analysis also highlights for utilities key legal requirements and risks that they must address in implementing CSR policies. It is not intended, on the other hand, to make recommendations either on how utilities *should* implement CSR policies or on how the EC should develop its own policies with respect to the Utilities Directive.

This chapter first briefly outlines the practical development and drivers for CSR in the supply chain, with particular reference to utilities (section 2) and then introduces the principles of the Utilities Directive (section 3). It then examines in detail the directive's implications for CSR in the supply chain (section 4). It also considers briefly the position of

---

[4] Except for undertakings subject to the Public Sector Directive which are subject to even greater constraints. On that directive's application to entities operating in the market, see S. Arrowsmith, *The Law of Public and Utilities Procurement*, 2nd edn (London: Sweet & Maxwell, 2005), at 15.8–15.9.

[5] Directive 2004/17/EC of the European Parliament and of the Council coordinating the procurement procedures of entities operating in the water, energy, transport and postal services sectors ('Utilities Directive') OJ 2004 No. L134/1.

[6] Communication on CSR, note 2 above.

utilities' procurement outside the directive (section 5). It then notes separately the particular issues that arise from increased globalisation and collaboration (section 6). Finally, based on the prior discussion, the chapter highlights the policy issues that need to be considered in developing policy in this area (section 7).

2. CSR and its relevance for utilities' supply chain policies

The proper role of a corporation as a creator of economic wealth principally for shareholders has been espoused by many, most famously by Friedman who claimed that 'few trends could so thoroughly undermine the foundations of our free society as the acceptance by corporate officials of a social responsibility other than to make as much money as possible for their stockholders'.[7] Following this principle, some would claim that social responsibility policies that are motivated merely by a concern for responsible behaviour have no place in corporate activity.

However, it is increasingly argued that adherence to CSR policies is *not* contrary to maximising shareholder value and to a large extent these now appear to be driven by concern for profitability. Commercial pressure to act in a socially responsible manner comes from three main sources, namely consumers of an entity's products or services, investors, and employees and potential employees.[8] Firms are also influenced by other factors, such as avoiding the greater burden of regulation that might result if they do not act on a 'voluntary' basis.[9] (For example, there is evidence that UK electricity companies changed their tough policy on disconnections because of the threat of action by the regulator.) Even to the extent that action is driven by genuine social concerns, the need for profitability may place constraints on what can be achieved.

The view that CSR is 'good for business' is contested by those who argue that corporations should not be 'second-guessing' true business drivers.[10] It is very difficult to measure the impact of CSR policies on profitability. Vogel, in a review of the empirical evidence of the financial

---

[7] M. Friedman, *Capitalism and Freedom* (University of Chicago Press, 1962).

[8] For a more detailed analysis of these drivers, see Vogel, note 3 above, especially chapter 3.

[9] In this respect, firms' behaviour can be seen as on the boundaries of a concept of CSR that is defined by reference to voluntary action in the sense of action not influenced by legal requirements.

[10] See recently, for example, E. Steinberg, 'Does Corporate Social Responsibility Make Good Sense?' minutes of the AEI; March 2006 available at http://www.aei.org/events/filter.all,eventid.1265/summary.asp.

impact of CSR, has concluded that it is 'inconclusive'[11] and suggests that its value may possibly be confined to businesses that make CSR a specific part of their drive to attract business.[12] However, despite this, there are clear indicators that the various drivers for including CSR policies in the everyday activities of major organisations are having a significant effect. Many large corporations now produce annual Corporate Responsibility Reports[13] and these have moved from being bland descriptions of sporadic company activities to being statistically thorough and independently audited accounts of progress.

Currently, nowhere is seeing more pressure than the supply chain, which is where major western corporations feel particularly vulnerable and where the most difficult issues arise. This is not surprising. The increase of outsourcing and the move to global sourcing, including from developing countries, has made CSR in the supply chain both more important and immeasurably more difficult. When the average notebook computer may include work by over 1,000 different suppliers, it is not surprising that corporations have traditionally chosen to deal with the issue of supply chain CSR at the end of the process rather than the beginning, focusing on 'top tier' suppliers who supply the major consumer-facing brand names rather than a myriad of smaller specialist companies.

Despite a reluctance to take CSR issues further into the supply chain, however, and the difficulties involved, the issue cannot be ignored permanently and there are now signs that firms are trying to effect change to supplier behaviour more broadly. Amongst the first to go down this route were garment and textile companies. These suffered the effects of bad publicity and consumer boycotts in the mid-1990s as a result of their perceived failures, especially in labour conditions, and reacted by setting up processes to impose standards on unwilling suppliers and to monitor and enforce compliance. These processes were largely aimed at the top levels of the supply chain, even though the garment retail industry generally has a fairly short supply chain. As the policies have spread into other industries, however, there have been major issues to resolve as many of these have deeper and more complex supply chains. Furthermore, the range of CSR issues has been increasing, to include areas such as bribery and corruption, occupational health and

---

[11] See, generally, Vogel, note 3 above, chapters 2 and 3.
[12] See, in particular, Vogel, note 3 above, chapter 3.
[13] See, for example, the CSR reports produced by BP and the BBC, a public sector organisation, available at www.bp.com and www.bbc.co.uk respectively.

development of sustainable industry. Thus the CSR agenda is growing and developing, with greater pressure upon purchasers and their supply chains.

Utilities are especially sensitive to public perception and pressure. This is, firstly, for historic reasons, with utilities traditionally regarded as part of the public sector and, until recently, mainly publicly owned. Second, there is fear that even the private utilities remain under state influence, with most of their fees from customers in part set or agreed by state regulators. Thirdly, the utilities face real public examination as a source of environmental pollution. Given this sensitivity it is unlikely that utilities would take a negative approach to CSR. Further, the supply chain was bound to become an issue given its importance economically to utilities and the extent of outsourcing.

This perception of developments is reinforced by specific company activity: the utilities have been devoting much energy and political capital to develop sound CSR policies, to put themselves in the top quartile of the various social accountability indices. Whether this is done for specific business reasons or as part of image building and social accountability is hard to elucidate. However this may be, large utilities clearly feel that it is strategically significant to do well in these indices. Further, many utilities are now publicly quoted, and these have been quick to pick up on the investment pressure for them to remain in the key Dow Jones Sustainability and FTSE4Good indices, believing that to drop out could have serious impacts on their share price and credibility. In addition, the growth in energy prices has led to interest in obtaining compensating cost reductions in procurement. National Grid has generally been at the top of the CSR pile for utilities for the last few years and has publicly indicated that it believes there are substantial strategic and profit related gains in this. CSR is also being used by some utilities as part of their overall strategy for risk management and for protecting their brand image. These areas are regarded as vital at a time of consolidation in the industry, when the opportunity to make politically sensitive acquisitions may hinge on the feelings of political and community leaders about an acquirer's CSR credentials.

As we have seen, the supply chain is important for CSR because of the size of utilities' spend and because of the difficulties it presents, especially as utilities look increasingly at sourcing in low-cost economies. This trend has been accelerated by two factors, namely the emergence of important new sources of supply, particularly India and China, and the growth in energy prices, leading to interest in procurement savings.

Larger companies are seeking to source more proactively in low-cost areas such as Eastern Europe, India and China. (One of the co-authors, Maund, has worked with several European utilities that have opened sourcing offices based in China and/or are using sourcing services to find and qualify Chinese suppliers using qualification processes that include CSR elements.) With the growth of low-cost country sourcing utilities have come to understand how their changing buying behaviour is creating new risks. These risks are not limited to companies seeking new supply sources; even those buying principally from traditional sources find that these sources are themselves increasingly outsourcing to low-cost countries or transferring work to factories or offices there.

Finally, the broadening of CSR to embrace new issues, as discussed above, has contributed to increasing concern over the EC procurement rules. The problems of the EC rules were less apparent when the issues related mainly to environmental care and health and safety, but as the areas covered by the CSR agenda have increased so has the importance of the legal constraints.

3. The EC Utilities Directive

Most corporations pursuing CSR policies are subject to few, if any, regulatory constraints. However, as mentioned, many utilities are subject to significant legal restrictions in their supply chain activities under the Utilities Directive. As chapter 2 explained, this forms part of the EC's regime to open up procurement to EC-wide competition. As elaborated there, the EC Treaty prohibits discrimination and certain other measures restricting access to public procurement and these Treaty prohibitions are supplemented by two directives, the Public Sector Directive and Utilities Directive. These directives require procuring entities to follow transparent award procedures for major contracts to ensure, in particular, that discriminatory behaviour cannot be hidden.

The current Utilities Directive has its origins in a directive adopted in 1990.[14] It covers[15] the contracts of certain entities that operate in four sectors: water – chiefly operation or provision of networks for transporting

---

[14] Council Directive 90/531/EEC on the procurement procedures of entities operating in the water, energy, transport and telecommunications sectors, OJ 1990 No. L297/1. Services were added in 1993 by Council Directive 93/38/EEC coordinating the procurement procedures of entities operating in the water, energy, transport and telecommunications sector, OJ 1993 No. L199/84.

[15] For details of coverage see Arrowsmith, note 4 above, chapter 15.

or distributing drinking water, and disposal and treatment of sewage; transport – chiefly operation or provision of railway, bus and tram networks, and provision of port and airport facilities; energy, notably provision and operation of networks for distributing gas, electricity and other heat sources and exploring for/extracting oil, gas and solid fuels; and postal services. These are utility sectors in which the EC considers there are significant risks of discriminatory behaviour, because the utilities involved do not operate in a fully competitive environment – for example, because of the high barriers to entry in setting up networks. (Where utilities do operate in a competitive market for an activity, because the market has been liberalised, the Commission may give an exemption from the directive.)[16]

As chapter 2 explained, the Public Sector Directive is largely confined to traditional public bodies, referred to as 'contracting authorities'.[17] The Utilities Directive, however, is not confined to contracting authorities that are subject to the Public Sector Directive.[18] It covers, in addition, two other categories, namely:

i) public undertakings, which are companies operating on the market that are subject to the dominant influence of a public authority,[19] and

ii) any utilities (including private utilities) that operate on the basis of special or exclusive rights granted by government – for example monopoly or other special licences.[20]

It is not common to subject state enterprises or private entities, even monopolies, to public procurement rules: the commercial nature of these bodies is considered both to require significant flexibility in purchasing and to provide some market discipline that reduces the need for bureaucratic regulation. However, EC regulation is justified by reference to the objective of the EC regime of preventing discriminatory behaviour:[21] the

---

[16] Under Article 30 of the Utilities Directive.

[17] See chapter 2, section 4.3.2. This directive has a very limited application to other entities (for example, some rules apply to works concessionaires and private firms awarded certain government-subsidised contracts).

[18] When they are involved in the activities covered by the Utilities Directive the Utilities Directive applies instead.

[19] See the definition in Article 2(1)(b) of the Utilities Directive. Some public undertakings are also covered by the public sector rules.

[20] See the definition in Article 2(3) of the Utilities Directive.

[21] The WTO's Government Procurement Agreement (GPA), which has similar objectives, covers some public companies but not purely private ones.

EC considers that there is a risk of discrimination because of the absence of commercial pressures combined with the susceptibility to governmental influence that arises from dependency on government for licences or other rights. Thus the Utilities Directive is applied to many organisations that are owned wholly or partly by private shareholders, and which seek to make profits for those shareholders. As discussed below, it is not clear how far the Treaty rules prohibiting discrimination by traditional public bodies apply also to these utilities, and thus the Utilities Directive has always included an explicit prohibition on discrimination (now found in Article 10) as well as requirements to follow transparent award procedures.[22]

As chapter 2 explained (in section 4.3.4), both procurement directives require entities to advertise their contracts in the *Official Journal of the European Union* and to award contracts through a prescribed competitive procedure. Under the Utilities Directive, a utility has a free choice between[23] the open procedure, restricted procedure and negotiated procedure with a notice. In this utilities have more flexibility than applies under the Public Sector Directive[24] – which generally requires use of the open or restricted procedure – and also have more flexibility in other respects, such as use of qualification systems (see section 4.6 below). The Explanatory Memorandum for the Commission's proposal for the original Utilities Directive justified this by the fact that 'industrial enterprises' engage more in organic and cooperative relationships, rather than one-off arms-length transactions, particularly in purchasing complex equipment central to their mission.[25] This leaves it unclear, perhaps, how far it is the nature of the purchases made rather than the nature of the organisation that is crucial. So far as the latter is concerned, more commercially motivated entities are less in need of strict regulation to eliminate discrimination, even if some regulation is necessary. In addition, some of these entities may in fact operate in an entirely commercial manner, and the directives may then have a detrimental impact on their ability to do so, which may need to be tolerated to achieve the directive's

---

[22] Such a general principle is now also stated in the Public Sector Directive, Article 2.

[23] Article 40(2) of the Utilities Directive. In limited cases defined in Article 40(3), such as extreme urgency, a utility may use a negotiated procedure without competition. On procedures see Arrowsmith, note 4 above, chapter 16.

[24] As to which see chapter 2, section 4.3.4.

[25] See European Commission, Proposal for a Council Directive on the procurement procedures of entities providing water, energy and transport services, COM (88) 377 final, *Bulletin of the European Communities 6/88*, Explanatory Memorandum, para. 79.

broader goals; in this case providing for flexibility reduces any detrimental effect.

As noted in chapter 2 (in section 4.3.3), in addition to the specific transparency rules, three general principles apply, namely equal treatment, non-discrimination and transparency. These are set out in Article 10 of the Utilities Directive.

4. The Utilities Directive's impact on CSR policies

4.1. Introduction

As already mentioned, the Utilities Directive restricts the freedom of regulated utilities to implement CSR policies in the same way as unregulated companies.[26] There has been much debate in academic literature on the Public Sector Directive's effect on socially responsible purchasing by government – in relation to which the term 'CSR', which originated to describe private sector activities, is now sometimes used.[27] However, there has been virtually no attention paid to the special position of utilities. To a great extent the same legal rules apply under both directives.[28] However, they do differ in some important respects, notably (as discussed below) in the rules on excluding suppliers and on qualification systems, and the implications of these differences for CSR have not been explored. For example, the European Commission's Interpretative Communication on social purchasing merely mentions that there is a 'wider' discretion in excluding suppliers under the Utilities Directive, but does not comment on what the differences are or on the difficult questions of interpretation that arise;[29] whilst the social purchasing guidance from the UK Office of Government Commerce (OGC) deals only with

---

[26] Except, as noted, undertakings subject to the public sector rules.
[27] The European Commission uses this term to embrace these issues in the public context in its Communication on CSR, note 2 above, and the term has become so widespread that many public sector organisations now have embraced the term CSR and even have job roles as CSR specialists.
[28] And the same interpretations apply: see, in particular, Case C–513/99, *Concordia Bus Finland* v. *Helsingin Kaupunki* ('*Concordia Bus Finland*') [2002] ECR I–7213.
[29] European Commission, Interpretative Communication on the Community law applicable to public procurement and the possibilities for integrating social considerations into public procurement, COM (2001) 566 final, p. 9. Likewise the Interpretative Communication on the Community law applicable to public procurement and the possibilities for integrating environmental considerations into public procurement, COM (2001) 274 final, does not specifically consider utilities.

the Public Sector Directive.[30] Further, the differing provisions have not yet been interpreted by the ECJ. There are also several important policy issues not yet considered in the public debate that arise for many utilities, particularly because of their private nature and the fact that many operate in a market, requiring them to be responsive to the concerns of their investors, customers and employees. It is also notable that the OGC and Commission guidance focuses on the kinds of social and environmental issues that concern the traditional public sector, and has little to say on, for example, issues relating to labour conditions in developing countries, which are of major concern to some utilities. Further, whilst the Commission's recent general Communication on CSR contains a brief section on 'Public Procurement',[31] this mainly refers back to the Commission's own Communications on procurement, which do not address utilities. This absence of debate perhaps reflects the relatively recent origins of the social dimension of utilities supply chain policy.

The analysis below will not duplicate the existing literature on socially responsible procurement[32] but will focus on issues specific to utilities. It will become apparent that some CSR activities are clearly permitted, whilst others, even those common in some private firms, are not. In many instances, however, as with the directives more generally, the exact requirements of the law are simply unclear. Thus for utilities wishing to implement CSR policies the question is often whether or not the benefits of a particular policy outweigh the legal risks.

4.2. Requirements concerning contract performance: technical requirements and 'special' conditions

4.2.1. Permitted requirements

The taxonomy of horizontal policies in chapter 3 made a distinction between measures relating to performance of the contract awarded, on the one hand, and measures not limited to that contract, on the other. One of the main mechanisms utilities use for implementing socially responsible procurement is the setting out of CSR requirements to be met in performing the contract itself, a mechanism that falls into the former category. These can be directed both at first-tier suppliers and at others in the supply chain, ensuring that the impact of the contract itself

---

[30] OGC, 'Social Issues in Purchasing' (February 2006), available at www.ogc.gov.uk.

[31] Communication on CSR, note 2 above, pp. 21–22.

[32] See chapters 1–4 of the present book and the literature cited there.

is positive, or at least neutral, from the perspective of social responsibility. Two major concerns, for example, are to safeguard the welfare of those employed on the contract, and to prevent the contract having a negative environmental impact.

As chapter 4 explained, under the Public Sector Directive entities may lay down social and environmental requirements relating to contract performance, which can be divided into two categories: technical requirements (such as a requirement for low energy light bulbs),[33] and special conditions under Article 26 (such as a requirement for suppliers to recruit long-term job seekers for the contract).[34] These same possibilities also apply under the Utilities Directive, which in Article 38 contains a parallel provision to Article 26 of the Public Sector Directive, stating that utilities may apply special conditions relating to performance of the contract. It appears that utilities could in principle include conditions for a main contractor to ensure that labour or environmental standards are met further down the supply chain, and specifically require suppliers to include equivalent conditions in subcontracts. Under Article 34 of the Utilities Directive utilities' contract requirements are subject to parallel controls to those under Article 23 of the Public Sector Directive, concerning transparency and other requirements for 'technical specifications', as discussed in chapter 4 in section 8.1.3.

These basic principles appear clear enough. However, as chapter 4 explained, there are question marks over how far an entity may impose conditions on work undertaken outside its own Member State, either in other EC Member States or in third countries, where the conditions go beyond merely requiring an undertaking to comply with the law or collective agreements of the state in which the work is carried out.[35] This issue may arise with supply contracts – for example, where a utility purchases transformers or protective clothing made in the developing world – or (increasingly) in relation to services contracts – for example, where a call-centre function is outsourced outside the EC. We saw in

---

[33] The 2004 directives also introduced a new *requirement* for regulated purchasers to design specifications for all users (Article 23(1) of the Public Sector Directive and Article 34(1) of the Utilities Directive), thus possibly imposing a social obligation beyond those applicable to other private companies and even to competitors (for example, those exempt from the directive because they operate in market conditions). See chapter 7, section 5.2 of this book and Arrowsmith, note 4 above, at 17.75.

[34] See chapter 4, section 8.

[35] That utilities (like the public sector) may require suppliers to comply with these is assumed in Article 39, which concerns provision of information on these matters to suppliers. See further the discussion of the public sector in chapter 4, section 8.1.1.

chapter 4 that the Commission has suggested that the EC Treaty may preclude conditions of this kind for supply contracts, apparently because of the potential impact beyond the contract – for example, by making it necessary to adapt production methods in a whole factory that produces goods for the contract.[36] This would seem to apply equally whether the business is organised by providing the goods and services directly or through subcontracting. If the Commission's view is correct, it will considerably restrict the scope for useful CSR policies that relate to, for example, labour conditions in developing countries. Chapter 4 suggested, however, that there are reasons to doubt the Commission's view, and it is not clear what approach the ECJ will take.[37]

As elaborated in chapter 4, in assessing whether a condition of this kind that hinders trade is justified the ECJ will consider whether the measure is suitable to achieve its objective. In the context of utilities, this raises several questions. One is whether the fact that the policy supports external norms, such as ILO standards, provides justification, without proving any concrete impact. The second arises from the fact that, as discussed, CSR requirements may have commercial motivations, whereby the utility's objective is not necessarily directly linked to the social impact of the policy but simply to the expectations of customers, investors etc. (expectations that may or may not be influenced by the actual social effects). As chapter 4 explained, the ECJ has repeatedly stated that economic objectives per se cannot suffice to justify hindrances to trade.[38] However, we suggested there that this applies only to a limited number of objectives that per se contravene free market principles.[39] Any such doctrine should not prevent concerns of profitability being relied on by corporations whose very objective is to make profits for shareholders, and which may compete with other entities that are not regulated in the same way. A third issue is the fact that a policy based simply on requirements for contract performance without supporting measures may be counter-productive. For example, prohibiting child labour without other measures concerned with schooling or alternative income sources may actually force those concerned into even more unsuitable occupations.[40] However, the Utilities Directive possibly limits the scope for utilities to take supportive measures that do not relate to the contract, as discussed at 4.3 below. It is not clear how the ECJ will deal with all these issues.

---

[36] See chapter 4, section 4.3.1.   [37] *Ibid.*   [38] See chapter 4, section 3.
[39] See chapter 2, section 3.   [40] See Vogel, note 3 above, pp. 98–99.

The ECJ is perhaps most likely to accept requirements embodied in international instruments such as the ILO Conventions, and may possibly do so regardless of their trade impact – and thus even for supply contracts. At the very least, it may accept them when a Convention has been ratified by the country in which the work is done, even though the standards have not been implemented into national law; and conditions relating to 'core' ILO standards[41] might even be accepted without ratification. Such standards may serve both to indicate a significant 'independent' justification for the content of the utility's requirement and to reduce the risk that it has been selected with discriminatory intent. The possibility of requiring compliance with ILO Conventions may also find indirect support in the procurement directives' recitals, which give as examples of permitted 'special conditions' requirements (when not implemented into national law) to comply with 'basic' ILO Conventions.[42] However, this admittedly does not rule out limits on the circumstances in which such standards may be set, and it is also not clear what is meant by 'basic' conventions. (If limited to certain core conventions it might even indicate a negative view on the possibility of imposing compliance with other Conventions.)[43] Further, whilst the recitals are relevant for interpreting the directives when ambiguous, the directives cannot authorise measures that contravene the Treaty.

EC law might not rule out even requirements going *beyond* ILO Conventions or other international treaties, even for supply contracts. If not, utilities may be able to require adherence to requirements that they have developed individually or in conjunction with other industrial partners, or to requirements reflected in industry standards such as SA8000 (a voluntary code developed by a group of large private-sector organisations and others (such as Amnesty International), which is based on, but goes beyond, ILO standards, including by requiring a 'living wage'). References

---

[41] These relate to freedom of association and the right to collective bargaining; the elimination of forced and child labour; and elimination of discrimination in employment: ILO Declaration on Fundamental Principles and Rights at Work, June 1998 available at www.ilo.org/dyn/declaris/DECLARATIONWEB.INDEXPAGE.

[42] Recital 44 of the Utilities Directive.

[43] Another argument that utilities may require suppliers to comply with ILO conventions is based on Article 59(4) of the Utilities Directive providing for EC action to exclude third countries from EC contracts when EC undertakings experience problems competing for contracts in those third countries because of non-observance of certain ILO standards listed in Annex XXIII. This assumes that it is not acceptable for EC undertakings to gain contracts through the fact that their own supply chain does not comply with these labour standards.

to such standards may help promote their use, as well as ensuring ethical performance of the utility's contracts. This is subject, however, to the important point *that utilities may not insist that suppliers or their facilities are certified* to external standard requirements, but merely that suppliers show, through certification *or* other means, that they are able to comply with the *substantive conditions* in the standard. This point is discussed at 4.6 below.

There is some scope for arguing that the Treaty's free movement obligations do not apply to all utilities, especially private utilities (see section 5 below). This could provide a basis for a more autonomous approach in CSR matters for some utilities than for other regulated purchasers, to take account of their commercial interests. However, if the ECJ decides that extra-territorial requirements indeed violate the Treaty, it might reach the same conclusion through interpreting the rules in the Utilities Directive, since, arguably, the directive seeks to mirror for utilities the principles applying to public bodies under the Treaty.[44]

As chapter 4 explained, CSR measures may also be restricted by the EC's agreements with third countries, most notably the World Trade Organization's Agreement on Government Procurement (GPA).[45] However, the GPA is of limited importance for utilities since it covers only public utilities and not those regulated by the Utilities Directive because they have special or exclusive rights.

4.2.2. Monitoring and enforcement

Introduction   Purchasers who lay down social or environmental requirements are not always concerned with monitoring and enforcement. Such requirements may be intended to be purely symbolic or to encourage by example, or may be implemented simply to gain political support or the support of consumers or investors; or the purchaser may lack commitment to the costs of enforcement.[46] For example, few social and environmental programmes in public sector procurement make provision for monitoring and enforcement[47] and in the private sector the OECD has found that two-thirds of codes in the garment industry contain no monitoring

---

[44] The fact that the Utilities Directive has always included a prohibition on discrimination to ensure this applies to utilities not covered by the Treaty possibly reflects an intention that any behaviour prohibited under the Treaty free movement rules is prohibited also for utilities.

[45] See chapter 4, section 16.   [46] On these costs see Vogel, note 3 above, pp. 92–96.

[47] S. Arrowsmith, G. Meyer and M. Trybus, 'Non-commercial Factors in Public Procurement', Report produced for the Office of Government Commerce (2000).

provisions.[48] However, some purchasers do implement monitoring and enforcement measures, or at least apply sanctions when violations come to light.

Exclusion for anticipated non-compliance: general principles As chapter 4 explained, regulated purchasers may – and indeed, must – reject a tenderer that does not accept a fundamental requirement laid down in the contract documents.[49] Even when the tenderer does accept the requirement, however, the purchaser may wish to exclude a tenderer that the purchaser believes will not comply. On this, chapter 4 explained that the Public Sector Directive makes a distinction between technical requirements and special conditions. That directive allows exclusion of a compliant tenderer only for lack of financial standing or technical or professional ability, and for specified reasons of 'honesty, solvency and reliability', including criminal convictions and grave misconduct. Inability to deliver various requirements concerning the works, supplies or services, referred to in chapter 4 as 'technical requirements', constitutes absence of technical or professional ability, but inability to meet special conditions (such as conditions concerning the workforce) does not.[50] Thus inability to meet the former can constitute grounds for exclusion whilst inability to meet the latter cannot. Which social or environmental requirements are technical requirements and which are special conditions under the Public Sector Directive was discussed in chapter 4 at 8.1.6.

The Utilities Directive merely states that utilities must select using 'objective rules and criteria',[51] and that objective criteria include the 'honesty, solvency and reliability' criteria of the Public Sector Directive.[52] Clearly 'objective' criteria also include, at least, economic and financial standing and technical or professional ability within the meaning of the Public Sector Directive, so that utilities clearly can exclude for anticipated non-compliance with matters that are technical requirements

---

[48] Citation from Vogel, note 3 above, p. 89.

[49] See chapter 4, section 8.1.3. Note, however, that utilities using a negotiated procedure may arguably be able to seek new offers without the condition, rather than recommencing a new award procedure.

[50] See chapter 4, section 8.1.4.

[51] Article 54(1) (open procedures) and Article 54(3) (restricted and negotiated procedures) of the Utilities Directive.

[52] Article 54(4) of the Utilities Directive, referring to Article 45 of the Public Sector Directive.

under that directive. However, it is not clear what other criteria are 'objective' criteria, including anticipated non-compliance with special conditions. The fact that the Utilities Directive does not contain the same precise list of grounds for exclusion as the Public Sector Directive and that, in general, the Utilities Directive's award procedures allow more discretion, suggests that grounds for exclusion for utilities are broader.[53] However, in the absence of judicial interpretation the grounds remain unclear. The European Commission Communication on social considerations confines itself mainly to the public sector rules: for utilities it merely suggests that 'their discretion in this respect is wider', without indicating how.[54]

The concept of an 'objective' criterion suggests, at least, it is submitted, a criterion suitable to achieve a legitimate policy of the utility.[55] It could also imply that any criterion must not confer an excessive degree of discretion, and that its application is capable of being verified – conditions that apply to award criteria and thus probably also to exclusion and selection criteria.[56] On this basis, several plausible interpretations can be constructed. These all provide a different balance between the objectives of the Utilities Directive – notably transparency – and utilities' commercial interests (see section 7). Some of these interpretations would allow utilities to exclude suppliers unable to comply with special conditions, but some would not. It is useful to set out these interpretations together:

  i) That a utility may exclude based on any consideration relating to the contract awarded, where done for reasons of commercial procurement. This could, for example, allow a utility to divide a procurement between two suppliers to avoid dependence on a single supplier, which might not be possible under the Public Sector Directive. However, it would generally not allow exclusion for anticipated non-compliance with special conditions.

 ii) That a utility may exclude based on any consideration relating to the contract awarded, where done for *any* reason related to its legitimate objectives in procurement, including social/environmental

---

[53] The current Public Sector Directive, unlike the previous directives, now uses the phrase 'objective criteria' in Article 44(3), but this merely refers back to the explicit and limited criteria set out in other Articles of the directive (which are all types of objective criteria) for the purpose of the disclosure rules.

[54] Note 29 above, Communication on social considerations, p. 9.

[55] This would exclude otherwise unlawful policies, such as national protectionism.

[56] See chapter 4, section 13.

objectives. This *would* generally allow the utility to exclude for anticipated non-compliance with any special conditions, without making a connection between the special conditions and commercial objectives.

iii) That a utility may exclude based on any consideration that relates to the contract awarded, where done for any reason connected with the utility's commercial objectives (and not merely for commercial *procurement*). This interpretation would allow exclusion for anticipated non-compliance with special conditions, but only when related to commercial, rather than purely social/environmental, objectives. In theory this would allow exclusion when the special conditions form part of the utility's commercial strategy based on attracting investment or consumers, for example. In reality, the scope for exclusion would depend on the degree of judicial scrutiny applied in assessing whether particular conditions really do form part of a commercial strategy and, in particular, whether the courts would require utilities to show evidence of commercial benefits. This may be almost impossible for utilities to do given the difficulty of proof for specific utilities and the limited general evidence, as discussed in section 2 above. However, they may be able to demonstrate a specific link between CSR and commercial objectives, such as where a policy is implemented to meet the criteria of particular investment funds.

iv) That a utility may exclude based on any consideration relating to the performance of the contract awarded, where connected with any legitimate policy of the utility. This interpretation, like interpretation (ii), could generally allow exclusion for anticipated non-compliance with special conditions, without showing any connection between the conditions and the utility's commercial objectives.

v) That a utility may exclude for any reason of commercial procurement, regardless of whether or not related to the performance of the contract awarded. This would, for example, allow a utility to exclude a supplier that already has significant work for the utility, to preserve competition for future contracts, even though this might not be allowed under the public sector rules;[57] or it might

---

[57] It might also allow the utility to consider a supplier's ability to undertake related follow-on contracts where there are benefits from one supplier performing both contracts.

allow utilities to take into account possibilities for collaboration in product development to limit the number of suppliers on a qualification system (see further 4.7 below). This would not, though, generally permit exclusion for non-compliance with special conditions.

vi) That a utility may exclude for any reason related to its legitimate objectives in procurement, including social objectives, whether or not these relate to performance of the contract awarded. This interpretation, as with (ii) and (iv), would generally allow exclusion for anticipated non-compliance with any special conditions, without connecting them with its commercial objectives.

vii) That a utility may exclude for any reason relating to its commercial objectives (and not merely its procurement objectives) whether or not relating to performance of the contract awarded. As with interpretation (iii), this would in principle allow exclusion for anticipated non-compliance with special conditions where linked to the utility's business strategy, but would raise the same problems of making the link in practice.

viii) That a utility may exclude for any reason connected to the utility's legitimate objectives, commercial or non-commercial, and regardless of any link to the performance of contracts being awarded. As with interpretations (ii), (iv) and (vi), this would allow the utility to exclude for anticipated non-compliance with special conditions, without connecting the conditions to the utility's commercial objectives.

Thus utilities, in contrast with the public sector, may be able to exclude for anticipated non-compliance with special conditions, either in general, based on interpretations (ii), (iv), (vi) and (viii), or where this is linked to their business strategy, based on interpretations (iii) and (vii). On the other hand, there are plausible interpretations, interpretations (i) and (v), which would not allow exclusion for anticipated non-compliance with special conditions. It is also not impossible that the ECJ could interpret the rules on exclusion as being the same as for the public sector. However, as noted above, the better view is that this is ruled out by the different wording of the directives.

In interpreting the Utilities Directive it is necessary to mention, in particular, Article 52(3). This provides, as does Article 48(2)(f) of the Public Sector Directive, that 'for works and services contracts, and only in appropriate cases, [procuring entities] may require, in order to verify the economic operator's technical abilities, an indication of the environmental measures which the economic operator will apply when carrying out the contract'.

In the Public Sector Directive the provision serves to authorise environmental management measures as evidence of technical ability that authorities may demand, since authorities may require only the evidence listed in the directive.[58] However, utilities are *not* limited to listed evidence and the provision's effect in the Utilities Directive is unclear. It might imply that evidence of environmental management measures may *only* be required in the cases referred to, namely for carrying out works and services contracts and of matters that relate to technical ability in the sense of the public sector rules. This could in turn possibly imply that *exclusion* for anticipated non-compliance with certain environmental requirements is permitted only when these are limited to the contract and concerned with technical ability in the sense of the Public Sector Directive (and not when concerned with special conditions). It might even be argued that this provision implies that grounds for exclusion more generally are limited to those applying under the Public Sector Directive.

However, it appears that, like some other provisions in the Utilities Directive, this provision has merely been carried over to the Utilities Directive almost verbatim without any consideration of its 'fit' with the scheme of the Utilities Directive, and without any intention to alter pre-existing rules. This, and the significant difference in wording and general approach between the two directives, suggests that the provision merely in fact confirms that what is possible for the public sector in seeking evidence and excluding suppliers is also possible for utilities, without ruling out any additional possibilities. Thus it is submitted that none of the interpretations of the Utilities Directive given above are ruled out by Article 52(3).

Exclusion based on non-compliance with existing or previous contracts If a supplier awarded a contract *does* fail to comply with any contractual conditions, the purchaser may wish to exclude it from future work. This may be considered necessary to prevent further violations. Further, the *threat* of exclusion could also serve to encourage compliance. Exclusion, or the threat of exclusion, is a particularly potent sanction when implemented in collaboration with other entities – for

---

[58] See chapter 4, section 8.1.6.

example, when entities implementing a common code of conduct for suppliers agree to exclude violators from contracts with all of the entities involved. Of course, as with the conditions themselves, exclusion may produce negative effects, such as loss of employment, both for those whom the policy is designed to protect and for others employed by the offending supplier, and consequent adverse publicity. This must be considered in deciding whether to implement any exclusions.

Does the Utilities Directive allow utilities to exclude suppliers from future work for not complying with CSR requirements under previous contracts?

A first question is whether the directives allow purchasers to terminate the *existing* contract for violating CSR requirements. As chapter 4 explained, the ECJ has not yet considered this point.[59] As explained there, the directives do not expressly limit contractual remedies, although their use is subject to the equal treatment and non-discrimination principles.[60] It was suggested that it is also arguable that, where special conditions are concerned, if a priori exclusion from contracts is permitted for past violations that are deliberate and/or serious (as discussed in chapter 4, section 10.3 and also below) termination might possibly also be confined to such conduct. This might make it particularly difficult to exclude for violations of the main contract that result not from actions of the main contractor but from actions of those further down the supply chain. However, chapter 4 suggested that the better view is that exclusion is permitted, even under the public sector rules, whenever a firm's contract has previously been terminated and that termination remedies are *not* themselves limited to serious and/or deliberate violations.

As to excluding from *future* contracts those who have violated CSR requirements in the past (whether technical requirements or special conditions), under both directives this is clearly possible (as mentioned) when the violation involves a criminal conviction or constitutes grave misconduct. Chapter 4 suggested that these grounds for exclusion need not involve any link with ability to perform the contract awarded.[61] If that is so, they offer a clear possibility for utilities to exclude firms to support CSR policies where a supplier has a relevant criminal conviction – for example, for criminal bribery, or for violating national laws on

---

[59] See chapter 4, section 8.1.4.
[60] These are important for utilities not covered by the Treaty's free movement rules (as to which see section 5 below) in covering the ground of those Treaty rules.
[61] See the discussion in chapter 4, section 11.2.

working conditions or environmental protection. Chapter 4 also suggested that the 'grave misconduct' ground permits exclusion for some serious criminal behaviour, such as bribery, even without a conviction and also for violations of professional codes of ethics.[62]

Chapter 4 also explained that violation of contract requirements might per se constitute 'grave misconduct', and that Advocate General Gulman has stated that at least *deliberate* contractual violations fall within this concept.[63] This might at least catch some direct violations of CSR obligations in the main contract, although it might not cover many violations occurring further down the supply chain. As argued above and in chapter 4, it also seems appropriate, however, to allow exclusions under the grave misconduct provision for *all* past violations that have given rise to termination of the same contract; it is anomalous to require utilities that terminate a contract to accept a new tender by the same supplier. Arguably *any* violation that led to termination of a previous contract should provide grounds for exclusion from future contracts, whether of the same procuring entity or others, but this may be more controversial.

This possibility of future exclusion for violations, even more so than cancellation of a contract, may provide an incentive for the supplier to comply with a requirement if the possibility is made clear to the supplier. On the other hand, there is a clear degree of legal risk involved in acting to exclude a supplier, given the uncertainty surrounding the scope of these provisions and the fact that, in contrast with exclusions by other private firms, any exclusion will be subject to judicial scrutiny.

To the extent that contractual violations do not constitute grave misconduct, it does not appear possible to exclude suppliers for these violations under the Public Sector Directive. Under the Utilities Directive, however, the power to exclude may be wider: as elaborated above, there is a general power to exclude for 'objective' reasons which is capable of various interpretations. Several of the interpretations suggested would allow a utility to exclude suppliers from future contracts, to motivate those suppliers to comply with contract requirements. This applies to interpretation (vi), allowing exclusions for matters relating to the utility's legitimate *procurement* objectives, and interpretation (viii), allowing exclusions for *any* of the utility's legitimate objectives. Interpretation

---

[62] See chapter 4, section 11.2.

[63] Case C–71/92, *Commission* v. *Spain* [1993] ECR I–5923, para. 95 of the Opinion, discussed in chapter 4, section 11.3.

(vii), permitting exclusion for any commercial objective, would allow exclusions for CSR policies when these are linked to the utility's business performance strategy.

There may, however, be difficulties in excluding for violations of similar requirements in a supplier's contracts with other organisations, as is discussed further in section 4.3 below.

Conclusion   In summary, there is some scope for utilities to lay down CSR requirements concerning contract performance. However, there are both constraints and uncertainties over the extent of the requirements permitted and the available enforcement mechanisms, which may inhibit CSR policies. In particular, it is not clear how far utilities may lay down requirements concerning working conditions and other matters outside the utility's own Member State. In relation to enforcement there is uncertainty, in particular, over whether utilities can exclude suppliers in anticipation of breach of special conditions, or for past contract violations; and even if this is possible, the possibility of judicial scrutiny over, for example, the 'grave' nature of any misconduct introduces an element of risk into exclusions that is absent for other private sector undertakings.

4.3. CSR policies that go beyond contract performance

4.3.1. Contract requirements that go beyond contract performance

We have so far considered CSR policies which are concerned with the impact of work on a utility's own contracts. However, as chapter 3 elaborated, entities may also seek to adopt measures relating to their supply chain that go beyond their own contracts. Utilities may, in particular, be concerned more broadly to ensure that their supply chain includes only socially responsible actors. For example, a utility might want to require its suppliers and their suppliers etc. to comply with ILO labour standards in all their activities, or require suppliers to implement general programmes to avoid wasting water.

At present there is a significant element of legal risk in including contract requirements that go beyond the contract awarded. This arises because of Article 38 of the Utilities Directive, which, like Article 26 of the Public Sector Directive, discussed in chapter 4,[64] states that entities

---

[64] See chapter 4, section 8.1.4.

'may lay down special conditions relating to the performance of a contract'.[65] As chapter 4 explained, Article 26 of the Public Sector Directive probably rules out conditions that are *not* limited to performance of the contract awarded.[66] It might be argued that the same applies to utilities under the parallel utilities provision.

However, the different context of the Utilities Directive might also support a different interpretation – in particular, the fact that that directive contains different exclusion provisions. If utilities cannot generally include contractual requirements that go beyond the contract awarded, it would seem that they also will not generally be able to *exclude* firms that do not meet norms unrelated to the contract, as discussed at 4.3.2 below. As explained there, this would substantially reduce the scope for any differences in the exclusion provisions in the two directives, in spite of the different wording. In this context, it could be argued that the provision on special conditions in the Utilities Directive merely clarifies that utilities have all the power to include special conditions that exists under the Public Sector Directive, but without *restricting* utilities' power to include contract conditions. On this approach, there is scope to argue that utilities have power to include special conditions that do not relate to the contract, in accordance with whichever of the interpretations of the exclusion power is accepted. For example, if we accept interpretation (vii), namely that a utility may exclude for any reason relating to its commercial objectives (and not merely its procurement objectives), whether or not this relates to performance of the contract awarded, this might lead to the conclusion that not only may a utility exclude for anticipated non-compliance with special conditions linked to its business strategy, but that it may also include any *contractual requirements* linked to its business strategy, regardless of whether these relate to the contract awarded.

However, the likelihood of the ECJ accepting contract requirements unrelated to contract performance is certainly diminished by the explicit provision on special conditions in the 2004 Utilities Directive. The fact that the directive's award criteria have been held by the ECJ (and now stated in the 2004 directive) to be limited to those relating to the subject matter of the contract (see section 4.5 below) may also indicate, by analogy, that contractual requirements are limited to contract-related matters.

[65] This is also referred to in Recital 44 of the Utilities Directive.
[66] See chapter 4, section 8.1.4.

Often it is, of course, artificial and difficult to separate the performance of contracts from the broader question of the ethical conduct of the supplier, particularly with contracts for standard supplies. As chapter 3 discussed, work under the contract may not be separate from other work, in that the same workers may be engaged on both, even in the same time period; or it may be possible to ensure compliance with the required standards only through a regime covering the whole workplace.[67] Further, limiting requirements to the contract only could produce inequitable differences of treatment between workers or different work by the same worker, giving rise to discontent. This may compel an organisation to apply the requirements to the whole organisation. As mentioned, the Commission considers that requirements relating to the performance of *supply* contracts are not generally justifiable under the Treaty because of their wide impact. If this is correct, then a fortiori requirements that go *beyond* the contract will contravene the Treaty, and probably also the Utilities Directive. However, as noted above and as chapter 4 discussed,[68] the position is not clear and the ECJ could adopt a much more nuanced approach. In that case, the scope for contract conditions under the Utilities Directive becomes more important.

If indeed a utility can lay down contractual requirements *only* in so far as these concern contract performance this significantly limits scope for CSR policies; whilst a utility may to an extent ensure that work for the utility itself is not 'tainted' with unethical conduct, it can do little about a supplier's behaviour outside the utility's own contracts. Further, such an approach may limit the scope for ancillary measures, such as requiring schooling for children excluded from contract work.

4.3.2. Excluding firms for non-compliance with norms that go beyond the contract being awarded

As noted above, if a utility cannot lay down contractual requirements unrelated to performance of the contract awarded, then it appears that 'objective' criteria for excluding suppliers do not include a supplier's failure to adhere to CSR requirements that are not confined to the utility's own contracts. (The Utilities Directive surely does not allow a utility to exclude suppliers for violating standards that the utility is not permitted to prescribe in the first place.) If that is the case, then if one of the interpretations (v) to (viii) applies – meaning that utilities may in principle exclude from contracts for reasons unrelated to the contract

[67] See chapter 3, section 3.3. [68] Chapter 4, section 4.3.2.

being awarded – that interpretation will need to be qualified to a significant extent, in that exclusion will not be possible simply because of non-compliance with requirements unrelated to contract performance. This would be significant. It would mean that utilities could not exclude, for example, for non-compliance with the utility's own labour codes, or general industry labour codes, even for commercial reasons (such as to avoid low ratings on investment indices). However, even with this qualification, interpretations (v) to (viii) give a broader scope for exclusions than the first four interpretations, in particular by allowing exclusions for past violations of the utility's own contracts that are not covered by the 'grave misconduct' provision.

As mentioned, whatever the general position on contractual requirements and exclusions unrelated to the contract, clearly it is possible to exclude suppliers for past non-compliance with social or environmental norms where there is a criminal conviction or where non-compliance constitutes grave misconduct. The grave misconduct provision was considered above, where it was pointed out that this might be invoked in practice where the utility's reason for wishing to exclude a supplier is its anticipated non-compliance with a special condition, or to penalise violations of the utility's own contracts. However, the utility does not need to make a link to its own contracts to invoke these provisions. Thus they may be invoked so that the utility can avoid associating itself with unethical conduct, whether for business reasons or simply to support the ethical standards in question.

This raises the question of how far the 'grave misconduct' provision can be invoked as an effective limit on any principle that the utility may not lay down conditions for a supplier's business that go beyond contract performance. If, for example, the provision can be invoked to exclude suppliers that have violated contracts with other utilities or other standards that the supplier has itself signed up to, or that have violated industry practices embodied in widely accepted codes, this will at least facilitate the scope for developing CSR policies through industry collaboration. This is important in the utility sector, particularly with the recent growth of shared qualification systems, as discussed at 4.7 below. However, accepting violations of norms of this kind as grave misconduct raises several problems. For example, excluding suppliers for not adhering to codes that suppliers themselves have accepted could lead to more favourable treatment for suppliers that refuse to accept such codes, and/or discourage suppliers from accepting them; whereas if grave misconduct is not limited to standards accepted by the supplier, there will be considerable difficulties in identifying 'objective' norms for defining grave misconduct.

4.3.3. Conclusion

Although Article 38 of the Utilities Directive refers expressly only to conditions concerning the contract to be awarded, there is scope to argue that utilities, perhaps differently from entities under the Public Sector Directive, may lay down requirements going beyond the contract work and, if that is possible, may exclude from contracts firms that cannot or do not adhere to such requirements. There are various possible interpretations of the precise scope for such conditions and exclusions, as discussed at 4.2.2 above. However, in practice, the new Article 38 in the 2004 Utilities Directive may make it less likely that the ECJ will accept measures going beyond the contract than would have been the case prior to 2004. If the ECJ does indeed take the view that utilities may neither lay down conditions unrelated to contract performance nor exclude firms that do not comply with such conditions, this will place a very significant constraint on utilities' ability to pursue the kind of CSR policies that are currently high on the agenda for ensuring the ethical behaviour of their supply chains.

4.4. Exclusion for offences of corruption, money laundering etc.

As mentioned, a growing concern in supply chain policy is corruption. In this context it is pertinent that, as examined in chapter 12, the 2004 procurement directives now *require* contracting authorities to exclude from contracts suppliers convicted of certain offences, including corruption.[69] Under the Utilities Directive the exclusion applies to contracting authorities carrying out utility activities but *not* to utilities covered merely because they are public undertakings or enjoy special or exclusive rights. This is one of the few cases in which the directive recognises that different treatment is appropriate for utilities that are not traditional public authorities – in this case to *limit* social responsibilities. The reason given for the different treatment was the greater difficulties for these bodies of accessing information.[70] However, it seems plausible that reluctance to impose bureaucratic burdens on commercial entities influenced the policy. A practical effect of the new provisions, however, may

---

[69] Article 45(1) of the Public Sector Directive and Article 54(4) of the Utilities Directive.
[70] The final provision differs on this point from the original proposal on the issue.

be to make it easier for all utilities to implement policies in this area in practice, should they choose to do so: it seems likely to result in increased efforts at national and EC level to provide accessible information for applying exclusions.[71]

4.5. Other mechanisms

Whilst utilities' interest in CSR has focused in practice on setting minimum standards of conduct for the supply chain, CSR policies can also be implemented in other ways. One issue is whether utilities selecting between suppliers that meet their minimum requirements when inviting tenders/offers[72] may select based on suppliers' policies on social and environmental issues. The directive requires utilities to make this selection based on 'objective' rules and criteria[73] and thus, in principle, the same range of criteria apply to selection as to exclusions[74] (although this does not mean that exactly the same criteria must be applied at each stage in each procurement). Thus the possibility for considering such policies at the selection stage depends on the scope of the power to exclude. For example, if a utility can always exclude for anticipated non-compliance with special conditions, then the capability of suppliers to meet such conditions can be considered at the selection stage, alongside technical and financial capabilities. This would mean that a utility tendering a contract for protective clothing that includes special conditions that the clothing must not be made using child labour or slave labour could, in choosing which of the qualified suppliers to invite, consider not merely suppliers' experience and reliability in meeting supply contracts of this size, but also their experience in monitoring for compliance with such special conditions. As we have seen at 4.2.2, however, the scope for considering special conditions in this respect is far from clear. On the other hand, we have seen that utilities may certainly exclude firms unable to comply with technical requirements, which (as chapter 4 explained)

---

[71] On the UK position, for example, see S. Arrowsmith, 'Implementation of the New EC Procurement Directives and the *Alcatel* Ruling in England and Wales and Northern Ireland: A Review of the New Legislation and Guidance' (2006) 15 *PPLR* 86, at pp. 121–123.

[72] This applies only in restricted or negotiated procedures. It is expressly permitted by Article 54(3) of the Utilities Directive.

[73] Article 54(3) of the Utilities Directive referring back to Article 52(1) and (2) which require use of objective criteria.

[74] For the Public Sector Directive, the ECJ has clarified this position: Case C–360/89, *Commission v. Italy* [1992] ECR I–3401.

include certain social and environmental requirements, such as requirements for minimum pollution in carrying out public works; thus, ability to manage requirements of this kind clearly may be considered in choosing between qualified firms.

Utilities might also wish to reserve some contracts exclusively for limited groups, such as firms owned by certain ethnic groups or small businesses. Their ability to do so will depend on whether excluding firms outside the targeted group is considered to be based on 'objective' criteria. If utilities may not, in general, lay down conditions unrelated to contract performance nor exclude suppliers for reasons unrelated to performance (as discussed at 4.3 above), then a fortiori it seems they may not reserve contracts for limited groups. If they *are* able to do so, it is possible that in justified cases they can also set aside contracts for limited groups, although subject to the EC Treaty and equal treatment principles, as discussed in chapter 4.[75] Regardless of the general position, however, it can be noted that Article 28 of the Utilities Directive expressly allows utilities to reserve contracts for sheltered employment workshops/programmes, as discussed in chapter 7 – a provision which also serves to limit the conditions for such set-asides.

Finally, as chapter 3 explained, CSR policies can be implemented by including social and environmental impacts as award criteria, to be weighed against price etc. (for example, by allowing a 10 per cent price preference for tenders offering social benefits), and are used this way by the public sector.[76] As chapter 3 also explained, this approach is valuable, in particular, to enable public bodies to balance price and other objectives and to set limits to the amount paid for social or environmental benefits. It does not appear,[77] however, to be a common approach for commercial utilities, whose concerns are largely limited to ensuring that their supply chains operate within minimum ethical standards that are not suitable for this kind of overt financial 'trade-off' (although such a trade-off almost inevitably operates at the stage of monitoring and enforcing the standards set). Should utilities wish to use award criteria to implement CSR policies, it appears that the principles are those applying in the public sector, since the rules on award criteria are

---

[75] See chapter 4, section 4.4.
[76] See S. Arrowsmith, J. Linarelli and D. Wallace, *Regulating Public Procurement: National and International Perspectives* (London and The Hague: Kluwer Law International, 2000), chapter 5.
[77] This observation is based on the authors' experience.

formulated, and are to be interpreted, in the same way.[78] As chapter 4 explained, these rules allow purchasers to use certain social and environmental criteria relating to the subject matter of the contract (for example, the noise or pollution level for buses purchased or used under a contract)[79] although it is not clear whether the rules permit award criteria concerned with the contract workforce.[80]

4.6. Evidence for proving compliance with CSR policies

We have so far examined the Utilities Directive's constraints on substantive CSR requirements. Also important, however, are the rules on evidence that utilities may require from suppliers. To address barriers to trade that result from procedural burdens on suppliers the Utilities Directive provides that in the qualification and selection process[81] utilities may not require tests or evidence that would duplicate objective evidence already available.[82] This means that utilities cannot require suppliers to provide evidence chosen by the utility to prove the supplier's compliance with CSR requirements: they must permit suppliers to offer any adequate evidence that the supplier has available (and must probably also make it clear that they will accept such alternative evidence).[83]

The principle is also stated more specifically for environmental management measures and quality assurance measures. Thus Article 52 of the Utilities Directive provides that entities cannot require suppliers to be certified by reference to EMAS or environmental management standards based on European or international standards, or to be certified in

---

[78] *Concordia Bus Finland*, note 28 above. It might possibly be argued that the rules on award for utilities are different in certain respects, however, because of the differences in the rules on exclusion, that are relevant to the overall context of the provisions on award.

[79] *Concordia Bus Finland*, note 28 above, concerning noise and pollution levels of buses in a contract for the provision of transport services.

[80] See chapter 4, section 13; C. McCrudden, *Buying Social Justice: Equality, Government Procurement, & Legal Change* (Oxford University Press, 2007), pp. 546–552.

[81] Article 52(1)(b). That does not expressly refer to open procedures but the same principle will apply by analogy. This requirement, like the rules on qualification criteria, is not as rigid as the comparable public sector rules which, in addition to this principle, also contain a detailed and limited list of evidence that can be even requested for proving certain aspects of technical and financial capability.

[82] Article 52(1)(b).

[83] Such an argument could be made on the basis of the transparency principle; it cannot be expected that suppliers will know of their rights to supply alternative evidence so as to rely on this even when the contract documents seem to imply that only the specified evidence will be accepted.

accordance with quality assurance systems based on European standards, but must accept evidence of 'equivalent' measures.[84]

The same principle is also stated for technical specifications. Utilities may set their specifications by reference either to certain recognised standards – such as those based on European standards – or to the functional or performance characteristics of the product/works/services.[85] In the former case, utilities cannot reject a tender simply because the offer does not comply with the standard, but must accept any offer that meets the substantive requirements 'in an equivalent manner'.[86] The directive here states expressly that the tenderer must prove equivalence 'to the satisfaction of the contracting entity, by whatever appropriate means'.[87] It seems likely that this same principle – that the burden is on tenderers to demonstrate compliance – also applies to other areas, including compliance with CSR requirements.

This general principle has important implications for CSR policies. Many private firms operate programmes that require suppliers to be certified under specific schemes, either based on international or European standards – such as those for environmental management – or set up by industry itself, as with SA 8000. The Utilities Directive does not, however, allow this approach: a utility cannot require any such certification, but must allow a supplier to demonstrate by other means that it can meet the utility's requirements relating to labour conditions, environmental impact etc. Such certifications are relevant only in that they provide one option for a supplier to show compliance (and here it may be helpful for utilities to indicate certain certificates that they will definitely accept).

From the point of view of balancing value for money, procedural efficiency and the effectiveness of CSR policies, an unregulated private firm may insist on certification: this limits the procedural burdens on the buyer itself, and can potentially provide a better guarantee of compliance than examining evidence on a case-by-case basis. From the utility's perspective, these advantages might outweigh any benefit from broadening the supply base to uncertified suppliers (especially if there are more than enough certified suppliers for adequate competition). The Utilities

---

[84] Article 52(2) and (3). These provisions also add to the general principles otherwise stated in the directive by requiring reference only to systems based on European standards when certifications are suggested as evidence; that is, the utility may not instead refer to other certification systems even as suggested evidence (although suppliers themselves could offer such certifications).

[85] Article 34(3).   [86] Article 34(3).   [87] Article 34(3).

Directive, however, constrains utilities' discretion in making this balance, in order to broaden access to markets and to limit discretion that could theoretically be abused to favour national suppliers. A rule that places the burden of proof on suppliers goes only part of the way towards addressing the problem of excessive procedural costs: it is still procedurally more burdensome for a utility than a rule that permits the utility to insist on certification, as the utility must itself examine the evidence in each case, and the risk of legal challenge may also make it difficult for utilities to insist on the level of proof that they would ideally like.

The Utilities Directive also states expressly that utilities may not impose administrative, technical and financial conditions on certain suppliers that are not imposed on others.[88] This appears to restate in this specific context the general equal treatment principle. This principle, as stated in *Fabricom*,[89] 'requires that comparable situations must not be treated differently and that different situations must not be treated in the same way, unless such treatment is objectively justified'.[90] One of the authors has already highlighted the uncertainty that this principle creates for everyday decision-making: it is difficult to anticipate both what courts will consider a comparable situation and what reasons will justify different treatment.[91] It raises a specific concern for utilities in the context of CSR: they may be nervous of imposing additional checks on some suppliers with operations in high-risk countries which might be considered to contravene this principle (especially as even an EC supplier may have a complex supply chain exposing the utility to significant risk), but equally nervous of a claim that they are imposing an unnecessary burden on suppliers from low-risk countries.

Utilities probably also cannot demand information beyond that needed to show compliance with requirements for participating in procurements. Merely to require suppliers to *provide* such information may contravene the directive, as it involves an unnecessary burden; and requiring irrelevant information may also create a presumption that this information has been *taken into account*. Thus utilities seeking

---

[88] Article 52(1)(a). Like Article 52(1)(b) this actually refers only to restricted and negotiated procedures, but the same rule will apply for open procedures.

[89] Joined Cases C–21/03 and C–34/03, *Fabricom* v. *État Belge* [2005] ECR I–1559.

[90] Para. 27 of the judgment. See also Advocate General Mischo in *Concordia Bus Finland*, note 28 above, point 149 of the Opinion.

[91] S. Arrowsmith, 'The Past and Future Evolution of EC Procurement Law: From Framework to Common Code?' (2006) 35 *PCLJ* 337, and chapter 4, section 6 of this book.

Can suppliers, however, be *required* to provide such information or to submit to such assessments at the time of registration as a condition of registration?

As discussed at 4.6, it is generally unlawful to require suppliers to provide information unrelated to the contract being awarded. In the context of qualification systems, it would appear that a parallel rule applies to that governing exclusions – suppliers cannot be required to provide information that is not relevant for registration on the system (or a particular classification within it), but such information would not need to be relevant for *every* contract.

Suppliers could also possibly be given a choice over whether to provide certain information or undertake certain assessments, but on the basis that without that information or those assessments they cannot be considered for later specific contracts for which the information/assessments are relevant. For example, a supplier could be given a choice over whether to provide information on environmental management measures, on the basis that if it does not it will not be considered for contracts for which these measures are relevant.

5. Utilities' procurement outside the Utilities Directive

Activities of the regulated utilities – as well as other state companies – may be affected by the Treaty rules as well as by the Utilities Directive. These Treaty rules are important for contracts outside the directive, including below-threshold contracts, and for concessions, which are excluded from the directive.[99] As chapter 2 explained, the free movement rules have become more important as a result of the ruling in *Telaustria*[100] stating that these rules imply a positive obligation of transparency.

Quite apart from the points already discussed above, notably the impact of the Treaty on measures affecting conduct outside the awarding state, the Treaty's significance for the CSR policies of utilities is not yet clear for two main reasons. The first is that, as chapter 2 discussed, the exact requirements of the transparency obligation are not yet clear.[101] The second is that the ECJ has yet to clarify whether the free movement

---

[99] Article 18. The directive is silent on supply concessions, leaving the position unclear.
[100] Case C–324/98, *Telaustria Verlags GmbH and Telefonadress GmbH* v. *Telekom Austria AG* [2000] ECR I–10745. On this see chapter 2, section 3.2.
[101] See chapter 2, section 3.2.

provisions apply to utilities that are public undertakings.[102] Whilst the legislator has provided for a broad application of internal market rules in certain secondary legislation, including under the Utilities Directive, by regulating all companies subject to dominant government influence as defined by ownership or control, it is not clear that the Treaty has such a broad application. Jurisprudence on state aid suggests that this might not be the case, and that only actual intervention in decision-making by government, or a real likelihood of this, will attract application of the Treaty.[103] Applying the Treaty broadly to state companies, particularly outside the sectors identified in the Utilities Directive as involving market access problems, is particularly problematic in procurement, given the Treaty's transparency obligations, since these can interfere with the ability of commercial undertakings to procure effectively. However, the position is unclear. It seems unlikely, though, that the Treaty's free movement rules will apply to private entities merely because they enjoy special or exclusive rights. There may, however, be a violation of Article 86 when a Member State itself encourages utilities that are public undertakings or have special or exclusive rights to act in a way that would violate the free movement rules if carried out by a Member State itself – for example, by limiting its procurements to national suppliers, or *requiring* them to include social clauses that would violate the Treaty if applied by the State.[104]

6. The problem of divergent regulatory regimes

A final important issue is the growing problem caused by the proliferation of regulatory regimes. Since the original Utilities Directive in 1990, both the nature of the utility industries and the nature of procurement have undergone great changes, as many utilities have been privatised and deregulated. For many years utilities were protected from major transformational change by state ownership or state control and/or an absence of competitive market conditions. However, privatisation and

---

[102] See Arrowsmith, note 4 above, at 4.23.

[103] See, in particular, Case C-482/99, *France* v. *Commission* [2002] ECR I-4397.

[104] It has been suggested that there may be a violation of Article 86 whenever a public undertaking or entity with special or exclusive rights acts in a way that would violate the Treaty if a Member State acted in the same way: J. Buendia Sierra, *Exclusive Rights and EC Monopolies under EC Law* (Oxford University Press, 1999), pp. 192–193 and the works cited there. However, the authors reject this view: see Arrowsmith, note 4 above, at 4.54–55.

liberalisation at Member State and EC level has meant takeover and merger activity has completely changed the landscape. In particular, there have emerged a smaller number of much larger utilities with clear international aspirations. This consolidation has been most apparent in the energy sector, although there has been some similar movement in other areas, such as transport and water. Consolidation has not been limited to private companies, with some of the most aggressive acquirers being state-owned energy companies such as EdF of France, which now owns utility assets in several European countries. These changes have had a major impact on procurement.

First, within individual utility groups the new transnational utilities are seeking to use their greater leverage and market position to improve their overall supply arrangements and are becoming large enough to enter into genuine global sourcing arrangements in the same way as the multinational oil and gas industry has long done. These generally take one of three forms: direct contracts with an individual user utility within the group, global sourcing arrangements awarded by the Head Office with call-offs by individual subsidiaries, and shared agreements between several subsidiaries.

Secondly, the growth of the companies has led to them diversifying out of their traditional activities, operating both in the EC and outside, and acting both in regulated and in non-regulated areas. As a result they are increasingly engaged in varying activities that are subject to different procurement rules. Thus, for example, a major German utility has found itself subject to the public sector regime for a public-private partnership deal, the utilities sector for its electricity network business, and potentially one of the Utilities Directive's derogations for its upstream gas business,[105] as well as operating several completely unregulated businesses, such as supply of consumer products, and activities outside the EC.

Finally, as mentioned above in looking at qualification systems, utilities are increasingly engaging in cooperative procurement arrangements, both to drive down costs and, more recently, to ensure effective implementation of CSR policies. This cooperation is carried on to a large extent with other regulated utilities, but also with both private and public bodies outside those sectors.

---

[105] Under Article 3 of Council Directive 93/38/EEC, an exemption preserved by the new directive.

By imposing regulatory constraints on utilities in the EC the Utilities Directive, and to a more limited extent the Treaty, may inhibit effective initiatives that span more than one country or sector, or which involve cooperation with non-regulated organisations. For example, a qualification system set up to cover both regulated and non-regulated activity must comply with the directive, potentially limiting its value for non-regulated organisations. The fact that individual utilities may carry out a diverse range of activities and operate in different regions that are subject to different regulatory regimes also creates confusion both within utilities – especially with activities such as IT purchasing that may cover a variety of projects – and amongst suppliers.

This problem barely exists for entities covered by the Public Sector Directive, since cooperation is largely limited to entities within the same Member State covered by the same regulatory regime. These entities may be affected, though, by the application of different regimes to the public and the utility sectors, which create obstacles to cross-sector cooperation. This has occurred in the UK, for example, where utility and public sector bodies have sometimes wished to use combined supplier databases. In addition, individual public authorities are sometimes covered by different directives for different activities.

7. Issues for the future

The discussion above has highlighted the legal position encountered by the regulated utilities that wish to implement CSR strategies relating to the supply chain.

It is apparent, first, that however the EC procurement rules are interpreted they place significant restrictions on regulated utilities' freedom of action in comparison with that of their non-regulated counterparts. This is more clearly so than it was prior to 2004, as the 2004 directive – particularly Article 38 on special conditions – has cast greater doubt on some of the previous possibilities for flexible interpretation. Secondly, the above discussion shows that the limits of discretion are not clear, and that there is very limited guidance from official sources, which have focused on the public sector rules. Utilities engaging in this area must carefully balance their interests in CSR against the legal risks involved.

Given the directive's impact, and the fact that it has not previously been much discussed in the public and institutional debates on CSR, there is clearly a need for further debate and further research. A number of questions and concerns need to be considered.

A first issue is whether there is a sufficient case for regulating utilities at all, at least those in the private sector. Is there sufficient recent evidence of the fact that utilities' behaviour in procurement operates as a barrier to trade to justify regulating such procurement (which is not generally regulated under other national and international regimes)? It is pertinent that the study of the economic impact of the internal market rules completed for the Commission in the late 1990s indicated that firms in the telecommunications industry were engaging in commercial procurement for reasons other than the influence of the directives, even though that industry was not yet fully competitive.[106] It is possible that for some sectors, at least, the problem no longer meets the threshold that justifies regulatory measures. However, in the recent reform of the directives a decision was taken to exclude only entities operating in fully competitive markets (under the Article 30 exemption and by a total exclusion of the telecommunications industry), and some utilities previously caught under the concept of special or exclusive rights (by narrowing the definition of that concept). It seems unlikely that this decision will be revisited in the short term, but research on this issue would be useful for ensuring that decisions on regulatory strategy in the longer term are made on the basis of full information. Assuming that regulation does continue, research on the extent of trade barriers and value of the directive's various rules would be equally useful for deciding precisely how to balance the competing concerns involved, as discussed below.

Assuming that the EC continues to regulate the procurement of private utilities and those that are public undertakings, the question is how the rules on CSR should be developed, whether through legislation, judicial interpretation or soft law, including guidance. To some extent the issues are the same as with the public sector. Key issues are the value of the directives' transparency rules for removing barriers to trade, and, assuming that those rules are of some value, how the internal market interests with which those rules are concerned should be balanced against their impact on national and EC-level policies on CSR. As chapter 1 emphasised,[107] the directives do not themselves seek to determine the proper balance between social and environmental concerns and other procurement objectives; policy in these areas remains in principle a matter for

---

[106] European Commission, *The Single Market Review* subseries III, *Dismantling of Barriers*, Volume 2, Public Procurement (1997).

[107] See chapter 1, section 5.

Member States. Such policies can only be implemented within the framework of rules laid down to achieve the EC's single market objectives, but in setting those rules the EC must take into account the adverse impact they may have on other interests. As elaborated in chapter 2, a number of commentators, and the European Parliament, have criticised the EC's current approach for the public sector as giving undue weight to the interests of the internal market, but in the recent reform process the same approach was largely maintained.

Irrespective of these criticisms of the public sector rules, are there reasons why utilities might anyway be treated differently? Several possible reasons can be identified. Some influenced the original decision to provide a more flexible regime for utilities, but some did not even exist at that time – or not to such a great extent – and/or are particularly relevant for CSR.

One is simply that the problem of procurement as a barrier to trade is not so great with the utilities, at least for some utilities, as with entities covered by the Public Sector Directive. Thus, the same degree of regulation may not be required to open markets, and this could justify allowing utilities more discretion – for example, to exclude suppliers. As already mentioned, utilities clearly enjoy more discretion in some areas, such as in using the negotiated procedure, and greater flexibility may possibly be justified also in the context of CSR. However, this argument is not particularly relevant for policies that go beyond the contract, which is based less on the desire to limit discretion than on the limiting effect of such policies on trade.

It can also be argued that, to the extent that CSR policies are part of the utility's commercial strategy, they are more important for many utilities than for many regulated entities, since they relate to what in many cases is the utility's core objective, namely commercial success. This is in contrast with some of the policies implemented by public sector bodies, which involve minimising the impact of the body's policies on unrelated areas of policy, or supporting policies unrelated to the entity's own mission. This argument may be less relevant if the public sector is regarded as a whole, rather than as a number of constituent parts. However, here it is relevant that there are alternative methods for implementing many of the policies promoted through procurement and that these methods may be more efficient, and this may be one consideration that has led the EC legislature and courts to take a strict approach (although neither has articulated this consideration). This is not, however, a consideration for utilities, whose commercial interests may be adversely affected if they cannot take account of CSR concerns in managing their supply chains.

Another similar consideration also arises from the fact that CSR policies may be driven by commercial motives. This is that, irrespective of whether alternatives are available, the Community's tolerance for adverse impact on the internal market may be influenced by the fact that the costs of implementing social or environmental policies through procurement may outweigh the substantive benefits, or even be counter-productive (as, for example, where policies to support a particular disadvantaged group lead that group to become dependent on government contracts and unable to compete in the broader economy); and the decision to implement them in Member States may be driven more by political concerns than a genuine assessment of costs and benefits. Again, this may result in less weight being placed on Member States' interests. The same concerns may also arise with utilities' policies – for example, where the immediate effect of prohibiting child labour has the effect of pushing the children concerned into even more unsatisfactory occupations. However, it is questionable whether this is so relevant for utilities, where the success of the policy from the perspective of the utility is often to be measured not at all (or, at least, not only) by its practical effects, but also by its impact on the utility's business. If this can affect the utility's competitiveness, is it a concern that should be given more weight than the political concerns of a Member State? Should policy makers then be less concerned – or not concerned at all – with the actual social or environmental impact of the policy when balancing the competing interests involved?

The fact that the drivers for CSR policies are often commercial also raises another question: how should policy makers deal with the fact that it is difficult to prove or disprove actual commercial benefits from CSR policies? Is this something that the courts, legislature or other policy makers should take into account and seek to judge or is it something that should be left to the utilities themselves? In this respect, it can be pointed out that the EC itself has placed increasing weight on the commercial reasons for CSR policies to justify its intervention in the field, although this does not mean that there are not also other reasons for Community action.[108]

Finally, it is relevant that the strictures of the directive are likely to have a greater adverse impact on utilities than on most of the public

---

[108] See Communication on CSR, note 2 above.

sector because of the increasingly international and collaborative nature of utility activity, and because of the problems of subjecting individual entities or different entities in corporate groups to divergent regulatory regimes, as discussed above. This is relevant both because it means that utilities may need to compete (for example, in global markets) against firms that are not regulated in the same way, and because the directive may prevent utilities from using efficient collaborative strategies, pushing up the costs of internal market regulation.

All these issues are relevant to any future debate and policy-making relating to CSR in the utility sectors. It is hoped that this chapter will serve to stimulate debate on the subject and to provide at least part of the legal and policy framework for conducting such a debate.

Coordinating public procurement to support EU objectives – a first step? The case of exclusions for serious criminal offences

SOPE WILLIAMS

1. Introduction

As chapter 1 explained, the main effect of the procurement directives on horizontal policies in public procurement is to restrict Member States' discretion to pursue their own policies because of the effect such policies have on trade. As discussed in earlier chapters, in particular in chapter 4, there is much debate over whether some of these restrictions can be justified, and some commentators argue that Member States should enjoy broader powers to pursue horizontal policies. This argument can be made both for policy areas of concern to the EU itself, and for areas of purely national concern.

In addition, as chapter 1 elaborated (in section 5.3), there have been calls for the EU not only to provide Member States with more freedom, but also itself to harness the power of public procurement in a proactive way to support the EU's own policies, and some steps have now been taken in this direction.

In this respect the 2004 procurement directives constituted a 'first' in including two sets of provisions that do this for the first time. One set of provisions is that requiring procuring entities to consider issues of accessibility for all users, including disabled persons, in designing specifications. This is considered further in chapter 7 on disability issues. The second set of provisions consists of those in Article 45 of Directive 2004/18/EC, the Public Sector Directive[1] and Article 54 of Directive 2004/17/EC,

---

[1] Directive 2004/18/EC of the European Parliament and of the Council on the coordination of procedures for the award of public works contracts, public supply contracts and public service contracts ('Public Sector Directive') OJ 2004 No. L134/114.

the Utilities Directive,[2] which *require* contracting authorities to exclude from contracts all firms convicted of offences relating to organised crime, corruption, fraud and money laundering. These provisions on mandatory exclusions are the subject of this chapter. In addition, as chapter 1 explained, there have also some been further proposals and measures requiring a proactive use of procurement to promote EU policy that apply in the environmental sphere, in particular on energy efficiency.

This chapter explains the policies involved in the mandatory exclusion provisions, and the way in which procurement has been used to support these policies in the directives, including the problems that arise in applying the provisions. The chapter will also comment briefly on the significance these provisions might have for future use of procurement for implementing horizontal policies in the EC.

The chapter begins with an explanation of the offences covered by the provisions, and a brief explanation of the rationale behind EC/EU policy in relation to these offences. Next the chapter briefly considers previous use of the procurement directives to exclude persons guilty of criminal and other misconduct from public procurement. It also considers the legislative history of the current mandatory exclusions, including the offences that were debated for inclusion but not eventually included. The chapter then examines practical and conceptual problems relating to the exclusion requirement, namely issues relating to the persons excluded, the nature of investigations required, the length of exclusions and the possibility for derogations from the exclusion requirement. It concludes with some brief observations on the possible significance of these provisions for future developments under the directives.

Before we examine the substance of the provisions, it should be pointed out that legislation imposing upon Member States an obligation to use procurement to promote horizontal policies must have an adequate legal basis. This requirement and its application in specific areas was examined in chapter 1 (in section 5.3). It was explained there that there are, in fact, serious doubts over whether the mandatory exclusion provisions have an adequate legal basis. The directives are based on Articles 47(2), 55 and 95 EC concerning free movement and the establishing and functioning of the internal market, and Arrowsmith and

---

[2] Directive 2004/17/EC of the European Parliament and of the Council coordinating the procurement procedures of entities operating in the water, energy, transport and postal services sectors ('Utilities Directive') OJ 2004 No. L134/1.

Kunzlik argue in chapter 1 that the mandatory exclusions do not appear related to these objectives; further, they question whether there is even any legal competence to adopt such mandatory exclusions under other Treaty provisions. This question was fully considered in chapter 1 and will not be addressed further here.

2. EU policy on serious criminal offences

While it may be too soon to talk about the creation of European criminal law,[3] due in part to the fact that coordination in criminal matters has its legal basis in the Third Pillar of the EU, under which any cooperation in criminal matters is intergovernmental and therefore limited,[4] EU policy against serious criminal offences has gained impetus in recent years. This is partly because as the Community strives towards completing the internal market, there is an awareness of the need to protect the internal market from criminal elements and undesirables.[5] The drive towards free movement does not enhance opportunities only for legitimate persons, capital, goods or services[6] – and the reduction of trade barriers generally, but in particular, in public procurement, may allow criminal elements access to Member States' procurement.

Apart from protecting the internal market from criminal activity, EU measures in the criminal sphere are also designed to block the legal loopholes arising from the incongruities between the criminal justice systems of Member States which are exploited by criminals.[7] Other reasons behind EU intervention in criminal law include the desire for

---

[3] P. Albrecht and S. Braum, 'Deficiencies in the Development of European Criminal Law' (1999) 5 *ELJ* 293.

[4] Article 29 Treaty of the European Union ('TEU'); Case C–176/03, *Commission* v. *Council of the European Union* [2005] ECR I–7879; Case 203/80, *Casati* [1981] ECR 2595, para. 27. See also S. White, 'Harmonisation of Criminal Law under the First Pillar' (2006) 31 *ELRev* 81.

[5] S. White (ed.), *Procurement and Organised Crime: An EU-wide Study* (Institute of Advanced Legal Studies, 2000), p. 3; S. Skinner, 'The Third Pillar Treaty Provisions on Police Cooperation: Has the EU Bitten off More than it Can Chew?' (2002) 8 *Colum J Transnat'l L* 203, p. 204.

[6] See, however, J. Zielonka, 'How New Enlarged Borders will Reshape the European Union' (2001) 39 *JCMS* 507.

[7] L. Ferola, 'The Fight against Organised Crime in Europe: Building an Area of Freedom, Security and Justice in the EU' (2002) 30 *IJLI* 53, p. 54; European Commission, The prevention of crime in the European Union: Reflection on common guidelines and proposals for Community financial support ('Communication on the prevention of crime'), COM (2000) 786 final.

harmonisation and need for coherence in tackling criminal activity with a European dimension. This section will consider the main policy considerations behind EU activity in the areas that are the subject of the mandatory procurement exclusions.

2.1. Organised crime

First, the new exclusions require authorities to exclude firms that have been convicted of participation in a criminal organisation,[8] as defined in Article 2(1) of Council Joint Action 98/733/JHA.[9] This defines such participation as conduct by a person who, with intent and knowledge of the aim of the organisation, takes part in the organisation's criminal activities or other activities that contribute to the furtherance of the organisation's criminal activities.

The EU's policy against organised crime is integral to its broader policy against serious crime. There are three rationales underpinning the policy against organised crime. The primary objective of the EU's intervention in the fight against serious crime, including organised crime, is to provide EU citizens with a high level of safety within an area of freedom, security and justice[10] by strengthening cooperation between Member States, and plugging legal loopholes that are exploited by crime syndicates.[11] Secondly, the EU's policy against organised crime is designed to complement the EU's fight against the types of crime that organised groups are involved in. The main features of organised crime are that it is an illegal enterprise using violence or the threat of violence to fulfil its aims,[12] and is a vehicle for the commission of serious crimes such as drug offences, money laundering, prostitution, human trafficking and

---

[8] Article 45(1)(a) of the Public Sector Directive.

[9] Council of the European Union, Joint Action adopted by the Council on the basis of Article K.3 of the Treaty on European Union, on making it a criminal offence to participate in a criminal organisation in the Member States of the European Union ('Joint Action against participating in a criminal organisation') OJ 1998 No. L351/1.

[10] See Article 29 and Article 31(e) TEU.

[11] S. White, note 5 above, at 3; European Union, Action Plan to combat organised crime ('Action Plan') OJ 1997 No. C251/1, Part I, chapter III, para. 6.

[12] C. Fijnaut, 'Transnational Crime and the Role of the United Nations in its Containment through International Cooperation: A challenge for the 21st century' (2000) *Eur J Crime Cr L Cr J* 119; L. Paoli, 'The Paradoxes of Organised Crime' (2002) 37 *Crime, Law & Social Change* 51. For a history of organised crime in the EU, see J. Solomon, 'Forming a More Secure Union: The Growing Problem of Organised Crime in Europe as a Challenge to National Sovereignty' (1995) 13 *Dickinson JIL* 623. See also Article 1, Joint Action against participating in a criminal organisation, note 9 above.

fraud. Thus, combating such serious crimes must include a strategy against organised crime. The EU has consequently devoted much attention to organised crime, and has adopted a myriad of instruments, initiatives and the creation of new institutions[13] to fight it. The EU's approach is centred on the harmonisation of definitions,[14] approaches[15] and prevention techniques,[16] but the policy is not designed to duplicate existing international efforts.[17] An important aspect of the approach is the confiscation of the profits of organised crime and the consequent reduction in the amount of criminal funds that can be laundered in domestic financial systems.[18] Thirdly, as suggested earlier, the opening up of the internal market and hard borders within Member States increases the fluidity of organised criminal groups,[19] and their ability to operate across national boundaries. This cross-border nature of organised crime makes it difficult to tackle purely at the domestic level without the cooperation of the Member States that may be involved,

[13] Action Plan, note 11 above; Joint Action against participating in a criminal organisation, note 9 above; Council of the European Union, Joint Action (97/827/JHA) establishing a mechanism for evaluating the application and implementation at national level of international undertakings in the fight against organised crime, OJ 1997 No. L344/7; European Union, The prevention and control of organised crime: a European Union strategy for the beginning of the new millennium, OJ 2000 No. C124/1; Council of the European Union, Resolution on the Prevention of organised crime with reference to the establishment of a comprehensive strategy for combating it, OJ 1998 No. C408/1; Council of the European Union and European Commission, Action Plan implementing the Hague Programme on strengthening Freedom, Security and Justice in the European Union, OJ 2005 No. C198/1; European Commission, Proposal for a Council Framework decision on the fight against organised crime, COM (2005) 6 final.

[14] See Joint Action against participating in a criminal organisation, note 9 above. See however C. Harding, 'The Offence of Belonging: Capturing Participation in Organised Crime' (2005) *CrimLR* 690.

[15] European Commission, Communication from the Commission to the Council and European Parliament: Developing a strategic concept on tackling organised crime, COM (2005) 232 final.

[16] For instance, the Action Plan raised the possibility of excluding from public contracts those committing offences connected with organised crime. See Action Plan, note 11 above, Part III, chapter II.

[17] Communication on the prevention of crime, note 7 above; Council Decision 2004/579/EC on the conclusion, on behalf of the European Community, of the United Nations Convention Against Transnational Organised Crime, OJ 2004 No. L261/69; European Commission, Proposal for a Council Framework decision on the fight against organised crime, note 13 above.

[18] European Union, The prevention and control of organised crime, note 13 above.

[19] L. Holmes, 'Crime, Corruption and Politics: International and Transnational Factors', in J. Zielonka and A. Pravada (eds.), *Democratic Consolidation in Eastern Europe*, Vol. 2 (Oxford University Press, 2001), pp. 192–230.

and EU intervention is necessary to secure the cooperation and participation of all affected Member States.

The relationship between organised crime and public procurement
occurs in the ability of organised criminal groups to infiltrate and
penetrate the public sector;[20] which if left unchecked may result in
state capture;[21] that is, organised groups may be able to influence government policies, law-making and law enforcement in their favour,
either because high-level government officials have been compromised
by organised groups or because organised groups are involved in political
campaign financing and electoral manipulation.[22]

Evidence collated by the United Nations suggests that a large proportion of organised criminal groups penetrate the legitimate economy.[23] As
a result, combating organised crime in public procurement is often
considered important to prevent the state being a party to the prosperity
of criminal groups, and to prevent these groups from using public
contracts to launder illicit funds. In addition, the participation of such
groups in public procurement may present security and moral problems
for a government, more so where that government develops a dependency on such groups participating in its procurement.

2.2. Corruption

Secondly, the new exclusions require contracting authorities to exclude
persons convicted of corruption.[24] Corruption here is defined by reference to Article 3 of Council Act of 26 May 1997[25] and Article 3(1) of
Council Joint Action 98/742/JHA.[26] Both these instruments criminalise
active corruption, i.e. the deliberate action of promising or giving an
undue advantage of any kind to another person so that the person may

---

[20] Action Plan, note 11 above, Part II, para.13.
[21] E. Buscaglia and J. van Dijk, 'Controlling Organised Crime and Corruption in the Public
Sector' (2003) 3 *Forum on Crime and Society* 23, p. 24.
[22] *Ibid.*
[23] UN Office of Drugs and Crime, *Global Programme against Transnational Organised
Crime: Results of a Pilot Survey of Forty Selected Organised Criminal Groups in Sixteen
Countries* (2002), p. 27.
[24] Article 45(1)(b) of the Public Sector Directive.
[25] Convention drawn up on the basis of Article K.3(2)(c) of the Treaty on European Union
on the fight against corruption involving officials of the European Communities or
officials of Member States of the European Union, OJ 1997 No. C195/2.
[26] Joint Action 98/742/JHA adopted by the Council on the basis of Article K.3 TEU on
corruption in the private sector, OJ 1998 No. L358/2.

refrain from acting in accordance with his duty in the public and the private sectors respectively.

EU policy against corruption has broadly shadowed international action against the same.[27] EU policy against corruption can be said to have three objectives. First, the policy is aimed at protecting Community finances,[28] possibly in response to the widespread corruption that appeared to characterise EU institutions.[29] Since then, the policy has expanded in scope and is now an integral part of EU internal and external trade policies.[30] Secondly, and similar to the main rationale for EU action against organised crime, EU measures against corruption are also intended to secure for EU citizens an area of 'freedom, security and justice'[31] devoid of activity such as corruption.

Thirdly, EU anti-corruption measures are intended to facilitate the liberalisation of the internal market.[32] Although there is no treaty provision linking corruption to market integration, corruption is at odds with the principles of non-discrimination and free competition advocated by the single market.[33] Eliminating corruption will facilitate competition by ensuring that corrupt practices do not interfere with free trade.[34] In a free

---

[27] OECD initiatives been influential in formulating EU policy against corruption. See OECD, Convention on Combating Bribery of Foreign Public Officials in International Business Transactions, 37 ILM 1; OECD, Recommendation of the Council on the Tax Deductibility of Bribes to Foreign Public Officials 35 ILM 1311; OECD, Revised Recommendation of the Council on Combating Bribery in International Business Transactions 36 ILM 1016.

[28] Article 280 EC Treaty; Convention drawn up on the basis of Article K.3 of the Treaty on European Union, on the protection of the European Communities' financial interests ('Convention on the protection of EC's interests') OJ 1995 No. C316/49; Council Regulation (EC, Euratom) No. 2988/95 on the protection of the European Communities' financial interests ('Regulation on the protection of EC's financial interests') OJ 1995 No. L312/1.

[29] Committee of Independent Experts, 'First Report regarding Allegations of Fraud, Mismanagement and Nepotism in the European Commission' (March 15, 1999). See www.europarl.eu.int/experts.

[30] Cotonou Partnership Agreement 2000/483/EC, OJ 2000 No. L317/3; European Economic and Social Committee, Opinion on development aid, good governance and the role of socio-economic interest groups, OJ 1997 No. C287/44.

[31] Article 29 TEU.

[32] European Parliament, Resolution on the communication from the Commission to the Council and the European Parliament on a Union policy against corruption, OJ 1998 No. C328/46.

[33] L. Ferola, 'Anti-Bribery Measures in the European Union: A Comparison with the Italian Legal Order' (2000) 28 IJLI 512; Joint Action 98/742/JHA, note 26 above; Council of the European Union, Council Framework Decision 2003/568/JHA on combating corruption in the private sector, OJ 2003 No. L192/54.

[34] Ferola, note 33 above, p. 515.

market, corruption may have cross-border implications, thus requiring supranational measures to combat it.

The relationship between public procurement and corruption policy takes the following form. Firstly, corruption in procurement can impede the objectives of Community procurement regulation by reducing competition and turning competitive bidding to 'competitive corruption'.[35] Secondly, the EU finances several projects within and outside Europe and must ensure that they are corruption-free. Third, corruption is a large facet of activities such as organised crime[36] and money laundering and tackling these crimes necessitates a comprehensive policy which includes combating such crimes in the area of public finances.[37] Finally, as mentioned above, open public procurement is an area with increased opportunities for criminal activity, and the EU has an interest in reducing the scope for corruption that may arise from liberalising public procurement markets.

2.3. Fraud

Thirdly, the new exclusions require authorities to exclude from public contracts persons convicted of fraud within the meaning of Article 1 of the Convention on the protection of the European Communities' financial interests.[38] This defines such fraud as any intentional act or omission relating to Community revenue or expenditure which results in the misapplication, misappropriation, illegal diminution or wrongful retention of such revenue or expenditure.[39]

The EU's policy against fraud has as its primary aim the protection of the Communities' financial interests.[40] The focus on Community finances is in response to the widespread fraud which was once estimated to consist of 10 per cent of the Communities' budget.[41] Fraud against the

---

[35] J. Moran, J. Pope and A. Doig, 'Debarment as an Anti-Corruption Means', available at www.u4.no.

[36] UN Office of Drugs and Crime, note 18 above, p. 25; Buscaglia and van Dijk, note 21 above, pp. 22–23.

[37] Note 15 above, p. 4.   [38] Article 45(1)(c) of the Public Sector Directive.

[39] Convention on the protection of EC's financial interests, note 28 above.

[40] S. White, *Protection of the Financial Interests of the European Communities: The Fight against Fraud and Corruption* (The Hague: Kluwer Law International, 1998). See also Case C–68/88, *Commission v. Greece* [1989] ECR 2965; Case C–186/98, *Nunes and de Matos* [1999] ECR I–4883.

[41] European Parliament, Questions to the Commission in cooperation to combat fraud in connection with the Community budget, OJ 1993 No. C155/12.

Communities' interests includes tax evasion, VAT fraud and fraud in relation to agricultural and other subsidies,[42] and the Community consequently defines fraud as acts or omissions which, inter alia, have as their effect the misapplication, wrongful retention or illegal diminution of Community funds.[43]

In an attempt to combat this fraud and circumvent the loopholes arising from multi-level jurisdiction over fraud cases,[44] the Commission created the European Anti-Fraud Office (OLAF)[45] and proposed the development of a *corpus juris*, comprising elements of substantive and procedural unification.[46] Although the *corpus juris* has not materialised, the Commission is committed to a system that will include the investigation and prosecution of offences against the Communities' financial interests at the Union level.[47]

A sub-rationale for the Union's policy against fraud is to limit the operation of criminal syndicates in public finances. There is evidence to suggest that some VAT fraud and fraud in relation to Community subsidies is carried out by organised groups.[48] Limiting the scope for this kind of fraud will have a consequential effect on the functioning and prosperity of these groups.

The relationship between EU anti-fraud policy and public procurement finds expression in the concern that funds for EU-financed projects are not fraudulently misapplied or diverted. As the directives apply to the EC institutions[49] and also where the EU finances a project

---

[42] B. Quirke, 'Fraud against European Public Funds' (1999) 31 *Crime, Law and Social Change* 173.

[43] Article 1, Convention on the protection of the EC's financial interests, note 28 above. See also Regulation on the protection of the EC's financial interests, note 28 above.

[44] Quirke, note 42 above, p. 183. See European Commission, Green Paper on criminal law prosecution of the financial interests of the Community and the establishment of a European prosecutor, COM (2001)715.

[45] European Commission, Decision establishing the European Anti-Fraud office, OJ 1999 No. L136/20.

[46] See Report of the House of Lords Select Committee on the European Communities, Prosecuting Fraud on the Communities Finances – the *Corpus Juris*, Ninth Report for the Session 1998–99 (HL 62), 26 May 1999; C. Harding, 'Exploring the Intersection of European Law and National Criminal Law' (2000) 25 *ELRev* 374, pp. 384–385; European Parliament, Resolution on the creation of a European legal and judicial area to protect the European Union's financial interests against organised crime, OJ 1997 No. C200, p. 157.

[47] European Commission, Protecting the Communities' financial interests, Fight against fraud action plan for 2004–2005, COM (2004) 544 final.

[48] Quirke, note 42 above, p. 173.

[49] Articles 104–106 of Council Regulation 1605/2002 on the financial regulations applicable to the General Budget of the European Communities, OJ 2002 No. L248/1.

but the process is conducted by a Member State, safeguarding public contracts against fraud will also safeguard the Community's financial interests.[50]

2.4. Money laundering

Finally, the new exclusions require contracting authorities to exclude firms convicted of money laundering.[51] Money laundering is defined as:

(a) the conversion or transfer of property, knowing that such property is derived from criminal activity ... for the purpose of concealing or disguising the illicit origin of the property or assisting any person ... to evade the legal consequences of his action;

(b) the concealment or disguise of the true nature, source, location, disposition, movement, rights with respect to, or ownership of property, knowing that such property is derived from criminal activity or from an act of participation in such activity;

(c) the acquisition, possession or use of property, knowing at the time of receipt that such property was derived from criminal activity or from an act of participation in such activity;

(d) participation in, association to commit, attempts to commit and aiding, abetting, facilitating and counselling the commission of any of the actions mentioned in the foregoing points.[52]

EU policy against money laundering has multiple rationales. First, it is clear that organised crime and corruption will only thrive if the proceeds of such crime may be utilised without alerting the authorities to its source,[53] which are therefore laundered to conceal their origins. Thus EU policy on money laundering is designed to complement its policy against organised crime (especially drug syndicates)[54] and

---

[50] Initiative of the Federal Republic of Germany with a view to the adoption of a Council Framework Decision on criminal law protection against fraudulent or other unfair anti-competitive conduct in relation to the award of public contracts in the common market, OJ 2000 No. C253/3.

[51] Article 45(1)(d) of the Public Sector Directive.

[52] Article 1(2)(a) to (d) of Directive 2005/60/EC of the European Parliament and of the Council on the prevention of the use of the financial system for the purpose of money laundering and terrorist financing ('Money Laundering Directive') OJ 2005 No. L309/15.

[53] A. Rizkalla, 'Money Laundering: The European Approach' (1998) 13 TECLF 111.

[54] W. Gilmore, 'International Initiatives', in T. Graham (ed.), Butterworths International Guide to Money Laundering: Law and Practice, 2nd edn (London: Butterworth, 2003), p. 116.

corruption[55] and make it more difficult for crime syndicates, terrorist groups and white-collar criminals to flourish.[56] Secondly, the policy aims at combating the cross-border nature of money laundering. Closer integration in relation to the free movement of capital has made it easier for criminal elements to conceal illicit funds across Member States,[57] and Community action is therefore necessary to address the cross-border elements of modern money laundering.[58] Thirdly, it is argued that the policy is designed to 'counter the distortion of competition ... caused by the introduction of illicit capital into the economic-financial circuits'.[59] The argument here is that criminal elements may achieve a monopolistic position in public or private enterprise if their activities are unchecked.[60] Fourthly, Community action against money laundering is designed to ensure that national measures in this sphere are not inconsistent with or contrary to the functioning of the internal market.[61] Lastly, EU policy is designed to accord with standards of international cooperation on money laundering issued by inter-governmental agencies such as the Financial Action Task Force on Money Laundering (FATF), of which the Community is a member.[62]

It has been mentioned above that criminal elements seek access to the legitimate public and private business sectors so that they can use the business opportunities provided to launder criminal proceeds.[63] The linkage between procurement regulation and Community policy against money laundering thus takes the form of the desire to prevent criminal elements from using Member States' public procurement systems to launder ill-gotten funds, in a region open to cross-border economic influences.

From the above, it can be seen that EU policy against the serious criminal offences which are the subject of the mandatory exclusions are interrelated and codependent for the fulfilment of the overarching goal of

---

[55] M. Tantam, N. Matthews and J. Traynor, 'UK Part III: Practical implementation of regulations and rules', in T. Graham (ed.) note 54 above, p. 45.

[56] See the Recitals to the Money Laundering Directive, note 52 above and European Convention on laundering, search, seizure and confiscation of proceeds from crime, ETS No 14.1, 30 ILM 148.

[57] B. Harte, 'Banking', in R. Parlour (ed.), *Butterworths International Guide to Money Laundering: Law and Practice* (London: Butterworth, 1995), p. 244.

[58] Recital 3 of the Money Laundering Directive, note 52 above.

[59] L. Ferola, note 7 above, p. 74.   [60] *Ibid.*

[61] Recital 2 of the Money Laundering Directive, note 52 above.

[62] Gilmore, note 54 above.

[63] European Union, The prevention and control of organised crime, note 13 above, p. 6.

EU intervention in criminal matters, which is to secure an area of 'freedom, security and justice' for EU citizens.

3. The use of procurement legislation to combat serious criminal offences

The use of exclusions against suppliers who have committed criminal offences is not a new concept in Community procurement regulation, and historically, the procurement directives have always contained provisions *permitting* Member States to exclude from public contracts firms that had engaged in criminal or even anti-social behaviour.[64] However, as was mentioned, the 2004 directives were the first instruments to include a provision making it mandatory for Member States to exclude firms guilty of serious offences.

It is interesting that the mandatory exclusions as eventually adopted are far less extensive than the proposals as amended by the European Parliament. So far as grounds of exclusion are concerned, the Commission initially proposed limited exclusions for participation in a criminal organisation, corruption and fraud. In addition, Member States were *allowed*, although not required, to exclude suppliers for: bankruptcy; offences regarding professional conduct; grave professional misconduct; breach of social security or taxation law; misrepresentation in contract tenders; and fraud or other illegal activity as defined by Article 280 EC.[65]

At the first reading of the proposals,[66] the scope of the mandatory exclusions was enlarged by the European Parliament to include money laundering, anti-competitive behaviour, breaches of employment legislation, bankruptcy and drugs-related offences. Apart from that relating to money laundering, the Council rejected these amendments[67] for various

---

[64] On the directive immediately prior to the 2004 directives see Article 20 of Directive 93/36/EEC OJ 1993 No. L199/1; Article 24 of Directive 93/37/EEC OJ 1993 No. L199/54; Article 29 of Directive 92/50/EEC OJ 1992 No. L209/1; on the current provisions see chapter 2, section 4.36 and chapter 4, section 10.2.

[65] S. Williams, 'The Mandatory Exclusions for Corruption in the New EC Procurement Directives' (2006) 31 *ELRev* 711.

[66] European Parliament, Position of the European parliament adopted at first reading on January 17, 2002 with a view to the adoption of the European and Council Directive.../.../EC on the coordination of procedures for the award of public supply contracts, public service contracts and public works contracts, OJ 2002 No. C271E/176.

[67] Council of the European Union, Common position adopted by the Council on March 20, 2003 with a view to the adoption of a directive of the European Parliament and of the Council on the coordination of procedures for the award of public supply contract, public service contracts and public works contracts: Statement of the Council's Reasons 11029/3/02 REV 3 ADD 1.

reasons, including the difficulty of integrating the exclusions for drug-related offences into the overall scheme of public procurement legislation.[68] In rejecting the proposal for exclusions for bankruptcy, the Council suggested that requiring exclusions for bankruptcy would lead to the 'systematic exclusion' of suppliers with arrangements with their creditors and 'condemn them to bankruptcy'.[69]

Whilst implementing the mandatory exclusions in their current limited form may be easier for national procurement systems, the Council's reasons for rejecting the Parliament's insertions are difficult to justify. Specifically, it is difficult to see how mandatory exclusions for corruption and money laundering may be properly integrated into the scheme of public procurement regulation, whilst exclusions for drug-related offences cannot. A better view is that the Council was wary of over-burdening the legislation with a plethora of exclusions which would hamper efficient national procurement.[70]

The adopted version of the provision as set out in Article 45 of the Public Sector Directive states:

> Any candidate or tenderer who has been the subject of a conviction by final judgement of which the contracting authority is aware for one or more of the reasons listed below shall be excluded from participation in a public contract:
>
> (a) participation in a criminal organisation as defined in Article 2(1) of Council Joint Action 98/733/JHA;
>
> (b) corruption, as defined in Article 3 of the Council Act of 26 May 1997 and Article 3 of Council Joint Action 98/742/JHA respectively;
>
> (c) fraud within the meaning of Article 1 of the Convention relating to the protection of the financial interests of the European Communities;
>
> (d) money laundering as defined in Article 1 of Council Directive 91/308/ EEC of 10 June 1991 on prevention of the use of the financial system for the purpose of money laundering.[71]
>
> Member states shall specify, in accordance with their national laws and having regard for Community law, the implementing conditions for this paragraph.
>
> They may provide for a derogation from the requirement referred to in the first subparagraph for overriding requirements in the general interest.

---

[68] Ibid.   [69] Ibid. See Williams, note 65 above, p. 718.   [70] Williams, note 65 above.
[71] Note that Directive 91/308/EEC on the prevention of the use of the financial system for the purpose of money laundering, OJ 1991 No. L166/77 which is the directive mentioned in Article 45(1)(d) has been repealed and replaced by Directive 2005/60/EC on the prevention of the use of the financial system for the purpose of money laundering and terrorist financing, OJ 2005 No. L309/15.

4. The procuring entities covered by the provisions

The mandatory exclusion provisions must be applied by all bodies that are 'contracting authorities' under the directives. With a few exceptions, the Public Sector Directive only regulates entities that are contracting authorities (state, regional and local authorities, bodies governed by public law and associations of these), as chapter 2 explained. The Utilities Directive, on the other hand, applies, as we saw in chapter 11,[72] also to public undertakings and certain private entities with special or exclusive rights,[73] but the exclusions do not apply to these last two categories[74] (although they may exclude on these grounds if they wish to do so).

5. The range of contractors subject to the exclusions

An important issue which Member States will have to address in implementation is the range of persons liable to be excluded. Specifically, the directives provide that the exclusion shall apply to any 'candidate or tenderer' convicted of the named offences, without specifying whether the exclusions will apply to persons or firms related to the convicted contractor. In the absence of specific provisions, it is uncertain how far a procuring entity must apply any exclusion to firms related to the convicted firm such as parent, subsidiaries or sister companies, and whether a firm must be excluded for a conviction received by, for example, a director.

Extending the exclusion to related firms may be necessary to make the mandatory exclusions effective.[75] Evidence from the United States, for example, shows that firms can avoid the effect of exclusions by tendering through related persons and companies in the same group.[76] Similarly, under the World Bank exclusion provisions, the Bank excludes any natural or legal person holding the majority of the excluded firm's capital, or any firm controlled by the excluded firm, where the subsidiary is formed or exists while the exclusion is in place.[77]

---

[72] Chapter 11, section 3.   [73] Article 2 of the Utilities Directive.
[74] Article 54(4) of the Utilities Directive.
[75] See also see S. Arrowsmith, 'Implementation of the New EC Procurement Directives and the *Alcatel* Ruling in England and Wales and Northern Ireland: a review of the New Legislation and Guidance' (2006) 15 *PPLR* 86, p. 119.
[76] F. Anechiarico and J. Jacobs, 'Purging Corruption from Public Contracting: The Solutions are Now Part of the Problem' (1995) 40 *NYLSLR* 172.
[77] Section 13(d) World Bank Sanctions Committee procedures (2001). See also S. Williams, 'The Debarment of Corrupt Contractors from World Bank-Financed Contracts' (2007) 36 *PCLJ* 277.

It is possible that to make the provisions effective the ECJ will interpret the mandatory exclusions as requiring exclusion of associated persons, possibly drawing on other EU jurisprudence concerned with similar issues of when to 'pierce the corporate veil'.[78] However, although extending exclusion to related companies may help to prevent firms from circumventing the effects of an exclusion, and as US experience of exclusions for corruption has shown, there are difficulties in achieving this objective, and the investigations needed for this may present serious financial and procedural burdens for the procurement process, as discussed in section 6 below.

Pending ECJ interpretation, it is difficult for Member States to know how to implement the provisions in this respect. It can be noted that under UK implementing regulations, procuring entities are enjoined to exclude the economic operator or its directors or any other person who has powers of representation, decision or control of the convicted firm.[79] Thus, the exclusion will be extended to directors and other natural persons who have obtained a conviction in their personal capacity as well as legal persons who have power to control the convicted contractor. However, the UK position is not necessarily indicative of how other Member States or the ECJ will interpret the exclusions.

These same difficulties of making exclusions effective without imposing unreasonable procedural burdens are also likely to arise, though perhaps to a different degree, in developing mandatory exclusions in other areas of activity.

6. The nature of investigations required

An issue with implications for, inter alia, whether exclusions will be applied in practice to related persons or firms is the nature and the depth of investigations that a procuring entity must carry out to discover whether a bidder has secured a relevant conviction. There are two issues. First, how does a procuring entity discover that a bidder has in fact obtained a relevant conviction and, second, must a procuring entity

---

[78] See Williams, note 65 above, pp. 720–725.
[79] Regulation 23, Public Contracts Regulations (England, Wales, Northern Ireland) SI 2006/5, and Regulation 23, Public Contracts (Scotland) Regulations, SSI 2006/1.

take any steps to discover whether a bidder is a façade for, or is closely related to, a firm that has previously been convicted or excluded?

Under the directives, a contracting authority has to be aware of the conviction before the obligation to exclude will arise,[80] and may request tenderers to furnish it with relevant documentation.[81] However, authorities are not obliged to require such documentation,[82] and are consequently not required to carry out checks or investigations on tenderers.[83] Such investigations may be necessary where the authority suspects that a firm closely related to the tenderer has been excluded or convicted of a relevant offence.[84] A propensity not to investigate will weaken the effect of the exclusions where a firm that conceals its convictions or tenders through a different corporate identity succeeds in obtaining a contract.

On the other hand, the resource implications of conducting investigations in every case, especially for firms in other Member States, may be significant for authorities and outweigh any benefits. Another potential problem is the delays that investigations may occasion to the procurement process. For instance, the UK Criminal Records Bureau takes ten to thirty days to furnish information on criminal convictions, depending on the information required.[85] A partial solution to the delay and difficulty of investigations, which is currently being debated, is the creation of a central register of convicted and excluded firms which is accessible to all Member States.[86]

---

[80] Article 45(1) of the Public Sector Directive.	[81] Ibid.

[82] The UK Office of Government Commerce has suggested that authorities may utilise a pre-selection or pre-qualification questionnaire to routinely elicit this information. See OGC, Mandatory Exclusions of Economic Operators, para. 3.2.

[83] See also Arrowsmith, note 74 above, at 19.83.	[84] Arrowsmith, note 75 above, p. 122.

[85] See www.crb.gov.uk

[86] See European Parliament, Report on the Initiative by the Federal Republic of Germany with a view to the adoption of a Council Framework Decision on criminal law protection against fraudulent or other unfair anti-competitive conduct in relation to the award of public contracts in the common market A5–0184/2002 final, p. 8; European Parliament, Resolution on aid effectiveness and corruption in developing countries, P6_TA(2006)0141. See also Office Européen de lutte anti-fraude (OLAF), Joint Transparency International-OLAF Policy Roundtable on Blacklisting: Protecting EU financial interests through management of effective and transparent debarment systems, OLAF/06/01; Transparency International, Recommendations for the development and implementation of an effective debarment system in the EU, available at www.transparency.org; European Commission, Proposal for a Council Framework Decision on the organisation and content of the exchange of information extracted from criminal records between Member States, COM (2005) 690 final.

7. Time limits

The directives are silent on the length of time for which a firm must be excluded from contracts after a conviction. The Commission's original proposals required that the conviction must have been obtained in the previous five years,[87] ensuring that firms were required to be disqualified for this period but that Member States were permitted to disregard any convictions older than five years. This requirement was, however, not included in the final directives. In implementing the provision, Member States thus have some discretion in deciding the length of the exclusion. This might lead to differences in treatment of convicted suppliers in different Member States. However, the ECJ will probably imply at least a certain minimum period of disqualification in order to render the provisions effective – for example, it would almost certainly not comply with the directive to limit exclusion to a short period such as one month from conviction. It can be noted that in the UK Public Contracts Regulations there is no prescribed length for exclusions;[88] there is thus the possibility that a tenderer may be excluded for an indeterminable period of time, and that the period of disqualification applied might vary between different UK authorities. However, it is arguable that Member States *must* specify the relevant period for their entities when implementing the directive. The lack of certainty and coherence in the current position in the directive may be criticised. Arguably it would be better to include a specific period for disqualification – either a uniform period or, at the very least, a minimum period – in the directive itself.

8. Derogations

Member States are permitted to derogate from the mandatory requirement to exclude for 'overriding requirements in the general interest'. Although 'general interest' is not defined, it seems clear that this derogation will be interpreted in line with Community jurisprudence, so that any derogation must be appropriate, necessary and proportionate to the objective sought, and must not be used to discriminate.[89]

---

[87] Article 46(1) of the Proposal for a Directive of the European Parliament and of the Council on the coordination of procedures for the award of public supply contracts, public service contracts and public works contracts, OJ 2001 No. C29E/11.

[88] Regulation 23(1) of the Public Contracts Regulations.

[89] Case C–318/86, *Commission* v. *French Republic* [1988] ECR 3559. See also Williams, note 65, p. 727.

Where these public interests are already the subject of specific derogations in the Treaty or directives, then it is likely that the derogations from
the exclusion requirement will be interpreted in a manner similar to
those more general derogations. This can be illustrated by reference to
the issue of security – for example, when an authority claims that it is
necessary to give military work to a convicted contractor on the basis that
only that contractor can maintain confidentiality. Two other kinds of
security exemptions apply to public contracts:[90] general exemptions
from the Treaty, including derogations from the free movement provisions on public security grounds;[91] and specific exemptions from the
directives, for contracts declared secret, contracts which must be accompanied by special security measures and other contracts as required by
the essential interests of a Member State.[92] In considering the security
exemption in the directives where military contracts are concerned, the
ECJ will examine whether the contract is one which falls within the
derogations[93] by determining whether it relates to the security interests
of a Member State, but apparently applies a low level of scrutiny to the
application of the provision and, in particular, will decline to examine
the availability of alternative measures that could have been utilised by
the Member State.[94] A similar approach can be expected with claims for
derogation from the mandatory exclusion provisions based on grounds
of military security.

Public health may also provide a reason for derogating from the
mandatory exclusions.[95] The preparatory documents to the directives
alluded to this in stating that derogations may apply in cases of public
health problems where the only available medicines are provided by a

---

[90] Note that the procurement directives exclude hard defence material: see chapter 2,
section 2 and note 1.
[91] Article 30 EC. On the standard of scrutiny see Case 72/83, *Campus Oil Ltd* v. *Minister for
Industry and Energy* [1984] ECR 2727, para. 36; Case C–398/98, *Commission* v. *Greece*
[2001] ECR I–7915; D. Akande and S. Williams, 'International Adjudication on National
Security Issues: What Role for the WTO?' (2003) 43 *VJIL* 365; M. Trybus, 'On the
Application of the EC Treaty to Armaments' (2000) 25 *ELRev* 663. Also relevant are
derogations for military hardware under Article 296 EC: see again chapter 2, section 2
and note 1.
[92] Article 14 of the Public Sector Directive.
[93] Case C–414/97, *Commission* v. *Spain* [1999] ECR I–5585; Case C–318/94, *Commission* v.
Germany [1996] ECR I–1949, para. 13.
[94] Case C–252/01, *Commission* v. *Belgium* [2003] ECR I–11859.
[95] Williams, note 65 above, 727.

convicted contractor.[96] Whilst there are no explicit derogations from the directives for public health, the recitals indicate that the directives do not preclude the application of measures necessary to protect public health that comply with the Treaty.[97]

It is not so clear whether derogations are permitted simply on grounds of cost, notably where turning to the second-best supplier would simply increase the price of the goods or services. As chapter 4 explained, a line of ECJ jurisprudence states that there can be no derogation from the EC Treaty on purely economic grounds, which might suggest that cost-based derogations might, likewise, be also ruled out here.[98] Arrowsmith suggests in chapter 4 that this alleged general rule may, in fact, need to be nuanced; but even if that is the case, the approach of the ECJ to other situations in which derogations have been claimed on grounds of cost indicate that such derogations will be allowed, at best, only when an exclusion would 'seriously undermine the financial balance'[99] of the procurement system.

9. The significance of the mandatory exclusions for future EC policy on public procurement

The mandatory exclusions for serious criminal offences represent a watershed in the use of procurement regulation to support Community objectives. Prior to the 2004 directives, Member States had traditionally been permitted, but not required, to exclude contractors for various reasons. The new requirement to exclude for certain criminal convictions, however, has now established the principle of using public procurement to achieve Community objectives in a manner that is not optional for Member States. The change may be evidence of an ideological shift from the use of EU procurement regulation solely to fulfil internal market objectives to the use of public procurement regulation to

---

[96] European Parliament, Legislative resolution on the Council common position with a view to adopting a European Parliament and Council directive coordinating the procurement procedures of entities operating in the water, energy, transport and postal services sectors, OJ 2004 No. C74E/445. Similar waivers in the US can be made in situations where only one contractor exists: Dept of Health and Human Services Acquisition Regulations 309.405(a)(1)(i).

[97] Recital 6 of the Public Sector Directive.

[98] E.g. Case 104/75, *Officier van Justitie* v. *de Peijper* [1976] ECR 613; Case C–120/95, *Decker* v. *Caisse de maladie des employés privés* ('*Decker*') [1998] ECR I–1831, para. 39; Case C–398/98, *Commission* v. *Greece* [2001] ECR I–7915; see chapter 4, section 3.

[99] Case C–120/95, *Decker*, note 98 above.

implement other EU goals, including through exclusions.[100] We noted in
the introduction to this chapter that further use of procurement to
promote EU policy goals has already been seen now in the environmental
sphere, although not involving the use of exclusions.

However, getting Member States to commit to mandatory requirements in other areas of endeavour may be more problematic. First, it can
be pointed out that in the case of the current mandatory exclusions, the
Community is merely requesting the enforcement of existing legal rules
and standards, and is not requiring from Member States new standards
that go beyond compliance with the general law. It may be more difficult
for Member States to agree on the use of procurement to promote
Community objectives in the latter case. Further, the Council's refusal
to adopt the other mandatory exclusions proposed by the European
Parliament[101] indicates that where there is a lack of harmony over the
importance (or lack thereof), value and weight attached to an objective,
the Community may be unable to implement such objectives through
mandatory exclusions in procurement instruments.

If in future Member States were, however, to pursue further the use of
procurement to support EU objectives, as well as establishing the *principle* of using mandatory exclusions for this, the new exclusion provisions might serve as a precedent for the *approach* to be adopted: future
mandatory exclusions follow the juristic format and limitations utilised
in the exclusions discussed in this chapter. For example, the limitation of
the exclusions only to procuring entities that are 'contracting authorities'– thus excluding many utilities – might be followed in other areas.
Similarly, the approach adopted to excluding companies and persons
that are merely associated with those convicted of relevant offences (such
as parent companies), both in the legislation itself and in the way it is
developed in the jurisprudence, might also provide a model for exclusion
provisions in other areas. On the other hand, if the exclusions included in
the 2004 directives prove to be unduly problematic or burdensome,
including because of the way they are interpreted by the ECJ, Member
States may be less willing in future to accept mandatory exclusions in
public procurement. For all these reasons, the experience at EC level and
in Member States in interpreting and implementing the new provisions is
likely to be watched with interest.

---

[100] Arrowsmith, note 75 above, p. 116.
[101] Note 66 above; note 67 above.

INDEX